Healthcare Politics and Policy in America

Healthcare Politics and Policy in America provides a comprehensive examination of the ways that health policy has been shaped by the political, socioeconomic, and ideological environment of the United States. The roles played by public and private, institutional and individual actors in designing the healthcare system are identified at all levels. The book addresses the key problems of healthcare cost, access, and quality through analyses of Medicare, Medicaid, the Veterans Health Administration, and other programs, and the ethical and cost implications of advances in healthcare technology. This fully updated fourth edition gives expanded attention to the fiscal and financial impact of high healthcare costs and the struggle for healthcare reform, culminating in the passage of the Affordable Care Act, with preliminary discussion of implementation issues associated with the new law as well as attempts to defund and repeal it. Each chapter concludes with discussion questions and a comprehensive reference list. Helpful appendices provide a guide to websites and a chronology. PowerPoint slides and other instructional materials are available to instructors who adopt the book.

Healthcare Politics and Policy in America

Fourth Edition

Kant Patel and

Mark E. Rushefsky

M.E.Sharpe
Armonk, New York
London, England

This book is dedicated to those fighting every day to make affordable healthcare available to every American.—K. P.

To my grandchildren, Echo, Damian, and Gabriel: May you grow up in a world where people do not have to worry about whether they can afford healthcare.—M.E. R.

The EuroSlavic fonts used to create this work are © 1986–2014 Payne Loving Trust. EuroSlavic is available from Linguist's Software, Inc., www.linguistsoftware.com, P.O. Box 580, Edmonds, WA 98020-0580 USA tel (425) 775-1130.

Library of Congress Cataloging-in-Publication Data

Patel, Kant, 1946–
   Healthcare politics and policy in America / by Kant Patel, Mark Rushefsky. — Fourth edition.
     pages cm
  Includes bibliographical references and index.
  ISBN 978-0-7656-2604-2 (cloth : alk. paper) — ISBN 978-0-7656-2605-9 (pbk. : alk. paper)
  1. Medical policy—United States. 2. Medical care—Political aspects—United States.
I. Rushefsky, Mark E., 1945– II. Title.

RA395.A3P285 2014
362.10973—dc23   2013035354

Printed in the United States of America

The paper used in this publication meets the minimum requirements of American National Standard for Information Sciences Permanence of Paper for Printed Library Materials, ANSI Z 39.48-1984.

AGC (c) 10 9 8 7 6 5 4 3 2 1
AGC (p) 10 9 8 7 6 5 4 3 2 1

CONTENTS

II

V

LIST OF TABLES AND FIGURES

TABLES

FIGURES

PREFACE

We are gratified by the reception *Healthcare Politics and Policy in America* has received since publication of the first edition. It has been well reviewed, it has sold well, and it has been adopted by many colleges and universities. The first edition was the first joint research project between Patel and Rushefsky. Since that time we have published several books on healthcare with M.E. Sharpe: *Politics, Power, and Policy Making: The Case of Health Care Reform in the 1990s; Health Care Policy in an Age of New Technologies; The Politics of Public Health in the United States;* and *Health Care in America: Separate and Unequal.* Patel began working on the first edition of the book while on a sabbatical in the spring of 1991. Rushefsky joined the project in 1994. It continues to be an interesting experience for both of us. We do not have the same kind of work habits. One of us (we won't tell you which one) is very meticulous and organized; the other is considerably more scattered and sloppy. This has sometimes led to noisy discussions and scampering to find things. This is the kind of book Felix and Oscar, the Odd Couple, might have written! One adjustment we did make was that the neat, meticulous one kept all the papers and files because the other misplaced his. That we remain close friends who share common interests in professional basketball (and computer games) helped the relationship. Patel, who is from Houston, roots for the Houston Rockets. Rushefsky, from New York, is a lifelong, avid, irrational Knicks fan. Patel retired from Missouri State University in 2011, and Rushefsky will retire in 2014.

Both of us have had a long involvement in healthcare, dating back to the 1970s. Rushefsky first became interested in healthcare when his wife, Cynthia, began teaching childbirth classes in rural Rocky Mount, Virginia. She trained some of the nurses and the wife of the administrator of the local rural hospital (about ten miles along winding mountain roads from where they lived), and that hospital maintained its maternity ward rather than closing it. That was fortunate for the Rushefskys when their second child, Leah, was born shortly after midnight on Halloween. They just made it those ten miles to the hospital. Had that hospital not maintained its birthing facilities, they would have had to go another twenty-five miles to Roanoke. Given the speed with which Leah was born (so fast that she beat the doctor to the delivery room!), Rushefsky half-jokingly says she would have been born in Boones Mill (about halfway between Rocky Mount and Roanoke), which had no hospital. Updating from the first edition of this book, Leah is now married and has given Rushefsky and his wife three grandchildren, Echo, Damian, and Gabriel, to whom he has dedicated this book. Echo and Damian were born prematurely, so the Rushefsky clan has had some close encounters with the American healthcare system.

Patel's interest in healthcare was developed more conventionally, as an academic. He has a lifelong belief that access to good healthcare is a right. The two of us agree that the healthcare system has problems; before publication of the first edition of this book, there was no text that addressed those problems from a political perspective.

This fourth edition has been considerably updated and reconceptualized. The three major events that have occurred since the third edition came out were the recapture of Congress by the Democrats in 2006, the election of Barack Obama in 2008 (and his reelection in 2012), and the passage of the Patient Protection and Affordable Care Act. The first four chapters of the book remain basically the same (with updates), providing background material and intensive discussions of Medicare and Medicaid. Chapter 5 is new to this edition, covering the Indian Health Service and the Department of Veterans Affairs. Chapter 6 focuses on the problems of the disadvantaged and holes in the healthcare safety net. Chapters 7 and 8 focus on healthcare costs. Chapter 7 sets out the problem of healthcare costs and spending and examines a variety of factors that have contributed to rising healthcare costs and expenditures. Chapter 8 follows with an exploration of various strategies for restraining costs and spending. Chapter 9 looks at contemporary issues such as technology, electronic medical records, the problem of undocumented immigrants, and reproductive issues. Chapter 10 focuses on the Patient Protection and Affordable Care Act. In chapter 11, we sum up the book and think about the future (one thing we have learned after decades of studying the American healthcare system is that change is continuous and predictions are hazardous).

ACKNOWLEDGMENTS

As is typical of any book, this text is not the product of its authors only. Patel would like to thank the Faculty Leave Committee at Southwest Missouri State University for the spring 1991 sabbatical that made the initial research for this project possible. We would also like to thank Patricia Kolb, vice president and editorial director at M.E. Sharpe, for her insightful judgment in continuing to support this project, along with the staff at M.E. Sharpe. We would also like to thank our graduate assistant, Monica Horton, for her great assistance in preparing the test bank for this edition. Of course, any remaining errors are ours.

Kant Patel
Mark E. Rushefsky

LIST OF ACRONYMS

AAHP	American Association of Health Plans
AAP	American Academy of Pediatrics
AAMC	Association of American Medical Colleges
AANS	American Association of Neurological Surgeons
AAPCC	Adjusted average per capita cost
AARP	American Association of Retired Persons
ABMS	American Board of Medical Specialities
ACA	Affordable Care Act
ACC	Alliance Cost Containment
ACE	Accelerated compensable event
ACF	Administration for Children and Families
ADR	Alternate dispute resolution
AdvaMed	Advanced Medical Technology Association
ACEP	American College of Emergency Physicians
AFDC	Aid to Families with Dependent Children
AFL-CIO	American Federation of Labor–Congress of Industrial Organizations
AHA	American Hospital Association
AHAPAC	American Hospital Association Political Action Committee
AHCA	American Health Care Association
AHCCCS	Arizona Health Care Cost Containment System
AHCPR	Agency for Health Care Policy and Research
AHIP	America's Health Insurance Plans
AHIP PAC	America's Health Insurance Plans Political Action Committee
AHN	Artificial hydration and nutrition
AHP	Accountable Health Plan
AHRQ	Agency for Healthcare Research and Quality
AI	Artificial insemination
AI/AN	American Indians and Alaska Natives
AIDS	Acquired immunodeficiency syndrome
ALTCS	Arizona Long-Term Care System
AMA	American Medical Association
AMPAC	American Medical Association Political Action Committee
ANA	American Nurses Association
ANAPAC	American Nurses Association Political Action Committee
ANCSA	Alaska Native Claims Settlement Act
AoA	Administration on Aging
APHA	American Public Health Association
APN	Advanced practice nurse
APRN	Advance practice registered nurse
ARRA	America Recovery and Reinvestment Act
ARTs	Assisted reproductive technologies
ATSDR	Agency for Toxic Substances and Disease Registry

BBA	Balanced Budget Act
BCBSM	Blue Cross and Blue Shield of Minnesota
BIA	Bureau of Indian Affairs
BRCC	Base Realignment and Closure Commission
CalPERS	California Public Employees' Retirement System
CARE	Community Based Abstinence Education
CBO	Congressional Budget Office
CCHP	Consumer Choice Health Plan
CCMC	Committee on the Costs of Medical Care
CDC	Centers for Disease Control and Prevention
CDER	Center for Drug Evaluation and Research
CDF	Children's Defense Fund
CDHCP	Consumer-driven health care plan
CDRH	Center for Devices and Radiological Health (FDA)
CEAP	Clinical Effectiveness Assessment Program (American College of Physicians)
CER	Cost-effectiveness research
CHAMPUS	Civilian Health and Medical Program of the Uniformed Services
CHAMPVA	Civilian Health and Medical Program of the Department of Veterans Affairs
CHCS	Center for Health Care Strategies
CHIP	Children's Health Insurance Program
CHIPRA	Children's Health Insurance Program Reauthorization Act
CLASS	Community Living Assistance Services and Supports
CMCS	Center for Medicaid and CHIP Services
CMS	Centers for Medicare and Medicaid Services
CNM	Certified nurse midwife
CNS	Clinical nurse specialist
COBRA	Consolidated Omnibus Budget Reconciliation Act
CON	Certificate of need
CPEs	Certified Public Expenditures
CPI	Consumer price index
CPRS	Computerized patient record system
CPS	Current Population Survey
CRNA	Certified registered nurse anesthetist
CT	Computerized tomography
DACA	Deferred Action for Childhood Arrivals
DATTA	Diagnostic and Therapeutic Technology Assessment
DCE	Designated compensable event
DDT	Dichlorodiphenyl trichloreothane
DHHS	Department of Health and Human Services
DMCA	Dependent Medical Care Act
DNC	Democratic National Committee
DOI	Department of the Interior
DOJ	Department of Justice
DRA	Deficit Reduction Act
DRGs	Diagnosis-related groups
DSH	Disproportionate Share Hospital

DSOB	Drug Safety Oversight Board
DTC	Direct-to-consumer
DVA	Department of Veterans Affairs
EFM	Electronic fetal monitor
EHR	Electronic health record
EKG	Electrocardiogram
EMR	Electronic medical record
EMTALA	Emergency Medical Treatment and Active Labor Act
EPSDT	Early and periodic screening, diagnosis, and treatment
ERISA	Employee Retirement Income Security Act
ESBs	Essential health benefits
ESI	Employer-sponsored insurance
ESRD	End-stage renal disease
FDA	Food and Drug Administration
FDCF	Florida Department of Children and Families
FEHBP	Federal Employees Health Benefits Program
FELA	Federal Employees Liability Act
FERA	Federal Emergency Relief Administration
FFS	Fee-for-service
FMA	Federal Medical Assistance Percentage
FPL	Federal poverty level
FSHCAA	Federally Supported Health Centers Assistance Act
FTC	Federal Trade Commission
FTCA	Federal Tort Claims Act
FY	Fiscal year
GAO	General Accounting Office
GAO	Government Accountability Office
GAR	Grand Army of the Republic
GATT	General Agreement on Tariffs and Trade
GDP	Gross domestic product
GIFT	Gamete intrafallopian transfer
GME	Graduate medical education
HBC	Health Benefits Coalition
HCA	Health Consumer Alliance
HCA	Hospital Corporation of America
HCAN	Health Care for Americans Now
HCBS	Home- and community-based services
HCCCCI	Health Care Cost and Coverage Crisis Index/Health Crisis Index
HCFA	Health Care Financing Administration
HDHP	High Deductible Health Insurance Plans
HEDIS	Healthcare Effectiveness Data and Information Set
HHA	Home Health Agency
HHCE	Home health care expenditures
HHS	Health and Human Services, Department of

HI	Hospital insurance
HIAA	Health Insurance Association of America
HIFA	Health Insurance Flexibility and Accountability Initiative
HIO	Health insuring organization
HIPAA	Health Insurance Portability and Accountability Act
HIV	Human immunodeficiency virus
HMOs	Health maintenance organizations
HOA	Health Opportunity Account
HRSA	Health Resources and Services Administration
HSA	Health Security Act
HSA	Health savings account
HSA	Health Systems Agency
HUGO	Human Genome Organization
ICU	Intensive care unit
IEDs	Improvised explosive devices
IGTs	Intergovernmental Transfers
IHCIA	Indian Health Care Improvement Act
IHS	Indian Health Service
IMSIHI	IMS Health Institute for Healthcare Information
IOG	Illness outcome group
IOM	Institute of Medicine
IPA	Independent practice association
IRA	Indian Removal Act
ISDEAA	Indian Self-Determination and Education Assistance Act
IUI	Intrauterine insemination
IVF	In vitro fertilization
JCAH	Joint Commission on Accreditation of Hospitals
KFF	Kaiser Family Foundation
LCWR	Leadership Conference of Women Religious
LEP	Limited English proficiency
LPN	Licensed practical nurse
LTC	Long-term care
LVN	Licensed vocational nurse
MAA	Medical Assistance for the Aged
MAI	Medical adversity insurance
MCCA	Medicare Catastrophic Coverage Act
MCOs	Managed care organizations
MDMA	Medical Device Manufacturers of America
Medi-Cal	California Medicaid program
MEG	Magnetoencephalography
MEPS	Medical Expenditure Panel Survey
MIC	Maternal and infant care
MICRA	Medical Injury Compensation Reform Act (California)

MMA	Medicare Modernization Act; See also MPDIMA
MMIA	Medical Malpractice Immunity Act
MPDIMA	Medicare Prescription Drug, Improvement, and Modernization Act
MRI	Magnetic resonance imaging
MSA	Medical savings account
NAFTA	North American Free Trade Agreement
NAIC	National Association of Insurance Commissioners
NAMIC	National Association of Mutual Insurance Companies
NAS	National Academy of Science
NCHC	National Coalition on Health Care
NCHCT	National Center for Health Care Technology
NCHSR	National Center for Health Services Research
NCI	National Cancer Institute
NCQA	National Committee for Quality Assurance
NCSL	National Conference of State Legislatures
NFIB	National Federation of Independent Businesses
NHI	National health insurance
NHS	National Health Service
NICA	(Birth-related) Neurological Injury Compensation Act
NIH	National Institutes of Health
NIOSH	National Institute for Occupational Safety and Health
NIS	National Institute of Science
NMEs	New molecular entities
NP	Nurse practitioner
NPDB	National Practitioner Data Bank
NRA	National Rifle Association
NSF	National Science Foundation
OBRA	Omnibus Budget Reconciliation Act
OECD	Organization for Economic Cooperation and Development
OHP	Oregon Health Plan
OHTA	Office of Health Technology Assessment
OIA	Office of Indian Affairs
OIG	Office of Inspector General
OMAR	Office of Medical Application of Research
OMB	Office of Management and Budget
OSHA	Occupational Safety and Health Administration
OTA	Office of Technology Assessment
OTC	Over-the-counter
OVT	Over-the-counter
PAC	Political Action Committee
PBM	Pharmaceutical benefit management
PCCM	Primary care case management
PCIP	Pre-existing condition insurance plan
PET	Positron emission tomography
P4P	Pay for performance

PGPs	Prepaid group plans
PHPs	Prepaid health plans
PhRMA	Pharmaceutical Research and Manufacturers of America
PHS	Public Health Service
PMA	Pharmaceutical Manufacturers of America
PMA	Premarket approval
PMPM	Per member/per month
POS	Point-of-service plan
POW	Prisoner of war
PPACA	Patient Protection and Affordable Care Act
PPOs	Preferred provider organizations
PPRC	Physician Payment Review Commission
PPRS	Pharmaceutical Price Regulation Scheme
PPS	Prospective payment system
PROs	Peer review organizations
PSN	Provider service network
PSO	Provider-sponsored organization
PSRO	Professional standards review organizations
PTSD	Post-traumatic stress disorder
PTSS	Post-traumatic stress symptoms
PRWORA	Personal Responsibility and Work Opportunity Reconcilation Act

QMBs	Qualified Medicare beneficiaries
QuIC	Quality Interagency Coordination Task Force

R&D	Research and development
RBRVS	Resource-based relative value scale
RN	Registered nurse
RVS	Relative value scale
RVU	Relative value unit
RWJF	Robert Wood Johnson Foundation

SAMHSA	Substance Abuse and Mental Health Services Administration
SCHIP	State Children's Health Insurance Program
SEIU	Service Employees International Union
SGR	Sustainable growth rate
SHCA	Society for Healthcare Consumer Advocacy
S/HMOs	Social health maintenance organizations
SLMBs	Specified low-income Medicare beneficiaries
SMI	Supplemental medical insurance
SSI	Supplemental Security Income
STIs	Sexually transmitted infections

TANF	Temporary Assistance to Needy Families
TBI	Traumatic brain injury
TEFRA	Tax Equity and Fiscal Responsibility Act
THCLA	Texas Health Care Liability Act

UCR	Usual, customary, and reasonable (fee payment system)
UHV	Universal health voucher
UIHOs	Urban Indian Health Organizations
UPC	Uniform Probate Code
USAID	United States Agency for International Development
USAMCO	USA Managed Care Organization
USPHS	United States Public Health Service
VA	Veterans Administration
VERA	Veterans Equitable Resource Allocation
VHA	Veterans Health Administration
VISNs	Veterans Integrated Service Networks
VistA	Veterans Health Information System and Technology Architecture
WHI	Women's Health Initiative
ZIFT	Zygote intrafallopian transfer

Healthcare Politics and Policy in America

1

HEALTHCARE POLITICS

Healthcare is one of the more difficult areas of policy making. Healthcare policymakers and providers must deal with a host of issues ranging from jurisdictional authority, financing, organization, and administration of health policy to issues of entrenched interests, ideological and partisan conflicts, value conflicts, equity and justice, access to and quality of care, and life and death (Gauld 2001). Policymakers must address a host of difficult questions: What are the goals of the healthcare system? What do we hope to accomplish with this policy? Should patient participation be voluntary or mandatory? Should there be intermediaries (organizations that accept funds from sponsors to coordinate benefits and provider activities) between healthcare sponsors and healthcare providers? If there are intermediaries, how many should there be, and should they be for-profit or not-for-profit? How many sponsors should there be, and should they be governmental or private organizations? How should healthcare be funded, organized, and administered (Dudley and Luft 1999)? In addition, policy making itself can be influenced by decision-making structures, that is, by the ways that policy-making institutions are organized and the rules by which they operate. It is very difficult to question and dramatically change decision-making structures and processes in healthcare, as in many other policy areas, because those with the greatest means and resources but not necessarily the best scientific evidence often are able to control the definition of what the "truth" is. We cannot ignore the power of money in decision- and policy-making processes in the field of healthcare (Tuulonen 2005).

Policy making in healthcare is often more art than science, since policy making involves struggles over ideas and values (Stone, Deborah 2011). This is illustrated by how numbers—statistics—are used by various actors in health policy making. Statistics are an important tool for policymakers. They often serve as a warning signal indicating the existence or worsening of a problem, and they may be used to measure and evaluate policy outcomes. However, numbers can also be strategically used to further particular political agendas. It is often not the magnitude of numbers but rather the *interpretation* of the numbers that influences policy making (Schlesinger 2004). Unfortunately, a great deal of the debate on healthcare policy is framed in terms of scientific, evidence-based medicine, as if policy decisions are going to be driven by facts rather than values. This is to assume that one can separate facts and values, that evidence is free of context and can be objectively weighed, and that health policy making is essentially an exercise in decision science (Russell et al. 2008). In the real world, however, policy making involves struggles over ideas and values. Debates over health policy are played out through the rhetorical use of language and the strategic portrayal of social situations. Policy making revolves around the naming and framing of a problem, the specification of problem boundaries, and the definition and negotiation of the ideas and values that guide the ways citizens create a shared meaning that motivates them to act (Russell et al. 2008).

It is also important to remember that health policymakers' decisions are influenced by the underlying "politics." Thus, to understand health policy it is important to understand the underlying politics surrounding various health policy issues. Awareness of political factors such as partisanship, voters' views, public opinion, political ideology, values and belief systems, the power of entrenched interest groups, and the nature of media coverage, along with constitutional requirements and institutional arrangements, is essential to understanding health policy making (Blendon and SteelFisher 2009; Theodoulou and Kofinis 2004; Weissert and Weissert 1996).

HEALTH POLICY MAKING IN THE UNITED STATES

Healthcare is the largest single industry in the United States (Skeen 2003). In 2010, the United States spent over $2.5 trillion on healthcare, which amounted to 17.9 percent of the gross domestic product (GDP) (Centers for Medicare and Medicaid Services, n.d.). If spending on healthcare alone guaranteed physical well-being, Americans would be the healthiest people in the world. Unfortunately, spending alone does not ensure a high level of care, as witnessed by the fact that the American healthcare system does not fare well compared to other countries on several indicators such as infant mortality rates and average lifespan. It is not too surprising that the American healthcare system is often described as inefficient and ineffective (Freddi 2009) or as scandalous and wasteful (Dentzer 1990; Taylor 1990).

Health policy making in the United States involves a complex web of decisions made by various institutions and political actors across a broad spectrum of public and private sectors. These institutions and actors include federal, state, and local governments in the public sector. In the private sector they include healthcare providers such as hospitals and nursing homes; healthcare professionals such as physicians; and healthcare purchasers such as insurance companies, industries, and consumers. In addition, a wide variety of interest groups influence and shape healthcare politics and policy making.

These institutions and actors are involved throughout the policy cycle. This cycle includes getting problems to the government and agenda setting; policy formulation and legitimation; budgeting, implementation of, evaluation of, and decisions about policy continuation; and modifications and/ or termination (Jones 1978; Rushefsky 2007). These institutions and actors interact at every stage of the policy cycle. No one institution or actor dominates any one stage of policy development. Each contributes to the process by providing input that often is designed to promote the individual institutions or the actor's own interests (Brown, Lawrence D. 1978).

Some of the problems in healthcare policy making are rooted in this diversity of institutions and actors. Any decision designed to affect the healthcare system generates immediate and heated responses. Any attempt to regulate the healthcare system also produces pressures from opponents of regulation who favor market-oriented approaches to the delivery of healthcare. Government regulations have often been thwarted by those being regulated as well as by actors in the system who oppose a strong government role (J.H.A. Brown 1978).

The development of a comprehensive and consistent healthcare policy is made difficult, if not impossible, by the shotgun approach followed by many policymakers, such as the president and Congress. For example, Congress deals with the most pressing problems one at a time and not in the framework of overall healthcare policy. Such an approach is often necessitated by the political realities of producing tangible results on a short-term basis for the purpose of reelection. Consequently, healthcare policy in the United States is in a constant state of fluidity. It lacks consistency and often encompasses a mishmash of programs involving conflicting values. Policymakers' discretion is often limited by a wide variety of restraints imposed by the policy environment. Just as a policy environment can help facilitate policy making, it can also hinder policy development by the number and types of constraints it imposes on policymakers. The constraints imposed by the policy environment make it difficult for the government to resolve issues in a new or innovative manner (Rosenbaum 1985). The health policy environment can be thought of as a total matrix of factors that influence and shape the health policy cycle. These factors include constitutional or legal requirements, institutional settings, shared understandings about the rules of the game, cultural values of a society, political ideology, economic resources, and technological innovations and their impact on the cost and delivery of healthcare services.

Section I of this book examines the healthcare politics and policy in the United States. Chapter 1 has two goals: to provide a detailed and systematic analysis of the health policy environment that shapes healthcare policy making and to examine the role played by key actors. Chapter 2 provides a historical perspective on the development of healthcare policy and the underlying politics in the United States. Section II of the book examines government's public health safety-net programs created to supplement the largely private U.S. healthcare system. Chapters 3 and 4 respectively examine the Medicaid and Medicare programs. Chapter 5 examines the role of the Indian Health Service and Veterans Health Administration (VHA) in meeting the healthcare needs of the American Indians and Alaska Natives (AI/AN) and veterans of the American wars. Section III looks at problems of access, cost, equality, and quality in the American health system. Chapter 6 examines the problem of the uninsured and the underinsured and healthcare disparities based on gender and race/ethnicity with respect to equality and quality of care. Section IV examines the problem of healthcare costs. In chapter 7 we examine the high cost of care and factors contributing to escalating healthcare costs; chapter 8 provides an analysis of efforts to contain rising healthcare costs by the public and private sectors. In section V, we examine contemporary issues in the American healthcare system. Chapter 9 examines the role of biomedical technology and the ethical dilemmas raised by such technologies; healthcare for undocumented immigrants; and emergency contraceptives. Chapter 10 provides a detailed analysis of the Affordable Care Act (ACA) of 2010, intended to overhaul the American healthcare system. Chapter 11 provides some concluding thoughts about healthcare politics and policy making in the United States and what we might expect in the future.

THE HEALTH POLICY ENVIRONMENT

Constitutional Environment

More than 200 years ago, the Founding Fathers established a constitutional system of government that had two purposes. First, it established a government with powers to act. But second, it also attempted to prevent a tyranny of the majority by creating a national government of limited powers. Having experienced the repressive measures of concentrated power under British rule, the Founding Fathers opted for a decentralized structure of government. The major features of the American system of government, discussed next, reflect these two conflicting objectives.

Separation of Powers, and Checks and Balances

The U.S. Constitution created a system that disperses political power and decision-making authority among various branches of government. The powers of the national government are divided among the legislative, executive, and judicial branches of government. This is known as the separation of powers. The powers of the three branches are not totally separated, however, and thus it is more accurate to describe this arrangement as three coequal branches of government sharing powers. For example, "war powers" are shared by the president and Congress. The Constitution makes the president the commander-in-chief of the armed forces and gives him the power to wage a war, but the power to declare war is given to Congress. The underlying principle behind such a sharing of powers was that it would lead to checks and balances among the three branches of government (Manning 2011). It is based on the assumption that other branches would check an attempt by one branch of government to assume too much power or abuse its powers. James Madison, one of the most influential delegates at the Constitutional Convention, argued in *The Federalist Papers* (No. 51) that "ambition must be made to counteract ambition" (Madison 1961a, 322).

A constitutional system of separation of powers and checks and balances with some exceptions creates constant competition among the three branches of government for preeminence in various policy areas. It necessitates lengthy negotiations and compromises and bargaining in policy making between the president and Congress. This makes it difficult to formulate a consistent and comprehensive set of policies. The result often is a government of deadlock and inaction. The problem becomes more pronounced during the periods of divided government, when different political parties control the White House and Congress. This includes divided control of the Congress itself. Between 1948 and 1992 we experienced divided government 59 percent of the time (twenty-six out of forty-four years) and between 1969 and 1992, 83 percent of the time (twenty out of twenty-four years) (Stanley and Niemi 2001). During the first six years of the Reagan administration (1981–86), the control of Congress itself was divided, with Republicans in the majority in the Senate and Democrats in the majority in the House. Divided government was the norm during the George H.W. Bush administration (1988–92) and the Clinton administration (1993–2000). During the first term of the George W. Bush administration (2001–4), for about a year and a half, Democrats controlled the Senate and Republicans the House. For two and a half years, there was a unified government. In the elections of November 2004, President Bush was reelected and the Republicans retained control of both the House and the Senate. Thus, the unified government continued in the second term of the Bush administration. However, in the election of 2006, the Democratic Party regained a majority in both houses of Congress. When Barack Obama, a Democrat, was elected president in 2008, we had a unified government for the first two years of his administration. However, in the 2010 congressional election, partly as a result of the Republican Party's opposition to the ACA and the passion generated by the conservative Tea Party movement, the Republican Party regained a majority in the House of Representatives, paving the way for a divided government again. While the Democratic Party retained its majority in the U.S. Senate, its majority was reduced. According to congressional expert Joseph Unekis (2011), a divided government is often the recipe for political gridlock, and he predicted that the 112th Congress elected in 2010 would not be an exception and that Congress would fail to accomplish much of anything.

Can presidents hope to be effective in policy making when Congress is controlled by the other party, that is, during a period of divided government? Some have tended to blame divided government for policy gridlock within Congress and between executive and legislatives branches of government (Galderisi, Herzberg, and McNamara 1996). One of the tests of the impact of divided government on legislative gridlock is to examine seriously considered, potentially important legislation that failed to pass under conditions of divided and unified government. Edwards, Barrett, and Peake (1997, 545), using regression analysis, concluded, "Presidents oppose significant legislation more often under divided government, and much more important legislation fails to pass under divided government than under unified government. Furthermore, the odds of important legislation failing to pass are greater under divided government." According to Badger (2010), divided government, more often than not, does not force parties to the center of the compromise and causes gridlock.

Some have argued that divided government may work better because it requires the president to reach out to members of the other party to create majority support for his programs. For example, Niskanen (2003) points to the fact that the Reagan tax laws of 1981 and 1986 were both approved by a House of Representatives controlled by the Democrats. He further argues that the rate of growth of real (inflation-adjusted) federal spending tends to be lower during periods of divided governments. Similarly, some of the policy successes of President Clinton, such as the North Atlantic Free Trade Agreement (NAFTA) and welfare reform, were the result of his success in getting support from Republicans in Congress (Galderisi et al. 1996; Niskanen 2003). In the health policy area, the passage of the State Children's Health Insurance Program (SCHIP) in 1997 and the Health Insurance and Portability and Accountability Act (HIPAA) in 1996 are examples of policy accomplishments during a period of divided government between a Republican-controlled

Congress and a Democratic president. Similarly, the passage of the Medicare Prescription Drug, Improvement, and Modernization Act (MPDIMA) of 2003 stands as an example of bipartisan cooperation between a Republican president, George W. Bush, and a Democrat-controlled Congress. Clearly, divided government in the past has produced some big accomplishments such as the Clean Air Act in the 1970s, tax reform in the 1980s, and welfare reform in the 1990s. However, during the 1960s and 1970s, 30 to 40 percent of the members of Congress were ideological moderates, which often made compromise on major important legislation possible. Increased partisanship in Congress had made such compromises more difficult.

Foley and Owens (1996) have argued that during the last three decades, the way in which Congress and presidents operate and interact has changed since the Republicans won control of Congress in 1994 and the advent of Newt Gingrich's "Contract with America." Conley (2003) makes a very persuasive argument that the conditions of "divided government" have changed significantly in recent years and recent administrations have faced a very different playing field than those in the earlier postwar years. This has happened because of changes in electoral politics that have reduced presidential coattails, lack of presidents' popularity in opposition members' districts, changes in institutional setting in Congress such as more assertive legislative majorities, changes in leadership structure, and increased party cohesion in voting. These changes have made it more difficult for the president to achieve his policy agenda in Congress. In response, to overcome such obstacles, presidents have come to rely on the use of presidential signing statements—written documents issued contemporaneously with the signing of a law in which the president states his objections to the law, including the reservation of the right not to enforce or comply with the law. Under the administration of George W. Bush, we witnessed a massive proliferation in the number of such presidential signing statements (Biller 2008).

Some scholars have taken a middle approach on the questions of divided government and legislative gridlock. For example, Ewing and Kysar (2011) have argued that, ironically, the constitutional division of authority between the three branches of government and the system of checks and balances it creates can constrain collective political action on the one hand, while on the other hand creating a system of "prods and pleas" in which policymakers in different branches of government can push each other to entertain collective political action when necessary. They further argue that the prods and pleas are a fail-safe mechanism for a limited government. Pandich (2007) has argued that the constitutional separation of powers and the resulting checks and balances do not always result in conflict and competition, because occasionally one branch of government shows considerable deference to another branch even in matters on which they might be expected to conflict. Nzelibe and Stephenson (2010) suggest that separation of powers does not necessarily induce gridlock or reduce the likelihood of policy change. Krehbiel (1996) has argued that gridlock occurs in divided and unified government alike.

Even during periods of unified government (when the same party controls the White House and the Congress), one of which occurred for a brief time after the 1992 elections (1992–94), institutional jealousies and prerogatives made policy making a problematic adventure. The Health Security Act (HSA) of 1993, designed to overhaul the U.S. healthcare system, failed partly because the Democrats themselves were divided over the Clinton plan. But more importantly, Republicans had no interest in compromising with the Democratic president, because they wanted to use the failure to pass healthcare reform as a campaign issue in the 1994 congressional election. Their political strategy worked, since this period of unified government lasted for only two years as the Republican Party gained control of both houses of Congress in the 1994 congressional elections, producing a divided government (Schantz 2001). American political parties are not strictly ideologically driven and are more like a coalition of different interests; a unified government does not guarantee success for the president, as demonstrated by difficulties of the Carter administration and the first two years of the Clinton administration (Galderisi et al. 1996). It is important to emphasize that over the last two decades or so, the Republican Party has become an ideologically more cohesive party as most of the moderate and liberal Republicans were driven out of the party or had decided not to run for reelection. The rise of the Tea Party movement has accelerated this trend. In contrast, the Democratic Party still largely remains an ideologically diverse party with liberals/progressives, moderates, and conservatives in its fold. Thus, even during the period of unified government during the first two years of the Obama administration, not only did the administration not receive any support from the Republicans, but also many conservative Democrats did not support President Obama's ACA (particularly in the House), and the administration had to rely on parliamentary maneuvering to pass the law by a slim majority (Mann and Ornstein 2006, 2012).

Federalism

A federal system of government is one in which the powers of the government are divided up between the national (central) government and its constituent units, that is, states. The national government and state governments share sovereignty. The Constitution gives exclusive authority over certain matters to the national government and over others to the states. Both levels of government are free to act in their areas of authority. Certain powers are shared by both levels of government. The residual or leftover powers are given to either the national government or the states. In a federal system, state government enjoys a considerable amount of autonomy and freedom. The actual balance of powers between the national and state governments may vary from one federal system to another. Examples of a federal system of government include the United States, Canada, and India. The advantages claimed for the federal system include regional autonomy and freedom, policy flexibility, innovations, and experimentation.

In a unitary system of government, the national government possesses all the power and is sovereign in all matters. It may delegate some of its powers to the states and may take them back. The state government enjoys only those powers that the national government delegates to it. The national government creates and is free to abolish them. Examples of a unitary system of government include Great Britain, Israel, France, and Finland. The advantages claimed for a unitary system include uniformity of laws and policies throughout the country, promotion of equality, and ability to act quickly and decisively. The reasons for a country to adopt a federal or unitary system of government depend on historical developments, shared experiences, practicality, and views about the use and exercise of power.

The U.S. Constitution, without even mentioning the word "federalism," created a federal system of government. An examination of various provisions in the Constitution reveals that it gives exclusive authority over certain subjects to the national government (e.g., foreign and defense matters), and state governments have the authority to legislate on all matters within their jurisdiction. States' "police power" does not arise from the Constitution but is viewed as an inherent characteristic of the states' territorial sovereignty (Thomas 2008). Certain powers, such as the power to tax, are shared by all levels of government. The Tenth Amendment to the Constitution specifies that powers not specifically given to the national government nor denied to the states are reserved for the states and its people. The Fourteenth Amendment to the Constitution also provides for the notion of dual citizenship, national and state.

Why did the Founding Fathers opt for a federal system of government? The U.S. federal system of government came about as a result of the Founding Fathers' desire to reconcile two strong but opposing forces: the need to give the national government more authority and at the same time distrust of a single sovereign power. The Founders realized that the Articles of Confederation had failed because under it, state government had too much authority and the national government was too weak to be effective in governing a new nation. On the other hand, Founders feared too strong and powerful a national government as a threat to individual liberty and freedom. Their solution was a federal system. The new Constitution gave the national government stronger powers and at the same time created a government of limited powers, protecting individual liberty and states' rights (Bovbjerg, Wiener, and Houseman 2003). The hope was that such a division of powers between the national and state government, like the idea of separation of powers, would create a system of checks and balances between the two levels (Nathan 2006). Despite the best efforts to divide up the power and authority between the national and state governments, some ambiguity in the allocation of power remained, creating a built-in tension between the levels of government.

Given that the Constitution was written and put into effect in the eighteenth century, perhaps it is not too surprising that there is no discussion of power over healthcare. However, two enumerated powers granted to the national government in the Constitution—Congress's power to tax and spend for the general welfare (James Madison viewed the "general welfare" clause as tied directly to national government's enumerated powers), and Congress's power to regulate interstate commerce—significantly influenced the development of health policy in the United States. The national government's power and responsibilities in the health area grew and expanded through various intergovernmental mechanisms such as grants-in-aid and healthcare financing, federal emergency relief to states, the national government's health safety-net programs such as Medicare, Medicaid, and SCHIP, and funded and unfunded mandates and regulations (Colby 2002).

Thus, perhaps it is not too surprising that the controversy over whether power and authority should be more centralized in the national government or more decentralized in state and local governments has been a perennial question in American politics. In addition, both the national and the state governments have often delegated important functions to thousands of units of local government. As a result, it is difficult to find many governmental activities that do not, to some extent, involve all three levels of government. Thus, despite the increased role of the federal government in the healthcare field during the 1960s, overall authority over health policy remains divided and shared among the national, state, and local governments. This is especially true with respect to implementation of many health policies and programs. In fact, the Reagan administration's desire to decentralize authority led to an increased role for state governments in the implementation of health programs (Thompson 1986). In 1995, the Republican-controlled Congress proposed shifting more authority over social programs, including healthcare, to the states. This devolution of authority to states in the health policy area was evident during the Clinton administration. The administration of George W. Bush continued this trend by giving states more discretion in a variety of policy areas such as education and welfare and, especially in the Medicaid program, by giving state governments more flexibility to experiment with the program (Dinan 2008; Thompson and DiIulio 1998). The controversy over the role of the state versus the national government in health policy, finance, and reform has been a steady staple of scholarly debate in American politics (Adler 2011; Beland and Vergniolle de Chantal 2004; DiIulio and Nathan 1994; France 2008; Greer and Jacobson 2010; Hackey and Rochefort 2001; Holahan, Weil, and Wiener 2003; Nathan 2005; Peterson 2001; Plein 2010; and Rich and White 1996).

To what extent do the constitutional arrangements such as federal structure of government influence the type of public policies in general and health policy in particular that are produced? Does federalism make a difference? Of course, as Banting and Corbett (2002) have suggested, political institutions alone are never determinative. Constitutional and institutional factors interact with other factors in shaping health policies. Thus, one can never assert that the federal structure of government leads to policy X. On the other hand, structures of governments are never completely neutral, because they make some outcomes easier than others. Experts and scholars are divided about whether the national or state government should have more powers and whether the federal structure of government has positive or negative effects on policy making. The arguments range from philosophical to practical.

Bovbjerg et al. (2003) provide an excellent analysis of arguments in favor of giving national or state government more powers. Those who advocate that state governments should be given more powers argue that geographically smaller governments know and represent citizens' values more, they know the unique nature of citizens' problems, and they can offer better solutions to those problems. In addition, they argue that interstate competition pressures states to improve their performance and attract and keep citizens and businesses. State governments can act as laboratories of democracy by experimenting with different policies, and such policies work better when implemented from the bottom up rather than the top down. On the other hand, proponents of giving more powers to the national government argue that national citizenship enjoys constitutional primacy and only the national government can provide uniformity and equality in areas such as civil rights because certain rights and responsibilities should not vary across states. Further they argue that interstate competition promotes a race to the bottom rather than a race to the top among states. Interstate competition can also lead to flight to the top, resulting in lower tax rates and revenue. Finally, proponents of giving more powers to the national government argue that certain problems are inherently national in scope, and solving them requires the greater fiscal capacity of the national government (Bovbjerg et al. 2003).

With respect to the impact of federal structure on policy making, some have argued that a federal system of government adds to the fragmentation of authority and thus increases complexity, jurisdictional competition, delays, duplication, finger pointing, and often the dodging of responsibilities by different levels of government in the health policy cycle. Attempts to reconcile many different geographical interests become problematic and tend to perpetuate a belief in organized chaos and flexible rules over central policy-making authority. The problem of regionalism and localism is accentuated by the need to satisfy the demands of a diverse and heterogeneous society. Thus, no single institution representing the nation as a whole defines the public interest and serves the public good. The result is a healthcare system made up of multiple "little governments" and "little empires" that pursue their own goals and interests. This, in turn, generates health policies that are vaguely defined and designed to serve "special publics" (Altenstetter 1974, 26–27). Another negative effect of the federal structure often mentioned is that the federal system makes government slow to respond to new challenges because of the cumbersome nature of decision and policy making as well as implementation structures (Nathan 2005). Others have argued that federal structure leads to state policy innovations and cooperation and work-sharing policies between different governments (Balducchi and Wander 2008).

The continuing debate in America politics for over a hundred years about the nature and meaning of American federalism suggests the tension and struggle between the national and state governments over power and authority to make and implement policies is likely to continue into the future. After examining the historical account of the founding of the federal system, Purcell (2009) observed that the Founders disagreed more and settled less with regard to federalism.

What is clear from the above discussion is that health policy making in the United States is a very complex process involving the private and public sectors, including multiple levels of government, and the distribution of authority and responsibility within the federal system does impact the making and implementation of health policy (Lee and Estes 1983).

Institutional Environment

The institutional environment consists of the rules, structures, and settings within which major institutions involved in policy making and implementation operate. These include the legislative, executive, and judicial branches of government. Congress is the primary policy-making institution, while the executive is primarily responsible for implementing policies. The judiciary's principal responsibility is to resolve constitutional and legal conflicts. Since the beginning of the twentieth century, however, these areas of responsibility have become increasingly blurred, with all three branches of government sharing powers in the areas of policy making, implementation, and adjudication.

The Congress

Policy making in Congress takes place in an environment of a decentralized and fragmented power structure where political power is dispersed among numerous committees and subcommittees in both chambers. This decentralization of power and authority in the committee structure has led some to describe Congress as a "kind of confederation of little legislatures" (Huitt 1970, 410). One of the consequences of this in health policy making is competition among committees within and between the Senate and the House. The second consequence for health policy making is bargaining and compromises. Thus, health policy formulation in Congress occurs in numerous subsystems with little coordination (Brown, Lawrence D. 1978). In the 104th Congress (1995–96), the Republican majority attempted to coordinate committee action under tight leadership control. House Speaker Newt Gingrich brought about more centralization of power in the House. He often stepped in and overruled committee chairmen on a range of significant legislation. This shift of power in the Speaker's office led at times to loss of autonomy of committee chairs. However, in general, the ability of an individual to maintain discipline over party members and exercise policy expertise is often found only in chairs of committees and subcommittees (Koszczuk 1995).

Senators and representatives are elected to represent their respective states and smaller congressional districts, which leads to an emphasis on pork-barrel politics to capture federal goods and services for their constituencies. This creates a tendency to promote state and local interests and less sensitivity to national interests and needs in healthcare policy making.

Recent research suggests that caucuses have become a critical feature of the congressional policy-making landscape. A caucus refers to members of Congress who form themselves into small groups because of shared interests and meet regularly to promote causes they believe in. For example, Burgin (2003), after examining the important role played by the Diabetes Caucus in successfully pushing diabetes-related legislation through Congress, suggests that the role of caucuses in policy making in Congress is unappreciated. Such caucuses may be based on race/ethnicity such as a "Hispanic" or "African American" caucus, or gender such as "Women's Caucus" or a specific issue such as the "Diabetes Caucus." She further argues that caucuses often act as a "policy entrepreneur" waiting for a window of opportunity to open to push their legislative agenda through Congress (Burgin 2003).

Research also suggests that policy making in Congress has become more problematic because of increased ideological polarization as well as increased partisanship, making it difficult to engage in bargaining, compromises, and consensus building. Members who are elected from safe congressional districts (districts with very little two-party competition) are more likely to engage in partisan conflict even though partisanship damages the collective reputation of the Congress as an institution (Harbridge and Malhotra 2011). Ramirez (2009), after examining the quarterly congressional-approval data from 1974 to 2000 to determine the consequences of partisan conflict on congressional approval, concluded that over time, changes in partisan conflict within the legislature have a direct and lasting effect on how citizens think about Congress. The increased ideological polarization and partisanship is also often accompanied by what Uslaner (1993) calls the decline of comity in Congress, that is, of the adherence to a set of norms including courtesy and reciprocity. In September 2009, during President Obama's speech to the joint session of Congress explaining his healthcare reform legislation, Republican Congressman Joe Wilson from South Carolina shouted, "You lie!" shocking many members of Congress and viewers. This is a perfect example of the decline in comity in Congress. This issue of partisanship and ideological polarization is discussed further in the section on consensus building.

One of the consequences of the unwillingness to compromise and bargain due to increased partisanship and ideological polarization is that Congress has come to rely on a full range of unusual special procedures and processes, such as filling the amendment tree (Senate), fewer conferences, more formal amendments, and earmarks and changes in the appropriation process. Sinclair (2012) refers to it as making nonincremental policy change through hyper-unorthodox procedures. She cites the Bush-Pelosi-Boehner Stimulus Bill of 2008, the America Recovery and Reinvestment Act (ARRA) of 2009, and the Patient Protection and Affordability Care Act (PPACA) of 2010 as recent examples of nonincremental policy changes made through hyper-unorthodox procedures. The chapter on healthcare reform further illustrates the use of such procedures.

The Executive

The Constitution assigns the president and the executive branch agencies (i.e., the bureaucracy) the role of implementing policies approved by Congress. In contrast to Congress, at least in theory, power in the executive branch is more centralized because the Constitution makes the president the chief executive. The executive branch is headed by one person, and the president is the highest official in the executive branch. Yet he does not directly control about 85 percent of the civil servants who work in the executive branch, because they are hired and promoted through a competitive civil service exam, and firing a civil servant is a slow and cumbersome process. The president appoints only about 15 percent of top "political executives"—executive department heads and the like who serve at the pleasure of the president. This institutional feature is designed to make bureaucracy provide continuity from one administration to the next and to make bureaucracy semi-independent and impartial and not subject to the whims of political bosses who are elected to office for a fixed term and do not hold their office permanently. Even though the president is the chief executive, there are constraints on his ability to significantly influence the executive branch. He can accomplish some changes through executive orders, but any major reorganization of the executive branch requires congressional approval.

When it comes to presidential policy making, it is said that the president proposes and Congress disposes; that is, the president proposes major policy initiatives and Congress acts on them by either accepting, modifying, or rejecting presidential initiatives. Presidents have been making policy since the time of George Washington and have become increasingly active in agenda setting, decision making, coalition building, and implementation of government policies (Light 2000). However, as Jones (1994) reminds us, the United States does not have a presidential system, and the president's impact on domestic policy is shaped by resources, advantages, and strategic position. Furthermore, in the last two decades or so, two changes in the policy process—what a president decides and how a president decides—have changed. Evidence suggests that domestic policy is becoming less responsive to presidential intent due to issue polarization that surrounds the presidential policy process and institutionalization and formalization; in other words, the bureaucratization of presidential policy making. There has been a balkanization of the White House policy process, and new problems are addressed by creating more structures and organizations (Light 2000). Krause (2004) suggests that the singular decline in presidential domestic policy making can be attributed to the increased size and scope of the institutional presidency. Suboptimal organizational size and scope of presidency have led to the deterioration of the president's advantages in policy making vis-à-vis Congress.

Increased partisanship, ideological and issue polarization, and divided government have made it difficult for the president and Congress to compromise and work together. This has led presidents to use techniques such as making recess appointments as a way to bypass the Senate's advice and consent role (Black et al. 2007), signing statements or conditions (Biller 2008), and adopting new "interpretations" of statutes to further their policy goals and agenda (Luton 2009).

It is also important to recognize the important role played by bureaucratic agencies in health policy making. Congress routinely delegates the authority for making many decisions to bureaucratic agencies. For example, Congress created the Occupational Safety and Health Administration (OSHA) and gave it the authority to write regulations concerning workers' health, safety, and privacy in the workplace. In addition, Congress often passes laws that are vague, very broad, or both, leaving bureaucratic agencies a significant amount of discretionary power to fill in the details of the law. Congress uses its legislative oversight and budgetary powers to exercise control over bureaucratic agencies. Nevertheless, the fact remains that congressional delegation of authority and discretionary power enjoyed by bureaucratic agencies gives them a significant role in health policy making and implementation.

As with Congress, power and authority in the bureaucracy is highly dispersed and fragmented. Various health policies are under the jurisdiction of many different federal agencies, which in turn creates overlapping jurisdictions, authority, and responsibilities. In addition, as we discussed earlier, in a federal system of government, state bureaucracies implement many federal programs either partially or totally. Such dispersal and fragmentation of authority creates competition and conflicts along both vertical and horizontal planes throughout the health policy cycle. Turf fighting over program implementation, authority, and resources becomes the name of the game. The health policy cycle operates in a dynamic environment of constantly changing alignments of bureaucratic agencies, congressional committees, policymakers, and various interest groups shaping and reshaping health policy.

In the health policy area during the 1960s, concerns about issues of access, quality, equity, and efficiency led Congress to create many programs such as Medicare and Medicaid to increase access. Creation of such programs was made possible through bargaining and compromises, and thus they were passed with bipartisan votes in Congress. Similarly, during the 1970s and 1980s, concerns over spiraling costs resulted in the creation of programs designed to contain those costs through planning, peer review, regulation, and encouragement of the development of new healthcare delivery organizations such as health maintenance organizations (HMOs). These policies often reflected ideological as well as partisan compromises. However, increased partisanship and the ideological divide beginning in the 1990s led to the demise of President Clinton's Health Security Act of 1993. The proposed reform designed to overhaul the U.S. healthcare system failed to get even an up or down vote in Congress because of internal divisions within the Democratic Party itself, as well as the Republican Party's unwillingness to compromise and give the president a major legislative victory during an election year. Similarly, the ACA of 2010 passed along a strong party-line vote in Congress. Only one Republican senator voted for the bill, and in the House it failed to receive a single Republican vote.

The Judiciary

The standard and general explanation of American government and policy making is that Congress makes the law, the executive branch agencies implement the law, and the courts apply the law as written as long as such laws are constitutional. In this explanation, courts and judges are viewed as influencing policy making and implementation only indirectly and only to a limited extent.

Courts and judges influence health policy making and implementation by the way in which they interpret the Constitution and laws. They make sure that implementation of laws meets constitutional standards and that administrative agencies discharge their assigned responsibilities. Federal courts are also responsible for enforcement of the Administrative Procedures Act, which governs administrative procedures in all federal agencies. In addition, individuals and groups who feel that the executive and legislative branches have failed to redress their grievances often resort to seeking help from the courts.

Miller and Barnes (2004) challenge this standard explanation of American government and policy making. They argue that no one dominant institution or even a consistent pattern of relationships exists among various players in the federal policy-making process. They argue that at different times and under different circumstances, all branches of government play a role not only in making public policy but also in enforcing and legitimizing public policies as well. Epstein and Knight (1998) suggest that justices realize that their ability to achieve their policy and other goals depends on the preferences of other actors and choices they expect others to make as well as the institutional context in which they act. Thus, they take such factors into account in their decision making. In fact, judicial process operates at the intersection of law and politics, and courts not only enforce norms and resolve disputes but also engage in policy making and shape the fundamental power relationships between various institutions in American politics (Porto 2009).

Thus, the view that American courts and judges are policymakers has become accepted wisdom among political scientists (Bloom 2001). In fact, Malcolm and Rubin (2000) argue that policy making is a standard and legitimate function of the modern courts. They provide a detailed analysis of how between 1965 and 1990, federal judges in almost all of the states handed down sweeping rulings that affected virtually every prison and jail in the United States. The federal courts formulated and implemented major prison reform policies. Law (2010) provides an analysis of the federal judiciary's role in the nation's immigration policy. Similarly, after examining the active role played by the courts in Medicaid nursing facility reimbursement, Miller (2008) concludes that neither the executive nor the judiciary acts in isolation, but instead they often serve as tandem institutions in guiding federal oversight of state policy making.

The federal courts in general and the U.S. Supreme Court in particular have come to play a significant role in policy making in certain aspects of the healthcare field. The Supreme Court's 1973 decision in *Roe v. Wade,* effectively legalizing abortion, was a major policy decision and a victory for groups supporting a woman's right to have an abortion. But a 1989 decision by the Supreme Court (*Webster v. Reproductive Health Services*), whereby the Supreme Court granted states authority to regulate and thus restrict abortions in public clinics, also suggests that the Court's position may change with changes in the composition of justices on the Court. Whether a more conservative Supreme Court in the future overturns *Roe v. Wade* remains to be seen.

Similarly, the impact of healthcare technology on the treatment and delivery of health services and the ethical concerns raised by medical technology have drawn state and federal courts into such varied topics as reproductive rights, organ transplants, stem cell research, healthcare surrogacy, quality of life, and the right to die with dignity, among others (see Patel and Rushefsky 2002).

What is interesting to note is that by the Supreme Court's decision in *Bush v. Gore*, which effectively ended the 2000 presidential election in favor of George W. Bush, the Supreme Court made itself the object of controversy, with opponents of the decision calling it "partisan" and "stealing the election" (Nicholson and Howard 2003). The decision had also shaken the faith of many in the legal academics in the Supreme Court because of the belief that the Court was motivated more by partisanship and not constitutional principle (Balkin 2001). After the decision, the perception of the U.S. Supreme Court changed dramatically among Americans based on their political party affiliation. According to Gallup polls, in September 2000 (prior to the decision), 70 percent of the Democrats, 60 percent of the Republicans, and 57 percent of the independents approved of the job the Supreme Court was doing. In January 2001 (post-Bush v. Gore decision), only 42 percent of the Democrats, 80 percent of the Republicans, and 54 percent of the independents approved of the Supreme Court's job performance. The Court's job approval rating dropped dramatically among Democrats while approval rating increased dramatically among Republicans. Despite this change in perception of the U.S. Supreme Court in the different segment of the population, the Court overall has continued to enjoy public legitimacy. In September 2009, 59 percent of Americans approved the job the U.S. Supreme Court was doing ("Rating of Supreme Court Improves as Partisans Switch Sides" 2009).

However, a different perception of the Supreme Court based on political party affiliation has continued. After the passage of the ACA, over twenty lawsuits were filed, including a lawsuit by twenty-six Republican state attorneys general challenging the constitutionality of the health insurance mandate and the law itself. There was a partisan divide among trial court judges who ruled on the law, fueling further partisan passion surrounding the healthcare reform law (Cunningham 2011; Mondics 2012; and Savage and Levey 2011). Many of these cases were combined into one major case which the U.S. Supreme Court agreed to hear.

The U.S. Supreme Court in March 2012, in the case of *National Federation of Independent Businesses, et al. v. Sebelius, Secretary of Health and Human Services, et al.*, heard three days of oral arguments challenging the constitutionality of the "individual mandate," expansion of the Medicaid program, and the whole law itself. Prior to the Court's ruling, in a Bloomberg National Poll, three-quarters of Americans stated that the U.S. Supreme Court will be influenced by politics when it rules on the constitutionality of the health insurance law. In fact, this sentiment ran across political party lines, with 80 percent of independents, 74 percent of Democrats, and 67 percent of Republicans expressing the belief that the Court will not base its ruling solely on legal merits, and politics will play a part in the Court's decision (Bykowicz and Stohr 2012).

The U.S. Supreme Court on June 28, 2012, announced its decision in the case. The Court ruled in favor of the law when it ruled by a vote of 5 to 4 that the individual mandate was constitutional under Congress's taxing power but not under Congress's power to regulate interstate commerce. The Court also ruled 7 to 2 that states must be allowed to opt out of the Medicaid expansion without losing their matching federal fund under the original Medicaid program.

In a poll conducted by ABC News/Washington Post between June 30 and July 1, 2012, 43 percent stated that they had a favorable opinion of the Court's ruling, while 42 percent expressed an unfavorable opinion. However, the poll revealed strong divisions along partisan and ideological lines about the Court's ruling. Seventy percent of Democrats and 65 percent of liberals expressed a favorable opinion of the Court's ruling, while 83 percent of Republicans and 69 percent of conservatives expressed a negative opinion of the ruling (ABC News/Washington Post Poll 2012). This again suggests that the American public has come to view the U.S. Supreme Court and its rulings through partisan and ideological lenses.

The discussion above points to the interconnection of federal judiciary and politics. Federal judges are appointed by the president and confirmed or rejected by the U.S. Senate. Among the many criteria considered by the president in his selection of candidates for the federal judiciary are nominee's party affiliation, political ideology, and judicial philosophy. That is why historically, Democratic presidents have largely nominated Democrats to the judiciary, and Republican presidents have largely nominated Republicans. Similarly, senators' own party affiliation and ideology plays a role in their decision to confirm or reject a nominee. Supreme Court nominations have failed to be confirmed by the Senate with some regularity since the early days of the Republic, but in recent years, increased partisan and ideological polarization has led to more gridlock between the president and the Senate over nominations to the federal judiciary. The possibility of divided government further exacerbates the difficulty of achieving cooperation by increasing uncertainty about both the benefits of cooperative behavior and the costs of retaliation (Law 2005).

Political Environment

The political environment includes a shared understanding among policymakers about how policy decisions should be made and of underlying values, political feasibility, electoral cycles, influence of organized interest groups, and political ideologies. The political environment itself is influenced and shaped by the constitutional, legal, institutional, economic, and technological environment of a given policy area.

Consensus Building

We have already discussed how the constitutional and institutional environments create diffused and fragmented systems of authority and responsibility in the health policy cycle. This in turn creates a political environment that is conducive to constant bargaining and compromises among major institutions and key actors in the health policy field. Since no single institution or actor is in a position to dominate the process, coalition building becomes inevitable. It also injects logrolling (trading votes to secure favors) and pork-barrel politics (obtaining government projects for one's legislative district) into the policy adoption and implementation stages. One of the consequences of this environment is that the policy-making process is invariably driven toward consensus building among diverse and conflicting interests, which often results in contradictory policies or policies that contain conflicting values (Allison 1971). Thus, the policy-making process, instead of being a science of creating policy that solves a problem, becomes an art of creating a consensus that holds conflicting and diverse interests together in order to create majority support for that policy. The political logic of coalition building in order to create a consensus creates a situation in which any measure that is successful, be it congressional or presidential, will have been changed in ways its proponents did not foresee or desire (Brown, Lawrence D. 1978). Attempts at comprehensive change, as in the healthcare reform debate of the 1990s and other attempts at national health insurance, often fail.

As we have mentioned earlier in this chapter, political compromises and consensus building between political parties in Congress and between the president and Congress have become more difficult in recent years due to increased political polarization in American society. This polarization is reflected in increased partisan differences in congressional voting behavior (voting along party line) and low-level or lack of party competition in congressional districts (McCarty, Poole, and Rosenthal 2009).

What are the causes of increased polarization? One often cited is partisan gerrymandering, in which congressional districts are drawn and redrawn by the majority party in state legislatures for partisan advantage. As congressional districts become less competitive and it becomes easy to get reelected, representatives no longer feel the need to reach out to moderate and independent voters. However, McCarty, Poole, and Rosenthal (2009) point out many problems with this explanation. First, they argue that the U.S. Senate has experienced polarization along with the U.S. House, and since gerrymandering is not an issue in U.S. Senate elections, it plays no role. They suggest that polarization in the House is the result of within-district divergence between the voting records of Democrats and Republicans (Republican representatives have compiled an increasingly more conservative record than Democrats have) and an increase in the congruence between a district's characteristics and the party of its representative (Republicans are more likely to represent a more conservative district). Along the same line, Quirk (2011) has argued that political polarization is more a function of what he calls "polarized populism," a condition of politics in which elected officials accord a great deal of deference to regular citizens, especially those who hold relatively extreme ideological views. In other words, increased partisan voting and ideological polarization in Congress simply reflects increased partisan and ideological polarization of the American electorate.

Gutmann and Thompson (2010) attribute the source of political polarization to the intrusion of campaigning into governing—the "permanent campaign" in which lines between campaigning and governing are blurred and campaigning becomes part and parcel of governing. Permanent campaigning encourages political attitudes and arguments that make compromises more difficult. They call this "uncompromising mindset." They argue that the uncompromising mindset marked by principled tenacity and mutual distrust is well suited for campaigning, but to govern a nation, what is needed is a compromising mindset characterized by principled prudence and mutual respect. To govern effectively, politicians (policymakers) must find ways to reach agreement with their political opponents across ideological and party lines. The most recent example of such an uncompromising mindset was the passage of the ACA of 2010. The debate surrounding the bill was one of the most intensely partisan legislative battles in many years. Very little, if any, compromises were made in the bill between Democrats and Republicans in Congress as it went through the legislative track and became the law (Frakes 2012).

Others have argued that partisan bickering is highlighted more today than in the past through traditional and nontraditional media outlets in the forms of radio and TV talk shows, blogs, newspapers, and magazines. In the television world, for example, FOX and MSNBC act respectively as a conservative and progressive/liberal voice. Some have blamed the increased political polarization on increased partisan and ideological news coverage by American media outlets (Frakes 2012). In fact, in recent years, there has been an increased blurring of lines between news, opinions, entertainment, and show business.

Regardless of the sources of increased partisanship and political polarization, one thing is clear. It has made the processes of policy making and governing through bargaining, compromises, and consensus building more difficult.

Incrementalism and Punctuated Equilibrium

Policymakers also share decision-making values that favor incremental policy making, that is, relatively small or incremental changes and modifications in existing policies. Thus, rather than consider all possible alternatives in a comprehensive manner, policymakers concentrate only on marginal values or relatively few alternatives that bring about marginal changes in existing policies, that is, incrementalism (Lindblom 1959). The incremental theory of policy making posits that the policy-making process should involve bargaining, delay, and compromises that lead to incremental change in public policies. Incrementalism itself is viewed as a natural by-product of a system of checks and balances in which policymakers disagree over policy goals and how best to achieve them (Hayes 2001, 2006).

Incremental policy making is politically attractive to policymakers because small policy adjustments reduce the impact of negative and politically risky consequences. Nevertheless, incremental policy making can also inhibit imagination, innovation, and fresh new approaches to the solution of problems (Rosenbaum 1985). Policymakers end up creating policies aimed at "satisfying" diverse interests, rather than problem solving. Herbert Simon (1957) first introduced the term "satisficing" to describe an outcome that is good enough. In other words, "satisficing" involves behavior that attempts to achieve some minimum level of a particular variable but does not strive to achieve its maximum possible value. He called this "bounded rationality."

While it is true that policy making in the United States largely follows a pattern of incremental changes, major and significant policy changes have occurred from time to time in American history, such as the creation of Social Security and welfare programs, Medicare and Medicaid, and the prescription drug coverage program. Incremental theory fails to explain such major policy changes. Recent research has suggested that the punctuated equilibrium theory better explains policy making and policy outcomes (Robinson and Carver 2006).

The theory of punctuated equilibrium was first presented by Baumgartner and Jones (1993, 2009) in their book *Agendas and Instability in American Politics* and further refined in the second edition. They draw our attention to forces in politics that create stability as well as forces that make dramatic changes and innovations in public policy possible. According to them, such punctuations come rarely, but they can produce long-lasting consequences. The political system, at times, creates opportunities and makes it possible for dramatic policy changes to occur occasionally. However, such changes are rare because most efforts to produce significant changes fail, and no single policy actor's behavior determines the outcome. Rather, the policy process depends on interaction and expectation of several players in the process. A sluggish political system can act suddenly if outside pressure becomes strong enough and reaches a tipping point, forcing a political system to act (Baumgartner 2006). For example, the Great Depression and resulting economic crisis led to the election of Franklin Roosevelt and created a receptive climate for the adoption of the New Deal programs. Determinants of policy change are characterized by positive and negative feedback. Since negative feedbacks threaten existing policies, entrenched interests that favor the status quo rise up to beat back the forces demanding change. Sources of negative feedback include structural and institutional as well as behavioral factors, such as division of powers between national and state governments in a federal system; separation and diffusion of power between and within political institutions such as the executive, legislative, and judicial branches of government; and the tendency of entrenched interests to mobilize to support the status quo and oppose policy change. This negative feedback must be counterbalanced with positive feedback. Sources of positive feedback include factors such as the bandwagon effect for a change, social learning, strong public opinion demanding change, and intense media attention paid to a policy issue. When a positive feedback force reaches a critical mass, or tipping point, forces of entrenched interests can be defeated, making major policy change and innovation possible (Repetto 2006).

Static, cross-sectional theory of incrementalism is challenged by punctuated equilibrium theory, which involves time-series analysis of dynamic processes in which an extended period of stability (incrementalism) is punctuated by short periods of instability during which major policy changes can take place, bypassing entrenched interests. In other words, public policies alternate between stasis and punctuation. The punctuated equilibrium theory itself has led to examination of the role of information processing in policy making (Breunig and Koski 2006; Givel 2010; Pump 2011; Robinson et al. 2007; Wood 2006; Workman and Jochim 2009).

Political Feasibility

Policymakers are also influenced and guided in their policy deliberations by political feasibility (Huitt 1970). This involves judgment about whether it is possible to enact a policy given the political realities. One of the major political realities that policymakers face is the potential public reaction to a proposed policy. All the major institutions and actors involved in policy making are influenced by considerations of political feasibility. This is especially true of elected public officials. Members of Congress are more apt to support and vote for a policy that is likely to be popular with their constituents than a policy that may produce a strong negative reaction from them. For example, members are more likely to support tax cuts over increased taxes. Throughout the book we have discussed how public opinion has shaped healthcare politics and policy.

Electoral Cycle

Policymakers are influenced in their deliberations by the electoral cycle and the necessity of reelection. Thus, policy decisions are viewed from the perspective of potential electoral consequences. This is all the more true near election time. The policy-making process is driven by the need to produce short-term tangible benefits. The fact that the president, senators, and representatives not only have different constituencies to serve but different term lengths in office makes electoral calculations a permanent fixture of the political environment. For example, healthcare reform came on the national agenda as a result of a special senatorial election held in Pennsylvania in 1991 in which incumbent Democratic U.S. senator Harris Wofford defeated Republican Dick Thornburg, a very popular former governor of the state, on the single issue of healthcare reform. As a result, in the presidential campaign of 1992, the Democratic nominee, Bill Clinton, governor of Arkansas, made healthcare reform a cornerstone of his campaign. However, the Clinton administration failed in its effort at healthcare reform (Rushefsky and Patel 1998). This failure was followed by few incremental, stopgap measures, such as the Health Insurance Portability and Accountability Act (HIPAA) of 1996 and the State Children's Health Insurance Program (SCHIP), enacted in 1997.

The issue of healthcare reform reemerged during the presidential campaign of 2004 due to the rising costs of healthcare and the increasing numbers of uninsured Americans. Both incumbent Republican president George W. Bush and the Democratic nominee, Senator John Kerry (D-MA), made healthcare a theme of their campaigns. Similarly, in the 2008 Democratic primaries, both Senators Hillary Clinton and Barack Obama made healthcare reform a major campaign issue. Obama, after winning the Democratic Party's nomination, ran on the promise of reforming the American health system if elected. After becoming president, Obama made healthcare reform a top priority of his administration. Congress in 2010, on a party-line vote, did pass the Affordable Care Act, reforming the American healthcare system. However, just as with President Clinton's effort to reform the healthcare system during 1993–1994, Republicans opposed the reform, refused to compromise, voted against the bill, and made it an issue in the 2010 congressional election, advocating repeal of the law. The controversy over the law also saw the rise of the Tea Party movement, which succeeded in electing to the House of Representatives many very conservative Republicans who had pledged to repeal the reform law. The House of Representatives on January 2011 did vote to repeal the law by a vote of 245 to 189 with only three Democrats voting for the repeal (Herszenhorn 2011). However, in February 2011, the Democratic-controlled Senate defeated a similar effort by a vote of 51 to 47 (Alphonse 2011). Since then, the Republican-controlled House has voted thirty-two times, largely along party lines, to repeal either all or part of the reform law (O'Keefe 2012).

Public Philosophy and Political Ideology

Political ideology is the set of political beliefs/attitudes and values by which policy actors in all policy arenas operate. Within the healthcare system it is possible to identify the ideology of the medical profession, healthcare administrators, planners, and policymakers. The term "public philosophy," in contrast, is a broader concept and can be defined as an outlook on public affairs shared by a wide coalition in a nation (Beer 1965). A public philosophy often may not be explicit, but the ideological debate on issues takes place within its confines.

The underlying principle in American public philosophy, resulting from constitutional guarantees of freedom of speech, expression, and petition, is that organized interests should have an important role in influencing public policies. The public philosophy in the United States was influenced greatly by the writing of John Locke, a seventeenth-century English philosopher. A central feature of Locke's argument is the belief that ultimate authority resides in the individual's inalienable right to seek his or her own self-preservation. According to Locke, people form a government to protect their natural right of self-preservation. For Locke, this right is closely associated with the right to acquire property, an idea that pervades American political thought and institutions (Bayes 1982).

The clearest integration of this Lockean idea is found in James Madison's "Federalist 10." According to Madison, a faction constitutes a number of citizens united by a common passion or interest adverse to the rights of other citizens or to the permanent and aggregate interests of the community. Madison argued that factions were evil and could lead to tyranny. Yet, elimination of the causes of factions was not a solution, because it could also destroy liberty. Therefore, Madison advocated controlling the effects of factions. Since American society is composed of a large number of geographic, ethnic, racial, economic, and religious groups, the way to control the negative effects of factions, according to Madison, was to create a representative form of government. In such a representative government, public views can be refined and enlarged by passing them through the medium of a chosen body of citizens (the legislature) whose wisdom can help determine the true interest of the country. Madison also asserted that a large republic was less susceptible to tyranny than a small one because in a large republic many different interests will exist, making it difficult for any one interest to regularly dominate all others (Madison 1961b).

This in turn helped to create a philosophy of liberalism, which argues that all interests should be able to penetrate the political arena. Theodore Lowi describes this philosophy as interest group liberalism (Lowi 1967). This is called a pluralistic system, which is characterized by many channels of access, with various interest groups exercising countervailing veto power. This system is justified in terms of equality and the openness that guarantees political freedom, which in turn can be used to achieve social and economic freedoms (Wilsford 1991).

The decentralized governmental structure based on separation of powers, checks and balances, and federalism is designed to give interest groups access throughout the policy cycle. Thus, ironically, a Madisonian system designed to prevent a tyranny of the majority and control the mischiefs of factions (interest groups) also gives these factions many opportunities for devilment. To formulate health policy under such a system requires public officials and institutions to reconcile the conflicting interests of many organized groups. In theory, the role of the government becomes one of neutral arbitrator resolving conflicts among organized groups. The broad and diffused distribution of political influences across numerous and diverse interest groups blurs the distinction between public and private power (Truman 1951).

Private interests battle with one another and define themselves in terms of the public interest. But because all interest groups do not have equal resources, those with more economic resources have greater access to channels of influence and thus more opportunities for engaging in mischief. As McConnell (1966) has persuasively argued, small groups monopolize political power by successfully defining their own narrow interests as the general public interest. For example, for many years, the American Medical Association (AMA) based its opposition to national health insurance on the ground that socialized medicine would be against the general public interest because it would deprive patients of their freedom of choice and would lead to poor-quality medical care. In a pluralistic system based on the public philosophy of interest-group liberalism, private economic, regional, and constituency interests are justified as public interests by appealing to values of individualism, constitution, democracy, freedom, and equality, which make up an important part of American culture and belief systems. Private interests as well as public officials often justify their narrow parochial interests as public interest. The consensus created from compromises and bargaining among competing interests gets defined as the public interest. The role of the government, according to the pluralistic formulation, becomes one of protecting these diverse and competing interests by creating a consensus through the give-and-take of politics.

The framework of pluralism assumes that multiple elites rule specific areas of public policy as a "subgovernment" or an "iron triangle." The concept of subgovernment or iron triangle presumes a small circle of participants, such as a couple of congressional committees (a few legislators), executive agencies (a few bureaucrats), and interest groups that become semiautonomous in policy making in a particular policy area (Mawhinney 2001). However, others have argued that while this scenario is true in explaining policy making prior to the 1970s, these concepts of rigid subgovernment or iron triangle no longer capture the role of interest groups in policy making (Heclo 1978). The interest group explosion of the 1970s has replaced the subgovernment or iron triangle model of policy making with the issue networks model of policy making. Issue networks are composed of a large number of participants with variable degrees of mutual commitment or dependence on others in the environment (Heclo 1978). Interest groups form networks and alliances with other groups for the purpose of working together to act as policy advocacy groups to achieve mutual objectives. This idea of issue networks has become widely accepted as an empirical description of how policy making takes place in the United States (Heaney 2004; Tichenor and Harris 2002/2003).

Reforming the present American healthcare system is difficult because every reform proposal gets trapped in pluralistic processes designed to safeguard all existing professional and organizational interests. Ideological conflicts between those who want to protect the professional monopoly and autonomy of the medical profession and those who want more healthcare planning and regulation are contained within a pluralistic institutional framework that prevents either side from generating enough power to bring about significant reforms designed to integrate and coordinate healthcare (Alford 1975). Market reformers blame bureaucratic interference and cumbersome regulations for the problems of the healthcare system. They call for less regulation and more incentive-based reforms to increase and diversify healthcare facilities and delivery of services. The libertarian ideology of distributive justice is most evident in arguments for competitive market reforms. According to this ideology, increased reliance on market competition for allocative decisions would result in a more efficient allocation of resources than we now have. Republicans in general and conservatives in particular support this position. Bureaucratic reformers blame market competition for the defects of the present system and call for more regulation and planning. This argument is based on egalitarian ideology, which emphasizes the just distribution of healthcare resources based on need. The concern is to provide equal access to decent-quality healthcare for everyone at a reasonable cost. Democrats in general, and liberals in particular, support this position (Berki 1983).

Thus the healthcare system exhibits a continuous conflict and strain between the values of efficiency, access, equality, rights, and freedom. This is reflected in the contradictions between people's expectations for equal access to decent-quality healthcare, the failure of the private sector to provide equal access, and the inability of the public sector to compensate completely for the inadequacies of the private sector.

Which health policies are pursued at a given point in time depends on which ideology is dominant at that time. During the 1960s and early 1970s, the dominance of egalitarian ideology resulted in bureaucratic reformers' success in creating health policies designed to increase access to healthcare and at the same time provide quality care at a reasonable cost through such policies as Medicare, Medicaid, healthcare planning, and regulation. The ascendancy of libertarian ideology during the 1970s, and particularly the 1980s, led to the creation of health policies—supported by market reformers—aimed at cost containment and economic efficiency. This was attempted through deregulation, cuts in federal funds, encouragement of development of alternative health delivery organizations such as health maintenance organizations (HMOs) and the establishment of a prospective payment system (PPS) of hospital payment for Medicare patients through diagnosis-related groups (DRGs). These policies were designed to induce diversity and competition in the healthcare system through market incentives. It should be noted that the PPS initiative itself was regulatory in nature.

Interest Groups, Lobbying, and Policy Making

Interest groups are generally seen as influencing public policy in two primary ways: through giving campaign contributions and through the distribution of information on subject matters they claim to have expertise or specialize in. The campaign contributions are seen as a way to get attention and to gain "access" to relevant policymakers (Austen-Smith 1993). Distribution of specialized information is seen as a way to influence the legislative policy-making process. In addition, interest groups use their economic resources to lobby for or against specific issues. Interest groups also sometimes fund policy research and use the research to influence policy process (Stone, Daniel 2011).

The rise and active participation of interest groups in policy making has been traced to government mobilization of interest groups during World War I because of government's need to coordinate industry to meet wartime production needs (Herring 1967). However, Truman (1951) has argued that the group mobilization that occurred during the Great Depression is an example of how economic crisis and social disturbances can give rise to interest groups and lobbying organizations. During the 1950s and 1960s, the civil rights movement, women's rights movement, and consumer and environmental activism also served as a catalyst for the rise of organized interests in American society (Walker 1991). However, prior to the 1950s, the lobbying community of organized interests in Washington, DC, was relatively small. The immense growth in the number of interest groups and their lobbying activities with the national government happened during the post–World War II period. These organized interests represented trade associations, business organizations, professional associations, and labor unions as well as citizens groups (Walker 1991). The 1960s saw a dramatic increase in citizens groups, often referred to as "public interest groups." The distinction that is often made between private interest groups and public interest groups is that the former represent/promote solely the private interest of its members (e.g., the National Rifle Association [NRA]), while the latter represent/promote the interest of the public at large (e.g., Common Cause). Interest groups often lobby on their own behalf or hire lobbyists/lobbying firms to represent their interests in the political arena.

How effective are interest groups in having their voices heard and influencing the policy-making process? Heinz et al. (1993) have argued that the social structure of interest representation lacks a center that could coordinate disparate and conflicting group demands, and that the relationships among and between interest groups within a policy domain differ from one another. They further argue that ideological differences and economic competition within the same ideological camp drive them apart, creating a hollow core in the interest-group system. Success in lobbying is relatively small, and interest groups are more successful in obstructing than in promoting new policy initiatives (Heinz et al. 1993). Negative lobbying is more effective than positive lobbying, and negative lobbying is a more powerful predictor of policy outcome than the level of conflict, the preferences of the majority of lobbyists, or the differences in interest-group resources (McKay 2012). Also, the proliferation of interest groups makes it difficult for any one group to yield tremendous power. Baumgartner and Leech (2001) have argued that despite the proliferation of interest groups, the number of them actively involved in a specific policy area remains relatively small. Interest groups' competition often can lead to conflicts or cooperation in the form of coalition building with other interest groups in order to be effective and successful in influencing policy process (Holyoke 2009). When advocates of a given issue finally succeed, policy can change significantly (Baumgartner et al. 2009).

A contrary perspective argues that during the early twentieth century, lobbyists began to use propaganda techniques, including false and misleading information, to assert a more prominent role in the policy-making process (Loomis 2009). Others have argued that interest-group membership represents upper-class bias because research shows that people with more income and education are more likely to join interest groups, and the interests of the poor and less educated, and thus unorganized, are not represented in the policy process. Also, citizens groups often cannot match the resources of business groups (Mills 1956; Schattschneider 1960). Lowi (1969) has described this as socialism for the organized and capitalism for the unorganized. Skopol (2004) has pointed to the demise of mass-membership organizations and voluntary organizations after the 1960s and the rise of professional lobby organizations that are divorced from regular citizens. Trevor (2006) has argued that contrary to conventional wisdom, a vast majority of groups, especially the poorest groups, simply do not have the resources to make noise, make news, and have their voices heard. Only the largest and well-funded groups have a place in the public debate. Thus, instead of a marketplace of pluralistic ideas in which every group's voice is heard, only the voice of a few powerful groups in each policy niche gets heard through the news media. In one of the more recent lobbying scandals related to Indian casino gambling interests, Jack Abramoff pleaded guilty in 2006 to three felony counts of conspiracy, fraud, and tax evasion and was sentenced to prison. One scheme hatched by Abramoff was to pay newspaper columnists and nonprofit organizations for editorials and press releases favorable to his clients (Loomis 2009).

The role played by interest groups in the health policy area can be seen in the MPDIMA of 2003, which added prescription drug coverage for Medicare, and the ACA of 2010, which overhauled the American healthcare system. Both Medicare and the Veterans Health Administration finance large outpatient drug programs. However, the VHA negotiates drug prices with drug companies for its patients, but the Medicare program does not. One of the ways to control Medicare spending is for the Centers for Medicare and Medicaid Services (CMS) to negotiate drug prices for Medicare patients. However, when Congress passed the MPDIMA, it prohibited CMS from negotiating drug prices because of pressure from the pharmaceutical interest groups (Frakt, Pizer, and Hendricks 2008). Some of the major interest groups involved in Medicare prescription drug policy were the American Association of Retired Persons (AARP), the American Medical Association (AMA), the Pharmaceutical Research and Manufacturers of America (PhRMA), the American Hospital Association (AHA), the Health Insurance Association of America (HIAA), and the American Association of Health Plans (AAHP), now known as America's Health Insurance Plans (AHIP), among others (Heaney 2006). Many interest groups also played a role in influencing and shaping the major provisions of the ACA of 2010 (Quadango 2011), and we discuss it in more detail in chapter 11.

Economic Environment

Decisions about healthcare policies are invariably intertwined with economics. The economic environment consists of a network of institutions, laws, and rules that deal with primary questions such as what goods and services to produce, how they should be produced, and for whom (Samuelson 1970). The economic point of view is also rooted in three fundamental assumptions: (1) resources are limited or scarce in relation to human wants, (2) resources have alternative uses, and (3) people have different wants and do not attach the same importance to them (Fuchs 1995). Because economic resources are limited and have alternative uses, decisions must be made with regard to how and for what purposes to use these resources. The concept of opportunity cost suggests that when deciding to use resources in a certain way, one loses the opportunity to obtain benefits of using resources in some other way.

The economic environment affects policy decisions in healthcare in a number of ways. At any given point in time, health policymakers are influenced in their decisions by the notion of economic feasibility. When an economy is growing at a healthy rate, making economic resources available, policymakers find it economically feasible to establish new programs. Such was the case during the 1960s and to an extent in the early 1970s, when a number of new programs designed to increase access to healthcare were created. But corresponding increases in healthcare costs, a slowed rate of economic growth, massive federal budget deficits, and an executive branch dominated by a conservative political philosophy during the 1980s not only made it economically difficult to establish new healthcare programs but also made it possible to cut expenditures on federal health programs (Sorkin 1986). If one accepts the assumptions of scarcity of resources and the existence of competing goals, then the question faced by health policymakers becomes how to bring about the optimum distribution of healthcare resources (Fuchs 1986). What is needed is not simply cost containment but a cost-effective healthcare system (Fuchs 1986). Former secretary of health, education, and welfare Joseph A. Califano Jr. (1988) has argued that one of the major problems with the American healthcare system is that it is less cost effective than healthcare systems in other industrialized countries. In a constrained economic environment, health policymakers are confronted with making choices and establishing priorities that are not easy to make.

One of the major issues in healthcare is that of deciding how to value health. An environment of limited resources and constantly changing healthcare needs requires value judgments by policymakers about priorities (Mooney 1986). How much of society's resources should be devoted to healthcare? What priorities should be assigned to different groups competing for the same healthcare resources? Should more priority be given to the healthcare needs of the elderly or to those of infants and children? Should everyone be entitled to an organ transplant, regardless of cost or the ability to pay? In recent years, a constrained economic environment has increased concerns about the values of cost effectiveness and efficiency. It has prompted some states to attempt healthcare rationing. This has generated significant controversy and public debate over the conflicting values of efficiency, access, and equality.

The interplay of economics and healthcare can be seen in the debate surrounding the ACA of 2010. One of the criticisms leveled by Republicans against the healthcare reform was that creating such a major and costly reform during a recession was a bad policy and it would only add to the federal government's deficit, while the defenders of healthcare reform argued that dramatically escalating healthcare costs were partly responsible for the deficits. They also stated that without the reform, the healthcare costs would rise even more, adding to the deficit, and the costs of the reform would be paid by savings in the Medicare program and added revenues. Thus, healthcare reform would actually help reduce deficits in the long run by controlling rising healthcare costs.

Technological Environment

Dramatic advances in healthcare technology in the past thirty years have revolutionized the nature and delivery of health services in the United States. The rapid pace with which new biomedical technologies are developed and the swiftness with which they are adopted have transformed many hospitals into very complex and resource-intensive institutions and have changed the very nature of medical practice (Cohen and Cohodes 1982).

New healthcare technologies have been linked to the problems of cost and quality of healthcare in the United States (Fineberg and Hiatt 1979). Since every change in technology involves costs and benefits, the formulation of a good public policy depends on an accurate assessment of the relative magnitudes of costs and benefits. The nature of technological change can have profound effects on resource requirements (Fuchs 1986).

The technological revolution in biomedicine also raises questions about what medical technology should be developed and what is the proper and appropriate level of medical intervention to treat an illness. Since healthcare costs make up an increasing part of the government budget, the role of the government becomes crucial with respect to allocation of healthcare resources. Should healthcare technologies be available to all persons on an equal basis? If not, what criteria should be used to decide who gets scarce health resources and who does not? Should government be involved in technology assessment and play a role in encouraging or discouraging the development of particular technology through its funding? Should the government establish legal and ethical guidelines not only with respect to biomedical research but also regarding application of biomedical technology? We explore these questions in chapter 9.

KEY HEALTH POLICY ACTORS

The key policy actors in the healthcare system include a variety of public and private institutions and groups such as healthcare providers, healthcare practitioners, healthcare purchasers, and health insurers. The remainder of this chapter examines the role of the key health policy actors.

Healthcare Purchasers

The simple fact that the federal, state, and local governments are involved in the development of health policy, funding healthcare, maintaining and improving public health, and delivery of health services makes them important policy actors in the healthcare field. Total government health spending by all three levels of governments specifically include expenditures for Medicare, Medicaid, SCHIP, healthcare for American Indians and Alaska Natives and veterans, contributions to private health insurance premiums and to the Medicare Hospital Insurance Trust Fund through payroll taxes, and a variety of other public health activities. Over the years, the health expenditures of all three levels of governments have continued to rise, absorbing an increasingly larger share of their budgets.

The Federal Government

Today the federal government is the largest purchaser of healthcare. In 2010, the federal government financed 29 percent of the $2.6 trillion total national health expenditures in the United States, which amounted to $8,402 per person or 17.9 percent of the nation's GDP. The federal share of 29 percent in 2010 is a significant increase from the 23 percent share in 2007. The federal government health spending growth rate slowed from 17.4 percent in 2009 to 8.6 percent in 2010, yet the federal share of national health expenditures increased from 27 percent in 2009 to 29 percent in 2010 due to a smaller share of spending by households, private businesses, and state and local governments ("National Health Expenditures 2010 Highlights" n.d.; "National Health Expenditures 2010: Sponsor Highlights" n.d.).

The majority of federal health spending is for health services provided to low-income individuals and others eligible through Medicaid, people over sixty-five years of age through Medicare, children (via SCHIP), military personnel and their dependents, veterans, federal civilian employees, and American Indians and Alaska Natives. Of these, the bulk of the expenditures are taken up by Medicaid and Medicare programs. Since 1990, the federal share of Medicaid has accounted for the largest portion of federal government spending on health. In 2010, the Medicaid share of federal health spending amounted to 37 percent. Medicare represents the second largest share of federal health spending, 35 percent in 2010 ("National Health Expenditures 2010 Highlights" n.d.; "National Health Expenditures 2010: Sponsor Highlights" n.d.).

All three major branches of government play a crucial role in the health policy cycle. The primary policymaking responsibility lies with Congress. Most federal programs are implemented by numerous bureaucratic agencies in the executive branch of government. This makes the president and the bureaucracy important actors, especially during the implementation stage of the health policy cycle.

The Department of Health and Human Services (DHHS) is the federal government's principal agency for carrying out federal health policies and programs. Medicare and Medicaid together provide healthcare insurance for one in four Americans. The department includes more than 300 programs administered by a variety of agencies and centers. The DHHS is headed by a secretary who is appointed by the president with Senate confirmation.

The secretary is responsible for administering federal healthcare programs and activities and for advising the president on health, welfare, and income security programs and policies of the federal government. For various divisions and offices located within the DHHS, see the organizational chart below.

The DHHS also contains eleven operating divisions that perform important functions related to health and human services. They include:

- Administration for Children and Families (ACF) is responsible for all issues pertaining to children, youth, and families, including things such as child support enforcement, developmental disabilities, and family assistance, among others [http://www.acf.hhs.gov/].

Figure 1.1 **U.S. Department of Health and Human Services Organizational Chart**

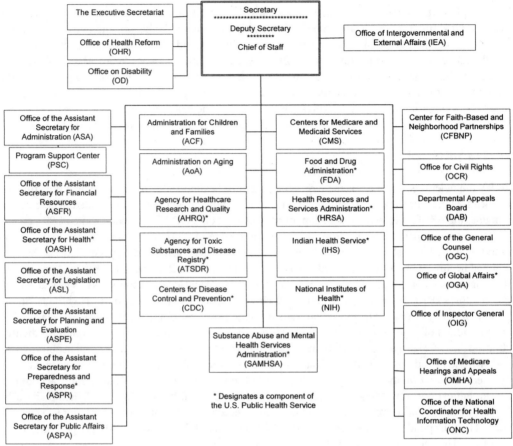

Source: U.S. Department of Health and Human Services, Washington D.C.: http://www.hhs.gov/about/orgchart/

- Administration on Aging (AoA) is responsible for all issues involving the elderly [http://www.aoa.gov/].
- Agency for Healthcare Research and Quality (AHRQ) is responsible for supporting research related to improving the quality of healthcare, reducing healthcare costs, and addressing issues of patient safety and medical errors [http://www.ahrq.gov/].
- Agency for Toxic Substances and Disease Registry (ATSDR) is responsible for prevention of exposure to toxic and hazardous substances [http://www.atsdr.cdc.gov/].
- Substance Abuse and Mental Health Services Administration (SAMHSA) is responsible for prevention and treatment of addictive and mental disorders [http://www.samhsa.gov/].
- Health Resources and Services Administration (HRSA) is responsible for making essential primary care services accessible to poor, uninsured, and geographically isolated persons [http://www.hrsa.gov/index.html].
- Indian Health Service (IHS) is responsible for providing comprehensive health services for American Indians and Alaska Natives [http://www.ihs.gov/].
- Centers for Disease Control and Prevention (CDC) is charged with the responsibility for protecting the public's health, preventing and controlling diseases, and responding to public health emergencies [http://www.cdc.gov/].

- Centers for Medicare and Medicaid Services (CMS) oversees the Medicare program, the federal portion of the Medicaid program, and the State Children's Health Insurance Program (SCHIP) [http://www.cms.hhs.gov/].
- Food and Drug Administration (FDA) is responsible for ensuring the safety of food, drugs, biological products, and medical devices [http://www.fda.gov/].
- National Institutes of Health (NIH) supports biomedical and behavioral research through its various institutes [http://www.nih.gov/].

State and Local Governments

Because of the federal system of government, state and local governments are important actors in the healthcare field. In 2010, the share of total national health care expenditures financed by state and local governments amounted to 16 percent. The state and local share of the total national health expenditures has actually continued to fall since 2007, when it was 18 percent. Medicaid spending accounted for 32 percent of the state and local spending in 2010. The state share of Medicaid spending has also declined from 39 percent in 2005 ("National Health Expenditures 2010 Highlights" n.d.; "National Health Expenditures 2010: Sponsor Highlights" n.d.).

Each state has a health department (name varies from state to state) that is led by a secretary of health or a state health commissioner who is typically appointed by the governor and is responsible for establishing and administering the state's health agenda. State health departments perform policy regulatory and administrative responsibilities and work closely with city and county health departments. State public health programs serve as an important link in the nation's health infrastructure by providing clinical services directly to individuals, collecting health surveillance data, monitoring population health, serving as a repository of information about vital health statistics, and coordinating the work of state and local health agencies. In addition, state laws also govern required reporting of communicable diseases, collecting and reporting such diseases, establishing health codes regulating aspects of sanitation and hygiene, and monitoring and preventing environmental hazards. State departments of health are also responsible for emergency preparedness and creating necessary infrastructure to deal with public health emergencies (Grott 2006; Perlin and Baggett 2010).

State health departments' regulatory responsibilities include regulating healthcare facilities such as hospitals, nursing homes, mental health facilities, ambulatory surgical centers, physician practices, and laboratory testing services. States' regulatory responsibilities also extend to the licensure of health services and healthcare professionals (Grott 2006; Perlin and Baggett 2010).

In recent years, state governments have also become involved in rate setting, negotiated or competitively bid fixed-price arrangements, and healthcare rationing to control healthcare costs. Some states have also been in the forefront of healthcare reform. In fact, the ACA is modeled after the Massachusetts health reform enacted in 2006 (Long, Stockley, and Dahlen 2012). State governments will play a crucial role not only in the implementation of the ACA but also in developing their own essential health benefit standards within guidelines set by the national government (Greer 2011; Levey 2012; Sparer 2011).

Local governments, that is, cities and counties, often play a critical role in administering state health programs and delivering health services. There are thousands of local health departments throughout the United States. They perform the important functions of health assessment, tracking population health, disease prevention, and development of community health services. In many communities, local health departments also provide primary and specialty services for mental health and sexually transmitted diseases. For example, public health laboratories of local health departments perform many important functions, including testing at the site of patient care, addressing local environmental health issues, and supporting missions of local health departments, as well as serving as conduits, collecting specimens for various state screening and disease control programs (Wilson, Gradus, and Zimmerman 2010). Local health departments also play a key role in leading immunization programs and often serve as provider of last resort for safety net services to the poor (Grott 2006; Perlin and Baggett 2010). However, financial strains have led to curtailment of such safety net programs.

Industries/Businesses

Large industries and businesses are also major purchasers of healthcare. Many major industries and firms provide health insurance coverage to their employees as part of a benefit package. Today a majority of workers in the United States are employed by firms that offer health insurance. Whether employers provide health insurance benefits or not often depends on employer size, nature and type of industry/business, and full-time work status of employees. In 2011, 60 percent of all firms (public and private) offered health insurance benefits to their workers, with 99 percent of large firms (200+ employees) compared to only 59 percent of small firms (3–199 employees) offering health benefits (Kaiser Family Foundation and Health Research and Educational Trust 2011). Many employers do not provide health insurance coverage to part-time or temporary workers. For example, in 2011, only 15 percent of small firms and 43 percent of large firms offered health benefits to part-time workers; and only 4 percent of small firms and 6 percent of large firms offered health benefits to their temporary workers (Kaiser Family Foundation and Health Research & Educational Trust 2011). The health insurance coverage provided by employer group insurance plans also varies widely with respect to the scope of covered services, conditions of eligibility, and the share of employees' contribution to the plan.

Major industries and businesses have become key actors in the healthcare system because of the cost they incur in providing health insurance for their workers. In addition, the cost of providing health insurance coverage has increased significantly since 2000 as premiums have increased. For example, from 2001 to 2004 insurance premiums increased by 59 percent—four years of double-digit premium increases (Gabel et al. 2004). In 2005, premiums increased another 9.2 percent (Gabel et al. 2005). The average annual health insurance premium for covered workers with family coverage increased from $7,056 (employees' contribution $1,787 and employers' contribution $5,269) in 2001 to $15,073 (employees' contribution $4,129 and employers' contribution $10,944) in 2011—a premium increase of 113 percent overall (Kaiser Family Foundation and Health Research & Educational Trust 2011).

Such dramatic increases in healthcare premiums have made businesses more conscious of their costs and have led them to use a variety of cost-cutting measures, such as encouraging or requiring employees to enroll in prepaid group plans such as health maintenance organizations (HMOs) or preferred provider organizations (PPOs) for health services; passing an increasing share of insurance costs to their workers by increasing their contribution to premiums, deductibles, and copayments; or dropping benefits completely. The percentage of businesses offering health insurance coverage to its workers dropped from 68 percent in 2001 to 60 percent in 2011, and the percentage of all workers covered by their employers' health benefits dropped from 65 percent to 58 percent over the same period. Employers have also increased the share of employees' deductibles and cost sharing. However, the increase in employees' deductibles and cost sharing depends on the type of health plan they are enrolled in (HMOs, PPOs, etc.) and the type of coverage (low deductible–high premium, services covered, etc.) (Kaiser Family Foundation and Health Research & Educational Trust 2011).

Some large employers still provide health insurance coverage to their retired workers. However, as businesses struggle to control rising healthcare costs, many employers are dropping health benefits for current or future retirees and are asking current retirees to pay more for their coverage. For example, among all large firms (200+ employees) that offer health benefits to active workers, the percentage that also offer retirees health benefits has dropped from 66 percent in 1988 to 37 percent in 2001 to 26 percent in 2011 (Kaiser Family Foundation and Health Research & Educational Trust 2011).

How the ACA affects the health insurance market in the long run remains to be seen. If the ACA dramatically helps to decrease the number of uninsured people will it solve the "free rider" problem (uninsured individuals who get treated in emergency rooms and the cost of their treatment is passed on to insured individuals), and ultimately lead to reduced health insurance premiums for everyone? Would total national health expenditures decline in the long run? Would a 35 percent tax credit lead more small businesses to provide health insurance coverage to their employees?

Since the law was enacted only in 2010 and because some of the important provisions are not scheduled to go into effect until 2014, it is impossible to make any assessment about the impact of the reform. Thus far, some anecdotal evidence does point to the fact that more small businesses are beginning to take advantage of the tax incentive by providing health insurance coverage to their employees (Levey 2010; Levey 2011; Ungar 2011).

Healthcare Providers

The major healthcare providers include institutions such as hospitals, nursing homes, and pharmacies, as well as professionals such as physicians, nurses, and dentists. They are important actors in the healthcare system because they not only deliver healthcare services but also influence the way in which services are delivered and the type of services that are delivered. The major feature of the U.S. healthcare system is its entrepreneurial nature. Pharmacies and manufacturers of pharmaceutical and medical equipment and suppliers are private, profit-making enterprises. Similarly, many nursing homes are for-profit institutions. Most physicians are private practitioners.

Hospitals

According to a 2010 survey by the American Hospital Association (AHA), there are 5,754 registered hospitals in the United States, with a total of 941,995 staffed beds. Registered hospitals are those that meet the AHA's criteria for accreditation as a hospital (American Hospital Association 2012). Of the total registered hospitals, 4,985 are community hospitals, of which 2,904 are nongovernmental not-for-profit hospitals, 1,013 are investor-owned for-profit hospitals, and 1,068 are state and local government hospitals. The remainder are made up of federal government hospitals, nonfederal psychiatric hospitals, nonfederal long-term care hospitals, and hospital units of institutions such as prison hospitals and college infirmaries. Also, of the 4,985 community hospitals, 1,987 are rural and 2,998 are urban community hospitals (American Hospital Association 2012). Hospitals have become the primary setting for the delivery of healthcare services because most of the sophisticated medical technology and equipment are located there. Hospitals vary by purpose and ownership.

Many not-for-profit hospitals (those that are community run or church affiliated) provide short-term care. States run psychiatric hospitals. The federal government operates veterans' hospitals. There is also an increasing number of proprietary or profit-making hospitals. A study conducted by Dr. P.J. Devereaux and colleagues at McMaster University in Hamilton, Ontario, reviewed medical studies on hospital care in the United States covering 350,000 patients and hundreds of for-profit hospitals. It concluded that U.S. hospitals owned by investors with the aim of making money are less cost-efficient and have higher death rates compared to nonprofit hospitals ("Study: For-Profit Hospitals Bill Bigger" 2004). A more recent study that examined the relationship between hospital ownership and technical efficiency in a managed care environment found that nonprofit hospitals were more efficient than for-profit hospitals (Lee, Yang, and Choi 2009). However, the trend in the increase in the number of for-profit hospitals has continued with hospital mergers and acquisitions. Nonprofit hospitals faced with cash flow problems and unable to improve and upgrade their facilities have eagerly sought to change from nonprofit to for-profit status by looking for profit suitors for mergers and acquisitions (Gold 2010). This trend is likely to continue in the future, because according to a report released by Moody's Investors Services (McCloud 2011) not-for-profit hospitals showed the lowest rate of growth in two decades. This in turn raises the question about the role of corporate medicine in the United States. Is for-profit ownership of hospitals good for patients, or does it result in overemphasis on profit, threatening the quality of care received by patients?

Paul Starr (1982), in his classic work *The Social Transformation of American Medicine,* warned about the coming of corporate medicine as it relates to hospitals. He argued that corporatization of American medicine was reflected in the movement from public planning and regulation to private/corporate planning and regulation and a shift in the prevalent discourse from "health centers" to "profit centers." Court and Smith (1999) provided a strong indictment of "corporate medicine" as practiced specifically by HMOs and HMO-owned hospitals. They argue that U.S. medicine has been taken over by a corporate marketplace that looks only for profits, a practice that endangers patients and leads to significant waste of healthcare resources. Similarly, Poduval and Poduval (2008) have argued that the medical-industrial complex has led to commercialization of healthcare that treats medicine as a business concern and is motivated by cost curtailments and profit margins.

Nursing Facilities

In 2012, there were about 15,690 nursing facilities, of which 54.8 percent were multi-facilities (multi-nursing-home chains have two or more homes under one ownership or operation), 45.2 percent were independent, and 6.3 percent were hospital-based. Of the total facilities, 67.8 percent were for profit, 25.3 percent were nonprofit, and 5.7 percent were government operated. Also, in terms of certification, 5 percent were Medicare only, 1.7 percent were Medicaid only, and 91.4 percent were both Medicare and Medicaid certified. These facilities had a total of 1,667,884 beds (American Health Care Association 2012a). They housed 1,387,727 patients, of whom 14.4 percent were Medicare patients, 63.6 percent were Medicaid patients, and 22 percent were other (private) payer patients (American Health Care Association 2012b).

Nursing facilities generally provide long-term care, and most of the people they serve are elderly. A sizable portion of their revenues comes from the government. Nursing facilities are also heavily regulated by state and local governments.

According to the U.S. Census Bureau, the number of people age sixty-five and over is expected to increase from 40 million in 2010 to 72 million by 2030 (Torpey 2011). The U.S. Bureau of Labor Statistics projects that this increase in the elderly population will result in significant job growth for a variety of occupations related to caring for the elderly, especially in nursing homes. Employment in nursing care facilities is expected to grow more than 24 percent between 2008 and 2018, an increase of more than 400,000 jobs (Torpey 2011). In 2009, nursing care facilities employed 609,440 nurse's aides, orderlies, and attendants; 212,990 licensed practical and licensed vocational nurses; 124,420 registered nurses; and more than 300,000 workers made up of maids, housekeeping cleaners, food preparation workers, cooks, recreational workers, dry cleaning workers, and food servers, among others (Torpey 2011). A study commissioned by American Health Care Association and conducted by the Moran Company (2011) found that because of economic conditions and government funding restrictions, skilled nursing facilities were in danger of falling into the red. According to the study, in 2009, nursing homes nationwide were operating at a margin of .075 percent of revenues. In recent years, private equity investors have targeted nursing home chains as investment opportunities, which, in turn, has raised concerns about quality of care, oversight, and accountability (Stevenson and Grabowski 2008).

Physicians

Physicians are key actors in the healthcare system because they are the primary caregivers. They enjoy considerable professional autonomy. In 2010, there were 850,085 physicians with an active license to practice medicine in the United States and the District of Columbia. Of these, 75.5 percent were doctors of medicine, and 6.9 percent were doctors of osteopathic medicine. Of the total number of physicians, 66.9 percent were male and 29 percent were female, and in 4.2 percent of cases, gender was unknown. Seventy-five percent were certified by an American Board of Medical Specialties (ABMS) specialty board, while 26 percent were not (Young et al. 2011).

A majority of physicians are specialists who conduct their practices in a hospital setting. Over the years, the number of generalists or family practitioners has declined considerably. Physicians work in one or more of several specialties, such as family and general medicine, general pediatrics, obstetrics and gynecology, surgery, and anesthesiology. There are over 180 specialties. In 2009, 58.9 percent of physicians were in the following top ten specialties: internal medicine, family medicine, pediatrics, obstetrics/gynecology, anesthesiology, psychiatry, general surgery, emergency medicine, diagnostic radiology, and orthopedic surgery (American Medical Association 2011).

Physicians play a pivotal role and occupy a unique position in the healthcare system. Since they not only diagnose an illness but also prescribe treatment, they control both the supply of and the demand for healthcare services. In the process, they exert substantial influence over the pattern of health resources utilization in general and hospital resources in particular. Doctors conduct their practices in private offices; hospitals; and federal, state, and local governments. Some work in outpatient care centers or educational services. An increasing number of physicians are partners or salaried employees of group practice or managed care organizations such as HMOs and preferred provider organizations (PPOs).

Starr (1982) suggests that with "coming of the corporation," more and more physicians will be working for large corporations in the near future. While there has been some movement of physicians into corporations, the extent of such a movement in the last two decades or so has been rather limited. Today, only about 25 percent of physicians work in corporate organizations. However, corporate influence on the physician practice is significant (Casalino 2004).

In addition, physician's assistants held about 63,000 jobs in 2002. They work under the supervision of a physician, and their duties are determined by the supervising physicians and by state law. Sometimes they may be the principal care providers in rural areas and inner-city clinics where a physician is present only a couple of days a week. They are formally trained to provide diagnostic, therapeutic, and preventive healthcare services, as delegated by a physician.

Nurses

The essential core function of nursing practice is to deliver holistic, patient-centered care. The nursing process involves a systematic assessment (collection and analysis of patient data), diagnostics (clinical judgment about the patient's response to actual or potential health conditions or needs), outcome/planning (setting measurable and achievable short- and long-term goals for the patient), implementation of a healthcare plan, and evaluation of patient and effectiveness of the nursing care ("The Nursing Process" n.d.).

Registered nurses (RNs) constitute the largest healthcare occupation, with 2.3 million jobs. Hospital nurses form the largest group of nurses. Most of them are staff nurses who provide bedside nursing care and carry out medical regimens. Office nurses care for outpatients in physicians' offices, clinics, and ambulatory surgical centers. Home healthcare nurses provide nursing services to patients at home, while nursing care facility nurses work in long-term care operations such as nursing homes. Public health nurses work in government and private agencies, including clinics, schools, and community settings, to improve the overall health of the community. Occupational health nurses (industrial nurses) provide nursing care at worksites ("What Nurses Do" n.d.).

Licensed practical nurses (LPNs) or licensed vocational nurses (LVNs) complement the health-care team by providing basic and routine care under the direction of physicians and registered nurses in a wide variety of settings.

Advanced Practice Registered Nurses (APRNs) are carving out a new role in healthcare delivery. The advanced practice nurse is an umbrella term given to a registered nurse who has met at least a master's degree in educational and clinical practice requirements beyond the years of basic nursing education required of all RNs. Advanced practice nurses can be classified under four types: nurse practitioner (NP), certified nurse midwife (CNM), clinical nurse specialist (CNS), and certified registered nurse anesthetist (CRNA). NPs are qualified to handle a wide range of basic health problems, and most of them have specialties, such as adult, family, or pediatric care. CNMs provide well-woman gynecological and low-risk obstetrical care. CNSs are qualified to handle a wide range of physical and mental health problems, and they provide primary care and psychotherapy. CRNAs administer more than 65 percent of all anesthetics given to patients each year ("What Nurses Do" n.d.).

In 2009, a total of 2,583,770 nurses were employed in a variety of settings. Fifty-seven percent of them were employed in general medical and surgical hospitals, 8.7 percent in doctors' offices, and the remainder in settings such as home healthcare services, nursing care facilities, outpatient care centers, specialty hospitals, government, and educational institutions. Federal, state, and local governments employed nearly 150,000 registered nurses in 2009. According to the Bureau of U.S. Labor Statistics, compared to other healthcare occupations, registered nursing was expected to see the greatest increase in absolute number of jobs—an increase of 582,000 jobs for registered nurses between 2008 and 2018 ("2009 Registered Nurses Employment and Earnings" 2010).

Third-Party Payers

The U.S. healthcare system over the years has undergone dramatic changes. One of the fundamental changes that have occurred since the early 1930s is the method of payment for healthcare services. Before the rise of the modern health insurance system, the nature of financial transactions between patient and healthcare provider was largely a direct one-on-one transaction. Under this system the patient paid for health services directly to the healthcare provider out of his or her own pocket. The birth of the modern health insurance system came in 1929 with the establishment of the Blue Cross plans for hospital insurance. A third-party-payer system was created under which a consumer paid monthly premiums to an insurance company. In return, the insurance company agreed to pay the healthcare provider for a specified range of health services received by the consumer. The Blue Shield plans, initiated by physicians, followed, based on a similar concept. Over the years, the number of private health insurance companies increased. Between 1930 and 1950, health insurance companies not only continued to cover more and more people under such plans but also expanded the scope of coverage. In 1965 the federal government entered the picture by creating two major insurance programs—Medicare for the elderly and Medicaid for the poor.

The United States has a largely private health system in which a majority of Americans receive their health insurance coverage through their employers. The public sector's role is confined to creating safety net programs such as Medicare, Medicaid, and SCHIP to provide health coverage to those who cannot get private health insurance coverage for a variety of reasons.

The private health insurance market can be divided into four categories. The first category is the large group market where large employers provide health benefits to their workers either through "self- funded" plans, which may be administered by a third party, or "fully insured" plans provided by an insurance carrier. The second category is the small-business-group insurance market.

However, this market is relatively small because small businesses (2–50 employees) often cannot get affordable insurance coverage because of the number of their employees. The third category is the individual insurance market. However, since individual insurance is not subsidized by an employer or through the tax code, each consumer is forced to pay the entire cost of the premium, which can be very expensive and often unaffordable. The fourth category is the health savings accounts (HSAs) and consumer-directed plans. Under this option, individuals, families, or employers are provided a comprehensive health insurance plan through an opportunity to save tax-deferred funds for qualified medical expenses ("Private-Market Health Insurance" n.d.).

In 2010, 49.9 million Americans were uninsured—16.3 percent of the population. Much of the increase in the number of uninsured can be attributed to the loss of employer-provided insurance and to sustained unemployment (Christie 2011). The increasing uninsured trend continued over the decade from 2000 to 2010. While public health insurance coverage through Medicaid and SCHIP filled in some of the gaps, it has not offset all the loss in private coverage (Holahan and Chen 2011). When the recession started in 2007, people began to put off elective health services, went to the doctors less, had fewer medical procedures, and purchased fewer drugs. Even after the recession ended in June 2009 and the economy started to recover, utilization continued downward. Health insurance premiums also witnessed only a modest increase of 3 percent to 6 percent from 2006 to 2010. However, premiums did jump 9 percent in 2011 (Altman 2010).

Cost increases and pressure from employers have led insurance companies to look for ways to cut costs as well as increase the premiums they charge. Many insurance companies have developed managed care systems. The concept of managed care involves arrangements with selected providers such as HMOs and PPOs to furnish a comprehensive set of healthcare services to its members, formal programs for ongoing quality assurance and utilization review, explicit standards for selection of healthcare providers, and financial incentives for members to use providers and procedures covered by the plan. The critics have charged that health insurance companies are engaging in "cream-skimming and cherry-picking" that eliminate or penalize firms and employees that could put the companies at risk of high payments, rather than offering coverage to all at rates that pool the risk. The role of health insurers has changed considerably since the advent of managed care and managed competition in the 1990s, and it will change even more dramatically under the ACA of 2010. It will also have a considerable impact on the private health insurance market by expanding access to private health insurance to millions of people and employees of small businesses through the establishment of state-based insurance exchanges. By March of 2012, thirteen states and the District of Columbia had established state-based insurance exchanges ("Establishing Health Insurance Exchanges" 2012).

Consumers

The public can exert influence on healthcare policies as purchasers of healthcare and by their perceptions, attitudes, values, and opinions about the American healthcare system. In 2010, the total household spending on healthcare amounted to $726 million, including out-of-pocket spending of $300 million—28 percent and 11 percent respectively—of the total national health spending of $2.6 trillion ("National Health Expenditures 2010: Sponsor Highlights" n.d.). Household spending for healthcare includes contributions to health insurance premiums as well as out-of-pocket costs such as copayments, deductibles, and amount not covered by insurance. By 2010, the household share of the total national healthcare spending had fallen to 28 percent compared to 37 percent in 1987.

Over the years, the proportion of healthcare costs paid directly by consumers has also declined. For example, in 1987, consumers' out-of-pocket payments accounted for 58 percent of total household healthcare spending, but by 2010 it had fallen to 41 percent. The introduction of Medicare Part D in

2006, which reduced out-of-pocket spending for prescription drugs, contributed to the overall decline in the out-of-pocket share of household spending on healthcare. Since 2010, healthcare spending by households has started to rise again due to faster growth in health insurance premiums and out-of-pocket spending ("National Health Expenditures 2010: Sponsor Highlights" n.d.).

The public's overall perception of the U.S. healthcare system has been consistently negative since the 1980s. This was clearly reflected in various public opinion polls conducted during the 1980s and 1990s. A study examining the public's feeling about healthcare systems found that of the ten countries included in the study, the lowest degree of satisfaction with healthcare systems was in the United States, and the highest was in Canada (Blendon et al. 1990). Surveys by the *Los Angeles Times* in March 1990, NBC in 1989, and Louis Harris and Associates in 1988 all showed that majorities of at least 61 percent of those polled supported establishing a Canadian-style comprehensive national health system. Despite escalating healthcare costs, the general public also shows a preference for more spending for healthcare, but they themselves do not want to pay the bill. They want the government to pay the cost of healthcare. In 1987 a Harris poll asked a random sample of 1,250 Americans whether some limit should be set, say $5 million, on what we can afford to spend to save a life. Fifty-one percent of the respondents said that no limit should be set (Morin 1990). Surveys also show that Americans want more healthcare, not less. About half of all Americans believe that the United States spends too little on healthcare. Polls also suggest that the public does not believe the increased healthcare costs have been matched by similar increases in the quality of treatment (Morin 1990).

Those who are dissatisfied with the current system cite the high cost of care and lack of access—lack of availability of healthcare or health insurance—as the primary reasons for their dissatisfaction. While a majority of Americans express a preference for a Canadian-style national health system, many also think that a government-run system would adversely affect their freedom of choice and provide a lower quality of care, and they express doubt that such a system would lower costs (Jajich-Toth and Roper 1990). The U.S. public still continues to express concern over problems with the U.S. healthcare system. In a series of public opinion polls conducted by the Kaiser Family Foundation, the public expressed concern over several healthcare issues. In a January 2000 poll, 54 percent favored building on the current system instead of switching to a system in which individuals would buy their own health insurance and receive a tax credit or subsidy to help them with the cost of the plan. In a poll conducted in February 2003, a slight majority of 52 percent expressed a willingness to pay more (either higher insurance premiums or higher taxes) to increase the number of Americans who have health insurance. In a January 2004 poll, 48 percent agreed with the statement that access to healthcare should be a right. In a poll conducted in February 2004, 82 percent listed lowering the cost of health insurance and prescription drugs as very important, while another 77 percent supported increasing the number of Americans covered by health insurance. Seventy-five percent of the respondents indicated that helping families with the cost of long-term care for the elderly and disabled was very important, while another 70 percent stated that improving the quality of medical care was very important (Kaiser Health Poll Report 2004).

An examination of data from twenty-two national polls during the 2004 presidential campaign indicated that healthcare ranked as the fourth most important issue to voters in the 2004 presidential elections. The top health issues of concern to the voters were the costs of healthcare and prescription drugs, the uninsured, and Medicare. However, the economy, the war in Iraq, and the war on terrorism were ranked higher by the voters (Blendon et al. 2004). In a Gallup Poll conducted between August 31 and September 2, 2009, the American public rated healthcare as the second most important problem facing the country after the economy (Jones 2009). Similarly, in another Gallup Poll, conducted between November 3 and 6, 2011, 59 percent of Americans rated the quality of healthcare in the United States as excellent to good, but when it came to healthcare coverage, only 33 rated it as excellent to good (Saad 2011).

Public dissatisfaction with the current healthcare system leads many Americans to support an overhaul of the U.S. healthcare system, but they are also ambivalent about the policy options that would change the system. In a New York Times/CBS News poll conducted in September 1993 before President Clinton formally proposed his plan to overhaul the U.S. healthcare system, a majority of Americans expressed a willingness to pay higher taxes to make health insurance secure and available to all. However, in the same poll, respondents expressed a great deal of skepticism about the ability of the government to achieve a successful overhaul of the system (Toner 1993). Public opinion initially showed strong support for President Clinton's reform effort. However, by the summer of 1994, public support for such a major reform had fallen considerably, and the reform effort died without a vote in Congress.

Similarly, as President Obama's healthcare reform bill advanced in Congress, public support for it slipped. Fifty-one percent of Americans in October 2009 had expressed support for President Obama's reform proposal. However, in a Gallup Poll conducted in March 2010, 48 percent of respondents indicated that they would urge their member of Congress to vote against the reform bill, and only 45 percent said they would want their member of Congress to vote for it (Grier 2009; Jones 2010). A year after the passage of the healthcare reform, Americans remain divided. In a Gallup Poll conducted in January 2011, 46 percent favored repealing the healthcare law, while only 40 percent favored letting the law stand (Jones 2011). In another Gallup Poll, conducted in March 2011, 39 percent of respondents expressed the belief that the ACA will improve medical care in the United States, while 44 percent say it will make it worse, with Democrats remaining highly positive and Republicans highly negative about the law (Newport 2011).

The American public seems to display a split personality when it comes to healthcare reform. They want healthcare reform/change but are unsure and apprehensive about its nature. They want more spending on healthcare by the government, but there is a limit as to how much more they are willing to pay. They want government to address the problems of the American healthcare system, but they are skeptical and cynical about government. A great deal of the divide on healthcare reform also splits along partisan and ideological lines. It is important to remember that simply because the public responds to questions asked in the opinion polls, it does not mean that their opinions are based on having accurate information, knowledge, and understanding of the topic on which they express an opinion. Polls also tend to show that the public is often confused and lacks clear understanding of the subject matter on which they express an opinion. Thus, the opinions they express may be based on lack of information/understanding or on misinformation, and are influenced more by partisan and ideological feelings and attitudes. An "interest" in a subject does not necessarily translate to "understanding" of the subject. For example, in poll that Pew Research Center Survey conducted in December 2009, the American public expressed the feeling that reform efforts in Congress were becoming more and more difficult for them to follow, and 59 percent of respondents agreed with the statement that "health reform is not getting any easier to understand (Grier 2009). On the two-year anniversary of the passage of the ACA, in a March 2012 poll conducted by the Kaiser Family Foundation (2012), 59 percent of respondents stated that they did not have enough information about the law to understand how it will impact them personally. The same poll also revealed an astounding amount of misunderstanding about the law. Thirty-six percent of respondents inaccurately believed that the law allows a government panel to make decisions about end-of-life care for people on Medicare, and another 20 percent did not know whether the law does this or not (including majorities of Republicans and independents).

Such shifting and often contradictory perceptions and attitudes on the part of the American public create interesting dilemmas and value conflicts for health policymakers, which makes meaningful reform more difficult to achieve. On the other hand, it also makes it possible for policymakers in Congress as well as interest groups opposed to reform to exploit, feed, and further fuel the public's confusion for partisan and ideological gains. Thus, rather than an objective and rational public discourse over the merits and demerits of reform proposals that helps enlighten and educate the public, public discourse is characterized by emotions, passions, and misleading or false claims and counter-claims. The mass media in general and twenty-four-hour cable news networks in particular further inflame such discourse by focusing on the "emotional drama" and "sound bites" and playing along by using labels such as "Hillarycare" and "Obamacare"—terms used by the opponents as a pejorative way to refer to reform proposals. It is ironic that the mass media has rarely used the actual name of the law to discuss President Obama's healthcare reform law, that is, the Affordable Care Act!

Interest Groups

The role of interest groups in U.S. politics has been debated intensely from the time of the founding of the Republic. The philosophy of interest-group liberalism has accorded interest groups a dominant role in U.S. politics. Proponents have praised interest groups for advancing the cause of U.S. democracy by providing access for citizen participation in the political process. Opponents have argued that special interests are stealing the United States (Navarro 1984) and destroying democracy (Bennett and DiLorenzo 1985). Regardless of how one feels about interest groups, there is no denying the fact that they have become important political power brokers in U.S. politics (Smith 1972).

Since healthcare affects everyone in society, a wide variety of interests—healthcare providers, purchasers, third-party payers, suppliers, consumers—are affected by what happens within its field. The universal nature of illness gives healthcare professionals, such as physicians, important psychological and political leverage. Given their prominent position, they are able to influence developments in the healthcare field. The introduction of government-sponsored health insurance programs such as Medicare and Medicaid has also made hospitals and skilled nursing facilities important players. The technical nature of modern medicine gives drug and medical supply companies significant leverage in the health field. Similarly, insurance companies as third-party payers have also come to play an important role (Bayes 1982).

One of the major ways interest groups try to influence the political process is by hiring lobbyists to represent them in the political arena. Interest groups and lobbyists spend a considerable amount of money on their lobbying efforts. From 1998 to 2011, the health sector spent $4,877,893,882 on lobbying and ranked no. 1 in this expenditure among all other sectors of American society. During the same time period, the pharmaceuticals/health products industry spent $2,323,394,297 on lobbying and ranked no. 1 within the health sector (Center for Responsive Politics n.d.).

Another way in which health interest groups try to influence the political process is by making campaign contributions through their political action committees (PACs). In the 2008 election cycle, 127 health PACs made a total of $49,226,365 in campaign contributions to federal candidates, with 55 percent of that amount going to Democrats and 45 percent to Republicans. In 2010, 135 health PACs contributed a total of $54,641,685 to federal candidates, again with 55 percent going to Democrats and 45 percent to Republicans (Center for Responsive Politics n.d.). From 2009 to 2010 when President Obama's healthcare reform proposal was being debated in the Congress, healthcare interest groups spent a considerable amount of money in lobbying efforts to influence the major components and the direction of the reform. For example, when a proposal was floated in both houses of Congress to levy a new excise tax on sugary drinks, Coke and Pepsi supersized their spending on lobbying to defeat such a proposal. In fact, in the first three quarters of 2009, the beverage trade group reportedly spent $8.7 on lobbying, including advertising, while PepsiCo spent $4.2 million and Coca Cola spent $4.6 million (Young 2009). In the first quarter of 2009, the five largest private insurers and the trade association group America's Health Insurance Plans (AHIP) spent a total of $6.2 million, the Pharmaceutical Research and Manufacturers of America (PhRMA) spent $6.4 million, and the American Medical Association (AMA) spent $4 million to influence the healthcare reform plan (Eggen 2009a, 2009b).

While it is impossible to discuss all the interest groups involved in the healthcare field, some of the major groups are discussed below. Many of them are professional or trade associations of key actors in the healthcare field.

American Medical Association (AMA)

The AMA was established in 1847, and today it is one of the largest and most influential health-related groups. It is a professional association of physicians, the voice of organized medicine, and as such it acts as an umbrella organization of U.S. medicine. Its main functions include representing the interests of its members; providing scientific and socioeconomic information; keeping data on the profession; and developing and maintaining standards of professional education, training, and performance (Campion 1984).

The AMA has grassroots political power and is very active in lobbying Congress on health-related issues. It is very well financed. It has one of the largest political action committees. The mission of the American Medical Association Political Action Committee (AMPAC) is to find and support candidates for congressional offices, whether a new candidate for office who will make physicians and patients a top priority, or a candidate running for reelection who has proved to be a friend of medicine. In the 2010 election cycle, AMPAC spent $2,345,491 on lobbying, of which $1,144,400 was spent on campaign contributions to federal candidates, with 57 percent going to Democrats and 43 percent going to Republicans (Center for Responsive Politics n.d.).

The AMA has acted as a voice of free enterprise and fee-for-service independent medical practice in the healthcare field. Much of its effort has been directed toward protecting the economic interests of its members and opposing policies that threaten those interests or threaten their professional autonomy. For example, for a long time the AMA successfully argued against a national health insurance program because of the fear of losing its professional autonomy and of a decline in physicians' income. But the organization has articulated its opposition to national health insurance not on the ground of protecting self-interest but by using the rhetoric of defending free enterprise and patients' freedom to choose their own doctors. It has argued that adoption of national health insurance would lead to lower quality of healthcare and services. The AMA has not been above using scare tactics to achieve its objectives, but over the years, it has softened its stand toward major healthcare reform.

The AMA is not the only physician group that has attempted to influence the political process. PACs representing groups such as physician assistants, clinical urologists, orthopedic surgeons, and emergency physicians have also contributed funds to political campaigns.

American Nurses Association (ANA)

The ANA is a professional organization that represents the interests of the country's 3.1 million registered nurses through its state organizations and organizational affiliates. It is the strongest voice of the nursing profession. Besides promoting advances in the nursing professions by fostering high standards of nursing practice, the ANA lobbies Congress and regulatory agencies on health-care issues affecting nurses and the general public. Through its legislative and political program, the ANA has taken positions on issues such as Medicare reform, patient rights, whistle-blower protection for healthcare workers, and access to healthcare. The association has advocated for an expanded role for RNs and APNs in the delivery of basic and primary healthcare (American Nurses Association n.d.). The American Nurses Association Political Action Committee (ANAPAC) in the 2010 election cycle spent $780,943 on lobbying, of which $582,911 was spent on campaign contributions to federal candidates, with 91 percent going to Democrats and 9 percent going to Republicans (Center for Responsive Politics n.d.). The ANAPAC is not as big a player in the area of lobbying and campaign contributions as some of the other groups.

American Hospital Association (AHA)

The National Hospital Superintendents' Association was created in 1899. Membership in this organization was limited to chief executive officers of hospitals. A few years after the organization's founding, its name was changed to the American Hospital Association (AHA). In 1917 it changed from an individual membership organization to an organization of institutions (Weeks and Berman 1985). Today, the AHA represents individuals and healthcare institutions including hospitals, healthcare systems, and pre- and post-acute healthcare delivery organizations. In addition to conducting research and education projects, it acts as the voice of hospitals and represents their interests in national health policy development. Its advocacy efforts have included lobbying executive and legislative branches of government (American Hospital Association n.d.).

The American Hospital Association Political Action Committee (AHAPAC) spent $3,440,670 in the 2010 election cycle on lobbying, of which $1,838,266 was spent on campaign contributions to federal candidates, with 65 percent going to Democrats and 35 percent to Republicans (Center for Responsive Politics n.d.).

America's Health Insurance Plans

America's Health Insurance Plans (AHIP) is the voice of U.S. health insurers. AHIP is the national association that represents nearly 1,300 member companies that provide health insurance coverage to more than 200 million Americans. The association represents the interests of its members on legislative and regulatory issues at the federal and state levels (America's Health Insurance Plans n.d.). In the 2010 election cycle, the America's Health Insurance Plans Political Action Committee (AHIP PAC) spent $511,017 on lobbying, of which $246,000 was spent on campaign contributions to federal candidates, with 40 percent going to Democrats and 59 percent to Republicans (Center for Responsive Politics n.d.).

Among the health insurers, the major commercial insurers are Blue Cross and Blue Shield. The Blue Cross plans were developed by the hospitals through the AHA, while the Blue Shield plans were developed by physicians through the AMA. The Blue Cross and Blue Shield plans are the nation's largest family of health benefit companies. Blue Cross Blue Shield provides coverage to more than 92 million people ("History of Blue Cross Blue Shield" n.d.).

Pharmaceutical Research and Manufacturers of America (PhRMA)

PhRMA represents the nation's major pharmaceutical research and biotechnology companies. Originally it started out as the Pharmaceutical Manufacturers of America (PMA) in 1958. In 1994, its name was changed to emphasize the research aspect of its work. The pharmaceutical and biotechnological research sector in America is the global leader in medical innovation. In the last decade, the FDA approved more than 300 new medicines (Pharmaceutical Research and Manufacturers of America n.d.). In 2010, of the $2.6 trillion spent on healthcare, spending for prescription drugs ranked third (10 percent) after hospital spending (31 percent) and physicians (20 percent) ("Breaking Down U.S. Health Care Spending" n.d.). This fact alone makes PhRMA an important player in the health policy field.

In the 2010 election cycle, PhRMA's political action committee, called the "Better Government Committee," spent $195,725 on lobbying, of which $124,800 was spent on campaign contributions to federal candidates, with 73 percent going to Democratic candidates and 26 percent to Republicans. This does not look like a great deal of money compared to some other groups. However, it is important to note that in the same election cycle, 109 PACs representing pharmaceuticals and health product companies combined spent $15,116,923 on political contributions to candidates running for federal office, with 54 percent going to Democratic and 46 percent going to Republican candidates (Center for Responsive Politics n.d.).

Medical Device Manufacturers of America (MDMA)

Created in 1992, MDMA is a national trade organization based in Washington, DC. It represents the interests of smaller medical technology companies. The organization is active in representing its members' interests before Congress, the FDA, CMS, and other federal agencies. It provides its members with educational and advocacy assistance. MDMA is relatively new and thus not as big a player as some other groups in the health policy fields (Medical Device Manufacturers of America n.d.).

Other Groups

The increase in the number of people enrolled in managed care plans has also led to a dramatic increase in the number of managed care organizations (MCOs). MCOs vary significantly in their structures, financing mechanisms, and benefit packages. A broad range of health insurers, medical groups, hospitals, and health systems are considered managed care organizations. MCOs can take the form of an HMO, a PPO, or a point-of-service (POS) plan. USA Managed Care Organization (USAMCO) is the largest, most comprehensive privately held Preferred Provider Organization in America (www.usamco.com/).

The increased cost of providing healthcare to employees has led many businesses and industries to form health coalitions to search for solutions to spiraling healthcare costs. Examples of the major health coalitions include Alliance Cost Containment (www.alliancecost.com/); the National Coalition on Healthcare (http://nchc.org/); and the Washington Business Group on Health (www. businessgrouphealth.org/).

There has also been significant growth in consumer/public interest groups in the field of healthcare. These groups essentially act as a voice and advocate for protecting and advancing consumers' interest in healthcare. Such groups include the Health Consumer Alliance (HCA) (http:// healthconsumer.org/); the Society for Healthcare Consumer Advocacy (SHCA) (www.shca-aha. org/); Families USA (www.familiesusa.org/); the American Health Care Association (AHCA) (www.ahcancal.org/); the Center for Health Care Strategies (CHCS) (www.chcs.org/); and the Children's Defense Fund (CDF) (www.childrensdefense.org/). They typically rely on methods such as coalition forming, litigation, lobbying, testifying before congressional committees, and participation in regulatory proceedings to influence healthcare policies.

Two of the most important private, nonpartisan foundations in the field of health are the Robert Wood Johnson Foundation (RWJF) (www.rwjf.org/) and the Kaiser Family Foundation (KFF) (www.kff.org/). The RWJF is the largest private philanthropy foundation devoted solely to the public's health and dedicated to the mission of improving the health and healthcare of all Americans. It does research as well as provides grants in healthcare field. The KFF serves as a nonpartisan source of information about health policy issues, and, unlike grant-making foundations, KFF runs its own research program, sometimes in partnership with other nonprofit organizations. Both are excellent sources of information on healthcare issues for policymakers, administrators, educators, students, and consumers.

CONCLUSION

Healthcare politics and policies in the United States are shaped by a variety of factors. Health policy reflects a combination of initiatives taken by institutions and actors in the public and private sectors. The health policy cycle is influenced and shaped by the constitutional, institutional, political, economic, ideological, and technological environment within which it operates. The public philosophy of interest-group liberalism combined with constitutionally guaranteed freedom of speech, association, and petition allow a variety of interest groups to promote policies for private profit and to successfully defeat policies they perceive as harmful to their interests. Interest groups promote their narrow private interests using the rhetoric of the common good. The consensus created through compromise and bargaining between narrow private interests is often defined as the public interest. Such a policy process makes the establishment of a comprehensive national health policy highly improbable, if not impossible. The result is a mishmash of public and private sector healthcare programs and policies that often reflects conflicting values of access, equality, quality of care, and efficiency.

Effective health policy often requires formulating policies based on research, scientific evidence, facts and rational public debate about the nature of the problem, available policy alternatives, and the best way to address a problem. However, this may become problematic because the scientific evidence is (a) nonexistent, (b) weak, and (c) inconclusive or contradictory, and (d) there is a disagreement over the nature and type of scientific evidence. Even when the scientific evidence is conclusive and strong, it may fail to inform policy making because it conflicts with other societal cultural, moral, or religious values. Thus, it may be ignored or twisted with misinformation and/ or falsehood for partisan, ideological, and electoral calculations. Witness the political controversy surrounding topics such as climate change, the theory of evolution, and stem cell research in American politics. Thus, more often than not, the science of policy making is substituted by the art of deal making. Health policies resulting from such deal making may turn out to be ineffective. However, to understand health policy in the United States, one must understand the health policy environment, including the underlying politics. Further, it is important to keep in mind that no one single factor in the health policy environment influences and shapes health policy making, but rather health policy making in the United States is often a product of a variety of complex but interrelated factors.

STUDY QUESTIONS

1. How does "politics" influence health policy making in the United States? What does one generally mean by politics? Give at least two specific examples where politics influenced health policy making.
2. What constitutes the health policy environment? What are some of the major factors in the health policy environment that influence health policy making in the United States?
3. Write an essay in which you discuss how some of the unique features of the American constitutional environment shape health policy making in the United States. Be sure to give specific examples.
4. How do some of the unique features of American institutions—Congress, the presidency, and the judiciary—shape health policy making in the United States? Give some specific examples.
5. What do the authors mean by "political environment," and what are major elements of this environment that help explain policy making in the United States?
6. What is the theory of incrementalism, and how does the theory of punctuated equilibrium advance our understanding of incremental and major policy changes?
7. Should health policy making in the United States be based solely on best available scientific evidence, or should factors such as public opinion and cultural/social/ and political values also play a role in health policy making? Why?
8. Discuss who some of the major public/government sector health policy actors are in the United States. What makes them major policy actors?

9. Who are some of the major private sector health policy actors in the United States? What makes them major policy actors?

10. Who are some of the major interest groups, and how do they exercise their influence in health policy making?

REFERENCES

ABC News/Washington Post Poll. 2012. "Public Divides on ACA Ruling, but Romney's Plans Fall Shorter." Online at www.langerresearch.com/uploads/1127a33FavorabilityNo33.pdf.

Adler, Jonathan H. 2011. "Cooperation, Commandeering, or Crowding Out? Federal Intervention and State Choices in Health Care Policy." *Kansas Journal of Law and Public Policy* 20, no. 2: 199–221.

Alford, Robert A. 1975. *Health Care Politics: Ideological and Interest Group Barriers to Reform.* Chicago: University of Chicago Press.

Allison, Graham. 1971. *The Essence of Decision.* Boston: Little, Brown.

Altenstetter, Christa. 1974. *Health Policy-Making and Administration in West Germany and the United States.* Beverly Hills, CA: Sage.

Altman, Drew. 2010. "The Falloff in Utilization: 'There Is Something Happening Here, What It Is Ain't Exactly Clear.'" Washington, DC: Henry J. Kaiser Family Foundation. Online at www.kff.org/pullingit-together/altman_falloff_utilization.cfm.

Alphonse, Lylah M. 2011. "Senate Votes Down Repeal of Health Care Law, Plus Five Affordable Care Act Myths Debunked." Online at http://shine.yahoo.com/work-money/senate-votes-down-repeal-of-health-care-law-plus-five-affordable-care-act-myths-debunked-2447757.html.

American Health Care Association. 2012a. *LTC Stats: Nursing Facility Operational Characteristics Report.* Washington, DC: Research Department, American Health Care Association.

———. 2012b. *LTC Stats: Nursing Facility Patient Characteristics Report.* Washington, DC: Research Department, American Health Care Association.

American Hospital Association. 2012. "Fast Facts on U.S. Hospitals." Chicago: American Hospital Association. Online at www.aha.org/research/rc/stat-studies/fast-facts.shtml.

———. n.d. "Vision and Mission." Chicago: American Hospital Association. Online at www.aha.org/about/mission.shtml.

American Medical Association. 2011. *Physician Characteristics and Distribution in the U.S., 2011.* Chicago: American Medical Association.

American Nurses Association. n.d. "Statement of Purpose." Silver Spring, MD: American Nurses Association. Online at http://nursingworld.org/FunctionalMenuCategories/AboutANA/ANAsStatementofPurpose.html.

America's Health Insurance Plans. n.d. "About Us." Washington, DC: America's Health Insurance Plans. Online at www.ahip.org/about/.

Austen-Smith, David. 1993. "Information and Influence: Lobbying for Agendas and Votes." *American Journal of Political Science* 37, no. 3: 799–833.

Badger, Emily. 2010. "Divided Government Usually Means Gridlock." Miller-McCune, *Idea Lobby.* Online at www.miller.mccune.com/politics/divided-government-usually-means-gridlock-25083.

Balducchi, David E., and Stephen A. Wander. 2008. "Work Sharing Policy: Power Sharing and Stalemate in American Federalism." *Publius* 38, no. 1: 111–36.

Balkin, Jack M. 2001. "Bush v. Gore and the Boundary Between Law and Politics." *Yale Law Journal* 110, no. 8: 1407–59.

Banting, Keith G., and Stan Corbett. 2002. "Health Policy and Federalism: An Introduction." In *Health Policy and Federalism: An Introduction,* ed. Keith G. Banting and Stan Corbett, 1–38. School of Policy Studies, Institute of Intergovernmental Relations, Social Union Series. Kingston-Ontario, Canada: Queens University. Online at www.queensu.ca/iigr/pub/archive/socialunionseries.html.

Baumgartner, Frank R. 2006. "Punctuated Equilibrium Theory and Environmental Policy." In *Punctuated Equilibrium and the Dynamics of U.S. Environmental Policy,* ed. Robert C. Repetto, 24–46. New Haven, CT: Yale University Press.

Baumgartner, Frank R.; Jeffrey M. Berry; Marie Hojnacki; David C. Kimball; and Beth L. Leech. 2009. *Lobbying and Policy Change: Who Wins, Who Loses, and Why.* Chicago: University of Chicago Press.

Baumgartner, Frank R., and Bryan D. Jones. 1993. *Agendas and Instability in American Politics.* Chicago: University of Chicago Press.

———. 2009. *Agendas and Instability in American Politics.* 2d ed. Chicago: University of Chicago Press.

Baumgartner, Frank R., and Beth L. Leech. 2001. "Interest Niches and Policy Bandwagons: Patterns of Interest Group Involvement in National Politics." *Journal of Politics* 63, no. 4: 1191–1213.

Bayes, Jane H. 1982. *Ideologies and Interest-Group Politics.* Novato, CA: Chandler and Sharp.

Beer, S.H. 1965. *Modern British Politics.* London: Faber and Faber.

Beland, Daniel, and François Vergniolle de Chantal. 2004. "Fighting 'Big Government': Frames, Federalism, and Social Policy Reform in the United States." *Canadian Journal of Sociology* 29, no. 2: 241–64.

Bennett, James T., and Thomas J. DiLorenzo. 1985. *Destroying America: How Government Funds Partisan Politics.* Washington, DC: Cato Institute.

Berki, S.E. 1983. "Health Care Policy: Lessons from the Past and Issues of the Future." *Annals of the American Academy of Political and Social Science* 468 (July): 231–46.

Biller, Sofia E. 2008. "Flooded by the Lowest Ebb: Congressional Response to Presidential Signing Statements and Executive Hostility to the Operation of Checks and Balances." *Iowa Law Review* 93, no. 3: 1067–1133.

Black, Ryan C.; Anthony J. Madonna; Ryan J. Owens; and Michael S. Lynch. 2007. "Adding Recess Appointment to the President's 'Tool Chest' of Unilateral Powers." *Political Research Quarterly* 60, no. 4: 645–54.

Blendon, Robert J.; Drew E. Altman; John M. Benson; and Mollyann Brodie. 2004. "Election 2004: Health Care in the 2004 Presidential Election." *New England Journal of Medicine* 351, no. 13 (September 23): 314–21.

Blendon, Robert J., and Gillian K. SteelFisher. 2009. "Commentary: Understanding the Underlying Politics of Health Care Policy Decision Making." *Health Services Research* 44, no. 4: 1137–43.

Blendon, Robert J.; Robert Leitman; Ian Morrison; and Karen Donelan. 1990. "Satisfaction with Health Systems in Ten Nations." *Health Affairs* 9, no. 2 (Summer): 185–92.

Bloom, Anne. 2001. "The Post-Attitudinal Moment: Judicial Policy Making Through the Lens of New Institutionalism." *Law & Society Review* 35, no. 1: 219–31.

Bovbjerg, Randall R.; Joshua M. Wiener; and Michael Houseman. 2003. "State and Federal Role in Health Care: Rationale for Allocating Responsibilities." In *Federalism and Health Policy*, ed. John Holahan, Allan Weil, and Joshua Weiner, 25–57. Washington, DC: Urban Institute Press.

"Breaking Down U.S. Health Care Spending." n.d. Washington, DC: Office of the Actuary, Centers for Medicare and Medicaid Services, U.S. Department of Health. Online at www.cms.gov/Research-Statistics-Data-and-Systems/Statistics-Trends-and-Reports/NationalHealthExpendData/Downloads/PieChartSourcesExpenditures2010.pdf.

Breunig, Christian, and Chris Koski. 2006. "Punctuated Equilibria and Budgets in American States." *Policy Studies Journal* 34, no. 3: 363–79.

Brown, J.H.A. 1978. *The Politics of Health Care.* Cambridge, MA: Ballinger.

Brown, Lawrence D. 1978. "The Formulation of Federal Health Care Policy." *Bulletin of the New York Academy of Medicine* 54, no. 1 (January): 45–58.

———. 1984. *Health Policy in the Reagan Administration: A Critical Appraisal.* Washington, DC: Brookings Institution.

Burgin, Eileen. 2003. "Congress, Health Care, and Congressional Caucuses: An Examination of the Diabetes Caucus." *Journal of Health Politics, Policy and Law* 28, no. 5: 789–821.

Bykowicz, Julie, and Greg Stohr. 2012. "Supreme Court Seen Influenced by Politics in Health-Care Ruling." New York: Bloomberg L.P. online at www.bloomberg.com/news/2012–03–15/supreme-court-seen-influenced-by-politics-in-health-care-ruling.html.

Califano, Joseph A. 1988. "The Health-Care Chaos." *New York Times Magazine,* March 20, 44.

Campion, Frank D. 1984. *The AMA and U.S. Health Policy Since 1940.* Chicago: University of Chicago Press.

Casalino, Lawrence P. 2004. "Physicians and Corporations: A Corporate Transformation of American Medicine?" *Journal of Health Politics, Policy and Law* 29, nos. 4–5: 869–83.

Center for Responsive Politics. n.d. "Lobbying Database." Center for Responsive Politics. Online at www.opensecrets.org/influence/index.php.

Centers for Medicare and Medicaid Services. n.d. "National Health Expenditures and GDP: Calendar Years 1960–2010." Washington, DC: U.S. Department of Health and Human Services. Online at www.cms.gov/NationalHealthExpendData/02_NationalHealthAccountsHistorical.asp#TopOfPage.

Christie, Les. 2011. "Number of People Without Health Insurance Climbs." CNN Money. Online at http://money.cnn.com/2011/09/13/news/economy/census_bureau_health_insurance/index.htm

Cohen, Alan B., and Donald R. Cohodes. 1982. "Certificate of Need and Low Capital-Cost Medical Technology." *Milbank Memorial Fund Quarterly/Health and Society* 60, no. 2 (Spring): 307–28.

Colby, David C. 2002. "Federal State Relations in United States Health Policy." In *Health Policy and Federal-*

ism: An Introduction, ed. Keith G. Banting and Stan Corbett, 143–72. School of Policy Studies, Institute of Intergovernmental Relations, Social Union Series. Kingston-Ontario, Canada: Queens University. Online at www.queensu.ca/iigr/pub/archive/socialunionseries.html.

Conley, Richard S. 2003. *The Presidency, Congress, and Divided Government: A Postwar Assessment.* College Station: Texas A&M University Press.

Court, Jamie, and Francis Smith. 1999. *Making a Killing: HMOs and the Threat to Your Health.* Monroe, ME: Common Courage Press.

Cunningham, Paige W. 2011. "Rebellious States Could Be Hazardous to Health Care Overhaul." *Washington Times,* August 26, 1.

Dentzer, Susan. 1990. "America's Scandalous Health Care." *U.S. News and World Report,* March 12, 25–30.

DiIulio, John J., Jr., and Richard R. Nathan, eds. 1994. *Making Health Reform Work: The View from the States.* Washington, DC: Brookings Institution.

Dinan, John. 2008. "The State of American Federalism 2007–2008: Resurgent State Influence in the National Policy Process and Continued State Policy Innovation." *Publius* 38, no. 3: 415–35.

Dudley, Adams R., and Harold S. Luft. 1999. "Goals, Targets, and Tactics: Making Health Care Policy Decisions Explicit." *Journal of Health Politics, Policy, and Law* 24, no. 4: 705–13.

Edwards George C., III, Andrew Barrett, and Jeffrey Peake. 1997. "The Legislative Impact of Divided Government." *American Journal of Political Science* 41, no. 2: 545–63.

Eggen, Dan. 2009a. "Lobbyists Spend Millions to Influence Health Care." *Washington Post,* July 21. Online at http://voices.washingtonpost.com/health-care-reform/2009/07/health_care_continues_its_inte. html.

———. 2009b. "Health-Care Lobbyists Continue Spending Spree." *Washington Post,* October 21. Online at http://voices.washingtonpost.com/health-care-reform/2009/10/health-care_lobbyists_continue. html.

Epstein, Lee, and Jack Knight. 1998. *The Choices Justices Make.* Washington, DC: Congressional Quarterly Press.

"Establishing Health Insurance Exchanges: An Overview of State Efforts." 2012. Washington, DC: Henry J. Kaiser Family Foundation. Online at http://healthreform.kff.org/tags/exchanges.aspx.

Ewing, Benjamin, and Douglas A. Kysar. 2011. "Prods and Pleas: Limited Government in an Era of Unlimited Harm." *Yale Law Review* 121, no. 2: 350–424.

Feeley, Malcolm, and Edward L. Rubin. 2000. *Judicial Policy Making and the Modern State: How the Courts Reformed America's Prisons.* Cambridge, MA: Cambridge University Press.

Fineberg, H.V., and H.H. Hiatt. 1979. "Evaluation of Medical Practices: The Case for Technology Assessment." *New England Journal of Medicine* 301, no. 20: 1086–91.

Foley, Michael, and John E. Owens. 1996. *Congress and the Presidency: Institutional Politics in a Separated System.* Manchester, NY: Manchester University Press.

Frakes, Vincent L. 2012. "Partisanship and (Un)compromise: A Study of the Patient Protection and Affordable Care Act." *Harvard Journal on Legislation* 49 no. 1: 135–49.

Frakt, Austin B.; Steven D. Pizer; and Ann M. Hendricks. 2008. "Controlling Prescription Drug Costs: Regulation and the Role of Interest Groups in Medicare and the Veterans Health Administration." *Journal of Health Politics, Policy and Law* 33, no. 6: 1079–1106.

France, George. 2008. "The Form and Context of Federalism: Meanings for Health Care Financing." *Journal of Health Politics, Policy and Law* 33, no. 4: 649–705.

Freddi, Giorgio. 2009. "Health Care as the Central Civic and Political Problem of the United States: A Comparative Perspective." *European Political Science* 8: 330–44.

Fuchs, Victor R. 1986. *The Health Economy.* Cambridge, MA: Harvard University Press.

———. 1995. *Who Shall Live? Health, Economics and Social Choice.* New York: Basic Books.

Gabel, Jon; Gary Claxton; Isadora Gil; Jeremy Pickreign; Heidi Whitmore; Erin Holve; Benjamin Finder; Samantha Hawkins; and Diane Rowland. 2004. "Health Benefits in 2004: Four Years of Double-Digit Premium Increases Take Their Toll on Coverage." *Health Affairs* 23, no. 5: 200–209.

———. 2005. "Health Benefits in 2005: Increases Slow Down, Coverage Continues to Erode." *Health Affairs* 24, no. 5: 1273–80.

Galderisi, Peter; Roberta Q. Herzberg; and Peter McNamara, eds. 1996. *Divided Government: Change, Uncertainty, and the Constitutional Order.* New York: Rowman and Littlefield.

Gauld, Robin. 2001. "Contextual Pressures on Health—Implications for Policy Making and Service Provision." *Policy Studies* 22, nos. 3–4: 167–79.

Givel, Michael. 2010. "The Evolution of the Theoretical Foundations of Punctuated Equilibrium Theory in Public Policy." *Review of Policy Research* 27, no. 2: 187–98.

Gold, Jenny. 2010. "Mergers of Profit, Non-Profit Hospitals: Who Does It Help?" *USA Today,* July 13. Online at www.usatoday.com/money/industries/health/2010–07–13-hospitalmergers13_CV_N. htm?csp=34money.

Greer, Scott L. 2011. "The States' Role Under the Patient Protection and Affordable Care Act." *Journal of Health Politics, Policy, and Law* 36, no. 3: 469–73.

Greer, Scott L., and Peter D. Jacobson. 2010. "Health Care Reform and Federalism." *Journal of Health Politics, Policy and Law* 35, no. 2: 203–26.

Grier, Peter. 2009. "As Health Care Reform Bill Advances, Public Support Slips." *Christian Science Monitor.* December 22, 1.

Grott, Catherine J. 2006. "The Development of the U.S. Health Care System and the Contemporary Role of the Public Health Department." *Journal of Health and Human Services Administration* 29, no. 3: 336–59.

Gutmann, Amy, and Dennis Thompson. 2010. "The Mindset of Political Compromise." *Perspectives on Politics* 8, no. 4: 1125–43.

Hackey, Robert B., and David A. Rochefort, eds. 2001. *The New Politics of State Health Policy.* Lawrence: University of Kansas Press.

Harbridge, Laurel, and Neil Malhotra. 2011. "Electoral Incentives and Partisan Conflict in Congress: Evidence from Survey Experiments." *American Journal of Political Science* 55, no. 3: 494–510.

Hayes, Michael T. 2001. *The Limits of Policy Change: Incrementalism, Worldview, and the Rule of Law.* Washington, DC: Georgetown University Press.

———. 2006. *Incrementalism and Public Policy.* Lanham, MD: University Press of America.

Health Insurance Association of America.1998. *Sourcebook of Health Insurance Data.* Washington, DC: Health Insurance Association of America.

Heaney, Michael T. 2004. "Issue Networks, Information, and Interest Group Alliances: The Case of Wisconsin Welfare Politics, 1993–99." *State Politics and Policy Quarterly* 4, no. 3 (Fall): 237–70.

———. 2006. "Brokering Health Policy Coalition, Parties, and Interest Group Influence." *Journal of Heath Politics, Policy, and Law* 31, no. 5: 887–944.

Heclo, Hugh. 1978. "Issues Networks and the Executive Establishment." In *The New American Political System,* ed. Anthony King, 87–124. Washington, DC: American Enterprise Institute Press.

Heinz, John P.; Edward O. Laumann; Robert L. Nelson; and Robert H. Salisbury. 1993. *The Hollow Core: Private Interests in National Policy Making.* Cambridge, MA: Harvard University Press.

Herring, Pendleton. 1967. *Group Representation Before Congress.* New York: Russell and Russell.

Herszenhorn, David M. 2011. "House Votes for Repeal of Health Law in a Symbolic Act." *New York Times,* January 19, 1.

"History of Blue Cross Blue Shield." n.d. Online at www.bcbs.com.

Holahan, John; Alan Weil; and Joshua M. Wiener. 2003. *Federalism and Health Policy.* Washington, DC: Urban Institute Press.

Holahan, John, and Vicki Chen. 2011. "Changes in the Health Insurance Coverage in the Great Recession, 2007–2010." Issue Paper, Kaiser Commission on the Medicaid and the Uninsured. Washington, DC: Henry J. Kaiser Family Foundation. Online at www.kff.org/uninsured/upload/8264.pdf.

Holyoke, Thomas T. 2009. "Interest Group Competition and Coalition Formation." *American Journal of Political Science* 53, no. 2: 360–375.

Huitt, Ralph. 1970. "Political Feasibility." In *Policy Analysis in Political Science,* ed. Ira Sharkansky, 399–412. Chicago: Markham.

Jajich-Toth, Cindy, and Burns W. Roper. 1990. "Americans' Views on Health Care: A Study in Contradictions." *Health Affairs* 9, no. 4 (Winter): 149–57.

Jones, Charles O. 1978. *An Introduction to the Study of Public Policy.* North Scituate, MA: Duxbury Press.

———. 1994. *The Presidency as a Separated System.* Washington, DC: Brookings Institution.

Jones, Jeffrey M. 2009. "Economy, Healthcare Top 'Most Important Problem List.'" Washington, DC: Gallup World Headquarters. Online at www.gallup.com/poll/122885/Economy-Healthcare-Top-Important-Problem-List.aspx.

———. 2010. "In U.S., 45% Favor, 48% Oppose Obama Healthcare Plan." Washington, DC: Gallup World Headquarters. Online at www.gallup.com/poll/126521/favor-oppose-obama-healthcare-plan.aspx.

———. 2011. "In U.S., 46% Favor, 40% Oppose Repealing Healthcare Law." Washington, DC: Gallup World Headquarters. Online at www.gallup.com/poll/145496/favor-oppose-repealing-healthcare-law. aspx.

Kaiser Family Foundation. 2012. "Kaiser Health Tracking Poll: Public Opinion on Healthcare Issues." Washington, DC: Henry J. Kaiser Family Foundation. Online at www.kff.org/kaiserpolls/8285.cfm.

Kaiser Family Foundation and Health Research and Educational Trust. 2011. "Employer Health Benefits: 2011 Annual Survey." Menlo Park: CA: Henry J. Kaiser Family Foundation.

Kaiser Health Poll Report. 2004, March–April Edition. Washington, DC: Henry J. Kaiser Family Foundation. Online at www.kff.org/healthpollreport/archive_April2004/1.cfm.

Koszczuk, Jackie. 1995. "Gingrich Puts More Power into Speaker's Hands." *Congressional Quarterly Weekly Report* 53, no. 39 (October 7): 3049–51.

Krause, George A. 2004. "The Secular Decline in Presidential Domestic Policy Making: An Organization Perspective." *Presidential Studies Quarterly* 34, no. 4: 779–92.

Krehbiel, Keith. 1996. "Institutional and Partisan Sources of Gridlock: A Theory of Divided and Unified Government." *Journal of Theoretical Politics* 8, no. 1: 7–40.

Law, Anna O. 2010. "Making Policy in the Margins: The Federal Judiciary's Role in Immigration Policy." *Juniata Voices* 10: 92–98.

Law, David S. 2005. "Appointing Federal Judges: The President, the Senate, and the Prisoner's Dilemma." *Cardozo Law Review* 26, no. 2: 479–523.

Lee, Keon-Hyung; Seung-Bum Yang; and Mankyu Choi. 2009. "The Association Between Hospital Ownership and Technical Efficiency in a Managed Care Environment." *Journal of Medical Systems* 33, no. 4: 307–15.

Lee, Philip R., and Carroll L. Estes. 1983. "New Federalism and Health Policy." *Annals of the American Academy of Political and Social Science* 468 (July): 88–102.

Levey, Noam N. 2010. "More Small Businesses are Offering Health Benefits to Workers." *Los Angeles Times,* December 27. Online at http:articles.latimes.com/2010/de/27/business/la-fi-health-coverage-20101227.

———. 2011. "Health Insurance Benefits Expand Among Small Businesses." February 7. Hudson, NH: Nashua Telegraph. Online at www.nashuatelegraph.com/business/904599–192/health-insurance-benefits-expand-among-small-businesses.html.

———. 2012. "Passing the Buck—Or Empowering States? Who Will Define Essential Health Benefits?" *Health Affairs* 31, no. 4: 663–66.

Light, Paul C. 2000. "Domestic Policy Making." *Presidential Studies Quarterly* 30, no. 1: 109–32.

Lindblom, Charles E. 1959. "The Science of Muddling Through." *Public Administration Review* 19 (Spring): 79–88.

Long, Sharon K; Karen Stockley; and Heather Dahlen. 2012. "Massachusetts Health Reform: Uninsurance Remains Low, Self-Reported Health Status Improves as State Prepares to Tackle Costs." *Health Affairs* 31, no. 2: 444–51.

Loomis, Christopher M. 2009. "The Politics of Uncertainty: Lobbyists and Propaganda in Early Twentieth-Century in America." *Journal of Policy History* 21, no. 2: 187–227.

Lowi, Theodore J. 1967. "The Public Philosophy: Interest Group Liberalism." *American Political Science Review* 61, no. 1 (March): 5–24.

———. 1969. *The End of Liberalism.* New York: Norton.

Luton, Larry S. 2009. "Administrative 'Interpretation' as Policy-Making." *Administrative Theory & Praxis* 31, no. 4: 556–76.

Madison, James. 1961a. "Federalist 51." In *The Federalist Papers,* ed. Clinton Rossiter, 320–25. New York: New American Library.

———. 1961b. "Federalist 10." In *The Federalist Papers,* ed. Clinton Rossiter, 77–84. New York: New American Library.

Mann, Thomas E., and Norman J. Ornstein. 2006. *The Broken Branch: How Congress Is Failing America and How to Get It Back on Track.* New York: Oxford University Press.

———. 2012. *It's Even Worse Than it Looks: How the American Constitutional System Collided with the New Politics of Extremism.* New York: Basic Books.

Manning, John F. 2011. "Separation of Powers as Ordinary Interpretation." *Harvard Law Review* 124, no. 8: 1941–2040.

Mawhinney, Hanne B. 2001. "Theoretical Approaches to Understanding Interest Groups." *Educational Policy* 15, no. 1 (January/March): 187–214.

McCarty, Nolan; Keith T. Poole; and Howard Rosenthal. 2009. "Does Gerrymandering Cause Polarization?" *American Journal of Political Science* 53, no. 3: 666–80.

McCloud, Pamela S. 2011. "Moody's Says Slowest Rate of Growth in 20 Years at Not-For-Profit Hospitals." Online at http://www.darkdaily.com/moodys-says-slowest-rate-of-growth-in-20-years-at-not-for-profit-hospitals-082211#axzz2nwnpF8JK.

McConnell, Grant. 1966. *Private Power and American Democracy.* New York: Knopf.

McKay, Amy. 2012. "Negative Lobbying and Policy Outcomes." *American Politics Research* 40, no. 1: 116–46.

Medical Device Manufacturers of America. n.d. "About MDMA." Washington, DC: Medical Device Manufacturers of America. Online at www.medicaldevices.org/about-mdma.

Miller, Edward Alan. 2008. "Federal Administrative and Judicial Oversight of Medicaid: Policy Legacies and Tandem Institutions Under the Boren Amendment." *Publius* 38, no. 2: 315–42.

Miller, Marc C., and Jeb Barnes, eds. 2004. *Making Policy, Making Laws: An Interbranch Perspective.* Washington, DC: Georgetown University Press.

Mills, Charles W. 1956. *The Power Elite.* New York: Oxford University Press.

Mondics, Chris. 2012. "Supreme Court Begins Three Days of Hearings on Obama's Health Care Overhaul Plan." *Philadelphia Inquirer,* March 27, A01.

Mooney, Gavin. 1986. *Economics, Medicine and Health Care.* Atlantic Highlands, NJ: Humanities Press.

Moran Company. 2011. *Assessing the Financial Implications of Alternative Reimbursement Policies for Nursing Facilities.* Arlington, VA: Moran Company.

Morin, Richard. 1990. "Americans Want Health Care to Save Lives Whatever the Cost." *Washington Post National Weekly Edition,* February 5, 11.

Nathan, Richard P. 2005. "Federalism and Health Policy." *Health Affairs* 24, no. 6: 1458–66.

———. 2006. "Updating Theories of American Federalism." Conference Papers. *American Political Science Association Annual Meeting.* August 31–September 3. Philadelphia, PA.

"National Health Expenditures 2010 Highlights." Washington, DC: U.S. Department of Health and Human Services, Centers for Medicare and Medicaid Services. Online at www.cms.gov/Research-Statistics-Data-and-Systems/Statistics-Trends-and-Reports/NationalHealthExpendData/Downloads/highlights.pdf.

"National Health Expenditures 2010: Sponsor Highlights." n.d. Washington, DC: U.S. Department of Health and Human Services, Centers for Medicare and Medicaid Services. Online at www.cms.gov/Research-Statistics-Data-and-Systems/Statistics-Trends-and-Reports/NationalHealthExpendData/Downloads/sponsors.pdf.

Navarro, Peter. 1984. *The Policy Game: How Special Interests and Ideologues Are Stealing America.* New York: Wiley.

Newport, Frank. 2011. "One Year Later, Americans Split on Healthcare law." Washington, DC: Gallup World Headquarters. Online at www.gallup.com/poll/146729/one-year-later-americans-split-healthcare-law.aspx.

Nicholson, Stephen P., and Robert M. Howard. 2003. "Framing Support for the Supreme Court in the Aftermath of Bush v. Gore." *Journal of Politics* 65, no. 3: 676–95.

Niskanen, William A. 2003. "A Case for Divided Government." *Cato Policy Report* 25, no. 2 (March/April): 2.

"The Nursing Process." n.d. Silver Spring, MD: American Nurses Association. Online at http://nursingworld.org/EspeciallyForYou/What-is-Nursing/Tools-You-Need/Thenursingprocess.html.

Nzelibe, Jide O., and Matthew C. Stephenson. 2010. "Complementary Constraints: Separation of Powers, Rational Voting, and Constitutional Design." *Harvard Law Review* 123, no. 3: 618–54.

O'Keefe, Ed. 2012. "House Has Voted 32 Times to Repeal All or Part of Health-Care Reform Law." Washington Post, July 11. Online at www.washingtonpost.com/blogs/2chambers/post/house-has-voted-32-to-repeal-all-or-part-of-health-care-reform-law-heres-the-full-list/2012/07/10/gJQAzoqgbW_blog.html#pagebreak.

Office of the Federal Register, National Archives and Records Administration.1990. *The United States Government Manual 1990/91.* Washington, DC: Government Printing Office.

Pandich, Scott C. 2007. "Six Out of Seven: The Missing Sin of Federalist 51." *Perspectives on Political Science* 36, no. 3: 148–52.

Patel, Kant, and Mark Rushefsky. 2002. *Health Care Policy in an Age of New Technologies.* Armonk, NY: M.E. Sharpe.

Perlin, Jonathan B., and Kelvin A. Baggett. 2010. "Government, Health and System Information." *Information Knowledge Systems Management* 8, nos. 1–4: 415–34.

Peterson, Mark A. 2001. Health Politics and Policy in a Federal System." *Journal of Health Politics, Policy and Law* 26, no. 6: 1217–22.

Pharmaceutical Research and Manufacturers of America. n.d. "About PhRMA." Washington, DC: Pharmaceutical Research and Manufacturers of America. Online at www.phrma.org/about/phrma.

Plein, Christopher L. 2010. "Federalism, Intergovernmental Relations, and the Challenge of the Medically Uninsurable: A Retrospective on High Risk Pools in the States." *Journal of Health and Human Services Administration* 33, no. 2: 135–57.

Poduval, Murali, and Jayita Poduval. 2008. "Medicine as a Corporate Enterprise: A Welcome Step?" *Mens Sana Monograph* 6, no. 1: 157–74.

Porto, Brian L. 2009. *May It Please the Court: Judicial Processes and Politics in America.* Boca Raton, FL: CRC Press/Taylor Frances Group.

"Private-Market Health Insurance." n.d. Washington, DC: America's Health Insurance Plans. Online at www.ahip.org/issues/private-market-health-insurance.aspx.

Pump, Barry. 2011. "Beyond Metaphors: New Research on Agendas in the Policy Process." *Policy Studies Journal* 39, no. 12: 1–12.

Purcell, Edward A. 2009. *Originalism, Federalism, and the American Constitution: A Historical Inquiry.* New Haven, CT: Yale University Press.

Quadango, Jill. 2011. "Interest-Group Influence on the Patient Protection and Affordable Care Act of 2010: Winners and Losers in the Health Care Reform Debate." *Journal of Health Policy, Policy and Law* 36, no. 3: 449–53.

Quirk, Paul J. 2011. "Polarized Populism: Masses, Elites, and Partisan Conflict." *Forum* 9, no. 1: 1–16.

Ramirez, Mark D. 2009. "The Dynamics of Partisan Conflict on Congressional Approval." *American Journal of Political Science* 53, no. 3: 681–94.

"Rating of Supreme Court Improves as Partisans Switch Sides." 2009. Washington, DC: Gallup World Headquarters. Online at www.gallup.com/poll121196/rating-supreme-court-improves-partisans-switch-sides.aspx.

Repetto, Robert C. 2006. Introduction. In *Punctuated Equilibrium and the Dynamics of U.S. Environmental Policy*, ed. Robert C. Repetto, 1–23. New Haven, CT: Yale University Press.

Rich, Robert F., and William D. White. 1996. *Health Policy, Federalism, and the American States.* Washington, DC: Urban Institute Press.

Robinson, Scott E., and Floun'say R. Carver. 2006. "Punctuated Equilibrium and Congressional Budgeting." *Political Research Qaurterly* 59, no. 1: 161–66.

Robinson, Scott E.; Floun'say R. Carver; Kenneth J. Meier; and Laurence J. O'Toole. 2007. "Explaining Policy Punctuations: Bureaucratization and Budget Change." *American Journal of Political Science* 51, no. 1: 140–50.

Rosenbaum, Walter A. 1985. *Environmental Politics and Policy.* Washington, DC: CQ Press.

Rushefsky, Mark. 2007. *Public Policy in the United States: At the Dawn of the Twenty-First Century.* Armonk, NY: M.E. Sharpe.

Rushefsky, Mark, and Kant Patel. 1998. *Politics, Power and Policy Making: The Case of Health Care Reform in the 1990s.* Armonk, NY: M.E. Sharpe.

Russell, Jill; Trisha Greenhalgh; Emma Byrne; and Janet McDonnell. 2008. "Recognizing Rhetoric in Health Care Policy Analysis." *Journal of Health Services Research and Policy* 13, no. 1: 40–46.

Saad, Lydia. 2011. "Americans Maintain a Negative View of U.S. Healthcare Coverage." Washington, DC: Gallup World Headquarters. Online at www.gallup.com/poll/150788/Americans-Maintain-Negative-View-Healthcare-Coverage.aspx.

Samuelson, Paul. 1970. *Economics.* New York: McGraw-Hill.

Savage, David G., and Noam N. Levey. 2011. "Obama Health Law Reaches High Court." *Los Angeles Times,* November 13, A24.

Schantz, Harvey L., ed. 2001. *Politics in an Era of Divided Government: Elections and Governance in the Second Clinton Administration.* New York: Routledge.

Schattschneider, E.E. 1960. *The Semi-Sovereign People.* New York: Holt, Rinehart, and Winston.

Schlesinger, Mark. 2004. "Health Policy by the Numbers." *Journal of Health Politics, Policy and Law* 29, no. 3: 347–57.

Silver, George A. 1998. "Health-Care Systems." *Grolier Multimedia Encyclopedia.* Grolier Online www.gme.grolier.com.

Simon, Herbert A. 1957. *Models of Man: Social and Rational; Mathematical Essays on Rational Behavior in Society Setting.* New York: Wiley.

Sinclair, Barbara. 2012. *Unorthodox Lawmaking: New Legislative Processes in the U.S. Congress.* Washington, DC: Congressional Quarterly Press.

Skeen, James W. 2003. "Health Care Fraud and Industry Structure in the United States." *Social Policy & Administration* 37, no. 5: 516–29.

Skopol T. 2004. *The Diminished Democracy: From Membership to Management in American Civic Life.* Norman: University of Oklahoma Press.

Smith, Judith G., ed. 1972. *Political Brokers: Money, Organizations, Power and People.* New York: Liveright.

Sorkin, Alan L. 1986. *Health Care and the Changing Economic Environment.* Lexington, MA: DC Heath.

Sparer, Michael S. 2011. "Federalism and the Patient Protection and Affordable Care Act of 2010: The Founding Fathers Would Not Be Surprised." *Journal of Health Politics, Policy and Law* 36, no. 3: 461–68.

Stanley, Harold W., and Richard G. Niemi. 2001. *Vital Statistics on American Politics, 2001–2002.* Washington, DC: CQ Press.

Starr, Paul. 1982. *The Social Transformation of American Medicine.* New York: Basic Books.

Stevenson, David G., and David C. Grabowski. 2008. "Private Equity Investment and Nursing Home Care: Is It a Big Deal?" *Health Affairs* 27, no. 5: 1399–1408.

Stone, Deborah A. 2011. *The Policy Paradox: The Art of Political Decision Making.* 3rd ed. New York: W.W. Norton.

Stone, Daniel. 2011. "A Signal-Jamming Model of Persuasion: Interest Group Funded Policy Research." *Social Choice and Welfare* 37, no. 3: 397–424.

"Study: For-Profit Hospitals Bill Bigger." 2004. Online at http://apolyton.net/showthread.php/116567-Study-says-For-Profit-hospitals-cost-more-than-non-profits.

Taylor, Humphrey. 1990. "U.S. Health Care Built for Waste." *New York Times,* April 17.

Theodoulou, Stella Z., and Chris Kofinis. 2004. *The Art of the Game: Understanding American Public Policy Making.* Belmont, CA: Thomson/Wadsworth.

Thomas, Kenneth R. 2008. *Federalism, State Sovereignty, and the Constitution: Basis and Limits of Congressional Power.* Congressional Research Service Report. Washington, DC: Federation of American Scientists.

Thompson, Frank J. 1986. "New Federalism and Health Care Policy: States and the Old Questions." *Journal of Health Politics, Policy and Law* 11, no. 4 (Tenth Anniversary Issue): 647–69.

Thompson, Frank J., and John J. DiIulio Jr. 1998. *Medicaid and Devolution: A View from the States.* Washington, DC: Brookings Institution Press.

Tichenor, Daniel J., and Richard A. Harris. 2002/2003. "Organized Interests and American Political Development." *Political Science Quarterly* 117, no. 4 (Winter): 587–612.

"Top 20 PAC Contributors to Federal Candidates, 2001–2002." n.d. Center for Responsive Politics. Washington, DC. Online at www.opensecrets.org.

Toner, Robin. 1993. "Clinton's Health Plan: Poll on Changes in Health Care Finds Support Among Skepticism." *New York Times,* September 23. Online at www.nytimes.com/1993/09/22/us/clinton-s-health-plan-poll-changes-health-care-finds-support-amid-skepticism.html?pagewanted=all&src=pm.

Torpey, Elka M. 2011. "Nursing Jobs in Nursing Homes." *Occupational Outlook Quarterly* 55, no. 1: 23–33.

Trevor, Thrall A. 2006. "The Myth of Outside Strategy: Mass Media News Coverage of Interest Groups." *Political Communication* 23, no. 4: 407–20.

Truman, David B. 1951. *Governmental Process, Political Interests and Public Opinion.* New York: Knopf.

Tuulonen, Anja. 2005. "The Effects of Structures on Decision-Making Politics in Health Care." *Acta Ophthalmologica Scandanavia* 83, no. 5: 611–17.

"2009 Registered Nurses Employment and Earnings." 2010. Silver Spring, MD: American Nurses Association. Online at www.nursingworld.org/MainMenuCategories/Policy-Advocacy/Positions-and-Resolutions/Issue-Briefs/RN-Employment-Earnings.pdf.

Unekis, Joseph. 2011. "Divided Government May Mean Gridlock Rules, Says Congressional Expert." Press release, Kansas State University. Online at www.k.state.edu/media/newsreleases/feb11/congressunekis21711.html.

Ungar, Rick. 2011. "More Small Businesses Offering Health Care to Employees Thanks to Obamacare." January 6. *Forbes Magazine.* Online at www.forbes.com/sites/rickungar/2011/01/06/more-small-businesses-offering-health-care-to-employees-thanks-to-obamacare/.

Uslaner, Eric M. 1993. *The Decline of Comity in Congress.* Ann Arbor: University of Michigan Press.

Vladeck, Bruce C. 1980. *Unloving Care: The Nursing Home Tragedy.* New York: Basic Books.

Wagner, Lynn. 1990. "Health PACs Modest Donors—Study." *Modern Healthcare* 20, no. 38 (September 24): 4.

Walker, J.L., Jr. 1991. *Mobilizing Interest Groups in America.* Ann Arbor: University of Michigan Press.

Ward, Paul D. 1979. "Health Lobbies: Vested Interests and Pressure Politics." In *Politics of Health,* ed. Douglas Carter and Philip R. Lee, 28–47. Huntington, NY: Robert F. Krieger.

Weeks, Lewis E., and Howard J. Berman. 1985. *Shapers of American Health Care Policy: An Oral History.* Ann Arbor, MI: Health Administration Press.

Weissert, Carol S., and William G. Weissert. 1996. *Governing Health: The Politics of Health Policy.* Baltimore: Johns Hopkins University Press.

"What Nurses Do." n.d. Silver Spring: MD: American Nurses Association. Online at http://nursingworld.org/EspeciallyForYou/What-is-Nursing/Tools-You-Need/RNsAPNs.html.

Wilsford, David. 1991. *Doctors and the State: The Politics of Health Care in France and the United States.* Durham, NC: Duke University Press.

Wilson, Michael L., Stephen Gradus, and Scott J. Zimmerman. 2010. "The Role of the Local Public Health Laboratories." *Public Health Reports* 125, Supplement 2:118–22.

Wood, Robert S. 2006. "The Dynamics of Incrementalism: Subsystems, Politics, and Public Lands." *Policy Studies Journal* 34, no. 1: 1–16.

Workman, Samuel, and Ashley E. Jochim. 2009. "Information Processing and Policy Dynamics." *Policy Studies Journal* 37, no. 1: 75–92.

Young, Aaron; Hamayoun J. Chaudhry; Janelle Rhyne; and Michael Dugan. 2011. "A Census of Actively Licensed Physicians in the United States, 2010." *Journal of Medical Regulation* 96, no. 4: 10–20.

Young, Jeffrey. 2009. "Coke. Pepsi Step Up Spending After being Targeted by Healthcare Reform Tax." The Hill.Com. November 26. Online at http://thehill.com/business-a-lobbying/69561-coke-pepsi-step-up-spending-after-being-targeted-by-tax.

2

HEALTHCARE POLICY IN
THE UNITED STATES

There are substantial differences in the healthcare systems of various countries. They differ with respect to financing, delivery of healthcare, and the role of the government. Today there are three primary models of healthcare. In a mostly private healthcare system, workers and their dependents are covered through private insurance, even though the insurance is generally bought through employers. Government provides public insurance programs for those not covered by private insurance. Mostly private hospitals and doctors deliver healthcare. The United States is an example of such a system (Hacker 2002).

Other countries have a healthcare system that is mostly public. Healthcare is paid out of general taxation or through payroll taxes. It is provided by publicly owned hospitals and salaried doctors. Examples of countries with such a system include Great Britain, Sweden, and Italy. The third model of healthcare system is a hybrid model. In such a system, healthcare is mostly publicly financed, generally through payroll taxes, but is delivered by private hospitals and doctors. Germany, Japan, Canada, France, and Holland exhibit variants of this model. Most countries incorporate public and private elements in their healthcare systems ("A Survey of Healthcare" 1991).

As mentioned, the U.S. healthcare system follows the model of the mostly private healthcare system. A majority of Americans are covered through private insurance, usually bought through their employers. The government provides public insurance programs to cover the healthcare needs of groups such as the poor, the disabled, the elderly, veterans, and children. Nevertheless, public insurance programs do not cover all uninsured Americans. Public programs do not cover a sizable number of individuals who cannot afford private health insurance for one reason or another.

The United States spends proportionately more money on healthcare than all other Western industrialized nations. Statistics compiled by the Organization for Economic Cooperation and Development (OECD) indicate that in 2009 total healthcare expenditures in the United States amounted to 17.4 percent of gross domestic product (GDP), compared to 11.6 percent for Germany, 11.8 percent for France, 11.4 percent for Canada, and 9.8 percent for Great Britain. Among the thirty member countries of the OECD, the United States ranked first in terms of percent of GDP devoted to healthcare expenditures. During the same year, the United States also spent more money per capita on healthcare than any other member country. In 2009, the United States spent $7,960 per capita on healthcare, compared to $4,218 in Germany, $3,978 in France, $4,363 in Canada, and $3,487 in Great Britain ("OECD Health Data" 2011).

Despite the fact that the United States spent more money per capita on healthcare, in 2008 it ranked lower than Germany, France, Canada, and Great Britain in male and female life expectancy. The United States also had higher infant mortality rates compared to Germany, France, Canada, and Great Britain ("OECD Health Data" 2011).

The United States also does not compare favorably with respect to some of the healthcare resources. For example, in 2009, the United States had 2.4 doctors per 1,000 population, compared to 3.3 in France, 3.6 in Germany, and 2.7 in Great Britain. The United States had 3.1 hospitals per 1,000 population compared to 6.6 in France, 8.2 in Germany, and 3.3 in Great Britain. The United States had more nurses—10.8 per 1,000 population compared to 8.2 in France and 9.7 in Great Britain ("OECD Health Data" 2011).

The U.S. healthcare system also has other problems. Healthcare costs continue to soar. The number of uninsured Americans continues to rise and is currently estimated to be around 48 million. By the early 1990s, many hospitals in large cities were reporting long waiting lines in emergency departments, with many Medicaid patients leaving in frustration without receiving treatment (Baker, Stevens, and Brook 1991; Bindman et al. 1991; Hilts 1991). Conditions in hospital emergency rooms have not improved since then. Annually, more than 100 million Americans end up in hospital emergency rooms for care and, according to the Centers for Diseases Control and Prevention, the American healthcare system is most likely to fail these individuals (Snyder 2006). According to the data from the American College of Emergency Physicians [www.acep.org/], the capacity of the country's emergency system has decreased by 14 percent since 1993 because more than a 1,000 hospitals have closed their emergency departments nationwide while demand for emergency hospital care has continued to increase (Snyder 2006). In 2006, a task force of the American College of Emergency Physicians issued a first-ever report card and gave a grade of C– to the country's emergency system. In fact, 60 percent of the national emergency system received a mediocre or failing grade (American College of Emergency Physicians 2006).

Of course, much of the demand for emergency care comes from the uninsured Americans because they receive less preventive care, are diagnosed with more advanced stages of illness, tend to receive less therapeutic care, and have a higher mortality rates. Because they have poorer general health, they end up in emergency rooms since they have nowhere else to go for care. Thus, the use of emergency room by primary patients at urban safety-net hospitals is very high (Lasser et al. 2012). Hospitals are required by federal law to provide emergency care to the uninsured without any federal funds, creating a cash problem for many hospitals. The biggest challenge facing the twenty-first-century emergency care system is how to meet increased demand in the face of inadequate system capacity (Committee on the Future of Emergency Care in the United States Health System 2007).

As mentioned in chapter 1, a majority of Americans express very low satisfaction with the U.S. healthcare system and believe that increased healthcare expenditures have not been matched by similar increases in the quality of treatment. Scholarly and journalistic literature has described the U.S. healthcare system as "broken" ("The Health Care System Is Broken" 1991), "still broken" (Davidson 2010), "sick" (Cohn 2008; Lewis 1991; Lynn 2004), "a disgrace" (Ehrenreich 1990), "wasteful" (Terris 1990), "built for waste" (Taylor 1990), "scandalous" (Dentzer 1990), "in crisis" (Ropes 1991), "deadly" (Moore 1995), "mismanaged" (Makover 1998), "accidental" (Reagan 1999), "licensed to steal" (Sparrow 2000), "an oxymoron" (Kleinke 2001), "in financial crisis" (Clark and McEldowney 2001), "fragmented" (McCarthy 2001; Elhauge 2010), "ailing" (Geyman 2002), "a mess" (Richmond 2005), "disorganized and irrational" (Mechanic 2004), "one nation, uninsured" (Quadagno 2005), in "critical condition" or "critical" (Barlett and Steele 2006; Daschle, Greenberger, and Lambrew 2008; Taurel 2005), and "unsystematic" (Budrys 2011).

The patients in the American healthcare system are often described as "suffering" (Downing 2006), "worried sick" (Hadler 2008), "falling through the safety net" (Geyman 2005), "stuck in the waiting room" (Smerd 2006), "overdosed" (Abramson 2004), "overtreated" (Brownlee 2007; Hadler 2008), "overdiagnosed" (Welch, Swartz, and Woloshin 2011), "suffering from too much medicine" (Gottfried 2009), and surrounded by the "wall of silence" (Gibson 2003) in which they are left to "heal themselves" (Veatch 2009).

According to some analysts, the truth is that the American healthcare system puts health against wealth in which corporate production of health goods for profit leads to multimillion-dollar PR campaigns designed to engage in "deadly spin" to mislead the press and the public and skew political debate, making true healthcare reform difficult (Anders 1997; Geyman 2010; Herzlinger 2007; Mechanic 2008; Potter 2010; Singer and Baer 2009; Starr 2011). The American healthcare system is suffering and needs "healing" (Cortese 2006; Downing 2006; Reed 2009) and "fixing" (Rangel 2009).

In this chapter we examine the historical development of healthcare policies in the United States. We discuss private and public sector policy initiatives and various factors that have shaped healthcare policy. The major emphasis is on the development of federal healthcare policies and how these policies have attempted to address the goals of equity, quality, and efficiency. The chapter also briefly explores the roles of state and local governments.

HEALTHCARE IN THE NINETEENTH CENTURY

The progress of medicine, or the "healing arts," was very slow in the 1700s and 1800s. Neither healthcare nor the biosciences received a great deal of popular support in the United States in the early 1800s. The biological sciences were not very popular with the general public. During the 1840s, a proposal for the establishment of a National Institute of Science, funded by the federal government, was rejected repeatedly by Congress. Finally, during the Civil War, the National Academy of Sciences was established in 1863 on the grounds of its usefulness to the Union armies (Hill 1976). During the Civil War the state of American medicine was very poor. The use of ether and chloroform was crude and often unavailable. Many surgical procedures were performed on the battlefield or in a field hospital without anesthesia (Rutkow 2005).

The American Medical Association (AMA) was formed in 1847. During the latter part of the nineteenth century, physicians and pharmacists were the sole dispensers of professionally recognized health services. Most physicians were trained through apprenticeships with practicing physicians. Physicians also established "diploma mills" to train several students at a time. Later, private and public schools set up medical schools to train physicians. Physicians made their living treating patients for fees and received very little money from the government. The same was true of pharmacists, who later developed drugstores to supplement their income from prescriptions. Thus, private practice and fee for service was firmly established in the early U.S. healthcare system (Anderson 1985).

During the nineteenth century, public health activities were devoted to preventing the spread of communicable diseases and were confined primarily to major cities until the Civil War. In response to epidemics, a city board or commission was appointed to establish regulations for the maintenance of a sanitary environment. Only after the Civil War did state boards of health become popular. By the end of the nineteenth century, boards of health had been established within the governments of most large cities and at the state level. Their functions were limited to enforcement of sanitary regulations and control of certain communicable diseases. The scope of the health departments did not expand until the turn of the century (Patel and Rushefsky 2005a; Roemer 1986). Public health services were separated from the private practice of medicine, and public health officers were not allowed to practice medicine (Patel and Rushefsky 2005a).

General hospitals, as we know them today, did not exist. Poorhouses and almshouses provided care for destitute persons. The origin of a hospital system in the United States is associated with the establishment of the first marine hospital in 1799 (Raffel 1980). Both the army and the navy had their own requirements for treating sickness, and they differed from those of the U.S. Marine Service. Between 1830 and 1860, marine hospitals proliferated. During the Civil War, the Marine Hospital Service was very much neglected and the number of hospitals decreased. In 1869, Congress reviewed the Marine Hospital Service and passed the first Reorganization Act in 1870. Under this law, the Marine Hospital Service was federalized and formally organized as a national agency with a central headquarters (U.S. Health Resources Administration 1976). The building of mental hospitals also preceded the development of personal health services. Mental hospitals were and continue to be largely publicly owned and operated.

The last quarter of the nineteenth century saw a steady advance in medical science (Stevens 2007; Stevens, Rosenberg, and Burns 2006; Warner and Tighe 2001). Antiseptic surgery was highly developed by 1875. The science of microbiology was introduced, and techniques of vaccination were developed. The advent of anesthesia and antisepsis made general hospitals a relatively safe place for surgery. Early general hospitals were established mostly by voluntary community boards and churches. The growing economy made it possible for hospitals to obtain capital funds from philanthropists and operating funds from paying patients. Voluntary hospitals, because of their charitable and nonprofit charters, were obligated to provide care for the poor. Physicians began to admit patients to hospitals for surgeries. Patients paid for hospital charges and physicians' fees. In return, hospitals provided physicians with their facilities to give free care to the poor. In 1875 there were very few general hospitals in the country. The number of hospitals grew tremendously in the nineteenth century. By the end of 2003 there were a total of 5,764 registered hospitals in the United States (American Hospital Association 2005).

THE TRANSFORMATION OF AMERICAN MEDICINE: 1900–1935

During the first decade of the twentieth century, the process of consolidation of medical education and the transformation of American medicine began to take shape. For a number of years, the AMA had been trying to force inferior medical schools to close in order to reduce the numbers of institutions competing for philanthropic support (Fox 1986). Reform of medical schools was the top priority of the AMA. The Council on Medical Education, established by the AMA in 1904, elevated and standardized requirements for medical education for physicians. In addition, in order to identify and pressure weaker institutions, the council began to grade medical schools and later extended its evaluation to include curriculum, facilities, faculty, and requirements for admissions (Starr 1982).

Philanthropic foundations often had power and influence, but they lacked authority. Their financial power was limited by their fear that legislatures that chartered them would restrict their power or tax them out of existence. Nevertheless, placing medical education on a more scientific basis had also become their top priority. Several foundations began to finance studies that recommended reorganization of medical education and medical care. The AMA Council invited an outside group, the Carnegie Foundation for the Advancement of Teaching, to investigate medical schools. Abraham Flexner, as a representative of the Carnegie Foundation, visited each of the medical schools in the country during 1909 and 1910. He saw a great discrepancy between medical science and medical education. His report, known as the Flexner Report, was published in 1910 and recommended adoption of the German model of medicine with scientifically based training, the strengthening of first-class medical schools, and the elimination of a great majority of inferior schools.

Following the Flexner Report, the process of consolidation of medical education proceeded at a rapid pace. By 1915, the number of medical schools had decreased from 131 to 95. Similarly, the number of graduates from medical schools dropped from 5,440 to 3,536. Mergers between class A and class B schools became common. The AMA Council became a national accrediting agency for medical schools, and many states came to accept its judgments regarding those schools. The new system increased the homogeneity and cohesiveness of the medical profession (Starr 1982). By the 1940s the AMA had become a powerful political force and a major player in shaping U.S. healthcare policy (Campion 1984).

Another significant development during this period was the rise of the third-party payment system in U.S. medicine. Prior to the 1930s, medical insurance programs were nonexistent. During the Great Depression of the 1930s, the incomes of hospitals and physicians declined. Many people could not afford to pay hospitals or physicians for their medical services. Realizing that they could operate better with a steady income, hospitals began to sponsor prepayment plans, which came to be known as the Blue Cross plans. Similarly, prepayment plans for physicians' services in the hospital, especially surgery, also began to appear. Sponsored by state medical societies, they became known as Blue Shield plans. Both the Blue Cross and the Blue Shield plans were very successful. During the 1940s, the federal government encouraged the development of private, voluntary insurance plans. For example, Congress gave voluntary plans a financial boost by legislating that health insurance and pensions were fringe benefits and exempt from a wartime freeze on wages. Thus, employers could offer their workers healthcare fringe benefits by paying for part or all of the cost of their insurance premiums. A ruling by the Internal Revenue Service in 1951 that employers' costs for premiums were a tax-deductible expense made large-scale development of private health insurance viable.

The rise of third-party payment led to increases in visits to physicians and admissions to hospitals. The third-party payment system replaced the financing system based on one-on-one financial transactions between patient and physician. Third-party payers insulated healthcare consumers from the realities of healthcare costs, leading to overconsumption, a problem called "moral hazard" by economists. Physicians and hospitals prospered. Since insurance companies reimbursed hospitals for the charges and/or costs of hospital services received by the patient, third-party payments made hospitals financially secure and independent because they could count on a steady income. Physicians prospered because they were paid by voluntary health insurance according to generous fee schedules negotiated by the Blue Shield plans.

THE ROLE OF THE FEDERAL GOVERNMENT

The Beginnings: 1800s

During much of the nineteenth century, the role of the federal government in healthcare was limited to providing public health services. In 1798 President John Adams signed into law an act that provided for the relief of sick and disabled seamen. This led to the development of marine hospitals during the nineteenth century. The American Public Health Association (APHA), composed mainly of social workers, was founded in 1872. Its main concern was the social and economic aspects of health problems. Following the Civil War, Congress in 1878 passed a National Quarantine Act for the purpose of preventing entry into the country of persons with communicable diseases. The period from 1870 to 1910 witnessed the maturation of the government's public health services. Health boards and health departments became widespread features of local and state governments; their functions were limited to the enforcement of sanitary regulations and control of communicable diseases. The AMA, which earlier had supported an expanded federal role in healthcare, came to view increased public health activities as a threat to economic interests of the physicians. The AMA began to attack all proposals designed to extend the role of government in healthcare.

Limited Federal Role: 1900s–1930s

During the late nineteenth and early part of the twentieth century, countries in Europe were establishing compulsory sickness insurance programs. Germany established the first national system of compulsory sickness insurance in 1883. Similar systems were established in Austria in 1888, Hungary in 1891, Norway in 1910, Britain in 1911, Russia in 1912, and the Netherlands in 1913. France and Italy required sickness insurance in only a few industries. Countries such as Sweden, Denmark, and Switzerland gave extensive state aid to voluntary funds and provided incentives for membership (Starr 1982).

The federal government in the United States, in contrast to happenings in Europe, took no action to subsidize voluntary funds or to make sickness insurance mandatory. This partly reflected existing political conditions and institutions in the United States, where, as a result of the influence of the public philosophy of classical liberalism, government was highly decentralized and played a very small role in regulation of the economy or in promoting social welfare.

Health insurance became a political issue in the United States on the eve of World War I. The progress of a workman's compensation (now referred to as worker's compensation) law between 1910 and 1913 encouraged reformers to believe that adoption of compulsory insurance against industrial accidents would lead to the adoption of compulsory sickness insurance. But the progressive reformers' hopes of strengthening government and adopting compulsory sickness insurance were soon dashed. Opposition from physicians and pharmaceutical and insurance companies defeated their reform proposals. In addition, both labor unions and business, fearing competition from government in social welfare programs, failed to support the reformers. By 1920, the movement for compulsory sickness insurance had faded from the political agenda.

Under pressure from the labor movement and children's advocates, Congress passed the Sheppard-Towner Act in 1921. It established the first federal grant-in-aid program for local child health clinics. But many local health departments refused to accept these grants because the AMA and local medical societies strongly opposed the program. Congress allowed the program to terminate in 1928 (Roemer 1984). Thus, the federal government's role in healthcare remained very limited during the nineteenth and early twentieth centuries.

Expanded Federal Role: 1930s–1960s

Increased Emphasis on Biomedical Research: 1930s

A number of significant developments took place in the healthcare field during the 1930s. One major development, as mentioned earlier, was the start of a third-party payment system with the establishment of the Blue Cross and Blue Shield insurance plans. This revolutionized healthcare financing and led to employer-based health insurance programs. A second development concerned advances in medical technology and the discovery of antibiotics. Antibiotics changed the focus of medical care from prevention of disease through inoculation and hygiene to cure of illnesses (Bernstein and Bernstein 1988). For the first time, sulfa drugs and penicillin gave physicians their true power to cure (Easterbrook 1987). The third development was the shift from local control of health and welfare issues to state and especially federal government control. Workman's compensation, pensions, unemployment insurance, and certain medical services came to be perceived by the people as the responsibility of the federal government (Greifinger and Sidel 1978). This was because of the Great Depression and the economic problems of state and local governments. The problems facing the country were too large for any but federal solutions.

The establishment of the National Cancer Institute in 1937, with a broad mandate for ascertaining the cause, prevention, and cure of disease, reflected the increased role of the federal government in healthcare in general and in public health services in particular. Later it paved the way for public funding of biomedical research through the National Institutes of Health (NIH) and later through the National Science Foundation (NSF). In 1934, during the Great Depression, the Federal Emergency Relief Administration gave the first federal grants to local governments for public assistance to the poor, including financial support for medical care.

During the depression, there was also an increased demand for social insurance as differentiated from insurance against specific risks. Most Western countries had placed a higher priority on establishing health insurance programs as a natural outgrowth of insurance against industrial accidents. Old-age pensions and unemployment insurance programs received a lower priority in these countries. In the United States, with millions of people out of work as a result of the depression, unemployment insurance and old-age pensions received the higher priority. Thus the United States, rather than move in the direction of providing free medical care or reimbursement for its costs, as many Western European countries had done, attempted to supply more general social security benefits.

The Social Security Act of 1935 provided for unemployment compensation, old-age pensions, and other benefits. The early planning of the legislation had initially included health insurance as part of the package. However, the Roosevelt administration did not want to jeopardize the enactment of the entire law because of strong opposition to health insurance by the medical profession. Therefore, national health insurance (NHI) was omitted from the final legislative proposal. The Social Security Act did extend the role of the federal government in healthcare by including provisions designed to strengthen public health services. These provisions called for federal matching grants-in-aid to states for maternal and infant care and diagnosis and treatment of crippled children. Federal grants were also made available for general public health purposes under the administration of the U.S. Public Health Service (USPHS), which had evolved in 1912 from the Marine Hospital Service.

In 1937 Congress passed the National Cancer Act. It established the National Cancer Institute (NCI) and set a national pattern for the federal support of biomedical research. The law authorized the NCI to conduct research in its own laboratories and to award grants to nongovernment scientists and institutions for training scientists and clinicians.

During 1935–36, the USPHS conducted a national health survey that revealed many untreated diseases in the population, especially in low-income groups. This led Senator Robert Wagner (D-NY), sponsor of the Social Security Act, to introduce an amendment to the act that would have provided federal grants to the states for the organization of health insurance plans covering workers and their dependents. The onset of World War II postponed any serious consideration of such a plan (Roemer 1986). Similar attempts to establish a health insurance program under the Truman administration were defeated during the 1940s. The medical profession had succeeded in defeating proposals for any national health insurance.

Expansion of Health Facilities and Services: 1940s

After the war, the Truman administration called for the expansion of hospitals, and more support for public health, maternal, and child health services, and federal aid for medical research and education. The administration's aim was to expand the country's medical resources and facilities, reduce the financial burden for their use, and in the process expand access to medical care (Starr 1982). One major problem was that no new hospital construction had taken place during the depression or World War II, a period of some sixteen years.

In 1946 Congress passed the National Hospital Survey and Construction Act, also known as the Hill-Burton Act. This program provided federal funds to subsidize construction of hospitals in areas of bed shortages, mainly in rural counties. State public health agencies were made responsible for surveying the hospital-bed supply in each state and for developing a master plan for the construction of new hospitals. They were also assigned the task of inspecting and licensing all hospitals and related facilities.

Physicians welcomed Hill-Burton funds and actively sought them for construction of new hospitals for reasons of prestige, convenience, and service. Many physicians did not have privileges to treat their patients in the limited number of hospitals that were in existence. These physicians, faced with a limited supply of hospitals and beds and restricted access to them, supported the construction of new hospitals in the hope that they would enjoy the privilege of treating their patients in newly constructed hospitals. In addition, local pressure favoring nearby facilities, tax-favored bonds, and assured income from insurance companies and later from Medicare contributed to the proliferation of hospitals (Bernstein and Bernstein 1988).

As the number of hospitals increased, a nongovernmental Joint Commission on Accreditation of Hospitals was established in 1952. Between 1947 and 1966, the number of voluntary, not-for-profit hospitals increased from 2,584 to 3,426. During the same period, state and local government general hospitals increased from 785 to 1,453. The total number of hospitals (for-profit, state and local government, and voluntary not-for-profit) increased from 4,445 to 5,736. The rate of hospital admissions per 1,000 population increased from 54 in 1935 to 129 in 1960 (Stevens 1989).

Congress, in 1946, also passed the National Mental Health Act. This law provided federal grants to states for research, prevention, diagnosis, and treatment of mental disorders. During the 1950s, there was also further expansion of public health services at the federal level. The NIH greatly expanded support of biomedical research. By the end of the 1950s, the role of the federal government in healthcare had increased significantly compared to its role in the early 1900s. There was a corresponding increase in the role of state and local governments in the field of public health services.

Increasing Access to Healthcare: 1950s–1960s

From the 1920s to the 1950s, efforts to establish a system of national healthcare or insurance for the entire population had failed because of charges from the medical profession and others that such plans would constitute "socialized medicine." The concept of socialized medicine went against the general public philosophy of classical liberalism, which advocates a limited role for government, and the specific philosophy of interest-group liberalism, wherein different interest groups exercise countervailing veto power over governmental policy decisions.

Faced with opposition to comprehensive change, advocates of a national system of healthcare or insurance changed their strategy and objectives and turned to an incremental strategy. They began to advocate increasing access to healthcare for the needy. Rather than push for universal coverage, under which the federal government would provide health insurance to all on a compulsory basis, they began to push for a limited system of health insurance for specific needy groups such as the elderly. The elderly were a perfect target group for providing help because of their greater medical need, inadequate financial resources, and loss of employment-based group medical insurance upon retirement. Additionally, the elderly were deemed worthy and were not stigmatized as a failed group, as were welfare recipients (Schneider and Ingram 2004). The healthcare problems of the elderly would be faced by most of us; almost everyone grows old, after all. This new approach also accommodated the federal structure of government by emphasizing that such programs would be administered by state governments with the federal government providing financial aid to states.

The result was the passage of the Kerr-Mills Act (also known as the Medical Assistance Act) by Congress in 1960. The law provided federal matching payments to states for vendor (provider) payments and allowed states to include the medically needy (i.e., elderly, blind, and disabled persons with low income who were not on public assistance). The act also suggested the scope of services to be covered, such as hospitals, nursing homes, physicians, and other health services. It also required each state to plan for institutional and noninstitutional care as a condition of federal cost sharing. State participation in the program was optional, and states were left free to determine eligibility and the extent of services provided. Most important, the act established the concept of "medical indigency."

The Kerr-Mills program proved to be neither effective nor adequate (Bernstein and Bernstein 1988). It failed to provide significant relief for a substantial portion of the elderly population. An investigation by the Senate Subcommittee on the Health of the Elderly in 1963 revealed that only 1 percent of the nation's elderly received help under the program. The report also highlighted several other problems such as stringent eligibility rules and high administrative costs of state governments

(U.S. Health Resources Administration 1976). Clearly, the issue of financing healthcare for the elderly had not been resolved and remained on the political agenda.

The Kennedy administration, on assuming office in 1961, was committed to increasing access to healthcare for millions of Americans. Having won a narrow victory in the 1960 presidential election, however, President Kennedy was not in a position to push for a universal insurance program. He faced a Congress that was not very amenable to his legislative proposals. He hoped that the 1962 congressional elections would produce a more receptive Congress. But he was able to keep the issue of healthcare needs of the elderly alive and on the political agenda (Fein 1986). On February 21, 1963, Kennedy delivered his "Special Message on Aiding Our Senior Citizens." The message contained thirty-nine legislative recommendations. The key proposal was Medicare to meet the medical needs of the elderly. It had two objectives. One was protection against the cost of serious illness. The other was to serve as a base of insurance protection on which supplementary private programs could be added (David 1985). The assassination of Kennedy in November 1963 left the task of carrying on the battle for Medicare to his successor, Lyndon Johnson.

Lyndon Johnson adopted most of Kennedy's unfinished legislative proposals and incorporated them into the Great Society's War on Poverty program. After civil rights, Medicare was second in the administration's priorities. Johnson saw Medicare as an essential part of his War on Poverty (David 1985). Johnson won a landslide victory in the 1964 presidential election, which allowed him to claim a public mandate for his programs. Equally important was the fact that Democrats also won major victories in congressional elections. The administration now had enough votes in the House and the Senate for the passage of its healthcare proposals.

Health insurance was at the top of the legislative agenda in 1965. The Johnson administration proposed compulsory hospital insurance for the elderly, financed through payroll taxes. Republicans offered a proposal for subsidized, voluntary insurance for the aged, including coverage for physicians' services financed through general revenues. The AMA opposed both plans and advocated expansion of the Kerr-Mills program of matching grants to the states for vendor payments for the needy. Both opponents and proponents used traditional concepts, symbols, and clichés in the debate. Opponents, especially the AMA and insurance companies, opposed the Johnson administration's proposal on the grounds that it was compulsory, it represented socialized medicine, it would reduce the quality of care, and it was "un-American." The proponents defended the plan as designed to help the needy by providing them with access to medical care and thus compatible with American ideals of equity and equality (Skidmore 1970).

In 1965 Congress passed the Medicare program for the elderly and the Medicaid program for the poor as amendments to the Social Security Act of 1935. This final product was a classic compromise between three competing proposals. It included a compulsory health insurance program for the elderly, financed through payroll taxes (Medicare Part A, the Johnson administration proposal), a voluntary insurance program for physicians' services subsidized through general revenues (Medicare Part B, the Republican proposal), and an expanded means-tested program administered by the states (Medicaid, the AMA proposal).

In addition to Medicare and Medicaid, a number of other health programs, such as Maternal and Infant Care (MIC), the Children Supplemental Feeding Program, and community health centers, were created during the 1960s as part of Johnson's War on Poverty.

The principal objective of the Medicare and Medicaid programs was to provide equal access to healthcare for the elderly and the poor. Both programs dramatically increased access to healthcare (Darling 1986). Medicare helped alleviate substantial financially related barriers to healthcare access that existed before the program's enactment (Long and Settle 1984). It greatly expanded financial access to acute care for the elderly and disabled (Aaron 1991).

In recent years, concerns over rising healthcare costs and efforts at cost containment have led to tradeoffs between cost containment and access to healthcare. This situation has created new problems and gaps in access to healthcare. The next section provides a brief overview of the federal government's efforts to contain healthcare costs. Chapter 8 provides a more detailed examination and evaluation of major policy initiatives undertaken by federal and state governments, as well as the private sector, to contain these costs.

Efforts at Healthcare Cost Containment: 1970s–1980s

The 1970s represented a decade of transition in the U.S. healthcare system. Prior to this time, federal healthcare policy was shaped by a number of assumptions. A major one was that the healthcare system suffered from too few healthcare facilities and services. The healthcare system needed more hospitals, physicians, technology, and biomedical research. Biomedical research was encouraged through federal funds for the National Institutes of Health, while new hospital construction was encouraged with federal funds provided through the Hill-Burton program. The second assumption was that one of the serious problems with the healthcare system was limited financial access to healthcare among disadvantaged citizens. The establishment of Medicare and Medicaid by the federal government was an effort to increase access to healthcare for the needy. The third assumption was that competitive markets and regulatory strategies do not work in the healthcare field (Brown 1986).

By the 1970s, these assumptions had come under increased scrutiny. As we discussed earlier in the chapter, the Hill-Burton program led to a significant expansion in the number of voluntary, not-for-profit, and state and local government hospitals. Policymakers came to recognize that the healthcare system was too large. This was in sharp contrast to the assumption before the 1960s that the healthcare system was too small. By the 1970s there was an increasing concern about the nation's sizable surplus of hospital beds and physicians. There was a realization that one of the reasons for increased healthcare costs was unconstrained diffusion of biomedical technology and an excess supply of hospitals and physicians, which encouraged excessive tests and treatments. Similarly, while Medicare and Medicaid had increased financial access to healthcare for the elderly and the needy, increased access had also led to increases in healthcare costs. From the beginning, outlays for Medicare and Medicaid greatly exceeded initial projections. When Medicare was established, the federal government had deliberately chosen to reimburse physicians in a generous manner to win their political support.

By the 1970s healthcare costs had risen dramatically. Total national healthcare expenditure increased from $27.1 billion in 1960 to $74.3 billion in 1970. During this same period, federal healthcare expenditures increased from $2.9 billion to $17.8 billion, while state and local governments' healthcare expenditures increased from $3.7 billion to $9.9 billion. Similar increases were evident in hospital care and physician services (Levit et al. 1994). From 1966 to 1970, Medicare expenditures increased from $1.6 billion to $7.1 billion, while Medicaid expenditures increased from $1.3 billion to $5.3 billion. Increases in medical care inflation outstripped overall inflation (Levit et al. 1994).

Consequently, policymakers' concerns began to shift from providing access and quality healthcare to containing rising healthcare costs. During the 1970s and 1980s, the federal government and the states undertook a number of regulatory and market-oriented policy initiatives in an effort to contain costs (Brown 1987; Field 2007). They are briefly described below. These policy initiatives and their results are examined in more detail in chapter 8, dealing with cost containment.

During his first two years in office (1968–1970), President Nixon signed into law various acts designed to extend community mental health centers, migrant health centers, and programs designed to support training of healthcare personnel, among others. In 1971, Senator Edward Kennedy (D-MA) introduced the Health Security Act in Congress, which called for a comprehensive program of free medical care and would have replaced all public and private health plans with a single federally operated health insurance system. Since Nixon was seeking reelection in 1972, he felt compelled to respond to Kennedy's political challenge by proposing the National Health Insurance Partnership Act, which consisted of two parts. The first part, the Family Health Insurance Plan, was a federally financed plan to provide health insurance for all low-income families. The second part, the National Health Insurance Standards Act, would be financed by private funds, would set standards for employer health insurance programs, and would require coverage of employees through an employer mandate. However, this plan failed to win the necessary support in Congress for passage (Norris 1984).

Beginning in 1971, the Nixon administration sought to curtail healthcare costs. In his health message to Congress on February 18, 1971, Nixon argued that costs had skyrocketed, and while we were investing more of nation's resources in the health of people we were not getting full return on our investment (Nixon 1971). Nixon sought curtailment in federal categorical health grant programs, vetoed legislation designed to renew and expand these programs, and impounded funds already appropriated. A struggle between the executive branch headed by a Republican president and a Congress controlled by Democrats ensued. The Democratic Congress was able to override some of Nixon's vetoes, and the battle over impoundment of funds ended up in the federal courts. It also ultimately led Congress in 1974 to enact the Congressional Budget and Impoundment Control Act, which Nixon signed into law a few days before he resigned from the presidency in the aftermath of the Watergate scandal. Despite Nixon's conflicts with Congress, a number of cost-containment initiatives were begun during this time.

PSROs and HMOs

One of the factors often cited as responsible for increased healthcare costs is the overutilization of healthcare resources. The rising costs of Medicare and Medicaid created concern in Congress about the cost as well as the quality of care provided in these programs. Congress created the Professional Standards Review Organizations (PSROs) through the Social Security Amendments Act of 1972. This was a regulatory mechanism to encourage efficient and economical delivery of healthcare in the two large public sector programs—Medicare and Medicaid. More than 200 local PSROs were created and staffed by local physicians to review and monitor care provided to Medicare and Medicaid patients by hospitals, skilled nursing homes, and extended-care facilities. The PSROs were given the authority to deny approval of payment to physicians who provided unnecessary or poor quality services to Medicare and Medicaid patients.

In addition, the Nixon administration wanted a plan to control healthcare costs that would look uniquely Republican. Nixon hoped to promote market-oriented reforms designed to encourage competition in the healthcare market as a way of controlling costs. He was interested in developing a health strategy that would create a more efficient healthcare system, balance the supply of healthcare resources and demands, and at the same time ensure equal access to healthcare.

The Nixon administration's key proposal was to provide federal funds for the development of health maintenance organizations (HMOs). In 1973, nearly three years after Nixon first sent his proposal to Congress, the Health Maintenance Organization Act was passed. It was a much more modest plan than originally conceived and reflected the necessity of bargaining and compromises between the president and Congress. For example, the first Senate bill had authorized $5.2 billion over three years for start-up costs. The version signed into law authorized $375 million over three years for projects more limited in scope (Falkson 1980; Norris 1984).

HMOs are a system in which enrollees pay a fixed fee (capitation) in advance, and in return they receive a comprehensive set of health services. The Nixon administration believed that HMOs would promote competition with traditional healthcare delivery systems by creating incentives for shifting health services utilization from more costly inpatient services such as hospitals and skilled nursing facilities to less costly outpatient services such as visits to doctors' offices.

Controlling Costs by Planning

During the late 1960s and the 1970s the federal government also emphasized health planning to contain rising healthcare costs. The rationale for planning was based on the argument that there was an abundance of healthcare facilities and services—too many hospitals, too many hospital beds, and too much medical equipment. Unnecessary expansion and duplication led to overutilization of healthcare resources. The Comprehensive Health Planning Act of 1966 was an attempt at healthcare-facilities planning through the states. Comprehensive health-planning agencies were to be established in every state and in local areas. Their principal focus was hospital planning. In 1974, Congress passed the National Health Planning and Resource Development Act, which replaced the Comprehensive Health Planning Act and other health planning programs such as the regional medical and Hill-Burton programs. The law required all states to adopt certificate-of-need (CON) laws by 1980. CON laws require hospitals to document community need to obtain approval for major capital expenditures for expansion of facilities and services. The law also established a network of health system agencies at state and local levels to administer the CON laws.

Jimmy Carter, as a Democratic candidate for president in the 1976 election, had pledged his support for a comprehensive national health insurance program. Nevertheless, after assuming office in January 1977, Carter was hampered by budget constraints and was less anxious to push for a national health insurance program (Iglehart 1978). From 1971 to 1974, under the Nixon-imposed Economic Stabilization Program, economy-wide wage and price controls were in effect. Hospital prices were subject to control under this program; however, this had a limited impact on controlling hospital costs. In 1977, the Carter administration proposed a series of all-payer revenue controls on hospitals, known as the hospital cost-containment proposal. The Carter administration argued that controlling hospital costs was necessary because traditional market forces would not keep those costs down. The proposal was strongly opposed by the medical community in general and hospitals in particular. It also did not receive enthusiastic support in Congress. After three years of legislative battles, the proposal was defeated in favor of a promised voluntary effort by hospitals to contain costs. In a June 1979 message to Congress, President Carter proposed National Health Plan legislation to expand health insurance coverage and to protect Americans from the cost of catastrophic illness. Under the plan, Medicare and Medicaid would have been consolidated in a single administrative structure. It would have also included an employer mandate. The plan advocated increased competition through development of HMOs and other alternative delivery-and-reimbursement systems (Carter 1979).

THE POLITICAL TRANSFORMATION OF THE AMERICAN HEALTHCARE SYSTEM: 1981–2008

From about 1981 to 2008, the American healthcare system underwent a significant transformation. It took place largely through the political and legislative process under the ascendency of a conservative political ideology. The period of the 1930s through the 1960s had witnessed a significant increase in the federal government's role in healthcare. Federal health policies encouraged expansion of federal health grants to states, expansion of biomedical research, and expansion of hospitals and healthcare facilities, along with greater access to healthcare through Medicare and Medicaid programs. The election of Richard Nixon in the 1968 election signaled an end to the liberal mandate and the rise of a conservative mandate. However, faced with a Democratic controlled Congress, Nixon was forced to compromise his conservative agenda. The election of Ronald Reagan to the presidency elevated conservative agenda. Under the conservatives, the period of 1981–2008 witnessed the initiation and implementation of several policy initiatives utilizing "managed competition" and "managed care" strategies to reduce the federal role in healthcare and expand the private sector role. The "managed" part of "competition" and "care" recognized some role for the government in managing competition and care. Major elements of this competitive approach to healthcare were to provide consumers with increased choice when they purchase insurance, the reduction and elimination of many regulatory approaches to cost containment, and new forms of prepaid healthcare delivery organizations to help contain costs (Ginsberg 1987).

The market approach to cost containment was designed to overcome perceived failures of the traditional system of health financing and services. These included (1) the lack of motivation on the part of consumers to forgo consumption of health services since they shared little or no cost of each service; (2) the traditional fee-for-service mechanism that rewarded health professionals for providing more, not fewer, medical tests and treatment; (3) lack of consumer knowledge about medical care, creating a dependence on healthcare providers that allowed them to control both demand and supply of services and thus the cost; and (4) that payments to hospitals and providers were based on the cost of care rather than on competitive prices (Oliver 1991). The goals of the market approach were to force consumers to share more of the cost of each medical procedure and health service and to emphasize competition between traditional fee-for-service organizations and alternative health delivery organizations (Oliver 1991).

As discussed in the previous section, the seeds of the market strategy were planted during the Nixon administration with the federal government encouraging the development of HMOs as an alternative healthcare delivery organization, but they developed deep roots during the period of 1980–2008. Health came to be treated more as a commodity than as a public good. Healthcare providers began to operate more like other businesses, relying on marketing strategies to attract new customers instead of outreach programs designed to bring needed health services to the community. The growing reliance on a market mechanism to address problems of the American healthcare system also led to the establishment of a medical-industrial complex consisting of a growing number of private for-profit hospitals, nursing homes, medical care organizations, and other businesses related to medical goods and services (Wallace and Estes 1989).

The Reagan Administration: 1981–1989

After campaigning on a platform of antiregulation and less government, Ronald Reagan became president in January 1981. Reagan sought to reduce expenditures for social programs, including healthcare. In this area, the Reagan administration reduced federal funding for preventive services, health professions education, community health centers, and Medicaid. The administration also shifted administrative and decision making in health programs by consolidating health services and preventive programs into block grant programs and, as a part of deregulation, eliminated health planning and PSRO programs, giving state and local governments more responsibility and discretionary authority. In addition, the administration promoted competitive strategies in the healthcare market (Davis 1981; Robbins 1983; Wing 1984). All resulted in the reexamination of the role of federal government in financing and administration of health services and a significant change in the healthcare sector.

During the first three years of the Reagan administration, funding for health planning and health maintenance organizations was eventually eliminated. The PSRO program was renamed Peer Review Organizations (PROs), and its funding was reduced from $58 million in 1980 to $15 million in 1983, effectively ending the program. The Reagan administration also succeeded in combining twenty-one categorical grant programs in the areas of prevention, mental health, maternal and child healthcare, and primary care into four block grants. Funding for Medicare and Medicaid was also reduced (Etheredge 1983; Ginsberg 1987).

Medicaid Waivers

Two types of waivers are available under the Medicaid program. Section 1115 of the Social Security Act gives the executive branch authority to experiment with alternative state approaches to program delivery. These are called demonstration waivers. The second type of waiver, called program waivers, was established under section 1915 of the Omnibus Budget Reconciliation Act of 1981 (Thompson and Burke 2008). This type of waiver gives the federal executive branch authority to allow states more freedom in their Medicaid programs in two areas. It gave states the opportunity to restrict the "freedom of choice" that beneficiaries had to select among Medicaid providers and adopt payment approaches other than fee-for-service. Using 1915(b) waivers, many states pursued various forms of managed care options for beneficiaries. The 1915(c) waivers, known as Home and Community-Based Services (HCBS) waivers, allow states to circumvent key requirements of the Medicaid law by providing alternatives to nursing home care in permitting states to offer home health benefits, such as personal assistance with daily living in a home or community setting, to the frail elderly or to young persons with disabilities. The administrations of both President Reagan and President George H. W. Bush made frequent use of such waivers. Between 1981 and 1991, the number of HCBS waivers in operation grew from 6 to 113 (Thompson and Burke 2008). The Reagan administration saw this as an important mechanism for returning program decision-making authority to states and giving state governments more flexibility.

Prospective Payment System for Medicare

The biggest innovation of the Reagan administration was the introduction in 1983 of the Prospective Payment System (PPS), mandated by the Deficit Reduction Act of 1982, for reimbursement to hospitals under the Medicare program in the hope of reducing Medicare costs and making hospitals more efficient. As discussed earlier, when Medicare was created, it provided for a generous reimbursement to hospitals on a retrospective, reasonable-cost basis for services provided to Medicare patients. Under the new system, illnesses are classified into one of 468 diagnosis-related groups (DRGs). Each category is assigned a treatment rate, and hospitals are reimbursed according to these rates. If hospitals spend more money on treatment, they have to absorb the additional costs. If they spend less money than the established rates, they can keep the overpayment as profit. The new system was phased in over a period of time and went into full effect in 1987.

Medicare Catastrophic Coverage

By the mid-1980s, it was also becoming clear that the Medicare program was unable to meet all the health expenses of its beneficiaries. Their out-of-pocket expenses for services covered by Medicare were on the rise. In addition, the Medicare program did not provide coverage for certain basic services such as outpatient prescription drugs, custodial care, and most of the cost of nursing home care. The Reagan administration tried to address this problem of "medigap." In his 1986 State of the Union message, President Reagan unveiled his proposal for an expansion of Medicare. Congress passed his proposal in 1988 as the Medicare Catastrophic Coverage Act.

The law modified both program benefits and financing, with changes to be phased in over a period of several years beginning in 1989. The act provided for coverage of outpatient prescription drugs such as home-administered intravenous antibiotics and other FDA-approved drugs, as well as mammography screening for disabled beneficiaries. The act also expanded coverage of inpatient hospital days from ninety to an unlimited number of days per year. Similarly, the act increased the number of days of coverage for skilled nursing facilities, home healthcare, and hospice care. The act also reduced the amount of deductibles and coinsurance for certain services. The new benefits were to be financed entirely by the beneficiaries themselves through supplemental premiums. The act increased monthly premiums for Part B of Medicare and increased the tax liability of higher-income beneficiaries.

The Medicare Catastrophic Coverage Act was very unpopular, particularly among the affluent elderly. One reason for their opposition was that they would shoulder most of the burden of financing the proposed changes through increases in their taxes. A second reason for the opposition was that many of the elderly were satisfied with the supplemental private insurance coverage they had purchased to cover the gaps in the Medicare program. Another major criticism of the act was that while it made modest changes in Medicare nursing home benefits, it did not extend Medicare coverage to long-term nursing home care (Rice, Desmond, and Gable 1990). Long-term care is the type of care most likely to financially devastate the elderly (Rice and Gable 1986).

A plethora of bills based on competitive and market strategies were proposed during the Reagan administration. Many of them did not make it out of the Democratic Party–controlled Congress, although several of the initiatives, such as a reduced federal role and reduced federal spending for healthcare, reduced regulations, giving state and local government more discretionary authority, and prospective payment system for Medicare patients, were successful.

The George H.W. Bush Administration: 1989–1993

George H.W. Bush was sworn in as president in January 1989. In November 1989 Congress repealed the Medicare Catastrophic Coverage Act due to significant protests against it. This defeat of one of the most significant expansions in the Medicare program since its creation in 1965 seemed likely to make Congress less enthusiastic about reforms in Medicare or undertaking any new initiatives with respect to long-term care (Rice, Desmond, and Gable 1990). Furthermore, the administration was too preoccupied by the Persian Gulf War (1990–1991) to undertake any major new initiatives in the area of healthcare. However, the Bush I administration did continue the practice started under the Reagan administration of granting Medicaid waivers to states.

Healthcare Reform

Polls in the early 1990s indicated that a majority of Americans had a negative view of the U.S. healthcare system and were in favor of reforming it. Healthcare reform emerged on the national policy agenda with the approaching presidential elections in November 1992. President Bush announced new healthcare initiatives in February 1992. He proposed a series of reforms, including tax credits of up to $3,750 per year for families with incomes of up to $70,000 and a voucher for the same amount for poor families. The estimated cost, about $100 billion, was to be paid for by placing limits on Medicare and Medicaid programs. Under the plan, the self-employed would receive a tax deduction equal to the size of the premiums. Small businesses would receive tax inducements. There was also a proposal for mild insurance reform (Barnes 1991; Bocchino and Wakefield 1992; Dentzer 1992; Kinsley 1992; Wines 1992).

The Bush I initiative was clearly in response to the coming presidential election and to the promise of Bill Clinton, Arkansas governor and Democratic candidate, that he would offer a plan for comprehensive reform of the U.S. healthcare system. By October 1992, both President Bush and Democratic presidential nominee Clinton had endorsed managed care as the centerpiece of their healthcare plans. Comprehensive reform of the U.S. healthcare system became one of the major campaign issues in the 1992 presidential election. Bill Clinton promised that, if elected, he would deliver a comprehensive reform of the U.S. healthcare system that would provide universal coverage to all Americans. Clinton won the presidency, but he had managed to garner only 43 percent of the popular vote in a three-candidate race.

The Clinton Administration: 1993–2001

President Clinton was a "post-conservative" leader in the sense that he led a left-of-center Democratic Party to victory after an extensive period of conservative rule. As a candidate for president, Clinton had run as a new kind of Democrat by disassociating himself from more traditional liberal rhetoric and policy preferences. Under pressure to reduce government spending, to reduce or eliminate the federal deficit, and to push citizens who received public assistance toward more self-reliance and personal responsibility, in many areas the Clinton administration followed a moderate to right-of-center path, including antifederal interventionist leanings (Bashevkin 2000). This was evident in the Clinton administration's preference for and use of Medicaid waivers and support for welfare reform.

Medicaid Waivers

The arrival of the Clinton administration in 1993 created a more receptive environment for both Medicaid demonstrations (section 1115) and program waivers (1915). During the Clinton years the number of HCBS waivers increased by almost 50 percent from 155 to 231, and the number of Medicaid enrollees covered by waivers increased by 225 percent from 236,000 to 768,000. The hallmark of the Clinton years with respect to Medicaid waivers was the approval of 17 comprehensive waivers that moved large number of Medicaid enrollees into managed care. Of the eighty-nine proposals, including renewals, submitted during the Clinton years, 57 percent were approved (Thompson and Burke 2007). It is important to note that granting program waivers to states by the federal authority has become an important policy tool in the American federal system (Thompson and Burke 2008).

Healthcare Reform

President Clinton had promised, if elected, to propose a plan for comprehensive healthcare reform. His plan to overhaul the American healthcare system was presented to the nation in a speech before the joint session of Congress in September 1993, and a bill was sent to Congress in October. The six general principles underlying the reform were: security, simplicity, savings, choice, quality, and responsibility (Skocpol 1994). The proposal, entitled the Health Security Act, was very comprehensive; it proposed a fundamental restructuring of the U.S. healthcare system. The bill provided universal coverage through an employer mandate. It also provided subsidies for poor persons and workers without insurance. The plan would provide a minimum benefits package covering a variety of services such as hospital, emergency, clinical preventive, mental health, substance abuse, family planning, pregnancy-related, hospice, home healthcare, extended care, outpatient laboratory, vision, hearing, and dental, among others (White House Domestic Policy Council 1993). "The healthcare plan that is always there" became the slogan for the Clinton plan (Clymer 1993). The plan was very much based on the concept of managed competition (Hanson 1994). Skocpol (1997, 41) described it as an ambitious plan for "inclusive managed competition."

The initial reaction to the Clinton plan was positive. Deliberation over healthcare reform in Congress did not begin until 1994, an election year. Several competing plans emerged in Congress on both sides of the aisle. The competing plans ranged from a more radical proposal of a single-payer system to proposals for only minor changes to the system, designed to deal with specific concerns. As the debate over these competing plans intensified, none of the plans managed to attract majority support. The initial positive reaction to the Clinton plan turned more negative as the plan was criticized and attacked by a variety of interest groups and Republicans in Congress. Republican leaders had made a strategic decision not to support the Clinton plan and to make the Clinton administration's failure to reform the healthcare system a campaign issue in the 1994 congressional elections. It was classic election-year politics. Public support for the Clinton plan as well as support for fundamental reform of the U.S. healthcare system also declined as the debate continued. Opponents of comprehensive reforms argued that the U.S. healthcare system was not facing a crisis requiring major changes and that the problems of the healthcare system could be addressed through incremental reforms.

Ultimately, this was the view that prevailed, and by late summer of 1994 President Clinton's Health Security Act was declared dead and buried. Some of the important reasons for this failure included the Clinton administration's miscalculation and mismanagement of the issue, attacks from interest groups opposed to the plan, partisan politics, election-year politics, a decline in President Clinton's popularity, and declining public support for comprehensive reform (Fallows 1995; Morin 1994; Patel 2003, Patel and Rushefsky 1998; Starr 1995). Another window of opportunity for reform of the U.S. healthcare system had opened and closed without any comprehensive changes (Brady and Buckley 1995; Brodie and Blendon 1995; Canaham-Clyne 1995; Jacobs and Shapiro 1995; Navarro 1995; Patel and Rushefsky 1998; Steinmo and Watts 1995; Thomas 1995).

Republicans used a three-pronged approach in the 1994 election campaign: develop a positive governing agenda, derail Clinton's agenda, and amass a large campaign war chest (Balz and Brownstein 1996). The Republican Party also came up with the Contract with America, a ten-point platform that included a balanced budget amendment, a line-item veto for the president, a crime bill, welfare reform, a family tax-cut plan, and parental rights in education. In addition, the Republican strategy of not cooperating with the president on the issue of comprehensive healthcare reform and then blaming President Clinton for its failure (on the basis that it was a bureaucratic, big-brother, big-government reform plan) paid handsome dividends in the 1994 congressional elections. The voters delivered the worst midterm repudiation that any president had received since Harry Truman in 1946. Republicans gained control of both the House and the Senate. The Republican victories extended to gubernatorial and state legislative races as well. A post-election survey conducted by President Clinton's pollster Stanley Greenberg identified the healthcare plan as the single item that directly linked Clinton with big government (Balz and Brownstein 1996). According to a survey of voters conducted on Election Day, President Clinton's failure to reform the healthcare system was a major reason Democrats suffered at the polls. Furthermore, polls also showed that the voters were strongly opposed to the comprehensive healthcare reform and instead favored an incremental solution to the nation's healthcare problems (Iglehart 1995).

Government Shutdown over Republican Proposal to
Cut Spending for Medicaid and Medicare

The Republicans came up with a budget plan and Congress adopted a budget resolution for fiscal year (FY) 1996. It promised to balance the budget within seven years. It called for a $245 billion tax cut. It advocated reducing projected spending (growth rate) on Medicare by $270 billion and on Medicaid spending by $182 billion over the next seven years. The Medicaid program was to be changed into a block grant and turned over to the states. The Democrats went on the offensive and portrayed themselves as the savior of the elderly (Medicare) and the poor (Medicaid) and argued that Republicans were willing to cut these programs to provide a tax cut for the wealthy. President Clinton refused to accept the Republican plan and was determined not to cave in to Republican demands. The stalemate between the president and the Republican Congress led to the partial shutdown of the government twice. This confrontation backfired on the Republicans, as they saw public support for the Contract with America decline sharply. No action was taken on the proposed reduction in spending for Medicare and Medicaid.

In 1996 legislation on the FY 1997 budget, the Republican leadership proposed block grants to replace the Medicaid and AFDC programs. President Clinton indicated that he strongly opposed turning Medicaid into a block-grant program, and twice he vetoed legislation that tried to transform both Medicaid and the AFDC program into block grants. Finally, the Republicans dropped their proposal to make Medicaid a block grant.

Welfare Reform

Republicans also wanted welfare reform, and President Clinton had indicated that he supported reforms. A welfare reform bill, after considerable bargaining between the president and congressional Republicans, did pass Congress, and President Clinton signed into law the bill known as the Personal Responsibility and Work Opportunity Reconciliation Act (PRWORA) of 1996. The new law included changes in welfare, supplemental security income, child support enforcement, and food stamps and social services. The main feature of the law is the Temporary Assistance to Needy Families (TANF) program, under which states are given a block grant to design their own welfare program. The Medicaid program was left virtually intact, but the linkage between Medicaid and welfare was broken.

Health Insurance Reform

Despite the partisan acrimony that dominated the 104th Congress in 1995 and 1996 over the issue of a balanced budget amendment, Congress did succeed in passing some incremental healthcare reforms. One of the crowning achievements of the 104th Congress was the passage of the Health Insurance Portability and Accountability Act (HIPAA) of 1996, which President Clinton signed into law in August. Two of the major provisions of the bill include placing limits on insurance companies' authority to deny coverage or to impose preexisting condition exclusions, and guaranteeing portability of insurance coverage when a person leaves his or her job voluntarily or involuntarily ("Kassebaum-Kennedy Health Insurance Bill Clears Congress" 1996).

Children's Health Insurance Program

President Clinton won an impressive reelection in 1996. The Republicans were able to retain their majorities in the House and the Senate with narrower margins. President Clinton and the Republican-controlled Congress managed to address another issue that had become an area of concern, the increased number of children who lacked health insurance coverage. The Balanced Budget Act of 1997 provided funds to expand health insurance coverage for children by creating the State Children's Health Insurance Program (SCHIP) as part of title XXI of the Social Security Act. State governments have taken advantage of this program and expanded health insurance coverage to uninsured children in their states (Congressional Budget Office 1998). When the program was reauthorized in 2009, it was renamed the Children's Health Insurance Program (CHIP).

When the SCHIP was passed, it was touted as enjoying broad bipartisan success. This bipartisan approach was symbolized by two of the cosponsors—Sen. Edward Kennedy (D-MA) and Sen. Orrin Hatch (R-UT). However, when the program came up for reauthorization in Congress in the summer and fall of 2007, a bitter partisan debate emerged over the intended purpose of the program. The Republicans argued that SCHIP should be a narrowly targeted means-tested program for poor, uninsured children. The Democrats argued that SCHIP should be expanded further to guarantee that all children and some adults have some type of healthcare coverage. The administration of George W. Bush vetoed reauthorization and issued a federal guidance restricting state flexibility around eligibility expansion (Gorin and Moniz 2007; Grogan and Rigby 2008). The SCHIP program is discussed in more detail in chapter 3 on Medicaid. The 1997 legislation also made significant changes in the Medicare program (see chapter 4).

Patient's Bill of Rights

The expansion of managed competition in the healthcare marketplace as a way to cut costs has led to a dramatic increase in the enrollment of millions of Americans in health maintenance organizations and preferred provider organizations (PPOs). This in turn has raised concerns about managed care plans that deny or limit provision of healthcare services to their members in order to cut costs. Some legislators and consumer advocates have suggested the passage of a patient's bill of rights to protect patients against unfair, arbitrary, and capricious decisions by managed care plans. President Clinton proposed such a bill, which would have allowed patients to sue their managed care plans and/ or managed care organizations such as HMOs and PPOs. Republicans in Congress proposed their own version of a patient's bill of rights, which did not allow patients to sue their healthcare plans or provider organizations. Under the George W. Bush administration, Congress failed to enact a patient's bill of rights. However, a great deal of patient's rights has been incorporated in the Affordable Care Act (ACA) passed by Congress and signed into law by President Obama in 2010.

The George W. Bush Administration: 2001–2009

George W. Bush won the presidency in the election of 2000 by receiving 271 votes (270 needed to win) in the Electoral College, even though his opponent, Democratic Party candidate Al Gore, received more than half a million more popular votes. Bush had articulated a conservative political agenda during his presidential campaign of 2000. One of the very first health issues he had to confront was federal funding for stem cell research.

Stem Cell Policy and Politics

Embryonic stem cell research has generated a significant amount of controversy and heated discussion among its supporters and opponents, especially over the question of whether the federal government should fund such research. Supporters of stem cell research have argued that it could lead to discovery of cures for diseases including Parkinson's, Alzheimer's, and diabetes. Such research, including therapeutic cloning, can help address problems of organ shortages and donor organ rejection. Supporters of stem cell research argue that such research is ethical because it promises to reduce human suffering and because thousands of frozen embryos are often discarded or destroyed at fertility clinics anyway. Opponents of stem cell research argue that this research is unethical and immoral because embryos are human and deserve the same full rights as humans, embryos should not be used to serve an instrumental value, taking life to prevent the suffering of others is unjustified, and research with embryonic stem cells so far is not very promising (Patel and Rushefsky 2005b).

Federal funding for embryonic stem cell research became a major issue in the 2000 presidential campaign. During the campaign, in order to attract the votes of Catholics and conservative evangelical Christians, George Bush indicated that he opposed federal funding for research that requires embryos to be destroyed or discarded. Upon assuming the presidency, Bush was confronted with the task of formulating a policy on the question of federal funding for stem cell research.

In August 2001, President Bush, in his first televised address to the nation, announced his policy decision. He argued that as a result of private research, more than sixty genetically diverse stem cell lines already in existence were created from embryos that were already destroyed. He further argued that these stem cell lines had the ability to regenerate themselves indefinitely, creating more opportunity for research. Thus, he argued that he would allow federal funds to be used for research only on these existing stem cell lines where the life and death decision had already been made.

President Bush's policy decision was essentially a political one designed to satisfy competing political interests and ethical values and was not based on any sound ethical principles, even though he tried to portray his decision as highly ethical (Patel and Rushefsky 2005b). The decision failed to satisfy completely either supporters or opponents of stem cell research. As Eric Cohen has pointed out, President Bush's decision is analogous to the Missouri Compromise, which permitted Missouri to enter the Union as a slave state and Maine as a free state. It sought to find a political compromise between competing interests and viewpoints (Cohen 2002). Furthermore, instead of more than sixty stem cell lines, in reality there were only about seventeen viable existing lines for researchers to work with because many of the other stem cell lines were damaged or lacked genetic diversity.

Given the fact that federal funding is limited to existing stem cells, embryonic stem cell research has turned into a state-by-state battle between proponents and opponents. Some states have moved ahead with stem cell research using only state funding. California voters in November 2004 approved a ballot initiative to spend $3 billion on stem cell research (Kasindorf 2004). State laws vary considerably on the topic of stem cell research. States such as California, Connecticut, Illinois, Iowa, Maryland, Massachusetts, New Jersey, and New York encourage embryonic stem cell research, while states such as South Dakota strictly prohibit stem cell research regardless of the source. Even states that permit such research have established guidelines for scientists to follow with respect to things such as consent requirements, an approval and review process for research projects, source of embryos for research, and cloning. For example, many states prohibit the sale of embryos or fetuses, while others prohibit research on live embryos; Arkansas, Indiana, Michigan, North Dakota, and South Dakota prohibit research on cloned embryos, while California, Connecticut, Illinois, Iowa, Massachusetts, New Jersey, New York, and Rhode Island prohibit human cloning only for the purpose of initiating a pregnancy, or reproductive cloning, but allow cloning for research. Some states limit the use of state funds for cloning or stem cell research. For example, Missouri law forbids the use of state funds for reproductive cloning but not for cloning for research ("Stem Cell Research: Undated January 2008" n.d.).

The federal government exercises control only over stem cell research that it funds. There are no restrictions on stem cell research carried on in the private sector. Citing lack of leadership by the federal government, the National Academy of Sciences has proposed ethical guidelines to govern research with human embryonic stem cells. Major guidelines include: (1) laboratories doing such research should run proposed studies past a review board made up of community members and scientists; (2) women who donate eggs for embryonic stem cell research should not be paid; (3) no human embryo should be grown in a lab for more than fourteen days; and (4) human embryonic stem cells may not be transplanted into an early human embryo. However, experiments in which human embryonic stem cells are transplanted into animals to study development and treatment of diseases is permitted with tight regulations ("Stem-Cell Guidelines: Ethics of a New Science" 2005; Wade 2005).

In 2005, the Republican-controlled House of Representatives passed a bill designed to expand federal funding for stem cell research beyond what President Bush's order allows. Bush had vowed to veto any measure that would expand federal financing of stem cell research (Stolberg 2005; Tumulty 2005). The Senate failed to act on the bill. President Obama in 2009 signed an executive order that allows federal tax dollars to be used for significantly broader research on embryonic stem cells ("Obama Ends Stem Cell Research Ban" 2009).

Medicaid Waivers

George W. Bush, like the Clinton administration, proved very receptive to HCBS waivers. In 2001, the administration announced the New Freedom Initiative, which called for the Centers for Medicare and Medicaid (CMS) to identify existing barriers to elderly and young people with disabilities in the community receiving health services. This initiative led to changes in some of the 1915(c) waiver practices. In 2002, the Bush administration started the Independence Plus initiative, under which waivers could be used for a cash payment and counseling. The number of 1915(c) waivers grew over 10 percent from the last year of the Clinton administration (Thompson and Burke 2008). The approval rate for Medicaid waivers increased considerably during the Bush administration. By August 2006, the administration had approved 72 percent of all waiver proposals and forty-four states and District of Columbia had obtained approval for 149 waivers (Thompson and Burke 2007). Virtually every aspect of the Medicaid program has been affected by the waivers. While broad and comprehensive reform of the Medicaid program has eluded national policymakers, waivers have allowed states to adopt smaller, incremental changes to the Medicaid program (Coughlin and Zuckerman 2008).

Effort to Turn Medicaid into Block Grant

In 2003, President George Bush proposed converting Medicaid from an entitlement to a block grant program. The proposal largely incorporated elements of similar but failed proposals by the Reagan administration in 1981 and congressional Republicans in 1995. Compared to categorical grants, block grants appeal to conservatives and Republicans since they are less restrictive, give states more flexibility, and eliminate the uncontrollable aspects of entitlement programs (Lambrew 2005). The proposal again failed to pass Congress.

Medical Liability Reform

President Bush also championed the cause of medical malpractice reform. Starting in 2003, in six consecutive State of the Union addresses he urged Congress to pass medical liability reform. The proposed reform urged the capping of pain-and-suffering awards at $250,000. He justified this proposal as a way to control rising healthcare costs. The reform campaign was conducted against the backdrop of rising insurance premiums for U.S. doctors ("U.S. Grapples with Solution to Preventable Medical Errors" 2009). Congress failed to pass such a reform.

Politics of Science and Reproductive Health

The term "reproductive health" is generally used to describe policies concerning abstinence, contraception, abortion, and assisted reproductive technologies. The topic of assisted reproductive technology and the court's role in dealing with ethical and legal issues raised by such a technology are discussed in chapter 9. The Bush administration played a major role in changing these policies in a more conservative direction.

Federal support for abstinence-only education flourished during the Bush administration, which launched a new abstinence program—Community Based Abstinence Education (CARE)—with more rigid guidelines. Under the program, grantees, often religious organizations, are required to teach that abstinence from sexual activity is the only way to avoid out-of-wedlock pregnancy and sexually transmitted diseases, and funded sex education curricula must accept the perspective that sexual activity outside marriage is likely to have harmful psychological and physical effects (McFarlane 2006). Under the Bush administration, annual funding for abstinence-only programs tripled from $60 million in 1998 to $176 million in 2006. The administration also altered performance measures to make the abstinence-only education program appear more successful. For example, outcome measures tracking pregnancy or sexual activity were replaced by measures of teenagers' attendance and attitudes. Abstinence-only programs also undermined more comprehensive sex education programs. The abstinence education movement was a key aspect of the Bush administration's attempt to promote a conservative moral framework and sexual ethic (Kulczycki

2007). Critics of the administration have argued that abstinence-only curricula blur religion and science, create stereotypes about boys and girls, and treat such stereotypes as scientific fact. For example, the curriculum teaches that women need financial support while men may need admiration and that women gauge their happiness/success by their relationships while men gauge their happiness/success by their accomplishments (Waxman 2006).

Given the Bush administration's commitment to abstinence, it also showed a great deal of ambivalence about the use of male condoms. Social conservatives have opposed efforts to support birth control by claiming that condoms are not very effective in protecting against sexually transmitted diseases. Administration officials, congressional lawmakers, and leaders of the religious right launched a series of campaigns that used partial or misleading information to cast doubt on the effectiveness of condoms (Kulczycki 2007). In 2002, the Centers for Disease Control and Prevention (CDC) replaced a comprehensive online fact sheet about condoms, which included sections on their proper use and the effectiveness of different types of condoms, with one lacking crucial information on condom use and effectiveness. As a result, critics accused the Bush administration of suppressing and/or distorting scientific evidence (Waxman 2006). The administration also pushed for more parental involvement in minors' contraceptive decisions (McFarlane 2006). The Bush administration also pressured the Food and Drug Administration (FDA) to first deny and then to postpone repeatedly its decision on over-the-counter availability of Plan B, which is a brand name for the most common form of emergency contraception. Opponents of Plan B tried to deny all women access to it over-the-counter. The agency in 2006 issued a compromise ruling that permitted over-the-counter status to Plan B, but only for women aged eighteen and older (Kulczycki 2007; McFarlane 2006).

The Bush administration also tried to restrict access to abortion. During the first term, the domestic abortion-related issue that received the most attention was partial birth abortion, which is not a medical term but a political one. President Bush signed the Partial Birth Abortion Ban Act into law on November 5, 2003. The law outlaws a specific abortion procedure medically called intact dilation and extraction (D&X). The law was challenged by opponents in courts and six federal courts ruled against the law on the grounds that it provided no exception for protection of women's health and its imprecise language. The Bush administration pursued the ban to the U.S. Supreme Court, which included two new Bush appointees. In April 2007 the Supreme Court upheld the law.

Consistent with its efforts to restrict domestic abortion, Bush also made two major changes in international abortion and family planning policy. He reinstated the "Mexico City policy" from the George H.W. Bush and Reagan era. Under the policy, the United States refuses to fund any foreign organization that provides abortion services (McFarlane 2006; Waxman 2006). Bush also signed a directive reviving the Global Gag Rule. This rule precludes awarding U.S. government money earmarked for international population assistance and funded by the U.S. Agency for International Development (USAID) to nongovernmental organizations in other countries that perform, counsel, or advocate for abortion services even in cases involving rape or incest (Kulczycki 2007).

Consumer-Driven Healthcare

Post the managed-care era, the Bush administration encouraged the idea of consumer-driven healthcare. Under this vision, patients are no longer just patients but take on the role of sophisticated consumers who use information and the Internet to comparison shop and make informed choices about their own healthcare and tailor their own custom-made health benefit packages. The major instruments of consumer-driven healthcare are high-deductible health insurance plans (HDHP) and health savings accounts (HSAs) used to pay for routine healthcare expenditures until deductibles are met, at which point the HDHP's catastrophic coverage kicks in. The concept behind consumer-driven healthcare is that it would make consumers more cost conscious, work against overinsurance and overutilization of health services, and lead to cost savings in healthcare (Oberlander 2006). The topics of managed competition, managed care, and consumer-driven healthcare are discussed in more detail in chapter 8, which deals with healthcare cost containment.

Medicare Modernization Act of 2003 and Prescription Drug Benefit

By early 2000, rapidly rising prescription drug costs and growing concern about the affordability of needed drugs had helped elevate this issue on to the national policy agenda. According to a comprehensive report issued by the federal government on the nation's health, during 2001–2004, 46.7 percent of Americans reported taking at least one prescription drug. During the same period, 20.2 percent of Americans reported taking at least three prescription drugs (National Center for Health Statistics 2012). The number of Americans taking prescription drugs has continued to increase in the United States.

Americans spend a considerable amount of money on prescription drugs; for example, in 2000 they spent $120.9 billion on these drugs (National Center for Health Statistics 2012). In 2002, prescription drugs constituted about 10.4 percent of total national healthcare spending. Three factors have contributed to the increases in prescription drug expenditures. The first is increased use—from 2 billion prescriptions in 1993 to 3.4 billion in 2003, an increase of 70 percent. A second factor is the proliferation of different kinds of drugs, with newer and higher-priced drugs replacing older ones. The FDA, on average, approves about thirty new drugs annually. The third factor is the almost 25 percent increase in manufacturers' prices for existing drugs. Retail prescription prices increased an average of 7.4 percent a year from 1993 to 2003, double the average inflation rate of 2.5 percent (Kaiser Family Foundation 2004).

The problem of the high cost of prescription drugs is most acute for many seniors, especially those with low incomes and/or with multiple health problems. They often must make a difficult choice between healthcare and other consumption needs. The problem is dire for seniors on Medicare with low fixed incomes. The original Medicare program did not provide coverage for prescription drugs. Seniors with very low income qualify for Medicaid. Many seniors purchase additional insurance to cover expenses that Medicare does not cover. Yet, about one-third of Medicare beneficiaries in 2003 did not have coverage for prescription drugs, and it was also becoming increasingly more expensive to obtain (Fan, Sharpe, and Hong 2003).

The Bush administration saw a political opening. Democrats had for years talked about providing drug benefits to Medicare recipients but had failed to deliver. With the presidential election only a year away, Republicans saw an opportunity to take the issue of Medicare away from the Democrats by proposing and passing the Medicare Modernization Act (MMA) in 2003 (Nather 2003). The law added Part D, often referred to as the prescription drug benefit plan, to Medicare and went in effect on January 1, 2006. Individuals are eligible for prescription drug coverage under a Part D plan if they are entitled to benefits under Medicare Part A and/or enrolled in Part B. Beneficiaries can obtain the Part D drug benefit either by joining a private prescription drug plan for drug coverage only, or under Medicare Part C by joining a Medicare Advantage plan that covers both medical services and prescription drugs. Chapter 4 provides a more detailed discussion of the politics surrounding the passage of the Medicare Modernization Act and the drug benefits provided under Part D.

The Barack Obama Administration: 2009–2017

Reauthorization of SCHIP

As discussed earlier, partisan differences regarding the goal of SCHIP had delayed authorization of the program. The election of 2008 ushered in two years of unified government with the Democratic

Party controlling both houses of Congress. One of the first actions undertaken by President Obama upon assuming office was to sign the Children's Health Insurance Program Reauthorization Act of 2009 (CHIPRA) on February 4, 2009. This legislation provides states with significant new funding, new program options, and a range of new incentives for covering children through Medicaid and the Children's Health Insurance Program (CHIP). CHIPRA also provides flexibility to states to expand healthcare coverage to children who need it. Under the law, the secretary of Health and Human Services (HHS) is tasked with developing standards by which states can measure the quality of the care that children receive.

Healthcare Reform: Affordable Care Act

By 2008, since the collapse of President Clinton's healthcare reform effort almost fifteen years earlier, a consensus was emerging that a solution for the U.S. healthcare system problems was overdue. The number of uninsured Americans had increased from 39.8 million in 2001 to 46.3 million in 2008 (Qazi 2009). There also appeared to be consensus across party lines that the American healthcare system serves too few, costs too much, harms too many, and is too inefficient. However, both the Democratic and Republican parties had different ideas about how to address these problems.

During the 2008 Democratic presidential primaries, both senators Hillary Clinton and Barack Obama endorsed healthcare reform plans that included expansion of Medicaid and SCHIP programs and some version of employer "play or pay," a system in which all but the smallest employers contribute to provide coverage to workers or pay a tax to a publicly funded plan to subsidize coverage for the remaining uninsured individuals. The only major difference between Clinton and Obama was whether the employer mandate should be supplemented by an individual mandate requiring all Americans to buy a health insurance policy. An individual mandate was the cornerstone of the Clinton plan, while Obama supported only a mandate to cover children (Flint 2008).

During the 2008 general election, both Barack Obama, the Democratic nominee, and Senator John McCain, the Republican, were in agreement on a few points. Both candidates advocated conversion to electronic medical records, greater transparency and consumer information, providing subsidies to low-to-moderate-income families for purchasing insurance, and more private insurance options. However, their agreements ended there. McCain's reform plan was more conservative. It opposed an individual mandate and advocated reforming the tax code to eliminate the bias toward employer-sponsored health insurance and to expand coverage through tax credits to families and individuals. To make insurance more affordable, McCain advocated expanding competition and expansion of Health Savings Accounts (Flint 2008).

Barack Obama's victory in the presidential election of 2008 set the stage for yet another major effort to reform the U.S. healthcare system. According to Skocpol (2011), the political terrain had shifted with the election of Obama, and there were many reasons to believe that his election had opened a door for more than just incremental reform. One reason was that Barack Obama had won the presidency handily by garnering 53 percent of the popular vote and 365 electoral votes compared to 47 percent of the popular vote and 173 electoral votes for McCain. Second, congressional Democrats had also strengthened their majority in both houses of the Congress. Third, the 2008 election was marked by the mobilization of a new bloc of voters, resulting in increased participation and enhanced support for the Democratic Party. Fourth, Obama assumed the presidency at a time when most Americans had become very disillusioned by his predecessor. Finally, during the campaign Obama had clearly articulated his desire to change the direction of federal social and fiscal policies from years of conservative dominance (Skocpol 2011).

President Obama made healthcare reform a top priority of his administration. However, he followed a different approach to reform than President Clinton had followed in the early 1990s. The Clinton administration had submitted to Congress a 1,342-page reform plan with specific details.

In contrast, the Obama administration outlined only general principles and let Congress work out the specifics and details of the reform plan. Obama's general principles were insurance market reform, shared responsibility, Medicaid expansion and tax credits, public health and workforce investments, lowering healthcare costs, and improving quality (Hayes 2011).

The Republican Party, just as it had done with the Clinton reform, decided to mount a strong opposition to Obama's reform plan. After more than a year of very partisan and divisive national and congressional debate, Congress passed and the president signed into law on March 23, 2010, the Affordable Care Act (ACA). The law aims to provide universal health insurance coverage through a combination of individual mandates, tax credits, insurance exchanges, expansion of Medicaid program, and several insurance market reforms. President Obama had finally broken a century-long logjam on healthcare reform. Chapter 10 provides a comprehensive account of the political and legislative history as well as the goals and major provisions of the law.

THE ROLE OF STATE AND LOCAL GOVERNMENTS IN HEALTHCARE

The topic of healthcare politics and policy in the United States is indivisible from the issues of American federalism (Peterson 2001). The distribution of authority and responsibility between different levels of government within a federal system is a topic of continuous debate. Healthcare policy has not been exempt from this debate (Rich and White 1996). Initially, the role of the federal government and of state and local governments was very limited. In the previous section we discussed how the federal government became increasingly involved in healthcare policy and how it plays a major role today with respect to access, quality, efficiency, and cost containment. This section briefly discusses the changing role of state and local governments in healthcare in our federal system.

During much of the nineteenth century, state and local governments confined their role to public health activities. The involvement of local governments in public health was stimulated by the great epidemics of the late eighteenth and early nineteenth centuries. Municipalities established health boards or health departments to deal with problems of sanitation, poor housing, and quarantine. Health departments were established in Baltimore in 1798, in Charleston, S.C., in 1815, in Philadelphia in 1818, and in Providence, R.I., in 1832 (Hanlon and Picker 1974).

Similarly, the states' role in public health was initially limited to special committees or commissions to control communicable diseases. The first state health department was established in Louisiana in 1855. State governments also played a significant role in personal healthcare through the establishment of state mental hospitals (Lee and Estes 1983).

By the beginning of the twentieth century, state and local governments were active in the delivery of personal health services. During the first decade of the century, state governments also began the regulation and licensure of hospitals. The Franklin Roosevelt administration dramatically expanded the role of the national government in social welfare through New Deal programs in the 1930s. At the end of World War II, detailed state regulations and licensure procedures for hospitals became more common (Rosenbloom 1983). The power and reach of the national government grew dramatically in the postwar period due to John F. Kennedy's New Frontier and Lyndon B. Johnson's Great Society—which included the Medicare and Medicaid programs enacted in 1965. The Great Society programs also brought new resources, rules, and enforcement from the national government to state and local governments (Peterson 2001). This also ushered in a period of cooperative federalism (Grodzins 1966) with national, state, and local governments working together as partners. In this new partnership, the national government took the lead, and state governments became avenues for innovations.

During the 1960s and 1970s, state governments took on many new functions; some of them fundamentally changed the traditional public health activities of subnational governments (Manning and Vladeck 1983). The federal health programs of the 1960s dramatically increased the role of state and local governments in healthcare. There was enhanced federal support for the delivery of healthcare services by institutions that traditionally served the poor (i.e., public hospitals and local health departments). The establishment of the joint federal-state Medicaid program also increased revenues available to public hospitals and local health departments. In the 1980s, state and local governments were not only heavily involved in traditional public health activities, such as health monitoring, sanitation, and disease control, but were also key participants in the financing and delivery of personal healthcare services, particularly to the poor through Medicaid and other programs. The traditional public health focus on sanitation and communicable diseases also expanded to cover a broad range of protection against human-made environmental and occupational hazards to personal health (Altman and Morgan 1983).

State governments are heavily involved in the regulation and licensure of healthcare facilities, such as hospitals and nursing homes, and in licensing healthcare professionals such as physicians and nurses. They also regulate hospital costs and prices through hospital rate setting. Furthermore, they have become important purchasers of healthcare services, especially for the poor. Thus, state and local governments play an important role, not only in public health activities, but in healthcare financing, delivery, and regulation of services as well.

The new federalism policies of the Nixon administration and especially the Reagan administration created new challenges for state and local governments. The Reagan administration placed heavy emphasis on decentralization, increased sharing of responsibilities and authority, and more discretion for state and local governments in the implementation of health programs. The diminishing federal responsibility for healthcare in the early 1980s resulted in increased cost shifting from the federal to state and local governments.

To some, the Reagan administration's new federalism strategy was largely a means of cutting the federal budget rather than sharing responsibilities (Nathan et al. 1982). The increased discretion granted to state governments in the implementation of health policy raises the question of the commitment, capacity, and progressivity of state governments. Conservatives have placed great emphasis on devolution of authority and financial responsibility back to the states, without much concern for adequate access to healthcare for all segments of the society (Thompson 1986). This concern is heightened by some evidence that state and local governments may be more susceptible to the influence of special interests than the federal government. Thus, compared to the federal government, some have argued that state governments are less likely to make decisions in the public interest (Lee and Estes 1983).

Federal budget reductions designed to contain rising healthcare costs left many states unable to meet the financial burden of meeting the healthcare needs of the poor under the Medicaid program. More stringent Medicaid eligibility rules also left a sizable number of poor people with no coverage under the program. Thus, the Medicaid program is increasingly confronted with a tradeoff between cost containment and access to healthcare (Holahan and Cohen 1986). State governments have increasingly felt the burdens of rapidly rising Medicaid costs. The Clinton and George W. Bush administrations continued the devolution of authority to state governments started under the Reagan administration.

During the 1990s, many state governments attempted innovative approaches to healthcare reform in general (Brown and Sparer 2001; Parmet 1993; Sparer 1998, 2004; Weil, Wiedner, and Holahan 1998) and Medicaid reform in particular (Coughlin and Zuckerman 2008; Daniels 1998; Davidson and Somers 1998; McEldowney and Jenkins 2005; Milgrom et al. 2010; Nietert, Bradford, and Kaste 2005) to deal with problems of rising healthcare costs and access to healthcare. Several state governments enacted market-based health insurance reforms in the 1990s (Barrilleaux and Brace 2007). Significant increase in the use of Medicaid waivers under the Clinton and George W. Bush administrations allowed state governments to experiment with different approaches to deliver health services under Medicaid. State governments are also playing a major role in providing health insurance coverage to children under the CHIP program. The role of state governments is examined in more detail in chapters 3 (Medicaid) and 8 (healthcare cost containment).

The ACA has significant implications for state governments and will play a crucial role in influencing the policy as well as its implementation (Dinan 2011). The healthcare reform relies heavily on Medicaid for achieving universal coverage. The law established a nationwide income floor at 133 percent of the federal poverty level, eliminating eligibility inequities across the states (Olson 2012). In December 2011, Kathleen Sebelius, the secretary of Health and Human Services, announced that states will be able to develop their own essential health benefit standards, throwing into doubt the notion that the federal government would ensure that health benefits across the country would offer consumers a minimum set of medical benefits. She touted this federalist approach as a way to give states more flexibility as they administer the massive health insurance coverage expansion (Levey 2012). However, the reliance on Medicaid to achieve universal coverage was thrown into uncertainty in July 2012 when the U.S. Supreme Court, by a vote of 7–2, ruled that the federal government cannot force states to adopt the Medicaid expansion. Given the fact that many Republican state attorneys general had unsuccessfully challenged the constitutionality of the ACA, it remains to be seen how many states opt out of the expansion of the Medicaid program (Von Drehle et al. 2012). A few Republican governors, such as those in Florida and Texas, have already announced that their state would opt out of Medicaid expansion. It is not yet clear how much partisan divide negatively impacts the expansion of Medicaid and thus the goal of achieving universal coverage. It also remains to be seen how many states will voluntarily establish their own health insurance exchanges as required under the ACA or whether the federal government will have to step in and establish such exchanges in states that fail to do so. Would the federal government follow a path of cooperation, commandeering, or crowding out as it tries to implement the various provisions of the ACA (Adler 2011)?

The U.S. Supreme Court, as its recent decision illustrates, after several decades of silence has reentered the debate over federalism. The central message in the Court's new federalism decisions involving the Tenth Amendment, the Eleventh Amendment, and the Interstate Commerce Clause is that the federal government should think twice before imposing federal regulations on states.

All this raises a concern about the impact of new federalism initiatives on the issue of access to quality healthcare by the elderly, the poor, and the uninsured. The liberals' vision of a national health insurance program is likely to remain elusive, confronted with the reality of enormous federal budget deficits and the anti-tax mood prevalent in the country.

Despite this, it should be noted that states have become major actors in health policy reform, from regulation to rationing to innovative competitive strategies to cut healthcare costs, including the cost of prescription drugs. This has become all the more true with some of the changes and incremental reforms passed by Congress and signed into law by President Clinton during the 1990s in the area of welfare reform, health insurance reforms, and children's health insurance. This devolution of authority to state governments has given them more autonomy and more freedom to innovate, and consequently they are likely to become even more important players in the future. State governments have already provided significant leadership in the area of expanding health insurance coverage to children and medical liability reforms. We consider these changes in later chapters.

CONCLUSION

Healthcare policy in the United States results from a combination of decisions made and initiatives undertaken by various levels of government and the private sector. Though the role of federal, state, and local governments in healthcare policy has expanded significantly in the twentieth century, U.S. healthcare remains a mostly private system. Policymakers in the United States have mainly followed a middle road between a totally private healthcare system and a publicly financed national healthcare system.

The federal government's health policy initiatives have focused on concerns about values of access (equality), quality of care, and cost efficiency. The federal role in healthcare has gone through four distinct stages. The first stage was characterized by policies designed to increase access through expansion of healthcare facilities, services, and resources; the second stage by policies specifically designed to provide equal access and quality care to needy groups such as the elderly and the poor; the third stage by policies designed to contain rising healthcare costs; and the fourth stage by the political transformation of the American healthcare system through managed care, managed completion, and consumer-driven healthcare.

The federal government in the past had always followed an incremental approach by creating specific policies such as Medicare, Medicaid, and numerous categorical grant programs targeted at narrowly defined groups or problems (Darling 1986). How the ACA changes the landscape of American healthcare system remains to be seen.

Medicare, Medicaid, CHIP, Medicare prescription drug benefit programs, and other federal grant-in-aid programs have increased access to healthcare by removing some of the financial obstacles facing needy groups. However, problems remain, and recent evidence suggests the emergence of new difficulties. The demise of the Medicare Catastrophic Coverage Act left many poor elderly with significant gaps in their Medicare coverage because they cannot afford to buy supplemental private insurance. This problem is likely to grow as the number of elderly in the population increases. One of the biggest problems is Medicare's failure to provide coverage for long-term care. Similarly, a significant number of poor people are not covered under Medicaid. More and more people are falling through the cracks in the healthcare safety net, as reflected in the increased number of uninsured Americans and the decline in employer-based health insurance. Moreover, hospitals in many major cities are facing a crisis situation (Beck et al. 1991; King 1990; Specter 1990).

Because government intervention in U.S. politics takes place within the context of the public philosophy of interest-group liberalism and cynicism about government regulation, governmental input has tended to occur at the margins rather than at the core of the problem (Mechanic 1981). Powerful interest groups have been able to exercise veto power over proposed policies. For example, since the 1920s, numerous attempts by the federal government to establish some form of national health insurance that would guarantee healthcare access to everyone have been defeated by powerful interests such as the AMA and insurance companies. Such groups have successfully defended and protected their narrow interests, even if they have done so in the name of protecting the public interest by appealing to the value of freedom to choose one's doctor and by raising the specter of "socialized medicine," which they argue would lower the quality of healthcare. In recent years, the issue of national health insurance has been pushed back on the legislative agenda because of an economic environment characterized by huge federal budget deficits and a protracted recession. In light of this past history, the passage of the ACA was a major historical achievement for the Obama administration.

Both liberals and conservatives have had difficulty in carrying out an ideologically faithful healthcare policy. For example, while the Nixon administration advocated a competitive market strategy and successfully pushed for federal support for the development of HMOs, it also had to accept increased federal government regulations in the form of peer review organizations. Similarly, the important innovation of the PPS for Medicare reimbursement under the Reagan administration relied on regulatory price-control mechanisms to encourage efficiency in the healthcare market. President George W. Bush, despite his strong conservative leanings, created the largest expansion of the Medicare program with the prescription drug benefits. President Clinton's efforts to overhaul the U.S. healthcare system through a national health insurance system failed to pass Congress.

Liberals and conservatives have also had to contend with powerful interest groups. For example, insurance companies, hospitals, and the medical profession have welcomed some regulatory relief, but they have not shown a great deal of enthusiasm for the conservative program of increased competition in the healthcare market (Starr 1982). Liberal efforts at major reforms to increase healthcare access were successfully thwarted by the same interest groups. Part of the reason for the success of the ACA was that the Obama administration from the very beginning courted and succeeded in winning over the support of some powerful interest groups through bargaining and achieving compromises. Also, it is important to remember that while Obama healthcare reform is a major accomplishment, the reform itself is modest. It did not create a single-payer universal healthcare system. Since undocumented individuals are not covered under the law, we can expect the number of individuals covered under health insurance to increase, but it will not achieve the goal of universal health insurance coverage. The law does not provide for a public option, and thus the American healthcare system will continue to remain a mostly private system despite opponents' charge that the law creates a "government controlled" and/or "government run" healthcare system.

The constitutional structure of separation of powers and checks and balances combined with the increased frequency of divided government has necessitated constant bargaining and compromises between the two houses of Congress and between the president and Congress. However, the increased partisanship and ideological divide between the two political parties has made bargaining and compromises more difficult. It is important to keep in mind that the ACA was passed largely on a party-line vote. Not a single Republican in the House voted for the law, while in the Senate only one Republican and two independents voted in favor with Democrats. The federal structure of government will continue to produce debate about the proper distribution of authority and responsibility between the different levels of government in health policy.

STUDY QUESTIONS

1. Discuss how healthcare evolved in the United States in the eighteenth and nineteenth centuries.
2. Discuss the most important factors/developments that helped transform American medicine between 1900 and 1935.
3. What factors contributed to the separation and the schism that developed between public health and private medicine in the early part of twenty-first-century America?
4. Discuss the evolution of the role of the federal government in healthcare from 1900 to the1960s. What was the single most important goal/purpose of federal government healthcare policies during this time period?
5. Why and how did the political transformation of the American healthcare system come about between 1970 and 2008? What factors contributed to this transformation?
6. The failure of the Clinton administration's (1993–2001) attempt to overhaul the U.S. healthcare system did lead to passage of some important incremental healthcare reforms during the Clinton years. What were they?
7. Write an essay in which you discuss the major conservative health policy initiatives of the administration of George W. Bush (2001–2009).
8. Discuss the role of state and local government in the healthcare field.

REFERENCES

Aaron, Henry J. 1991. *Serious and Unstable Condition: Financing America's Health Care.* Washington, DC: Brookings Institution.

Abramson, John. 2004. *Overdosed America: The Broken Promise of American Medicine.* New York: Harper Collins.

Adler, Jonathan H. 2011. "Cooperation, Commandeering, or Crowding Out? Federal Intervention and State Choices in Health Care Policy." *Kansas Journal of Law and Public Policy* 20, no. 2: 199–221.

Altman, Drew E., and Douglas H. Morgan. 1983. "The Role of the State and Local Government in Health." *Health Affairs* 2, no. 4 (Winter): 7–31.

American College of Emergency Physicians. 2006. *The National Report Card on the State of Emergency Medicine.* Washington, DC: American College of Emergency Physicians. Online at www.acep.org/ assets/0/16/648/1994/00FA9DFA-9B89–4DA8-A3D8–5FBD37DD858D.pdf.

American Hospital Association. 2005. *AHA Hospital Statistics.* Chicago: Health Forum Publishing.

Anders, George. 1997. *Health Against Wealth: HMOs and the Breakdown of Medical Trust.* Thorndike, ME: G.K. Hall.

Anderson, Odin W. 1985. *Health Services in the United States: A Growth Enterprise Since 1875.* Ann Arbor, MI: Health Administration Press.

Baker, David W.; Carl D. Stevens; and Robert H. Brook. 1991. "Patients Who Leave a Public Hospital Emergency Department Without Being Seen by a Physician." *Journal of the American Medical Association* 266, no. 8 (August 28): 1085–90.

Balz, Dan, and Ronald J. Brownstein. 1996. *Storming the Gates: Protest Politics and the Republican Revival.* Boston: Little, Brown.

Barlett, Donald L., and James B. Steele. 2006. *Critical Condition: How Health Care in America Became Big Business and Bad Medicine.* New York: Broadway Books.

Barnes, Fred. 1991. "Rude Health." *New Republic* 205, no. 23 (December): 9–10.

Barrilleaux, Charles, and Paul Brace. 2007. "Notes from the Laboratories of Democracy: State Government Enactments of Market- and State-Based Health Insurance Reforms in the 1990s." *Journal of Health Politics, Policy and Law* 32, no. 4 (August): 655–83.

Bashevkin, Sylvia. 2000. "Rethinking Retrenchment: North American Social Policy During the Early Clinton and Cheretien Years." *Canadian Journal of Political Science* 33, no. 1 (March): 7–36.

Beck, Melinda; Daniel Glick; Nadine Joseph; and Peter Katel. 1991. "State of Emergency." *Newsweek,* October 14,

Bernstein, Merton C., and Joan Broadshaug Bernstein. 1988. *Social Security: The System That Works.* New York: Basic Books.

Bindman, Andrew; Kevin Grumbach; Dennis Keane; Loren Rauch; and John M. Luce. 1991. "Consequences of Queuing for Care at a Public Hospital Emergency Department." *Journal of the American Medical Association* 266, no. 8 (August 28): 1091–96.

Bocchino, Carmella A., and Mary K. Wakefield. 1992. "Capitol Commentary: The Health Care Reform Debate: Competition vs. Government Control." *Nursing Economics* 10, no. 5 (September–October): 360–61.

Brady, David, and Kara M. Buckley. 1995. "Health Care Reform in the 103d Congress: A Predictable Failure." *Journal of Health Politics, Policy and Law* 20, no. 2 (Summer): 447–54.

Brodie, Mollyann, and Robert J. Blendon. 1995. "The Public's Contribution to Congressional Gridlock on Health Care Reform." *Journal of Health Politics, Policy and Law* 20, no. 2 (Summer): 403–10.

Brown, Lawrence D. 1986. "Introduction to a Decade of Transition." *Journal of Health Politics, Policy and Law* 11, no. 4: 569–83.

———. 1987. *Health Policy in Transition: A Decade of Health Politics, Policy, and Law.* Durham: Duke University Press.

Brown, Lawrence D., and Michael S. Sparer. 2001. "Window Shopping: State Health Reform Politics in the 1990s." *Health Affairs* 20, no. 1 (January/February): 50–68.

Brownlee, Shannon. 2007. *Overtreated: Why Too Much Medicine Is Making Us Sicker and Poorer.* New York: Bloomsbury.

Budrys, Grace. 2011. *Our Unsystematic Health Care System.* 3rd ed. Lanham, MD.: Rowman & Littlefield.

Campion, Frank D. 1984. *The AMA and U.S. Health Policy Since 1940.* Chicago: Chicago Review Press.

Canaham-Clyne, John P. 1995. "Clinton's Folly—The Health Care Debacle." *New Politics* 5, no. 2 (Winter): 27.

Carter, Jimmy. 1979. "National Health Plan Legislation." *Challenge* 22, no. 3 (July–August): 11–16.

Clark, Cal, and Rene McEldowney, eds. 2001. *The Health Care Financial Crisis: Strategies for Overcoming an "Unholy Trinity."* Huntington, NY: Nova Science.

Clymer, Adam. 1993. "Clinton Asks Backing for Sweeping Change in the Health System." *New York Times,* September 23.

Cohen, Eric. 2002. "Bush's Stem Cell Ruling: A Missouri Compromise." In *The Future Is Now: America*

Confronts the New Genetics, ed. William Kristol and Eric Cohen, 316–18. Lanham, MD.: Rowman & Littlefield.

Cohn, Jonathan. 2008. *Sick: The Untold Story of America's Health Care Crisis—and the People Who Pay the Price.* New York: HarperCollins.

Committee on the Future of Emergency Care in the United States Health System. 2007. *Hospital-Based Emergency Care: At the Breaking Point.* Washington, DC: National Academies Press.

Coughlin, Teresa A., and Stephen Zuckerman. 2008. "State Responses to New Flexibility in Medicaid." *Milbank Quarterly* 86, no. 2 (June): 209–40.

Congressional Budget Office. 1998. "Expanding Health Insurance Coverage for Children Under Title XXI of the Social Security Act." February and August. Online at www.cbo.gov/ftpdocs/3xx/doc353/kids-hi.pdf.

Cortese, Denis A. 2006. "Healing America's Health Care System." *Mayo Clinic Proceedings* 81, no. 4 (April): 492–96.

Daniels, Mark R., ed. 1998. *Medicaid Reform and the American States: Case Studies of Managed Care.* Westport, CT: Auburn House.

Darling, Helen. 1986. "The Role of the Federal Government in Assuring Access to Health Care." *Inquiry* 23, no. 1 (Fall): 286–95.

Daschle, Thomas, Scott S. Greenberger, and Jeanne M. Lambrew. 2008. *Critical: What We Can Do About the Health Care Crisis.* New York: Thomas Dunne.

David, Sheri I. 1985. *With Dignity: The Search for Medicare and Medicaid.* Westport, CT: Greenwood Press.

Davidson, Stephen M. 2010. *Still Broken: Understanding the U.S. Health Care System.* Stanford, CA: Stanford University Press.

Davidson, Stephen M., and Stephen A. Somers, eds. 1998. *Remaking Medicaid: Managed Care for the Public Good.* San Francisco: Jossey-Bass.

Davis, Karen. 1981. "Reagan Administration Health Policy." *Journal of Public Health Policy* 2, no. 4 (December): 312–32.

Dentzer, Susan. 1990. "America's Scandalous Health Care." *U.S. News and World Report,* March 12.

———. 1992. "Work-Care." *New Republic* 206, no. 22 (June): 18–21.

Dinan, John. 2011. "Shaping Health Reform: State Government Influence in the Patient Protection and Affordable Care Act." *Publius* 41, no. 3 (June): 395–420.

Downing, Raymond. 2006. *Suffering and Healing in America: An American Doctor's View from Outside.* Seattle: Radcliffe.

Easterbrook, Gregg. 1987. "The Revolution in Medicine." *Newsweek,* January 26.

Ehrenreich, Barbara. 1990. "Our Health-Care Disgrace." *Time,* December 10.

Elhauge, Einer, ed. 2010. *The Fragmentation of U.S. Health Care: Causes and Solutions.* New York: Oxford University Press.

Etheredge, Lynn. 1983. "Reagan, Congress and Health Spending." *Health Affairs* 2, no. 1 (Spring): 14–24.

Falkson, Joseph L. 1980. *HMOs and the Politics of Health Service Reform.* Chicago: American Hospital Association.

Fallows, James. 1995. "A Triumph of Misinformation." *Atlantic Monthly* 275, no. 1 (January): 26–37.

Fan, Jessie X.; Deanna L. Sharpe; and Goog-Soog Hong. 2003. "Health Care and Prescription Drug Spending by Seniors." *Monthly Labor Review Online* 126, no. 3 (March).

Fein, Rashi. 1986. *Medical Care, Medical Costs: The Search for a Health Insurance Policy.* Cambridge, MA: Harvard University Press.

Field, Robert E. 2007. *Health Care Regulations in America: Complexity, Confrontation, and Compromise.* New York: Oxford University Press.

Flint, Samuel S. 2008. "Health Care Reform in the 2008 Presidential Primaries." *Health & Social Work* 33, no. 2 (May): 93–96.

Fox, Daniel M. 1986. *Health Policies, Health Politics: The British and American Experience: 1911–1965.* Princeton, NJ: Princeton University Press.

Geyman, John P. 2002. *Health Care in America: Can Our Ailing System Be Healed?* Boston: Butterworth-Heinemann.

———. 2005. *Falling Through the Safety Net: Americans Without Health Insurance.* Monroe, ME: Common Courage Press.

———. 2010. *Hijacked: The Road to Single Payer in the Aftermath of Stolen Health Care Reform.* Monroe, ME: Common Courage Books.

Gibson, Rosemary. 2003. *Wall of Silence: The Untold Story of the Medical Mistakes That Kill and Injure Millions of Americans.* Washington, DC: LifeLine Press.

Ginsberg, David L. 1987. "Health Care Policy in the Reagan Administration: Rhetoric and Reality." *Public Administration Quarterly* 11, no. 1 (Spring): 59–70.

Goozner, Merrill. 2004. *The $800 Million Pill: The Truth Behind the Cost of New Drugs.* Berkeley: University of California Press.

Gorin, Stephen H., and Cynthia Moniz. 2007. "Why Does President Bush Oppose the Expansion of SCHIP?" *Health and Social Work* 32, no. 4 (November): 243–46.

Gottfried, Dennis. 2009. *Too Much Medicine: A Doctor's Prescription for Better and More Affordable Health Care.* St. Paul, MN: Paragon House.

Greifinger, Robert B., and Victor William Sidel. 1978. "Three Centuries of Medical Care." In *Medical Care in the United States,* ed. Eric F. Oatman, 12–26. New York: H.W. Wilson.

Grodzins, Morton. 1966. *The American System: A New View of Government in the United States.* Chicago: Rand McNally.

Grogan, Colleen M., and Elizabeth Rigby. 2008. "Federalism, Partisan Politics, and Shifting Support for State Flexibility: The Case of the U.S. State Children's Health Insurance Program." *Publius* 39, no. 1 (December): 47–69.

Hacker, Jacob S. 2002. *The Divided Welfare State: The Battle Over Public and Private Social Benefits in the United States.* Cambridge, MA: Cambridge University Press.

Hadler, Nortin M. 2008. *Worried Sick: A Prescription for Health in an Overtreated America.* Chapel Hill: University of North Carolina Press.

Hanlon, John T., and George E. Picker. 1974. *Public Health: Administration and Practice.* St. Louis, MO: C.V. Mosby.

Hanson, Russell L. 1994. "Health Care Reform, Managed Competition and Subnational Politics." *Publius* 24, no. 3 (Summer): 49–68.

Hayes, Katherine. 2011. "Overview of Policy, Procedure, and Legislative History of the Affordable Care Act." *National Academy of Elder Law Attorneys* 7, no. 1 (March): 1–9.

"The Health Care System Is Broken and Here Is How to Fix It." 1991. *New York Times,* July 22.

Herzlinger, Regina. 2007. *Who Killed Health Care? America's $2 Trillion Medical Problem—and the Consumer-Driven Care.* New York: McGraw Hill.

Hill, Lister. 1976. "Health in America: A Personal Perspective." In *Health in America: 1776–1976,* ed. U.S. Department of Health, Education, and Welfare, 3–15. Washington, DC: Government Printing Office.

Hilts, Philip J. 1991. "Many Leave Emergency Room Needing Care." *New York Times,* August 27.

Holahan, John F., and Joel W. Cohen. 1986. *Medicaid: The Trade-Off Between Cost-Containment and Access to Care.* Washington, DC: Urban Institute Press.

Iglehart, John K. 1978. "The Carter Administration's Health Budget: Charting New Priorities with Limited Dollars." *Milbank Memorial Fund Quarterly* 56, no. 1 (Winter): 51–77.

———. 1995. "Health Policy Report: Republicans and the New Politics of Health Care." *New England Journal of Medicine* 332, no. 14 (April 6): 972–75.

Jacobs, Lawrence R., and Robert Y. Shapiro. 1995. "Don't Blame the Public for Failed Health Care Reform." *Journal of Health Politics, Policy and Law* 20, no. 2 (Summer): 411–23.

Kaiser Family Foundation. 2004. "Prescription Drug Trends." Fact-Sheet #3057–03. Online at www.kff.org.

Kasindorf, Martin. 2004. "States Play Catch-up on Stem Cells." *USA Today,* December 17.

"Kassebaum-Kennedy Health Insurance Bill Clears Congress." 1996. Washington, DC: Families USA, August. Online at www.epn.org/families/Kafeka.html.

Kaufman, Marc. 2005. "FDA Plans New Board to Monitor Drug Safety." *Washington Post,* February 16: A01.

King, Peter. 1990. "The City as a Patient." *Newsweek,* February 19.

Kinsley, Michael. 1992. "Quack." *New Republic* 206, no. 9 (March): 4.

Kleinke, J.D. 2001. *Oxymorons: The Myth of a U.S. Health Care System.* San Francisco: Jossey-Bass.

Kulczcki, Andrzej. 2007. "Ethics, Ideology, and Reproductive Health Policy in the United States." *Studies in Family Planning* 38, no. 4 (December): 333–51.

Lambrew, Jeanne M. 2005. "Making Medicaid a Block Grant Program: An Analysis of the Implications of Past Proposals." *Milbank Quarterly* 83, no. 1: 41–64.

Lasser, Karen E.; Andrea Kronman; Howard Cabral; and Jeffrey H. Samet. 2012. "Emergency Department Use by Primary Care Patients at a Safety-Net Hospital." *Archives of Internal Medicine* 172, no. 3: 278–90.

Lee, Philip R., and Carroll L. Estes. 1983. "New Federalism and Health Policy." *Annals of the American Academy of Political and Social Science* 468 (July): 88–102.

Levey, Noam N. 2012. "Passing the Buck or Empowering States? Who Will Define Essential Health Benefits?" *Health Affairs* 31, no. 4: 663–66.

Levit, Katherine R., et al. 1994. "National Health Expenditures, 1993." *Health Care Financing Review* 16, no. 1 (Fall): 247–94.

Lewis, Anthony. 1991. "A Sick System." *New York Times,* June 3.

Long, Stephen H., and Russell F. Settle. 1984. "Medicare and the Disadvantaged Elderly: Objectives and Outcomes." *Milbank Memorial Fund Quarterly/Health and Society* 62, no. 4 (Fall): 609–56.

Lynn, Joanne. 2004. *Sick to Death and Not Going to Take It Anymore! Reforming Health Care for the Last Years of Life.* Berkeley: University of California Press.

Makover, Michael E. 1998. *Mismanaged Care: How Corporate Medicine Jeopardizes Your Health.* Amherst, NY: Prometheus Books.

Manning, Bayless, and Bruce Vladeck. 1983. "The Role of State and Local Government in Health." *Health Affairs* 2, no. 4 (Winter): 134–40.

McCarthy, Michael. 2001. "Fragmented U.S. Health-Care System Needs Major Reform." *Lancet* 357, no. 9258: (March 10): 782.

McEldowney, Rene, and Carol Jenkins. 2005. "Efforts to Reform Medicaid in a Time of Fiscal Stress: Are We Merely Shuffling Chairs on the Deck of the Titanic?" *Journal of Health and Social Policy* 21, no. 2: 1–16.

McFarlane, Deborah R. 2006. "Reproductive Health Policy in President Bush's Second Term: Old Battles and New Fronts in the United States and Internationally." *Journal of Public Health Policy* 27, no. 4: 405–26.

Mechanic, David. 1981. "Some Dilemmas in Health Care Policy." *Milbank Memorial Fund Quarterly/Health and Society* 59, no. 1 (Winter): 1–14.

———. 2004. "The Rise and Fall of Managed Care." *Journal of Health and Social Behavior* Supplement 1, no. 45 (December): 76–81.

———. 2008. *The Truth About Health Care: Why Reform Is Not Working in America.* New Brunswick, NJ: Rutgers University Press.

Milgrom, Peter; Rosanna S. Lee; Colleen E. Huebner; and Douglas A. Conrad. 2010. "Medicaid Reform in Oregon and Suboptimal Utilization of Dental Care by Women of Childbearing Age." *Journal of the American Dental Association* 14, no. 6 (June): 688–95.

Moore, Thomas J. 1995. *Deadly Medicine: Why Tens of Thousands of Heart Patients Died in America's Worst Drug Disaster.* New York: Simon & Schuster.

Morin, Richard. 1994. "A Health Care Reform Post-Mortem." *Washington Post National Weekly Edition,* September 12–18.

Nathan, Richard P., et al. 1982. "Initial Effects of the Fiscal Year 1982 Reductions in Federal Domestic Spending." In *Reductions in U.S. Domestic Spending: How They Affect State and Local Governments,* ed. John W. Ellwood, 315–49. New Brunswick, NJ: Transaction.

Nather, David. 2003. "GOP Hones 'Can Do' Pitch to Party Base, Swing Voters." *Congressional Quarterly Weekly* 61, no. 48 (December 13): 3062–64.

National Center for Health Statistics. 2012. *Health United States, 2011: With Special Features on Socioeconomic Status and Health.* Hyattsville, MD.

Navarro, Vicente. 1995. "Why Congress Did Not Enact Health Care Reform." *Journal of Health Politics, Policy and Law* 20, no. 2 (Summer): 455–62.

Nietert, Paul J; David W. Bradford; and Linda M. Kaste. 2005. "The Impact of an Innovative Reform to the South Carolina Dental Medicaid System." *Health Services Research* 40, no. 4: 1078–91.

Nixon, Richard M. 1971. "Message to Congress." *Weekly Compilation of Presidential Documents.* Washington, DC: Office of the Federal Register, February 18.

Norris, Jonas. 1984. *Searching for a Cure: National Health Policy Considered.* New York: PICA Press.

"Obama Ends Stem Cell Research Ban." 2009. CBS News, June 18. Online at www.cbsnews.com/2100–503767_162–4853385.html.

"OECD Health Data." 2011. Available online at www.oecd.org.

Oberlander, Jonathan. 2006. "The Political Economy of Unfairness in U.S. Health Policy." *Law and Contemporary Problems* 69, no. 4 (Autumn): 245–64.

Oliver, Thomas R. 1991. "Health Care Market Reform in Congress: The Uncertain Path from Proposal to Policy." *Political Science Quarterly* 106, no. 3: 453–78.

Olson, Laura K. 2012. "Medicaid, the States and Health Care Reform." *New Political Science* 34, no. 1 (March): 37–54.

Parmet, Wendy E. 1993. "Regulation and Federalism: Legal Impediments to State Health Care Reform." *American Journal of Law and Medicine* 19, nos. 1–2: 121–45.

Patel, Kant. 2003. "Presidential Rhetoric and the Strategy of Going Public: President Clinton and the Health Care Reform." *Journal of Health and Social Policy* 18, no. 2: 21–42.

Patel, Kant, and Mark Rushefsky. 1998. "Health Policy Community and Health Care Reform in the United States." *Health: An Interdisciplinary Journal for the Social Study of Health, Illness and Medicine* 2, no. 4 (October): 459–84.

———. 2005a. *The Politics of Public Health in the United States.* Armonk, NY: M.E. Sharpe.

———. 2005b. "President Bush and Stem Cell Policy: The Politics of Policy Making." *White House Studies Journal* 5, no.1 (Special issue): 37–52.

Peterson, Mark A. 2001. "Editor's Note: Health Politics and Policy in a Federal System." *Journal of Health Politics, Policy and Law* 26, no. 6 (December): 1217–22.

Porter, Eduardo. 2004. "Do New Drugs Always Have to Cost So Much?" *New York Times,* November 14.

Potter, Wendell. 2010. *Deadly Spin: An Insurance Company Insider Speaks Out on How Corporate PR Is Killing Health Care and Deceiving Americans.* New York: Bloomsbury Press.

Qazi, Khalid J. 2009. "Healthcare Reform in the United States: Fact, Fiction and Drama." *British Journal of Medical Practitioners* 2, no. 4: 5–7.

Quadagno, Jill. 2005. *One Nation, Uninsured: Why the U.S. Has No National Health Insurance.* New York: Oxford University Press.

Raffel, Marshall W. 1980. *The U.S. Health System: Origins and Functions.* New York: Wiley.

Rangel, Charles B. 2009. "Fixing America's Health Care System." *New York Amsterdam News* 100, no. 34 (August 20): 12.

Reagan, Michael D. 1999. *The Accidental System: Health Care Policy in America.* Boulder, CO: Westview Press.

Reed, T.R. 2009. *The Healing of America: A Global Quest for Better, Cheaper, and Fairer Health Care.* New York: Penguin Press.

Rice, Thomas; Katherine Desmond; and Jon Gable. 1990. "The Medicare Catastrophic Coverage Act: A Post-Mortem." *Health Affairs* 9, no. 3 (Fall): 75–87.

Rice, Thomas, and Jon Gable. 1986. "Protecting the Elderly Against High Health Care Costs." *Health Affairs* 5, no. 3 (Fall): 5–21.

Rich, Robert F., and William D. White, eds. 1996. *Health Policy, Federalism, and the American States.* Washington, DC: Urban Institute Press.

Richmond, Julius B. 2005. *The Health Care Mess: How We Got Into It and What It Will Take to Get Out.* Cambridge, MA: Cambridge University Press.

Robbins, Anthony. 1983. "Can Reagan Be Indicted for Betraying Public Health?" *American Journal of Public Health* 73, no. 1 (January): 12–13.

Roemer, Milton I. 1984. "The Politics of Public Health in the United States." In *Health Politics and Policy,* ed. Theodore J. Litman and Leonard S. Robins, 261–73. New York: Wiley.

———. 1986. *An Introduction to the U.S. Health Care System,* 2nd ed. New York: Springer.

Ropes, Linda B. 1991. *Health Care Crisis in America: A Reference Handbook.* Santa Barbara, CA: ABC-CLIO.

Rosenbloom, David. 1983. "New Ways to Keep Old Promises in Health Care." *Health Affairs* 2, no. 4 (Winter): 41–53.

Rutkow, Ira M. 2005. *Bleeding Blue and Gray: Civil War Surgery and the Evolution of American Medicine.* New York: Random House.

Schneider, Ann L., and Helen M. Ingram. 2004. *Deserving and Entitled: Social Constructions and Public Policy.* New York: State University of New York Press.

Singer, Merrill, and Hans Baer, eds. 2009. *Killer Commodities: Public Health and the Corporate Production of Harm.* Lanham: AltaMira Press.

Skidmore, Max J. 1970. *Medicare and the American Rhetoric of Reconciliation.* University: University of Alabama Press.

Skocpol, Theda. 1994. "From Social Security to Health Security? Opinion and Rhetoric in U.S. Social Policy Making." *PS: Political Science and Politics* 27, no. 1 (December): 21–25.

———. 1997. *Health Care Reform and the Turn Against Government.* New York: W.W. Norton.

———. 2011. "Obama and the Transformation of U.S. Public Policy: The Struggle to Reform Health Care." *Arizona State Law Journal* 42, no. 4 (Winter): 1203–32.

Smerd, Jeremy. 2006. "Stuck in the Waiting Room—Part 1 and 2." *Workforce Management* 85, no. 18 (September 25): 25–28.

Snyder, Don. 2006. "In U.S. Hospitals, Emergency Care in Critical Condition." May 1. Online at www.foxnews.com/story/0,2933,193883,00.html.

Sparer, Michael S. 1998. "Devolution of Power: An Interim Report Card." *Health Affairs* 17, no. 3 (May/June): 7–17.

————. 2004. "States and the Politics of Incrementalism: Health Policy in Wisconsin During the 1990s." *Journal of Health Politics, Policy and Law* 29, no. 2 (April): 269–92.

Sparrow, Malcolm K. 2000. *License to Steal: Why Fraud Plagues America's Health Care System.* Boulder, CO: Westview Press.

Specter, Michael. 1990. "Putting Michigan Hospitals on the Critical List." *Washington Post National Weekly Edition,* June 4–10.

Starr, Paul. 1982. *The Social Transformation of American Medicine.* New York: Basic Books.

————. 1995. "What Happened to Health Care Reform?" *American Prospect,* no. 20 (Winter): 20–31.

————. 2011. *Remedy and Reaction: The Peculiar American Struggle over Health Care Reform.* New Haven, CT: Yale University Press.

Steinmo, Sven, and Jon Watts. 1995. "It's the Institutions, Stupid! Why Comprehensive National Health Insurance Always Fails in America." *Journal of Health Politics, Policy and Law* 20, no. 2 (Summer): 329–72.

"Stem-Cell Guidelines: Ethics of a New Science." 2005. *Time,* May 9.

"Stem Cell Research: Undated January 2008." n.d. National Conference of State Legislatures, Washington, DC. Online at www.ncsl.org/issues-research/health/embryonic-and-fetal-research-laws.aspx.

Stevens, Rosemary A. 1989. *In Sickness and in Wealth: American Hospitals in the Twentieth Century.* New York: Basic Books.

————. 2007. *The Public-Private Health Care State: Essays on the History of American Health Care Policy.* New Brunswick, NJ: Transaction Publishers.

Stevens, Rosemary A., Charles E. Rosenberg, and Lawton R. Burns. 2006. *History and Health Policy in the Unites States.* New Brunswick, NJ: Rutgers University Press.

Stolberg, Sheryl G. 2005. "In Rare Threat, Bush Vows Veto of Stem Cell Bill." *New York Times,* May 21. Online at www.nytimes.com/2005/05/21/politics/21stem.html.

"A Survey of Health Care: Surgery Needed." 1991. *Economist* (July 6): 4–5.

Taurel, Sidney. 2005. "Critical Condition: The Ills of America's Health Care System and How We Can Heal Them." *Executive Speeches* 19, no. 6 (June–July): 106.

"Tauzin to Head Pharmaceutical Lobbying Group." 2004. *Washington Post,* December 15. Online at www.washingtonpost.com.

Taylor, Humphrey. 1990 "U.S. Health Care: Built for Waste." *New York Times,* April 17.

Terris, Milton. 1990. "A Wasteful System That Doesn't Work." *Progressive* 54, no. 10 (October): 14–16.

Thomas, W. John. 1995. "Clinton Health Care Reform Plan: A Failed Dramatic Presentation." *Stanford Law and Policy Review* 7, no. 1: 83–104.

Thompson, Frank J. 1986. "New Federalism and Health Care Policy: States and the Old Questions." *Journal of Health Politics, Policy and Law* 11, no. 4 (Tenth Anniversary Issue): 647–69.

Thompson, Frank J., and Courtney Burke. 2007. "Executive Federalism and Medicaid Demonstration Waivers: Implications for Policy and Democratic Process." *Journal of Health Politics, Policy and Law* 32, no. 6 (December): 971–1004.

————. 2008. "Federalism by Waiver: Medicaid and the Transformation of Long-Term Care." *Publius* 39, no. 1: 22–48.

Tumulty, Karen. 2005. "Stem Cells: Why Bush's Ban Could Be Reversed." *Time,* May 23, pp. 26–30.

U.S. Census Bureau. 1996. *Statistical Abstract of the United States, 1996.* Washington, DC: Government Printing Office.

"U.S. Grapples with Solution to Preventable Medical Errors." 2009. *Canadian Medical Association Journal* 180, no. 7 (March 31): E4-E5.

U.S. Health Resources Administration. 1976. *Health in America: 1776–1976.* Rockville, MD: U.S. Department of Health, Education, and Welfare.

Veatch, Robert M. 2009. *Patient, Heal Thyself: How the New Medicine Puts the Patient in Charge.* New York: Oxford University Press.

Von Drehle, David; Alex Altman; Michael Crowley; Michael Grunwald; and Michael Scherer. 2012. "Here's What We Know for Sure: Obama's Health Care Reform Is Constitutional, Congress May Not Hold States Hostage to Its Every Whim." *Time* 180, no. 3 (July 16): 30–41.

Wade, Nicholas. 2005. "Group of Scientists Draft Rules on Ethics for Stem Cell Research." *New York Times,* April 27. Online at www.nytimes.com/2005/04/27/health/27stem.html

Wallace, Steven P., and Carroll L. Estes. 1989. "Health Policy for the Elderly." *Society* 26, no. 6 (September–October): 66–75.

Warner, John H., and Janet A. Tighe. 2001. *Major Problems in the History of American Medicine and Public Health: Documents and Essays.* Boston: Houghton Mifflin.

Waxman, Henry A. 2006. "Politics and Science: Reproductive Health." *Health Matrix: Journal of Law-Medicine* 16, no. 1 (Winter): 5–25.

Weil, Alan; Joshua M. Wiedner; and John Holahan. 1998. "Assessing the New Federalism and State Health Policy." *Health Affairs* 17, no. 6 (November/December): 162–64.

Welch, Gilbert H.; Lisa Swartz; and Steve Woloshin. 2011. *Overdiagnosed: Making People Sick in the Pursuit of Health.* Boston: Beacon Press.

White House Domestic Policy Council. 1993. *The President's Health Security Act: The Clinton Blueprint.* New York: Times Books.

Wines, Michael. 1992. "Bush Announces Health Plan, Filling Gap in Re-Election Bid." *New York Times,* September 23.

Wing, Kenneth R. 1984. "Recent Amendments to the Medicaid Program: Political Implications." *American Journal of Public Health* 74, no.1 (January): 83–84.

3

MEDICAID AND CHILDREN'S HEALTH INSURANCE PROGRAMS

Healthcare for the Poor and the Disabled

The establishment of Medicare and Medicaid in 1965 was the result of a lengthy debate during the early part of the twentieth century over the role of the federal government in financing healthcare. The debate among policymakers focused on two competing models. Under the universal coverage model, the federal government would provide health insurance to all people on a compulsory basis, financed by taxes on earnings. The second model envisioned a more limited role for the federal government, providing assistance only to needy groups in society. Throughout the twentieth century, all federal healthcare laws followed the second model (Ginsburg 1988). The political environment, institutional structures, and legislative processes made such an incremental approach feasible.

In the 1930s, President Herbert Hoover established the Committee on the Costs of Medical Care (CCMC). This committee's assessment of U.S. healthcare specifically focused on challenges facing low-income Americans in obtaining care. Prior to the passage of Medicaid in 1965, a hodgepodge of poorly funded federal programs existed for meeting the healthcare needs of the poor (Goldfield 2003). The 1950 amendments to the Social Security Act authorized matching grants to the states for direct vendor (provider) payments for treatment of individuals on public assistance. During the late 1950s, the debate focused on the problem of hospital costs faced by the aged, which had doubled over the decade. Support increased for addressing this problem because the aged were presumed to be both needy and deserving (Starr 1982). In 1960, Congress passed the Kerr-Mills Act, creating the Medical Assistance for the Aged (MAA) program. This act expanded federal matching funds to the states for vendor payments, and, more importantly, it allowed states to include the "medically needy"—that is, elderly, blind, and disabled persons with low incomes who were not on public assistance. However, many states moved very slowly or failed to move at all to take advantage of the Kerr-Mills Act.

The Democratic Party's sweep of the 1964 elections guaranteed further action with respect to the role of the federal government in healthcare. Lyndon Johnson was elected to the presidency with an overwhelming popular vote. The Democrats gained a two-to-one majority in the House of Representatives. This made it possible for Congress in 1965 to create the Medicare and Medicaid programs. Both were in the forefront of Lyndon Johnson's Great Society programs designed to help the poor and the disadvantaged (Davis and Reynolds 1977). Medicare was established as a program for the elderly, Medicaid as a program for the poor. The final shape of both programs represented compromises among competing models and approaches. The Democratic plan for a compulsory hospital insurance program, financed through payroll taxes under Social Security, became Part A of Medicare. The Republican-supported plan of a government-subsidized, voluntary insurance program financed through general revenues to cover physicians' bills became Part B of Medicare. The AMA opposed both plans and pushed a plan of its own to expand the Kerr-Mills program to the needy. An expanded means-tested program for the poor administered by the states became the Medicaid program.

The generally accepted political explanation for the creation of Medicaid is that the program was created almost as an afterthought to Medicare (Grannemann and Pauly 1983). Medicaid was intended to "pick up the pieces" left over by Medicare. It was designed to cover deductibles and coinsurance for indigent Medicare patients. The program was intended to pay for services not covered, or covered only inadequately, by Medicare (i.e., outpatient and nursing home care), and to pay the cost of medical care of indigent persons other than the elderly (Brown 1984).

Although Medicare and Medicaid were adopted at the same time, there are fundamental differences between the two. First, the Medicare program has enjoyed public popularity and legitimacy because it is tied to Social Security, a program that is contributory in nature (i.e., through Social Security taxes paid by workers). In contrast, from the beginning, Medicaid has been burdened by the stigma of being a public assistance (i.e., welfare) program. Second, Medicare has uniform national standards for eligibility and benefits. In sharp contrast, Medicaid, to a large extent, lets states decide on eligibility and benefit standards. Third, physician reimbursement under Medicaid is lower than under Medicare or private insurance; consequently, fewer physicians participate in the Medicaid program (Starr 1982). Fourth, Medicare is financed and administered solely by the federal government, while Medicaid is financed by both the federal and state governments on a matching basis. Fifth, Medicare is administered by the federal government, while Medicaid is administered by the state governments.

PROGRAM OBJECTIVE AND STRUCTURE

The primary objective of Medicaid is to provide the poor with financial assistance to meet their medical needs. State governments are given the responsibility for establishing program requirements. States were also given the option of making the administration of the program a local rather than state responsibility.

Although federal law created the program, the intent was to encourage state governments to set up a "unified system of healthcare" for certain low-income individuals (Schneider 1988). The federal government encourages state participation and compliance with the program in several ways. The federal government provides matching funds to encourage states to expand their existing medical assistance programs. The federal government pays a certain percentage of program expenditures to states in the form of matching funds, the Federal Medical Assistance Percentage (FMAP). The FMAP varies by state based on criteria such as per capita income in the state. Thus, poorer states receive a larger percentage of federal matching funds. Today, the FMAP varies from a minimum of 50 percent to a maximum of 75 percent. The average state FMAP is about 57 percent. To account for factors such as inflation and other fluctuations in the economy, FMAPs are adjusted for each state on a three-year cycle. The FMAP is published annually in the *Federal Register* ("Medicaid and CHIP Program Information" n.d.).

The Medicaid program was created as a partnership between federal and state governments to improve access and quality of healthcare for the poor. The national government establishes broad program guidelines, promotes and monitors program development, and provides financial assistance through matching grants. State governments are given significant control over important aspects of the scope and structure of the program. For example, state governments enjoy discretionary authority for establishing eligibility standards, the nature and scope of benefits provided, and mechanisms used to reimburse healthcare providers.

The Centers for Medicare and Medicaid Services (CMS) issues program guidelines in the form of letters to state Medicaid directors and state health officials. The CMS also issues regulations to codify policies based on legislative provisions. It does this through issuing notices of proposed rulemaking, seeking inputs on proposed rules, and issuing interim and final rules. The Center for Medicaid and CHIP Services (CMCS), created in 2000, also uses informational bulletins to communicate with state officials and other stakeholders in the Medicaid program ("Medicaid and CHIP Program Information" n.d.).

Medicaid is an excellent example of how the federal structure of government shapes the dynamics of policymaking and implementation. On the one hand, the federal structure, with its multiple governments, shared authority, political autonomy, and constitutional ambiguities, has allowed states to act as laboratories for innovation and experimentation in the Medicaid program. On the other hand, the same federal structure of government produces overlapping jurisdictions and duplications, encourages the promotion of narrow and parochial interests, and creates inefficiencies and inequities. Instead of a "unified system of healthcare" for low-income individuals as originally envisioned, the Medicaid program varies a great deal from state to state with respect to eligibility, services, and benefits creating many inequities in the program. It allows one level of government to pass the buck or to blame another level of government by playing the federalism game.

MEDICAID: ELIGIBILITY AND COVERAGE, SERVICES AND BENEFITS

Eligibility and Coverage

Medicaid provides medical assistance to poor persons who fit into one of the designated groups. Today, Medicaid serves low-income pregnant women, children, nondisabled adults, some seniors age 65 and over, and individuals with disabilities. Some seniors are enrolled in both the Medicaid and Medicare program because they qualify for both programs by criteria of low income (Medicaid) and age (Medicare), such individuals are referred to as "dual eligible." In order to participate in Medicaid, the federal government requires states to cover certain population groups called "mandatory eligibility groups." States are also given the flexibility to cover other populations called the "optional eligibility groups."

The "mandatory eligibility groups" include:

- Pregnant women and children under age six with family income below 133 percent of the Federal Poverty Level (FPL);
- Children age six to eighteen below 100 percent of FPL;
- Parents below states' July 1996 welfare eligibility levels (often below 50 percent of FPL); and
- Most elderly and persons with disabilities who receive Supplemental Security Income (SSI), a program for which income eligibility equates to 75 percent of FPL for an individual (Kaiser Commission on Medicaid and the Uninsured 2010).

The "optional eligibility groups" include, among others:

- Pregnant women, children, and parents with income exceeding the mandatory thresholds;
- Elderly and disabled individuals up to 100 percent of FPL;
- Working disabled individuals up to 250 percent of FPL;
- Persons residing in nursing facilities with income below 300 percent of the SSI standard;
- Individuals who would be eligible if receiving institutionalized care, but who are receiving care under home and community-based services waivers; and
- "Medically needy" individuals who cannot meet the financial criteria but have high health expenses relative to their income, and who belong to one of the categorically eligible groups (Kaiser Commission on Medicaid and the Uninsured 2010).

There are several factors that go into establishing eligibility. Since the program is designed to serve the poor, one of the primary factors in defining eligibility is income. For many eligibility groups, income is calculated in relation to a percentage of the federal poverty level (FPL), which is adjusted annually. In 2012, 100 percent of the FPL for a family of four was $23,050 ("2012 HHS Poverty Guidelines" 2012). For other groups, income standards are based on other nonfinancial criteria of programs such as Supplemental Security Income (SSI). Some of the nonfinancial criteria used to determine Medicaid eligibility include federal and state requirements regarding residency, immigration status, and documentation of U.S. citizenship. The Affordable Care Act of 2010 would have required all states to expand their Medicaid program to cover more uninsured persons and established a minimum Medicaid income eligibility level across the country. Beginning in 2014 the law would have made individuals under the age of sixty-five with income below 133 percent of FPL eligible for Medicaid. However, the U.S. Supreme Court in 2012 ruled by a vote of 7–2 that the states cannot be forced to expand their Medicaid coverage and are free to opt out of such an expansion. This is discussed in more detail later in the chapter.

Services and Benefits

States are required to cover certain "mandatory benefits" in their Medicaid programs. These benefits include inpatient and outpatient hospital services; physician services; nursing facility services; rural health clinic services; prenatal care; vaccines for children; family planning services and supplies; and laboratory and X-ray services, among others. States can also receive federal matching funds if they elect to provide other "optional benefits" such as diagnostic and clinic services, intermediate care facilities for the mentally retarded, prescribed drugs and prosthetic devices, optometrist services and eyeglasses, transportation services, rehabilitation and physical therapy services, and home and community-based care for certain persons with chronic impairment (see Table 3.1).

Medicaid also provides coverage for a host of long-term care services to beneficiaries in a variety of settings. For example, Medicaid pays for most of the cost of nursing home care once a person living in a nursing home has exhausted all of his/her own financial resources/assets to pay for such care. Nursing home care is very expensive, ranging from $5,000 to $8,000 a month or more, and can easily deplete the lifelong savings of an elderly couple if one of them has to live in a nursing home. In 1988, Congress enacted provisions called "spousal impoverishment," to prevent a spouse living at home in the community with little or no income or resources. Under the provision, a certain amount of the couple's combined resources is protected for the spouse living at home in the community. The resources and incomes that can be protected for a spouse living in a community in 2011 ranged from a minimum of $21,920 to a maximum of $109,560 ("Medicaid and CHIP Program Information" n.d.). The topic of long-term care is discussed in more detail later in the chapter.

MEDICAID AND STATE FINANCING, REIMBURSEMENT, AND COST SHARING

State Financing Sources

States' share of Medicaid expenditures comes from state legislative appropriations, intergovernmental transfer of funds (IGTs), certified public expenditures (CPEs), and permissible taxes and provider donations. States are permitted to restrict the amount of services per beneficiary. For example, a state may limit the number of days in hospitals or number of visits to physicians per year that it would cover.

Table 3.1

Medicaid Benefits

Mandatory Benefits	Optional Benefits
• Inpatient hospital services • Outpatient hospital services • Early and periodic screening, diagnostic, and treatment (EPSDT) services • Nursing facility services • Home health services • Physician services • Rural health clinic services • Federally qualified health center services • Laboratory and X-ray services • Family planning services • Nurse midwife services • Certified pediatric and family nurse practitioner services • Freestanding birth center services (when licensed or otherwise recognized by the state) • Transportation to medical care • Tobacco cessation counseling for pregnant women • Tobacco cessation	• Prescription drugs • Clinic services • Physical therapy • Occupational therapy • Speech, hearing, and language disorder services • Respiratory care services • Other diagnostic, screening, preventive, and rehabilitative services • Podiatry services • Optometry services • Dental services • Dentures • Prosthetics • Eyeglasses • Chiropractic services • Other practitioner services • Private-duty nursing services • Personal care • Hospice • Case management • Services for individuals age 65 or older in an institution for mental disease (IMD) • Services in an intermediate care facility for the mentally retarded • State plan Home and Community Based Services—1915(i) • Self-Directed Personal Assistance Services—1915(j) • Community First Choice Option—1915(k) • TB-related services • Inpatient psychiatric services for individuals under age 21 • Other services approved by the secretary[1]

[1]This includes services furnished in a religious nonmedical health care institution, emergency hospital services by a non–Medicare-certified hospital, and critical access hospital (CAH).

Source: Centers for Medicare and Medicaid Services, Baltimore, MD. 2012. Online at www.medicaid. gov/Medicaid-CHIP-Program-Information/By-Topics/Benefits/Medicaid-Benefits.html.

Provider Taxes

State governments have increasingly come to rely on provider taxes as a way to increase their share of Medicaid matching funds. The National Conference of State Legislatures reported that in 2011, forty-six states plus the District of Columbia had some type of Medicaid-related provider tax for fiscal year 2011 (Daly 2012). Today, forty-seven states have at least one provider tax in place.

Provider taxes are any mandatory payments required by states in which at least 85 percent of the burden falls on healthcare providers. This includes licensing fees or assessments. Federal regulations list nineteen different classes of healthcare services, such as inpatient hospital services, nursing facilities services, and the like. Current federal law allows states to use the revenue from provider taxes to help make up the state share of Medicaid. CMS requires that such provider taxes be broad-based and uniformly imposed. Thus, provider taxes allow states to produce revenues that go into the state treasury, and then that revenue is directly appropriated to the state Medicaid agency (Kaiser Commission on Medicaid and the Uninsured 2011a).

Provider taxes give states two advantages. One, as states are faced with ever increasing costs of the Medicaid program and tight budgets, provider taxes generate added revenue to pay for their share of the program costs. Second, by coming up with more money for Medicaid, states receive more federal matching funds. In fact, the federal stimulus law adopted in 2009 gave states added incentive to raise provider taxes. The stimulus law provided an extra $87 billion in Medicaid funding to help states during the recession, and, at least temporarily, it raised the federal matching share nationwide to more than 63 percent from its normal national average of 57 percent (Miller 2010).

Disproportionate Share Hospital Payments

Federal law requires state Medicaid programs to make Disproportionate Share Hospital (DSH) payments to qualifying hospitals that serve a large number of Medicaid and uninsured persons. The federal government annually allocates DSH payments to the states. The allocations for each state are established by law. In order to receive such payments, states must submit an independent certified audit and annual report to the secretary of the Department of Health and Human Services (DHHS) explaining the DSH payments made to each of their DSH hospitals. In December 2008, CMS published a final rule to implement this federal law and outlined specific elements and verifications required for states to include in their certified audits ("Medicaid and CHIP Program Information" n.d.).

Medicaid DSH payments are the largest source of federal funding for uncompensated hospital care provided to Medicaid beneficiaries and uninsured individuals. States are required to make supplemental payments or adjustments to the DSH payment rates. The federal government distributes the DSH allocation to states based on a formula, and states in turn use this money to cover the costs of hospital care they are required to provide to low-income individuals and that are not covered by other payers such as Medicaid, Medicare, and CHIP. The expectation is that state payment rates will be sufficient to enlist enough providers to make services available to the general population within that geographic area. Providers participating in Medicaid must accept Medicaid rates as payment in full. Payment rates are often updated based on factors such as an economic index or an inflation index ("Medicaid and CHIP Program Information" n.d.).

The DSH payments vary considerably from state to states. Qualifying hospitals are defined as those that meet minimum criteria established by the law and include hospitals that have a Medicaid inpatient utilization rate in excess of one standard deviation or more above the mean for all hospitals in the state or a low-income utilization rate exceeding 25 percent. States can include other hospitals in their designation of DSH hospitals as long as hospitals meeting the minimum criteria are included ("Medicaid Disproportionate Share Hospital (DSH) Payments" 2009).

State Medicaid Reimbursement

States enjoy significant discretion with respect to the method and rate of payment to healthcare providers. Medicaid operates as a vendor payment program. States can establish their own Medicaid provider payment rates within federal guidelines. For example, states can pay healthcare providers directly on a fee-for-service basis or through a variety of managed care arrangements.

The 1981 Omnibus Budget Reconciliation Act (OBRA-81) eliminated altogether the federal requirement for reasonable-cost reimbursement. Under this act, states were required to pay only the "reasonable and adequate" rates needed to meet the costs of "efficiently and economically operated facilities." This was also known as the Boren Amendment, named after Senator David Boren (D-OK). States had to consider only the special needs of institutions serving a disproportionate number of poor persons and to ensure "reasonable access" to services and "adequate quality."

State governments facing budget problems changed their rate-setting formulas to reduce reimbursements to hospitals and nursing homes. This in turn led hospitals and nursing homes to file lawsuits against states to force them to increase Medicaid payments to levels that more closely reflect what it costs to treat patients. Not only did the number of Medicaid lawsuits increase, but the legal and political complexities involved in such lawsuits also increased (Durda 1991). In a decision handed down in June 1990, the U.S. Supreme Court upheld the right of hospitals and other providers to sue the states for higher Medicaid payments (Pear 1990).

In many states, judges have ruled that Medicaid payments to healthcare providers do not meet the standards of "reasonable and adequate" compensation under the law. Judges in several states have also concluded that states often base their payments simply on budget considerations. Federal and state spending for Medicaid increased by several billion dollars a year as a result of court judgments, settlements, and rate increases granted by states in anticipation of lawsuits (Pear 1991a, 1991b). As mentioned previously, the Balanced Budget Act of 1997 repealed the Boren Amendment, which gave states more flexibility to set payment levels for nursing home care (Grabowski et al. 2004). Between 2003 and 2008, Medicaid reimbursement for physicians' fees increased 15.1 percent on average (Zuckerman, Williams, and Stockley 2009). Yet Medicaid's physician fees have not kept up with Medicare, which explains the lower rate of physician participation in the Medicaid program and the difficulty Medicaid beneficiaries face in getting physician services ("Medicaid Rates Have Not Kept Up with Medicare's" 2009).

Cost Sharing

States, at their discretion, are allowed to charge premiums and to establish out-of-pocket spending (cost sharing) requirements for Medicaid enrollees. The out-of-pocket costs can include copayments, coinsurance, deductibles, and other similar charges. However, certain vulnerable groups such as children and pregnant women are exempted from most out-of-pocket charges. Similarly, copayment and coinsurance cannot be charged for certain services. States often use out-of-pocket charges to encourage most cost-effective use of services. Thus, for example, to encourage the use of lower-cost drugs, states can establish different copayments for generic versus name-brand drugs. Similarly, states can impose higher copayments for enrollees who use hospital emergency departments for non-emergency services ("Medicaid and CHIP Program Information" n.d.).

In summary, Medicaid was originally viewed as a limited entitlement program for the poor. Over time, the scope of the program has expanded considerably. Congress imposed various federal mandates requiring states to expand Medicaid coverage to women and children during the 1980s. During the 1990s and 2000s, both presidents Clinton and George W. Bush granted many waivers to allow state governments to experiment with their Medicaid program. Today, Medicaid is the most heterogeneous insurance program in the country, providing insurance coverage to a diverse group of beneficiaries with a diverse range of services. Finally, a variety of institutions such as public hospitals, children's hospitals, community health centers, and public clinics depend on the Medicaid program for their survival (Mann and Westmoreland 2004).

MAJOR TRENDS IN THE MEDICAID PROGRAM

Program Expenditures

Table 3.2 presents Medicaid expenditure data at five-year intervals from 1966 to 2010. Medicaid has experienced significant increases in program costs from the time of its creation in 1965. Total Medicaid expenditures increased from $1.3 billion in 1966 to $401.4 billion in 2010. During the same period, Medicaid as a percent of total national health expenditures increased from 2.8 percent in 1966 to 15.5 percent in 2010. Both the federal and state governments experienced significant increases in program costs. From 1966 to 2010, federal expenditures for Medicaid increased from

Table 3.2

Medicaid Expenditures: 1966–2010 (in $ millions and percent)

	1966	1970	1975	1980	1985	1990	1995	2000	2005	2010
Total national health expenditures	46,253.8	74,853.5	133,584.9	255,782.5	444,623.3	724,282.3	1,027,456.8	1,377,185.1	2,029,147.5	2,593,644
Medicaid expenditures	1,303.9	5,289.7	13,445.6	26,032.5	40,937.4	73,660.8	144,862.2	200,482.8	309,538.5	401,417.7
Medicaid as % of NHE	2.8%	7.1%	10.1%	10.2%	9.2%	10.2%	14.1%	14.6%	15.3%	15.5%
Federal expenditures	631.6	2,842.3	7,408.6	14,521.3	22,594	42,607.2	85,945.5	116,919.2	177,639.2	269,504.5
% of total Medicaid	48.4%	53.7%	55.1%	55.8%	55.2%	57.8%	59.3%	58.3%	57.4%	67.1%
State/local expenditures	672.3	2,447.3	6,037	11,511.2	18,343.4	31,053.7	58,916.7	83,563.6	131,899.3	131,913.2
% of total Medicaid	51.6%	46.3%	44.9%	44.2%	44.8%	42.2%	40.7%	41.7%	42.6%	32.9%

NHE = National health expenditures.
Source: National Center for Health Statistics, Centers for Medicare and Medicaid Services, Baltimore, Maryland. 2012. Online at www.cms.gov/Research-Statistics-Data-and-Systems/Statistics-Trends-and-Reports/NationalHealthExpendData/NationalHealthAccountsHistorical.html.

$631.6 million to $269.5 billion, while the state Medicaid expenditures increased form $672 million to $131.9 billion.

In the early years of the program, the primary reason for increases in program cost was the growth in the number of eligible beneficiaries/recipients. Thus, Medicaid expenditures increased from $1.3 billion in 1966 to $13.4 billion in 1975, while Medicaid as a percent of total national health expenditures increased from 2.8 percent to 10.1 percent during the same time period and remained at 10.2 percent from 1975 to 1980.

The election of a conservative Republican, Ronald Reagan, to the presidency heralded a significant policy shift affecting healthcare for the poor. The Omnibus Budget Reconciliation Act of 1981 contained three major changes affecting Medicaid. First, the federal contribution to Medicaid was directly reduced by 3 percent in 1982, 4 percent in 1983, and 4.5 percent in 1984. Second, changes in federal welfare eligibility policy reduced welfare rolls and thereby the number of eligible Medicaid recipients. Third, the law allowed states to pay healthcare providers on a basis other than reasonable cost (Altman 1983). In addition, OBRA-81 restricted coverage for the "categorically needy," and states were also given new discretion to restrict coverage to "medically needy" individuals (Grogan and Patashnik 2003b). The act also gave states wide discretion to limit Medicaid recipients' freedom to choose their doctors or hospitals and made it easier to use new kinds of healthcare providers such as health maintenance organizations (HMOs). The act also gave states wide discretion in deciding whom they would cover under Medicaid. The Tax Equity and Fiscal Responsibility Act (TEFRA) of 1982 created new financing initiatives that allowed shifting costs to beneficiaries and third parties by allowing the states to require Medicaid beneficiaries to pay nominal fees for medical services. The Deficit Reduction Act of 1984 required Medicaid beneficiaries to assign to the states any rights they had to other health benefit programs. This allowed the states to collect from such programs any available payments for medical care for the covered beneficiaries.

As a result of these policy changes, as the data in Table 3.2 demonstrate, Medicaid expenditures as a percent of total national health expenditures dropped from 10.2 percent in 1980 to 9.2 percent in 1985.

However, the Democrat-controlled Congress between 1984 and 1990 succeeded in imposing many federal mandates leading to incremental expansion of Medicaid coverage (Lykens and Jargowsky 2002). Thus, for example, under the Deficit Reduction Act of 1984, Congress required states to broaden their Medicaid coverage to include more low-income women during their first pregnancy, pregnant women in two-parent families in which the principal breadwinner was unemployed, and poor children up to the age of five in two-parent families. The Consolidated Omnibus Budget Reconciliation Act of 1985 (COBRA) required coverage under Medicaid of all remaining pregnant women meeting Aid to Families with Dependent Children (AFDC) financial standards (Grogan and Patashnik 2003b).

The Omnibus Budget Reconciliation Act of 1986 gave states the option to extend Medicaid coverage to pregnant women and to infants up to the age of one year who were members of households with incomes as high as 100 percent of the federal poverty level (Grogan and Patashnik 2003b). The Omnibus Budget Reconciliation Act of 1987 required states to provide coverage to all children up to age seven born after September 30, 1983, who met AFDC eligibility standards. States were also given the option to cover all children up to age eight born after September 30, 1983, with a family income up to 100 percent of the federal poverty level (Grogan and Patashnik 2003b). In 1988, Congress passed the Medicare Catastrophic Coverage Act (MCCA), under which states were given the option of allowing Medicaid coverage to all pregnant women and infants with family income up to 185 percent of the federal poverty level (Grogan and Patashnik 2003b).

The Omnibus Budget Reconciliation Act of 1989 required coverage of pregnant women and infants under age one with incomes of less than 100 percent of the federal poverty level (Grogan and Patashnik 2003b). It also mandated provision of all Medicaid-allowed treatments to correct problems identified during early and periodic screening, diagnosis, and treatment (EPSDT), even if the treatment was otherwise not covered under the state Medicaid plan. The act also required periodic screening under EPSDT if medical problems were suspected. The Budget and Reconciliation Act of 1990 required Medicaid coverage of children under the age of eighteen if the family income was below 100 percent of the federal poverty line (Grogan and Patashnik 2003b).

The expansion in Medicaid eligibility from 1984 to 1990 discussed above combined with a slowdown in the economy caused additional individuals to qualify for Medicaid, leading to increased expenditures (Letsch et al. 1992). As the data in Table 3.2 indicate, Medicaid expenditures as a percent of total healthcare expenditures increased from 9.2 in 1985 to 10.2 in 1990 and to 14.1 by 1995. From 1995 to 2010, Medicaid expenditures as a percent of total national health expenditures remained relatively stable around 14–15 percent.

State governments have also experienced significant increases in their program costs. The combined cost of state/local governments for Medicaid increased from $672 million in 1966 to $131.9 billion in 2010 (see Table 3.2). Another interesting point to observe from Table 3.2 is how states' proportionate share of the total Medicaid expenditures has declined from 51.6 percent in 1955 to 32.9 percent in 2010, while the federal share has increased from 48.4 percent to 67.1 percent. Thus, since the inception of the program, the federal government has taken on the increased burden of financing the program.

Needless to say, program costs, eligibility standards, and benefit levels vary significantly among the states. The amount of optional services (those beyond the ones mandated by the federal government) and the mix of services provided by the state governments also vary a great deal.

Since states enjoy significant discretion in setting eligibility and benefit standards, it is not surprising that there is considerable variation in how much individual states spend on the Medicaid program. What factors explain this variation? Kousser (2002) analyzes the impact of political and socioeconomic factors to explain state spending decisions. The early literature (Key 1949; Lockard 1959) tended to attribute great significance to political factors, especially political party structure, in influencing states' spending on social services. However, during the 1960s, several scholars (Dawson and Robinson 1963; Dye 1966; Hofferbert 1966) argued that the socioeconomic and demographic factors in individual states influenced the level of spending on social services, while party structure and party control, had little effect. Most such studies failed to differentiate between the portion of state expenditures mandated by the federal government and that which is authorized by state policymakers themselves. Kousser (2002), in his analysis, focuses only on states' discretionary spending on Medicaid from 1980 to 1993, a variable that truly reflects the decisions of state policymakers. He concludes that political party control strongly influences levels of state spending for Medicaid. States with Democrat-controlled legislatures tend to fund their Medicaid programs more generously than those controlled by Republicans. While economic conditions do affect states' optional spending levels, they have a much weaker impact than party control.

Table 3.3 provides data on annual Medicaid expenditures from 2000 to 2010. Several observations are in order. First, total Medicaid expenditure as a percentage of total national health expenditures has remained stable, ranging between 14.2 percent and 15.5 percent. Second, the federal share of total Medicaid expenditures increased from 58.3 percent in 2000 to 67.1 percent in 2010, while the state share declined from 41.7 percent to 32.9 percent. Third, the annual percent change in Medicaid expenditure has fluctuated considerably for both the federal and state governments. Such fluctuations can be attributable to changes in the economy, general and medical inflation, changes in eligibility leading to an increase or decrease in the number of Medicaid beneficiaries, cutbacks in benefits and/or duration of the benefits, changes in the financial commitments of the state government, changes in the federal share of the contribution, and the like. Fourth, the most dramatic change occurred

Table 3.3

Medicaid Expenditures: 2000–2010 (in $ millions and percent)

	2000	2001	2002	2003	2004	2005	2006	2007	2008	2009	2010
Total national health expenditures	1,377,185	1,494,116	1,636,416	1,774,297	1,900,045	2,029,148	2,162,410	2,297,098	2,403,938	2,495,842	2,593,644
Total Medicaid expenditures	200,482.8	224,236.4	248,217.6	269,104.8	290,916.8	309,538.5	306,839.9	326,370.8	343,813.5	374,433.4	401,417.7
% of total NHE	14.6%	15.0%	15.2%	15.2%	15.3%	15.3%	14.2%	14.2%	14.3%	15.0%	15.5%
% change from previous year		11.8%	10.7%	8.4%	8.1%	6.4%	-0.9%	6.4%	5.3%	8.9%	7.2%
Federal expenditures	116,919.2	132,288.1	145,339.4	160,894.8	172,437.3	177,639.2	174,035.3	185,857	202,856.9	247,456.5	269,504.5
% of total Medicaid	58.3%	59.0%	58.6%	59.8%	59.3%	57.4%	56.7%	56.9%	59.0%	66.1%	67.1%
% change from previous year		13.1%	9.9%	10.7%	7.2%	3.0%	-2.0%	6.8%	9.1%	22.0%	8.9%
State/local expenditures	83,563.6	91,948.3	102,878.2	108,210	118,479.5	131,899.3	132,804.6	140,513.8	140,956.7	126,976.9	131,913.2
% of total Medicaid	41.7%	41.0%	41.4%	40.2%	40.7%	42.6%	43.3%	43.1%	41.0%	33.9%	32.9%
% change from previous year		10.0%	11.9%	5.2%	9.5%	11.3%	0.7%	5.8%	0.3%	-9.9%	3.9%

NHE = national health expenditures.

Source: National Center for Health Statistics, Centers for Medicare and Medicaid Services, Baltimore, Maryland. 2012. Online at www.cms.gov/Research-Statistics-Data-and-Systems/Statistics-Trends-and-Reports/NationalHealthExpendData/NationalHealthAccountsHistorical.html.

between 2008 and 2009 when federal government expenditures for Medicaid increased 22 percent while the state governments' expenditures declined almost 10 percent.

What explains this dramatic change? Between December 2007 and December 2009, the economic recession dramatically increased Medicaid enrollment by 14 percent, driving Medicaid expenditures upward. To help the states with their mounting enrollment and costs, the federal government stepped in. President Obama signed into law two important pieces of legislation designed to help states with their healthcare coverage. First, the Children's Health Insurance Program Reauthorization Act (CHIPRA) provided $33 billion in additional federal funds to extend and expand the program. Second, the American Recovery and Reinvestment Act (ARRA) provided an additional $87 billion in federal funding from the economic stimulus package for Medicaid. Consequently, federal Medicaid expenditures increased by 22 percent, while state expenditures declined by 10 percent between 2008 and 2009 (Galewitz 2011; Kaiser Commission on Medicaid and the Uninsured 2011b; Rowland 2009).

The percent change in federal expenditure decreased to 8.9 percent in 2010 from 22 percent in 2009 as the stimulus money ran out. Consequently, since 2010, state governments have been scrambling to make up for the end of billions of dollars in federal stimulus funding. They are actively reducing benefits, cutting fees paid to health providers, or both. For example, in fiscal years 2011 and 2012, eighteen states eliminated, reduced, or restricted certain benefits; nineteen states increased copayments or imposed new ones; forty-one states added more Medicaid recipients covered by private managed care companies; and thirty-nine states reduced provider payments (Galewitz 2011). In an effort to bend the trend in Medicaid spending growth, state governments are also trying to make the program more efficient and cost-effective through investment in care management and pay for performance, providing economic incentives to managed care organizations (MCOs), and putting more emphasis on effective prevention programs ("States 'Bend the Trend' in Medicaid Spending Growth" 2009).

Overall, three factors have contributed to the steady growth in program expenditures. First, since Medicaid is an "entitlement" program, individuals who meet eligibility criteria are automatically covered. Thus, program costs increase any time the size of the population in need increases. Second, Medicaid, like other health insurance systems, pays healthcare providers and not the recipients who receive treatment. Thus, overall healthcare costs directly influence Medicaid expenditures. During the 1970s and 1980s, the cost of medical care increased annually by an average of 8.5 percent. Some of the increases in the Medicaid expenditures are attributable to general medical cost inflation (Schneider 1988). Throughout the 1990s, medical costs increased at a much higher rate than the overall consumer price index. Third, the creation of the State Children's Health Insurance Program (SCHIP) in 1997 provided health insurance coverage to millions of children, adding to the cost of the Medicaid program. Under the new program, the federal government began to provide matching funds to assist states in providing health insurance coverage for uninsured children (Rosenbaum et al. 1998). When the program was reauthorized in 2009, the name of the program was changed to Children's Health Insurance Program (CHIP). Throughout the book, we refer to the program as CHIP except when use of SCHIP is appropriate in the context of the discussion. The CHIP program and its impact are discussed in greater detail later in this chapter.

Program Beneficiaries

Medicaid has experienced a steady growth in the number of beneficiaries. Those receiving Medicaid nationwide increased from 22 million in 1975 to 62.3 million in 2009 (see Table 3.4). It is important to note that the number of recipients has fluctuated over time. In the early years of the program's history, the number increased because eligibility for Medicaid increased. Paul Ginsburg cites four main reasons for this: states increased their needs standards for AFDC, making more people eligible for Medicaid; the number of female-headed households (i.e., those categorically eligible for AFDC) increased as this demographic trend continued during the 1980s; organizations mounted public information campaigns to increase awareness and participation in the program; and additional states initiated Medicaid programs (Ginsburg 1988).

The number of beneficiaries declined slightly and/or remained steady during the early 1980s (1981–83), began to rise again beginning in 1984, and continued to rise during the 1990s. The decline in the number of recipients can be attributed to the fact that from 1980 to 1984, eligibility for Medicaid was either directly or indirectly limited as a result of budget cuts by the Reagan administration. Factors contributing to this decline included failure to update state income standards, changes in Medicaid eligibility policy, and federal and state changes in AFDC eligibility policy (Davis et al. 1990).

By 1985, however, this downward trend in the number of Medicaid beneficiaries was reversed, and the number of recipients began to increase. This was largely caused by new federal mandates imposed by Congress between 1984 and 1990. Most of these mandates significantly expanded Medicaid eligibility for children and pregnant women. Between 1989 and 1991, the number of recipients increased by 4.4 million, with a significant portion of the increase attributable to federal mandates. For example, about one-half of the 3 million additional recipients qualifying for Medicaid between 1990 and 1991 were eligible because of mandated program expansions. The major beneficiaries of the mandated program expansions were children (Letsch et al. 1992). The creation of SCHIP in 1997 expanded the number of beneficiaries, as more children were provided health insurance coverage through Medicaid in many states. For example, the number of Medicaid beneficiaries increased by 5.2 million, from 34.8 million to 40.1 million between 1997 and 1998. The number of Medicaid beneficiaries has continued to increase at a very steady pace since 2000 (see Table 3.4).

One of the major contributing factors to the rising number of Medicaid beneficiaries between 2000 and 2009 was the economic recessions in 2000–2001 and 2007–2009. For example, from 2007 to 2009 Medicaid monthly enrollment rose by nearly 6 million, about 14 percent (Kaiser Commission on Medicaid and the Uninsured 2011b). Millions of individuals turned to Medicaid for support during this period as they lost their jobs and experienced a drastic decline in their income (Sack 2010). As insured workers lose their jobs, they often also lose their job-based health insurance coverage and turn to Medicaid for help. It is estimated that every 1-percentage-point increase in the national unemployment rate translates to an additional 1 million Americans turning to Medicaid for health insurance coverage and another 1.1 million becoming uninsured because they do not qualify for Medicaid (Rowland 2009).

The Medicaid beneficiaries include a varied group of individuals—the elderly, people with disabilities, low-income families with children, poor adults, and children. The various groups who are beneficiaries of the Medicaid program have different political characteristics. For example, the elderly in their sixties and early seventies have the highest voting rates among all age groups. In sharp contrast, those receiving Temporary Assistance to Needy Families (TANF) generally have below-average educations, low incomes, and low rates of voting. Children are at a special disadvantage in getting policymakers to pay attention to their needs because they are not political participants. The advancement of children's interests depends on policymakers' own goals, interest groups that speak on their behalf, and the altruism of voters. Since the mid-1990s, people with disabilities have become more active in interest groups. Also, Medicaid eligibility standards for low-income groups are transitory, while for other groups, such as the elderly, they are permanent and fixed, making it easier to politically mobilize the elderly compared to low-income beneficiaries (Kronebusch 1997).

Policymakers are more likely to respond to the needs of those groups that are politically mobilized and have high levels of political participation. Thus Democrats, who draw support from

Table 3.4

Number of Medicaid-Served Persons (Beneficiaries), by Eligibility Group: Fiscal Years 1975–2009 (in $ millions and percent)

Year	Total served	Children[1] served	% Served	Adults served	% Served	Aged served	% Served	Disabled served	% Served	Unknown served	% Served
1975	22,007	9,598	43.6	4,529	20.6	3,615	16.4	2,464	11.2	1,801	8.2
1976	22,815	9,924	43.5	4,773	20.9	3,612	15.8	2,669	11.7	1,837	8.1
1977	22,832	9,651	42.3	4,785	21.0	3,636	15.9	2,802	12.3	1,958	8.6
1978	21,965	9,376	42.7	4,643	21.1	3,376	15.4	2,718	12.4	1,852	8.4
1979	21,520	9,106	42.3	4,570	21.2	3,364	15.6	2,753	12.8	1,727	8.0
1980	21,605	9,333	43.2	4,877	22.6	3,440	15.9	2,911	13.5	1,044	4.8
1981	21,980	9,581	43.6	5,187	23.6	3,367	15.3	3,079	14.0	766	3.5
1982	21,603	9,563	44.3	5,356	24.8	3,240	15.0	2,891	13.4	553	2.6
1983	21,554	9,535	44.2	5,592	25.9	3,372	15.6	2,921	13.6	134	0.6
1984	21,607	9,684	44.8	5,600	25.9	3,238	15.0	2,913	13.5	172	0.8
1985	21,814	9,757	44.7	5,518	25.3	3,061	14.0	3,012	13.8	466	2.1
1986	22,515	10,029	44.5	5,647	25.1	3,140	13.9	3,182	14.1	517	2.3
1987	23,109	10,168	44.0	5,599	24.2	3,224	14.0	3,381	14.6	737	3.2
1988	22,907	10,037	43.8	5,503	24.0	3,159	13.8	3,487	15.2	721	3.1
1989	23,511	10,318	43.9	5,717	24.3	3,132	13.3	3,590	15.3	754	3.2
1990	25,255	11,220	44.4	6,010	23.8	3,202	12.7	3,718	14.7	1,105	4.4
1991	27,967	12,855	46.0	6,703	24.0	3,341	11.9	4,033	14.4	1,035	3.7
1992	31,150	15,200	48.8	7,040	22.6	3,749	12.0	4,487	14.4	674	2.2
1993	33,432	16,285	48.7	7,505	22.4	3,863	11.6	5,016	15.0	763	2.3
1994	35,053	17,194	49.1	7,586	21.6	4,035	11.5	5,458	15.6	780	2.2
1995	36,282	17,164	47.3	7,604	21.0	4,119	11.4	5,858	16.1	1,537	4.2

1996	36,118	16,739	46.3	7,127	19.7	4,285	11.9	6,221	17.2	1,746	4.8
1997	34,872	15,791	45.3	6,803	19.5	3,955	11.3	6,129	17.6	2,195	6.3
1998	40,096	18,969	47.3	7,895	19.7	3,964	9.9	6,637	16.6	2,631	6.6
1999	40,184	18,837	46.9	7,511	18.7	3,774	9.4	6,698	16.7	3,365	8.4
2000	42,763	19,723	46.1	8,750	20.5	3,731	8.7	6,889	16.1	3,671	8.6
2001	45,766	21,064	46.0	9,758	21.3	3,810	8.3	7,107	15.5	4,026	8.8
2002	49,329	23,227	47.1	11,255	22.8	3,887	7.9	7,408	15.0	3,552	7.2
2003	51,971	24,831	47.8	11,691	22.5	4,041	7.8	7,669	14.8	3,739	7.2
2004	55,002	26,459	48.1	12,244	22.3	4,318	7.9	7,933	14.4	4,048	7.4
2005	57,349	27,096	47.2	12,461	21.7	4,370	7.6	8,165	14.2	5,257	9.2
2006	57,181	27,438	48.0	12,490	21.8	4,330	7.6	8,254	14.4	4,669	8.2
2007	56,821	27,527	48.4	12,405	21.8	4,044	7.1	8,427	14.8	4,418	7.8
2008	58,771	28,071	47.8	12,947	22.0	4,147	7.1	8,694	14.8	4,912	8.4
2009	62,363	29,848	47.9	14,447	23.2	4,195	6.7	9,036	14.5	4,837	7.8

[1]Includes nondisabled children and foster care children.

Note: Beginning in fiscal year 1998, a Medicaid-eligible person who, during the year, received only coverage for managed care benefits was included in this series as a person served (beneficiary). Beneficiaries covered under SCHIP are excluded from Medicaid.

Sources: Centers for Medicare and Medicaid Services, Center for Medicaid and State Operations: Statistical Report on Medical Care: Eligibles, Recipients, Payments, and Services (HCFA-2082); and the Medicaid Statistical Information System (MSIS); data development by the Center for Strategic Planning, 2012.

blue-collar workers and people having lower incomes and less formal education, are more likely to support higher expenditures for social programs compared to Republicans, who draw their support more from upper-income groups and people with higher levels of education who work in managerial and professional occupations. Similarly, when it comes to program cutbacks, those groups that are difficult to mobilize and have low participation rates might see their benefits cut more than other groups. Economic factors may also influence spending. "Welfare recipients" are expected to work, while there are no such general expectations about children. Furthermore, programs for children are viewed as investments with long-term payoffs (Kronebusch 1997). Medicaid spending may reflect a variety of these factors.

Changes in the Composition of Medicaid Beneficiaries

Over the years, the composition of the Medicaid clientele has changed. This in turn has affected patterns of Medicaid expenditures and enrollments. Between 1975 and 2009, the percentage of aged beneficiaries declined from 16.4 percent to 6.7 percent. During the same time period the percentage of children and disabled people increased. In 1975, disabled persons accounted for 11.2 percent of the total Medicaid population; in 2009, they accounted for 14.5 percent. Similarly, the proportion of children in the Medicaid program increased from 43.6 percent of total beneficiaries in 1975 to 47.9 percent in 2011. The number of adults served increased from 20.6 percent in 1975 to 23.2 percent in 2011 (see Table 3.4). Today, children constitute the largest and fastest-growing component of the Medicaid population.

The elderly and the disabled are the most costly beneficiaries covered by the program. Medicaid per person payment in 2011 was $15,337 per aged beneficiary, $15,670 for the disabled beneficiary. In contrast, Medicaid per person payment in 2011 was $3,144 for adults and $2,146 for children. The average for all recipients in 2011 was $5,225 (Centers for Medicare and Medicaid Services 2011).

Most of the Medicaid money is spent on providing healthcare for elderly, blind, and disabled individuals. Although children and adults make up more than 70 percent of Medicaid enrollees, they account for less than 30 percent of spending. In contrast, the aged, blind, and disabled make up less than 25 percent of the Medicaid rolls, yet they account for more than 70 percent of the program cost (Matthews 2003). Needless to say, the elderly and disabled individuals often suffer from more chronic health conditions and often have more pressing and complex healthcare needs than children or adults. Medicaid plays a crucial role in providing healthcare and supportive services for disabled, chronically ill, and individuals with special needs. The needs of such individuals cover a wide range of acute and long-term care services. Some of the most recent trends in meeting the needs of these individuals have been the growth in noninstitutional care alternatives, private financing options, and consumer-directed service delivery models (Wallack, Sciegaj, and Long 2002). The issue of long-term care is discussed in more detail under the section on state Medicaid reforms.

Medicaid Pay-for-Performance

In recent years, one of the major trends in the Medicaid program is the adoption of pay-for-performance (P4P) programs by the healthcare industry to manage and improve the quality of care. Over 150 P4P programs exist in the United States. The program's main targets are hospitals and physicians by providing them financial incentives to achieve assigned quality goals. The most common financial incentives are bonuses or add-on per diem rates. Most such programs are sponsored by private health insurance plans and employer purchasing cooperatives. The enthusiasm for P4P has spread to the Medicaid program, and more than twenty-eight state Medicaid agencies have either adopted or plan to adopt P4P programs in the coming years (Young et al. 2010). In nursing homes Medicaid P4P has become more common (Airling, Job, and Cooke 2009).

The jury is still out on the success/failure of such programs. At present, very little evidence exists about their impact on quality improvement. The evidence that does exist thus far suggests that such programs have minimal short-term effect on quality improvement. Two of the primary barriers to P4P identified for safety-net-setting providers are the limitations of financial incentives as motivation and complex patient care requirements, especially in safety-net settings of elderly and disabled patients suffering from complicated medical conditions (Young et al. 2010).

MEDICAID REFORMS AT THE STATE LEVEL: LABORATORIES OF EXPERIMENTS?

Medicaid Reforms: 1980s–1990s

The decentralization of the Medicaid program under the Reagan, George W. Bush, and Clinton administrations on the one hand and the expansion of the program through federal mandates between 1984 and 1990 on the other raise a fundamental question: Can state governments contain the rising cost of the Medicaid program and still provide increased access and high-quality care to the poor? How states respond to this challenge will shape the future course of Medicaid policy.

By the early 1980s, Medicaid cost containment had emerged as a major issue for state and local governments. Confronted with more discretionary authority and the need to reduce Medicaid expenditures, state governments responded to new federal initiatives of the 1980s and 1990s in a variety of ways (Patel 1996). The story of Medicaid reform varies considerably from state to state (Daniels 1998). The discussion that follows focuses on some of the major state responses and trends.

Use of Medicaid Waivers

Medicaid waivers are the primary tool that state governments have used to reform and experiment with their own programs. Through such waivers, state governments can try new approaches to delivery and financing of health service to Medicaid beneficiaries. President Clinton (1993–2000) pursued his own vision of Medicaid devolution (Thompson 1998). The Clinton administration allowed states more flexibility on Medicaid funds and supported states' efforts at innovation and experimentation. For example, President Clinton ordered the federal government to make it easier for states to use Medicaid funds to introduce new healthcare programs for the poor. Upon assuming office in 1993, the Clinton administration began to provide states with waivers to experiment with their Medicaid programs. The Health Care Financing Administration (HCFA), relying upon the demonstration authority embedded in section 1115 of the Social Security Act, approved dramatic changes in the Medicaid programs of many states.

Waivers can be divided into four major types:

- Section 1115 Research and Demonstration Project Waivers: This type of waiver allows states to experiment with new or existing approaches to financing and delivering health services under Medicaid and CHIP.
- Section 1915(b) Managed Care Waivers. This type of waiver allows states to provide services through managed care delivery systems or to limit beneficiaries' choice of providers.
- Section 1915(c) Home and Community-Based Services Waivers. This type of waiver allows states to provide long-term care services in home and community settings rather than institutional settings.

- Concurrent Section 1915(b) and 1915(c) Waivers: States can simultaneously implement both types of waivers to provide a continuum of services to the elderly and people with disabilities as long as all federal program requirements are met.

State governments made frequent use of these waivers during the 1980s and 1990s to reform their Medicaid programs. The major types of reforms are discussed below.

Cutbacks in Eligibility, Benefits, and Coverage

During the 1980s, in response to federal cuts in matching funds, in an attempt to reduce state Medicaid expenditures, many states turned to strategies such as placing limits on income eligibility standards, reducing coverage of optional groups, and reducing the amount of services covered. States selected options that were easy to implement and promised the quickest savings.

Some states attempted Medicaid cuts by reducing the number of people on the program, reducing benefits for those covered, or both (Altman and Morgan 1983). These are attractive options for state governments because state agencies are the ones that make such decisions, and they have the machinery to calculate the amount of savings that can be generated. Of course, these cost-saving methods are most likely to affect low-income patients adversely (Altman 1983).

In a nationwide survey, the Intergovernmental Health Policy Project at George Washington University found that in 1981 alone, more than thirty states reduced Medicaid benefits or limited Medicaid eligibility. By January 1982, twenty-four states had restricted use of medical services by placing limits on the number of visits to doctors, emergency rooms, and outpatient facilities. Eleven states had placed limits on the number of hospital days covered under Medicaid, while another eight states had eliminated some optional services (Altman 1983). Many states used a combination of stringent income criteria and limited optional service coverage to constrain enrollments and outlays.

By 1982, most of the states had made only small increases or none at all, in AFDC benefit levels thereby allowing inflation to raise earnings of employed welfare recipients above the eligibility ceiling. People between the ages of eighteen and twenty-one were declared ineligible for AFDC in several states. Some states, such as California and Washington, reduced medically needy patients' coverage by increasing the amount that recipients must "spend down" before Medicaid eligibility begins. Thus, by 1982 most states had reduced eligibility (Bovbjerg and Holahan 1982). The number of total Medicaid recipients declined from 22 million in 1981 to 21.6 million in 1982.

Similarly, states were active in reducing service coverage. States including Illinois, Massachusetts, Michigan, Missouri, and Rhode Island placed limits or increased existing limits on hospital days, eliminating weekend admissions, reducing the coverage of preoperative days, and ending payment for inpatient surgery when the service could be provided on an outpatient basis. California, Connecticut, Illinois, New Jersey, and North Carolina directly limited physician visits to "lock in" overutilizing patients or to "lock out" providers found to deliver too many services or poor quality care. Several states also added controls on the number of nursing home days (in either skilled nursing or intermediate-care facilities) they would pay for. Several states extended limits on drug coverage. Other states placed limits on optional services such as dentists, chiropractors, and optometrists, or eliminated coverage for such services completely (Johnson 1983).

As we discussed earlier in the chapter, federal mandates imposed between 1984 and 1990 designed to expand coverage to women and children greatly increased the number of Medicaid beneficiaries. The result is that despite state governments' attempts to reduce program costs and enrollments, both increased dramatically in the late 1980s and early 1990s. While federal mandates have helped increase access to the healthcare system, especially for poor women and children, they have also significantly increased program costs at both the federal and state levels. Again, we were faced with the conflicting values of access versus cost.

Increased Use of Copayments for Medicaid Services

During the 1980s, use of copayments became common in many states (Johnson 1983). The assumption here is that copayments force the beneficiary to ask whether the care is really worth paying for and thus make him or her more cost-conscious. Some view copayments as an ideal mechanism for eliminating services not highly valued by Medicaid recipients. Others fear that even small copayments will result in drastic reductions in the use of healthcare services by the poor. Some early studies have suggested that copayments do indeed reduce expenditures on medical services. More importantly, the effects of copayments, at least with income-related upper limits, did not vary significantly with the family income of those participating in these studies. Thus, supporters of use of the copayment approach argued that the fear of reduced use of health services by the poor because of copayments was unfounded (Newhouse et al. 1981). However, it should be noted that states that have received 1915(b) and 1115 waivers are now significantly restricted in their use of copayments.

Competitive Bidding: Contractual and Prudent Buyer Arrangements

Another approach—a competitive strategy—used by the states is to attempt a fundamental reform in their approach to Medicaid. This involves replacing a fee-for-service system with negotiated or competitively bid fixed-price arrangements for Medicaid services. The 1981 OBRA also greatly expanded state authority by allowing states to purchase in bulk durable medical equipment, lab tests, and X-ray services. Some states are using bulk purchase arrangements for goods such as eyeglasses, hearing aids, and laboratory services. The objective is to buy from the lowest bidder rather than to reimburse every retail seller at his or her price.

For example, California's Medicaid Program—Medi-Cal—relies on negotiated fixed-price arrangements. Medi-Cal established selective contracting with hospitals in 1983. During that year the state negotiated all-inclusive per diem rates on an individual basis with eligible hospitals. Once the rate was determined, hospitals had to absorb costs that exceeded the negotiated level. Medi-Cal patients are required to go to a contracting hospital, and contracting facilities must treat patients coming to them. Contracting applied to more than half of California's hospitals and more than 75 percent of its Medicaid hospitalizations (Holahan 1988).

Similarly, the Arizona Health Care Cost Containment System (AHCCCS), implemented in 1982, relies on provider bidding for the delivery of healthcare to the indigent. The Arizona Medicaid program puts out various types of care for per capita bids, and counties as well as private-sector providers compete for prepaid contracts. In such a prepaid, capitated system, financial risk bearing is shifted, partially from the consumer and totally from the third-party insurer, to the provider. According to proponents, such a system internalizes economic incentives (Vogel 1984).

Competitive bidding is also becoming increasingly popular for healthcare services such as clinical laboratory services, home healthcare, and mental healthcare (McCombs and Christianson 1987). In the mid-1990s, Tennessee made history when it replaced its traditional Medicaid program by implementing TennCare. Under this program it extended coverage to uninsured and uninsurable adults and children. The program provides a wide range of medical services that include inpatient and outpatient hospital care, physician services, prescription drugs, laboratory and X-ray services, medical supplies, home healthcare, and hospice care, among others. All beneficiaries are served by capitated managed care organizations that are HMOs (Larson and Williams 2003). TennCare also channeled all Medicaid recipients into managed care programs (Bonnyman 1996). However, a survey of physicians found that dissatisfaction with TennCare was very high (72 percent), and 46 percent of physicians thought that quality of care had actually declined under TennCare (Sloan 1999).

Rationing of Medicaid Services

The state of Oregon implemented an innovative approach to address problems of cost and access in its Medicaid program. In 1987, the state decided to stop financing most organ transplants for Medicaid patients and to use the money instead for prenatal care for pregnant women. In 1990, the state produced a more revolutionary Medicaid plan. A large number of poor people do not have access to Medicaid because they do not meet eligibility criteria. The state proposed that under its plan, Medicaid would cover all poor people in the state but may not cover all medical services. In other words, the plan proposed a tradeoff—increased access in return for reduced benefits. The state ranked most medical services as more or less economically worthwhile to treat under the plan. If money ran out before all services were covered, the lowest-priority services would not be covered. In March 1993, the HCFA under the Clinton administration granted the state of Oregon a waiver from federal statutes to implement the Oregon Health Plan (OHP). Critics charged that the plan targets the poor—mainly women and children, who make up most of the Medicaid population (Kosterlitz 1990). They also argued that such a meat-ax approach to healthcare would inevitably lead to gross misallocation of resources (Schwartz and Aaron 1985, 1990).

Use of Medicaid Managed Care

OBRA-81 gave states more flexibility to design managed care plans. In addition, the HCFA—now CMS—allowed states to experiment with innovative approaches to Medicaid through research and demonstration projects.

In response to problems of cost and access, most state governments increasingly turned to managed care systems as a tool for cost containment. States are expanding contracts with managed care plans for the most costly Medicaid beneficiaries—the aged and the disabled (Iglehart 2011). The Medicaid managed landscape is shaped by recipients, healthcare providers, and labor unions that generally oppose managed care plans for fear of job loss (Pracht 2007).

Many state governments have also moved in the direction of "privatization" of their Medicaid programs. States and the federal government continue to fund the program jointly, but the day-to-day control of health plans for the poor is being turned over to managed care organizations or private insurers. Many states require Medicaid recipients to enroll in some form of MCO. Case managers or primary-care physicians are assigned to watch Medicaid patients' health. They act as gatekeepers to control and coordinate the delivery of health services in a cost-conscious manner. As a way of reducing costs, the emphasis is on low-cost preventive care, outpatient services, and less reliance on emergency hospital care and costly specialists (Anders 1993).

As of 2010, all states except Alaska, New Hampshire, and Wyoming were operating comprehensive Medicaid managed care programs. Thirty-six states, including the District of Columbia, contract with MCOs, and thirty-one states operate a Primary Care Case Management (PCCM) program. Over 26 million Medicaid beneficiaries are enrolled nationwide in MCOs and another 8 million are enrolled in PCCM (Kaiser Commission on Medicaid and the Uninsured 2012a). Medicaid and Medicare managed care programs as cost-saving tools are discussed in more detail in chapter 8 dealing with healthcare cost containment.

New Approaches to Reimbursing Providers

Payments to Physicians. States have generally enjoyed significant discretion over Medicaid payments to physicians. The Medicaid program has traditionally paid physicians much less than Medicare or private insurers do. For example, under the Medicaid program, states are mandated to pay physicians "usual, customary, and reasonable" fees (the UCR payment system). The Medicaid statute, however, never imposed any specific method of payment on the states except that the fee should be high enough to ensure reasonable access to care for Medicaid beneficiaries.

Through waivers, states can pay physicians a set fee or capitation payment rather than a fee-for-service. States also can establish case management programs linking patients to solo or group practice physicians or to an HMO (Kern, Windham, and Griswold 1986). States may, under a waiver program, enroll Medicaid patients in an HMO and restrict their use of other providers.

Several state Medicaid programs imposed significant limits or ceilings on physician payments. Some states turned to the use of fee schedules. The average Medicaid payment for a visit to a physician is estimated to be only 65 percent of the average charge for visits of other patients. Medicare pays about 84 percent on the average. The result is that many physicians do not accept Medicaid patients (Ginsburg 1988); the willingness to accept them varies with the level of Medicaid payments (Sloan, Mitchell, and Cromwell 1978). This raises questions about Medicaid recipients' access to physicians. When Medicaid cuts have to be made, state programs often attempt to impose further restrictions on physicians' fees. Such efforts are often misguided. In general, physicians' fees constitute a very small percentage of total Medicaid spending. Thus, trying to save money by limiting payments to physicians may not be the best way to reduce program costs. In fact, reduced physician participation may drive many beneficiaries to substitute services at a greater cost to Medicaid.

The physician participation rates in Medicaid vary significantly across the country. To increase physician participation in the Medicaid program, several states increased physician payment rates. Between 1998 and 2003, physicians' fees increased by an average of 27.4 percent nationwide. Yet, in most states, Medicaid reimbursement rates still remained below Medicare reimbursement rates. Thus, despite the fee increase, the physician participation rate in the Medicaid program, as measured by a national average, increased only slightly, from 61 percent in 1997 to 62 percent in 2001 ("Medicaid Physician Fees Rise Sharply" 2004). Despite small gains, the relative attractiveness of Medicaid patients to physicians has not improved much over a longer term (Zuckerman, McFeeters, Cunningham, and Nichols 2004).

Payments to Hospitals. In contrast to physician payment, Medicaid has generally been required to pay hospitals on the same basis as Medicare, using a "reasonable cost" reimbursement method. With the 1972 amendments to the Social Security Act, however, there has been a gradual trend toward paying less than the actual cost. The amendments allowed states, with approval from HHS, to use alternate (to Medicare) payment methods for Medicaid.

OBRA-81 gave states more flexibility to develop and implement new Medicaid hospital payment methods as long as those payments were reasonable and adequate to meet the costs of "efficiently and economically operated facilities." The only requirements were that payment levels take into consideration the circumstances of hospitals serving a disproportionate number of low-income persons and that payments be sufficient to ensure Medicaid patients reasonable access to adequate-quality services (Bovbjerg and Holahan 1982).

Faced with reduced revenues and increased healthcare costs, state governments tried various strategies to contain costs. By 1982, seventeen states had legislation requiring the disclosure, review (such as health system agencies [HSAs] and certificate-of-need [CON]), or regulation of hospital rates or budgets. One major alternative payment method used by state governments is rate setting. Many states have adopted some form of hospital rate review or prospective reimbursement system. In some states, rate setting applies only to Medicaid, while in others the rate applies to all payers (Grannemann and Pauly 1983). Rate-setting programs fall into three broad strategies to control Medicaid costs: multiple-payer rate setting, Medicaid-only prospective payment, and selective contracting (Holahan 1988).

State rate-setting programs have produced mixed results. Proponents have argued that some mandatory prospective rate-setting programs have been successful in reducing hospital expenditures per patient day, per admission, and per capita (Coelen and Sullivan 1981). Other studies have also demonstrated that states have achieved modest success in containing Medicaid payments to hospitals under different rate-setting strategies—multiple-payer rate setting, Medicaid-only rate setting, and selective contracting—with some being more effective than others (Holahan 1988). States that use all-payer rate setting are able to force down hospital prices for all payers. In states where the payment systems apply only to Medicaid, savings appear to be temporary and may not be sustained over a long period (Davis et al. 1990).

Medicaid Reforms: 2001–2010

Upon his taking office in 2001, the George W. Bush administration changed the name of the Health Care Financing Administration to the Centers for Medicare and Medicaid Services as well as announced its willingness to allow states to reinvent their Medicaid programs (Thompson and Burke 2007). The CMS also made it easier for states to use additional federal money to fund their 1115 waivers initiatives. One initiative was the Medicaid disproportionate share hospital program. The federal government made disproportionate share money more fungible. The CMS also gave states more discretion over CHIP funds. The waivers of the early 2000s permitted greater enrollee cost sharing and more restricted service packages. By 2006, the CMS had approved more than 72 percent of waiver proposals submitted by states (Thompson and Burke 2007). Another major initiative of the George W. Bush administration was the Health Insurance Flexibility and Account-ability Initiative (HIFA), a demonstration waiver policy making the waiver process quicker and easier. Between 2001 and 2006 the CMS approved section 1115 waivers from over two-thirds of the states (Coughlin and Zuckerman 2008).

Another major policy that gave states new authority to make changes in their Medicaid programs was the Deficit Reduction Act (DRA) of 2005. The main goal was to reduce federal Medicaid spending. Thus, the DRA gave states authority to require certain Medicaid beneficiaries to pay premiums and to share costs and to offer beneficiaries a "benchmark benefit package" in lieu of a "standard benefit package," and allowed up to ten states to open Health Opportunity Accounts (HOAs) modeled after Health Savings Accounts (HSAs). HOAs permit states to establish accounts for beneficiaries to pay for healthcare services, and when the beneficiaries have exhausted their HOA, states can impose cost sharing on them. The DRA provisions allow states to make many of these changes by simply amending their state Medicaid plans (Coughlin and Zuckerman 2008).

As a result of these policy initiatives, thirty-five states reformed their Medicaid programs either through use of waivers or by taking advantage of the provisions of the DRA. Consequently almost every aspect of the Medicaid programs has been impacted by reforms. However, the reforms or changes have not been uniform. Some reforms have been simply extensions or variations of reforms adopted during the 1980–1990 period, while others have been new approaches.

One example of a new approach is the very ambitious new healthcare initiative that Oregon has proposed for its Medicaid program. This new initiative would create "coordinated care organiza-tions" throughout the state. These organizations would manage all mental, physical, and dental care for all of its low-income patients in the state's Medicaid program, called Oregon Health Plan. The initiative would focus on the sickest patients with the highest cost. Coordinated care orga-nizations would operate on a fixed budget and invest heavily on preventive care to keep patients healthy in order to avoid costly hospitalization. The state hopes to prove that its approach can save billions in Medicaid and not sacrifice quality of care. The Obama administration has bought into Oregon's initiative and tentatively agreed to contribute $1.9 billion over the next five years to get the program off the ground (Cooper 2012).

Some states have reduced or eliminated certain Medicaid benefits, capped enrollments, and/or imposed premiums and other cost-sharing measures. In contrast, a few other states have actually extended Medicaid to groups previously not eligible by expanding their Medicaid programs. For example, between 2001 and 2008, seventeen states sought to gain benefit flexibility, twenty-three states introduced premiums and cost sharing, eleven states have capped their Medicaid enrollments, nine states have revamped Medicaid financing, while twenty-four states expanded eligibility for coverage (Coughlin and Zuckerman 2008).

Previously, federal rules governing Medicaid mandated that all enrollees be eligible for all services provided by the state—mandatory as well as optional. Under the new federal rules that provide more benefit flexibility, several states have either eliminated or restricted coverage. On the other hand, some other states have used benefit flexibility to expand their coverage to a greater population. However, to pay for the expansion of enrollees, these states have used cost sharing extensively. The state of Tennessee has disenrolled several hundred thousand beneficiaries from its Medicaid program. States such as Massachusetts, Florida, and Vermont have relied heavily on managed care, while other states have promoted Medicaid privatization via public-private partnerships through premium assistance programs by subsidizing individuals' employer-sponsored insurance (ESI) premiums (Coughlin and Zuckerman 2008).

One of the major reform trends is the increased use of managed care, competition, consumer choice models, and privatization of Medicaid program. For example, Florida was one of the first states to implement a competitive consumer choice model in its Medicaid reform. Fiscal analysis of Florida's initial demonstration program indicated that although the program saved the state of Florida a significant amount of money, it was very difficult to establish precise reasons for the savings. The state also experienced a significant amount of delay and difficulty in establishing new delivery organizations—Provider Service Networks (PSN) (Duncan et al. 2008). Another study of the demonstration program, after examining the entire Medicaid population, found that the reforms had little impact on per member/per month (PMPM) expenditures (Harman et al. 2011). A study of Medicaid recipients enrolled in the reform program also found that 30 percent were not aware that they were enrolled in the program, and more than 50 percent had difficulty understanding the information provided about the plan they were enrolled in (Coughlin et al. 2008).

Whether reforms discussed in this section, including efforts at privatization, have helped reduce the cost of Medicaid or improve the quality of services for the beneficiaries is still open to debate. However, one thing is clear from the above discussion. Medicaid 1115 waivers have not galvanized universal coverage in any one state. In incremental fashion, waivers have bolstered access to health services in some states, while in others there has been some retrenchment (Thompson and Burke 2007).

Critics of states' Medicaid reforms have leveled many criticisms at their approaches. One criticism is that giving states more authority in setting Medicaid policy has led them to pursue short-term goals, such as cost containment, increasing the chance of harming the welfare of the beneficiaries rather than behaving as laboratories of innovations (Holahan 2003). A second criticism is that since Medicaid expenditures are a major part of most states' budgets, when faced with budget shortfalls and constraints, many states have relied heavily on one-time funding sources such as tobacco settlement monies and traditional cost-control mechanisms such as reducing program eligibility and freezing provider reimbursement rates. Such short-term solutions are more likely to be simply "shuffling the chairs on the deck of the *Titanic*" (McEldowney and Jenkins 2005).

Third, many of these approaches are motivated not as much by potential cost savings but by greater paternalism, based on the belief that an emphasis on personal responsibility (as in the welfare program) might help Medicaid beneficiaries lift themselves out of poverty or at least into better health. However, such an approach is unlikely to work, because the key features of the Medicaid program are very different from the cash benefits elements of the welfare program (Hermer 2008).

Fourth, the implementation of Medicaid managed care plans creates new winners and losers among patients and providers. It also raises serious questions about the administrative capacity of state health bureaucracies to preserve the safety net providers, to serve the poor and disabled, and at the same time introduce new competition to challenge traditional models of financing and delivering care to program enrollees. State officials face many challenges in building provider networks, educating beneficiaries about managed care, enrolling beneficiaries in managed care plans, developing new payment methodologies, and developing information systems to monitor the quality of patient care among others. State officials may not possess the necessary skills to deal with these (Daniels 1998; Davidson and Somers 1998). It remains to be seen whether state health bureaucracies are capable of devising and implementing new cost-effective health services delivery systems without harming the healthcare needs of the vulnerable population.

Similarly, many unanswered questions remain about the implementation of market-oriented, consumer-driven choice models, and privatization of the state Medicaid programs. The advantages proponents claim for market-oriented approaches are potential Medicaid program cost savings, giving beneficiaries more choices, and improving beneficiaries' satisfaction level due to more choices (Coughlin and Zuckerman 2008). However, critics point out that there are several drawbacks to market-oriented approaches. Research seems to suggest that Medicaid was not more expensive than private insurance, and thus the cost-saving potential of market-oriented approaches is likely to be minimal (Hadley and Holahan 2003; Holahan and Ghosh 2005). Second, shifts to market approaches increase administrative costs. Third, the assumption of the market-oriented approach that individuals would make informed healthcare choices is very doubtful, because information that allows one to make informed choices is often not available. Research also indicates that nearly half of Americans have difficulty understanding and using such information (Lee and Tollen 2002; Institute of Medicine 2004).

LONG-TERM CARE IN TRANSITION: FROM INSTITUTION TO COMMUNITY/HOMEWARD BOUND

Over time, institutional long-term care for the frail elderly has shifted from local government funding and administration to state-level oversight to a shared federal-state concern. Like so many other policy areas, nursing home care policy in the United States is a reflection of American federalism—a system that encourages differences among states and in the process creates inconsistent policies between and among states. Long-term care has often been referred to as Medicaid's eight-hundred-pound gorilla because of the growing costs of institutional care and its impact on state budgets (Olson 2010).

Long-term care policy in the United States has undergone several phases. During the seventeenth century, colonial statutes assigned the responsibility for taking care of the impoverished frail elderly and disabled to local governments funded by the local poor tax. From the late 1800s to early 1900s, public almshouses became the primary residence for the elderly and were funded by public funds, and the state governments played a primary role in providing long-term care. Following the Great Depression, the federal government's role in long-term care began to grow as the federal intergovernmental grant system expanded and the federal government became more involved in financing services for the elderly. With the passage of the Social Security Act, several states moved to close their almshouses. The 1954 amendments to the Hill-Burton Act allowed federal grants to public and nonprofit entities for nursing homes and rehabilitation services. The 1965 Medicaid law mandates certain basic medical services that include "skilled nursing home" care. The law also includes a provision for long-term care for those receiving any kind of cash welfare benefits from federal programs. This provision provided a backdoor entryway for elders into nursing home care. Most states quickly moved to access this new source of funding (Ogden and Adams 2009). Consequently, the nursing home population and costs started to rise.

The Omnibus Budget Reconciliation Act of 1980 included the Boren Amendment, which linked Medicaid's nursing home payment policy with minimum federal and state quality-of-care standards and required that Medicaid nursing home rates be "reasonable and adequate." State Medicaid officials had opposed the Boren Amendment because they felt that it would cause states to spend too much on nursing home care (Grabowski et al. 2004). In order to maximize federal Medicaid dollars, many states adopted a nursing home provider tax. States with more powerful nursing home lobbies, a lower proportion of private-pay nursing home residents, worse fiscal health, weaker fiscal capacity, broader Medicaid eligibility, and nursing home supply restrictions were most aggressive in adopting nursing home provider taxes (Miller and Wang 2009).

During the 1980s and 1990s, Medicaid had become the major financier for all U.S. nursing home patient days (Grogan and Patashnik 2003a). The annual private-pay nursing home prices grew by 7.5 percent annually from $8,645 in 1977 to $60,249 in 2004. The Medicaid nursing home prices grew by 6.7 percent annually from $9,491 in 1977 to $48,056 in 2004 (Stewart, Grabowski, and Lakdawalla 2009).

As the data in Table 3.5 indicate, between 1970 and 1980, nursing home costs had become a sizable portion of total Medicaid expenditures, raising concern among policymakers at all levels. Total nursing care facilities expenditures grew from $1.7 billion in 1966 to $15.3 billion by 1980, while Medicaid's percentage share of total nursing care facilities expenditures jumped 11.7 percent in 1966 to 47.5 percent in 1975. In 1980, it declined slightly to 46.2 percent. Total home healthcare expenditures grew from $107.8 million in 1966 to $2.4 billion in 1980, while Medicaid's percentage share of total home healthcare increased from 1.5 percent in 1966 to 11.7 percent in 1980.

In response to the increased financial burden of long-term care and specifically the burden of nursing home care costs on Medicaid, section 2176 of the Omnibus Budget Reconciliation Act of 1981 allowed states to seek Medicaid 1915(c) waivers from the Department of Health and Human Services for a variety of home-and community-based services provided to certain individuals—the elderly, the physically disabled, the developmentally disabled, and the mentally ill—who would otherwise require nursing home care. States that have approval from HHS can receive matching funds. The objective of section 2176 was to encourage a move away from the use of more expensive treatment in nursing homes and other long-term care facilities and toward less expensive home-and community-based services when appropriate.

Such waiver programs became popular with many states and grew rapidly. This trend continued in the 1990s due to political pressure on long-term care policymakers to expand home-and community-based services under Medicaid. By 1997, every state was participating in the 1915(c) waiver program (Miller et al. 2001). During the 1990s, there was a 285 percent increase in waiver participants (Kitchener et al. 2005). The political popularity of waiver programs is partly explained by the fact that waivers provide states with a way to secure additional federal funding for services that otherwise would have to be funded entirely through state revenues (Laudicina and Burwell 1988).

The Balanced Budget Act of 1997 repealed the Boren Amendment and gave states more flexibility to set payment for nursing home care (Grabowski et al. 2004). Long-term care policymakers have continued to face mounting pressures to expand Medicaid home-and community-based services (Kitchener et al. 2005). States' efforts to expand access to community-based services depend heavily on the success of state policies that encouraged decreased use of institutional care and increased use of community-based care (Miller et al. 2006).

As a result of the 1915(c) waivers and the repeal of the Boren Amendment in 1997, there has been a major shift in Medicaid's long-term care policy, away from an acute-care program for the disabled, poor adults, and children toward a long-term care program for the elderly and chronically ill. Today, state governments increasingly employ home-and community-based services (HCBS) in Medicaid to support long-term care. States are shifting Medicaid spending on long-term care

Table 3.5

Total Nursing Care Facilities[1] and Home Healthcare Expenditures: 1966–2010 (in $ millions)

	1966	1970	1975	1980	1985	1990	1995	2000	2005	2010
Total national health expenditures	46,253.8	74,853.5	133,584.9	255,782.5	444,623.3	724,282.3	1,027,456.8	1,377,185.1	2,029,147.5	2,593,644
Total Medicaid expenditures	1,303.9	5,289.7	13,445.6	26,032.5	40,937.4	73,660.8	144,862.2	200,482.8	309,538.5	401,417.7
Total nursing care facilities[1] expenditures	1,732.3	4,033.8	8021.9	15,269.6	26,253.5	44,890.3	64,478	85,119.9	112,454.8	143,077.6
Medicaid (Title XIX) $	203.5	940.3	3,809.9	7,055.4	10,694.8	16,433.2	24,515.9	31,859.2	41,131.5	45,086.4
Medicaid % of NCFE	11.7%	23.3%	47.5%	46.2%	40.7%	36.6%	38.0%	37.4%	36.6%	31.5%
Federal $	98.3	504.8	2,093.8	3,984.1	5,881.9	9,247.4	13,683.1	18,510.4	23,210.5	30,624.4
State and local $	105.2	435.5	1,716.1	3,071.2	4,812.9	7,185.8	10,832.8	13,348.8	17,921	14,462.1
Total home healthcare expenditures	107.8	219.5	622.6	2,378.1	5,647.3	12,566.9	32,358.1	32,425.1	48,709.6	70,172.3
Medicaid (Title XIX) $	1.6	14.7	86	277.3	885.7	2,143.6	4,313.1	6,771.3	15,113.1	26,190
Medicaid % of HHCE	1.5%	6.7%	13.8%	11.7%	15.7%	17.1%	13.3%	20.9%	31.0%	37.3%
Federal $	0.8	7.3	48	148.5	465.1	1,146.9	2,301.7	3,656.5	8,163.2	17,248.5
State and local $	0.8	7.4	38	128.8	420.7	996.7	2,011.4	3,114.8	6,949.9	8,941.5

[1]Includes nursing care and continuing care retirement communities.

NCFE = Nursing care facilities expenditures; HHCE = Home healthcare expenditures.

Source: National Center for Health Statistics, Centers for Medicare and Medicaid Services, Baltimore, Maryland. 2012. Online at www.cms.gov/Research-Statistics-Data-and-Systems/Statistics-Trends-and-Reports/NationalHealthExpendData/NationalHealthAccountsHistorical.html.

and institutional services to home-and community-based services. This often is referred to as rebalancing (Kaye 2012; Robison et al. 2012).

Several factors have contributed to states' increased reliance on HCBS and less reliance on nursing facilities for long-term care services in their Medicaid programs. First, many older persons prefer the HCBS alternative because it gives them more privacy and control over their own lives. Second, the U.S. Supreme Court in its 1999 *Olmstead v. L.C.* ruling supported seniors' preference for HCBS by prodding states to reduce their reliance on nursing facilities institutionalization and to their integration of seniors in the community. Third, HCBS alternatives are generally less expensive per resident in the long run (Lockhart, Giles-Sims, and Klopfenstein 2009). Fourth, HCBS options have broad-based ideological appeal. Conservative states like HCBS waivers as a relatively inexpensive way to provide services to a narrowly defined group of recipients. Liberal states like waivers, especially for the very expensive special-needs population, because they view such waivers as part of their policy tool kit to expand services (Thompson and Burke 2009).

States enjoy significant discretion in setting Medicaid payment methods and rates. The three primary payment methods used by states for nursing home care are: retrospective, prospective, and a combination of both. Under a retrospective method, Medicaid payments are determined after the services are provided based on costs incurred by the facility. Under a prospective method, rates are set in advance of care regardless of actual costs to the facility. Prospective rates can be flat rate, facility specific, resident specific, or a combination facility and resident specific. A combination method uses both retrospective and prospective methods (Grabowski et al. 2004).

The long-term landscape is changing as a result of the shift from institutional/nursing facilities care to more focus on home-and community-based long-term services. Expenditures for these services have increased significantly. Medicaid HCBS expenditures increased from $17 billion in 1999 to $45 billion in 2008, while the number of HCBS participants increased from 1.9 million in 1999 to 3.1 million in 2008 (Kaiser Commission on Medicaid and the Uninsured 2011c).

Tables 3.5 and 3.6 present a similar story using slightly different data and format. Table 3.5 presents total nursing care facilities and home health services expenditures from 1966 to 2010 using five-year intervals. Several trends stand out. First, the overall expenditures for nursing care facilities increased from $1.7 billion in 1966 to $143 billion 2010 while the expenditures for home healthcare increased from $107.8 million to $70 billion during the same period. Second, the impact of the shift in Medicaid's long-term care services from nursing facilities to home-and community-based care during the 1980s is clear. Medicaid's share of the total nursing facilities expenditures dropped from 46.2 percent in 1980 to 36.6 percent in 1990 to 31.5 percent in 2010. Third, correspondingly, Medicaid's share of home healthcare expenditures increased from 11.7 percent in 1980 to 17.1 percent in 1990 to 37.3 percent in 2010. The most dramatic increases occurred between 1995 and 2010.

Table 3.6 presents annual total nursing care facilities and home healthcare expenditures from 2000 to 2010. Between 2000 and 2010, total expenditures for nursing care facilities increased from $85 billion in 2000 to $143 billion in 2010, while total expenditures for home healthcare increased from $32 billion to $70 billion during the same time. Medicaid's share of total nursing facilities expenditures decreased from 37.4 percent in 2000 to 31.5 percent in 2010, while Medicaid's share of total home healthcare expenditures increased from 20.9 percent in 2000 to 37.3 percent in 2010.

Approximately 12.7 million individuals in the United States need long-term care, of which about 10.9 million are community residents, while 1.9 million are nursing home residents. The number of people who need long-term care increases with age. This fact leads many to assume that a large majority of the population that needs long-term care must be elderly people over the age of sixty-five. However, such is not the case. About half of the community residents requiring long-term care are younger than sixty-five. Community-based long-term care services are paid

Table 3.6

Total Nursing Care Facilities[1] and Home Healthcare Expenditures: 2000–2010 (in $ millions)

	2000	2001	2002	2003	2004	2005	2006	2007	2008	2009	2010
Total national health expenditures	1,377,185.1	1,494,115.8	1,636,416.1	1,774,297.1	1,900,044.8	2,029,147.5	2,162,409.5	2,297,098.2	2,403,938.2	2,495,842	2,593,644
Total Medicaid expenditures	200,482.8	224,236.4	248,217.6	269,104.8	290,916.8	309,538.6	305,839.9	326,370.8	343,433.4	374,433.4	401,417.7
Total nursing care facilities[1] expenditures	85,119.9	90,780.8	94,479.8	100,307.7	105,745.6	112,454.8	117,283.1	126,437.3	132,660.5	138,670	143,077.6
Medicaid (Title XIX) $	31,859.2	34,529.2	35,481.9	37,762.4	39,614.6	41,131.5	41,290.1	42,061.6	43,757.8	44,903.7	45,086.4
Medicaid % of NCFE	37.4%	38.0%	37.6%	37.6%	37.5%	36.6%	35.2%	33.3%	33.0%	32.4%	31.5%
Federal $	18,510.4	21,205.8	21,515.3	22,126.5	22,946.7	23,210.5	23,257.2	23,705.9	25,648.7	29,982.2	30,624.4
State and local $	13,348.8	13,323.5	13,966.6	15,635.9	16,667.9	17,921.0	18,032.8	18,355.7	18,109.1	14,921.6	14,462.1
Total home healthcare expenditures	32,425.1	34,419.6	36,628	39,797.6	43,808.5	48,709.6	52,591.1	57,771.7	61,463.4	66,103.7	70,172.3
Medicaid (Title XIX) $	6,771.3	8,282.7	9,791.2	11,521.7	13,617.7	15,113.1	17,214.8	20,144.4	22,254.6	24,293.6	26,190
Medicaid % of HHCE	20.9%	24.1%	26.7%	29.0%	31.1%	31.0%	32.7%	34.9%	36.2%	36.8%	37.3%
Federal $	3,656.5	4,486.5	5,295.3	6,475.1	7,538.0	8,163.2	9,298.2	10,890.3	12,597.7	15,793	17,248.5
State and local $	3,114.8	3,796.2	4,495.9	5,046.6	6,079.7	6,949.9	7,916.6	9,254.2	9,656.8	8,500.6	8,941.5

[1]Includes continuing retirement care communities.

NCFE = Nursing care facilities expenditures; HHCE = Home healthcare expenditures.

Source: National Center for Health Statistics, Centers for Medicare and Medicaid Services, Baltimore, Maryland. 2012. Online at www.cms.gov/Research-Statistics-Data-and-Systems/Statistics-Trends-and-Reports/NationalHealthExpendData/NationalHealthAccountsHistorical.html.

by Medicaid or Medicare, and nursing home stays are paid primarily by Medicaid (Kaye, Harrington, and LaPlante 2010). A great deal of long-term care services are provided informally by family caregivers and are not paid. Most formal long-term care services are paid by government sources (Ng, Harrington, and Kitchener 2010). For example, a large majority of older Americans with cognitive or physical disabilities live at home and are taken care of by their spouses or adult children (Olson 2010). Some of the new consumer-directed service delivery approaches adopted by states have given individuals with disabilities and their families greater choice and control over publicly funded long-term care services (Doty, Mahoney, and Sciegaj 2010).

The transition of long-term care services seems to be successfully achieving its goals. First, the number of HCBS participants has increased over the years. Second, more choices with respect to delivery setting are available to long-term care recipients. Third, Medicaid's share of total nursing home care expenditures has declined.

However, the transition from institutional to home-and community-based care still faces many challenges. First, despite this shift in long-term care from an institutional nursing home care setting to home-and community-based care setting, the overall cost for long-term care has continued to increase. More importantly, Medicaid payment rates have continued to grow, straining state budgets. Ironically, the widespread use of nursing home provider taxes, which allow states to increase federal matching dollars, may have contributed to this development (Grabowski et al. 2008). Second, the costs of nursing home care and assisted living remain high. In 2011 the average annual cost for nursing home care was over $78,000, while for assisted living it was about $48,000 (O'Shaughnessy 2012). Clearly, the cost of assisted living is much lower compared to nursing home care. However, states vary a great deal in their spending on HCBS. Third, many states have a waiting list for home and community-based care (O'Shaughnessy 2012). Fourth, shortages of affordable and accessible housing, especially for those needing specialized services, remain an obstacle to a successful transition from nursing home to HCBS. This is particularly true for rural areas where there is also a shortage of direct-care health workers (Reinhard 2012). A great deal of success in cost savings will depend on states' ability to increase their home-and community-based care capacity to successfully transition people on the waiting list. Fifth, the number of persons in need of long-term care services is likely to grow with aging of the population. Sixth, the quality of care and inequities in ability to access long-term care based on income strata could also become a major challenge in market-driven reforms in long-term care services (Smith and Feng 2010).

The Affordable Care Act of 2010 has three important voluntary provisions for the expansion of HCBS under Medicaid. A state can offer a community a first-choice option to provide attendant care services and support, amend the state plan to provide optional HCBS benefits, and rebalance its spending on long-term services by increasing its community-based portion (Harrington et al. 2012).

Long-term care will continue to remain a major issue as a result of the aging of American society. Yet, Americans continue to underestimate their chances of needing long-term care as they get older, and few have engaged in long-term care planning. According to a poll conducted in 2012 of people over forty, three in ten Americans indicated they would rather not think about getting old at all, and only a quarter of respondents thought that they will personally need help in getting around or caring for themselves in their senior years (Neergaard and Agiesta 2013).

CHILDREN'S HEALTH INSURANCE PROGRAM (CHIP)

The Origins and Evolution of CHIP

The failed attempt at comprehensive reform of the U.S. healthcare system under the Clinton administration in 1993–94 led advocates of reforms to push for incremental changes. In the past,

Medicare and Medicaid programs had targeted specific groups of Americans for protection. Following this model, the advocates of reforms argued that the next logical group that needed government protection was uninsured individuals. The result was the passage of the Health Insurance Portability and Accounting Act (HIPAA) of 1996, which provided some protection to uninsured adult Americans by placing limits on insurance companies' ability to deny coverage for preexisting conditions and by allowing portability of insurance from one job to the next.

The next logical group to target was the large number of children who lacked any health insurance (Flint 1997). The issue of health insurance coverage for children has been an important topic for policymakers, as children are uniquely vulnerable because of their dependent status, that is, their health insurance status often generally depends on the economic status of their parents. Consequently there was a bipartisan support for expansion of children's health insurance programs. This was exemplified from the mid to late 1980s when Congress passed several mandates requiring states to expand their Medicaid program to cover more children (Cunningham and Kirby 2004). As a result the number of poor children with public coverage increased, and the uninsured rate among poor children declined for those living in families whose income was up to 100 percent of the federal poverty level. However, the uninsurance rate continued to increase for low-income children whose family income was between 100 and 200 percent of the federal poverty level and thus not poor enough to be eligible for Medicaid coverage.

To address the coverage gap problem for these low-income children, Congress created the State Children's Health Insurance Program (SCHIP) in 1997 as part of Title XXI of the Social Security Act under the 1997 Balanced Budget Act (Cunningham and Kirby 2004). When the program was reauthorized in 2009, its name was changed to the Children's Health Insurance Program (CHIP). Hence, we use the name Children's Health Insurance Program (CHIP) throughout the book except when the use of SCHIP is appropriate in the context of the discussion.

Initially, states were given three options to expand health insurance coverage to children: expanding their Medicaid program to cover more children by raising their Medicaid income-eligibility standards; developing new or expanding insurance programs for children; or using a combination of the first two options (Congressional Budget Office 1997). Under the first option, states build on existing institutional structures and make very few program modifications. Many advocates favored this approach because Medicaid already provides a comprehensive benefit package for children. However, opponents argued that some low-income families may not apply for coverage because of the perceived stigma associated with the Medicaid program. Under the second option, states could create an alternative new insurance program, separate from Medicaid, with the CHIP funds. Such an approach was attractive to states that already had such a program in place funded by state and local governments. This option also gave such states the advantage of not having to satisfy all the federal requirements of the Medicaid program, such as the mandatory benefits and limits on cost sharing. Since such a program is not an individual entitlement, program outlays can be capped. Under the third option, states could use a combination of the first two approaches.

Within three years of its establishment, all states had implemented the program (Rosenbaum and Budetti 2003). Today, the first option of expanding Medicaid is used by seven states, Washington, DC, and five US territories. Seventeen states have created a separate children's health insurance program, while twenty-six states use a combination of the first two options.

When CHIP was passed, it was touted as enjoying broad bipartisan success because the legislation was cosponsored by Sen. Edward Kennedy (D-MA) and Sen. Orrin Hatch (R-UT). However, when the program came up for reauthorization in Congress in summer and fall of 2007, a bitter partisan debate emerged over the program's intended purpose. Republicans argued that CHIP should be a narrowly targeted means-tested program for poor, uninsured children. The Democrats argued that CHIP should be expanded further to guarantee that all children and some adults could have some type of healthcare coverage (Grogan and Rigby 2009). President George W. Bush vetoed reauthorization and issued a federal guidance restricting state flexibility around eligibility expansion (Gorin and Moniz 2007; Grogan and Rigby 2009).

In February 2009 President Obama signed the Children's Health Insurance Program Reauthorization Act (CHIPRA) extending the program through October 2015. The act provided states with more flexibility, significant new funding, programmatic options, and new incentives for covering children, and it helped states develop strategies to identify, enroll, and retain children who were eligible for Medicaid or CHIP but were not yet enrolled/covered. The new strategies include approaches such as an express lane eligibility in which states can enroll children in Medicaid or CHIP through information available through other programs and databases; automatic eligibility for children whose mothers are already covered through Medicaid or CHIP; and performance bonuses to offset some of the cost associated with states' success in enrolling more children. Several states received millions of dollars in bonuses from the federal government between 2009 and 2011 ("Children's Health Insurance Program Reauthorization Act" n.d.).

CHIP Funding, Eligibility, Coverage, Benefits, and Cost Sharing

Funding

Each state designs its own CHIP program, including eligibility, benefits, premiums, cost sharing, and application and renewal procedures.

Just as in the Medicaid program, state governments are responsible for administering CHIP, but it is funded jointly by the federal and state governments. The federal match rate is about 15 percent higher than the state match rate for Medicaid. Thus, the overall average federal matching rate is about 71 percent, that is, the federal government funds about 71 percent of the total program costs. Each fiscal year CMS determines the federal share of the program funding and allocates funds to states. The ACA extends the CHIP through most of 2015, and starting in October of that year, the federal matching rate will be increased by almost 23 percent. Thus, the federal match rate will become 93 percent and will continue until September 2019 ("Children's Health Insurance Program" n.d.).

Eligibility and Coverage

Most states provide Medicaid to children with family incomes above the minimum 100 percent of the FPL. Many states have expanded their coverage to children with higher income through CHIP. The minimum FPL in 2012 for a family of four was $20,050. The ACA would create a national minimum Medicaid eligibility level of 133 percent of the FPL. The Medicaid and CHIP upper-income eligibility level varies by state (Children's Health Insurance Program" n.d.). For example, in fiscal year 2011, forty-seven states and the District of Columbia covered children with incomes up to 200 percent of the FPL. In fact, eighteen of those states covered children with income up to 300 percent of the FPL. During the same year, twenty-three states qualified for a total of $300 million in performance bonuses ("Connecting Kids to Coverage: Continuing the Progress" n.d.).

Benefits

Each state is free to decide on the benefits provided under CHIP within federal guidelines. Thus, benefits provided in CHIP vary by state. However, all states cover health services such as routine checkups, immunizations, hospital care, dental care, and lab and x-ray services. Children get free preventive care, but low premiums and other cost sharing may be required for other services.

States that expanded their Medicaid programs to cover additional children (Medicaid Expansion CHIP) provide the standard Medicaid benefit package, including early and periodic screening, diagnostic and treatment services, which include all medically necessary services like mental health and dental. States that created separate CHIP programs can provide benchmark coverage, benchmark-equivalent coverage, or HHS secretary-approved coverage ("Children's Health Insurance Program" n.d.). Benchmark coverage must be based on one of the following: (1) the standard Blue Cross/Blue Shield preferred provider organization service benefit plan offered to federal employees, (2) state employees' coverage plan, or (3) the HMO plan that has the largest commercial, non-Medicaid enrollment within the state. Benchmark-equivalent coverage must be actuarially equivalent and include inpatient and outpatient hospital services, physician's services, surgical and medical services, laboratory and x-ray services, and well-baby and well-child care, including immunizations. Secretary-approved coverage can include any other health coverage deemed appropriate and acceptable by the secretary of the U.S. Department of Health and Human Services ("Children's Health Insurance Program" n.d.).

Cost Sharing

States have discretionary authority to impose limited enrollments fees, premiums, deductibles, coinsurance, and copayments for children and women enrolled in CHIP. Cost sharing is limited to 5 percent of a family's annual income and is prohibited for services such as well-baby and well-child visits ("Children's Health Insurance Program" n.d.).

CHIP Expenditures and Enrollment Trends

Table 3.7 presents data on CHIP expenditures, enrollment, and percent of uninsured children under the age of eighteen. It is important to note that the expenditure and enrollment data are for the CHIP program only and do not include children covered under the Medicaid program.

Several observations are warranted based on the data. First, between 1998 and 2010, total CHIP expenditures grew from $400 million in 1998 to $11.6 billion in 2010. Second, CHIP expenditures and enrollment rates have fluctuated dramatically between 1998 and 2010. Third, the percent of uninsured children has also fluctuated considerably during this time period, even though the overall the percentage of uninsured children dropped from 12.5 percent in 1998 to 10 percent in 2010.

Fluctuations in expenditure and enrollment growth rates and the percent of uninsured children are explained by several factors. CHIP was endangered in 2003 and 2004 by budget problems faced by state governments. This was largely due to the national economic recession from 2001 to 2002 (Kaiser Commission on Medicaid and the Uninsured 2011d) and by the "CHIP dip" provision in the original legislation that reduced federal matching funds during fiscal years 2002 through 2004. In August 2003, Congress passed the "CHIP fix," which allowed states to use $2.7 billion in unspent CHIP money that was scheduled to revert to the federal treasury (Park and Oliver 2004). Two annual surveys of fifty states released by the Kaiser Commission on Medicaid and the Uninsured showed that between April 2003 and July 2004, twenty-three states took actions that made it more difficult to secure and retain health coverage for children and families. The actions included freezing enrollment for varying periods, more stringent enrollment and retention procedures, and premium hikes (Smith et al. 2004). The result was that the nationwide rate of CHIP enrollment growth slowed considerably during 2004 and 2005 and some states actually experienced enrollment declines (Park and Oliver 2004).

Growth rate in CHIP expenditures and enrollment slowed again considerably between 2008 and 2010 as the economic recession took hold in 2007 and 2008 (Kaiser Commission on Medicaid and

Table 3.7

CHIP Expenditures, Enrollment, and Uninsured Children: 1998–2010 (in $ millions and percent)

	1998	1999	2000	2001	2002	2003	2004	2005	2006	2007	2008	2009	2010
Total national health expenditures[1]	1,209,038.1	1,286,622	1,377,185.1	1,494,115.8	1,636,416.1	1,774,297.1	1,900,044.8	2,029,147.5	2,162,409.5	2,297,098.2	2,403,938.2	2,495,842	2,593,644
CHIP (Title XIX and Title XXI) $	400.3	1,679.2	3,015.4	4,169.4	5,474.6	6,282.8	7,145.9	7,549.2	8,334.1	9,116.1	10,208.4	11,122.4	11,667.8
% Change[2]		319.5%	79.6%	38.3%	31.3%	14.8%	13.7%	5.6%	10.4%	9.4%	12.0%	9.0%	4.9%
Federal $	276.7	1,167.1	2,099.7	2,915.2	3,825.1	4,397.4	4,966.9	5,241.7	5,731.7	6,315.8	7,124.6	7,825.1	8,147.2
State and local $	123.6	512.1	915.7	1,254.1	1,649.5	1,885.4	2,179	2,307.5	2,602.5	2,800.3	3,083.8	3,297.3	3,520.6
CHIP enrollment[3]	660,351	1,966,716	3,369,747	4,581,418	5,336,593	5,984,772	6,102,784	6,156,249	6,745,194	7,097,684	7,355,746	7,659,264	7,705,723
% Change[2]		197.8%	71.3%	36.0%	16.5%	12.1%	2.0%	0.9%	9.6%	5.2%	3.6%	4.1%	0.6%
% Uninsured children under age 18[4]		12.5	11.6	11.3	11.2	11.0	10.5	10.9	11.7	11.0	9.9	10.0	10.0

[1]Data from National Center for Health Statistics, Centers for Medicare and Medicaid Services, Baltimore, Maryland. 2012. Online at www.cms.gov/Research-Statistics-Data-and-Systems/Statistics-Trends-and-Reports/NationalHealthExpendData/NationalHealthAccountsHistorical.html.
[2]Percent change from previous year.
[3]Data from Center for Medicaid and CHIP Services (CMCS), Centers for Medicare and Medicaid Services, Washington, DC. 2012. Online at http://medicaid.gov/CHIP/CHIP-Program-Information.html.
[4]Data from "Annual Social and Economic Supplements," U.S. Census Bureau, Washington, DC: Online at www.census.gov/hhes/www/hlthins/data/historical/index.html.

the Uninsured 2011d). However, the percentage of uninsured children did not drop and remained relatively steady, largely due to the fact that CHIPRA of 2009 provided states with more flexibility, incentives, and new funds to expand health insurance coverage to more children ("Children's Health Insurance Program Reauthorization Act" n.d.).

Assessment of CHIP

It is clear from the above discussion that the CHIP program has helped cover more children under public health insurance programs. Both CHIP and Medicaid have provided a crucial safety net for low-income children.

CHIP has been successful in reducing the number of uninsured children (Coles 2003; Dick et al. 2004; Kronebusch and Elbel 2004a, 2004b; "Report Gives SCHIP Good Marks" 2003; Selden, Hudson, and Banthin 2004). CHIPs administered as Medicaid expansions have been more successful than either separate CHIP plans or combination plans in enrolling children (Kronebusch and Elbel 2004a).

The CHIP program has also been credited with producing cost savings over the long term. One study found that Minnesota saved about $60 million in uncompensated care over five years through its MinnesotaCare program—a combination of CHIP and Medicaid. The state of New York found that simplifying the enrollment process reduced the administrative costs of Medicaid and CHIP and saved the state $112 per form (Park and Oliver 2004).

Despite these successes, CHIP suffers from several shortcomings and faces numerous challenges. First, the incremental nature of CHIP, combined with layering it on top of existing programs, has often created problems of coordination and equity. Second, inequities are produced across states by the fact that those states that had already expanded Medicaid coverage to children could not receive the higher CHIP matching rates for those children. Third, CHIP has substituted for private insurance coverage to some extent. Fourth, some CHIP-eligible children are still uninsured. Fifth, use of CHIP funds to cover adults by some states has introduced trade-offs by taking away some resources that could have been used to cover more children (Kenney and Chang 2004). Sixth, waiting periods and premiums, combined with stringent welfare reforms introduced in several states, have often acted as barriers to enrollment (Kronebusch and Elbel 2004a, 2004b). Seventh, CHIP continues to remain very vulnerable to changes in the national economy, individual state economies, and state budgetary constraints. Considerable variations in the social safety net for children remain among different states. For example, between June 2010 and June 2011, CHIP enrollment grew in thirty-seven states, but enrollment declined in fourteen states, with five states experiencing an enrollment decrease of 5 percent or more. During this period, the largest enrollment decline—43 percent—occurred in Arizona due to an enrollment freeze enacted by the state in December 2009 because of budget pressures (Kaiser Commission on Medicaid and the Uninsured 2012b).

MEDICAID EXPANSION UNDER THE AFFORDABLE CARE ACT OF 2010

Over the years, a variety of reform proposals have been floated at the national level to fundamentally alter the structure and/or financing mechanisms of the Medicaid program. Reform proposals have included ideas such as returning Medicaid to its original purpose by making poverty the sole criterion for Medicaid eligibility; changing the federal funding formula; federalizing Medicaid; dividing Medicaid into two programs—one program dealing with acute care and the other dealing with long-term care; and merging Medicaid and Medicare in part or in whole and using the market share created by the merged programs to achieve greater economies of scale (de Alteriis 1992).

In 2003, the administration of George W. Bush proposed turning Medicaid into a block grant program that gives states fixed sums of money or block grants, instead of basing federal Medicaid payments on actual costs and enrollment (Baker 2005). However, that proposal backfired, as states and consumer advocates argued that it would create further hardship for the poor and jeopardize state finances (Fong and Tieman 2004; Pear 2005). Despite increased Republican majorities in both the House and the Senate after the 2004 elections, Bush's proposal failed to pass Congress. While attempts to dramatically reform Medicaid failed at the national level, the scope of the program has expanded considerably since its origins through various incremental reforms.

The Affordable Care Act (ACA) passed in 2010 will impact many aspects of the Medicaid program in a variety of ways (Guterman et al. 2010; Landers and Leeman 2011). We have discussed some of these throughout this chapter. A more detailed analysis of ACA is provided in chapter 10.

One of the major goals of the ACA is to reduce the number of uninsured persons in the country by making affordable health insurance available to everyone. This is to be accomplished by following two strategies: (1) requiring virtually all Americans to have basic health insurance coverage or pay a penalty in the form of a tax beginning in 2014, and (2) by expanding the Medicaid program to cover a large number of uninsured low-income individuals who are currently not eligible for Medicaid. Our focus here is on this second strategy.

The law in effect would create a national eligibility standard for Medicaid instead of each state establishing its own eligibility standards constrained only by the minimum federal guidelines, as currently is the case. Under the law, effective January 2014, all states would be required to cover all adults (under sixty-five) with income below 133 percent of the FPL—plus a standard 5 percent point deduction—raising the total level to 138 percent of the FPL (Ku 2010). Because Medicaid imposes certain categorical restrictions at present, it covers only about two out of five "poor" Americans, as defined by the federal poverty standards. The ACA establishes a new mandatory eligibility group and ends Medicaid's exclusion of individuals from coverage based on family status (Landers and Leeman 2011). The law provided states with both a carrot and a stick to expand their Medicaid program. The federal government would pick up all the costs associated with Medicaid expansion for at least five years and at least 90 percent of the cost after that. States' share would slowly rise to 10 percent by 2020. However, the law also threatened that if states refused to participate in the expansion, they could lose not only the federal funding relating to the expansion but also all of their federal Medicaid dollars, including their funding for the existing program (Pear and Cooper 2012). If all the states had implemented the Medicaid expansion, it is estimated that around 14 million low-income uninsured individuals would receive health insurance under the expanded Medicaid (Ku 2010).

From the very beginning, however, a great deal of political controversy has surrounded the ACA in general and Medicaid expansion in particular. The law itself was passed along party lines, with almost all Republicans voting again the law and a majority of Democrats voting for it. The partisan and ideological divide was also clear in the debate over the Medicaid expansion in Congress, with most Republicans and conservatives opposing it. In fact, many Republican governors also expressed their strong reservations and/or opposition to the proposed expansion. Republican and conservative opposition to Medicaid expansion was based largely on the grounds that in the federal system, the national government did not have the authority to coerce states to implement federal policy goals and objectives because states enjoy considerable autonomy and freedom. Several lawsuits were filed challenging the constitutionality of the whole law itself, as well as individual mandate and the Medicaid expansion.

One of the lawsuits, from a Florida district court, included twenty-six states, two private citizens, and the National Federation of Independent Businesses and ultimately reached the U.S. Supreme Court. After hearing oral arguments, the Supreme Court in June 2012, by a 5–4 majority, upheld the constitutionality of the law and the individual mandate under Congress's power to tax. However, by a 7–2 majority, the court ruled that requiring states to expand their Medicaid program was unconstitutional and that the states are free to voluntarily join or to opt out of the expansion without fear of losing federal matching funds for the original Medicaid program. The ruling has created a great deal of uncertainty about the future of Medicaid expansion itself and about the goal of moving toward a system of universal health insurance coverage. It is guaranteed to generate more debate, especially in Republican-leaning red states and states with Republican governors and/or Republican controlled state legislatures, over whether to join the Medicaid expansion under the law (Brownstein 2012).

If a significant number of states decide to opt out of the Medicaid expansion, millions of Americans would be left without health insurance under the ACA. Initially Republican officials in more than a half-dozen states have already stated that they oppose the Medicaid expansion or at least have serious reservations about it (Pear and Cooper 2012). Republican governors of two of the largest states—Texas and Florida—indicated that they were likely to opt out of the Medicaid expansion (Kilff 2012; Koppelman 2012). Others have argued that the financial deal the federal government is offering for Medicaid expansion is too good to refuse for many states, particularly for the red states, because they get the best deal under the law. An example is Texas, which has a stingy Medicaid program at present; the federal government will pick up the bill for insuring millions of uninsured people in the state (Klein 2012). Similarly, Potter (2012) argued that states with Republican governors would embrace Medicaid expansion after the November 2012 elections because they would be under intense political pressure from the health insurance industry in their states, which will stand to make a great deal of money under ACA and the proposed Medicaid expansion. To a great extent, this has turned out to be true. Several Republican governors who had initially indicated their opposition to Medicaid expansion have changed their mind and come out in favor of it. These includes governors of Arizona, North Dakota, Ohio, Michigan, New Mexico, Nevada, and Florida (Beaumont 2012; Christie 2013; Goodnough and Pear 2013; Nather 2013; Young 2013a). Thus far, Republican governors of Texas, Idaho, and South Carolina have remained steadfast in their opposition to Medicaid expansion (del Bosque 2013; Young 2013b). Only time will tell how many Republican governors continue to oppose Medicaid expansion.

CONCLUSION

The future of Medicaid remains clouded. Regardless of what shape Medicaid reform takes, one thing is certain: Medicaid will continue to occupy a vital role in the U.S. healthcare system because the program is essential to cover those priced out of the private insurance market (Mann and Westmoreland 2004).

Medicaid policy has, in a sense, come full circle. The Reagan administration, in the early 1980s, used the conservative rhetoric of decentralization as a way of giving states more discretionary authority and reducing Medicaid enrollment. In the process, the administration also attempted to reduce the federal costs of the program and pass along some of its financial burden to the states. The Democrats in Congress during the mid-1980s used the liberal rhetoric of equal access, equality, and quality of care to expand the Medicaid program incrementally through the use of federal mandates that led to an increased number of beneficiaries and higher costs. The period of the 1990s to 2000s again witnessed significant decentralization of the Medicaid program under the Clinton and George W. Bush administrations, leading to expansion in some states and contraction in others. The ACA 2010 is an attempt by the Democrats to expand the Medicaid program to provide health insurance coverage to more low-income individuals.

Concerned with the dramatically rising cost of a program that is consuming an ever-larger portion of their budgets, state governments have experimented with innovative ways to respond to the access and healthcare financing problems. State governments have tried to expand coverage and at the same time control rising costs (Coughlin 1994). The results of these experiments have been mixed. With few exceptions, the overall cost of the program continues to rise both at the federal and the state levels. Managed care, privatization, rationing, and use of consumer choice models have led to concerns about reduced access and quality of care.

State governments alone are not likely to solve the problems of Medicaid and its cost because of fundamental impediments in the federal system. As Stone (1992) has argued, state governments lack sufficient autonomy from the federal government in the area of healthcare financing. Nor do they have sufficient power over private insurers, doctors, and hospitals. The problem is too big and too complex for state-based solutions (Stone 1992).

The Medicaid program has been described as the "workhorse" of the U.S. healthcare system because whenever policymakers want to provide health insurance to new population groups, they turn to Medicaid (Weil 2003). However, Medicaid has also been described as the "Pac-Man" of the state budgets because it crowds out other state spending (McDonough 2003). Some have attributed the fiscal crisis of Medicaid to state overspending in general and generous and excessive spending on Medicaid. However, others have argued that the real cause of the Medicaid fiscal crisis is a combination of tax cuts adopted by state governments in the 1990s, a growing weakness in state tax structures, and state requirements of balanced budgets. They argue that it is not the spending growth in Medicaid but a real decline in state revenues that has generated the fiscal crisis. According to this argument, the Medicaid program is not the bogeyman that it is made out to be (Miller 2003). Others have argued that Medicaid gets very little respect because, like Cinderella, the program has ended up in the wrong household—state governments. While state governments may not be the "evil stepmother," the reality is that the financial condition of state governments is linked to that of the U.S. economy, and health sector spending tends to be countercyclical. This means that health sector spending rises fastest when the economy experiences a downturn. Such was the case during recessions of the mid-1970s, the early 1990s, the late 1980s/early 1990s, and the early 2000s (McDonough 2003).

Republicans and Democrats have pursued very different strategies with different political agendas. Republicans, since the early 1980s, have followed a long-term strategy aimed at dramatically changing entitlements in the United States. Significant budget cuts in federal grant-in-aid programs during the Reagan administration and Republican attempts to turn Medicaid into a block grant program reflect this strategy. On the other hand, Democrats have attempted to broaden Medicaid to expand healthcare coverage to additional groups. President Clinton, in his budget battle with Republicans in Congress during the 1990s, portrayed Medicaid as essential for protecting the elderly from large nursing home expenses and suggested that Medicaid was not just a safety net program designed to protect the poor but also a broad-based entitlement that protected all Americans. Thus, the politics of Medicaid has turned into a "campaign mode" of legislative politics in the context of partisan mobilization (Smith 2002). Whether Medicaid is an entitlement program or not remains one of the most contentious questions. Support for entitlement can be found in the fact that the program has been repeatedly ratified. Opposition to the idea of entitlement rests on the argument that it has encouraged too much growth (Smith and Moore 2008).

Medicaid policy reflects the dictum that the more things change, the more they stay the same. The Medicaid policy process is driven to a significant extent by the forces of federalism that often produce policies geared toward short-term, patchwork answers, rather than long-term solutions. All the new state experiments and innovations have failed to produce any consensus on how best to contain costs. These experiments have yielded different models of cost containment but none that is satisfactory to all parties, nor have they resulted in significant overall cost containment in the program. The Medicaid program, in many ways, represents the best and the worst of American politics. It reflects the best of the American tradition of helping the poor and disadvantaged groups who cannot help themselves. It also reflects the worst of American politics and policy making— that of an incremental, patchwork approach to policy making—influenced by the vagaries of electoral and economic cycles and partisan and ideological battles that often produce irrational and incomprehensible public policy.

STUDY QUESTIONS

1. What factors contributed to the successful passage of Medicare and Medicaid in 1965? What are some of the fundamental differences between the two programs?
2. Write an essay in which you discuss the objective, structure, eligibility/coverage requirements, and benefits and services provided by Medicaid.
3. Who are the main beneficiaries of the Medicaid program, and how has the composition of beneficiaries changed over the years?
4. Since its creation in 1965, what have been some of the major trends in the Medicaid program?
5. Compare and contrast the role of the federal vs. state governments with respect to administration, financing, cost sharing, and setting eligibility requirements and benefit standards in the Medicaid program.
6. In the American federal system, state governments are often heralded as laboratories of experiments. Write an essay in which you discuss how different state governments experimented with the Medicaid program with respect to financing, cost containment, administration, and service delivery.
7. How successful have state governments been in reforming Medicaid to contain costs, and what are the major criticisms of such reforms?
8. Discuss long-term care policy in the United States. How has it changed over the years? What are some of the major challenges confronting long-term care in the United States?
9. What role has the Children's Health Insurance Program (CHIP) played in addressing the problem of uninsured children? How successful has CHIP been in increasing children's access to healthcare? What are some of challenges confronting CHIP?
10. Both the Medicare and Medicaid programs were created to increase access to healthcare and meet the healthcare needs of specific groups—Medicare for the elderly, and Medicaid for poor adults, children, the elderly, and the disabled. Yet, Medicare has been one of the most popular programs and has enjoyed public support while Medicaid has been very unpopular and has enjoyed much less public support. Write an essay in which you discuss why this has been the case. What factors help explain this difference in public popularity and support?

REFERENCES

Airling, Greg; Carol Job; and Valerie Cooke. 2009. "Medicaid Nursing Home Pay for Performance: Where Do We Stand?" *Gerontologist* 49, no. 5 (October): 587–95.

Altman, Drew E. 1983. "Health Care for the Poor." *Annals of the American Academy of Political and Social Sciences* 468 (July): 103–21.

Altman, Drew E., and Douglas H. Morgan. 1983. "The Role of the State and Local Government in Health." *Health Affairs* 2, no. 4 (Winter): 7–31.

Anders, George. 1993. "Many States Embrace Managed Care System for Medicaid Patients." *Wall Street Journal,* June 11.

Baker, Al. 2005. "Pataki Aides Sketch $1 Billion in Proposed Cuts in Health Care and Medicaid Spending." *New York Times,* January 18.

Beaumont, Thomas. 2012. "In a Switch, GOP Governors Back Expanding Medicaid." Associated Press, February 8. Online at http://news.yahoo.com/switch-gop-governors-back-expanding-medicaid-204320515—election.html.

Bonnyman, G. Gordon, Jr. 1996. "Stealth Reform: Market-Based Medicaid in Tennessee." *Health Affairs* 15, no. 2 (Summer): 306–14.

Bovbjerg, Randall R., and John Holahan. 1982. *Medicaid in the Reagan Era: Federal Policy and State Choices.* Washington, DC: Urban Institute.

Brown, Richard E. 1984. "Medicare and Medicaid: Band-Aids for the Old and Poor." In *Reforming Medicine: Lessons of the Last Quarter Century,* ed. Victor W. Sidel and Ruth Sidel, 50–76. New York: Pantheon.

Brownstein, Ronald. 2012. "Why the Health Care Decision Means More Conflict in the States." *National Journal,* June 28. Online at http://decoded.nationaljournal.com/2012/06/why-the-health-care-decision-m.php. www.cms.hhs.gov/statistics/nhe/historical/t7.asp.

Centers for Medicare and Medicaid Services. 2011. *Medicare and Medicaid: Statistical Supplement, 2011.* Baltimore, MD: Centers for Medicare and Medicaid Services.

"Children's Health Insurance Program." n.d. Maryland: Centers for Medicare and Medicaid. Online at http://medicaid.gov/CHIP/CHIP-Program-Information.html.

"Children's Health Insurance Program Reauthorization Act." n.d. Maryland: Centers for Medicare and Medicaid. Online at http://medicaid.gov/Medicaid-CHIP-Program-Information/By-Topics/Childrens-Health-Insurance-Program-CHIP/CHIPRA.html.

Christie, Bob. 2013. "Arizona Gov. Opts for Federal Medicaid Expansion." Associated Press, January 14. Online at http://news.yahoo.com/arizona-gov-opts-federal-medicaid-expansion-235535133.html.

Coelen, Craig, and Daniel Sullivan. 1981. "An Analysis of the Effects of Prospective Reimbursement Programs on Hospital Expenditures." *Health Care Financing Review* 1, no. 3 (Winter): 62–73.

Coles, Adrienne. 2003. "SCHIP: Meeting the Health Care Needs of Children." *NEA Today* 21, no. 5 (February): 19.

Congressional Budget Office. 1997. *Expanding Health Insurance Coverage for Children Under Title XXI of the Social Security Act.* Washington, DC: Congressional Budget Office.

"Connecting Kids to Coverage: Continuing the Progress." n.d. 2011 CHIPRA Annual Report. Washington, DC: U.S. Department of Health and Human Services. Online at www.insurekidsnow.gov/chipraannualreport.pdf.

Cooper, Jonathan J. 2012. "Feds to put up $1.9B for Oregon's Health Overhaul." Associated Press. May 5. Online at http://news.yahoo.com/feds-put-1-9b-oregon-health-overhaul-161426061—finance.html.

Coughlin, Teresa A. 1994. *Medicaid Since 1980: Costs, Coverage, and the Shifting Alliance Between the Federal Government and the States.* Washington, DC: Urban Institute.

Coughlin, Teresa A; Sharon K. Long; Timothy Triplett; Samantha Artiga; Barbara Lyons; Paul R. Duncan; and Allyson G. Hall. 2008. "Florida's Medicaid Reform: Informed Consumer Choice?" *Health Affairs* 27, no. 6 (November supplement): 523–32.

Coughlin, Teresa A., and Stephen Zuckerman, 2008. "State Responses to New Flexibility in Medicaid." *Milbank Quarterly* 86, no. 2 (June); 209–40.

Cunningham, Peter, and James Kirby. 2004. "Children's Health Coverage: A Quarter-Century of Change." *Health Affairs* 23, no. 5 (September/October): 27–38.

Daly, Rich. 2012. "Provider Tax Feud." *Modern Healthcare* 42, no. 25 (June): 6–9.

Daniels, Mark R., ed. 1998. *Medicaid Reform and the American States: Case Studies on the Politics of Managed Care.* Westport, CT: Auburn House.

Davidson, Stephen M., and Stephen A. Somers, eds. 1998. *Remaking Medicaid: Managed Care for the Public Good.* San Francisco: Jossey-Bass.

Davis, Karen; Gerard F. Anderson; Diane Rowland; and Earl P. Steinberg. 1990. *Health Care Cost Containment.* Baltimore, MD: Johns Hopkins University Press.

Davis, Karen, and Roger Reynolds. 1977. *The Impact of Medicare and Medicaid on Access to Medical Care.* Washington, DC: Brookings Institution.

Dawson, R.E., and J. Robinson. 1963. "Interparty Competition, Economic Variables, and Welfare Policies in the American States." *Journal of Politics* 25, no. 1 (February): 265–89.

De Alteriis, Martin. 1992. "Medicaid's Role Moves Toward Universal Health Care." *Policy Studies Review* 11, nos. 3–4 (Autumn–Winter): 203–21.

del Bosque, Melissa. 2013. "Rick Perry's Refusal to Expand Texas' Medicaid Program Could Result in Thousands of Deaths." *Texas Observer,* January 2. Online at www.texasobserver.org/rick-perrys-refusal-to-expand-texas-medicaid-program-could-result-in-thousands-of-deaths/.

Dick, Andrew W; Cindy Brach; R. Andrew Allison; Elizabeth Shenkman; Laura P. Shone; Peter G. Szilagyi; Jonathan D. Klein; and Eugene M. Lewit. 2004. "SCHIP's Impact in Three States: How Do the Most Vulnerable Children Fare?" *Health Affairs* 23, no. 5 (September–October): 63–65.

Doty, Pamela; Kevin J. Mahoney; and Mark Sciegaj. 2010. "New State Strategies to Meet Long-Term Care Needs." *Health Affairs* 29, no. 1 (January): 49–56.

Duncan, Paul R; Christy H. Lemak; W. Bruce Vogel; Christopher E. Johnson; Allyson G. Hall; and Colleen K. Porter. 2008. "Evaluating Florida's Medicaid Provider Services Network Demonstration." *Health Services Research* 43, no. 1 (Pt. 2) (February): 384–400.

Durda, David. 1991. "Number of Medicaid Lawsuits Belies Complexities Involved in Such Filings." *Modern Health Care* 21, no. 8 (February 25): 31–32.

Dye, Thomas. R. 1966. *Politics, Economics, and the Public Policy Outcomes in the American States.* Chicago: Rand McNally.

Flint, Samuel S. 1997. "Insuring Children: The Next Steps." *Health Affairs* 16, no. 4 (July/August): 79–81.

Fong, Tony, and Jeff Tieman. 2004. "Politics Front and Center." *Modern Healthcare* 34, no. 2 (January 12): 26–28.

Galewitz, Phil. 2011. "State Medicaid Spending Skyrockets." *Kaiser Health News,* October 27. Washington, DC: Kaiser Family Foundation. Online at www.kaiserhealthnews.org/stories/2011/october/27/state-medicaid-spending-increase.aspx?referrer=search

Ginsburg, Paul B. 1988. "Public Insurance Programs: Medicare and Medicaid." In *Health Care in America: The Political Economy of Hospitals and Health Insurance,* ed. H.E. Frech III, 179–215. San Francisco: Pacific Research Institute for Public Policy.

Goodnough, Abby, and Robert Pear. 2013. "Governors Fall Away in G.O.P. Fight Against More Medicaid." *New York Times,* February 21. Online at www.nytimes.com/2013/02/22/us/politics/gop-governors-providing-a-lift-for-health-law.html.

Goldfield, Norbert. 2003. "The Crisis Confronting Medicaid." *Journal of Ambulatory Care Management* 26, no. 4 (October–December): 277–84.

Gorin, Stephen H., and Cynthia Moniz. 2007. "Why Does President Bush Oppose the Expansion of SCHIP?" *Health and Social Work* 32, no. 4 (November): 243–246.

Grabowski, David C.; Zhanlian Feng; Orna Intrator; and Vincent Mor. 2004. "Recent Trends in State Nursing Home Payment Policies." *Health Affairs,* Web exclusive W4 (January–June): 363–73.

———. 2008. "Medicaid Nursing Home Payment and the Role of Provider Taxes." *Medical Care Research & Review* 65, no. 4 (August): 514–27.

Grannemann, Thomas W., and Mark V. Pauly. 1983. *Controlling Medicaid Costs: Federalism, Competition, and Choice.* Washington, DC: American Enterprise Institute for Public Policy Research.

Grogan, Colleen M., and Eric M. Patashnik. 2003a. "Universalism Within Targeting: Nursing Home Care, the Middle Class, and the Politics of the Medicaid Program." *Social Service Review* 71, no. 1 (March): 51–71.

———. 2003b. "Between Welfare Medicine and Mainstream Entitlement: Medicaid at the Political Crossroads." *Journal of Health Politics, Policy and Law* 28, no. 5 (October): 821–38.

Grogan, Colleen M., and Elizabeth Rigby. 2009. "Federalism, Partisan Politics, and Shifting Support for State Flexibility: The Case of the U.S. State Children's Health Insurance Program." *Publius* 39, no. 1 (December): 47–69.

Guterman, Stuart; Karen Davis; Kristof Stremikis; and Heather Drake. 2010. "Innovation in Medicare and Medicaid Will Be Central to Health Reform's Success." *Health Affairs* 29, no. 6 (June); 1188–93.

Hadley, Jack, and John Holahan. 2003. "Is Health Care Spending Higher Under Medicaid or Private Insurance?" *Inquiry* 40, no. 4: 323–42.

Harman, Jeffrey S.; Christy H. Lemak; Mona Al-Amin; Allyson G. Hall; and Paul R. Duncan. 2011. "Changes in Per Member Per Month Expenditures After Implementation of Florida's Medicaid Reform Demonstration." *Health Services Research* 46, no. 3 (June): 787–904.

Harrington, Charlene; Terence Ng; Mitchell LaPlante; and Stephen H. Kaye. 2012. "Medicaid Home-and Community-Based Services: Impact of the Affordable Care Act." *Journal of Aging and Social Policy* 24, no. 2 (April/June): 169–87.

Hermer, Laura D. 2008. "Personal Responsibility: A Plausible Social Goal, but Not for Medicaid Reform." *Hastings Center Report* 38, no. 3 (May/June): 16–19.

Hofferbert, R.I. 1966. "The Relations Between Public Policy and Some Structural and Environmental Variables." *American Political Science Review* 60, no. 1 (March): 73–82.

Holahan, John. 1988. "The Impact of Alternative Hospital Payment Systems on Medicaid Costs." *Inquiry* 25, no. 4 (Winter): 519–20.

———. 2003. "Variation in Health Insurance Coverage and Medical Expenditures: How Much Is Too Much?" In *Federalism and Health Policy,* ed. John Holahan, A. Weil, and J.M. Weiner, 111–44. Washington, DC; Urban Institute Press.

Holahan, John, and Arunabh Ghosh. 2005. "Understanding the Recent Growth in Medicaid Spending, 2000–2003." *Health Affairs* 24 (January/June): 52–62. Online at http://content.healthaffairs.org/content/early/2005/01/26/hlthaff.w5.52.

Iglehart, John K. 2011. "Desperately Seeking Savings: States Shift More Medicaid Enrollees to Managed Care." *Health Affairs* 30, no. 9 (September); 1627–29.

Institute of Medicine. 2004. *Health Literacy: A Prescription to End Confusion.* Report Brief, April. Washington, DC: Institute of Medicine. Online at www.iom.edu/Reports/2004/Health-Literacy-A-Prescription-to-End-Confusion.aspx.

Johnson, Kathryn. 1983. "Major Surgery for Ailing Medicaid Program." *U.S. News and World Report,* October 17.

Kaiser Commission on Medicaid and the Uninsured. 2010. *Medicaid: A Primer—Key Information on Our Nation's Health Coverage Program for Low-Income People.* Washington, DC: Kaiser Family Foundation.

———. 2011a. *Medicaid Financing Issues: Provider Taxes.* Washington, DC: Kaiser Family Foundation. Online at www.kff.org/medicaid/upload/8193.pdf.

———. 2011b. *Medicaid Spending Growth and the Great Recession, 2007–2009.* Washington, DC: Kaiser Family Foundation. Online at www.kff.org/Medicaid/Upload/8157.pdf.

———. 2011c. *Medicaid Home and Community-Based Service Programs: Data Update.* Washington, DC: Kaiser Family Foundation. Online at www.kff.org/medicaid/upload/7720–05.pdf.

———. 2011d. *Changes in Health Insurance Coverage in the Great Recession, 2007–2009.* Washington, DC: Kaiser Family Foundation. Online at www.kff.org/uninsured/upload/8264.pdf.

———. 2012a. *Medicaid Managed Care: Key Data, Trends, and Issues.* Washington, DC: Kaiser Family Foundation. Online at www.kff.org/medicaid/upload/8046–02.pdf.

———. 2012b. *CHIP Enrollment: June 2011 Data Snapshot.* Washington, DC: Kaiser Family Foundation. Online at http://kff.org/medicaid/issue-brief/chip-enrollment-june-2011-data-snapshot/.

Kaye, Stephen H. 2012. "Gradual Rebalancing of Medicaid Long-Term Services and Support Saves Money and Serves More People, Statistical Model Shows." *Health Affairs* 31, no. 6 (June): 1195–1204.

Kaye, Stephen H.; Charlene Harrington; and Mitchell P. LaPlante. 2010. "Long-Term Care: Who Gets It, Who Provides It, Who Pays, and How Much?" *Health Affairs* 29, no. 1 (January): 11–21.

Kenney, Genevieve, and Debbie I. Chang. 2004. "The State Children's Health Insurance Program: Successes, Shortcomings, and Challenges." *Health Affairs* 23, no. 5 (September–October): 51–62.

Kern, Rosemary G., and Susan R. Windham, with Paula Griswold. 1986. *Medicaid and Other Experiments in State Health Policy.* Washington, DC: American Enterprise Institute for Public Policy Research.

Key, V.O. 1949. *Southern Politics.* New York: Knopf.

Kilff, Sarah. 2012. "Six Governors Say They Will Opt out of Medicaid: How Long Will They Hold Out?" *Washington Post,* July 9. Online at http://decoded.nationaljournal.com/2012/06/why-the-health-care-decision-m.php.

Kitchener, Martin; Terence Ng; Nancy Miller; and Charlene Harrington. 2005. "Medicaid Home and Community-Based Services: National Program Trends." *Health Affairs* 24, no. 1 (January–February): 206–12.

Klein, Ezra. 2012. "The Affordable Care Act's Big Giveaway to Stingy Red States." *Washington Post,* July 2. Online at www.washingtonpost.com/blogs/ezra-klein/wp/2012/07/03/the-affordable-care-acts-giveaway-to-stingy-red-states/.

Koppelman, Andrew. 2012. "Uninsured Still Being Screwed." Salon.com, July 2. Online at www.salon.com/2012/07/02/uninsured-still-suffer/.

Kosterlitz, Julie. 1990. "Rationing Health Care." *National Journal* 22, no. 26 (June 30): 1590–95.

Kousser, Thad. 2002. "The Politics of Discretionary Spending, 1980–1993." *Journal of Health Politics, Policy, and Law* 27, no. 4 (August): 639–71.

Kronebusch, Karl. 1997. "Medicaid and the Politics of Groups: Recipients, Providers, and Policy Making." *Journal of Health Politics, Policy and Law* 22, no. 3 (June): 839–78.

Kronebusch, Karl, and Brian Elbel. 2004a. "Enrolling Children in Public Insurance: SCHIP, Medicaid, and State Implementation." *Journal of Health Politics, Policy and Law* 29, no. 3 (June): 451–89.

———. 2004b. "Simplifying Children's Medicaid and SCHIP: What Helps? What Hurts? What's Next for the States?" *Health Affairs* 23, no. 3 (May–June): 233–46.

Ku, Leighton. 2010. "Ready, Set, Plan, Implement: Executing the Expansion of Medicaid." *Health Affairs* 29, no. 6 (June): 1173–77.

Landers, Renee M., and Patrick A. Leeman. 2011. "Medicaid Expansion Under the 2010 Health Care Reform Legislation: The Continuing Evolution of Medicaid's Central Role in American Health Care." *National Academy of Elder Law Attorneys Journal* 7, no. 1: (March); 143–64.

Larson, Celia, and Jannie Williams. 2003. "Sociological Context of TennCare: A Public Health Perspective." *Journal of Ambulatory Care Manager* 26, no. 4 (October–December): 315–21.

Laudicina, Susan S., and Brian Burwell. 1988. "Profile of Medicaid Home and Community-Based Care Waivers, 1985: Findings of a National Survey." *Journal of Health Politics, Policy and Law* 13, no. 3 (Fall): 525–46.

Lee, Jason S., and Laura Tollen. 2002. "How Low Can You Go?: The Impact of Reduced Benefits and Increased Cost Sharing." *Health Affairs Web Exclusive* w2: (July/August): 229–41.

Letsch, Suzanne W.; Helen C. Lazenby; Katharine R. Levit; and Cathy A. Cowan. 1992. "National Health Expenditures, 1991." *Health Care Financing Review* 14, no. 2 (Winter): 1–30.

Lockard, Duane. 1959. *New England State Politics.* Princeton, NJ: Princeton University Press.

Lockhart, Charles; Jean Giles-Sims; and Kristin Klopfenstein. 2009. "Comparing States' Medicaid Nursing Facilities and Home and Community-Based Services Long-Term Care Programs: Quality and Fit Inclination, Capacity, and Need." *Journal of Aging and Social Policy* 21, no. 1 (January/March): 52–74.

Lykens, Kristine A., and Paul A. Jargowski. 2002. "Medicaid Matters: Children's Health and Medicaid Eligibility Expansion." *Journal of Policy Analysis and Management* 21, no. 2 (Spring): 219–39.

Mann, Cindy, and Tim Westmoreland. 2004. "Attending to Medicaid." *Journal of Law, Medicine & Ethics* 32, no. 3 (Fall): 416–25.

Matthews, Trudi. 2003. "Trends in Medicaid Cost Control in the States." *Spectrum: Journal of State Governments* 76, no. 2 (Spring): 10–15.

McCombs, Jeffrey S., and Jon B. Christianson. 1987. "Applying Competitive Bidding to Health Care." *Journal of Health Politics, Policy and Law* 12, no. 4 (Winter): 703–21.

McDonough, John E. 2003. "The Clouded Future of Medicaid." *Journal of Ambulatory Care Management* 26, no. 4 (October–December): 369–72.

McEldowney, Rene, and Carol L. Jenkins. 2005. "Efforts to Reform Medicaid in Times of Fiscal Stress: Are We Merely Shuffling the Chairs on the Deck of the Titanic?" *Journal of Health and Social Policy* 21, no. 2: 1–16.

"Medicaid and CHIP Program Information." n.d. Centers for Medicare & Medicaid Services. Baltimore, MD. Online at www.medicaid.gov/Medicaid-CHIP-Program-Information/Medicaid-and-CHIP-Program-Information.html.

"Medicaid Disproportionate Share Hospital (DSH) Payments." 2009. *National Health Policy Forum,* June 15. Washington, DC: George Washington University. Online at http://www.idilus.com/_docs/informational_articles/medicaid%20disproportionate%20share%20payments-illinois.pdf.

"Medicaid Physician Fees Rise Sharply but Still Trail Medicare in Most States." 2004. *Modern Health Care* 34, no. 38 (September 20): 30.

"Medicaid Rates Have Not Kept Up with Medicare's." 2009. *State Health Watch* 16, no. 8 (August): 10–11.

Miller, Andy. 2010. "States Weigh Taxes to Help Fund Medicaid—And Raise Federal Contributions." *Kaiser Health News,* March 17. Washington, DC: Kaiser Family Foundation. Online at www.kff.org/medicaid/upload/8193.pdf.

Miller, Edward A., and Lili Wang. 2009. "Maximizing Federal Medicaid Dollars: Nursing Home Provider Tax Adoption: 2000–2004." *Journal of Health Politics, Policy and Law* 34, no. 6 (December): 899–930.

Miller, Michael. 2003. "The Policy and Political Context of Defending Medicaid." *Journal of Ambulatory Care Management* 26, no. 4 (October–December): 307–14.

Miller, Nancy A; Andrea Rubin; Keith T. Elder; Martin Kitchener; and Charlene Harrington. 2006. "Strengthening Home and Community-Based Care Through Medicaid Waivers." *Journal of Aging and Social Policy* 18, no. 1: 1–16.

Miller, Nancy A.; Sarah Ramsland; Elizabeth Goldstein; and Charlene Harrington. 2001. "Use of Medicaid 1915(c) Home- and Community-Based Care Waivers to Reconfigure State Long-Term Care Systems." *Medical Care Research and Review* 58, no. 1 (March): 100–119.

Nather, David. 2013. "Kasich's Obamacare Flip Burns Conservatives." Politico.com, February 4. Online at www.politico.com/story/2013/02/john-kasich-obamacares-biggest-red-state-catch-87143.html.

Neergaard, Lauran, and Jennifer Agiesta. 2013. "Long-Term Care in Aging U.S.: Not for Me, Poll Says." Yahoo.News, April 24. Online at http://news.yahoo.com/long-term-care-aging-us-not-poll-says-174856514--politics.html.

Newhouse, Joseph P., et al. 1981. "Some Interim Results from a Controlled Trial of Cost Sharing in Health Insurance." *New England Journal of Medicine* 305, no. 25 (December): 1501–7.

Ng, Terence; Charlene Harrington; and Martin Kitchener. 2010. "Medicare and Medicaid in Long-Term Care." *Health Affairs* 29, no. 1 (January): 22–28.

Ogden, Lydia L., and Kathleen Adams. 2009. "Poorhouse to Warehouse: Institutional Long-Term Care in the United States." *Publius* 39, no. 1(Winter): 138–63.

Olson, Laura K. 2010. *The Politics of Medicaid.* New York: Columbia University Press.

O'Shaughnessy, Carol V. 2012. *National Spending for Long-Term Services and Supports (LTSS).* National Health Policy Forum. Washington, DC: George Washington University. Online at www.nhpf.org/library/the-basics/Basics_LongTermServicesSupports_02–23–12.pdf.

Park, Hy Gia, and Leah Oliver. 2004. "Is SCHIP Shipshape?" *State Legislatures* 30, no. 5 (May): 16–19.

Patel, Kant. 1996. "Medicaid: Perspectives from the States." *Journal of Health and Social Policy* 7, no. 3: 1–20.

Pear, Robert. 1990. "Ruling May Lead to Big Rise in States' Medicaid Costs." *New York Times,* July 5.

———. 1991a. "U.S. Moves to Curb Medicaid Payments for Many States." *New York Times,* September 11.

———. 1991b. "Suits Force U.S. and States to Pay More for Medicaid." *New York Times,* October 29.

———. 2005. "Bush Nominee Wants States to Get Medicaid Flexibility." *New York Times,* January 19. Online at http://www.nytimes.com/2005/01/19/national/19leavitt.html?

Pear, Robert, and Michael Cooper. 2012. "Reluctance in Some States over Medicaid Expansion." *New York Times*, June 29. Online at www.nytimes.com/2012/06/30/us/politics/some-states-reluctant-over-medicaid-expansion.html.

Potter, Wendell. 2012. "Why GOP Governors will Embrace Obamacare's Medicaid Expansion—After the Election." *Huffington Post,* July 16. Online at www.huffingtonpost.com/wendell-potter/why-gop-governors-will-em_b_1676056.html.

Pracht, Etienne E. 2007. "State Medicaid Managed Care Enrollment: Understanding the Political Calculus That Drives Medicaid Managed Care Reforms." *Journal of Health Politics, Policy and Law* 32, no. 4 (August): 685–731.

Reinhard, Susan C. 2012. "Money Follows the Person: Un-burning Bridges and Facilitating a Return to Community." *Generations* 36, no. 1 (Winter): 52–58.

"Report Gives SCHIP Good Marks for Covering Uninsured Children." 2003. *Congress Daily,* April 8: 13.

Robison, Julie; Noreen Shugrue; Martha Porter; Richard H. Fortinsky; and Leslie A. Curry. 2012. "Transition from Home Care to Nursing Home: Unmet Needs in a Home- and Community-Based Program for Older Adults." *Journal of Aging and Social Policy* 24, no. 3 (July/September): 251–70.

Rosenbaum, Sarah H., and Peter Budetti. 2003. "Low-Income Children and Health Insurance: Old News and New Realities." *Pediatrics* supplement 2, no. 112 (December): 551–53.

Rosenbaum, Sarah H.; Kay Johnson; Colleen Sonosky; Anne Markus; and Chris DeGraw. 1998. "The Children's Hour: The State Children's Health Insurance Program." *Health Affairs* 17, no. 1 (January/February): 75–89.

Rowland, Diane. 2009. "Health Care and Medicaid—Weathering the Recession." *New England Journal of Medicine* 360, no. 13 (March 26): 1273–75.

Sack, Kevin. 2010. "Recession Drove Many to Medicaid Last Year." *New York Times*, September 30. Online at www.nytimes.com/2010/10/01/health/policy/01medicaid.html.

Schneider, Saundra K. 1988. "Intergovernmental Influences on Medicaid Program Expenditures." *Public Administration Review* 48, no. 4 (July/August): 756–63.

Schwartz, William B., and Henry J. Aaron. 1985. *Health Care Costs: The Social Tradeoffs.* Washington, DC: Brookings Institution.

———. 1990. "The Achilles Heel of Health Care Rationing." *New York Times,* July 9.

Selden, Thomas N.; Julie L. Hudson; and Jessica S. Banthin. 2004. "Tracking Changes in Eligibility and Coverage Among Children, 1996–2002." *Health Affairs* 23, no. 5 (September–October): 39–50.

Sloan, Frank A. 1999. "Physician Participation and Non-Participation in Medicaid Managed Care: The TennCare Experience." *Southern Medical Journal* 92, no. 11 (November): 1064–70.

Sloan, Frank A.; Janet Mitchell; and Jerry Cromwell. 1978. "Physician Participation in State Medicaid Programs." *Journal of Human Resources* 13 (Supplement): 211–45.

Smith, David B., and Zhanlian Feng. 2010. "The Accumulated Challenges of Long-Term Care." *Health Affairs* 29, no. 1 (January): 29–34.

Smith, David G. 2002. *Entitlement Politics: Medicare and Medicaid, 1995–2001.* New York: Aldine de Gruyter.

Smith, David G., and Judith D. Moore. 2008. *Medicaid Politics and Policy: 1965–2007.* New Brunswick: Transaction.

Smith, Vernon; Rekha Ramesh; Kathleen Gifford; Eileen Ellis; Robin Rudowitz; and Molly O'Malley. 2004. *The Continuing Medicaid Budget Challenge: State Medicaid Spending Growth and Cost Containment in Fiscal Years 2004 and 2005: Results from a 5-State Survey.* Washington, DC: Henry J. Kaiser Family Foundation.

Starr, Paul. 1982. *The Social Transformation of American Medicine.* New York: Basic Books.

"States 'Bend the Trend' in Medicaid Spending Growth." 2009. *State Health Watch* 16, no. 2 (February): 4–5.

Stewart, Kate A.; David C. Grabowski; and Darius N. Lakdawalla. 2009. "Annual Expenditures for Nursing Home Care: Private and Public Payer Price Growth." *Medical Care* 47, no. 3 (March): 295–301.

Stone, Deborah A. 1992. "Why the States Can't Solve the Health Care Crisis." *American Prospect,* no. 9 (Spring): 51–60.

Thompson, Frank J. 1998. "The Faces of Devolution." In *Medicaid and Devolution: A View from the States,* ed. Frank J. Thompson, 15–55. Washington, DC: Brookings Institution.

Thompson, Frank J., and Courtney Burke. 2007. "Executive Federalism and Medicaid Demonstration Waivers: Implications for Policy and Democratic Processes." *Journal of Health Politics, Policy and Law* 32, no. 6 (December): 971–1004.

———. 2009. "Federalism by Waiver: Medicaid and the Transformation of Long-Term Care." *Publius* 39, no. 1 (Winter): 22–46.

"2012 HHS Poverty Guidelines." 2012. Washington, DC: U.S. Department of Health and Human Services. Online at http://aspe.hhs.gov/poverty/12poverty.shtml.

Vogel, Ronald J. 1984. "An Analysis of Structural Incentives in the Arizona Health Care Cost-Containment System." *Health Care Financing Review* 5, no. 4 (Summer): 13–32.

Wallack, Stanley S., Mark Sciegaj, and Linda Long. 2002. "Short- and Intermediate- Term Trends Affecting Medicaid Policy for Persons with Disability, Chronic Illness, and Special Needs." *Journal of Disability Policy Studies* 12, no. 4 (Spring): 236–42.

Weil, Alan. 2003. "There Is Something About Medicaid." *Health Affairs* 22, no. 1 (January–February): 13–30.

Young, Jeffrey. 2013a. "North Dakota Medicaid Expansion Favored by Republican Governor." *Huffington Post,* January 15. Online at www.huffingtonpost.com/jeffrey-young/north-dakota-medicaid-exp_b_2481572.html.

———. 2013b. "Idaho Medicaid Won't Expand Under Obamacare: GOP Governor Says." *Huffington Post,* January 7. Online at www.huffingtonpost.com/2013/01/07/idaho-medicaid-obamacare-governor_n_2426983.html.

Young, Gary; Mark Meterko; Bert White; Karen Sautter; Barbara Bokhour; Errol Baker; and Jason Silver. 2010. "Pay-for-Performance in Safety Net Settings: Issues, Opportunities, and Challenges for the Future." *Journal of Healthcare Management* 55, no. 2 (March/April): 132–42.

Zuckerman, Stephen; Aimee F. Williams; and Karen E. Stockley. 2009. "Trends in Medicaid Physician Fees, 2003–1008." *Health Affairs* 28, no. 3 (May/June): 510–19.

Zuckerman, Stephen; Joshua McFeeters; Peter Cunningham; and Len Nichols. 2004. "Changes in Medicaid Physician Fees, 1998–2003: Implications for Physician Participation." *Health Affairs Web Exclusive* w4 (January–June): 374–84.

4

MEDICARE

Healthcare for the Elderly

Much of the current debate is about Medicare's future mistakes, what Medicare is, and what it is designed to achieve. Medicare isn't just a trust fund. Medicare isn't just a certain kind of health care system called fee for service. And Medicare is a lot more than just another number in the federal budget debate. Medicare is designed, at bottom, for two purposes. First, Medicare helps assure that older Americans and those with disabilities have access to the same standard of quality health care services as most Americans. Second, Medicare is an essential part of economic security. It is an insurance system that protects beneficiaries and their families from the high and unpredictable costs of health care services

—John C. Rother (n.d.)

Medicare is the largest public sector healthcare program in the United States, in terms of both dollars and numbers of people covered. It began as an alternative to national health insurance and remains one of the most popular government programs. Despite its popularity, it continues to be a target for those seeking to curtail government spending and shrivel what government does. The 1990s and the 2000s saw legislation that both expanded Medicare benefits and threatened the very nature of the program itself. Cost and coverage problems remain an issue, as does the lack of coverage for long-term care. The passage of the Patient Protection and Affordable Care Act, formally known as the Affordable Care Act (ACA), in 2010 presented new changes and challenges to the program.

In this chapter, we closely examine Medicare. We begin by looking at its origin and structure. We then look at some of the changes and problems with the program and how those problems have been addressed. We next turn to the problem of long-term care and how that has been addressed in the United States. We conclude the chapter by considering the impact of the ACA on Medicare and proposals to reform it.

THE ORIGINS OF MEDICARE

As mentioned in chapter 2, national health insurance (NHI) was first mentioned in the early twentieth century during the presidential elections of 1912. But the onset of World War I, the linkage between NHI and Germany (which was the first to adopt NHI), and opposition to national health insurance on the part of the American Medical Association (AMA) killed the program. During the development of what eventually became the Social Security Act of 1935, policy formulators considered and rejected the idea of adding a national health insurance provision. They believed, based on responses to the mere mention of it, that including national health insurance would sink the entire Social Security bill (Marmor 2000; Oberlander 2003; Starr 1982). Beginning in 1939, bills for national health insurance were introduced in Congress (e.g., the Murray-Wagner-Dingell legislation). Marmor (2000, 7) points out that, though the Democrats had a numerical majority, they did not have a "programmatic majority" to enact the legislation. That is, there was insufficient unity within the majority Democratic Party, a problem that was repeated in 1994 during the Clinton administration. The 1948 Democratic national platform called for national health insurance. Despite Truman's victory in that election, the Murray-Wagner-Dingell proposal died, never coming out of committee in Congress.

Advocates of national health insurance then tried an alternative strategy. The new strategy was incremental in nature, focusing on a group or groups that could garner sympathy but could not afford health insurance. The ideal group was the elderly. Marmor (2000, 15) describes the politics behind the new strategy:

> The concentration on the burdens of the aged was a ploy for sympathy. The disavowal of aims to change fundamentally the American medical system was a sop to AMA fears, and the exclusion of physician services benefits was a response to past AMA hysteria. The focus on the financial burdens of receiving hospital care took as given the existing structure of the private medical care world, and stressed the issue of spreading the costs of using available services within that world. The organization of healthcare, with its inefficiencies and resistance to cost-reduction, was a fundamental but politically sensitive problem which consensus-minded reformers wanted to avoid when they opted for 60 days of hospitalization insurance for the aged in 1951 as a promising "small" beginning.

The above quote contains several important points. It shows the attempt to accommodate potential opposition, primarily the medical profession. It did this in several ways. This incremental strategy excluded coverage of physician services (though Medicare as enacted did include such coverage but treated it differently from hospital care). It limited the number of hospital days covered, the "small beginning," a feature that remains an integral part of Medicare. Finally, it left the structure of American medicine alone. That structure was the private practice of physicians and the fee-for-service system (Krause 1977). Some of these features would eventually be changed beginning in the 1980s, but they were at least partly responsible for some of the problems that Medicare has faced. The finance committees in Congress held hearings on Medicare from 1958 to 1965 (Marmor 2000).

In 1960 Congress passed the Kerr-Mills bill, which provided federal assistance (50–80 percent) to states to help with hospital care for the aged poor. In other words, Kerr-Mills was a welfare program, with all the accompanying problems and stigma of means-tested (income-based) programs. Few states made any effort to implement the program (Starr 1982).

John F. Kennedy's campaign platform in 1960 included health insurance for the aged. Attempts were made to push a narrow program for the elderly from the beginning of the Kennedy administration. The conservative coalition (Republicans and southern Democrats) that had long opposed liberal legislation was able to delay enactment of the program, but the great electoral victory of Lyndon Johnson in 1964 accompanied by a large liberal Democratic majority in Congress allowed passage of a number of programs, part of the Johnson administration's Great Society. For our purposes, the important bill was Medicare, passed in 1965.

The law (Title 18 [XVIII] amendments to the 1935 Social Security Act) was broader than envisioned under the incrementalist strategy following the defeat of national health insurance during the Truman administration. It included physician services and covered a large section of the aged population, not just those who were poor but also those covered by Social Security. Thus it embodied a social insurance concept whereby subscribers made contributions, rather than assistance to the poor, which required means testing, though means testing for premiums would eventually be incorporated into the program. Medicare would cover a large portion of the population, and virtually all would contribute and benefit. It was, effectively, national health insurance for the elderly and eligible disabled (Reid 2009).

PROGRAM OBJECTIVES AND STRUCTURE

Objectives

The original design or theory of the program has been aptly stated by Thompson: "If Washington paid mainstream rates to providers for delivering medical care to the elderly, they would receive increased amounts of needed care" (1981, 155).

The problem facing the elderly was that, for several reasons, they could not afford health insurance. First, health insurance was available to individuals and families largely through the workplace. As retirees, the elderly were in most cases no longer eligible to receive health insurance benefits. Second, because retirees were no longer part of a larger group through their jobs, they would not be able to gain the benefits of group insurance. Individual insurance rates are considerably higher than group rates. Finally, the elderly were (and remain) more at risk of needing medical care (more likely to experience periods of illness, especially extended illness) and more expensive care than those of working age. The combination of these three factors meant that few private health insurance companies would offer a policy to retirees, and those that were offered were prohibitively expensive. In 1963, only about 54 percent of the elderly (sixty-five years and older) had hospital insurance (calculated from U.S. Bureau of the Census 1966).

Medicare resolved many, but not all, of these problems. In 2009, 98.7 percent of those sixty-five or older were covered by insurance. By comparison, nearly 15 percent of those under eighteen had no health insurance (U.S. Bureau of the Census 2012). Medicare had achieved its primary goal of providing health insurance for the elderly. Whether it was adequate is another story.

Structure

Medicare is open to those over sixty-five years of age, those disabled and receiving Social Security cash benefits, and those suffering from end-stage renal disease (ESRD, or kidney failure) or amyotrophic lateral sclerosis (ALS, also known as Lou Gehrig's disease) ("Medicare: A Primer" 2010).

Medicare originally had two parts (A and B), with Part C added in 1997 (and modified in 2003), and Part D in 2003. The hospital insurance (HI, or Part A) program covers inpatient hospital expenses for specified periods. Recipients are covered for up to ninety days for a benefit period and have a lifetime reserve of sixty hospital days. Payment is made for room and board in semiprivate rooms and for such hospital services as nursing and pharmaceuticals. Part A also pays for hospice services, home healthcare, and limited skilled nursing care ("Medicare: A Primer" 2010). Table 4.1 lists the services covered under Part A.

The second part of Medicare is the supplemental medical insurance (SMI), or Part B program. It is a voluntary program, though most Medicare recipients (just above 92 percent, calculated from "Medicare: A Primer" 2010) subscribe to it. SMI covers a wide range of physician and outpatient services, including diagnostic and surgical procedures and radiology. It also covers ambulance services, medical supplies, clinical services, and blood transfusions. Table 4.2 lists the services covered under Part B.

The third part of Medicare, Part C, focuses on alternative delivery systems. Under the Balanced Budget Act (BBA) of 1997, the new program was entitled "Medicare+Choice." Under the 2003 Medicare Prescription Drug, Improvement, and Modernization Act, also known as the Medicare Modernization Act or MMA, Part C was renamed "Medicare Advantage." It is through this program that Medicare recipients enroll in managed care programs such as health maintenance organizations (HMOs) as an alternative to what is now called traditional Medicare (see below).

Table 4.1

Medicare Part A: Hospital Insurance–Covered Services for 2014

Services	Benefit	Medicare Pays	Recipient Pays
Hospitalization: Semiprivate room and board, general nursing, and other hospital services and supplies	First 60 days 61st–90th day 91st–150th day[1] Beyond 150th day	All but $1,156 All but $289 a day All but $578 a day Nothing	$1,156 $289 per day $578 per day All costs
Skilled nursing facility: Semiprivate room and board, general nursing, skilled nursing, and rehabilitative services and other services and supplies[2]	First 20 days Additional 80 days Beyond 100 days	100% of approved amount All but $144.50 a day Nothing	Nothing Up to $144.5 a day All costs
Home health care: Part-time or intermittent skilled care, home health aide services, durable medical equipment and other supplies, and other services	Unlimited as long as recipient meets Medicare conditions	100% of approved amount; 80% of approved amount for durable equipment	Nothing for services; 20% of approved amount for durable equipment
Hospice care	For as long as doctor certifies need	All but limited costs for outpatient drugs and inpatient respite care	Limited costs for outpatient drugs and inpatient respite care

[1]This 60-day-reserve benefit may be used only once in a lifetime.
[2]Neither Medicare nor private Medigap insurance will pay for most nursing home care.
Source: www.medicare.gov.

The final, and newest, part of Medicare is Part D. Under the MMA, Medicare recipients beginning in January 2006 were eligible for prescription drug coverage. We will discuss this legislation in more detail below.

As important as what is covered is what is not covered. In two major areas Medicare coverage is extremely limited: catastrophic coverage, that is, coverage of hospital stays that exceed the specified limits, and long-term care coverage. We will address these issues later in this chapter.

FINANCING MEDICARE

Medicare is financed through a combination of subscriber and tax payments. The hospital insurance and supplemental medical insurance programs are financed differently. We begin with the hospital program.

The bulk of funds for the hospital insurance trust fund comes from the payroll tax (2.90 percent), a part of the Social Security tax that employees and employers pay (1.45 percent each) (Baicker and Chernew 2011; "Medicare Spending and Financing: Fact Sheet" 2011). In addition, there are deductibles (initial out-of-pocket costs before Medicare pays anything) and copayments when Medicare recipients use hospital services. There is a one-time deductible (paid before Medicare starts paying) equal to the average cost of one day in the hospital. For 2014, that amount was

Table 4.2

Medicare Part B: Medical Insurance–Covered Services for 2014

Services	Benefit	Medicare Pays	Recipient Pays
Medical expenses: doctors' services, inpatient and outpatient medical and surgical services and supplies, physical and speech therapy, diagnostic tests, durable medical equipment, and other services	Unlimited if medically necessary	80% of approved amount (after $147 deductible); 50% of approved charges for most outpatient mental services	$147 deductible[1] plus 20% of approved amount and limited charges above approved amount
Clinical laboratory services and screenings: blood tests, urinalysis, and more	Unlimited if medically necessary	100% of approved amount; 80% of approved amount for durable equipment	Nothing for services; 20% of approved amount for durable equipment
Home health care: part-time or intermittent skilled care, home health aide services, durable medical equipment and other supplies, and other services	Unlimited as long as recipient meets Medicare conditions	100% of approved amount; 80% of approved amount for durable equipment	Nothing for services; 20% of approved amount for durable equipment
Outpatient hospital treatment: services for the diagnosis or treatment of illness or injury	Unlimited if medically necessary	Medicare payment to hospital based on hospital cost	20% of billed amount (after $147 deductible)
Blood[2]	Unlimited if medically necessary	80% of approved amount (after $147 deductible and starting with 4th pint)	First 3 pints plus 20% of approved amount for additional pints (after $147 deductible)

[1]Once recipient has had $147 of expenses-covered services in 2014, the Part B deductible does not apply to any further covered services received for the rest of the year.

[2]Cost is based on whether blood is obtained from a blood bank.

Source: www.medicare.gov. 2014 Part B monthly premium: $104.90 (higher income recipients pay higher amount).

$1,156 for each benefit period (Centers for Medicare and Medicaid Services 2013). Medicare then pays for the entire cost of hospitalization for the next fifty-nine days. If the hospitalization lasts longer than sixty days, there is a copayment equal to one-quarter of a hospital day ($304 as of 2013) for days sixty-one through ninety. Each Medicare recipient has a reserve equal to sixty hospital days, which can be used past day ninety. Under Part A, Medicare also pays for hospice and home healthcare with very limited deductibles. Approved home healthcare services do not have a deductible, and there is a 20 percent copayment for durable medical equipment, such as oxygen and wheelchairs. Those eligible for skilled nursing home services do not have to pay a deductible for the first twenty days. For the next eighty days, the deductible is $152 per day as of 2013 (Centers for Medicare and Medicaid Services 2013).

The supplemental insurance program, or Part B, is financed through a combination of general federal revenues and Medicare subscriber premiums. Premiums and tax contributions were approximately equal in 1971; since that time, tax contributions have dwarfed premiums. The federal government pays 75 percent of the costs, and premiums cover the remaining 25 percent ("Medicare: A Primer" 2010). That is why, even given the cost increases in Part B copayments, SMI remains a bargain.

As mentioned above, most Medicare recipients are enrolled in the supplemental insurance program (Part B). The 2014 premium (the amount paid each month) was $104.90, though it could rise to as much as $335.70 for those at the highest range of income or $353.60 (depending on income and whether the unit is an individual or a couple) and is deducted from Social Security checks (Centers for Medicare and Medicaid Services 2013). There is also a $147 deductible as of 2014, and a 20 percent copayment for Part B services (with the exception of some preventive services), with Medicare paying 80 percent of those services (Centers for Medicare and Medicaid Services 2013). Physician charges are determined under the physician fee scale phased in beginning in 1992. Physicians elect each year whether to accept full assignment, that is, whether to accept the Medicare fee schedule (participating). If the physician does accept the fee schedule, Medicare is billed by the physician and the recipient pays the balance. Physicians do not have to accept full assignment. They can charge up to 115 percent of the Medicare fee schedule.

An example may help explain the fee schedule. Assume that you are a Medicare recipient who needs to visit a doctor for a Medicare-approved service. Your doctor would normally charge $200, given the services provided. According to the Medicare physician fee schedule, the visit is worth $142. Medicare then will pay 80 percent of the $142, or $113.60. Now it gets complicated. Consider these two cases: In case 1, the physician accepts full assignment, or the $142. He or she then sends in the paperwork to Medicare and receives a reimbursement of $113.60. You, the Medicare patient, pay the balance, or $28.40, to the doctor. Now take case 2: The physician does not accept full assignment. He or she can charge up to 115 percent of the $142, or $163.30. The physician bills the patient for the entire amount. The patient pays the doctor and files for reimbursement from Medicare. The Medicare recipient receives $113.60 from Medicare and has to pay the physician $49.70. From the standpoint of the recipient, using a physician who does not accept full assignment would cost an additional $21.30, an increase in the copayment of 75 percent. It obviously pays the Medicare recipient to use physicians who accept assignment.

Over time, Medicare cost-sharing has become a significant proportion of the elderly's expenses. One definition of those who are underinsured, who have insurance but whose healthcare costs still total a significant portion of a person's budget, is that 10 percent or more of a person's or family's expenses are spent on healthcare. By that definition, many Medicare beneficiaries are underinsured. On average, in 2010, Medicarie beneficiaries spent 14.7 percent of their income on healthcare, with premiums being the largest part (Cubanski et al. 2012). For those whose income is at the lower end (relying primarily on Social Security), the burden is higher. Indeed, employing a definition of poverty that takes into account the cost of medical care, the poverty rate among the elderly increases from 9 percent (in 2010) under the more traditional measure to 15.9 percent (Komisar 2012).

SUPPLEMENTING MEDICARE

Because of the substantial and growing cost-sharing provisions (premiums, deductibles, and copayments) and coverage gaps, many Medicare recipients have looked for ways to supplement their Medicare plans. As of 2009, 92.7 percent of the elderly population had some kind of health coverage in addition to Medicare. Of these, 31.3 percent were covered through a current or former employer, 21.3 percent owned individual coverage (e.g., a medigap policy), 12 percent were also Medicaid beneficiaries (dual eligibles), and 27.3 percent participated in HMOs or other private plans (Medicare Payment Advisory Commission 2012).

Medicaid Buy-In

For Medicare beneficiaries who are also eligible for Medicaid (i.e., low-income individuals), known as dual eligibles, there is state buy-in coverage. In 2009, about 12 percent of Medicare recipients, about 4.8 million people, were partially or fully eligible for both programs (Medicare Payment Advisory Commission 2012). States pay Part B premiums and any cost sharing. What is covered under Medicare is paid for by Medicare, and what is covered under Medicaid (such as long-term care) is paid for by Medicaid. A sizable proportion of the dual eligibles are disabled and under sixty-five years of age. Dual eligibles tend to be sicker than the overall Medicare population, and many of them are in long-term care institutions. Seventy-three percent of the dual eligibles have incomes less than 125 percent of the federal poverty line (Jacobson, Neuman, and Damico 2012; Medicare Payment Advisory Commission 2012; Young et al. 2012). Dual eligibles are disproportionately female and minority (Hispanic and African American). They are also more likely to be in poorer health. Spending on them is much higher than for nondual Medicare and Medicaid recipients (Jacobson, Neuman, and Damico 2012; Young et al. 2012).

There are three groups of Medicare beneficiaries who qualify for the Medicaid buy-in. One group are those who are either categorically (eligible for programs such as Supplemental Security Income) or medically needy. Additionally, there are two low-income groups that also qualify for the buy-in: those whose income is below the poverty line with limited assets (qualified Medicare beneficiaries, or QMBs) and those whose income is just over the poverty line (120 percent of poverty) with limited assets (specified low-income Medicare beneficiaries, or SLMBs). QMBs are limited to help with paying for Part B premiums and cost sharing, while SLMBs are limited to help with Part B premiums (Young et al. 2012).

The state buy-ins changed somewhat beginning in 2006, when the Medicare Modernization Act's prescription drug benefit took affect. The law requires that states pay for their Medicaid/ Medicare beneficiaries (see below).

Medigap

Another alternative is private supplemental medical insurance, so-called medigap policies. Such policies are provided by insurance companies or group organizations such as the American Association of Retired Persons (AARP). In 2011, over 20 percent of Medicare recipients purchased such policies ("The Diversity of Dual Eligible Beneficiaries" 2012). Medigap policies raise the average cost of healthcare because policyholders pay the full cost of that insurance, which includes administrative and advertising costs plus profits for insurance (Moon 1996). Such policies, as might be expected, are expensive. There are ten standardized medigap policies, labeled A through N, with different policies and benefits. The monthly premiums vary depending on the plan chosen and can range from about $150 to $350 a month.

Employment Retiree Benefits

A third way that beneficiaries can supplement Medicare coverage is through their former employers. A number of those companies that insure their workers also insure their retirees. As of 2010, some 28 percent of Medicare enrollees were in employer retirement plans (Cubanski et al. 2010).

However, there has been a major drop in such coverage. Large employers, the ones most likely to cover workers and retirees, significantly decreased their coverage of retirees, from 66 percent in 1988 to just 36 percent five years later (Cubanski et al. 2010). This is part of a larger trend of reducing employer coverage, primarily due to the cost problems.

TRANSFORMING MEDICARE

Parts A and B compose what is now called traditional Medicare, as it was designed in the 1965 legislation. But Congress has tinkered with the program since then, with some of the changes being fairly significant. This illustrates the incrementalist nature of American public policy making. It is rare that a piece of legislation is the final say. We continually visit and revisit programs. Indeed, since 1997, Medicare has been affected by ten pieces of legislation, included the Patient Protection and Affordable Act of 2010, the Medicare Modernization Act of 2003, and the Deficit Control Act of 2011 (Cubanski et al. 2010).

In this section, we focus on the two newest parts of Medicare, C and D, and changes from 1995 to 2012. The changes are profound and have transformed Medicare into something quite different from its original design. We might label this process as "Ending Medicare as We Know It" (Rushefsky 2004; see also Oliver, Lee, and Lipton 2004).

In the 1980s, Medicare began enrolling recipients in managed care organizations (MCOs), such as HMOs, as a means of restraining cost increases while maintaining quality of care for recipients. In addition, it was hoped that Medicare recipients would gain access to the same range of services as other patients (Brown et al. 1993). The plans often offered important additional services that Medicare did not at that time, such as prescription drugs. The plans also did not originally charge for their services and allowed Medicare beneficiaries to avoid the high costs of medigap policies (Freudenheim 1997).

A major move toward Medicare managed care and greater choice came in 1997 (see Marmor 2000; Oberlander 2003; Palazzolo 1999; Rushefsky and Patel 1998). To understand what happened, we need to go back to 1995. The Republicans gained control of Congress following the 1994 off-year elections. Their policy agenda, most of which was stated in the Contract with America, was to balance the federal budget and to cut taxes. Doing so required significant budget cuts. Medicare (and Medicaid) was an important target because of their size. The fiscal year (FY) 1996 budget that Congress passed called for $270 billion in savings over a seven-year period (Marmor 2000; Rushefsky and Patel 1998).

Here we have an interesting play of semantics and politics. The Republican proposal called for cuts in projected spending increases. It did not call for actual reductions in Medicare spending, at least on the surface. Managed care and HMOs would be one way to reduce spending increases, by making the system more efficient; at least, so claimed the Republicans (Rushefsky and Patel 1998).

Democrats, especially President Clinton, saw the proposed cuts as real, not just a slower increase in spending. The reasoning here was twofold. First, as the population ages, Medicare enrollment will increase. By definition, then, Medicare spending will have to increase, even if spending per beneficiary is kept constant or decreases. And Medicare spending per beneficiary was, in fact, decreasing.

In politics, sometimes things can get topsy-turvy. One of the provisions of the Affordable Care Act calls for savings from Medicare spending—again, a decrease in the increase rather than an actual decrease in spending. But now the political roles were reversed. Republicans, who unanimously opposed ACA, argued that it cut spending, while Democrats, who mostly supported it, argued that it only cut the increases and focused on waste (Kessler 2011).

From our perspective, the most important part was the creation of Part C and its focus on managed care. Enrollment in these alternative plans was slow. One reason might be that there was insufficient choice among types of plans. Prior to the BBA of 1997, the choice was between traditional Medicare and HMOs. The BBA of 1997 expanded choice through the Medicare+Choice program.

Under the BBA, Medicare recipients had a choice of seven different types of plans. Recipients would now be able to have a selection of plans that would rival that of private employer-based plans. The Medicare+Choice program (Part C) undermined traditional or regular Medicare. It attempted to fragment the Medicare community. The idea that everybody had the same plan, an idea that underlay the consensus about Medicare (Oberlander 2003), was eliminated. The proponents of choice hoped to wean beneficiaries away from Medicare, modernize Medicare, and move Medicare to more efficient healthcare plans. The plans were to be competitive, based on price and quality (Newman and Langwell 1999).

As subsequent data showed, the program did not work as planned. For one thing, enrollment in managed care plans declined in 2000 and 2001. HMOs withdrew from some areas, leaving recipients without any similar health plan. In 2001, nearly one million recipients lost their health-care plan (Gold 2001). Further, plans that remained became less generous to their beneficiaries. More of them were requiring premiums and fewer were covering prescription drugs (Gold 2001; see also Biles, Dallek, and Nicholas 2004).

One of the more interesting aspects of the debate over Medicare+Choice and the withdrawal of plans, one that also affected the 2003 and 2010 legislation, had to do with payments to plans by Medicare. The Health Care Financing Administration (HCFA, now the Centers for Medicare and Medicaid Services, or CMS) reasoned that HMOs would be able to save money serving their clientele. Because of this reasoning, the reimbursement rate for HMOs was set at 95 percent of the average spending on Medicare beneficiaries (adjusted average per capita cost, or AAPCC). Paradoxically, both HCFA and HMOs claimed that they were losing money on the deal. The HCFA's claim was based on HMOs' enrolling healthier segments of the Medicare population, whose costs would be less than average. The HMOs' claim was based on recipients making more use, particularly of the prescription drug benefit, than anticipated.

The next stage came in 2003.

The Medicare Prescription Drug, Improvement, and Modernization Act of 2003 (MPDIMA)

Medicare, when it was adopted and throughout most of its existence, had some important gaps. A major one was in prescription medications. Medicare pays for such medications while the recipient is in a hospital or a skilled-nursing home. It did not, traditionally, pay for outpatient prescription drugs. The 1988 Medicare Catastrophic Coverage Act provided for the addition of such a benefit. But because of the politics surrounding it (Marmor 2000; Oberlander 2003), the law was repealed the next year. In 2003 a new law was enacted that provided a prescription drug benefit, plus much more. The politics surrounding that new law and the policy implications of what that law has done, represented the greatest change in Medicare since the 1997 Balanced Budget Act and possibly since the origin of Medicare itself (Oliver, Lee, and Lipton 2004; Rushefsky 2004).

The Need for Prescription Drug Coverage

Before we look at the history of drug coverage proposals and the 2003 proposals in particular, we should examine why such an addition to Medicare was necessary. Much of the biomedical revolution in the late twentieth and early twenty-first centuries was in the area of pharmaceuticals. One measure of the revolution in the use of pharmaceuticals can be seen in national health expenditure data. Overall spending on prescription medications rose fairly rapidly, especially in the 1999–2003 period. For 2002, spending on prescription medications accounted for 11 percent of all national healthcare expenditures, but also represented 16 percent of the *increase* in expenditures in 2002 (Levit et al. 2004). Further, one set of projections suggested that spending on prescription medications would increase from $162.4 billion in 2002 to $483.2 billion in 2021 (Keehan et al. 2012).

One reason this is important is that the elderly population (sixty-five plus) makes higher use of prescription medications than younger people because they are more likely to have chronic conditions that require such use. Xu's (2003) analysis finds that the nonelderly are more likely to rate their health as good or excellent than the elderly. The elderly are also more likely than the nonelderly to have chronic conditions such as cancer, asthma, and arthritis (HIV/AIDS is the one area where the younger group has a higher incidence of chronic conditions). Of course, spending on prescription medications is not uniformly distributed among the elderly; average spending is misleading. Those with fewer or no chronic conditions will spend considerably less than those who have chronic or more serious conditions (Steinberg et al. 2000). We can see this pattern in what is known as concentration of healthcare expenses. Looking at 2010 data, we find that 28 percent of enrollees accounted for 74 percent of spending on prescription medications outside the hospital and 9 percent accounted for 44 percent of such spending (Part D) (Medicare Payment Advisory Commission 2012). This spending pattern is supported in an earlier study by Thomas, Ritter, and Walleck (2001). The elderly with high prescription drug use accounted for a significant and growing proportion of total healthcare spending. In 1997, those spending more than $3,000 a year on prescription medications accounted for 20 percent of total healthcare spending; by 2000, they accounted for 42 percent. Putting it in a slightly different way, those spending more than $6,000 a year on prescription medications made up 1.7 percent of the elderly population but accounted for 10.5 percent of total healthcare spending (Thomas, Ritter, and Walleck 2001). There are three reasons for projected increases in prescription medication spending: increasing prices of medications, the increasing size of the beneficiary population, and the Part D coverage of outpatient prescriptions.

Further, studies have shown that those who have no insurance or poor insurance coverage for prescription medications are less likely to use them or adhere to the prescribed regimen than those who do (Mojtabai and Olfson 2003). Seniors with chronic illnesses, such as diabetes and hypertension, who have no prescription drug coverage are more likely to skip using their medications than similar seniors who do have such coverage (Newman 2004).

Of course, most seniors now have prescription drug coverage (see Table 4.3), largely because of the 2003 legislation. A couple of points need to be made about Table 4.3. First, the percentage of retirees who have employer- or union-sponsored plans has declined. In 2003, the year the MMA was passed but three years before it was fully implemented, 34 percent of Medicare beneficiaries had such drug coverage. By 2010, that was down to 18 percent. Second, in 2003, 10 percent of beneficiaries had medigap policies with prescription drug benefits. The MMA eliminated that benefit, so now no beneficiaries have such policies. Similarly, the MMA eliminated drug coverage by Medicaid for the dual eligibles. Finally, the percentage of beneficiaries with no drug coverage declined from 22 percent in 2003 to 10 percent in 2010 (Lundy 2010; Newman 2004).

The Road to Change

The Clinton administration made two efforts to include prescription drug coverage within Medicare. The first came in the context of the proposal for national health insurance, the Health Security Act. The failure of the Clinton plan (or any other) to be passed during this period (1993–94) meant that the proposed benefit was still missing. Near the end of the Clinton administration and as the 2000 elections approached, there was renewed activity over the benefit. The Clinton proposal contained elements of what became the Medicare Modernization Act three years later. The proposal would have created a Part D (Part C was the Medicare+Choice program created in the 1997 BBA). There was considerable cost sharing, such as beneficiaries paying all costs after the first $5,000 and the use of pharmacy benefit management (PBM) companies (Oliver, Lee, and Lipton 2004).

Some important perspectives on the Clinton proposal crop up in the 2003 legislation. The pharmaceutical industry was not very supportive of the proposal. While the new benefit would have likely increased the use of its products (the intent of the program), it might also have led to price controls. There was also concern about how the proposal would affect employer-retiree

Table 4.3

Sources of Prescription Drug Coverage for the Elderly, 2010

Type of Plan	Percentage of Medicare Beneficiaries
Stand-alone	38
Medicare Advantage	21
Employer/union retiree	18
VA and other	13
No coverage	10

Source: Lundy (2010).

plans. The fear was that such a new proposal would lead employers to drop such coverage, putting more pressure on Medicare.

Republicans began offering their version of a plan, and presidential politics became involved. The Republican plan was based on subsidizing private insurance companies that would then offer drug benefits to Medicare recipients (Pear 2000). Both Vice President Al Gore and Texas governor George W. Bush offered plans during the 2000 presidential campaign. The Gore plan was essentially the Clinton plan. Gore's plan would allow Medicare to negotiate prices with the pharmaceutical companies (Serafini 2000).

The Bush plan was a more modest one that relied on the states for the first four years of the program to offer a benefit to their seniors. The plan included payments to the states and subsidies for low-income recipients. States would participate in the program on a voluntary basis. The more permanent program would be based on private plans offering the benefit and subsidies for low-income seniors. Federal spending would be capped at $6,000 per beneficiary ("The Bush Prescription Drug Plan" 2000). The idea was that competition among the plans would be a way to control costs. Further, the purpose of the Bush plan was to move more Medicare recipients into HMOs (Dao 2000). Serafini (2000) described the goals of the Bush plan as follows:

> Overall, Bush has focused on making Medicare less of a one-size-fits-all program. He wants to strengthen Medicare by providing more choice and more private-sector alternatives. In particular, he supports the idea of seniors opening medical savings accounts—tax-free accounts from which they can pay their healthcare bills. And, after they had spent a certain amount of money in any one year, a catastrophic health insurance policy would kick in.

In July 2001, President Bush presented his Medicare proposal. It included a discount-card transitional program and changing Medicare to be more like private insurance plans (i.e., HMOs) (Kaisernetwork.org 2001).

The push for a prescription benefit took a back seat after the September 11, 2001, terrorist attacks against the United States. Democrats and Republicans disagreed on the specifics of a prescription drug plan, and the focus turned to the response to the terrorist attacks and the war on terrorism (Welch 2001). Additionally, HMOs continued dropping their participation in Medicare, claiming that their reimbursements were too low (see, for example, Pear 2001). Many HMOs that stayed in the program either eliminated the prescription drug benefit or severely restricted it (Kaisernetwork.org 2002).

In 2002, Bush offered a new version of his plan, including discount cards, assistance to states that offer help to their low-income seniors, and a modest plan directed at low-income seniors. The plan would cost an estimated $77 billion over ten years and cover about 3 million Medicare recipients. Another $190 billion would be used to reform Medicare B (Feder 2002). That started a concern about whether there was sufficient money in the Bush plan for the prescription drug benefit. Both congressional Democrats and Republicans argued that it was not nearly enough. Numbers between $300 and $700 billion were bandied about as more appropriate ("In 'Rare' Agreement" 2002). In 2002, congressional Republicans offered a bill that would cost an estimated $350 billion over ten years, employ discount cards during the transitional period, cover low-income seniors, and provide coverage for very high costs for others. The plan would rely on private insurance companies ("GOP to Unveil Drug-Benefit Plan" 2002). Democrats offered a more generous bill (Pear 2002). Throughout 2002 and 2003, Bush continued to push for the legislation (see, for example, Guggenheim 2002). A House Republican bill contained increased payments to a variety of providers ("House GOP Unveils Final Version" 2002).

Apart from differences in the costs and generosity of the House Republican and Democratic proposals ($350 billion for the Republican proposal, $800 billion for the Democratic proposal), how the benefits would be delivered indicated philosophical differences about the role of government in general and Medicare in particular, a difference that percolates with Paul Ryan's "Path to Prosperity" proposal (see below). Democrats preferred that the benefit be part of Medicare, similar to Part B. Republicans wanted the benefits to be delivered by private insurance companies, on the grounds that they were more efficient than government programs and competition would help control costs (Toner 2002). While the House succeeded in passing a Republican bill, the Senate, controlled by Democrats, was not able to pass the legislation (Hook 2002; Oliver, Lee, and Lipton 2004).

A Bill Becomes a Law

That set the stage for action in 2003. Fueled by the war on terrorism and the coming war with Iraq, Republicans regained control of the Senate that they had lost in 2001 because of the defection to the Democrats of Vermont Senator Jim Jeffords. With control of both houses of Congress and the presidency in Republican hands, it was inevitable that a Republican version of a Medicare prescription drug benefit would pass. Republican control of the House, though not large, was firm. Republican control of the Senate was much smaller. Also, given the rules of the Senate, where minorities have a greater ability to thwart a small majority, the House and Senate would pass somewhat different legislation. And it would take a fair amount of finagling to produce the final bill, similar to what occurred during the legislative proceedings over the Affordable Care Act (see chapter 10). The Bush administration position was that it wanted a bill before 2004 and was willing to approve almost anything (Oliver, Lee, and Lipton 2004). One important aspect of the Bush proposal was that only those who opted for the private plan would be offered a drug benefit. Both Republicans and Democrats opposed this position, and it was not included in the final legislation (Oliver, Lee, and Lipton 2004).

The House and Senate versions were passed in June 2003. Because the two versions were different, a conference committee was necessary to reconcile differences. Negotiations took some four months and required considerable compromises. Oliver, Lee, and Lipton (2004) note that "sweeteners" were placed in the bill to help it assuage different groups, typical of the legislative process and something that we saw with the passage of the ACA and that opponents of the 2010 legislation, i.e., Republicans, complained about (see chapter 10). These included some provision for obtaining benefits while staying in regular Medicare. Various interest groups also made out well, including providers, drug companies, and employers.

In order to gain passage, at least five unusual maneuvers were necessary, again paralleling the passage of the Affordable Care Act. The first had to do with how the conference committee operated. Members of both houses are appointed to the committee by the respective house leaders from both parties. The normal "Congress makes a law" view of how things are done is that there would be negotiations among the members. However, Republicans, who controlled Congress, held their own set of negotiations with almost no Democratic input. Then the resultant compromise was presented to the entire conference committee, with majority Republican control, and approved by the committee (Cohen, Victor, and Baumann 2004). One of the strongest supporters of the original Senate bill was Edward Kennedy (D-MA). After the compromise he found that the changes were so significant that he could no longer support it. In 2010, Republicans, who were in the minority in both houses of Congress, complained that they were left out of the process of passage of the ACA, though they had less to complain about than the Democrats in 2003.

One could see the differences in the titles of the three bills. The Senate bill was titled the "Prescription Drug and Medicare Improvement Act of 2003." The House bill was titled the "Medicare Prescription Drug and Modernization Act of 2003." The bill produced by the conference committee, the final version, was titled the "Medicare Prescription Drug, Improvement, and Modernization Act of 2003" (Health Policy Alternatives 2003).

As one example of the change from the House and Senate bills to the conference bill, consider the status of dual eligibles, low-income seniors who are also eligible for Medicaid. Under the Senate bill, those dual eligibles receiving coverage under a Medicaid program would not be eligible for the Medicare Part D coverage. Under the House bill, dual eligibles could enroll in Part D coverage. State obligations to provide drug coverage would be gradually eliminated, and states could require dual eligibles to enroll in Part D. Under the conference bill, states would no longer be reimbursed for drugs covered under Part D (the states would have to transfer funds into Part D) (Caplan and Housman 2004). In essence, dual eligibles would only be able to get coverage under Part D (Health Policy Alternatives, Inc. 2003).

A second intriguing manipulation concerned the vote in the House on the conference bill. According to House rules, floor votes normally take fifteen minutes. However, the leadership did not have sufficient votes to pass the bill during that fifteen-minute period. In a virtually unprecedented maneuver, they kept voting open for three hours, searching for votes (Cohen, Victor, and Baumann 2004).

A third and related element was how the leadership apparently got one of its votes. Nick Smith's (R-MI) son was campaigning for office to replace the retiring congressman. Smith asserted that he changed his "no" vote to "yes" after threats and promises of campaign assistance by Tom DeLay (R-TX) (see Green 2005) for his son seeking to replace him. Smith later said that it did not happen, but there is every reason to believe he was offered a bribe on the floor of the House (Center for American Progress 2004; Chait 2004). As a sidenote, Smith's son lost the election (Noah 2004).

The fourth event was related to the estimated costs of the prescription benefit. When Governor Bush began proposing a prescription benefit, the costs were quite modest. When he was president, Bush's proposal was in the $170 billion range. After he agreed to sign a proposal, his one condition was that it not cost more than $400 billion over a ten-year period, and those were the estimates used in considering the bill. However, an actuary for the Centers for Medicare and Medicaid Services (CMS) estimated that the bill might cost as much as $540 billion over the ten-year period. The importance of this estimate is that conservative Republicans were unhappy about the original $400 billion estimate. The extra $140 billion in estimated costs might have resulted in more Republican votes against the bill. Tom Scully, then the administrator of CMS, ordered the actuary not to submit his estimate to Congress and threatened to fire him if he did (Center for American Progress 2004). So Congress considered the bill with the smaller estimate.

A last example of manipulation took place after the legislation was passed and signed. The administration was concerned about criticism of the new law and also wanted credit for having passed a prescription benefit. It hired a lobbyist to promote the law through advertising using public funds. Part of the campaign included a video story sent to local television stations that was used as if it were actual news (i.e., the speaker appearing to be a reporter). According to the Government Accountability Office, this was illegal (Chait 2004).

What Is in the Law: The New Drug Benefit (Part D)

The Medicare Prescription Drug, Improvement, and Modernization Act of 2003 (or Medicare Modernization Act, abbreviated as MMA) is a complex piece of legislation. The first portion of the new law was a transitional discount card program until the benefit became effective in January 2006.

The major part of the Medicare legislation is the drug benefit itself, the new Part D. The benefit is available to seniors on a "voluntary" basis. Voluntary is used advisedly, because those who do not meet the exceptions (for example, being part of an employee-retirement program that offers a prescription drug benefit at least as good as Medicare's) and not enrolled by January 2006 face a 1 percent penalty for each month they do not enroll if they choose to do so later. It could be argued that Part D is effectively an individual mandate for Medicare beneficiaries, similar to what is contained in the ACA.

Seniors have some choices to make even before they get to choose a plan. To receive the Part D benefits, they will either have to join a preferred provider organization (PPO) or HMO (a Medicare Advantage plan) and get all their healthcare, including prescription drugs, from them. Alternatively, seniors could stay with Medicare but enroll in a private insurance plan that only offers a prescription drug benefit. And some seniors will have coverage through an employer or union retiree plan, although, as we have seen, this benefit has declined.

Seniors pay a monthly premium and a deductible. The premiums depend on the type of plan chosen. For stand-alone plans, the monthly premium in 2011 averaged $38.29. This represents a 48 percent increase since the start of the program, though only a 3 percent increase from the previous year. For those in the MA-PD (Medicare Advantage-Part D) plans, the premiums averaged $12.26 (Hoadley et al. 2011). In a complex architecture, benefits and copayments rise and fall and rise again depending on the level of spending on the part of the individual. Under the original 2003 legislation, beneficiaries would have to pay a $250 deductible and then copayments of 25 percent up to $2,500. Then comes the famous "doughnut hole," between $2,250 and $5,100, where the seniors would pay all the costs. After that, copayments would be 5 percent. The reason for this complex structure was to keep the costs of the program within the $400 billion cap that President Bush insisted upon (even though the administration knew that it would cost much more than that). Subsidies are available for low-income seniors.

Seniors have a choice of at least two plans, and formularies must include at least two drugs from each category. In the event that no plans are available in a particular area, Medicare itself will provide the benefit, the "fallback" provision (Oliver, Lee, and Lipton 2004).

One interesting part of the new drug benefit, because of the politics involved, concerns dual enrollees and the states. Under the new law, the states have to pay Medicare for the prescription drug costs of covering those enrolled in both Medicare and Medicaid. Some states have calculated that they will be paying for a federal service and will pay more than they spent on the benefit for their enrollees. As a result, some states have decided not to make the payments. For example, Texas Governor Rick Perry, Bush's Republican successor, vetoed legislation in 2005 that would have appropriated money for that purpose (Pear 2005; see also Smith, Gifford, and Kramer 2005).

The Affordable Care Act modifies parts of the prescription drug legislation. An important provision is to gradually reduce, by 2020, the copayments in the doughnut hole from 100 percent to 25 percent ("Summary of Key Changes to Medicare in 2010 Health Reform Law" 2010).

Subsidies for the Favored

Another part of the legislation involves subsidies and other favors. One set of favors concerns provider reimbursement. Historically, the federal government has tried restraining the costs of

Medicare by reducing payments to providers (we come back to this below). Doctors and hospitals are on fee schedules that have been the subject of negotiations over the years. For example, the 1997 Balanced Budget Act significantly reduced payments to providers. This has created the problem that physicians are becoming more reluctant to accept Medicare patients. The 2003 Medicare law included increases, rather than the proposed decreases, in payments to providers (Altman 2004).

A second related feature is centered around health plans, such as PPOs and HMOs. Recall that in the late 1990s and early 2000s, some HMOs exited the Medicare field, claiming that they were losing money on Medicare recipients. The new legislation provided for additional payments to those plans, some $14 billion. As Oliver, Lee, and Lipton (2004) pointed out, this means that these healthcare plans would be getting more per Medicare enrollee than Medicare on average would normally spend.

Third, employers who offer healthcare benefits for their retirees would also get subsidies. The subsidy amounts to about $81 billion and was intended to provide an incentive for employers to maintain their coverage. Interestingly, employers who reduced their coverage would still get the subsidy (Antos and Calfee 2004).

If there is an overall winner in the legislation, it is the pharmaceutical industry, which has historically opposed the addition of a drug benefit for fear that it would lead to price controls. The MMA alleviated all such fears. Under the law, Medicare cannot negotiate drug prices. The states do engage in such negotiation under Medicaid, as does the Department of Veterans Affairs, but Medicare cannot. It will be up to the private plans to engage in the negotiations. Further, the legislation banned the reimportation of drugs from other countries. Under the law, the Food and Drug Administration will explore drug importation from Canada (Oliver, Lee, and Lipton 2004).

Medicare Advantage

The story of Part C is another thread in the transformation of Medicare. In 1982, Medicare enabled participation of health maintenance organizations (HMOs) in Medicare as an alternative to what is now called traditional Medicare. Private plans were also a way to make greater use of markets, according to advocates, and control costs. Growth of Medicare beneficiary enrollment in the private plans, however, was small. That bring us to the Balanced Budget Act of 1997.

The BBA created Part C, Medicare+Choice. Medicare beneficiaries could choose among seven plans, including traditional Medicare and medical savings account (a high-deductible plan with Medicare paying for catastrophic expenses).

HMOs were thought to be more efficient than traditional Medicare in the sense that they could deliver the same services for less cost. This was because such plans are generally paid on a per capita (capitation) rather than fee-for-service basis. On a fee-for-service system, providers are paid for each service delivered. In a capitation system, the organization is paid a certain amount for each of its members. In that sense, private plans were effectively assuming the risk of enrollee illness. Congress took these ideas into consideration, and Medicare, as we saw above, paid HMOs 95 percent of what, on average, Medicare spends per beneficiary. Further, enrollees would not have to pay extra. Plans would cover Part A and Part B services, cost-sharing such as deductibles and copayments, plus some would offer additional services.

The program did not work out as planned, which laid the groundwork for the 2003 legislation. A four-year evaluation found that risk plans (whereby the plan would not get more money from the Health Care Financing Administration if its costs increased) tended to enroll healthier-than-average Medicare recipients. Those enrolled in risk plans had 20 percent lower Medicare reimbursements than those not so enrolled. Further, they were less likely to be disabled or have chronic health problems than those enrolled in risk plans. Such a pattern of enrollment, called favorable selection, has often been charged to HMOs. The evaluation study estimated that, given favorable selection, costs to Medicare were actually 5.7 percent higher than with the fee-for-service system (Brown et al. 1993; see also Biles, Dallek, and Nicholas 2004; Congressional Budget Office 1997; Oberlander 1997).

On the other hand, HMOs do tend to reduce the length of hospital stays compared to the fee-for-service system, though they do not reduce the number of admissions. For other services, HMOs tend to reduce the intensity of services (the number of services provided) by 10–20 percent (Congressional Budget Office 1997). The effects are greatest for those who are chronically ill (Oberlander 1997). Quality of care for HMO Medicare recipients is about equal to that of fee-for-service Medicare recipients (Brown et al. 1993).

One question that could be asked is how satisfied Medicare recipients are with managed care plans. A study by Nelson (1997) found that most Medicare HMO enrollees were satisfied with their access to care, such as being admitted to a hospital, seeing a specialist, making an appointment, or receiving desired home healthcare. Most were able to select their primary care physician and had received enough information to obtain care. Those more likely to report access problems were from "vulnerable subgroups" (Nelson 1997, 151–52), such as the nonelderly disabled, those whose health was less than good, the oldest beneficiaries, and those with functional disabilities. African Americans seemed less satisfied with their HMOs than whites. Even so, most of these groups said they would recommend the plan to others with health problems. Adequacy of home healthcare services appears more likely under Medicare fee-for-service than under managed care.

In the late 1990s and early 2000s, Medicare+Choice plans began to drop out of the market and avoid rural areas. By 2003 some 2.4 million HMO enrollees had been dropped by their plans (Peck 2003). This obviously caused disruptions for beneficiaries, as they had to find another plan or, more likely, enroll in traditional Medicare. Further, HMOs and PPOs limited the availability of physicians. Only those providers who were included in the plan or network were available to beneficiaries (going outside plans costs beneficiaries more money), a phenomenon that recurred in 2013 with the rollout of the ACA. Disenrollment—beneficaries dropping plans—was also a problem. Disenrollees tended to be sicker, had more chronic conditions, and were older than those who stayed (Riley, Ingber, and Tudor 1997). One can see the impact of disenrollment and dropping beneficiaries. In 1999, 6.9 million Medicare recipients, 18 percent of all Medicare recipients, were in private plans. By 2003, that number had declined to 5.3 million people, 13 percent of Medicare recipients (Gold et al. 2012).

The 2003 Medicare Modernization Act sought to fix this problem. The legislation, including the new prescription drug benefit (Part D) discussed above and health savings accounts (HSAs), sought to move Medicare beneficiaries to private plans.

Medicare+Choice was renamed Medicare Advantage (MA) (employing the symbolic use of names to describe a program). More importantly, it changed Medicare payments to private plans from the 95 percent average per capita Medicare spending as it was under the Balanced Budget Act to 113 percent. This was designed to encourage private plans to return or stay with Medicare. The extra money could be used to provide additional benefits, including prescription medications.

Beneficiaries began to move to MA plans. By 2012, 13.1 million beneficiaries or 27 percent were enrolled in a Medicare Advantage plan. Most of them (65 percent) were in traditional health maintenance organizations, 21 percent were in local preferred provider organizations, 7 percent in regional preferred provider organizations, and 4 percent in private fee-for-service plans (Gold et al. 2012). There are also HMO Point of Service Plans, which pay a higher rate for out-of-network care than do traditional HMOs. Another alternative was medical savings account plans. Under such plans, the federal government puts money into an account that can be used to pay for needed services ("Different Types of Medicare Advantage Plans" 2012.)

Complaints on the part of those opposed to private plans cropped up almost immediately after the passage of the Medicare Modernization Act. A major objection was to the higher payments to the plans, with the result that Medicare is spending more than it otherwise might, an estimated $157 billion more from 2009 to 2019 (Jaffe 2009).

Additionally, according to the majority (Democratic) staff of the U.S. House Committee on Energy and Commerce, administrative costs are much higher for private plans than for traditional Medicare. These costs include marketing, profits, and so on (Committee on Energy and Commerce 2009). Further, such plans paid out less for services than traditional Medicare. As an extreme case, one MA plan spent only 36 percent of what it received from Medicare on services (what is called the medical loss ratio). Many of the companies had a medical loss ratio of nearly 85 percent, a figure contained in the Affordable Care Act. Further, MA plans tended to advertise for (try to attract) health beneficiaries (see Cai et al. 2008).

The Affordable Care Act (2010), as it did with Part D, made some changes to Part C. The additional payments will be phased out through 2017, and the medical loss ratio will be mandated at 85 percent (Potetz, Cubanski, and Neuman 2011).

Lessons from the Medicare Modernization Act

One last consideration about the Medicare Modernization Act: there are parallels between it and the ACA. One already mentioned is that the MMA is effectively an individual mandate for Medicare beneficiaries, similar to the individual mandate in the ACA. Under the MMA, a Medicare beneficiary who is not enrolled in some type of drug benefit plan must, upon enrollment, pay a penalty equal to 1 percent of the premiums for each month the person was not enrolled. The ACA, likewise, contains a penalty (officially a tax) for not having health insurance.

Second, the private drug benefit plans under the MMA are effectively the equivalent of the health exchanges contained in both the 2006 Massachusetts plan (see chapter 10) and the ACA.

Third, implementation of the prescription drug benefit plan under the MMA was very bumpy. Beneficiaries were confused about the program and did not understand it well. Over the years, the confusion has diminished and the program has worked better, though there are still some problems. One problem was that the helpline for the program did not always provide accurate information. Further, a large number of beneficiaries signed up for the program on the last day of 2005, and when they went to purchase their medications in early 2006, there was no record of them in the system (Kliff 2013).

Fourth, Medicare Part D was very unpopular when it passed and as it approached the 2006 implementation year. Indeed, it was even more unpopular in 2005 and 2006 than the ACA was in 2013 (Kliff 2013).

Of course, there are differences between the two programs. The ACA is more complex and covers much more of the population than Medicare. There was less political opposition to Part D than there has been for the ACA. Medicare, as a federal program, did not rely on the states for implementation as ACA does with the Medicaid expansion and the health exchanges. Nevertheless, there are lessons from Part D that can be applied to the implementation of the ACA (see chapter 10).

CONTROLLING COSTS

From the beginning, a chief concern about the Medicare program was cost. Several dimensions of cost play a role. One discussed earlier is costs to the Medicare beneficiary. Here we can look at the copayments and deductible that recipients have to pay under Parts A and B and premiums under Part B (and the new Parts C and D). We have also looked, to a certain extent, at the problem of cost through HMOs and medigap policies.

A second major dimension of cost control is cost to the federal government. As Medicare became more expensive for a variety of reasons, federal administrators and policymakers sought ways to curb those costs. Some of it could be done by raising premiums and deductibles for Medicare recipients. By far the largest target of cost control was providers: physicians, hospitals, and so forth. From the beginning, the politics of Medicare revolved around the issue of provider payment, beginning with hospitals and then expanding to doctors (Feder 1977; Thompson 1981). In addition, the size of the Medicare program made it a tempting target for those seeking to cut government spending and/or reduce the budget deficit. Medicare played a key role in the 1995–97 budget debates, debates that ultimately led to significant changes in the program. The enormous budget deficits that appeared beginning in 2007 renewed the debate over the role of Medicare in the federal budget. Table 4.4 presents data on Medicare expenditures for selected years.

Third, and related, are questions about the long-term viability of the program. The trust fund, which affects Part A, is predicted to be depleted by 2024 and to be inadequately funded through 2021 (Boards of Trustees 2012; Cubanski 2009).

Consider, first, the increase in expenditures and enrollments in Medicare (see Table 4.4). Medicare expenditures in 1970 were about $7.7 billion, almost 42 percent of federal health expenditures and 10.3 percent of total personal health expenditures. In 1995, Medicare expenditures were about $184.43 billion, representing just over 50 percent of federal personal healthcare expenditures and almost 18 percent of total personal healthcare expenditures. By 2010, Medicare expenditures were over $500 billion, representing almost 50 percent of federal health expenditures and over 20 percent of total personal health expenditures (calculated from Centers for Medicare and Medicaid Services 2012b). As fast as overall health expenditures were increasing, Medicare expenditures were increasing ever more rapidly. Considering the concern about overall increases in healthcare, such rapid increases in Medicare could not help but raise alarms.

One of the reasons for the increase in program expenditures was the increase in the number of Medicare beneficiaries (see Table 4.5). When the program began operation in 1966, it had a little over 19 million enrollees. By 1970, that number had increased to over 20 million. The 1972 amendments to the Social Security Act added the disabled and those suffering from end-stage renal disease (kidney failure). By 1995, there were just over 37 million Medicare enrollees, 4.4 million of whom were disabled. That represents an increase of about 83 percent in total recipients. By 2010, there were nearly 47 million beneficiaries, including almost 8 million disabled (Centers for Medicare and Medicaid Services n.d.). This represents an increase of 26 percent in the number of beneficiaries since 1995.

Another reason is the growing generosity of Medicare in the sense that cost-sharing on the part of Medicare recipients has become relatively smaller. In 1980, cost-sharing amounted to about 19.6 percent of total expenditures. By 2010, the number had decreased to 17.6 percent (calculated from Centers for Medicare and Medicaid Services 2011a). Even with these numbers, Medicare recipients still pay a sizable portion of their income on healthcare. Other reasons for greater expenditures include general inflation, healthcare inflation over and above general inflation, and changes in the technology of healthcare.

When policymakers began to seriously consider imposing cost-control measures on Medicare, they focused first on hospitals. As is true for overall national healthcare expenditures, hospitals accounted for the largest single portion of Medicare expenditures. In 2010, hospital inpatient services cost $226.5 billion, approximately 43 percent of total Medicare payments. By contrast, physician services accounted for $114.6 billion, approximately 22 percent of total payments (calculated from Centers for Medicare and Medicaid Services 2011b).

When Medicare began, it contained the usual compromise provision that "the federal insurance program would not interfere in the practice of medicine or the structure of the medical care industry" (Feder 1977, 1; Krause 1977). But it was inevitable that the federal government would

Table 4.4

Medicare Expenditures, Selected Years, 1970–1995 (in $ billions)

1970	$7.67	1997	$210.37
1975	$16.34	1998	$209.21
1980	$37.39	2000	$224.34
1985	$71.83	2005	$338.77
1990	$110.18	2010	$524.55
1995	$184.39		

Source: Centers for Medicare and Medicaid Services (2012b).

Table 4.5

Medicare Beneficiaries, Selected Years, 1970–2010 (in millions)

	Total Enrollees	Aged	Disabled
1970	20.4	20.4	
1975	25.3	22.5	2.2
1980	28.1	25.1	3.0
1985	29.6	26.7	2.9
1990	33.7	30.5	3.3
1995	37.1	32.7	4.4
2000	39.2	33.8	5.4
2005	42.0	35.3	6.7
2010	46.9	39.0	7.9

Source: Centers for Medicare and Medicaid Services (n.d.).

have to take steps as the program became relatively more expensive. One way to understand that inevitability is to consider the theory of imbalanced political interests and its application to Medicare (Marmor, Wittman, and Heagy 1983).

At the beginning of the program, Medicare amounted to a relatively small percentage of federal expenditures. In FY 1970, five years after it was established, Medicare accounted for 3.7 percent of federal expenditures. Hospitals and physicians were faced with concentrated benefits and costs of payment and regulatory policies. The program was too small in the early years for the federal government to give it much concern. By 1980, Medicare as a percentage of total federal spending had nearly doubled to 6.1 percent. By 2010, Medicare accounted for 15.2 percent of federal spending (calculated from Office of Management and Budget 2011). As Medicare spending continued to increase faster than overall spending, the federal government developed its own set of interests in cost containment that would counterbalance provider interests. Additionally, there was, and is, the continual concern that the hospital trust fund will eventually become insolvent. In the early 1980s, the federal government looked at hospital cost containment in Medicare. During the latter part of the decade, it turned to physician payments. Eventually, other providers, such as nursing homes and home healthcare agencies, were covered by prospective payment.

Prospective Payment System

With the enactment of Medicaid and Medicare in the mid-1960s, the federal government became a major purchaser of services in the healthcare market. Part of the increase in overall healthcare costs is attributed to dramatic increases in the cost of Medicaid and Medicare. By 1980, spending had reached about $61.2 billion, constituting about 27.8 percent of total national health spending—financing healthcare for about 50 million people (Levit et al. 1994). At the same time, hospital costs were also rising dramatically, from $28 billion in 1970 to $102.7 billion in 1980 (Levit et al. 1994). From 1977 to 1982, Medicare hospital expenditures grew at an average annual rate of 18 percent compared to a 14.6 percent increase in overall hospital spending (Gibson et al. 1984).

The burden on the federal health budget created the political environment for federal regulation of hospital costs (Marmor, Wittman, and Heagy 1983; Steinwald and Sloan 1981). Advocates of regulation argued that cost controls on hospitals would limit waste and inefficiency without sacrificing quality of care.

President Carter, in response to rising hospital costs, proposed hospital cost-containment legislation designed to constrain the rate of increase in hospital charges and to limit the rate of increase in hospital revenues. Not surprisingly, the hospital industry strongly opposed such a measure and proposed a voluntary plan to control costs on its own. The controversy surrounding both plans led to their demise in 1979.

As mentioned earlier, President Reagan came to office in 1981 with the express intention of eliminating federal regulatory healthcare programs in favor of a market-oriented, competitive strategy to contain healthcare costs. Federal funding was cut for health planning programs, and the Professional Standards Review Organizations (PSROs) program was renamed Peer Review Organizations (PROs) and given reduced funding. Budget cuts were made in Medicaid and Medicare, and new federal grants for health maintenance organizations startups were eliminated.

Minor changes were made in Medicare by the Omnibus Budget Reconciliation Act of 1981. This included tightening Medicare reimbursement payments. The 1982 Tax Equity and Fiscal Responsibility Act (TEFRA) limited the increase in Medicare hospital payment rates, created an early basis for prospective payment based on a case-mix index, and called for incentive payments to hospitals defined as efficient. TEFRA required that the Department of Health and Human Services (HHS) design a new plan for the Medicare program. That new system, implemented in 1983, was the Prospective Payment System (PPS) for Medicare reimbursement to hospitals. The PPS was based on the New Jersey diagnosis-related groups (DRGs) program. This is an example of the federal government embracing a program originally implemented at the state level.

Under the PPS, hospitals are paid according to a schedule of preestablished rates linked to over 500 DRGs, effectively a form of price regulation. The categories depend on the type of case or what is called case mix. Case mix includes such factors as the severity of the disease, the amount of resources needed to treat the patient, and the prognosis.

Each category is assigned a treatment rate. Hospitals are reimbursed according to these rates. There are economic incentives in the form of rewards and punishments built into the system. If a hospital spends more money than the preestablished rate for a particular diagnostic treatment, the hospital must absorb the additional cost. If the hospital spends less money than the preestablished rate, it is still paid the preestablished rate and can keep the overpayment as profit. The HCFA (now the CMS) within the HHS was assigned the responsibility of establishing the DRG payment schedule. To safeguard against reduction in quality of care as a result of the PPS, Congress assigned PROs the responsibility of monitoring the quality and appropriateness of care for Medicare patients. If a PRO finds inappropriate or substandard care, the hospital may be denied Medicare payment. If a pattern of inappropriate or substandard care is discovered, the hospital's Medicare provider agreement may be terminated.

The rationale behind replacing the retrospective (fee-for-service or FFS) payment system was that under that system, hospitals had no incentive to economize in their use of healthcare resources in treating Medicare patients. If anything, such a system tended to encourage overutilization of health resources, since hospitals were assured that they would be reimbursed for all reasonable costs incurred. The PPS was based on the assumption that, given built-in incentives, hospitals would be forced to consider cost factors in treatment and would be encouraged to be economically more efficient. Thus, inefficient hospitals would be forced to close. An economically more efficient hospital sector would help contain increases in hospital costs. The PPS was viewed as a method of influencing hospital activities, creating cost-containment constraints, and introducing incentives into hospital payments (Shaffer 1983). The cost-control incentive was the primary purpose in establishing the PPS (Quade 1989). As we saw above in chapter 4, additional Medicare prospective payment mechanisms were imposed on physicians in 1989 and on nursing homes, home healthcare agencies, and hospice agencies in 1997 (the latter as a result of the 1997 Balanced Budget Act).

How well has the prospective payment system constrained hospital and other cost increases? Our analysis of national health expenditure data (available at cms.gov) shows significant declines in the rate of increase in Medicare hospital expenditures in the first three years of the DRG system. Additionally, increases in Medicare hospital expenditures prior to the implementation of the prospective payment system were higher than overall hospital expenditures, but lower afterward. Though there has been some variation from year to year, the general trend remains that such Medicare hospital expenditures are lower than overall hospital expenditures. In the later years, some of the difference might be at least partly a function of the move toward managed care plans within Medicare.

One way of looking at the impact of the PPS is to consider PPS margins, effectively a measure of profits and the balance of revenue and expenses. Data from 1999 to 2010 (Medicare Payment Advisory Commission 2012) shows that the margins declined from 13.7 percent in 1999 to –0.3 percent in 2004. Since then, the margins have remained under zero.

Between 1984 and 1991, the PPS payment per caseload rose at an annual rate of 6.4 percent (2.5 percent faster than the CPI). Between 1991 and 1995, the PPS payment per case had decelerated to 4.2 percent per year. The PPS cost per case actually declined in 1994 and again in 1995 (Guterman 1998). Medicare payments per hospital discharge were flat from 1996 to 2000 and then began a steep rise in 2001 and 2002 (Medicare Payment Advisory Commission 2004). The most recent data indicate that over the past several years the hospital industry has managed to improve the balance of revenue and expenses in the face of strong pressure from private payers. Hospital inpatient margins were negative in 1991 (–2.4 percent), reached a peak in 1997 (16.7 percent), and declined significantly through 2002 (4.7 percent). The overall margin (including most institutional care) declined from 10.3 percent in 1996 (the first year for which such data were collected) to 1.7 percent in 2002 (Medicare Payment Advisory Commission 2004). From 2004 to 2011 (the latest year data available), hospital inpatient margins were consistently negative, reaching a low of –4.7 percent in 2008 (Medicare Payment Advisory Commission 2013). Cost shifting to outpatient care has occurred. The prospective payment system has had similar effects on physicians (after 1989) and nursing homes, home healthcare agencies, and hospices with the passage of the Balanced Budget Act in 1997.

There have been criticisms of the payment system. Some suggest that hospitals seek ways to limit the impact of the new hospital regulations (see, for example, Lave 1984). Because price regulation is a tax on hospital behavior, it affects not only price but also hospital output and quality and quantity of services. Hospitals respond by attempting to reduce the use of affected services or resources by modifying their practices and products (Cook et al. 1983). Hospitals modify the cost of regulation by seeking an area unaffected by the regulation, that is, the "unregulated margin." Organizations respond to regulation through institutional, managerial, and technical changes (Parsons 1956). Hospitals altered services, influenced practices, and changed the products offered to decrease the impact of regulation at the expense of Medicare patients. They also changed the mix of services offered in the inpatient Medicare market and expanded the surgical market because surgical DRGs are more profitable than medical DRGs. Often, services were cut (Gay et al. 1989).

Controlling Physician Costs

The Prospective Payment System focused on hospitals, but it also had an indirect effect on doctors. Hospitals are the structure or framework, but doctors decide medical or surgical treatment. The PPS, by creating a ceiling on hospital reimbursements, caused hospitals to pressure doctors so as to limit hospital expenditures. But physicians had independent effects on Medicare expenditures and government budgets.

General revenues make up a significant portion of Part B expenditures. After the 1972 Social Security amendments, increases in premiums were limited by increases in Social Security beneficiary payments. Thus, whereas in 1972 beneficiary premiums almost equaled general revenue contributions, by 1995 beneficiary premiums accounted for a little over 27.4 percent of Part B program payments (calculated from Moon [1996, 38] and "Medicare and Medicaid Statistical Supplement" [1998, 28 and 37]. With hospital expenses easing a bit, attention naturally turned to expenditures on the next biggest item, physicians. By 1995, such expenses accounted for 21.7 percent of total Medicare spending (Levit, Lazenby, and Stewart 1996).

In some ways, though Medicare based payments on usual and customary fees, the process was administratively complex and created inequities in physician income and dissatisfaction among physicians. In 1984, Congress froze Medicare physician reimbursements and then limited balance billing (the amount doctors could charge above Medicare). Further, there were significant increases in Medicare beneficiary cost-sharing above increases in Social Security benefits. A final factor leading to change was the passage and implementation of the Prospective Payment System for hospitals. As Oliver points out, PPS "demonstrated that health cost containment was both technically feasible and politically feasible" (Oliver 1993, 120).

Although the Reagan administration did not consider a physician payment schedule program, Congress acted. It froze physician fees in Medicare and ordered the Office of Technology Assessment to evaluate different payment schemes. In 1985, Congress created the Physician Payment Review Commission (PPRC), through an omnibus budget reconciliation act, and ordered it to make recommendations regarding a payment system. It simultaneously ordered the Department of Health and Human Services to develop a fee schedule, based on a resource-based relative value scale (RBRVS). Such a scale was adopted in 1989, again through an omnibus budget reconciliation act. HCFA began implementing the fee schedule in 1992, and it was fully implemented in 1996 (Moon 1996).

A relative value scale (RVS) compares the complexity and time of services offered (Moon 1996). Thus a simple office visit would have a lower RVS than a coronary bypass operation. The fee schedule also contains adjustments for geography, and there is a conversion factor that translates the results into dollar amounts. Additionally, volume standards help in establishing growth rates in physician payments (Moon 1996).

The impact of the fee schedule varied, depending on the kind of service. Fees for office and hospital visits were generally increased; fees for surgery were significantly reduced. It is no wonder that physicians and their associations were unhappy with the fee schedules. Political pressure by interest groups, Congress, and the Bush administration led HCFA to liberalize the fee schedule (Oliver 1993). In 1998, HCFA began using a single conversion factor for all physician services, effectively raising the conversion factor for primary care and nonsurgical care and lowering it for surgical services ("Victory" 1997). The 1997 Balanced Budget Act called for changes in the fee schedule components to be fully implemented by 2002 (Physician Payment Review Commission 1997). By FY 2004, physician spending was down to 17.4 percent of total Medicare spending (Centers for Medicare and Medicaid Services 2004b).

The figures through 2002 show the impact of cost controls, especially the Balanced Budget Act of 1997. Consider the 1998–2002 period by comparison. Overall health expenditures increased by about 35 percent, and federal health expenditures increased by about 37 percent. Medicare expenditures, on the other hand, grew by only about 27 percent during the same time period (Centers of Medicare and Medicaid Services 2004b).

The Balanced Budget Act of 1997 also focused on physician reimbursement and created a problem that remains to this day, known as the sustainable growth rate (SGR). The idea behind this was to put a leash on physician payments (Part B) as part of the reimbursement rates that CMS sets each year. SGR has resulted in cutbacks in physician payments. The problem, apart from the impact on physicians, is that the cutbacks actually made each year have been less than those targeted under the program. The differences become cumulative. So by 2010, physician reimbursement should have been cut by 21 percent (American Medical Association 2009).

Each year Congress is faced with the decision of whether to allow the scheduled cuts to take place or to change the reimbursements. Naturally, physicians and their organizations such as the American Medical Association oppose the cuts. Physicians are unhappy with the Medicare program because of the relatively low reimbursement rates, higher than Medicaid but lower than for privately insured patients. Congress has responded by either not allowing the cuts to take place or, in some cases, increasing reimbursements to physicians (American Medical Association 2009). This yearly ritual is known as the "doc fix." But each year that Congress delays action, the targeted cuts get bigger. Recall the 2010 cumulative figure. For 2013, the cumulative cuts would be 27 percent (Congressional Budget Office 2012). Actually allowing the SGR reimbursement cuts to take effect would reduce Medicare spending by over $200 billion (Walker 2011).

What Congress needs is a permanent solution, rather than a yearly one, to this problem. However, while there are steps that could be taken, including repealing or resetting the sustainable growth rate (see Congressional Budget Office 2012; Walker 2011), no such solution is in sight. In late 2013, there was some inkling that Congress might permanently address the issue in 2014 (Rovner 2013).

Reorganizing Payment Mechanisms and Service Delivery

Another possible set of reforms would reorganize how services are delivered. One such reform, which the Centers for Medicare and Medicaid Services is currently experimenting with, is bundled payments. Under such a system, similar to DRGs but broader, when a patient experiences a health incident, such as a heart attack, Medicare would pay one amount for all the care by all the providers. This would end or trim fee-for-service.

A second reorganizational reform, similar in some ways to the bundle payment idea, is accountable care organizations. Here the organization would be responsible for the care of the patient through the entire range of services, such as hospital and post-hospital. Both reforms were included in the Affordable Care Act.

THE PROBLEM OF LONG-TERM CARE

Although the impetus behind the nation's quest for health care reform is public dissatisfaction over glaring deficiencies in America's acute-care health system—primarily excessive cost and the inability of millions of Americans to get health insurance—the way the nation provides for the financing and delivery of long-term care (LTC) may be even more badly in need of reform. Strong considerations, both public policy and moral, argue for addressing health care for the uninsured first, before long-term care. Yet no other part of the health care system generates as much passionate discontent as does long-term care. (Weiner and Illston 1994, 17)

As we saw in the discussion of the Medicare Catastrophic Coverage Act, one of the important gaps in Medicare pertains to long-term care. We begin this section by looking at some of the data concerning long-term care.

A first point is the significant increase in expenditures on nursing homes. In 1970, about $4 billion was spent on nursing homes. By 1997, that figure had risen to $74.4 billion, an increase of 1,860 percent. In 2010, nursing home expenditures rose to $143.1 billion, an increase of more than 192 percent over the 1997 figure (Centers for Medicare and Medicaid Services 2011b).

Second, Medicare (and most private medical insurance) focuses on short-term or acute care. It provides limited coverage for skilled nursing care, and then only after a hospital episode on physician orders. The bulk of spending on nursing homes is from Medicaid and out-of-pocket expenditures. Of the $143.1 billion spent on nursing homes nationally in 2010, Medicare accounted for only about 22 percent. By contrast, Medicaid accounted for almost 32 percent, and out-of-pocket payments accounted for a little over 28 percent of nursing home expenditures (calculated from Centers for Medicare and Medicaid Services 2011b).

Having looked at expenditure data, we can look at the population likely to need long-term care. The number of elderly (those sixty-five and over) is growing rapidly, and the segment of the elderly population growing the fastest is eighty-five and older. Thus there are projections that the need for long-term-care services, especially nursing homes, will double over the next twenty to thirty years. For example, one projection is that the nursing home population will increase to 3.5 million people by 2030 (Administration on Aging n.d.). Similar increases are projected for the use of home healthcare and hospice services. One reason is the growth in the number of the elderly population and their increased life span. Another reason is the surge in disabilities among the elderly. This includes the rising number of people with AIDS who survive the disease because of medications, the increasing prevalence of obesity and the chronic diseases that accompany it, and the increasing incidence of asthma within the population (Gittler 2009).

The nursing home industry was born of two actions by the federal government. One, in 1950, was an amendment to the Social Security Act prohibiting payments to residents living in institutional settings, such as boardinghouses, that did not provide healthcare. The other major development was the establishment of Medicaid. Though Medicaid does not pick up all the nursing home costs, it does pay for the medically indigent in nursing homes. These two developments created a situation in which long-term care became synonymous with nursing homes.

Despite the relatively small number of the elderly in nursing homes, the threat of a nursing home stay is that it can wipe out lifetime savings. In 2011, the national median daily rate for a semiprivate room in a nursing home was $200, or $71,200 a year. Nor is home healthcare cheap, costing about $19 an hour. Adult day healthcare has a median cost of $61 a day, over $21,000 a year. The median cost of living in an assisted living facility is $39,000 (Genworth Financial 2012). The impact of these high costs should be compared to the income available to the elderly. While the baby boomer generation is relatively better prepared for retirement than previous (and perhaps future) generations, they are hardly wealthy. Just over half of elderly Social Security beneficiaries depend on the program for more than half of their income, especially minority groups (Caldera 2012). Social Security benefits are not overly generous. The average monthly benefit for a retired worker in 2012 was $1,230, with a maximum monthly benefit of $2,513 (Social Security Administration 2012). To put this into perspective, compare the above numbers on the cost of long-term care with the yearly benefits from Social Security: its average is $14,760 and the maximum is $30,156, less than the cost of living in an assisted living facility and much less than the cost of living in a nursing home. And those who receive the maximum are more likely to have other sources of income, such as retirement accounts and pensions, than those at the lower end.

Long-term care thus presents several problems at different levels. At the level of the individual, the problem is financial: being able to afford long-term care, or in some cases being able to arrange it. From the standpoint of government, the problem is long-term care's ever-increasing costs. From a societal standpoint, the problem is the increasing demand for long-term care in the twenty-first century.

Much care for the elderly is given in the home by relatives, that is, unpaid informal assistance. This includes meals, transportation, and home healthcare. Only a small minority of the elderly at any one time live in a nursing home. Relatives (mainly spouses and children) caring for the elderly need help and understanding as they deal with work and home conflicts (Tilly, Goldenson, and Kasten 2001). One way that these informal caregivers, the overwhelming majority of whom are women, can be assisted is by employers (both public and private) providing options for their employees that will help them assist their disabled relatives, such as stronger medical and family leave policies.

An alternative to informal home care and nursing homes (institutionalization) is the use of home healthcare agencies. Under Parts A and B, Medicare will pay for services if the enrollee is "under the care of a physician, confined to home, and need[s] skilled nursing services on an intermittent basis" (Moon 1996, 79; see also Centers for Medicare and Medicaid Services 2004a, 27). Since 1989, after a Supreme Court decision, Medicare has relaxed eligibility requirements for home healthcare. Medicare will pay 100 percent of home healthcare visits and 80 percent of durable equipment costs (Centers for Medicare and Medicaid Services 2012a). The result has been a massive increase in use of services and increased costs. In 2004, total home healthcare expenditures were $43.8 billion, of which Medicare paid $15.5 billion or 35.8 percent. By 2010, total home healthcare expenditures had increased to $70.2 billion, of which Medicare paid $31.5 billion or 44.9 percent (calculated from Centers for Medicare and Medicaid Services 2011a, 2011b).

The major change that occurred in regard to home healthcare agencies came in the Balanced Budget Act of 1997. It called for a prospective payment system, similar to what already existed for hospital and physician services, for nursing homes, home healthcare agencies, and hospice services.

Long-Term Care Insurance

One policy alternative for addressing the cost of long-term care is long-term care (LTC) insurance. LTC is an indemnity type policy. It pays a certain amount per day that the recipient is in a facility, usually with some limits on how long the policyholder will be covered (Congressional Budget Office 2004). Insurance could be sold to the elderly, say when they become sixty-five years old, or to younger people where they work so that a reserve fund could be established.

Long-term care insurance is not cheap, and its premiums depend on the age of the holder at the time the policy is purchased. A forty-year-old, on average, would pay an annual premium of $1,741 (2008 numbers). A sixty-year-old would pay, on average, $2,329, and a seventy-year-old would pay, on average, $4,515 (Tumlinson, Aguiar, and Watts 2009). The difference in costs is due to the greater likelihood that older people would need the benefit than younger people.

There are other issues with long-term care insurance. Those purchasing such insurance undergo risk evaluations and as many as twenty percent of applicants are denied coverage based on health risks. The policies are complex to understand and there is a long period between the time when one purchases the policy and when one needs to make use of it, as long as several decades (Tumlinson, Aguiar, and Watts 2009). Often the payments from the policy last for three years at most. The result of all this (along with the unwillingness on the part of many to think about the issue) is that only a small percentage (10 percent) of the senior population has such coverage (Andrews 2010).

The Affordable Care Act of 2010 contained a provision that addressed the long-term care insurance issue. The Community Living Assistance and Services and Supports (CLASS) Act would have created a voluntary program whereby workers would enroll in long-term care policies through the workplace (implying that people with serious disabilities would not be part of the program). Unlike private insurance, benefits would be for the lifetime of the purchaser, and there would be subsidies for low-income purchases ("CLASS Act Provision of Health Care Reform" 2011).

Several provisions of the law led the Obama administration to decide not to implement it. One was that participating in the program was voluntary, a problem that the ACA in general had to face (see chapter 10). Those most likely to need the benefit are also those most likely to participate, an issue known in the insurance world as adverse selection. And the resulting premiums would be much less than for private LTC insurance, between $235 and $391 a month. A third feature is the lifetime benefit versus the normal three-year benefit of private plans. Finally, the subsidies for low-income people would have been substantial.

POLICY OPTIONS: TRANSFORMING MEDICARE

Oberlander (2003) views the process leading to the Medicare Modernization Act as the end of the consensus about what Medicare was supposed to be. Indeed, the process that began with the 1997 Balanced Budget Act led to drastic changes in the nature of Medicare. As we discussed earlier, Medicare represents a significant portion of federal spending at a time when the economy is still recovery from the severe recession (2007–2009) and the deficit is large (though declining). The large baby boomer generation (those born between 1946 and 1964 or so) is entering its retirement stage, healthcare costs continue to increase, and Medicare benefits have improved (especially for outpatient prescription drugs and subsidies to private plans). Johnson and Kwak (2012; see also Wessel 2012) argue that healthcare costs in general are the major problem behind long-term deficits. Because Medicare is such a large part of the federal deficit, it is only natural that thought would given as to how to rein in the future costs of the program, what is called "bending the curve."

Before we look at reform proposals, we should point out that the problems that Medicare faces are at least partly a function of how the American healthcare system is constructed. Because Medicare is specifically designed for the elderly, demographic changes loom large. The baby boomer generation is the largest generation in American history, some seventy-five million people. As that generation moves into the Medicare-eligible age, obviously, the number of Medicare recipients, dramatically increases. It is a shock to the system. A national health system of some sort (see Reid 2009) would not experience this kind of shock because everyone is already enrolled. Even if Medicare is able to control costs per capita, there will be more per capitas. That presents a major public policy problem for the program itself and for the federal government's budget.

Some of the reform proposals are fairly straightforward, amounting to incremental change or tinkering. Such policy tools would include some combination of reducing demand, increasing revenue, and reducing provider reimbursements. Others would fundamentally change the nature of Medicare. Having said that, none of the proposals for change is politically easy to do. Some would affect the beneficiaries. But seniors are a potent political force and would likely push back on policies that would adversely affect them. Others would affect providers, also obviously not a group to be taken lightly. And the future of Medicare became tied to the 2012 presidential race.

Incremental Policy Alternatives

The simplest way to control costs is to raise the age of eligibility for Medicare, currently at sixty-five. Social Security, a program that in some ways resembles Medicare, has raised the full retirement age to sixty-seven. The argument for it is obvious. If people are on Medicare for a shorter period of time, say two years less, Medicare will spend less money on them.

But simple, straightforward, and easy is not necessarily the same as a good or effective policy. There are several reasons why such a change might have little effect. One is that younger seniors, sixty-five to sixty-seven, are generally healthier than older seniors. One thing we know about Medicare, and healthcare spending in general, is that a small percentage (10 percent) of the senior population accounts for a large percentage (42 percent) of Medicare expenditures (Cubanski et al. 2010. Raising the eligibility age will not change this. Aaron (2011) points out that Medicare premiums are based on average costs. Taking out the lower-costing recipients would lead to higher premiums for the beneficiaries.

Further, there is the concern over how those in the two additional years before eligibility will be covered. Many of them might spend those years without coverage, or perhaps be covered by Medicaid, raising that program's costs.

A second possibility is to raise premiums for Part B and Part D. To some extent this has already been done for higher-income beneficiaries, effectively income-related or means-tested premiums. But as Stuart Butler (AARP Public Policy Institute 2012) notes, premiums for the higher-income beneficiaries would need to be higher to pay the full costs of their benefits, and the income threshold for designating the higher-income should be lowered somewhat. A variation on this is to raise premiums on all beneficiaries. This is one example of cost-shifting, asking some (if not all) beneficiaries to pay more.

One question that can be raised is where the threshold should be. If the threshold is lowered, as Butler suggests, then more recipients will face the considerably higher premiums. If the threshold is frozen, then more and more recipients' income will exceed the threshold in future years. Another concern is that higher-income beneficiaries might decide that Parts B and D are not worth it to them and pay for that coverage themselves. This would, again, make premiums higher for the many remaining in the program.

Another possibility is to generate additional revenue by raising the payroll tax. The total Medicare payroll tax is 2.9 percent, split between employer and employee (or the full 2.9 percent for self-employed people). Unlike Social Security, there is no cap or limit on how much of earned income is subject to the Medicare payroll tax. An increase of the total tax to 3.9 percent would eliminate much of the Part A trust fund deficits (AARP Public Policy Institute 2012).

But raising taxes is difficult in the United States, even if by a relatively modest amount (see Wessel 2012). Congress and the Obama administration cut the Social Security payroll taxes in 2010 through 2012, going the other way in a program with a similar trust fund problem. Butler (AARP Public Policy Institute 2012) argues that increasing taxes would slow economic growth and the burden of taxation would be on younger people (because they would be in the workforce the longest). He also argues that raising taxes would eliminate any incentive on the part of Congress to make needed changes in the program.

Another possibility would be to increase cost-sharing, including deductibles (how much recipients have to pay before Medicare begins paying for a service) and copayments (how much of the remaining part of the bill recipients would have to pay). Some have suggested that increased cost-sharing could be combined with limits on out-of-pocket expenses, which currently do not exist. Increased cost-sharing does tend to reduce the use of services. The combined impact of these effects would be sizable. A major problem with this proposal is that it would adversely affect lower-income beneficiaries who would reduce their use of necessary services (AARP Public Policy Institute 2012).

Of course, the most common approach to controlling Medicare costs has focused on provider reimbursements, as we discussed above. The two major examples of this focus are prospective payment systems (applied to hospitals, doctors, nursing homes, etc.) and the sustainable growth rate issue. CMS could certainly reduce provider payments. The problem is that as provider payments are reduced, and begin to approach the levels of reimbursement that Medicaid pays, providers will be increasingly reluctant to take on Medicare patients. That is one reason why the SGR issue has not yet been resolved (the other is the impact of eliminating the SGR on the federal budget).

Another possibility is to require Medicare beneficiaries to enroll in managed care plans. As of 2012, about one-quarter of Medicare beneficiaries were in Medicare Advantage plans. It is not clear whether such plans produce savings or are more efficient than the current system.

One set of incremental plans comes from the National Commission on Fiscal Responsibility and Reform, better known as the Bowles-Simpson report, named after the chairs of the commission, former Wyoming Republican Senator Alan K. Simpson and Erskine Bowles, former chief of staff in the Clinton White House. The commission was formed by President Obama, with members nominated by Obama and Democratic and Republican leaders in both houses of Congress. The purpose of the commission was to develop a set of proposals to address the fiscal problems (slow recovery from the recession, large federal government debts and deficits). While the commission was unable to gain the supermajority needed to adopt the proposals, they did address Medicare. One reason for doing this is that Medicare and Medicaid represent growing slices of the federal budget. Resolving, or at least alleviating, the cost increases would go a long way toward facing those fiscal challenges.

The commission made seven recommendations to restrain cost increases in Medicare (National Commission on Fiscal Responsibility and Reform 2010). The first recommendation, one of the smaller in terms of monetary impact (an estimated $9 billion in savings through 2020), is to reduce fraud in the program by enhancing CMS oversight of Medicare and providing more resources to achieve these savings.

The second recommended change, with a much larger impact ($110 billion through 2020), focuses on cost-sharing. The commission points out that cost-sharing provisions in Medicare are complicated and confusing. The recommendation would replace all the different types of cost-sharing with a simpler plan that would have a single $500 deductible for Parts A and B and a 20 percent coinsurance rate after that. The commission recommended a cap or limit on cost-sharing by lowering the coinsurance to 5 percent after $5,500 of out-of-pocket costs and no cost-sharing after expenses exceed $7,500. Cost-sharing for Part D (the prescription drug benefit) would not be changed (though it was reduced by the ACA).

The remainder of the recommendations collectively are smaller. The third recommendation would prohibit medigap (or supplementary policies) from paying for the first $500 of expenses and also require that such plans pay for no more than half of the next $5,000 of expenses. Recommendation number 4 would extend prescription drug rebates under Medicaid to those Medicare recipients eligible for both programs (dual eligibles). The fifth recommendation would reduce payments to hospitals that engage in medical education. The sixth recommendation, following the practice of private insurance companies, over a period of time would terminate payment to providers for bad debts. The final recommendation suggests accelerating home healthcare cost savings called for by the ACA. The savings from these seven recommendations total $298 billion through 2020.

Ultimately, both House Republicans and President Obama rejected Bowles-Simpson, though not necessarily because of the Medicare provisions. The Republicans, including 2012 Republican vice presidential candidate Paul Ryan, rejected the report because it called for tax increases (though dwarfed by spending reductions). The president's concern were cuts to Social Security and a cap on federal spending (Pianin 2011).

Comprehensive Policy Alternatives

The biggest proposed change is to transform Medicare into a premium-support program. This was a policy favored by a majority of commissioners of the National Bipartisan Commission on the Future of Medicare. As of mid-2012, there were at least five premium support proposals. There is a distinctive political edge to such proposed reforms. For the most part, premium support proposals are supported by Republicans, including the 2012 Republican presidential nominee Mitt Romney and especially his vice presidential running mate, Paul Ryan, chair of the House Budget Committee.

The idea behind premium support is that Medicare beneficiaries would choose from a number of plans and receive some portion of the plans' premiums as a subsidy from the federal government. There would be some regulation of the plans and, depending on the proposal, some minimum or common level of benefits. The federal government's contribution would be a fixed amount. Depending on the proposal, traditional Medicare (i.e., fee-for-service) would stay in some form or be replaced entirely (Fuchs and Potetz 2011).

From the standpoint of the Medicare beneficiary, she would be faced every year with a choice of plans. The beneficiary would choose the plan that would meet her needs as well as be affordable. Some plans will offer more benefits and less cost-sharing, while others will offer fewer benefits and more cost-sharing. Premiums for the former would be greater than premiums for the latter. The beneficiary would also want to know what doctors and other providers are included in the plan. Under premium support, the federal government would pay some percentage of the average premium of all plans, perhaps 80 percent. Plans would likely include some additional cost-sharing, such as deductibles and copayments.

Premium support proposals, according to its advocates, have several advantages over Medicare as it currently exists. One is that it would create conditions under which competitive markets could operate. In this case the competition is among plans rather than providers. Certainly one of the problems of the healthcare system is that it operates much differently than other markets, such as those for automobiles or shoes (for the classic discussion of market failures in healthcare, see Arrow 1953). Creating those conditions would, hopefully, restrain costs, either through reducing use of services or reducing the price for services (Fuchs and Potetz 2011).

A second advantage of such plans is that they reduce the federal government's role in the healthcare sector. The federal government, through Medicare, Medicaid, employee health benefits (the Federal Employees Health Benefits Program [FEHBP]), and the Department of Veterans Affairs, is the single largest purchaser/provider of healthcare services. Especially with Medicare, the federal government is involved in rate setting, quality control, and so forth. Recall the discussion about DRGs and SGR. Under the more radical premium support plans, government's role would be very much constrained.

A third advantage of premium support plans may be even more significant than the other two. Under the current program, Medicare is largely an uncontrolled expense for the federal government. Expenditures depend on a combination of utilization and prices. As the baby boomer generation ages, utilization will increase and expenditures will go up. That is a large part of the problem that Medicare causes the federal budget.

Under premium support, the uncontrollable becomes the controllable. One way of understanding this is to think about the difference between a defined-benefit plan and a defined-contribution plan (Aaron 2011). Medicare and most pension plans (private as well as public such as Social Security) are defined-benefit plans. Beneficiaries are guaranteed a certain set of benefits, and the plan pays for all or part of the cost of those services or benefits. If more services are used, then the plan pays more. That has been the experience with Medicare (of course, the cost of healthcare has risen so that also plays a major role).

Under a defined-contribution plan, on the other hand, the plan is limited to paying a specific portion of, in this case, premiums. Utilization of services then becomes less important. The expense is controllable and knowable in advance because we know how many people will be on Medicare.

Further, premium support proposals allow the federal government to control future expenses. Let's say that premiums, on average, go up by 6 percent next year (a lower than normal amount for many plans) and the federal government's program pays 80 percent of the average premium for all plans. The federal government could decide to maintain its 80 percent rate, or it could decide to allow only a portion of the increase, so the effective premium support might be 77 percent.

The most prominent recent plan is Representative Paul Ryan's (R-WI) proposal, "The Path to Prosperity: Restoring America's Promise." Ryan was the chair of the House Budget Committee, so his proposal drew a great deal of attention ("Proposed Changes to Medicare in the 'Path to Prosperity'" 2011). The Ryan plan took center stage when, in August 2012, he was chosen to be the vice presidential running mate by Mitt Romney; media attention on Medicare greatly increased after Ryan's selection.

Under Ryan's plan, the eligibility age would gradually rise to sixty-seven. In the 2011 version of the plan, new beneficaries as of 2022 could only choose private plans, and the federal government would pay the support to the plans. Under the 2012 revision, new beneficiaries would have a choice between the premium support programs and traditional Medicare (House Budget Committee 2012). Those currently in Medicare or entering it before 2022 could choose between private plans or traditional Medicare. Beneficiaries would go to virtual markets—private exchanges—to pick plans, similar to what is done with Part D plans, the California Public Employees' Retirement system (CalPERS), the Federal Employees Health Benefits Program (FEHBP), the Massachusetts plan, and the healthcare exchanges or marketplaces under the ACA. The Centers for Medicare and Medicaid Services would regulate the plans ("Comparison of Medicare Premium Support Proposals" 2012).

Premiums would be adjusted depending on age, income, and health of the recipient (Fuchs and Potetz 2011; "Proposed Changes to Medicare in the 'Path to Prosperity'" 2011). The premium support payment or voucher would be paid to the plans. Those whose income was below the federal poverty line would receive a medical savings account with $7,500 deposited in it. Those whose income is between 100 and 150 percent of the federal poverty line would receive seventy-five percent of that amount. The deposits would be indexed to the consumer price index ("Proposed Changes to Medicare in the 'Path to Prosperity'" 2011).

An important element of the plan is how the premiums would increase over time. The key to the plan is that competition, a "competitive bidding process" (House Budget Committee 2012, 53), would keep growth under control. Under the original Ryan plan, government's contribution would be based on increases in the consumer price index. Other proposals would be based on changes in gross domestic product (GDP). The modified Ryan plan would base increases, as a backup in case competitive bidding does not work, on GDP plus one-half of a percent. Because healthcare costs exceed either indicator, over time the relative value of the premium support would decrease ("Proposed Changes to Medicare" 2011).

Not surprisingly, there have been many critics of the premium support proposals. One of the more interesting critics is Henry Aaron, an economist with the Brookings Institution. In 1995, Aaron and another economist, Robert Reischauer, coined the phrase "premium support" (Aaron 2011). They wanted to distinguish premium support from the similar concept of vouchers. Voucher proposals would be based not on the cost of services but on government budget considerations. But Aaron thought three changes were necessary to make the proposal stronger and move from a voucher to premium support.

The first change would be to link increases in the value of the voucher (and medical savings account deposits) to increases in the cost of healthcare, rather than linking them to either changes in gross domestic product or overall price changes. The second change would be to create what are effectively regulated insurance markets, providing information so that consumers can make appropriate choices. Third, premiums should be adjusted for factors such as health risk and age. By these standards, Aaron continued, all such premium support proposals had some defects.

For example, Aaron (2011) notes that if the original Ryan plan had been in force over the last twenty years, recipient benefits would have been nearly 50 percent lower than they are now. But that, of course, is the point of such plans.

An analysis of the original Ryan plan by the Kaiser Family Foundation ("Proposed Changes to Medicare in the 'Path to Prosperity'" 2011) found that the plan would not, according to the Congressional Budget Office, reduce the cost of healthcare spending on the elderly. What it would do is constrain government spending on Medicare. Under the current system and projecting to 2022, healthcare spending for a sixty-five-year-old would average $13,500; the federal government's share would be just over 59 percent, and the beneficiary's share would be about 41 percent. Under the original Ryan plan, healthcare spending for a sixty-five-year-old that same year would average $20,500; the federal government's share would drop to about 39 percent, and the beneficiary's share would rise to about 61 percent. It follows that under the Ryan plan, beneficiaries would be paying a larger amount of their income than under the current Medicare program. According to the Kaiser report, the typical sixty-five-year-old in 2022 would have an average income of $25,000. Under the current plan, healthcare costs would amount to about 22 percent of her income. Under the original Ryan plan, it would amount to nearly 50 percent of her income ("Proposed Changes to Medicare" 2011).

The next question then becomes, why would healthcare spending on the elderly increase by so much under the Path to Prosperity Plan? Aaron (2011) and the Kaiser study ("Proposed Changes to Medicare" 2011) provide the same answer. Private plans have substantially higher administrative costs than Medicare, including marketing and sales, and also pay providers at higher rates than Medicare.

While not true for all who propose premium support/voucher programs, Park et al.'s comment about an earlier proposal rings true for some:

> In short, while the idea of introducing more competition into Medicare through the expanded use of private plans has been promoted as a "reform" that can restrain rising Medicare costs, the reality is that the legislation *increases* Medicare costs by overpaying private plans in order to induce more beneficiaries to enroll in them. Examination of the details of the legislation indicates that the ideological goal of privatizing more of Medicare trumped the stated goal of using "competition" to restrain the rate of growth in Medicare costs. (Park et al. 2003, 5)

Alice Rivlin suggests a compromise. She notes the inconsistency of Republican and Democratic arguments. "Ironically, Democrats favor competiton among private plans in the ACA, but oppose it in Medicare, while Republicans push competition in Medicare but want to repeal the ACA. But who expects campaign politics to be logical?" (2012).

Paul Ryan teamed up with Democratic Senator Ron Wyden (Oregon) to propose the "Guaranteed Choices" plan (Wyden and Ryan 2011). The plan, which Rivlin endorses and indeed called for a similar measure, would be a hybrid, similar to Ryan's 2012 revision. New seniors in 2022 would have a choice of traditional Medicare (changes proposed by Democrats) and private plans. Should the program not restrain cost increases, a cap of GDP plus 1 percent would be put in place in 2023. If the cap is exceeded, reductions in payments to providers and pharmaceutical companies would be made, among other changes. It should be pointed out that this element of the plan gives it one year to succeed before taking these other measures, a goal that is nearly impossible. But Rivlin's point is an interesting one, and it falls into the tradition of compromise that can be seen back to the founding of the republic.

MEDICARE AND THE AFFORDABLE CARE ACT

In March 2010, Congress passed and President Obama signed the ACA. The legislation impacts much of the healthcare system, including Medicare. We discuss the ACA in detail in chapter 10; here we briefly summarize the legislation's provisions concerning Medicare. Some of the changes provide additional benefits to Medicare recipients (and increase expenditures), and some seek to control costs.

One important change provided in the ACA is the shrinking of the "doughnut hole" that is part of Part D. Recall that after a certain point ($2,250), Medicare recipients would pay for their entire drug costs up to about $5,100. That "hole" will began to shrink in 2010 with small rebates, and by 2020 recipients would have to pay only 25 percent of drug costs in the hole ("Summary of Key Changes to Medicare in 2010 Health Reform Law" 2010).

A second change is to eliminate cost-sharing for specified prevention benefits. A third set of changes is designed to either provide for more revenue for the program or reform or cut provider payments. One change, mentioned above, is reduction of payments to Medicare Advantage plans. Another change is in provider payments, with some reductions in payments to specialists but increases in payments to primary care physicians. Income-related premiums will be instituted for the Part D benefit as will a higher payroll tax for the Part A trust fund targeted at high-income wage earners.

Other changes focus on payment structure and reorganization. These include bundled payments (discussed above) and accountable care organizations ("Summary of Key Changes to Medicare in 2010 Health Reform Law" 2010).

CONCLUSION: THE POLITICS AND POLICY OF MEDICARE

> The challenges posed by rising costs today combined with the future burdens that will arise from an aging population will require that changes be made in Medicare. But we should not begin this process of reassessment under the mistaken claim that the program is a failure. (Moon n.d.)

Financial considerations have been an important part of the politics and policy deliberations surrounding Medicare since the program's inception. One such problem, already mentioned, is the sheer size of the program combined with its rapid growth and its impact on the federal budget. Another aspect is that the increase in the size of Medicare beneficiary population (especially as the massive baby boom generation begins to retire) places increased pressure on Medicare. This is most clearly seen in estimates that the Hospital Insurance (Part A) Trust Fund is expected to be depleted by 2024 (Boards of Trustees 2012). The trust fund and budget impacts of Medicare came together in the politics of balanced budgets in the twenty-first century.

On the one hand, there have been enhancements of Medicare benefits. The Medicare Modernization Act, however controversial, represents a major, but not the only, example. Beginning January 1, 2005, there were new preventive benefits, such as physical exams and screening for diabetes, elevated blood pressure, and hearing and vision losses (Rainey 2004). On the other hand, there are continual warnings that the financial future of Medicare is bleak. Not all researchers are quite as alarmed as the authors of these reports. Haase (2004) points out that long-range projections are notoriously inaccurate (see also Johnson and Kwak 2012). He also notes that the aging of the population is only a small factor in increased medical costs. Increased utilization of services and medical price inflation are more important factors. These two factors affect all costs, not just Medicare (see chapter 7).

Medicare remains a popular program among the population at large. This can be seen in public opinion polls during the 2012 election. The selection of Paul Ryan as the Republican vice presidential candidate placed his Medicare premium support proposal and Medicare in general front and center on the public agenda. An August 2012 poll found that majorities from both parties supported Medicare as it currently existed over the premium support plan. Further, Medicare was considered a more important issue than the ACA. Only the cost of healthcare exceeded Medicare as a concern ("Public Opinion on Health Care Issues" 2012; Viebeck 2012). And Medicare has done a better job of controlling costs than the healthcare system as a whole and private insurance in particular (Miller 2012).

But problems remain in both the long and the short term. First, the cost of Medicare and the increases in those costs affect both recipients and the federal government. Second, as the baby boom generation began retiring in 2010–11, additional pressures were placed on the program. Additionally, Medicare has significant gaps in its coverage, particularly in long-term care. Even with the new prescription drug benefit, financial pressure on beneficiaries will remain. One estimate is that retirees will need about $108,000 to pay for medical costs not covered by Medicare if they live to be eighty and $300,000 if they live to be ninety-five (Bowman 2005).

The past four plus decades have seen significant change in the structure of Medicare. The 1980s saw the imposition of fee schedules for hospitals and physicians and the beginning of Medicare managed care. The Balanced Budget Act of 1997 brought more potentially fundamental restructuring of Medicare. It extended fee schedules to other providers (e.g., home healthcare agencies) and instituted the Medicare+Choice program, which increased the types of plans beneficiaries could choose, even giving some (the wealthier ones) an opportunity to effectively drop out of the program. The 2003 Medicare Modernization Act created even more changes and challenges. It provided a prescription drug benefit, however limited it might be, and revamped the managed care program (Medicare Advantage). At the same time, it increased the fiscal pressure through the new benefits and provisions that create new threats (the 45 percent cap on general revenue funding). The ACA also promises changes, including savings to the program.

The consensus that had existed from the beginning of the program about what Medicare would be is dissolving. Oberlander (1997, 2003) argues that the politics of Medicare up to 1994 led to a consensus, first that Medicare would be a public program, one that was operated by the federal government. The other element of the consensus was that the politics of Medicare was bipartisan, supported by Republicans and Democrats. The politics of Medicare subsequent to the November 1994 elections saw the unraveling of the consensus. Medicare was depicted by some as a failure, a throwback to the 1960s Great Society programs, and a problem of intergenerational equity (younger people paying for older people). Medicare+Choice was the result, with its medical savings accounts and private fee-for-service provisions. This has been supplanted by the MMA.

One simple example will show the changing nature of Medicare. From its beginning until the mid-1990s, Medicare was the equivalent of a universal national health insurance program for the elderly (Reid 2009). All seniors were eligible, and all had the same benefits, regardless of residence (unlike Medicaid). The MMA changed this by making it more of (though not nearly entirely) a means- or income-tested program, more like Medicaid or welfare. This is done by giving subsidies and more generous benefits to low-income recipients and by having higher Part B premiums for higher-income seniors (Moon 2004; Pauly 2004).

The Balanced Budget Act of 1997 had, for a while, protected the fiscal future of Medicare. This was combined with a vibrant economy in the late 1990s and the brief reappearance of federal budget surpluses during the Clinton administration. But the new legislation and the reappearance of substantial budget deficits in the twenty-first century have placed Medicare in a more precarious financial position.

A variety of proposals have been suggested that would affect Medicare in the twenty-first century, from the incremental, tinkering type to dramatically changing the nature of the program. The debate over the future of Medicare is part of a larger debate, about not only government deficits and balanced budgets, but also the role of government in American society.

The twenty-first-century Medicare program is being built around the ideas found in the Balanced Budget Act of 1997, the Medicare Modernization Act of 2003, and the Affordable Care Act of 2010. We live in a brave and scary new world.

STUDY QUESTIONS

1. Medicare as it is currently configured is the product of accommodations made over the years, starting from the original 1965 legislation. What were those accommodations? Who was accommodated? Why were they accommodated? What has been the impact of those accommodations?

2. A number of researchers/experts have argued that Medicare (along with Medicaid) will have an important negative impact on federal budget deficits. Why might that be the case? Do you agree that Medicare will lead to increased federal budget deficits? Republicans and Democrats disagree on the potential impact of Medicare on federal budget deficits. What are their disagreements? Who do you agree with? Why?

3. Write an essay in which you discuss the objective, structure, eligibility/coverage requirements, and benefits and services provided by Medicare.

4. The chapter has the following statement: "Ending Medicare as we know it." What does this mean? What are the nature of the changes? Have they strengthened or improved Medicare?

5. In the chapter on the safety net (chapter 6), we offer the following definition of the concept "underinsured": individuals and families who spend at least 10 percent of their income on healthcare (including premiums). By that definition, many Medicare beneficiaries are underinsured. Do you think this is a problem that should be addressed? Why? If so, what changes would you recommend?

6. A frequently suggested Republican proposal to reform Medicare is to transform it into a voucher or premium support program (defined contribution program). What are the advantages and disadvantages of this proposal? Why do you think Republicans rather than Democrats have proposed this? If it were adopted, how would it affect Medicare beneficiaries?

REFERENCES

Aaron, Henry J. 2011. "Medicare Reform: Rhetoric Versus Substance." Washington, DC: Brookings Institution.

AARP Public Policy Institute. 2012. "Options for Reforming Medicare." Washington, DC: AARP.

Administration on Aging. n.d. "Aging into the Twenty-First Century." Washington, DC: U.S. Department of Health and Human Services. Online at www.aoa.gov/AoARoot/Aging_Statistics/future_growth/aging21/health.aspx#Nursing.

Altman, Drew E. 2004. "The New Medicare Prescription-Drug Legislation." *New England Journal of Medicine* 350, no. 1 (January 1): 9–10.

American Medical Association. 2009. "Medicare Physician Payment System: Permanently Reforming the Sustainable Growth Rate (SGR)." Washington, DC: American Medical Association.

Andrews, Michelle. 2010. "Few Senionrs Have Long-Term Care Insurance." Kaiser Health News.

Antos, Joseph, and John E. Calfee. 2004. "Of Sausage-Making and Medicare." *Health Policy Outlook* (January–February). Washington, DC: American Enterprise Institute for Public Policy Research. Online at www.aei.org.

Arrow, Kenneth J. 1953. "Uncertainty and the Welfare Economics of Medical Care." *American Economic Review* 53, no. 5: 941–973.

Baicker, Katherine, and Michael E. Chernew. 2011. "The Economics of Financing Medicare." *New England Journal of Medicine* 10, no. 1056 (July 28): e7(1)–e7(3).

Biles, Brian; Geraldine Dallek; and Lauren Hersch Nicholas. 2004. "Medicare Advantage: Déjà Vu All Over Again?" *Health Affairs* (December 15): W4–586–W4–597. Online at www.healthaffairs.org.

Boards of Trustees, Federal Hospital Insurance and Federal Supplementary Medical Insurance Trust Funds. 2012. "2012 Annual Report of the Boards of Trustees, Federal Hospital Insurance and Federal Supplementary Medical Insurance Trust Funds." Washington, DC.

Bowman, Lee. 2005. "Older Americans Fear Health Costs." *Detroit News,* June 29.

Brown, Randall S.; Dolores G. Clement; Jerold W. Hill; Sheldon M. Retchin; and Jeanette W. Bergeron. 1993. "Do Health Maintenance Organizations Work for Medicare?" *Health Care Financing Review* 15, no. 1 (Fall): 7–23.

"The Bush Prescription Drug Plan." 2000. *New York Times,* September 11.

Cai, Xiaomei, et al. 2008. "Pitching Private Medicare Plans: An Analysis of Medicare Advantage and Prescription Drug Plan Advertising." Menlo Park, CA: Kaiser Family Foundation.

Caldera, Selena. 2012. "Social Security: Who's Counting on It?" Washington, DC: AARP Public Policy Institute.

Caplan, Craig, and Lori Housman. 2004. "Redefining Medicare's Long-Term Financial Health: A Closer Look at the 'Medicare Funding Warning' in the Trustees' Report." Public Policy Institute Issue Brief #67 (June). Washington, DC: AARP.

Center for American Progress. 2004. "Administration Threatened Truth-Teller on Medicare Bill." March 12. Online at americanprogress.org.

Centers for Medicare and Medicaid Services. n.d. "Medicare Enrollees." Washington, DC: Centers for Medicare and Medicaid Services.

———. 2004a. *Your Medicare Benefits.* Washington, DC: Centers for Medicare and Medicaid Services.

———. 2004b. "2004 CMS Statistics." Washington, DC: Centers for Medicare and Medicaid Services.

———. 2011a. "Medicare and Medicaid Statistical Supplement, 2011." Washington, DC: U.S. Department of Health and Human Services.

———. 2011b. "National Health Expenditures 2011." Washington, DC: U.S. Department of Health and Human Services.

———. 2012a. "Medicare and Home Health Care." Washington, DC: U.S. Department of Health and Human Services.

———. 2012b. "National Health Expenditures by Type of Service and Source of Funds: Calendar Years 1960 to 2010." Washington, DC: Centers for Medicare and Medicaid Services.

———. 2013. "Medicare 2013 & 2014 Costs at a Glance. Washington, DC: Centers for Medicare and Medicaid Services.

Chait, Jonathan. 2004. "Power from the People: The Case Against George W. Bush, Part II." *New Republic* 231, no. 4671 (July 26): 15–19.

"CLASS Act Provision of Health Care Reform Depicts a Practical but Disappointing Reality." 2011. Online at www.news-medical.net/news/20111105/CLASS-Act-provision-of-health-care-reform-depicts-a-practical-but-disappointing-reality.aspx.

Cohen, Richard E.; Kirk Victor; and David Baumann. 2004. "The State of Congress." *National Journal* 36, no. 2 (January 10): 82–105.

Committee on Energy and Commerce. 2009. "Profits, Marketing, and Corporate Expenses in the Medicare Advantage Market." Washington, DC: U.S. House of Representatives, Committee on Energy and Commerce, Majority Staff.

"Comparison of Medicare Premium Support Proposals." 2012. Menlo Park, CA: Kaiser Family Foundation.

Congressional Budget Office. 1997. *Predicting How Changes in Medicare's Payment Rates Would Affect Risk Sector Enrollment and Costs.* Washington, DC: Congressional Budget Office.

———. 2004. "Financing Long-Term Care for the Elderly." Washington, DC: Congressional Budget Office (December).

———. 2012. "Medicare's Payments to Physicians: The Budgetary Impact of Alternative Policies Relative to CBO's March 2012 Baseline." Washington, DC: Congressional Budget Office.

Cook, Karen, et al. 1983. "A Theory of Organizational Response to Regulation: The Case of Hospitals." *Academy of Management Review* 8, no. 2 (April): 193–205.

Cubanski, Juliette. 2009. "Update on Medicare Spending and Financing and Highlights from the 2009 Medicare Trustees' Report." Menlo Park, CA: Kaiser Family Foundation.

Cubanski, Juliette, et al. 2010. "Medicare Chartbook: Fourth Edition 2010." Menlo Park, CA: Kaiser Family Foundation.

———. 2012. "Health Care on a Budget." Menlo Park, CA: Kaiser Family Foundation.

Dao, James. 2000. "On the Streets of Baltimore, the Word on Medicare is 'Expand,' Not 'Overhaul.'" *New York Times,* September 8.

"Different Types of Medicare Advantage Plans." 2012. Washington, DC: Centers for Medicare and Medicaid Services.

"The Diversity of Dual Eligible Beneficiaries: An Examination of Services and Spending for People Eligible for both Medicaid and Medicare." 2012. Menlo Park, CA: Kaiser Commission for Medicaid and the Uninsured.

Feder, Barbara. 2002. "Prescription Plan Wouldn't Cover All." *San Jose Mercury News,* January 30.

Feder, Judith M. 1977. *Medicare: The Politics of Federal Hospital Insurance.* Lexington, MA: DC Heath.

Freudenheim, Milt. 1997. "Medicare H.M.O.'s to Trim Benefits for the Elderly." *New York Times,* December 2.

Fuchs, Beth, and Lisa Potetz. 2011. "The Nuts and Bolts of Medicare Premium Support Proposals." Menlo Park, CA: Kaiser Family Foundation.

Gay, E. Greer, et al. 1989. "An Appraisal of Organizational Response to Fiscally Constraining Regulation: The Case of Hospitals and DRGs." *Journal of Health and Social Behavior* 30, no. 1 (March): 41–55.

Genworth Financial. 2012. "Genworth 2012 Cost of Care Survey." Richmond, VA: Genworth Financial.

Gibson, Robert M., et al. 1984. "National Health Expenditures, 1983." *Health Care Financing Review* 6, no. 2 (Winter):1–29.

Gittler, Josephine. 2009. "Government Regulation and Oversight of Nursing Homes: Improving Quality of Care for Nursing Home Residents and Protecting Residents from Abuse and Neglect." PowerPoint presentation delivered to the Geriatric Grand Rounds, Institute on Aging, Iowa Geriatric Education Center.

Gold, Marsha. 2001. "Medicare+Choice: An Interim Report Card." *Health Affairs* 20, no. 4 (July/August): 120–38.

Gold, Marsha, et al. 2012. "Medicare Advantage 2012 Data Spotlight: Enrollment Market Update." Menlo Park, CA: Kaiser Family Foundation.

"GOP to Unveil Drug-Benefit Plan." 2002. Associated Press, May 1.

Green, Joshua. 2005. "The Hammer Falls." *Rolling Stone* (June 2): 35–39.

Guggenheim, Ken. 2002. "Bush Pushes for Medicare Changes." Associated Press, May 18.

Guterman, Stuart. 1998. "The Balanced Budget Act of 1997: Will Hospitals Take a Hit on Their PPS Margins?" *Health Affairs* 17, no. 1 (January/February): 159–188.

Haase, Leif Wellington. 2004. "The Debate over Medicare Costs: A Primer." New York: Century Foundation. (September 24).

Health Policy Alternatives. 2003. "A Side-by Side Comparison of the Prescription Drug Coverage Provisions of S. 1 and H.R. 1, and the Conference Report." Prepared for the Henry J. Kaiser Family Foundation (November 26).

Hoadley, Jack, et al. 2011. "Analysis of Medicare Prescription Drug Plans in 2011 and Key Trends Since 2006." Menlo Park, CA: Kaiser Family Foundation.

Hook, Janet. 2002. "Senior Drug Plans Killed." *Los Angeles Times,* July 24.

House Budget Committee. 2012. "The Path to Prosperity: A Blueprint for American Renewal: Fiscal Year 2012 Budget Resolution." Washington, DC: U.S. House of Representatives, House Budget Committee.

"House GOP Unveils Final Version of Medicare Package." 2002. Kaisernetwork.org, June 18.

"In 'Rare' Agreement, Republicans, Democrats Say Bush's Proposed Allocation for Medicare Drug Benefit Not Enough." 2002. Kaisernetwork.org, February 26.

Jacobson, Gretchen; Tricia Neuman; and Anthony Damico. 2012. "Medicare's Role for Dual Eligible Beneficiaries." Menlo Park, CA: Kaiser Commission on Medicaid and the Uninsured.

Jaffe, Susan. 2009. "Health Policy Brief: Medicare Advantage Plans." *Health Affairs* (April 29).

Johnson, Simon, and James Kwak. 2012. *White House Burning: The Founding Fathers, Our National Debt, and Why it Matters to You.* New York: Pantheon Books.

Kaisernetwork.org. 2001. "Bush Lays Out Proposals for Medicare Reform, Prescription Drug Plan." July 13. Online at kaisernetwork.org.

———. 2002. "Many M+C Plans Dropping Prescription Drug Benefits or Charging More." January 25. Online at kaisernetwork.org.

Keehan, Sean P., et al. 2012. "National Health Expenditure Projections: Modest Annual Growth Until Coverage Expands and Economic Growth Accelerates." *Health Affairs* 31, no. 7 (June 12): 1600–1612.

Kessler, Glenn. 2011. "Fact Checking the GOP Debate: $500 Billion in Cuts to Medicare." *Washington Post,* June 15.

Kliff, Sarah. 2013. "Part D Was Less Popular Than Obamacare When It Launched." *Washington Post,* June 21.

Komisar, Harriet. 2012. "Key Issues in Understanding the Economic and Health Security of Current and Future Generations of Seniors." Menlo Park, CA: Kaiser Family Foundation.

Krause, Elliott A. 1977. *Power and Illness: The Political Sociology of Health and Medical Care.* New York: Elsevier.

Lave, Judith R. 1984. "Hospital Reimbursement under Medicare." *Milbank Memorial Fund Quarterly/Health and Society* 62, no. 2 (Spring): 251–78.

Levit, Katharine R., et al. 1994. "National Health Spending Trends: 1960–1993." *Health Affairs* 13, no. 5 (November): 14–31.

Levit, Katharine R.; Helen C. Lazenby; and Madie W. Stewart. 1996. "DataView: National Health Expenditures, 1995." *Health Care Financing Review* 18, no. 1 (Fall): 175–214.

Levit, Katharine, et al. 2004. "Health Spending Rebound Continues in 2002." *Health Affairs* 23, no. 1 (January/February): 147–59.

Lundy, Janet. 2010. "Prescription Drug Trends." Menlo Park, CA: Kaiser Family Foundation.

Marmor, Theodore. 2000. *The Politics of Medicare,* 2d ed. Chicago: Aldine.

Marmor, Theodore R.; Donald A. Wittman; and Thomas C. Heagy. 1983. "The Politics of Medical Inflation." In *Political Analysis and American Medical Care,* ed. Theodore R. Marmor, 61–75. Cambridge: Cambridge University Press.

"Medicare: A Primer." 2010. Menlo Park, CA: Kaiser Family Foundation.

"Medicare and Medicaid Statistical Supplement, 1997." 1998. Washington, DC: Health Care Financing Administration.

Medicare Payment Advisory Commission. 2004. *Healthcare Spending and the Medicare Program: A Data Book.* Washington, DC: Medicare Payment Advisory Commission.

———. 2012. *Health Care Spending and the Medicare Program: A Data Book.* Washington, DC: Medicare Payment Advisory Commission.

———. 2013. *Health Care Spending and the Medicare Program: A Data Book.* Washington, DC: Medicare Payment Advisory Commission.

"Medicare Spending and Financing: Fact Sheet." 2011. Menlo Park, CA: Kaiser Family Foundation, August.

Miller, Mark. 2012. "Top Six Myths About Medicare." Online at Reuters.com.

Mojtabai, Ramin, and Mark Olfson. 2003. "Medication Costs, Adherence, and Health Outcomes Among Medicare Beneficiaries." *Health Affairs* 22, no. 4 (July/August): 220–29.

Moon, Marilyn. n.d. "Ensuring a Future for Medicare." Online at www.aarp.org/monthly/medicare3/viewmm.htm.

———. 1996. *Medicare Now and in the Future,* 2d ed. Washington, DC: Urban Affairs Press.

———. 2004. "Medicare Means-Testing: A Skeptical View." *Health Affairs* (December 8): W4–558–W4–560. Online at www. healthaffairs.org.

National Commission on Fiscal Responsibility and Reform. 2010. "The Moment of Truth." Washington, DC: National Commission on Fiscal Responsibility and Reform.

Nelson, Lyle. 1997. "Access to Care in Medicare HMOs, 1996." *Health Affairs* 16, no. 2 (March/April): 148–56.

Newman, Patricia. 2004. "The New Medicare Prescription Drug Benefit: An Overview." PowerPoint presentation. Kaiser Family Foundation (February).

Newman, Patricia, and Kathryn M. Langwell. 1999. "Medicare's Choice Explosion? Implications for Beneficiaries." *Health Affairs* 18, no. 1 (January/February): 150–60.

Noah, Timothy. 2004. "Brad Unbound." Online at slate.com.

Oberlander, Jonathan B. 1997. "Managed Care and Medicare Reform." *Journal of Health Care Politics, Policy and Law* 22, no. 2 (April): 595–631.

———. 2003. *The Political Life of Medicare.* Chicago: University of Chicago Press.

Office of Management and Budget. 2011. "Historical Tables; Budget of the U.S. Government, Fiscal Year 2012." Washington, DC: Executive Office of the President.

Oliver, Thomas R. 1993. "Analysis, Advice and Congressional Leadership: The Physician Payment Review Commission and the Politics of Medicare." *Journal of Health Politics, Policy and Law* 18, no. 1 (Spring): 113–74.

Oliver, Thomas R.; Philip R. Lee; and Helene L. Lipton. 2004. "A Political History of Medicare and Prescription Drug Coverage." *The Milbank Quarterly* 82, no. 2 (June): 283–354.

Palazzolo, Daniel J. 1999. *Done Deal? The Politics of the 1997 Budget Agreement.* New York: Chatham House.

Park, Edwin; Melanie Nathanson; Robert Greenstein; and John Springer. 2003. "The Troubling Medicare Legislation." Washington, DC: Center on Budget and Policy Priorities (December 8).

"Part B Costs." 2012. Washington, DC: Centers for Medicare and Medicaid Services.

Parsons, Talcott E. 1956. "Suggestions for a Sociological Approach to a Theory of Organizations." *Administrative Science Quarterly* 1, no. 1 (June): 63–85.

Pauly, Mark V. 2004. "Means-Testing in Medicare." *Health Affairs* (December 8): W4–546–W4–557. Online at www.healthaffairs.org.

Pear, Robert. 2000. "Drug Benefits for Medicare Are Proposed by Democrats." *New York Times,* May 11.

———. 2001. " H.M.O.'s Plan to Drop Medicare, Calling Fees Too Low." *New York Times,* September 21.

———. 2002. "Drug Plans For Elderly Are Unveiled by 2 Parties." *New York Times,* May 1.

———. 2005. "States Rejecting Demand to Pay for Medicare Cost." *New York Times,* July 4.

Peck, Benjamin. 2003. "Private Insurance Plans & Medicare: The Disappointing History." Washington, DC: Public Citizen.

Physician Payment Review Commission. 1997. "A New Law Changes Practice Expense." *PPRC Update* no. 24 (August).

Pianin, Eric. 2011. "Super Flaw: If Only Obama Had Upheld Bowles-Simpson." *Fiscal Times,* November 22.

Potetz, Lisa, Juliette Cubanski, and Tricia Neuman. 2011. "Medicare Spending and Financing: A Primer." Menlo Park, CA: Kaiser Family Foundation.

"Proposed Changes to Medicare in the 'Path to Prosperity': Overview and Key Questions." 2011. Kaiser Family Foundation. Menlo Park, CA: Kaiser Family Foundation.

"Public Opinion on Health Care Issues." August 2012. Menlo Park, CA: Kaiser Family Foundation.

Quade. E.S. 1989. *Analysis for Public Decisions*, 3rd ed. New York: Elsevier.

Rainey, Richard. 2004. "Medicare Adds Preventive Benefits." *Los Angeles Times,* November 10.

Reid, T.R. 2009. *The Healing of America: A Global Quest for Better, Cheaper, and Fairer Health Care.* Farmington Hills, MI.: Gale Group.

Riley, Gerald F.; Melvin J. Ingber; and Cynthia G. Tudor. 1997. "Disenrollment of Medicare Beneficiaries from HMOs." *Health Affairs* 15, no. 5 (September/October): 117–24.

Rivlin, Alice M. 2012. "The Great Medicare Compromise." Online at brookings.edu.

Rother, John C. n.d. "A Medicare in the 21st Century." Online at www.aarp.org/monthly/medicare3/viewjr.htm.

Rovner, Judith. 2013. "Congress Posed to Permanently Fix its Medicare Payment Glitch. *National Public Radio* (December 19).

Rushefsky, Mark E. 2004. "Ending Medicare as We Know It?" Paper presented at the annual meeting of the American Political Science Association, September 2–5, Chicago.

Rushefsky, Mark E., and Kant Patel. 1998. *Power and Policy Making: The Case of Health Care Reform in the 1990s.* Armonk, NY: M.E. Sharpe.

Serafini, Marilyn Werber. 2000. "Medicare Reforms May Be Too Expensive." *National Journal* 23, no. 39 (September 23): 2980–81.

Shaffer, Franklin A. 1983. "DRGs: History and Overview." *Nursing and Health Care* 4, no. 7 (September), 388–89.

Smith, Vernon; Kathleen Gifford; and Sandy Kramer. 2005. "Implications of the Medicare Modernization Act for States." Menlo Park, CA: Henry J. Kaiser Foundation.

Social Security Administration. 2012. "Frequently Asked Questions." Online at http://ssa-custhelp.ssa.gov/app/home.

Starr, Paul. 1982. *The Social Transformation of American Medicine.* New York: Basic Books.

Steinberg, Earl P. et al. 2000. "Beyond Survey Data: A Claims-Based Analysis of Drug Use and Spending by the Elderly." *Health Affairs* 19, no. 2 (March/April): 198–211.

Steinwald, Bruce, and Frank A. Sloan. 1981. "Regulatory Approaches to Hospital Cost Containment: A Synthesis of the Empirical Evidence." In *A New Approach to the Economics of Health Care,* ed. Mancur Olson, 273–308. Washington, DC: American Enterprise Institute for Public Policy.

"Summary of Key Changes to Medicare in 2010 Health Reform Law." 2010. Menlo Park, CA: Kaiser Family Foundation.

Thomas, Cindy Parks; Grant Ritter; and Stanley S. Walleck. 2001. "Growth in Prescription Drug Spending Among Insured Elders." *Health Affairs* 20, no. 5 (September/October): 265–77.

Thompson, Frank J. 1981. *Health Policy and the Bureaucracy: Politics and Implementation.* Cambridge, MA: MIT Press.

Tilly, Jane; Susan Goldenson; and Jessica Kasten. 2001. *Long-Term Care: Consumers, Providers, and Financing; A Chartbook.* Washington, DC: Urban Institute.

Toner, Robin. 2002. "The Nation: The Prescription Drug Debate." *New York Times,* June 23.

Tumlinson, Anne; Christine Aguiar; and Molly O'Malley Watts. 2009. "Closing the Long-Term Gap: The Challenge of Private Long-Term Care Insurance." Menlo Park, CA: Kaiser Commission on Medicaid and the Uninsured.

U.S. Bureau of the Census. 1966. *Statistical Abstract of the United States, 1966.* Washington, DC: U.S. Government Printing Office.

———. 2012. *Statistical Abstract of the United States, 2012.* Washington, DC: U.S. Department of Commerce.

"Victory: Family Physicians Make Gains in Medicare Fee Schedule." 1997. *AAFD Directors' Newsletter* (November 13). Online at www.aafp.org/dn;/971113dl/2.html.

Viebeck, Elise. 2012. "New Poll Finds Medicare More Important to Voters Than Healthcare Reform Law." Online at thehill.com.

Walker, Emily. 2011. "Medicare Commission Votes to Scrap SGR Pay Formula." *MedPage Today* (October 6). Online at www.medpagetoday.com/PublicHealthPolicy/Medicare/28919.

Weiner, Joshua M., and Laurel Hixon Illston. 1994. "How to Share the Burden: Long-Term Care Reform in the 1990s." *Brookings Review* 12, no. 2 (Spring): 16–21.

Welch, William M. 2001. "Attacks Prompt Lawmakers to Reorder Their Priorities." *USA Today,* September 17.

Wessel, David. 2012. *Red Ink: Inside the High-Stakes Politics of the Federal Budget.* New York: Crown Business.

Wyden, Ron, and Paul Ryan. 2011. "Guaranteed Choices to Strengthen Medicare and Health Security for All: Bipartisan Options for the Future." Washington, DC: U.S. Congress. Online at www.budget.house. gov/bipartisanhealthoptions.

Xu, K. Tom. 2003. "Financial Disparities in Prescription Drug Use Between Elderly and Nonelderly Americans." *Health Affairs* 22, no. 5 (September/October): 210–21.

Young, Katherine, et al. 2012. "Medicaid's Role for Dual Eligible Beneficiaries." Menlo Park, CA: Kaiser Commission on Medicaid and the Uninsured.

5

HEALTHCARE FOR AMERICAN INDIANS, ALASKA NATIVES, AND VETERANS

AMERICAN INDIANS AND ALASKA NATIVES

In the 2000 Census, for the first time individuals were given the option to self-identify with more than one race, a practice that was continued in the 2010 Census. American Indian and Alaska Native respondents who identified themselves with only one race are referred to as the "American Indians and Alaska Natives alone" while those who identified themselves with more than one race are referred to as "American Indians and Alaska Natives combination population" (U.S. Census Bureau 2012). Because of this change, the 2000 and 2010 census data on race are not directly compatible with the 1990 and earlier censuses. The term "American Indians or Alaska Natives" refers to people having origins in any of the original people of North and South America (including Central America), and who maintain tribal affiliation or community attachment (U.S. Census Bureau 2012).

Population Characteristics and Trends

In comparison to African Americans and Hispanics, American Indians and Alaska Natives constitute a very small minority in American society. In the 2010 census, 2.9 million people (0.9 percent) identified themselves as American Indians and Alaska Natives alone. In addition, another 2.3 million people (0.7 percent) identified themselves as American Indian and Alaska Native in combination with one or more other races, that is, combination population. Thus, the total population of American Indians and Alaska Natives alone or in combination with one or more other races totaled 5.2 million or 1.7 percent of the U.S. population in 2010 (U.S. Census Bureau 2012).

The term Alaska Natives refers to all indigenous groups who live in the state of Alaska. Alaska Natives constitute about 16 percent of the state's population and include the three primary groups of Eskimo, Indian, and Aleut. The majority of rural residents in Alaska are Alaska Natives who live in small villages (Barnhardt 2001). For the remainder of this chapter, American Indians and Alaska Natives together are referred to as AI/AN.

According to the 2010 Census, 41 percent of the AI/AN alone or in combination population live in the West. The second largest concentration of AI/AN is in the South, followed by the Midwest and the Northeast. Ten states with the largest AI/AN alone or in combination population are California, Oklahoma, Arizona, Texas, New York, New Mexico, Washington, North Carolina, Florida, and Michigan. Between 2000 and 2010, states that experienced the most growth in AI/AN population were Texas (46 percent), North Carolina (40 percent), and Florida (38 percent). Overall, between 2000 and 2010, the AI/AN population declined in the West and increased in the South. The multiple-race AN/AN population is geographically more dispersed in the United States than the AI/AN-alone population (U.S. Census Bureau 2012).

AI/AN as a group enjoy lower socioeconomic status compared to non-Hispanic whites. Socioeconomic status is generally determined by one's level of education, occupation, and income. For example, in 2010, 77 percent of AI/AN age twenty-five and over had at least a high school diploma compared to 90 percent of non-Hispanic whites. Only 13 percent of AI/AN age twenty-five and over had a bachelor's degree compared to 31 percent of non-Hispanic whites. Similarly 31 percent of AI/AN age fifteen and over worked in management and professional occupations compared to 39.6 percent of non-Hispanic whites. The median family income of AI/AN in 2010 was $39,664 in comparison to $54,620 for non-Hispanic whites. Twenty-eight percent of AI/AN in 2010 lived at the federal poverty level compared to 9.9 percent of non-Hispanic whites ("American Indian/ Alaska Native Profile" n.d.).

There are 565 federally recognized AI/AN tribes and more than 100 state-recognized tribes. Twenty-two percent of AI/AN live on either reservations or other trust lands. Sixty percent of AI/AN live in metropolitan areas. Federally recognized tribes are provided health and educational assistance through the Indian Health Service (IHS) within the U.S. Department of Health and Human Services (DHHS). The majority of those who receive services from the IHS live on reservations and in rural communities. AI/AN living in urban areas receive health services through Urban Indian Health Organizations (UIHOs) funded by the IHS ("American Indian/ Alaska Native Profile" n.d.). Healthcare for members of AI/AN is delivered from a system that is separate from that of mainstream America. This system has evolved from the unique and complex history of interaction between the various AI/AN tribes and the United States government (Shelton 2004).

HISTORICAL BACKGROUND

The immigration from Europe that began in the sixteenth century impacted the historical sovereignty of American Indian tribes and healthcare for their people. The colonizing nations of Europe used the doctrine of discovery as a first step in obtaining the right to land from the local native population. Under this doctrine, the first discoverer had the right to control the land it discovered. The right of the local Indians was relegated to mere occupancy, that is, the right to be on the land without being found guilty of trespassing. Treaties of peace and treaties of war were used to eliminate the right of American Indians to own the land. In return, tribes were provided with some medical supplies and physician services (Shelton 2004). The doctrine of conquest was used to remove Indians who were not willing to move from their land. It claimed that when a nation defeats another nation in a war, it gains the right to the defeated nation's land and control of its people. The United States was born into this established legal tradition based on the doctrines of discovery and conquest (Shelton 2004).

Prior to any contacts with the European immigrants, the North American Indians lived a very healthy lifestyle that included a good diet and natural exercise. The European colonizers introduced many infectious diseases among the native populations, such as measles, cholera, diphtheria, and smallpox. Epidemics of such diseases often wiped out whole tribes, leading to the ultimate subjugation of Native people (Pfefferbaum et al. 1995/1996).

Colonial powers used imperial medicine—European or Western medicine—as an important tool in colonies established by conquest, occupation, and settlement for further colonial expansion. For example, as early as 1780s, Catholic missionaries used live smallpox virus to inoculate Native Americans in Guatemala and southern Mexico. The first recorded inoculation of an American Indian occurred in 1797 (Pearson 2004). Thomas Jefferson ordered Meriwether Lewis to use smallpox vaccine as a diplomatic tool on the Lewis and Clark expedition. One of the major goals of the expedition was to use imperial medicine to advance colonization among the indigenous population by gaining diplomatic and political access to American Indians (Pearson 2004).

LEGAL AND CONSTITUTIONAL STATUS OF
AMERICAN INDIANS AND ALASKA NATIVES

American Indians

Upon gaining independence, the United States assumed the role previously held by England with respect to American Indians. The commerce clause (Article I, section 8, clause 3) and the treaty clause (Article II, section 2, clause 2) of the U.S. Constitution grants the federal government exclusive authority to regulate commerce and to make treaties with Indian tribes on behalf of the United States. The four most basic principles of federal Indian law established early in the United States were: (1) tribes retain all of their inherent sovereignty that the federal government has not encroached upon; (2) the federal government, and not states, is in charge of Indian affairs; (3) the federal government deals only with tribes it has recognized; and (4) the United States has assumed trust responsibility toward the Indian nations (Shelton 2004).

As America's original people, AI/AN hold a distinct legal, cultural, and historical position in American society. Many AI/AN people are entitled to certain services of the federal government as a result of, first, their membership in sovereign Indian nations and negotiated treaties, agreements, legislative enactments, and compacts signed between the various tribes and the federal government and, second, as citizens of local, state, and the federal government (Pfefferbaum et al. 1995/1996). The federal government's responsibility toward the AI/AN originates from a variety of sources, including specific treaties through which land and other resources were given up by Indians in exchange for promises of health and other services such as education. However, the federal government's obligation is often not clearly defined with respect to specific rights and responsibilities and is influenced by courts' interpretations and rulings. For example, courts have ruled that benefits provided to AI/AN by the government are provided voluntarily rather than in response to the federal government's trust responsibility for the Indian tribes; that is, the government's trust responsibility alone cannot constitute a basis for claim against the government nor does it constitute a legal entitlement to benefits. On the other hand, Congress has passed laws that require the federal government to provide the best possible health status to Indians and to provide all resources necessary to the Indian Health Service (IHS) to make that possible (Pfefferbaum et al. 1995/1996; Pfefferbaum et al. 1997).

Alaska Natives

The United States acquired Russia's rights to Alaska in 1867. The Treaty of Cession provided that Alaska Natives would be treated the same as aboriginal peoples in the rest of the United States (Shelton 2004). Between 1778 and 1871 almost 400 treaties were negotiated between the U.S. government and Indian nations. Alaska Natives were not part of these treaties since Alaska did not become part of the United States until 1867. The U.S. government never negotiated treaties with Alaska Natives, and few reservations were created in Alaska. The federal government did not initially deal with Alaska Natives as dependent Indian communities, and it was not until 1905 that a distinction was made between Native and non-Native residents of the territory for the purpose of education (Barnhardt 2001).

Initially, Congress placed responsibility for Alaska Natives under the Bureau of Education, the sole federal agency responsible for Alaska Native services. In 1931, responsibility for Alaska Natives was shifted to the Office of Indian Affairs (OIA) and later to the Bureau of Indian Affairs (BIA) (Huhndrof and Huhndorf 2011). The federal government, through the Bureau of Indian Affairs, pursued its relationship with Alaska Natives on a village-by-village basis. Since the 1930s Alaska Natives have generally been subject to the same policies and are eligible for the same programs as the American Indians (Huhndorf and Huhndorf 2011).

It wasn't until the Alaska Native Claims Settlement Act of 1971 (ANCSA) that the land claims of Alaska Natives were addressed. Native corporations were created to hold settlement funds and lands. In general, the regional Native nonprofit corporations provide healthcare to Alaska Native people (Shelton 2004).

EVOLUTION OF HEALTH POLICY

The federal government's relationship with the AI/AN has always reflected a great deal of ambivalence. As a result, the government's policy toward the AN/AN has vacillated between aggression and paternalism, reflecting two images of the American Indians in the mind of white people: "noble savage" and "ignoble savage" (Pfefferbaum et al. 1995/1996). A vague sense of obligation has guided successive generations of policymakers and often has led to a great deal of fluctuation and inconsistent policies that have been described as "a great patchwork quilt pieced together with fragments of faded, long-abandoned programs and bright, new policies cut from shiny, new cloth" (Pfefferbaum et al. 1995/1996, 366).

Nineteenth Century

At the beginning of the 1800s, primary administrative responsibility for Indian healthcare was assigned to the War Department (Pfefferbaum et al. 1997). The main efforts in the area of healthcare were designed to prevent the spread of infectious diseases such as smallpox. Army physicians undertook emergency measures to curb such infectious diseases among Indians living in the vicinity of military posts (Pfefferbaum et al. 1995/1996; Bergman et al. 1999). In 1824, the Bureau of Indian Affairs (BIA) was created within the War Department and charged with the overall responsibility for overseeing treaty negotiations, administering trade with the Indians, managing Indian schools, as well as handling all expenditures and correspondence concerning Indian affairs.

In 1832, Congress appropriated $12,000 to hire physicians and to provide vaccinations to American Indians (Pfefferbaum et al. 1995/1996). This was the first large-scale smallpox vaccination authorized by Congress, aimed more at protecting American soldiers than protecting American Indians (Bergman et al. 1999). Some health services were also provided through general educational appropriations made available to religious and philanthropic organizations engaged in the "civilization of" Indians (Shelton 2004). In 1849, the BIA was transferred to the newly created Department of the Interior, and thus Indian healthcare passed from military to civilian control (Kunitz 1996; Shelton 2004).

By the early 1830s the U.S government's relationships with Indian tribes had changed and President Andrew Jackson had come to view the tribes as obstacles to American expansion. Consequently, the Indian Removal Act was signed into law by President Jackson in 1830, authorizing him to negotiate with the Indians in the southern United States for their removal to federal territories west of the Mississippi in exchange for their homeland. The BIA enthusiastically advocated the "civilization" of Indians through the creation of the reservations system by negotiating with the tribes for their settlement on the reservations. By 1840, despite the opposition to the act by some of the Christian missionaries, the BIA and the U.S. military had removed and relocated about forty Indian tribes to the west of the Mississippi. Thousands of American Indians, often by force, were made to emigrate to the West.

The Indian Removal Act (IRA) was strongly supported in the South, where states were eager to gain access to land inhabited by the Five Civilized Tribes. States such as Virginia, North Carolina, and South Carolina sought to make Indian land available to white farmers. During the antebellum period (pre–Civil War) the primary factors that contributed to the dispossession of southern Indians were greed, racism, and political posturing (Perdue 2012). One of the common strategies used in the southern states was to categorize Indians as "colored," insisting that intermarriage with African

Americans had tainted native Indian people's blood, thus closing "white" facilities to them and refusing to record them as Indian on official documents (Perdue 2012). As a way of maintaining white power and authority as well as justifying slavery and the dispossession of Indian land, "race" was systematically categorized by rules governing identity, that is, the amount of blood required to be Indian or black. Individuals belonging to several of the Southeast's tribal nations were often reclassified and their collective identity disbanded (Gonzales, Kertesz, and Tayac 2007).

However, the Indian removal policy of the 1830s designed to rid the South of Indian nations with communal land and sovereign powers had fallen short. Following the Civil War, to deal with the federal government's "Indian problem," a policy of assimilation gained favor over the policy of eradication and removal. The main goal of the policy was to try to assimilate Indians into the mainstream of American society by encouraging them to abandon their way of life (Shelton 2004). Under the Indian Appropriation Act of 1871, making treaties with Indian tribes was discontinued. The major tool used for implementation of the assimilation policy was the General Allotment Act of 1887, under which the group title of a tribe to the land on its reservation was abolished in favor of providing individual land ownership. The law also provided U.S. citizenship to allottees via the Fourteenth Amendment (Shelton 2004; Pfefferbaum et al. 1995/1996). By the end of the nineteenth century, the number of Indian tribes had decreased and they were geographically dispersed and isolated.

Toward the end of the nineteenth century, a more organized health service structure for AI/AN was established in the country. By 1880, the BIA was operating four hospitals and employed seventy-seven physicians to serve the Indian population (Pfefferbaum et al. 1995/1996). However, westward expansion and removal of Indians to reservations also produced harmful health effects on them because of a shift away from traditional diet. Many of the health problems faced by the AI/AN today, such as diabetes, cancer, and heart disease, are related to this change. Many traditional healthcare activities were prohibited, and detaining of "medicine men" was authorized. The development of federal healthcare for AI/AN during the period of assimilation helped establish the early framework for the modern AI/AN healthcare system (Shelton 2004).

Twentieth Century

Congress began formally appropriating funds for BIA healthcare services in 1910. In 1912 President Taft sent a special message to Congress summarizing the results of several surveys that described the deplorable conditions of health and sanitation on Indian reservations (Shelton 2004). Congressional appropriations for Indian health services increased from $200,000 in 1914 to $300,000 in 1915 and 1916, to $350,000 in 1917 (Pfefferbaum et al. 1995/1996). World War I delayed further advancement in AI/AN health policy, and it was not until the 1920s that Indian health needs again received serious public attention (Pfefferbaum et al. 1995/1996). The 1921 Snyder Act provided formal legislative authorization for Indian healthcare and provided for regular congressional appropriations (Pfefferbaum et al. 1997). Under the law, formal federal health services were established within the War Department (Bergman et al. 1999). This was Congress's first explicit legislative authorization for federal provision of healthcare services to members of all federally recognized American Indian tribes and for the conservation of the health of Indian communities (Roubideaux 2002).

The Merriam Report, published in 1928 by the nongovernmental Institute for Government at the request of the secretary of the interior, described the devastation caused by land allotment, the failure of Indian education, and the dreadful health status of American Indians. This set the stage for an era of reorganization of health services for AI/AN (Shelton 2004). The Johnson-O'Malley Act of 1934 authorized the secretary of the interior to contract with states and territories for the provision of services, which allowed the BIA to contract for provision of Indian health services.

The Indian Reorganization Act of 1934 encouraged economic development and provided for Indian tribes' self-determination (Shelton 2004; Gonzales, Kertesz, and Tayac 2007).

By the early 1950s, an assimilation policy reemerged. The prevailing political philosophy was that the interests of AI/AN would be served best by assimilating them into the larger American society (Bergman et al. 1999). The Hoover Commission's Task Force on Indian Policy had advocated this policy. Thus, assimilation policy became the formal federal Indian policy during the Eisenhower years (Kunitz 1996). However, assimilation was to be accomplished by terminating federal recognition of Indian tribes, eliminating their reservations, and encouraging the relocation of Indians from reservations to cities, and ultimately the weakening and dismantling of the BIA (Kunitz 1996). Thus, this policy has also been referred to as the policy of termination because congressional acts terminated the special federal-tribal trust relationship with 109 tribes and bands (Shelton 2004). This move was promoted as a way to "free" Indians from supervision and control by the BIA. The result was a marked increase in the Indian population in cities across the country.

In 1954, the Transfer Act moved responsibility for Indian health to the Public Health Service, which at that time was part of the Department of Health, Education, and Welfare (Shelton 2004). The Indian Health Service was established as an agency under the Public Health Service in 1955. Today, the IHS within the Public Health Service is part of the U.S. Department of Health and Human Services (DHHS). The IHS is the main federal agency with primary responsibility for fulfilling the United States' trust obligation to provide healthcare for AI/AN people (Shelton 2004). At the time of the transfer of responsibilities to IHS, Congress had identified four major functions for the IHS: advocacy for Indian health, providing comprehensive health services, providing training and technical assistance, and coordinating health resources between federal, state, and local programs for the benefit of AI/AN (Pfefferbaum et al. 1995/1996; Kunitz 1996).

The American Indian Movement of the 1960s and 1970s brought about a shift from a policy of assimilation/termination toward a policy of self-determination for American Indian tribes. President Nixon specifically rejected the "forced termination" policy of the Eisenhower years in a message to Congress on the grounds that (1) federal responsibility was not simply an act of generosity toward a disadvantaged people but a solemn obligation, (2) the practical result of forced termination had been clearly harmful in instances where it has been tried, and (3) the fear of one extreme policy, forced termination, had produced the opposite extreme, excessive dependence on the federal government (Kunitz 1996). The Nixon administration's Indian policy was embodied in two major pieces of legislation passed by Congress: the Indian Self-Determination and Education Assistance Act (ISDEAA) of 1975 and the Indian Health Care Improvement Act (IHCIA) of 1976.

The Indian Self-Determination and Education Assistance Act of 1975 directed the secretary of the Interior and the secretary of Health and Human Services, upon the request of any Indian tribe, to enter into self-determination contracts or compacts with tribal organizations for planning, conducting, and/ or administering programs that are provided by the federal government for the benefit of Indians.

The Indian Health Care Improvement Act of 1976 contained many provisions designed to increase the quantity and quality of Indian health services and to improve the participation of Indians in planning and providing these services, with the national goal of establishing the highest health conditions for Indians and providing existing Indian health services with all necessary resources to effect that policy. For the first time, the law authorized Medicare and Medicaid reimbursement for services performed at Indian health facilities. The primary goal of the act was to improve the health status of AI/AN. It also authorized services for AI/AN living in urban areas, including establishment of urban health centers (Pfefferbaum et al. 1995/1996). Charles Trimble, the executive director of the National Congress of American Indians from 1972 to 1978, called those years the golden era of Indian policies (Bergman et al. 1999).

The 1992 amendments to the IHCIA of 1976 (a) reauthorized the Indian Self-Determination Act, (b) provided for tribal self-governance demonstration projects through the IHS, and (c) authorized the secretary of Health and Human Services to negotiate and implement a compact of Self-Governance and Annual Funding with tribes participating in demonstration projects (Pfefferbaum et al. 1995/1996).

President Clinton, in 1994, issued executive orders to facilitate tribal involvement in the administration of Indian programs. One of the initiatives undertaken by the Clinton administration was called "compacting." Compacting involves a looser arrangement than contracting and gives tribes more flexibility in their use of government funds. Indian and Alaska Native corporations differ greatly in their use of contracting and compacting with the IHS. Some tribal corporations have participated a great deal in such arrangements, while others have not. The Navajo tribe, for example, has been reluctant to engage in contracting. However, the reality is that they are forced to undertake contracting and compacting in the fear that if they do not, a larger share of the limited funding available through the IHS budget will be absorbed by those willing to engage in such arrangements. Thus, even though contracting and compacting are supposed to be a matter of free choice for tribal governments, the reality is that if they do not engage, they risk losing IHS funding. The result is increased competition not only between tribes but also within tribes for limited federal resources (Kunitz 1996). In 1998, Clinton issued an executive order that further defined the policy of requiring executive departments and agencies to consult with tribal governments. The administration of George W. Bush has continued the policy of tribal consultation (Shelton 2004), as has the Obama administration.

Today, under the broad authorization of the 1921 Snyder Act, Congress every year appropriates funds to the IHS to fulfill the federal government's trust responsibility to provide health services to AI/AN people.

INDIAN HEALTH SERVICE: ORGANIZATION AND STRUCTURE

The Indian Health Service has evolved from a very centralized and regionalized service at the time of its creation in 1955 to a highly decentralized service today involving contracting and compacting (Bergman et al. 1999). The IHS is a division of the Department of Health and Human Services. The division consists of local administrative units called service units. These units provide healthcare in their designated areas, generally centered on a reservation or on multiple small reservations. In Alaska, service units provide healthcare where there is a concentration of Alaska Natives. Service units are grouped into larger jurisdictions administered by area offices. Each area office is responsible for overseeing the operation of IHS programs within its jurisdictions. The heavy reliance on service units reflects the high degree of decentralization that exists in today's IHS (Pfefferbaum et al. 1997).

In addition to health programs administered by IHS area offices, several tribes operate their own health programs and urban projects. There are 12 area offices and 157 IHS and tribally managed service units. Tribal facilities are operated under the authority of the Indian Self-Determination and Education Assistance Act of 1975, Titles I and V, and subsequent amendments. There are 82 Title V compacts funded through 107 funding agreements representing 337 tribes—about 60 percent of all federally recognized tribes. In addition, there are about 231 tribes and tribal organizations that contract under Title I ("IHS Year 2012 Profile" n.d.).

Healthcare facilities consist of hospitals, health centers, clinics, and health stations. The IHS operates 29 hospitals while another 16 hospitals are operated by tribes. Similarly the IHS runs about 68 health centers, while tribes run another 258. The IHS also operates 41 health stations, while tribes operate another 74. In Alaska, tribes operate all 166 village clinics ("IHS Year 2012 Profile" n.d.).

With respect to staff and personnel, the IHS has a total of 15,920 employees of which 70 percent are IA/AN. This includes about 2,590 nurses, 860 physicians, 660 pharmacists, 640 engineers/

sanitarians, 340 physician assistants and/or nurse practitioners, and about 310 dentists ("IHS Year 2012 Profile" n.d.).

Congress's fiscal year 2012 budget appropriation for the IHS was $4.3 billion. Over half of the IHS budget appropriation is administered by tribes through self-determination contracts or self-governance compacts. The IHS's annual budget request is a result of a consultation process involving the IHS and Indian health program representatives ("IHS Year 2012 Profile" n.d.).

INDIAN HEALTH SERVICE: DELIVERY OF HEALTH SERVICES

The federal government, in order to fulfill its responsibility for healthcare of AI/AN, has established a separate system of healthcare. AI/AN are entitled to certain health services as a result of treaty provisions and a long legislative history. There are also certain health services for which they qualify as U.S. citizens and state residents (Pfefferbaum et al. 1997).

The IHS provides a comprehensive range of health services that include traditional public health services along with inpatient and ambulatory clinical services. The IHS places great emphasis on community and preventive medicine. It administers a variety of programs. For example, IHS's Environmental Health Services program provides services in the areas of injury prevention and institutional environmental health. The program helps identify environmental hazards and risk factors in tribal communities and proposes preventive measures. The Sanitation Facilities Construction Program is designed to provide safe drinking water and sewerage systems. The Behavioral Health Program focuses on problems of alcohol and substance abuse, mental health disorders, suicide, violence, and behavior-related chronic diseases in AN/AN communities. The Injury Prevention Program promotes building the capacity of tribes through increased understanding of preventable injuries and finding effective solutions. The HIV/AIDS Program focuses primarily on the care of individuals and facilitating a preventive approach to reduce the impact of HIV/AIDS in AI/AN communities. Since AI/AN have the highest rates of type 2 diabetes in the United States, the IHS Division of Diabetes Treatment and Prevention conducts extensive diabetes treatment and prevention programs and activities ("IHS Year 2012 Profile" n.d.).

IHS is primarily a rural healthcare delivery system. There are three major ways in which the IHS delivers health services. First, the IHS uses its own hospitals, outpatient health centers, and smaller health stations. Second, the IHS contracts with tribes under the Indian Self-Determination and Education Act to operate its hospitals, health centers, and health stations. Third, the IHS purchases services not available through its own facilities from nontribal, private sector hospitals and health practitioners. IHS services are provided free of charge to eligible AI/AN people (Forquera 2001). However, the IHS has a limited reach because eligibility for its services does not extend to all AI/AN for two reasons. First, IHS services are available only to members of federally recognized tribes. Thus, AI/AN who are not members of federally recognized tribes are ineligible to receive IHS services (Katz 2004). Second, IHS services are provided only to AI/AN living on or near reservations. However, today, a majority (over 60 percent) of AI/AN people live in metropolitan areas ("American Indian/Alaska Native Profile" n.d.). These two factors combine to considerably limit the IHS service population (Forquera 2001).

It is important to keep in mind that historically the migration of AI/AN to urban areas was the direct result of the federal government's "relocation" policy in effect during the 1950s. More than 160,000 AI/AN were forcibly moved from their reservations into cities to promote their assimilation into American society. As a result, many Indians including those who are members of federally recognized tribes, lost access to healthcare and other benefits granted to them when they lived on reservations.

As the urban Indian population increased, in part due to the government's relocation program, the need for health services for Indians living in urban areas also increased. Several cities, particularly those designated as relocation sites, independently developed health services for urban Indians. The Indian Health Care Improvement Act of 1976, in recognition of the plight of urban

Indians who lacked access to health services, provided for the creation of an urban Indian health program (Bergman et al. 1999). This was a major departure for the IHS because previously it had not included Indians living outside IHS service areas. The purpose was to make outpatient health services available to urban Indians directly or by referrals. The IHS administers a program of grants and contracts to nonprofit organizations, controlled by urban Indians often called Urban Indian Health Organizations. This is also referred to as urban Indian health program (Forquera 2001).

Urban Indian Health Organizations provide outpatient health services and referrals to urban Indians on an income-based, sliding-scale fee schedule. Thus, this service is not free. The patients are asked to pay what they can afford. Most Urban Indian Health Organizations receive their income from patient fees, public and private insurers, tribal funds, and a mix of public and private grants, including funding from IHS contracts. More than half of the UIHOs are certified as federally qualified health centers, making them eligible for additional federal funds (Renfrew 2006). The services at urban health centers are restricted to primary care, and referrals for inpatient hospital care, specialty services, diagnostics, and the like are at the patient's expense (Forquera 2001).

Today, IHS programs for Indians who live in urban areas include a range of ambulatory medical, dental, mental health, social support, and referral services. IHS urban projects do not provide hospital care directly but give referrals to an IHS hospital located in the area. It is important to note that Urban Indian Health Organizations authorized and funded under the IHCIA of 1976 and its 1992 amendments operate separately from reservation-based IHS programs. Such projects receive funding from IHS as well as non-IHS sources (Pfefferbaum et al. 1997).

Urban Indians, like other American citizens, are eligible for health coverage under Medicaid, Medicare, or the State Children's Health Insurance Program (SCHIP) if they meet the eligibility requirements. However, some Indians do not enroll in public programs because they believe the federal government is obligated by treaty and laws to pay for their healthcare and they should not have to enroll in healthcare programs for the general population. Despite this reluctance, many urban Indians are enrolled in public programs (Forquera 2001). Since UIHOs are recognized by law as federally qualified health centers, they have an opportunity to enroll eligible urban Indians in Medicaid. In their benefit package, state Medicaid programs are required to cover the services provided by federally qualified health centers and such centers are entitled to payments for these services at a specified rate under the law (Forquera 2001).

One of the major changes made by the IHCIA of 1976 was a provision that allowed IHS to bill Medicaid for services provided to Medicaid-eligible patients. This was not the case prior to 1976. Since Medicaid is a joint federal-state program funded on a matching basis, this would have increased costs to the state government. To limit state resistance to this provision, Congress provided in the law a 100 percent federal medical assistance percentage (FMAP). This opened a new stream of federal funding for IHS. However, the Centers for Medicare and Medicaid Services (CMS) has narrowly interpreted this provision to provide 100 percent federal reimbursement only for care provided inside IHS facilities. State and tribal advocates have sought to apply this provision to healthcare services offered to AI/AN through IHS programs outside of IHS facilities. State governments have challenged CMS's narrow interpretation of this statutory provision in courts. Healthcare advocates for AI/AN have argued that the 100 percent federal medical assistance provision should be interpreted broadly to provide full funding for transportation to and from IHS facilities, referrals from IHS facilities, and care provided in urban UIHOs with IHS contracts (Renfrew 2006; A. Schneider 2005).

ACCOMPLISHMENTS OF THE IHS

Since the establishment of the IHS in 1955, there have been considerable improvements in the health status of AI/AN, and healthcare disparities between AI/AN and the general U.S. population have narrowed somewhat. Mortality rates for AI/AN have declined and life expectancy has improved. There have also been major improvements in infant and child mortality and a decline in infectious diseases. In the first twenty-five years of IHS, infant mortality rates dropped 82 percent, maternal death rates declined 89 percent, mortality rates from tuberculosis declined by 96 percent, and deaths from diarrhea and dehydration declined by 93 percent (Bergman et al. 1999).

Between 1940 and 1990 life expectancy at birth among AI/AN men increased by 17.8 years to 69.1 years. During the same time, life expectancy at birth for IN/AN women increased by 25.6 years to 77.5 years. The most significant decline in mortality is for two infectious diseases—tuberculosis and gastroenteritis (Young 1997).

The IHS has been effective in reducing preventable and treatable conditions/diseases but has not had much impact on certain chronic conditions such as diabetes and certain types of cancers (Kunitz 1996). While the burden of mortality and morbidity has decreased since World War II, the relative contribution of various diseases and health conditions has changed, reflecting what might be called epidemiologic transition (Young 1997). Furthermore, despite some of the successes, it is clear that AI/AN still experience significant healthcare disparities when it comes to health status/ outcome, access to healthcare, and quality of healthcare in comparison not only to whites but also to the general U.S. population. In certain areas, AI/AN fare even worse than do African Americans or Hispanics. The topic of healthcare disparities and AI/AN is discussed further in chapter 6.

HEALTH STATUS AND TRENDS

When Columbus arrived in the Western hemisphere, he found American Indians to be clean, fit, and without illness. Today, American Indians have higher occurrences of diseases than other racial/ethnic minorities (Ambler 2003). For example, American Indians have a higher prevalence of disease risk factors such as obesity, hypertension, high cholesterol, and tobacco smoking than other racial/ethnic minorities (Liao, Tucker, and Giles 2003). According to a report issued by the U.S. Commission on Civil Rights (2004, 7–8), "Native Americans are 770 percent more likely to die from alcoholism, 650 percent more likely to die from tuberculosis, 420 percent more likely to die from diabetes, 280 percent more likely to die from accidents, and 52 percent more likely to die from pneumonia or influenza than the rest of the United States, including white and minority population." For all health behaviors and status measures, AI/AN elders report greater risk factors than white elders (Denny et al. 2005). Mortality data also show an excessive overall mortality among AI/AN as well as excesses for specific causes of death (Mahoney and Michalek 1998). Within AI/AN communities, males' death rates exceed those of females of every age up to seventy-five years and from six of the eight leading causes of death (Rhoades 2003).

AI/AN have the highest prevalence of diabetes among all racial/ethnic groups in the United States, and their mortality attributable to diabetes is three to four times higher. They also have the highest rate of premature death from heart diseases among all racial/ethnic groups (O'Connell et al. 2012).

About 18 percent of AI/AN individuals suffer from two or more chronic health conditions. Around 27 percent of AI/AN are smokers, and about 19 percent are binge drinkers. Such risky behaviors are related to cancer, chronic liver disease, unintentional injuries, diabetes, and other heart problems. About 47 percent of unintentional injuries are due to motor vehicle accidents (James, Schwartz, and Berndt 2009).

AI/AN living in cities continue to face a host of health problems. The infant mortality rate among urban AI/AN is 33 percent higher than that of the general population. The death rate due to accidents is 38 percent higher; diabetes is 54 percent higher; and chronic liver disease is 126 percent higher than the general population. The rate of alcohol-related deaths is 178 percent higher compared to the general population (Urban Indian Health Commission 2007).

Table 5.1 shows data about the leading causes of death among AI/AN for 1980 and 2008. It demonstrates that some significant changes have taken place in the ranking of causes of death within the AI/AN community. For example, diabetes mellitus was the sixth leading cause of death

Table 5.1

Leading Causes of Death for American Indians and Alaska Natives: 1980 and 2008

Rank	1980	2008
1	Diseases of the Heart	Malignant Neoplasms
2	Malignant Neoplasms	Diseases of the Heart
3	Unintentional Injuries	Unintentional Injuries
4	Chronic Liver Diseases & Cirrhosis	Diabetes Mellitus
5	Cerebrovascular Diseases	Chronic Liver Diseases & Cirrhosis
6	Diabetes Mellitus	Chronic Lower Respiratory Diseases
7	Pneumonia and Influenza	Cerebrovascular Diseases
8	Certain Conditions Originating in Prenatal Care	Influenza and Pneumonia
9	Nephritis, Nephrotic Symptoms, & Nephrosis	Nephritis, Nephrotic Symptoms, & Nephrosis
10	Homicide	Alzheimer's Disease

Source: National Center for Health Statistics, 2012. *Health United States, 2011.*

in 1980, but by 2008 it had become the fourth leading cause. Two of the top ten leading causes of death in 1980—certain conditions related to prenatal care, and homicide—had dropped out of the top ten in 2008 and were replaced by chronic lower respiratory diseases (ranked sixth) and Alzheimer's disease (ranked tenth). Diseases of the heart had dropped from the top leading cause of death in 1980 to second in 2008. Unintentional injury continues to be a major problem in the AI/AN community. It was ranked the third leading cause of death in 1980 and also in 2008.

Diabetes is one of the most serious health problems confronting AI/AN and is responsible for significant morbidity and mortality rates among AI/AN. Most AI/AN with diabetes have type 2 diabetes, also known as adult onset diabetes, which is characterized by high levels of blood glucose stemming from impaired insulin secretion and/or the body's resistance to the action of insulin. Native Americans have the highest prevalence of diabetes in the world. Furthermore, the rate of diabetes among AI/AN has increased at almost epidemic proportions. In some AI/AN communities, more than half of the adult population suffers from diabetes (U.S. Commission on Civil Rights 2004). For example, a cross-sectional study of men/women ages forty-five to seventy-four in thirteen American Indian tribes or communities in Arizona, Oklahoma, and South and North Dakota, found that Arizona had the highest age-adjusted rates of diabetes—65 percent in men and 72 percent in women. The study also found that in all the communities included in the study, diabetes was more prevalent in women than in men. According to the study, diabetes rates were positively associated with age, amount of Indian ancestry, parental diabetes status, and level of obesity (Lee et al. 1995).

What is troubling is that the incidence of diabetes is increasing among AI/AN at an alarming rate. For example, the number of AI/AN aged younger than thirty-five with diabetes diagnosed through IHS more than doubled from 6,001 in 1994 to 12,313 in 2004. While the rates of diabetes increased among both males and females, the prevalence of diabetes was greater among females than males in all age groups ("Diagnosed Diabetes" 2006).

Diabetes is related to obesity, and American Indians of all ages and both sexes have a high prevalence of obesity. Obesity has become a major health problem in American Indians in the past one to two generations. Obesity is believed to be associated with the relative abundance of high-fat foods and the rapid changes in AI/AN lifestyle—from an active to a more sedentary lifestyle (Story et al. 1999; Welty 1991).

One of the leading causes of mortality in the AI/AN community is heart disease, and the largest percentage of deaths from heart disease is caused by diabetes. Another startling fact is that in recent years, type 2 diabetes has become a significant threat to Native American children. Type 2 diabetes in the past was largely confined to adults. IHS has documented a 54 percent increase since 1996 in the prevalence of diagnosed diabetes among Native American youth fifteen to nineteen years of age (U.S. Commission on Civil Rights 2004; "Diagnosed Diabetes" 2006; Fagot-Campagna, Pettitt, and Engelgan 2000). Perhaps related to the high rate of diabetes in the AI/AN population is the fact that the AI/AN community also suffers from a higher prevalence of visual impairment and normal-tension glaucoma compared to other racial/ethnic groups (Mansberger et al. 2005).

The diabetes rate for AI/AN is more than twice that for whites. Native Americans are 2.6 times more likely to be diagnosed with diabetes than non-Hispanic whites of similar age. From 1994 through 1996, the IHS age-adjusted rates for diabetes were 350 percent greater than the rates for the rest of the U.S. population (U.S. Commission on Civil Rights 2004).

Cardiovascular disease is another major health problem confronting AI/AN communities. In the past, heart disease and strokes were rare among AI/AN. While the general population has experienced a 50 percent decrease in heart disease, it has increased among AI/AN, which has helped widen healthcare disparities. For example, cardiovascular disease rates among AI/AN are twice that of the general population. The soaring rates of cardiovascular disease can be traced to the high rates of diabetes, high blood pressure, and the presence of other risk factors such as poor diet and a more sedentary lifestyle (U.S. Commission on Civil Rights 2004). While the death rates from strokes remain relatively lower for AI/AN (39.7 percent) than the national death rate (61.8 percent), the data point to future problems because at lower age brackets, the risk is two times higher for AI/AN (U.S. Commission on Civil Rights 2004).

AI/AN have the highest rates of smoking by adults among all ethnic groups (U.S. Department of Health and Humans Services 2000). According to a national telephone survey conducted by the Centers for Disease Control and Prevention (CDC) (2000), a sizable percentage of AI/AN suffered from specific risk factors such as high blood pressure (22 percent), high cholesterol (16 percent), and obesity (21.5 percent). In addition, 30.8 percent of AI/AN were smokers. Having more than one risk factor for heart disease is also more common among older AI/AN.

Unintentional injuries are another leading cause of death for AI/AN under the age of forty-four. The age-adjusted injury death rate for AI/AN is about 250 percent higher than for the total U.S. population. The financial costs of treating these injuries are also very high (U.S. Commission on Civil Rights 2004). As Table 5.1 shows, overall unintentional injuries were the third leading cause of death for AI/AN in 1980 and remained so in 2008.

AI/AN are consistently overrepresented among the high-need population in mental health services. According to a report by the Surgeon General of the United States, this overrepresentation may be associated with high rates of homelessness, incarceration, alcohol and drug abuse, and stress and trauma (Satcher 2001). An examination of the prevalence of trauma in two large American Indian communities revealed that members of both tribes witnessed traumatic events, experienced trauma to loved ones, and were victims of physical attacks more often than in the overall U.S. population (Manson et al. 2005).

The most significant public health concerns in AI/AN communities are substance abuse, depression, anxiety, violence, and suicide. Up to 30 percent of AI/AN suffer from depression (Urban Indian Health Commission 2007). American Indians experience the highest rate of suicide of all racial/ethnic groups in the United States (Olson and Wahab 2006). The suicide rate for AI/AN continues to escalate and is now 190 percent of the rate of the general population. Between 1985 and 1996, AI/AN children committed suicide at a rate two and one-half times that of white children. The highest suicide rate for the general U.S. population is found among individuals seventy-four years old and older. In sharp contrast, among AI/AN the highest suicide rate is found within the fifteen to thirty-four-year old age group (U.S. Commission on Civil Rights 2004). At the same time, research also shows that many suicidal young people avoid asking for help. For example, in a study of a sample of 101 American Indians between the ages of fifteen and twenty-one who had thought about or attempted suicide, seventy-four participants indicated that they had avoided seeking help because of largely internal factors, such as embarrassment, lack of problem recognition, or a belief that nobody could help. Participants rarely cited structural factors such as lack of money or service availability as reasons for not seeking help (Freedenthal and Stiffman 2007). Research also suggests that suicide attempts among AI/AN youths are associated with factors such as friends or family members having attempted or succeeded in committing suicide, somatic symptoms, physical or sexual abuse, substance abuse, gang involvement, and availability of guns (Borowsky et al. 1999).

Alcohol abuse is also a significant concern in AI/AN communities and contributes to mental health problems. Studies show that drinkers in the highest risk category for alcohol dependence are also more likely to report drug use disorders, mood/anxiety disorders, alcohol-related physical disorders, and a lower quality of life (Novins et al. 2006).

Overall, little is known about effective mental healthcare services among AI/AN because of the lack of culturally appropriate models of mental health in the AI/AN community (Johnson and Cameron 2001). What is clear is that despite a significant demand for mental health services, there are only approximately 101 mental health professionals available per 100,000 AI/AN compared with 173 per 100,000 whites (U.S. Commission on Civil Rights 2004).

Cancer is another growing concern among AI/AN. While AI/AN have lower cancer incidence and mortality rates than whites, cancer has become the leading cause of death for Alaska Native and American Indian women. Also, the ratio of cancer deaths to new cancer cases is higher for AI/AN than the ratio for all other races (U.S. Commission on Civil Rights 2004). AI/AN have the poorest cancer-survival rates among any racial group in American society. Furthermore, among AI/AN there has been a steady increase in cancer incidence and mortality. Nevertheless, malignant disease is not generally recognized as a leading cause of death among AI/AN (Clegg et al. 2002; Mahoney and Michalek 1999; Sugarman, Dennis, and White 1994).

The most common types of cancer among AI/AN are breast, colon, rectum, and lungs. In eight of the nine IHS areas, death caused by lung cancer is the most common, and 87 percent of all lung cancer deaths can be linked to tobacco smoking (UCLA Center for Health Policy Research 2004). AI/AN have a high rate of tobacco use, especially cigarette smoking, compared to the general population. Epidemiological data from a population-based, cross-sectional study of Southwestern and Northern Plains American Indians ages fifteen to fifty-four years found that 19 percent of Southwestern men, 10 percent of Southwestern women, 49 percent of Northern Plains men, and 51 percent of Northern Plains women smoked regularly (Henderson, Jacobsen, and Beals 2005). It is important to point out that racial misclassification and undercounting are often major obstacles to obtaining accurate and informative data on the AI/AN populations (Swan et al. 2006). In reality, cancer rates among the AI/AN population are shown to be considerably higher when more accurate methods are used to estimate the incidence of cancer (Puukka, Stehr-Green, and Becker 2005).

The good news is that the tuberculosis rate among AI/AN is declining. Between 1993 and 2002, the rates declined 40.4 percent in the AI/AN population. Nonetheless, tuberculosis continues to be a significant public health problem for the AI/AN population (E. Schneider 2005; Young 1997).

CHALLENGES CONFRONTING THE IHS AND HEALTHCARE POLICY FOR AI/AN

The health status of IA/AN is the result of a variety of health determinants such as exposure to risk factors, affordability, availability and accessibility of health services, social factors, and individual behavioral factors. AI/AN have a high poverty rate with nearly one-third of nonelderly living in families with income below the federal poverty level and nearly half living in families with income below 200 percent of the federal poverty level (James, Schwartz, and Berndt 2009). As a result, more than 25 percent of AI/AN are eligible for Medicaid, but only 17 percent report that they are covered by Medicaid or any other public program (Urban Indian Health Commission 2007). Part of the reason is that some AI/AN do not apply for Medicaid even when eligible, and the reach of the Medicaid program to childless adults is limited due to eligibility restrictions (James, Schwartz, and Berndt 2009). One in five AI/AN live in families without a worker. Also one in five AI/AN adults do not have a high school diploma. Among those under the age of sixty-five, AI/AN have the lowest rate of private health insurance coverage of any racial/ethnic groups, and one in three nonelderly AI/AN are uninsured or depend solely on services provided by the IHS (James, Schwartz, and Berndt 2009).

Increasing Funding for the IHS

Critics have argued that one of the major shortcomings of the IHS in providing healthcare services is that it is critically underfunded (Lillie-Blanton 2005; Noren, Kindig, and Sprenger 1998; Warne 2007). In 2003, per capita expenditure for AI/AN health services was only $1,914. In contrast, per capita expenditure for Medicaid recipients was $3,879 in 2003, for Medicare recipients $5,815, for Veterans Administration beneficiaries $5,214; and for federal inmates in the Bureau of Prisons it was $3,803 (Warne 2007). The IHS budget for FY 2012 was $4.3 billion, which amounts to per capita personal healthcare expenditure of $2,741 for AI/AN compared to $7,239 for the total U.S. population ("IHS Year 2012 Profile" n.d.).

One of the consequences of this low level of expenditures is that IHS hospitals provide a more limited range of diagnostic and therapeutic services than community hospitals do in general. Because of the underfunding of IHS and tribal programs and the fact that a significant number of AI/AN are poor, IHS and tribal programs have become heavily dependent on third-party revenue sources such as Medicaid (Warne 2007).

Underfunding also affects the ability to recruit and retain competent healthcare providers, which in turn has a direct bearing on the quality of care received by AI/AN. Overworked staff develop burnout, resulting in high turnover rates, which also negatively affects the quality of care provided. It has been well documented that, historically, the IHS has experienced shortages of doctors, dentists, pharmacists, and nurses. The IHS also faces problems in recruiting and retaining healthcare providers because of the remoteness of some of the health clinics. It is difficult to recruit and retain healthcare providers who are willing to live and work in remote tribal communities (U.S. Commission on Civil Rights 2004). The problem is further compounded by factors such as a lack of parity in pay, insufficient or inadequate housing, lack of jobs for spouses, and insufficient opportunities for continuing education. It is clear that a shortage of healthcare providers negatively affects the quality of care for AI/AN (U.S. Commission of Civil Rights 2004).

Another problem caused by high provider-turnover rates is that AI/AN patients do not receive consistent care from the same provider. This, combined with a lack of resources and the remoteness of healthcare facilities, often leads to misdiagnosis or late diagnosis of diseases, which can negatively affect health outcomes. For example, early detection of cancer can increase the patient's chance of survival, while late diagnosis decreases the chances. Unfortunately, in AI/AN communities, misdiagnosis of a disease is too common (U.S. Commission on Civil Rights 2004).

Thus, the most important challenge is to increase funding for AI/AN healthcare services since it affects access to care as well as the quality of care received. The IHS has been underfunded over the years, and increases in funding would go a long way toward improving the quality of health services provided to AI/AN.

Increasing Access to Healthcare Services

A second important policy challenge for AI/AN healthcare is increasing access to healthcare services and increasing funding for the IHS and tribal programs may help. Research has shown that a lack of health insurance negatively affects people's health because they are less likely to receive preventive care, are more likely to be hospitalized for avoidable health problems, and are more likely to be diagnosed in the late stages of disease. AI/AN have the lowest rate of private health insurance coverage among all racial/ethnic groups in American society. Those who lack health insurance coverage are more financially vulnerable to the high cost of care and end up paying more out-of-pocket costs for care. In contrast, having health insurance improves overall health and could reduce mortality rates of those currently uninsured by 10–15 percent (Kaiser Commission on Medicaid and the Uninsured 2006). Having health insurance coverage increases the chances of having a "medical home" and thus improves access to preventive screening, medical care for acute illness, and ongoing care for chronic medical conditions (Kaiser Commission of Medicaid and the Uninsured 2006).

Availability of medical providers, place of residence, travel time, and financial factors are some of the other major factors strongly associated with the use of healthcare services by AI/AN (Cunningham and Cornelius 1995). High rates of poverty, low rates of other health insurance coverage, and the lack of private providers in many areas inhabited by AI/AN also contribute to less access and utilization (Cunningham and Altman 1993).

The U.S. Commission on Civil Rights (2004), in its report *Broken Promises: Evaluating the Native American Health Care System,* found that structural factors such as high staff turnover and loss of continuity of care, long distances to travel to receive even primary care, lengthy waiting lines upon arrival, and many outdated health facilities act as added barriers to healthcare access.

The U.S. Government Accountability Office (2005) conducted a study of the availability of health services for AI/AN and whether they were accessible to AI/AN in the IHS facility area. The study found that the availability of primary care—medical, dental, and vision service—largely depended on the extent to which AI/AN were able to gain access to the services offered at the thirteen IHS-funded facilities. While IHS facilities generally offered primary care services, access to these services was not assured because of factors such as waiting times between the call to make an appointment and the delivery of service, and long travel distances to facilities or lack of transportation. Waiting times often ranged from two to six months for certain types of appointments, and some Native Americans were required to travel over ninety miles one way to obtain care. The study further found that certain services were not always available to Native Americans. Gaps in services were found in diagnosis and treatment of nonurgent conditions such as arthritis, knee injuries, and chronic pain. Gaps were also found in specialty dental and behavioral healthcare.

Providing Culturally Competent Care

Racial/ethnic minorities often have cultural values that may differ from the mainstream cultural values and influence perceptions about health and illness, healing, and treatment, and can affect nutrition and lifestyle behaviors. This is also true in the case of AI/AN communities. The cultural values shared by AI/AN certainly influence their lifestyle and risk and health behaviors.

In contrast to AI/AN and African Americans, many other ethnic groups voluntarily emigrated to the United States and assimilated into the majority American culture. In the case of American Indians, the majority culture forced its beliefs, values, and practices on them and removed them from their ancestral lands. In addition, many American Indians continue to reside on geographically remote reservations isolated from mainstream culture (Herman-Stahl, Spencer, and Duncan 2003). Perhaps more than any other ethnic groups in American society, traditional AI/AN have consistently resisted acculturation into mainstream society. Many traditional American Indian cultural values such as sharing, cooperation, importance of the group, and harmony and balance with nature are in sharp contrast to the mainstream European-American values of domination over nature, competition and aggression, winning, individualism, the nuclear family, and a preference for scientific explanations of everything (Garrett and Garrett 1994).

Consequently, traditional AI/AN often encounter difficulties when dealing with Western medicine and practices and the mainstream healthcare system. For example, American Indians' emphasis on a nonverbal communication style, avoiding direct eye contact, respect for authority figures, speaking slowly and softly, and the like, may be misinterpreted by mainstream healthcare providers as slow, lazy, uncooperative, passive, withdrawn, and nonassertive. This creates communication barriers and room for misunderstanding between healthcare providers and patients (Garrett and Garrett 1994). AI/AN in general do perceive various barriers to obtaining social and health services based on a mutual misinterpretation of cultural norms and etiquette (Kramer 1992).

Research also suggests a high incidence of behavioral risk factors such as substance and alcohol abuse in the AI/AN communities (Herman-Stahl, Spencer, and Duncan 2003). Such behavioral risk factors are often found to be associated with the cultural values and belief system.

For centuries, many indigenous cultures in America have used nonpharmacologic methods such as sleep deprivation, drumming, pain, and fasting to achieve altered mind states. Prior to contact with the Europeans, mind-altered states were viewed as a social good in cultures of the Plains Indians, associated with a quest for enlightenment, powers of healing, and facilitation of war-making. In more contemporary times, it is common to see the use of alcohol in an Iroquois vision quest as well as the use of nonalcoholic psychotropic substances such as jimsonweed, peyote, and tobacco. The use of such substances and the states they induced occur under the umbrella of religious and social sanctions (Frank 2000).

Some scholars have also traced the roots of the epidemic of alcohol-related problems among AI/AN to a cultural response to the European arrival and the use of alcohol in frontier society. It has been suggested that Native Americans' responses to alcohol were heavily influenced by the example of white frontiersmen who drank a lot and engaged in unacceptable behavior while drunk. Whites also deliberately pressed alcohol upon the natives because it was a very profitable trade good. Alcohol was used as a tool of "diplomacy" in official dealings between authorities and natives. Alcohol was also used as a bargaining chip in the appropriation of traditional land holdings (Frank 2000).

Another area where cultural values play a role among AI/AN is in the use of healers such as herbalists, spiritual healers, and medicine men to deal with their health problems (Marbella et al. 1998). The U.S. Commission on Civil Rights (2004) found that social and cultural factors such as a healthcare system that is insensitive to AI/AN peoples' unique culture, bias among healthcare workers, disproportionate poverty, and low levels of education among AI/AN acted as significant barriers to Native Americans' access to healthcare and contribute to healthcare disparities.

Thus, the third challenge is to increase the number of culturally competent healthcare providers. This would include providing necessary training to healthcare professionals currently serving AI/AN communities as well as increasing the number of AI/AN healthcare professionals. It would require a coordinated educational policy that encourages young AI/AN to enter healthcare profession education by providing more scholarships. Currently there is a significant shortage of minority, especially AI/AN, health professionals and researchers. African American, Hispanics/ Latinos, and AI/AN together make up more than 25 percent of the population, but they make up less than 9 percent of nurses, 6 percent of physicians, and 5 percent of dentists. If fewer and fewer minorities enter health professions, it is likely to negatively impact availability and quality of healthcare services for minorities (Warne 2009). AI/AN's long history of nonparticipation in research processes and policy development has often crated misunderstanding and mistrust about motivations of researchers and policymakers. It is important to include AI/AN in the research agenda for dealing with their health status, as well as in policy discussions and developments that arise out of research findings (Warne 2009).

CONCLUSION

In comparison to African Americans and Hispanics, American Indians and Alaska Natives (AI/AN) constitute a very small minority in American society, but they experience some of the worst health status. Healthcare for members of American Indian tribes and Alaska Natives is delivered from a system that is separate from that of mainstream America. This separate healthcare delivery system has evolved from the unique and complex history of interaction between the various tribes and the U.S. government. The Indian Health Service (IHS) is primarily responsible for delivering health services to the AI/AN populations.

Since its establishment in 1955, the IHS has accomplished a lot and significant progress has been made in improving the health status of AI/AN in certain areas such as life expectancy, infant mortality, and reducing the incidence of certain preventable diseases. Yet, many challenges remain. The AI/AN community suffers some of the worst health indicators compared to other racial/ethnic groups in American society. Inconsistent and often conflicting policies pursued toward AI/AN, such as relocation, assimilation, eradication, and self-determination, combined with apprehension and ambiguities in dealings with AI/AN, have often produced negative health consequences. In the last several decades, policies to enhance self-determination and empowerment of AI/AN are steps in the right direction.

Critics have argued that one of the reasons for the healthcare disparity is that the IHS is critically underfunded. Consistent underfunding of health programs is negatively impacting healthcare access, quality of care, and health status of AI/AN communities and remains a threat to undermining any progress already made. The fact that AI/AN constitute a very small minority in American society, that they do not participate in large numbers in political processes, and that they have very little representation of their community in policymaking institutions of government speaks to their lack of political power that makes them more invisible and vulnerable.

HEALTHCARE FOR VETERANS

Population Characteristics and Trends

As of September 2010, the total veteran population seventeen years and older was 22.7 million. Of the total veteran population, 8.1 percent were female and 91.9 percent were male. The racial makeup of the veterans consisted of about 11 percent blacks, 6 percent Hispanics, and the remaining 83 percent were of all other races. Overall, the veteran population seventeen years and older is expected to decline to under 15 percent by 2035. The projected trends also suggest that the number of female veterans will increase to about 15 percent, blacks to about 15 percent, and Hispanics to over 8 percent by the year 2035 ("Veterans Population Projections: FY 2000 to FY 2036" 2010). Of the total veteran population, about 7.4 million served during the Vietnam era, 5.8 million during the Gulf War, 5.7 million during peacetime only, 2.3 million in the Korean War, and another 1.7 million during the World War II era ("Department of Veterans Affairs Statistics at a Glance" 2012).

In 2009, the median age of male veterans was sixty-four compared to forty-nine for female veterans. Almost 68 percent of male veterans were married, compared to 47.4 percent of female veterans ("Profile of Veterans: 2009" 2011).

The breakdown by occupation of employed veterans in 2009 was management/professional 34 percent, production/transportation 18.8 percent, sales/office 17.4 percent, service 13.9 percent, and all others 15.9 percent. The breakdown for female employed veterans was management/professional 47.1 percent, sales/office 29.8 percent, service 15.1 percent, production/transportation 5.9 percent, and all others 1.9 percent. The fact that more female veterans were employed in management/professional occupations compared to male veterans is perhaps not too surprising given the fact that female veterans were more likely to have had a higher level of educational attainment compared to their male counterparts. For example, 47.5 percent of female veterans had some college education, compared to 35.4 percent of male veterans. Eighteen percent of female veterans had a college degree and 11.6 percent had an advanced degree, compared to 15 and 9.9 percent of male veterans respectively. Yet the median earning of year-round full-time employed male veterans was $51,230 compared to $41,441 for female veterans ("Profile of Veterans: 2009" 2011).

Overall unemployment rates among veterans eighteen years and older is lower compared to nonveterans. This has been the case since the 2000. For example, in 2009, the unemployment rate among veterans was around 8 percent compared to over 9 percent for nonveterans. There was no appreciable difference in unemployment rates between male and female veterans ("Unemployment Rates of Veterans: 2000 to 2009" 2010). Similarly, the poverty rate among population 18 years and older has been much lower among veterans compared to non-veterans. In 2009, the poverty rate among veterans was 6.3 percent compared to 11.9 percent among non-veterans ("Health Insurance Coverage, Poverty, and Income of Veterans: 2000 to 2009" 2011).

However, it is important to note that veterans are overrepresented among the homeless population in the country. In 2010, veterans accounted for 10 percent of the total population but composed about 13 percent of the sheltered homeless adults and 16 percent of the total homeless adult population. Of the total sheltered homeless individuals veterans in 2010, 93.4 percent were male, 52.6 percent were non-Hispanic white, 41.1 percent were between the ages of thirty-one and fifty, and 51.2 percent were disabled ("Profile of Sheltered Homeless Veterans for Fiscal Years 2009 and 2010" 2012). While the total veteran population has been declining since 1985, the number of veterans with a service-connected disability has been on the rise. Since 1973 the lowest number of disabled veterans was recorded in fiscal year 1990. However, since 1990 there has been a 46 percent increase in service-connected disabled veterans. The rate of increase in cash payment is outpacing the growth in the number of veterans with a service-connected disability ("Trends in Veterans with a Service-Connected Disability: 1985 to 2010" 2012).

In 2009, 7.2 percent of veterans nineteen years and older were without any health insurance coverage. The percentage of insured veterans covered by government health programs was 60 percent. This is attributable to two factors: many older veterans are eligible for Medicare and accessibility to VA healthcare ("Health Insurance Coverage, Poverty, and Income of Veterans: 2000 to 2009" 2011). According to a 2010 national survey of veterans, 41 percent stated that they had a good understanding of veterans benefits, while 35 percent reported that they had a good understanding of their healthcare benefits. Enrolled veterans reported greater understanding of their entitled VA healthcare benefits. Overall, young veterans (eighteen to thirty years old) reported greater understanding of their VA healthcare coverage ("2010 National Survey of Veterans: Understanding and Knowledge of VA Benefits and Services" 2011). Forty-two percent of veterans cited lack of awareness about healthcare benefits as the reason for not applying or using VA benefits and services ("Department of Veterans Affairs: Veteran Surveys and Studies" 2011).

HISTORICAL BACKGROUND: DEVELOPMENT
OF VETERANS BENEFITS

The United States has a very comprehensive veterans benefit system. The origins of this system can be traced back to 1636 when pilgrims of the Plymouth Colony passed a law supporting disabled soldiers in the war with the Pequot Indians. In 1778, the first national pension laws were passed for soldiers who fought in the American Revolution (Kizer, Demakis, and Feussner 2000). In 1811, the federal government authorized the first domiciliary and medical facility for veterans. During the nineteenth century, veterans benefits and pension programs were expanded to include not just veterans but also their widows and dependents ("History—VA History" n.d.).

In 1862, President Lincoln signed a law authorizing the creation of the National Cemeteries system for veterans, and in 1865, he signed another law creating the National Home for Volunteer Soldiers in Maine. Homes for disabled Civil War veterans were subsequently opened in several states (Kizer, Demakis, and Feussner 2000).

After the Civil War (1861–1865) there were significant increases in veterans' benefits due to two factors. One was the fact that their claims for increased benefits were legitimized by their patriotic service to the country. Second, veterans had become a large and well-organized interest group with political clout and were able to successfully lobby for increased benefits (Holcombe 1999). After the Civil War, veterans made up 5 percent of the total population, but due to the limited franchise (eligible voters) at the time, they made up a much larger fraction of the voting population. In 1865, the United States Soldiers' and Sailors' Protective Society was organized to help veterans. In 1866, the Grand Army of the Republic (GAR) was formed as a political group to lobby for veterans benefits. Laws passed by Congress between 1865 and 1868 helped define federal benefits to Civil War veterans. Under these acts, pension payments were made to disabled veterans and surviving widows and their children of those killed in the war. Veterans who survived the war uninjured were not entitled to a pension. Another act by Congress in 1868 specified that to be eligible for a disability pension, the disability had to have occurred in the line of duty (Holcombe 1999). The Arrears Act of 1879 specified that veterans benefits started from the time of discharge from the army or for dependents from the time of the death and not at the time of application as was the case previous to the act. In 1890 veterans benefits were broadened to provide benefits to disabled veterans and survivor benefits to widows of veterans regardless of whether they were injured in the war and regardless of need. Under this policy, veterans who became physically or mentally disabled after the war were entitled to a pension as were their widows (Holcombe 1999).

When the United States entered World War I in 1917, Congress established a new system of veterans benefits that included programs for disability compensation, insurance for service persons and veterans, and vocational rehabilitation for the disabled. In 1930, President Hoover signed a law consolidating many separate veterans programs into an independent federal agency called the Veterans Administration ("History—VA History" n.d.; Kizer, Demakis, and Feussner 2000). The Servicemen's Readjustment Act of 1944, famously known as the "GI Bill of Rights," offered low-interest loans for veterans to purchase homes, farms, or small businesses, unemployment benefits, and financial assistance for education as well as for healthcare and rehabilitation services. In 1988, President Reagan established a new cabinet-level department—the Department of Veterans Affairs (DVA) (Kizer, Demakis, and Feussner 2000). In 2009, President Obama announced a major initiative focused on transforming the DVA into a high-performing organization under three guiding principles—people-centric, result-driven, and forward-looking ("History—VA History" n.d.).

Overall, veterans benefits have always included some healthcare. However, such benefits were initially limited to infirmary-type services and were provided by the U.S. Public Health Service. After World War I, Congress authorized hospital inpatient care as a veteran benefit and transferred several U.S. Public Health Service hospitals to the agency known at that time as the Veterans Bureau. The massive numbers of veterans produced by World War II overwhelmed the Veterans Administration's capabilities, and Congress in 1946 authorized the creation of a formal veterans healthcare system (Kizer, Demakis, and Feussner 2000).

VETERANS HEALTH POLICY DEVELOPMENT

In January 1946 Congress passed and President Truman signed into law Public Law 293 formally creating the Veterans Health Administration (VHA) within the Veterans Administration (now the Department of Veterans Affairs). Veterans Affairs hospitals immediately sought affiliation with university medical schools in order to improve the quality and the quantity of physicians. This helped establish a very successful partnership between the VA and the country's medical schools, allowing the veterans healthcare system to grow rapidly during the 1940s and 1950s. The addition of more than seventy new hospitals, combined with the establishment of university medical school affiliations and teaching programs, dramatically expanded research activities as well as new avenues of care for the veterans. During this time period, most emphasis was placed on providing hospital inpatient care for veterans, with healthcare provided by medical specialists (Kizer and Dudley 2009).

In 1956, the Dependents Medical Care Act provided the Department of Defense the authority to provide civilian healthcare to eligible dependents of military service members. The Civilian Health and Medical Program of Uniformed Services (CHAMPUS) was established in 1966 for family members of those on active duty and was later extended to retired service members and their dependents. This program provided supplemental care in addition to what was available in both the military and the Public Health Service (PHS), inpatient as well as outpatient care, and pharmacy benefits (Jackonis, Deyton, and Hess 2008).

As the veterans healthcare system grew, it also became more complex and bureaucratic. During the 1970s and 1980s, the media reported several embarrassing incidents involving the poor quality of healthcare received by veterans in several VA hospitals. Also, the number of Vietnam War veterans needing healthcare increased significantly during this time. Many of these veterans became alienated by what they perceived as a lack of response from the VA to their healthcare needs. Several veterans service organizations sought higher status for veterans programs. In response, President Reagan in March 1989 elevated the Veterans Affairs to the cabinet-level Department of Veterans Affairs (Kizer and Dudley 2009). However, by the early 1990s, the veterans healthcare system had come to be perceived as very dysfunctional, fragmented, disjointed, and insensitive to individual veterans' needs. This popular sentiment was often captured in movies such as *Article 99* and *Born on the 4th of July* (Kizer and Dudley 2009).

In 1991, the Physicians' Pay Bill substantially raised physicians' salaries and helped attract high-quality staff to the VHA (Oliver 2007). Under the authority of the CHAMPUS Reform Initiative of 1988, several reforms were introduced in the CHAMPUS program and implemented in 1993. The thrust of the reform initiatives was to bring the military healthcare system in line with the emerging concept of managed care. The revised program was named TRICARE, and it incorporated financial, practice management, and provider network aspects of managed care in most healthcare delivered directly at military treatment facilities. Active duty service members are automatically enrolled in the managed care program (TRICARE Prime), while other beneficiaries can voluntarily enroll in it or can use the Preferred Provider Option (TRICARE Extra), or they can rely on traditional fee-for-service (TRICARE Standard) (Jackonis, Deyton, and Hess 2008). Since its creation, TRICARE has undergone several changes, including realignment of TRICARE contract regions for better coordination and delivery of services; base realignment and closure; the addition of TRICARE for Life benefits for Medicare-eligible individuals; and expansion of the program to military reservists (Jackonis, Deyton, and Hess 2008).

By 1994, a consensus had emerged that the veterans healthcare system needed a major overhaul. A plan to dramatically transform the veterans healthcare system was developed during 1994–1995 under the VHA leadership of Kenneth Kizer, who was appointed undersecretary for health, the chief executive officer of the VHA. Kizer wrote two reports. In *Vision for Change* (Kizer 1995), he outlined his vision for reorganizing the VHA. In *Prescription for Change* (Kizer 1996), he outlined the underlying principles and strategic objectives for accomplishing the transformation of VHA. Based on these two reports Congress in 1996 passed the Veterans Eligibility Reform Act, which went into effect on October 1, 1998.

Under the Veterans Eligibility Reform Act, veterans benefits were expanded. For example, it made the VHA more accessible for the nonindigent and for those without service-related disabilities, and it also offered access to pharmaceuticals in outpatient care. The VHA keeps the cost of prescription drugs low by using its bargaining powers with pharmaceutical companies. Ironically, the Centers for Medicare and Medicaid Services is explicitly prohibited by congressional law from bargaining with drug companies for lower prices for its Medicare and Medicaid patients (Oliver 2007).

The Veterans Eligibility Reform Act dramatically changed the VHA. It relied on five major strategies to bring about the change. First, to create an accountable management structure and management control system within the VHA, the law established twenty-two Veterans Integrated Service Networks (VISN), implemented a new performance management system, and decentralized decision making. Second, to integrate and coordinate services, the VHA created a number of primary care projects and changed its focus from inpatient hospital care to outpatient care for veterans in any medically appropriate setting. Third, to improve the quality of care received by veterans, a performance-based management system was implemented and promoted the use of evidence-based clinical guidelines. Also a Patient Safety Initiative was launched in 1997. Fourth, to align system finances to desired outcomes, a new global fee-based resource reallocation system called the Veterans Equitable Resource Allocation (VERA) was developed to allocate funds based on actual service needs to VISNs and not to individual hospitals or clinics. Fifth, to modernize its information system, the VHA upgraded its information technology infrastructure and implemented a nationwide Computerized Patient Record System (CPRS) platform in 1997. When the CPRS was combined with a new graphical interface, the VHA's new electronic health record (EHR) became known as the Veterans Health Information System and Technology Architecture or VistA. The CPRS/VistA was implemented in all VHA medical centers over the years (Kizer and Dudley 2009). All these changes transformed the VHA into a model integrated healthcare system. Research evidence points to improved quality of care and clinical performance, higher levels of service satisfaction, greater operational efficiency, an improved information management system, and improved research and education programs (Kizer and Dudley 2009).

In October 2000, the National Institutes of Medicine issued a report linking exposure to Agent Orange (an herbicide used by the U.S. military in Vietnam) to onset of diabetes among Vietnam veterans. In response to this report, the VA defined diabetes as service-connected disability for veterans who served in the Vietnam War beginning in 2001. The defining of diabetes as a service-connected disability does not apply to Vietnam-era veterans who did not serve in Vietnam. This policy change increased the number of Vietnam veterans enrolled in the veterans disability compensation program (Duggan, Rosenheck, and Singleton 2010).

In interviews conducted by the Department of Veterans Affairs in August 2004, seriously wounded recuperating soldiers at the Walter Reed Army Medical Center in Washington, DC, expressed anger and a great deal of frustration in dealing with the hospital bureaucracy. They also reported substandard living conditions at the facility. In 2005, the Base Realignment and Closure Commission (BRCC) recommended closing down the hospital and moving its staff and services to the National Naval Medical Center (Blum and Fee 2008).

The *Washington Post*, in a series of articles published in February 2007, exposed the shortcomings and deficiencies at Walter Reed Army Medical Center involving substandard living conditions, inadequate management of outpatient care, insufficient resources, and poor leadership (Jackonis, Deyton, and Hess 2008). President George W. Bush appointed a bipartisan commission to investigate the matter. The commission recommended creation of recovery coordinators, restructuring the disability and compensation system, and improving the prevention, diagnosis, and treatment of post-traumatic stress disorder and traumatic brain injury (United States President's Commission 2011). An independent review group appointed by the U.S. Secretary of Defense, Robert

Gates, submitted a report, *Rebuilding the Trust* (2007), concluding that a variety of factors such as the decision to close Walter Reed by BRCC, pressure to outsource traditional military service functions, military-to-civilian personnel conversions, inadequate facilities, inattentive leadership, combined with the increased number of soldiers returning from wars in Iraq and Afghanistan, had contributed to the shortcomings and failures at Walter Reed. Finally in 2011, under the order from the Department of Defense, Walter Reed Army Medical Center was merged and integrated with the National Naval Medical Center and renamed Walter Reed Bethesda. Today, Walter Reed Bethesda is the largest state-of-the-art military treatment facility in the Department of Defense, and it integrates Army, Navy, and Air Force medical expertise into one tertiary care facility (Regan and Hobbs 2012).

VETERANS HEALTH ADMINISTRATION (VHA)

Mission

The VHA has a fivefold mission. Its primary mission is to provide medical care to eligible veterans, especially those with service-connected health conditions. Its second mission is to train healthcare professionals. Almost 50 percent of all American medical students and one-third of all postgraduate physician residents receive their training at VA facilities every year. The VHA's third mission is to conduct medical research in basic biomedical sciences, rehabilitation, health service delivery, and quality of care aimed at improving care for the veterans. The fourth mission is to provide contingency support to the military healthcare system and to the Department of Homeland Security. The fifth mission of the VHA is to serve homeless veterans. About one-third of adult homeless men in the United States are veterans (Kizer and Dudley 2009; Kizer, Demakis, and Feussner 2000).

Organization and Structure

The Department of Veterans Affairs (DVA) includes three administrative offices—the Veterans Health Administration, the Veterans Benefits Administration, and the National Cemetery Administration. The deputy secretary of the DVA is the second in command and serves as the chief executive officer of the VHA. Various program offices within the VHA help carry out the mission of the agency. The Office of Academic Affiliation provides information about higher education programs and opportunities for veterans. The National Center for Ethics addresses complex problems pertaining to ethical issues that arise in patient care. The Office of Health Information supports the computer information needs of VHA clinical and administrative staff. The Office of Medical Inspector examines healthcare issues raised by veterans and conducts surveys. The Office of Patient Care Services oversees VHA's clinical programs. The National Center for Patient Safety deals with patient safety issues. The Office of Public Health protects the health of the veterans through research and new initiatives. The Office of Policy and Planning coordinates various aspects of national health policy development and programs. The Office of Quality and Performance supports the VHA mission of providing high-quality care to veterans. The Office of Research and Development publishes research articles and reports. The Office of Research Oversight oversees safety and protection of human subjects in research activities. Finally the financial staff deals with budget formulation and execution of VHA programs ("VHA Program Offices" n.d.).

The VHA is the United States' largest integrated healthcare system, providing comprehensive healthcare to about 8.57 million veterans every year out of a total veteran population of over 22.2 million. The VHA's healthcare system consist of 152 medical centers (VA hospitals), about 817 community-based outpatient clinics, 300 VA Vet Centers, plus many community living centers, and domiciliaries ("Department of Veterans Affairs Statistics at a Glance" 2012). Medical centers/VA hospitals provide traditional hospital-based services such as surgery, critical care, mental health, pharmacy, and radiology. Community-based outpatient clinics provide common outpatient services such as health and wellness visits. Community living centers are essentially skilled nursing facilities. Vet centers provide readjustment counseling and outreach services to veterans who served in combat zones. Domiciliaries provide medical, psychiatric, vocational, educational, and other services to veterans in a homelike setting. These facilities employ more than 53,000 independent licensed healthcare practitioners The United States is divided into twenty-two Veterans Integrated Service Networks, that is, regional healthcare centers ("About VHA" n.d.).

The VHA employs a staff of 255,000 and has academic affiliations with 107 academic health centers. Over 65 percent of all physicians in the United States have trained in VA facilities. Over the last fifteen years or so, the VHA has reinvented itself into a model healthcare system ("Department of Veterans Affairs 2010 Organizational Briefing Book" 2010).

In 1988, the Women Veterans Health Program was established to streamline services for women veterans. At present, women veterans constitute about 8 percent of the total veteran population, and this number is on the rise. The program addresses the healthcare needs of women veterans, working to ensure that timely and equitable healthcare services are provided to women veterans in a sensitive and safe environment at VHA health facilities ("About VA Women's Health" n.d.).

Eligibility and Enrollment

In principle, all veterans are eligible for lifetime VA medical treatment, but in reality, of the total veteran population of about 22.2 million, only about 8.57 million (about 38.9 percent) veterans are enrolled in the veterans healthcare system. The VA rations care based on its annual appropriations. Approximately 3.4 percent of veterans receive VA disability compensation ("Department of Veterans Affairs Statistics at a Glance" 2012).

It is also important to remember that many veterans constitute a dual-enrolled population, that is, they can be enrolled in a veterans health benefit program and at the same time can be enrolled in a Medicaid program if they are poor and meet Medicaid's eligibility criteria. Similarly, since many veterans are older than 65 years of age, they can be enrolled in veterans health benefits as well as Medicare. In 1999, 10.2 percent of the VA's annual patient load was made up of the VA-Medicaid dual-enrolled population, while 53 percent of VA patients were also enrolled in Medicare (Hendricks et al. 2010).

Any individual who served in the active military, naval, or air service and who was discharged and released honorably may qualify for VA health benefits. Reservists and national guards may also qualify if they were called to active duty by a federal order and completed the full period for which they were called or ordered to active duty ("Health Benefits: Federal Benefits for Veterans, Dependents, and Survivors" n.d.).

Applying for enrollment is the first step of entry into the VA health system for most veterans. Once enrolled, veterans can receive health services at any VA healthcare facility in the country. During enrollment, each veteran is assigned a priority group. This is done in order to balance demand with resources. The priority groups range from one to eight, with priority group one receiving the highest priority and priority group eight receiving the lowest priority for enrollment. Priority groups are based on factors such as severity of service-connected disability, household income, prisoner of war (POW) status, veterans awarded service-related medal, and certain health conditions related to service in combat. For example, priority group one consists of veterans with service-connected disabilities rated 50 percent or more and determined to be unemployable due to their disabilities, while priority group 8 includes veterans enrolled as of January 15, 2003, with gross household income and/or net worth above the VA national income threshold ("Health Benefits: Federal Benefits for Veterans, Dependents, and Survivors" n.d.).

Four categories of veterans who are not required to enroll but are urged to enroll for better planning of healthcare resources include: (1) veterans with a service-connected disability of 50 percent or more, (2) veterans seeking care for a disability incurred or aggravated in the line of duty within 12 months of discharge but who have not been yet rated, (3) veterans seeking care for a service-connected disability only, and (4) veterans seeking care for exposure to ionizing radiation, Agent Orange, Gulf War/Operation Iraqi Freedom, and depleted uranium ("Health Benefits: Federal Benefits for Veterans, Dependents, and Survivors" n.d.).

Healthcare Benefits and Services

The VA provides a comprehensive health benefits package to all enrolled veterans. It includes a full range of preventive outpatient and inpatient health services within the VA healthcare system. Once enrolled, a veteran can seek health services at any VA facility in the country. All VA patients receive comprehensive care from a primary care team. Throughout the country, VA healthcare facilities offer a broad range of medical, surgical, and rehabilitative care for acute and chronic health conditions. A variety of specialized care suited for individual needs of the patient is also offered, such as prosthetic devices, rehabilitative services for spinal cord injury, post-traumatic stress disorder, psychological counseling for war-related trauma, as well as rehabilitative services for veterans suffering from alcoholism, drug abuse, and homelessness (Vadenberg, Bergofsky, and Burris 2010).

The VA also maintains several health registries, and certain veterans can participate in a VA health registry and receive free medical examinations that include laboratory and other diagnostic tests considered necessary by the examining health clinician. For example, the Gulf War Registry was established for veterans who served on active military duty in Southwest Asia during the Gulf War. It was established to identify possible diseases resulting from serving in that part of the world. Similarly, the Agent Orange Registry was established for veterans possibly exposed to dioxin and other toxic substances in herbicides used during the Vietnam War. Other health registries maintained by the VA include the Depleted Uranium Registry and the Ionizing Radiation Registry ("Health Benefits: Federal Benefits for Veterans, Dependents, and Survivors" n.d.).

For older veterans, the VA provides a wide range of institutional and noninstitutional long-term care services. Institutional long-term care is provided through VA Community Living Centers, that is, nursing homes, community nursing homes, state veterans homes, and domiciliaries (Vandenberg, Bergofsky, and Burris 2010). In 1998, expert external review of VA management of older veterans concluded that the system was much too dependent on institutional long-term care and recommended that the VA should make noninstitutional care alternatives to long-term care widely available (Shay and Yoshikawa 2010). Today, older veterans have a broad range of noninstitutional home and community-based services available to them, including hospice and palliative care, respite care, geriatric evaluation and management care, community residential care, home-based primary care, adult day healthcare, and homemaker/home health aide services (Vandenberg, Bergofsky, and Burris 2010).

The VA's Women Health Services Office addresses the healthcare needs of women veterans and offers gender-specific comprehensive primary care such as cervical cancer screens, breast cancer screens, birth control counseling, and hormone replacement therapy at every VA facility. Specialty care provided includes management and screening of chronic conditions such as heart disease, diabetes, and sexually transmitted diseases, along with reproductive healthcare including maternity care and infertility evaluation ("About VA Women's Health" n.d.).

The VA also provides a comprehensive range of health services for blind and visually impaired veterans, mental health services, a suicide prevention lifeline for veterans experiencing an emotional distress/crisis, and outpatient dental care. Finally, under the Civilian Health and Medical Program of the Department of Veterans Affairs (CHAMPVA), certain dependents and survivors can receive reimbursement for most medical expenses ("Health Benefits: Federal Benefits for Veterans, Dependents, and Survivors" n.d.).

Financing and Expenditures for Veterans Health Services

Veterans health services are funded through a regular congressional appropriations process. The VHA's resources have been increasingly devoted to programs designed to meet the healthcare needs of returning soldiers, especially those who have suffered traumatic brain injury (TBI) and post-traumatic stress disorder (PTSD), the need for prosthetics and burn care, and healthcare requirements of young female veterans (Jackonis, Deyton, and Hess 2008).

Most veterans who are not receiving VA disability compensation or pension payments are required to provide information about their gross household income and net worth to determine if they are below the annually adjusted financial threshold. Some veterans are required to make copays to receive VA healthcare and/or medications. Some low priority group enrollees are required to make a copayment for inpatient care. For outpatient care, a three-tiered copay system is utilized. Copayment is limited to a single charge per visit regardless of number of providers seen in a day. No copayment is required for most of the preventive care services such as screening and immunization ("Health Benefits: Federal Benefits for Veterans, Dependents, and Survivors" n.d.).

Table 5.2 provides some data on veterans healthcare expenditures for selected years from 1990 to 2010. The total spending on veterans health services has increased from $11.5 billion in 1990 to $47.3 billion in 2010. The data in Table 5.2 attest to the success of the Veterans Eligibility Reform Act's emphasis on shifting veterans care from inpatient hospitals to outpatient care and from long-term nursing home care to home healthcare and other community-based care. The expenditures for inpatient hospital care as a percent of total veterans healthcare expenditures declined from 52.5 percent in 1990 to 21.4 percent in 2010. Similarly, expenditures for outpatient hospital care increased from 25.3 percent in 1990 to 52.5 percent in 2010. Expenditures for nursing home care declined as a percent of total expenditures from 9.5 percent in 1990 to 7.4 percent in 2010. In 1990, there were 22,602 outpatient visits, and that number had jumped to 79,457 by 2010. Another fact to note is that expenditures for veterans with a service-connected disability as a percent of total veterans healthcare expenditure increased from 38.9 percent in 1990 to 43.5 percent in 2010. This is consistent with the fact that since 1990 there has been a 46 percent increase in service-connected disabled veterans, which has led to an increase in cash payments to veterans with service-connected disability ("Trends in Veterans with a Service-Connected Disability: 1985 to 2010" 2012).

HEALTH STATUS OF VETERANS

Veterans as a whole are more likely to be homeless and to lack health insurance coverage than the general population. Factors responsible for this include difficulty in transitioning from military to civilian employment, higher incidence of mental health and substance abuse problems, and the fact that single men are generally ineligible for Medicaid. Furthermore, the all-volunteer military draws on younger, working-age persons, who disproportionately come from households with lower income, yet their income is not low enough to qualify them for Medicaid or VA healthcare (Jackonis, Deyton, and Hess 2008). Research shows that a veteran's decision to use the VA healthcare facility is largely dependent on whether the individual has some type of health insurance or not (Hisnanick and Gujral 1996). In addition, characteristics of neighborhoods that veterans live in are related to their health status. For example, veterans living in lower socioeconomic neighborhoods have poorer health status and a higher risk of mortality than veterans living in upper socioeconomic neighborhoods. This is independent of individual characteristics and healthcare access (Nelson et al. 2011).

Table 5.2

Department of Veterans Affairs Healthcare Expenditures, Selected Fiscal Years, 1990–2010

Health Care Expenditures	1990	1995	2000	2005	2010
All Expenditures (Amounts in millions)	11,500	16,126	19,327	30,291	47,290
All Services (Percent distribution)	100.0	100.0	100.0	100.0	100.0
Inpatient Hospital	57.5	49.0	37.3	24.3	21.4
Outpatient Hospital	25.3	30.2	45.7	53.4	52.5
Nursing Home Care	9.5	10.0	8.2	8.4	7.4
All Other	7.7	10.8	8.8	13.9	18.8
Health Care Use (Number in thousands)					
Inpatient Hospital Discharges	1,029	879	579	614	656
Outpatient Visits	22,602	27,527	38,370	57,169	79,457
Nursing Home Discharges	75	79	91	61	67
Inpatients (Number in thousands)					
Total	598	527	417	488	532
Total (Percent distribution)	100.0	100.0	100.0	100.0	100.0
Veterans with Service-Connected Disability	38.9	39.3	34.3	37.8	43.5
Veterans without Service-Connected Disability	60.3	59.9	64.7	61.5	55.6
Nonveterans	0.8	0.8	0.9	0.9	0.9
Outpatients (Number in thousands)					
Total	2,564	2,790	3,657	5,077	5,631
Total (Percent distribution)	100.0	100.0	100.0	100.0	100.0
Veterans with Service-Connected Disability	38.8	37.5	30.7	31.6	38.6
Veterans without Service-Connected Disability	49.8	50.5	60.8	62.7	56.4
Nonveterans	11.8	12	8.5	5.7	5.1

Source: National Center for Health Statistics 2012.

As we mentioned in our discussion of veterans' population characteristics, veterans are overrepresented among the homeless population in the country. In 2010, veterans accounted for 10 percent of the total population, but they composed about 13 percent of the sheltered homeless adults and 16 percent of the homeless adult population. Homeless veterans tend to be male, non-Hispanic white, between the ages of thirty-one and fifty, and disabled ("Profile of Sheltered Homeless Veterans for Fiscal Years 2009 and 2010" 2012). Homeless veterans have many health problems that can be classified into four categories: addiction, psychosis, vascular disorders, and generalized medical and psychiatric illness. Factors most closely associated with homelessness appear to be sociodemographic factors such as age, ethnicity, and employment status. Psychosis, especially schizophrenia and substance abuse, typically seem to precede the onset of homelessness. However, the stereotype that all homeless veterans suffer from PTSD or alcohol or drug abuse is not true. Some homeless veterans have significant medical illness without accompanying psychiatric disorder. Some have major substance abuse problems, while others have some form of mental illness. The health status of homeless veterans is a complex problem that defies a single explanation (Goldstein et al. 2010).

One of the consequences of war is the physical injuries suffered by soldiers in combat. The "war on terror" launched by the United States following the September 11, 2001, terrorist attack on the U.S. soil has resulted in continuous combat that has lasted over a decade and led to the wounding of over 50,000 troops in wars waged in Iraq and Afghanistan. Blast injuries resulting from the use of improvised explosive devices (IEDs) by the enemy have included loss of limbs, traumatic brain injuries, and severe burns suffered by soldiers. About 1,400 service members have lost one or more of their limbs, requiring use of prosthetic limbs (Rizzo 2012). The number of soldiers suffering from a service-related disability has also increased dramatically along with the cost of the disability compensation program. The number of pending rating-related claims handled by the DVA has increased 66 percent since the year 2000 (Katel 2007).

A record number of American soldiers have been wounded in the fighting in Iraq and Afghanistan—by far the highest wounded-to-killed ratio in U.S. military history. For example, more than 50,000 soldiers have suffered nonmortal wounds, and more than 3,000 soldiers have been killed in war in Iraq and Afghanistan—a ratio of 16 to 1. In contrast, the wounded-to-killed ratio for Desert Storm/Desert Shield was 1.2 to 1; Vietnam War 2.6 to 1; Korean War 2.8 to 1; World War II 1.6 to 1; World War I 1.8 to 1; Civil War (Union) 0.7 to 1; War of 1812 0.5 to 1; and the Revolutionary War 0.7 to 1. If one uses the Pentagon's narrower definition of wounded personnel, the killed-to-wounded ratio for Iraq and Afghanistan wars is 8 to 1, still much higher than any other wars in U.S. history (Katel 2007).

Among the many consequences of wars are the psychological stress and toll that soldiers suffer. According to a recent study, more than one-third of army and marine troops have consulted mental health professionals after returning from Iraq, and 19 percent screened positive for mental health concerns (Hoge, Auchterlonie, and Milliken 2006). According to a task force appointed by the Pentagon, as many as one-half of active duty and reserve troops deployed to combat zones reported various mental health symptoms, including possible post-traumatic stress disorder (PTSD) and traumatic brain injury (TBI). In addition, one of the major reasons cited for not seeking help and/ or reporting mental health issues was the negative responses they received from their superiors ("An Achievable Vision" 2007). Forty-nine percent of National Guard service members, 38 percent of the army, and 31 percent of the marines reported suffering from psychological symptoms within 120 days of returning from combat ("An Achievable Vision" 2007). The Department of Defense has documented almost 250,000 cases of TBI since year 2000 and more than 60 TBI programs have been created at military medical treatment facilities at U.S. bases to address the problem (Rizzo 2012).

Another health concern related to the psychological stress and post-combat mental health problems is the problem of suicide among soldiers. Until 2008, neither the VA nor the Pentagon kept track of suicides among veterans. Thus, the only available data was suicide among active-duty service members. In 2006, ninety-nine active-duty army troops, mostly in Iraq, committed suicide, which was up from eighty-eight in 2005 ("High Rates of Suicide Seen in Soldiers" 2007). The rate of suicide among those serving in the military has been on the rise. A mental health diagnosis is a very strong suicide risk factor (Hyman et al. 2012). In 2008, the DVA implemented a suicide event reporting system designed to collect standardized information on all suicide attempts reported to VA clinicians. Since then, the VA has collected information on about 46,000 suicide attempts ("Surveillance of Suicide and Suicide Attempts Among Veterans" 2012). Preventing suicide has become a high priority issue for the military and specifically the VHA, given the fact that the rate of suicide among active duty soldiers has doubled since 2005 ("Preventing Suicide by Preventing Lethal Injury" 2012). In July 2012, soldiers killed themselves at a rate faster than one per day— there were 38 deaths either confirmed or suspected as suicide. The army suicide rate in 2012 has surpassed the rate in 2011. Furthermore, a new pattern emerged in 2012 when there were more suicides among veteran soldiers than among younger GIs (Zoroya 2012).

A study that examined the mental and physical health of veterans within one year of returning from war zone deployment found that their mental health functioning was significantly worse compared with the general population. Almost 14 percent screened positive for probable post-traumatic stress disorder, 39 percent for probable alcohol abuse, and 3 percent for probable drug abuse. Men reported more alcohol and drug abuse than women (Eisen et al. 2012).

Women veterans comprise about 8.1 percent of the total veteran population. Furthermore, projected trends also suggest that the number of female veterans will increase to about 15 percent by the year 2035 ("Veterans Population Projections: FY 2000 to FY 2036" 2010). Thus, the health status of female veterans and their health services needs has become an important topic in the veterans healthcare system. Women have been involved in many military conflicts in a variety of roles, and they have suffered deaths and injuries just like their male counterparts. Overall, most women veterans report good to excellent health. However, evidence suggests that for female veterans, military service is associated with increased risks of suffering from a variety of physical conditions and illnesses. For women veterans, in-service sexual assaults and sexual harassment have long-term health implications. Research shows that psychosocial health complications of sexual assault include increased risk of suicide, depression, alcohol and drug abuse, sexual dysfunction, and PTSD. Similarly, in-service sexual harassment is also demonstrated to be related to adverse psychiatric outcomes such as depression, anxiety, and PTSD (Murdoch et al. 2006). Women veteran VA patients also suffer as heavy a burden of physical and mental illness as do men in the VA system (Frayne et al. 2006).

Finally, research also shows that elderly veterans enrolled in the VHA healthcare system suffer from a substantial disease burden with major impairments across several dimensions of health. Understanding the health status of elderly veteran enrollees is very important for geriatric research, practice, and education. The VHA has not only been a leader in implementing innovative programs for geriatric care, it has also been an important training site for geriatric care throughout the nation (Selim et al. 2004).

CHALLENGES CONFRONTING THE VA HEALTHCARE SYSTEM

The veterans' healthcare system has undergone a major organizational and management transformation since the passage of the Veterans Eligibility Reform Act, which went into effect on October 1, 1998. It has led to improved patient safety and quality of care. However, the veterans healthcare system faces some challenges that it needs to address.

One of the challenges is addressing the problem of perceived racial disparity in the VA's healthcare system. Among veterans, perceived discrimination is more prevalent among patients who use Veterans Affairs facilities than among those who do not (Hausmann et al. 2009). There continues to be a gap in clinical outcomes between African American and white veterans (Trivedi et al. 2011). Racial/ethnic discrimination during military service is also strongly associated with lower physical health. Better mental health among minority veterans also seems to be related to satisfaction with healthcare providers' sensitivity toward the racial/ethnic background of patients (Sohn and Harada 2008). Part of the problem in studying racial-ethnic disparities with respect to veterans is that VHA databases used to study this problem do not necessarily capture all care received by VHA patients (Halanych et al. 2006).

The second challenge confronting the VA healthcare system is reducing the pervasive number of uninsured persons. Poor, less-educated, and minority veterans are more likely to receive all their healthcare at VA healthcare facilities, and a large number of veterans who could use VA services are uninsured (Nelson, Strakebaum, and Reiber 2007). A number of military families rely on Medicaid to supplement their military health service benefits. While, the availability of Medicaid coverage addresses lack of financial barriers to accessing affordable healthcare services, there is a lack of participating providers to meet all the healthcare needs (Jackonis, Deyton, and Hess 2008).

The third challenge is to coordinate access to comprehensive short- and long-term care for persons with serious, chronic physical and mental health conditions. One of the major new challenges for the VHA is to help transition sick and wounded service members (especially those deployed in Iraq and Afghanistan) from active service to civilian life. This will require the Departments of Defense, Veterans Affairs, and Health and Human Services to improve and better coordinate their federal resources (Jackonis, Deyton, and Hess 2008).

Addressing the unique healthcare needs of the increasing number of women veterans is the final challenge confronting the VHA. Even though, technically, women are barred from serving in combat specialties, the reality is that women are serving in forward positions in combat in larger numbers. Their increased involvement has resulted in increased physical and mental health risks (Resnick, Mallampalli, and Carter 2012). Conducting research on women veterans, identifying their unique healthcare needs and meeting these needs, is important given the fact that they are a rapidly growing segment of the total veteran population (Washington 2004).

CONCLUSION

Inscribed on the wall of the Department of Veterans Affairs headquarters in Washington, DC, is a quotation from Abraham Lincoln, "To care for him who shall have borne the battle, and for his widow and his orphan" (quoted in Oliver 2007, 13). Unfortunately, that has not been the case throughout our history. Benefits for veterans (including healthcare benefits) and their dependents have slowly and steadily expanded only after political struggles and political lobbying and pressure group politics. But, even today, not all veterans or their dependents receive healthcare benefits through the veterans healthcare system because enrollment is based on a priority rating system designed to balance resources with needs. Poor and minority veterans have come to rely exclusively on the veterans' healthcare system to meet all their healthcare needs. A significant number of veterans still lack health insurance coverage, and homelessness is a major problem confronting many veterans. Many also suffer from psychological stress and mental health problems and are at higher risk for suicide and alcohol and substance abuse. Many have found transition from military to civilian life difficult after returning from battlefields.

The wars in Iraq and Afghanistan have dramatically increased the number of soldiers who are physically wounded, have lost their limbs, and suffer from service-related disabilities. As a result, increased financial strain is placed on the Disability Compensation program. Also meeting the healthcare needs of the increased number of women veterans continues to be an important challenge.

Since the establishment of the Veterans Health Administration in 1946, the veterans' healthcare system has come a long way. It has improved considerably from the scandal-plagued days from the 1970s and 1980s and the scandal involving Walter Reed Army Medical Center in the mid-2000s. The Veterans Eligibility Reform Act, passed in 1996 and implemented in 1998, not only expanded veterans' health benefits but fundamentally and dramatically helped revolutionize the veterans' healthcare system. Today, the veterans' healthcare system is the largest integrated healthcare system in the United States and is being held as a model of envy by many. Many opponents of President Obama's healthcare reform, the Affordable Care Act, falsely portrayed it as government takeover of healthcare, that is, it would lead to a government-run, government financed, and government-controlled healthcare system. Yet, what is ironic is the fact that the current veterans healthcare system that is being held up as a model by many is the only true government-run, government-financed, and government-controlled healthcare system in the United States today!

STUDY QUESTIONS

1. Discuss the legal and constitutional status of American Indians and Alaska Natives in the United States.
2. Discuss the evolution of U.S. health policy for American Indians and Alaska Natives.
3. Discuss the role of the Indian Health Service (IHS) in providing healthcare for American Indians and Alaska Natives. Be sure to include in your discussion the organization of IHS and its role in service delivery.
4. What are the major accomplishments of the IHS? What are major challenges confronting the IHS?
5. Discuss the trends and health status of American Indians and Alaska Natives. What factors help explain their relatively poor health status compared to white Americans?
6. Discuss how U.S. health policy for the veterans has evolved over the years.
7. Discuss the mission and organization of the Veterans Health Administration (VHA) and its role in delivering health services to the veterans.
8. Discuss the eligibility requirements for veterans to receive health services. What are some of the major trends in veterans' enrollment? What health services and benefits are they entitled to?
9. Discuss the health status of veterans compared to nonveterans in American society. What are some of the unique health issues confronted by American veterans of wars?
10. What are some of the problems confronted by the VHA? What are some of the challenges facing the VHA? How has the VHA changed over the years?

REFERENCES

"About VA Women's Health." n.d. Washington, DC: U.S. Department of Veterans Affairs. Online at www.womenshealth.va.gov/womenshealth/about.asp.

"About VHA." n.d. Washington, DC: U.S. Department of Veterans Affairs. Online at www.va.gov/health/aboutVHA.asp.

"An Achievable Vision: Report of the Department of Defense Task Force on Mental Health, June 2007." 2007. Falls Church: Virginia. Defense Health Board Task Force on Mental Health. Online at www.health.mil/dhb/mhtf/mhtf-report-final.pdf.

Ambler, Marjane. 2003. "Reclaiming Native Health." *Tribal College Journal* 15, no. 2 (Winter): 8–9.

"American Indian/Alaska Native Profile." n.d. Office of Minority Health, U.S. Department of Health and Human Services. Rockville, MD. Online at http://minorityhealth.hhs.gov/templates/browse.aspx?lvl=2&lvlID=52.

Barnhardt, Carol. 2001. "A History of Schooling for Alaska Native People." *Journal of American Indian Education* 40, no. 1: 1–30.

Bergman, Abraham B.; David C. Rossman; Angela M. Erdrich; John G. Todd; and Ralph Forquera. 1999. "A Political History of Indian Health Service." *Milbank Quarterly* 77, no. 4: 571–604.

Blum, Nava, and Elizabeth Fee. 2008. "Critical Shortcomings at Walter Reed Army Medical Center Create Doubt." *American Journal of Public Health* 98, no. 12 (December): 2159–60.

Borowsky, Iris W.; Michael D. Resnick; Marjorie Ireland; and Robert W. Blum. 1999. "Suicide Attempts Among American Indian and Alaska Native Youths." *Archives of Pediatric and Adolescent Medicine* 153, no. 6 (June): 573–80.

Centers for Disease Control and Prevention. 2000. *Facts about Heart Disease and Stroke among American Indians and Alaska Natives*. Online at www.cdc.gov.

Clegg, Limin X.; Frederick P. Li; Benjamin F. Hankey; Kenneth Chu; and Brenda K. Edwards. 2002. "Cancer Survival Among U.S. Whites and Minorities." *Archives of Internal Medicine* 162, no. 17: 1985–93.

Cunningham, Peter J., and Barbara M. Altman. 1993. "The Use of Ambulatory Health Care Services by American Indians with Disabilities." *Medical Care* 31, no. 7 (July): 600–16.

Cunningham, Peter. J., and L.J. Cornelius. 1995. "Access to Ambulatory Care for American Indians and Alaska Natives: The Relative Importance of Personal and Community Resources." *Social Science & Medicine* 40, no. 3 (February): 393–407.

Denny, Clark H.; Deborah Holtzman; Turner Goins; and Janet B. Croft. 2005. "Disparities in Chronic Disease Risk Factors and Health Status Between American Indian/Alaska Native and White Elders: Findings from a Telephone Survey, 2001 and 2002." *American Journal of Public Health* 95, no. 5 (May): 825–27.

"Department of Veterans Affairs Statistics at a Glance." 2012. Washington, DC: National Center for Veterans Analysis and Statistics, U.S. Department of Veterans Affairs. Online at www.va.gov/vetdata/docs/Quickfacts/Homepage_slideshow_FINAL.pdf.

"Department of Veterans Affairs 2010 Organizational Briefing Book." 2010. Washington, DC: Office of Human Resources and Administration, Office of Administration. Online at www.va.gov/ofcadmin/docs/vaorgbb.pdf.

"Department of Veterans Affairs: Veteran Surveys and Studies." 2011. Washington, DC: National Center for Veterans Analysis and Statistics, U.S. Department of Veterans Affairs. Online at www.va.gov/vetdata/docs/QuickFacts/Surveys-slideshow.pdf.

"Diagnosed Diabetes Among American Indians and Alaska Natives Aged <35 Years–United States, 1994–2004." 2006. *Morbidity & Mortality Weekly* 55, no. 44 (November 10): 1201–3.

Duggan, Mark; Robert Rosenheck; and Perry Singleton. 2010. "Federal Policy and the Rise in Disability Enrollment: Evidence for the Veterans Affairs' Disability Compensation Program." *Journal of Law and Economics* 53, no. 2 (May): 379–98.

Eisen, Susan; Mark R. Schultz; Dewne Vogt; Mark E. Glickman; Rani Elwy; Mari-Lynn Drainoni; Princess E. Osei-Bonsu; and James Martin. 2012. "Mental and Physical Health Status and Alcohol and Drug Use Following Return from Deployment in Iraq or Afghanistan." *American Journal of Public Health* 102, no. S1 (Supplement): S66-S73.

Fagot-Campagna, A.; D.J. Pettitt; and M.M. Engelgan. 2000. "Type 2 Diabetes Among North American Children and Adolescents: An Epidemiologic Review and a Public Health Perspective." *Journal of Pediatric* 136, no. 5 (May): 664–72.

Forquera, Ralph. 2001. *Urban Indian Health*. Washington, DC: Henry J. Kaiser Family Foundation.

Frank, John W. 2000. "Historical and Cultural Roots of Drinking Problems Among American Indians." *American Journal of Public Health* 90, no. 3 (March): 344–51.

Frayne, Susan M; Victoria A. Parker; Cindy L. Christiansen; Susan Loveland; Margaret R. Seaver; Lewis F. Kazis; and Katherine M. Skinner. 2006. "Health Status Among 28,000 Women Veterans." *Journal of General Internal Medicine* 21, no. 3 Supplement (March): S40-S46.

Freedenthal, Stacey, and Arlene R. Stiffman. 2007. "They Might Think I Was Crazy: Young American Indians' Reasons for Not Seeking Help When Suicidal." *Journal of Adolescent Research* 22, no. 1 (January): 58–77.

Garrett, J.T., and M.W. Garrett, 1994. "The Path of Good Medicine: Understanding and Counseling Native American Indians." *Journal of Multicultural Counseling and Development* 22, no. 3 (July): 134–44.

Goldstein, Gerald; James F. Luther; Gretchen Haas; Cathleen Appelt; and Adam Gordon. 2010. "Factor Structure and Risk Factors for the Health Status of Homeless Veterans." *Psychiatric Quarterly* 81, no. 4 (December): 311–23.

Gonzales, Angela; Judy Kertesz; and Gabrielle Tayac. 2007. "Eugenics as Indian Removal: Sociohistorical Processes and the De(con)struction of American Indians in the Southeast." *Public Historian* 29, no. 3 (Summer): 53–67.

Halanych, Jewell H.; Fie Wang; Donald R. Miller; Leonard M. Pogach; Hai Lin; Dam R. Berlowitz; and Susan M. Frayne. 2006. "Racial/Ethnic Differences in Diabetes Care for Older Veterans: Accounting for Dual Health System Use Changes Conclusions." *Medical Care* 44, no. 5 (May): 439–45.

Hausmann, Leslie R.; Kwonho Jeong; James E. Bost; Nancy R. Kressin; and Said A. Ibrahim. 2009. "Perceived Racial Discrimination in Health Care: A Comparison of Veterans Affairs and Other Patients." *American Journal of Public Health* 99, no. S3 (November): S718-S724.

"Health Benefits: Federal Benefits for Veterans, Dependents, and Survivors." n.d. Washington, DC: U.S. Department of Veterans Affairs. Online at www.va.gov/opa/publications/benefits_book/benefits_chap01. asp.

"Health Insurance Coverage, Poverty, and Income of Veterans: 2000 to 2009." 2011. Washington, DC: National Center for Veterans Analysis and Statistics, U.S. Department of Veterans Affairs. Online at www. va.gov/vetdata/docs/SpecialReports/HealthIns_FINAL.pdf

Henderson, Patricia N.; Clemma Jacobsen; and Janette Beals. 2005. "Correlates of Cigarette Smoking Among Selected Southwest and Northern Plains Tribal Groups: The AL-SUPERRFP Sud." *American Journal of Public Health* 95, no. 5 (May): 867–72.

Hendricks, Ann; John Gardner; Austin Frakt; Daniel Gilden; Julia Prentice; Lynn Wolfsfeld; and Steven Pizer. 2010. "What Can Medicaid Data Add to Research on VA Patients?" *Journal of Rehabilitation Research and Development* 47, no. 8: 773–88.

Herman-Stahl, Mindy; Donna L. Spencer; and Jessica E. Duncan. 2003. "The Implications of Cultural Orientation for Substance Use Among American Indians." *American Indian & Alaska Native Mental Health Research* 11, no. 1: 46–66.

"High Rates of Suicide Seen in Soldiers." 2007. *Los Angeles Times,* August 11, A13.

Hisnanick, John J., and Surinder S. Gujral. 1996. "Veterans' Health Insurance Status and Their Use of VA Medical Facilities: A Joint-Choice Analysis." *Social Science Quarterly* 77, no. 2 (June): 393–406.

"History—VA History." n.d. Washington, DC: U.S. Department of Veterans Affairs. Online at www.va.gov/ landing2_about.htm.

Hoge, Charles W.; Jennifer L. Auchterlonie; and Charles S. Milliken. 2006. "Mental Health Problems, Use of Mental Health Services, and Attrition from Military Service After Returning from Deployment to Iraq or Afghanistan." *Journal of the American Medical Association* 295, no. 9 (March): 1023–32.

Holcombe, Randall G. 1999. "Veterans Interest and the Transition to Government Growth: 1870–1915." *Public Choice* 99, nos. 3–4: 311–26.

Huhndorf, Roy M., and Shari M. Huhndorf. 2011. "Alaska Native Politics Since the Alaska Claims Settlement Act." *South Atlantic Quarterly* 110, no. 2 (Spring): 385–401.

Hyman, Jeffrey; Robert Ireland; Lucinda Frost; and Linda Cottrell. 2012. "Suicide Incidence and Risk Factors in an Active Duty U.S. Military Population." *American Journal of Public Health* 102, no. S1 (Supplement): 38–46.

"IHS Year 2012 Profile." n.d. Washington, DC: Indian Health Service, Department of Health and Human Services. Online at www.ihs.gov/PublicAffairs/IHSBrochure/Profile.asp.

Jackonis, Michael J; Lawrence Deyton; and William J. Hess. 2008. "War, Its Aftermath and U.S. Health Policy: Toward a Comprehensive Health Program for America's Military Personnel, Veterans and Their Families." *Journal of Law, Medicine, and Ethics* 36, no. 4 (Winter): 677–89.

James, Cara; Karyn Schwartz; and Julia Berndt. 2009. *A Profile of American Indians and Alaska Natives and Their Health Coverage.* Washington DC: Henry J. Kaiser Family Foundation.

Johnson, Jeannette L., and Mark C. Cameron. 2001. "Barriers to Providing Effective Mental Health Services to American Indians." *Mental Health Services Research* 3, no. 4 (December): 215–23.

Kaiser Commission on Medicaid and the Uninsured. 2006. *The Uninsured: A Primer. Key Facts about Americans Without Health Insurance.* Washington, DC: Henry J. Kaiser Family Foundation.

Katel, Peter. 2007. "Wounded Veterans." *Congressional Quarterly Researcher* 17, no. 30 (August): 699–706.

Katz, Ruth J. 2004. "Addressing the Health Care Needs of American Indians and Alaska Natives." *American Journal of Public Health* 94, no. 1 (January): 13–14.

Kizer, Kenneth W. 1995. *Vision for Change: A Plan to Restructure the Veterans Health Administration.* Washington, DC: Department of Veterans Affairs.

Kizer, Kenneth W. 1996. *Prescription for Change: The Guiding Principles and Strategic Objectives Underlying the Transformation of the Veterans Health Care System.* Washington, DC: Department of Veterans Affairs.

Kizer, Kenneth W., and Adams R. Dudley. 2009. "Extreme Makeover: Transformation of the Veterans Health Care System." *Annual Review of Public Health* 30, no. 1: 313–39.

Kizer, Kenneth W.; John G. Demakis; and John R. Feussner. 2000. "Reinventing VA Health Care: Systematizing Quality Improvement and Quality Innovation." *Medicare Care,* Supplement 38, no. 6 (June): I-7–I-16.

Kramer, Josea B. 1992. "Cross-Cultural Medicine: A Decade Later." *Western Journal of Medicine* 157, no. 3: 281–85.

Kunitz, Stephen J. 1996. "The History and Politics of U.S. Health Care Policy for American Indians and Alaskan Natives." *American Journal of Public Health* 96, no. 10 (October): 1464–73.

Lee, Elisa T.; Barbara V. Howard; Peter J. Savage; Linda D. Cowan; Richard R. Eabsitz; Arvo J. Oopik; J. Yeh; O Go; D.C. Robbins; and Y.K. Welty. 1995. "Diabetes and Impaired Glucose Tolerance in Three American Indian Populations Aged 45–74 Years. The Strong Heart Study." *Diabetes Care* 18, no. 5 (May): 599–610.

Liao, Y.; P. Tucker; and W.H. Giles. 2003. "Health Status of American Indians Compared with Other Racial/ Ethnic Minority Population." *Morbidity & Mortality Weekly Report* 52, no. 47: 1148–52.

Lillie-Blanton, Marsha. 2005. "Understanding and Addressing the Health Care Needs of American Indians and Alaska Natives." *American Journal of Public Health* 95, no. 5 (May): 759–61.

Mahoney, Martin C., and Arthur M. Michalek. 1998. "Health Status of American Indians/Alaska Natives: General Patterns of Mortality." *Family Medicine* 30, no. 3: 190–95.

———. 1999. "The Health Status of American Indians and Alaska Natives: 2. Lessons for Cancer Educators." *Journal of Cancer Education* 14, no. 1 (Spring): 23–27.

Mansberger, Steven L.; Francine C. Romero; Nicole H. Smith; Chris A. Johnson; George A. Cioffi; Beth Edmunds; Choi Dongseok; and Thomas M. Becker. 2005. "Causes of Visual Impairment and Common Eye Problems in Northwest American Indian and Alaska Natives." *American Journal of Public Health* 95, no. 5 (May): 881–86.

Manson, Spero M.; Janette Beals; Suzell A. Klein; and Calvin D. Croy. 2005. "Social Epidemiology of Trauma Among 2 American Indian Reservation Populations." *American Journal of Public Health* 95, no. 5 (May): 851–59.

Marbella, Anne M.; Mickey C. Harris; Sabina Diehr; Gerald Ignace; and Georginna Ignace. 1998. "Use of Native American Healers Among Native American Patients in an Urban Native American Health Center." *Archives of Family Medicine* 7, no. 2 (March–April): 182–85.

Murdoch, Maureen; Arlene Bradley; Susan H. Mother; Robert E. Kline; Carole L. Turner; and Elizabeth M. Yano. 2006. "Women at War." *Journal of General Internal Medicine* 21, no. 3, Supplement (March): S5-S10.

National Center for Health Statistics. 2012. *Health, United States, 2011: With Special Feature on Socioeconomic Status and Health.* Centers for Disease Control and Prevention, Hyattsville, MD. Online at www.cdc.gov/nchs/data/hus/hus11.pdf.

Nelson, Karin M.; Gordon A. Strakebaum; and Gayle E. Reiber. 2007. "Veterans Using and Uninsured Veterans Not Using Veterans Affairs (VA) Health Care." *Public Health Report* 122, no. 1 (January-February): 93–100.

Nelson, Karin M.; Leslie Taylor; Nicole Lurie; Jose Escarce; Lynne McFarland; and Stephan Finn. 2011. "Neighborhood Environment and Health Status and Mortality Among Veterans." *Journal of General Internal Medicine* 26, no. 8 (August): 862–67.

Noren, Jay; David Kindig; and Audrey Sprenger. 1998. "Challenges to Native American Health Care." *Public Health Reports,* 113, no. 1 (January/February): 22–33.

Novins, Douglas K.; Janette Beals; Calvin Croy; Anna E. Baron; Paul Spicer; and Dedra Buchwald. 2006. "The Relationship Between Patterns of Alcohol Abuse and Mental and Physical Health Disorders in Two American Indian Populations." *Addiction* 101, no. 1 (January): 69–83.

O'Connell, Joan M.; Charlton Wilson; Spero M. Manson; and Kelly J. Acton. 2012. "The Cost of Treating American Indian Adults with Diabetes Within the Indian Health Service." *American Journal of Public Health* 102, no. 2 (February): 301–8.

Oliver, Adam. 2007. "The Veterans Health Administration: An American Success Story?" *Milbank Quarterly* 85, no. 1: 5–35.

Olson, Lenora M., and Stephanie Wahab. 2006. "American Indians and Suicide: A Neglected Area of Research." *Trauma, Violence & Abuse* 7, no. 1 (January): 19–33.

Pearson, Diane J. 2004. "Medical Diplomacy and the American Indian: Thomas Jefferson, the Lewis and Clark Expedition, and the Subsequent Effects on American Indian Health and Public Policy." *Wicaza Sa Review* 19, no. 1: 105–30.

Perdue, Theda. 2012. "The Legacy of Indian Removal." *Journal of Southern History* 78, no. 1: 3–36.

Pfefferbaum, Betty; Rennard Strickland; Everett R. Rhoades; and Rose L. Pfefferbaum. 1995/1996. "Learning How to Heal: An Analysis of the History, Policy, and Framework of Indian Health Care." *American Indian Law Review* 20, no. 2: 365–97.

Pfefferbaum, Rose L.; Betty Pfefferbaum; Everett R. Rhoades; and Rennard J. Strickland. 1997. "Providing for the Health Care Needs of Native Americans: Policy, Programs, Procedures, and Practices." *American Indian Law Review* 21, no. 2: 211–58.

"Preventing Suicide by Preventing Lethal Injury: The Need to Act on What We Already Know." 2012. *American Journal of Public Health* 102, no. S1 (Supplement): e1–e2.

"Profile of Sheltered Homeless Veterans for Fiscal Years 2009 and 2010." 2012. Washington, DC: National Center for Veterans Analysis and Statistics, U.S. Department of Veterans Affairs. Online at www.va.gov/vetdata/docs/SpecialReports/Homeless_Veterans_2009–2010.pdf.

"Profile of Veterans: 2009." 2011. Washington, DC: National Center for Veterans Analysis and Statistics, U.S. Department of Veterans Affairs. Online at www.va.gov/vetdata/docs/SpecialReports/Profile_of_Veterans_2009_FINAL.pdf.

Puukka, Emily; Paul Stehr-Green; and Thomas M. Becker. 2005. "Measuring the Health Gap for American Indians/Alaska Natives: Getting Closer to the Truth." *American Journal of Public Health* 95, no. 5 (May): 838–43.

Regan, Ann-Francis C., and Loretta M. Hobbs. 2012. "Walter Reed Bethesda—Much More than Changing Name." *OD Practitioner* 44, no. 3 (Summer): 31–36.

Rebuilding the Trust: Report on Rehabilitative Care and Administrative Processes at Walter Reed Army Medical Center and National Naval Medical Center. 2007. Arlington, VA: Independent Review GROUP/.

Renfrew, Megan J. 2006. "The 100% Federal Medical Assistance Percentage: A Tool for Increasing Federal Funding for Heath Care for American Indians and Alaska Natives." *Columbia Journal of Law and Social Problems* 40, no. 2 (Winter): 173–224.

Resnick, Eileen M; Monica Mallampalli; and Christine L. Carter. 2012. "Current Challenges in Female Veterans' Health." *Journal of Women's Health* 21, no. 9 (September): 895–900.

Rhoades, Everett R. 2003. "Health Status of American Indians and Alaska Native Males." *American Journal of Public Health* 93, no. 5 (May) 774–78.

Rizzo, Jennifer. 2012. "The Medical Legacy of a Decade at War." Online at http://security.blogs.cnn.com/2012/09/11/the-medical-legacy-of-a-decade-at-war/.

Roubideaux, Yvette. 2002. "Perspectives on American Indian Health." *American Journal of Public Health* 92, no. 9 (September): 1401–6.

Satcher, David. 2001. *Mental Health: Culture, Race, and Ethnicity—A Supplement to Mental Health: A Report of the Surgeon General.* Washington, DC: U.S. Department of Health and Human Services.

Schneider, Andy. 2005. "Reforming American Indian/Alaska Native Health Care Financing: The Role of Medicaid." *American Journal of Public Health* 95, no. 5 (May): 766–68.

Schneider, Eileen. 2005. "Tuberculosis Among American Indians and Alaska Natives in the United States, 1993–2002." *American Journal of Public Health* 95, no. 5 (May): 873–80.

Selim, Alfredo J.; Dan R. Berlowitz; Graeme Fincke; Cong Zhongxiao; William Rogers; Samuel C. Haffer; Zinhua S. Ren; Austin Lee; Shirley X. Qian; Donald R. Miller; Avron Spiro; Bernado J. Selim; and Lewis E. Kazis. 2004. "The Health Status of Elderly Veteran Enrollees in the Veterans Health Administration." *Journal of the American Geriatric Society* 52, no. 8 (August): 1271–76.

Shay, Kenneth, and Thomas T. Yoshikawa. 2010. "Overview of VA Healthcare for Older Veterans: Lessons Learned and Policy Implications." *Journal of the American Society on Aging* 34, no. 2 (Summer): 20–28.

Shelton, Brett L. 2004. *Legal and Historical Roots of Health Care for American Indians and Alaska Natives in the United States.* Washington, DC: Henry J. Kaiser Family Foundation.

Sohn, Linda, and Nancy D. Harada. 2008. "Effects of Racial/Ethnic Discrimination on the Health Status of Minority Veterans." *Military Medicine* 173, no. 4 (April): 331–38.

Story, Mary; Marguerite Evans; Richard R. Fabsitz; Theresa E. Clay; Bonnie Holy Rock; and Brenda Broussard. 1999. "The Epidemic of Obesity in American Indian Communities and the Need for Childhood Obesity-Prevention Programs." *American Journal of Clinical Nutrition* 69, no. 4 (April): 747–54.

Sugarman, Jonathan R.; Leslie K. Dennis; and Emily White. 1994. "Cancer Survival Among American Indians in Western Washington State (United States)." *Cancer Causes and Control* 5, no. 5 (September): 440–48.

"Surveillance of Suicide and Suicide Attempts Among Veterans: Addressing a National Imperative" 2012. *American Journal of Public Health* 102, no. S1 (Supplement): e4–e5.

Swan; Judith; Nancy Breen; Linda Burhansstipanov; Delight E. Satter; William W. Davis; Timothy McNeel; and Matthew C. Snipp. 2006. "Cancer Screening and Risk Factor Rates Among American Indians." *American Journal of Public Health* 96, no. 2 (February): 340–50.

"Trends in Veterans with a Service-Connected Disability: 1985 to 2010." 2012. Washington, DC: National Center for Veterans Analysis and Statistics, U.S. Department of Veterans Affairs. Online at www.va.gov/vetdata/docs/QuickFacts/SCD_quickfacts_FY2011_FINAL.pdf.

Trivedi, Amal N; Regina C. Grebla; Steven M. Wright; and Donna L. Washington. 2011. "Despite Improved Quality of Care in the Veterans Affairs Health System, Racial Disparity Persists or Important Clinical Outcomes." *Health Affairs* 30, no. 4: 707–15.

"2010 National Survey of Veterans: Understanding and Knowledge of VA Benefits and Services." 2011. Washington, DC: National Center for Veterans Analysis and Statistics, US Department of Veterans Affairs. Online at www.va.gov/vetdata/docs/SpecialReports/2010NSV_Awareness_FINAL.pdf.

UCLA Center for Health Policy Research. 2004. "American Indian and Alaska Native Cancer Fact Sheet." Los Angeles, CA. Online www.healthpolicy.ucla.edu.

"Unemployment Rates of Veterans: 2000 to 2009." 2010. Washington, DC: National Center for Veterans Analysis and Statistics, U.S. Department of Veterans Affairs. Online at www.va.gov/vetdata/docs/SpecialReports/Unemployment_Rates_FINAL.pdf.

United States President's Commission. 2011. *Serve, Support, Simplify: Report of the President's Commission on Care of America's Wounded Heroes.* Memphis, TN: Books LLC.

Urban Indian Health Commission. 2007. *Invisible Tribes: Urban Indians and Their Health in a Changing World.* Seattle: Urban Indian Health Commission.

U.S. Census Bureau. 2012. *The American Indian and Alaska Native Population: 2010.* Washington, DC: Economics and Statistics Administration, U.S. Department of Commerce.

U.S. Commission on Civil Rights. 2004. *Broken Promises: Evaluating the Native American Health Care System.* Washington, DC: U.S. Commission on Civil Rights.

U.S. Department of Health and Human Services. 2000. *Healthy People 2010: Understanding and Improving Health.* Washington, DC: Government Printing Office.

U.S. Government Accountability Office. 2005. *Indian Health Service: Health Care Services Are Not Always Available to Native Americans.* Report to the Committee on Indian Affairs, U.S. Senate. Washington, D.C.: U.S. General Accountability Office.

Vandenberg, Patricia; Linda R. Bergofsky; and James F. Burris. 2010. "The VA's System of Care and the Veterans Under Care." *Journal of American Society on Aging* 34, no. 2 (Summer): 13–19.

"Veterans Population Projections: FY 2000 to FY 2036." 2010. Washington, DC: National Center for Veterans Analysis and Statistics, U.S. Department of Veterans Affairs. Online at www.va.gov/vetdata/.

"VHA Program Offices." n.d. Washington, DC: Department of Veterans Affairs. Online at www.va.gov/health/orgs.asp.

Warne, Donald. 2007. "Policy Challenges in American Indian/Alaska Native Health Professions Education." *Journal of Interprofessional* Care, supplement, vol. 21, Supplement 2 (October 7): 11–19.

———. 2009. "The State of Indigenous America Series." *Wicazo Sa Review* 24, no. 1 (Spring): 7–23.

Washington, Donna L. 2004. "Challenges to Studying and Delivering Care to Special Populations—The Example of Women Veterans." Guest Editorial. *Journal of Rehabilitation Research and Development* 41, no 2: vii–ix.

Welty, T.K. 1991. "Health Implications of Obesity in American Indians and Alaska Natives." *American Journal of Clinical Nutrition* 53, no. 6 Supplement (June): 1616–20.

Young, T. Kue. 1997. "Recent Health Trends in America Indian Population." *Population Research and Policy Review* 16, nos. 1–2 (April): 147–67.

Zoroya, Gregg. 2012. "Army Suicide Rate in July Hits Highest One-Month Tally." *USA Today*, August 16. Online at http://usatoday30.usatoday.com/news/military/story/2012–08–09/army-suicides/57096238/1.

6

FALLING THROUGH THE SAFETY NET

The Disadvantaged

By 1970, healthcare policy in the United States had reached its maturity. Medicare and Medicaid were passed in 1965; private insurance covered most of working America. But healthcare costs grew dramatically beginning in the mid-1960s, and portions of the population were left out of the system. Two of the major problems of the healthcare system are cost increases and access. We consider the problem of cost increases in the next chapter. This chapter focuses on the problem of access and the disadvantaged.

We concentrate on issues of access to the healthcare system, the problem of the uninsured and the underinsured, low-income groups, and minorities and women. To some extent, these problems overlap. While a good portion of the uninsured are low-income people, some are not. While minorities in general have lower incomes than whites, not all the problems of minorities and healthcare result from lower incomes. Rural areas have access problems with healthcare in the same way that inner cities do: lack of providers. We spell out these interrelationships as we go along.

Perhaps the underlying issue in looking at the disadvantaged and healthcare is equality and equity. We begin this chapter by considering this issue.

EQUALITY AND EQUITY

Equality means that we should treat people who are in the same situation the same way or treat people who are in different situations differently. That is, we should not discriminate against someone on account of race, religion, age, sex, ethnic group, and so forth. One reality of the healthcare system, to be discussed later in the chapter, is that there is discrimination based on income or at least based on health insurance. Those with private insurance plans, especially very generous ones, tend to get better service than those on public plans (such as Medicaid); those without health insurance tend to get the worst care (Berk and Schur 1998). Some have argued that the United States has a two-tiered healthcare system, one for most of us and another for the poor. In Krause's words,

> we have, combining the doctors and the office and hospital settings, a two-class medical care system. On the one hand, few practitioners and a few public settings for the poor in either the ghetto or rural areas; on the other hand, many practitioners and voluntary nonprofit hospitals for the middle class and the upper class in the suburbs. (Krause 1977, 146)

This leads us to the notion of equity, an extension of the concept of equality. Equity is related to another concept, social justice. Both ideas suggest that, given that some are disadvantaged in the healthcare system, an extra effort should be made to help overcome those disadvantages. This is, in a sense, the idea behind Medicaid (and to a lesser extent, Medicare). Medicaid recipients pay a minimal amount in copayments, if anything, for their healthcare. To compensate, their healthcare is subsidized by the larger community (taxpayers) and to some extent by providers and their patients in the sense that Medicaid reimbursements are lower than for privately insured patients and costs are shifted to privately insured patients. Education programs such as Head Start, where we devote more resources to children from impoverished backgrounds, are another example of equity-based programs.

A number of philosophical concepts support extending access to heathcare services to those who do not have it. Daniels, Light, and Caplan (1996) argue that the appropriate philosophical ground is *fairness*. To the authors, fairness is related to social justice and equal opportunity, or what they call fair equal opportunity. This concept—not especially well defined, in our opinion—sees healthcare as instrumental in that it allows people to function normally. The lack of healthcare services, according to their reasoning, shortens people's lives or makes it more difficult for them to function normally and therefore to live on a level playing field with other people. They write:

> A commitment to fair equality of opportunity thus recognizes that we should not allow people's prospects in life to be governed by correctable, morally arbitrary, or irrelevant differences between them, including those that result from disease and disability. . . . By designing a health care system that keeps *all* people as close as possible to normal function-ing, given reasonable resource constraints, we can in one important way fulfill our moral and legal obligations to protect equality of opportunity. (Daniels, Light, and Caplan 1996, 22; emphasis in original)

Notice at the end of the quote the reference to resource constraints. Their view of fairness is balanced by a concern for liberty, social productivity, and efficiency (Daniels, Light, and Caplan 1996).

The bulk of their book develops ten benchmarks of fairness to evaluate healthcare policy and then applies those benchmarks to the system as it existed at the time, the Clinton plan in 1993 and 1994, and managed care. Their benchmarks include universal access, equitable financing, value for money, public accountability, comparability, and degree of consumer choice. Their evaluation of the 1993–94 proposals gives the highest marks to the single-payer plan, lower marks to the Clinton proposal, and lowest marks to a market-oriented plan. Daniels et al. also conclude that the trend toward managed care and system integration would move the United States further away from fairness than any of the proposals considered in the 1993–94 period.

Baird (1998) uses the concept of justice, in this case gender justice, to evaluate the U.S. health-care system. Baird summarizes the gender justice framework as follows:

> The framework of gender justice includes the principles of self-determination, which is composed of the criteria of self-development, recognition, and democratic freedom; equality of gendered consequences; and diversity. (Baird 1998, 114)

Self-development refers to a policy's ability to help people develop their capabilities. Recogni-tion is accepting women's needs and experiences as legitimate, and respecting women. Democratic freedom refers to participating in or determining actions that affect one's life. Equality of gen-dered consequences asks whether public policies, even those that are seemingly neutral, promote equality. Diversity recognizes differences between men and women, but also differences among women (minority versus white).

Others argue for the concept of a *right to healthcare*. Cust (1997) contends that there is a moral right to healthcare, what he calls a just minimum. He writes that the moral right to healthcare is based on the fact that it can mean the difference between living and dying, and that it also affects a person's quality of life. The notion of rights, he continues, asserts an obligation to fulfill those rights. However, Cust, like Daniels et al., notes that because of resource constraints and the ever-increasing demand for heathcare, the right is not unlimited. Thus, he balances the moral right to healthcare with the notion of a just minimum.

One aspect of this underlying issue is whether healthcare is a right, in the same way that there is a right to education (a state mandate). In most industrialized countries, healthcare is indeed considered a right. The United States is the only Western industrialized country without a national healthcare system (see Graig 1999; Reid 2009; and White 1995). And as we shall see, one of the problems to be discussed is the increasing number of people without health insurance.

Watson (1994) argues that, at least for minorities, civil rights issues are at the base of healthcare inequities. He points to significant noneconomic barriers that lead to less access to healthcare and thus poorer healthcare and healthcare outcomes for minorities. Thus, he advocates new civil rights legislation that would forbid discriminatory practices, including unintentional ones, "if they are not necessary to the provision of health care and if their goals cannot be substantially accomplished through less discriminatory alternatives" (Watson 1994, 132).

A human rights approach to healthcare, with similarities to the ideas discussed above, also provides justification for expanding access to health insurance and healthcare services. Chapman (1994) defines human rights as those rights people inherently have because they are human. Human rights exist within the context of a community (see the discussion of community below) and are given high, though not absolute, priority. Chapman writes that these rights are "regarded as essential to the adequate functioning of the human being within the context of community, and (society) accepts responsibility for its promotion and protection" (Chapman 1994, 5). Thus there is the obligation on the part of society to fulfill those rights, though again there are limits to how much those rights, like some of the others we have discussed, are fulfilled. Like Daniels et al., Chapman holds that healthcare as a human right would be limited to those services that would allow a person to function in society and to achieve his or her potential. Chapman goes further when she states:

> The litmus test in this model of human rights is the extent to which the rights of the most vulnerable and disadvantaged individuals and groups are assured by these arrangements. A human rights standard assumes a special obligation or bias in favor of the needs and rights of the poor, the disadvantaged, the powerless, and those at the periphery of society. (Chapman 1994, 7)

Aday (1993b) argues that we should not base our healthcare system on a right to healthcare, which is within the individualistic, liberal tradition of American politics (see chapter 1). Instead, we should employ the notion of the common good, that it is in the best interest of the community, of society, not just the individual, that all its members have access to healthcare.[1] Kari, Boyte, and Jennings (1994) argue that healthcare should be seen as a civic question, where all participate in policy deliberations and emphasis should be placed on preventing disease and promoting health.

Stone (1993) contends that in recent years, and for good financial reasons, the private insurance market has moved away from notions of community embodied in the civics and communitarian approach of Kari et al. Insurance was originally intended as a means to spread the risk of individual misfortune among the larger community. Private insurers have increasingly sought to fragment the market, however, searching for those who are good health risks and placing more of the burden of financing care on those who are poor risks. This undermines the idea of community.

The debates over national health insurance, Medicare, Medicaid, and healthcare reform are, in a sense, marked by notions of community. Do we help those who are vulnerable or disadvantaged, or is everyone on his or her own? The implications of the two choices are not trivial.

Jecker (1993), likewise, suggests that the link between employment and health insurance itself creates injustices, an argument that Enthoven (2003) makes in a different context. Jecker argues that there is discrimination in the distribution of jobs, focusing on gender-based discrimination, and that this creates discrepancies in the availability of health insurance. As one example, consider that women are less likely to be employed in jobs that offer health insurance than men are.[2]

Thus, access to healthcare raises important ethical issues. What we must do now is document that the problems indeed do exist.

UNINSURED AND UNDERINSURED

As noted, most people in the United States with health insurance have it through their jobs. In 2010, 83.7 percent of the population were covered by health insurance, down from the almost 87 percent in 2000. About 31 percent were insured by public programs. Comparing the 2010 numbers with 2000, we see that dependence on private insurance has gone down. Private insurance is generally linked to employment. Table 6.1 indicates that 55.3 percent of the population had employer-based insurance in 2010, compared to 65.1 percent in 2000. Coverage by employer-sponsored insurance in 2010 was 55.3 percent, a decline from 65.1 percent in 2000. This is partly, though not entirely, a function of the recession in 2001 and the slow job recovery for several years after that and then the Great Recession from 2007 to 2009 and the slow recovery from that.

Table 6.1 also presents data about the number and percentage of uninsured persons. Note that the percentage of persons without insurance increased from 1999 to 2003. For 2010, the number of uninsured persons was almost 50 million. These numbers give an incomplete picture of the uninsurance problem. The data are, in a sense, a snapshot, a picture of those without insurance. A number of people experience spells of uninsurance during the year. According to the Centers for Disease Control and Prevention, about 59 million people lacked health insurance for some part of the year (Fox 2010).

The question to be raised is, why has health insurance coverage decreased?[3] This is an important question, given two facts. One is that much health insurance coverage, as noted earlier, is linked to jobs. This is the uniqueness of healthcare in the United States, a combination of public and private coverage, what Hacker (2002) calls the "divided welfare state." Second, such coverage decreased in the 1990s, even as job expansion was impressive. As noted above, job growth in the 2000s has been slower, with slow recoveries from the two recessions (2001–2002, 2007–2009). Coverage has continued to decline ("The Uninsured: A Primer" 2011a). An important related factor is the cost of healthcare and its reflection in the cost of health insurance. Employers try to shift more costs to employees or not cover employees at all. The individual market is so expensive that many either cannot afford it or are discouraged from getting it.

One way of looking at this is to consider employment-based insurance for children. In 1988, about 73.6 percent of children were covered under private insurance, most of that through a parent's employer. By 2010, that number had declined to 54.8 percent (U.S. Bureau of the Census 2004; 2011). It should be noted that the number of children without any coverage has declined because of expansions in Medicaid (and the Children's Health Insurance Program—from 20.5 percent of all children in 1999 to 34.8 percent in 2010 [U.S. Bureau of the Census 2011]), though a number of Medicaid-eligible children are not covered. The numbers show that the unique basis of medical insurance in the United States is declining (Gould 2004). Why?

The answer lies partly in the restructuring of the American economy. Insurance coverage is linked to size and type of firm (Claxton et al. 2004). The largest firms, those with 200 or more employees, are much more likely to offer health insurance to their employees than smaller firms are. During the period from 1999 to 2010, an average of 99 percent of such firms offered the health

Table 6.1

Sources of Health Insurance Coverage, 1999–2010

	Percent of population insured by all sources	Percent of population insured by employer	Percent of population insured by public insurance	Percent of population with nongroup insurance	Percent of population without health insurance	Number of people uninsured (in millions)
2010	83.7	55.3	31.0	9.8	16.3	49.9
2009	83.9	56.1	30.6	9.6	16.1	48.9
2008	85.1	58.9	29.1	9.5	14.9	44.8
2007	85.3	59.8	27.8	9.5	14.7	44.1
2006	84.8	60.3	27.1	9.8	15.2	45.2
2005	85.4	60.7	27.3	9.9	14.6	43.0
2004	85.7	61.1	27.3	10.0	14.3	41.8
2003	85.4	61.5	26.4	10.0	14.8	41.9
2002	86.1	62.8	25.5	10.2	13.9	39.8
2001	86.5	63.8	24.9	10.1	13.5	38.0
2000	86.9	65.1	24.4	10.2	13.1	36.6
1999	86.4	64.1	24.2	10.6	13.6	37.7

Note: Public insurance includes Medicare, Medicaid, and military. Some people have coverage under more than one type of insurance (i.e., Medicare and Medicaid, or Medicare plus retiree insurance).

Source: U.S. Bureau of the Census, "Health Insurance Historical Tables—HIB Series" Online at census.gov.

insurance benefit in good times and bad. For small firms (3–199 workers), the percentage offering health insurance declined from 65 percent in 1999 to 59 percent in 2010. A bit less than 49 percent of the smallest of firms, three to nine workers, offered health insurance to their employees (Claxton et al. 2011). The major reasons that smaller firms are less likely to cover their employees are the cost of the coverage and the greater inability of such firms to absorb these costs.

Another reason for erosion in employer-based health insurance has to do with the sectors of the economy that are growing and shrinking. Manufacturing firms and unionized firms (with much overlapping) are more likely to offer insurance than service-based or agricultural firms (Holahan and Ghosh 2004). For example, 96 percent of unionized firms offer health insurance to their employees compared to 61 percent of nonunion firms (Claxton et al. 2004). The service sector has experienced considerable growth, while the manufacturing sector and unionization have shrunk (Thorpe 1997).

Consider the following numbers. In 1970, some 20.7 million workers were in the manufacturing sector. In 2010, the number had shrunk to 14.1 million. By contrast, 20.4 million workers were in the service sector in 1970; in 2010 that number had jumped to almost 76 million. Another way of looking at this is to compare the relative shares of manufacturing and service workers. In 1970, the share of workers in manufacturing was 26.4 percent; in 2010, that share had declined to 10.1 percent. The share of workers in the service sector in 1970 was 25.9 percent, a little less than the manufacturing share. But by 2010, the service-sector share of jobs had increased to 54.6 percent (calculated from U.S. Bureau of the Census 1997, 2012). Thus, if there is less likelihood that the service sector will offer health insurance than the manufacturing sector will, it is understandable why fewer workers have health insurance.

Walmart, the largest employer in the United States, is a good example of these tendencies and problems. It has been criticized for failing to provide healthcare benefits for many of its employees. Most of those not receiving insurance were the lower-level and less well-paid workers. Almost half of the children of Walmart employees were either in Medicaid programs or remained uninsured (Abelson 2005). Indeed, a study commissioned by the company found that the presence of Walmart stores in a community tended to depress wages both for its employees and for other workers in the communities and to increase spending on Medicaid ("Wal-Mart Conference" 2005). In 2009, Walmart covered 52 percent of its workforce. In 2011, it announced that because of the continuing high increases in insurance premiums, new part-time employees working less than twenty-four hours a week will not receive coverage, and new employees who work twenty-four to thirty-three hours will not be able to get spousal coverage (Greenhouse and Abelson 2011).

A related problem concerns younger retirees, those between fifty-five and sixty-five. Many such retirees once maintained their healthcare plans with their former companies. Larger firms (and unionized firms) are more likely to offer health insurance to their retired workers than are smaller and nonunionized firms. However, even the larger firms are less likely to cover retirees. In 1988, 66 percent of large firms (200 or more workers) offered such a benefit. By 2011, the number was 26 percent (Claxton et al. 2011).

There are three other components to our understanding of the growth of the uninsured population. First is the growth in part-time or temporary workers. They are also unlikely to have health insurance, even if they work in firms that offer it to their full-time employees (Thorpe 1997). Full-time, year-round employees had an uninsurance rate of 15.1 percent in 2010 compared to 27.1 percent of year-round part-time employees ("The Uninsured: A Primer" 2011b). Second, a number of uninsured workers are covered as dependents under their spouses' health insurance. To the extent that this is the case, the fact that not all firms offer health insurance is not quite as much of a problem. In 2003, 77.5 million workers had health insurance and another 78.6 million people had insurance as dependents of other workers (Fronstin 2011). Some of these 78.6 million are workers in jobs that offer health insurance. On the other hand, this amounts to a subsidy from firms that offer health insurance to firms that do not. Additionally, because of the changing job structure, sectors that provide dependent coverage are also shrinking, so it is not just those with insurance-covered jobs but the dependents in non–insurance-covered jobs who are losing coverage.

Another part of the explanation for the uninsurance problem is that Medicaid, the healthcare program for the poor, covers only about 48 percent of those with incomes under the federal poverty level (calculated from Fronstin 2011, Figure 18). As we explained in chapter 3, Medicaid eligibility is set by states, and Medicaid is a costly program for them, even though the federal government picks up over half the costs. Medicaid increases combined with other budget pressures, including spending on crime and education, tight fiscal circumstances, and resistance to tax increases, led to efforts to constrain spending (see chapter 3). Despite expansion of Medicaid coverage for children and the establishment of the Children's Health Insurance Program (CHIP) (see chapter 3), 48 percent of uninsured children (about 3.9 million) live in families with income under the federal poverty line, and another 26 percent of uninsured children (about 2.1 million) live at 100 to 199 percent of the federal poverty line (Kaiser Commission on Medicaid and the Uninsured 2012).

But there is a more fundamental reason for people's being uninsured: health insurance is expensive, an issue we discuss in the next chapter. This is one of the reasons, discussed earlier, that smaller firms are less likely to offer health insurance. This is the issue that confronts larger companies such as General Motors and Walmart. If it is difficult for small firms to afford insurance because of the small pool of workers, then it is even more difficult for individuals to afford it. Such plans not only are costly in terms of premiums but also are likely to have significant cost-sharing provisions.

One last aspect remains. The section heading refers to the uninsured and the underinsured. The underinsured are those who have health insurance but whose insurance is inadequate for their present or future needs. A commonly used measure of underinsurance is when family healthcare costs exceed 10 percent of family income; for low-income families, the underinsurance threshold is 5 percent. This refers especially to those who may have illnesses such as AIDS or multiple sclerosis, chronic diseases that are potentially expensive to cover. Adding in the underinsured to the uninsured, one estimate is that as many as 81 million people are at some financial risk (Schoen 2011).

PROFILING THE UNINSURED

The obvious picture of the uninsured is that they are poor. Insurance coverage is linked to income: those with lower incomes are less likely to be insured than those with higher incomes ("The Uninsured: A Primer" 2011a). In terms of income, in 2010, 44 percent of nonelderly adults living in families with income under $20,000 lacked health insurance, compared to nearly nine percent for the same group with family income at $40,000 or more ("The Uninsured: A Primer" 2011b). Among age groups, the youngest adults were less likely to have health insurance than older, nonelderly adults ("The Uninsured: A Primer" 2011b).

A sizable percentage (about 82 percent) of uninsured people were in households where there were workers, and this was affected by whether family income was above or below 200 percent of the poverty line and whether the household had one or two full-time workers, or whether the primary worker worked part-time ("The Uninsured: A Primer" 2011a). Only 8.5 percent of families with two full-time workers were uninsured. Part-time workers had very high uninsurance rates. Minorities and foreign-born people (especially noncitizens) had high uninsurance rates ("The Uninsured: A Primer" 2011b).

CONSEQUENCES OF UNINSURANCE AND UNDERINSURANCE

There is a simple and easy, though not pleasant, answer to the question of what the consequences are of inadequate or no insurance. That answer is that such people are at higher risk of disease and death and are less likely to receive the services that they need when they need them than are those who have insurance. This section documents that claim.

One clearly important consequence is the linkage between health insurance coverage and mortality. In 2002, the Institute of Medicine (IOM) estimated that nearly 18,000 people died in 2000 because of lack of health insurance coverage, what is called excess deaths (Committee on the Consequences of Uninsurance 2002; Dorn 2008). Updating the IOM study, Dorn (2008) estimated the number of excess deaths between 2000 and 2006 at between 137,000 and 165,000 (the different numbers reflect somewhat different methodologies).

The uninsured are five times less likely than the insured to have a regular physician (Committee on the Consequences of Uninsurance 2002; "The Uninsured: A Primer" 2011a). Those with chronic health conditions who are uninsured are also less likely than those with health insurance to get the care they need, including the preventive care that would keep the chronic condition from worsening (Hoffman and Schwartz 2008). In general, the uninsured are less likely to get preventive care than the insured ("The Uninsured: A Primer" 2011a).

One interesting question focuses on the use of hospital emergency departments by the uninsured. There are political aspects to the question, because if the uninsured are crowding emergency departments, care becomes extremely costly. Based on our reading of the literature, we conclude the following. The uninsured are much more likely to make use of emergency departments for care than the insured. According to a study by the Center for Healthcare Research and Transformation (cited by Greene 2011), about 10 percent of the uninsured (Michigan data) use EDs for primary care compared to only 3 percent of the insured. Further, the uninsured are much more likely to utilize walk-in urgent care centers than the insured. But some have argued that it is insured patients, whether privately insured or on Medicaid, who really crowd the EDs and that blaming the uninsured is a myth. Data from the National Center for Health Statistics seem to support this finding (Garcia, Bernstein, and Bush 2010; LaCalle and Rabin 2010). Both statements appear to be correct.

The seemingly contradictory findings are easily reconcilable. The key is that the uninsured are a small portion, about 17 percent, of the population. So while the uninsured are more likely to use EDs than the insured, the insured population is more than five times as large. So we would expect that most of the people using ED services would be insured. Further, there is a convenience factor involved. While waiting times may be long for those going to EDs with non-life-threatening issues, it is still easier to see a doctor there than to see a family's regular family physician. Consider a family with a young child who develops an ear infection late Friday night. The parents are more likely to take the child to the ED on Saturday than to wait until Monday to call the child's pediatrician and hope to get in that day.

One result of delaying needed physician visits is that Medicaid patients and those without insurance are more likely than those with private insurance to be hospitalized for conditions that could be avoided or treated outside hospitals ("The Uninsured: A Primer" 2011a). Uninsured hospital patients are more likely to enter hospitals sicker and have shorter stays and fewer procedures performed on them than privately insured patients. They also have a higher death rate than insured patients (Committee on the Consequences of Uninsurance 2002).

Perhaps the most important impact is on children. Children whose families lack health insurance are less likely to see a physician than children in families with insurance and less likely to get the same quality of care as those who are insured (Children's Defense Fund 1998; "The Uninsured: A Primer" 2011a). Typical and treatable maladies of childhood, such as ear and throat infections, may go untreated and worsen (Quintana, Goldmann, and Homer 1997).

Further, barriers other than lack of insurance may hinder needed physician visits. These include cost-sharing provisions, lack of transportation, and lack of child care (Stoddard, St. Peter, and Newacheck 1994). The General Accounting Office (now the Government Accountability Office) expressed the problem this way:

> But having health insurance is no guarantee that children will get appropriate, high-quality care. Some children live in families that do not understand the need for preventive care or do not know how to seek high-quality care. Some live in neighborhoods that have few health care providers, where they have to travel further and wait longer for care. Some live in families in which most of the members do not speak English or defer getting care because they have had difficulty getting care previously. Some children have health insurance that does not cover some of the services they need the most—such as dental care or physical therapy for the developmentally disabled. . . . Such barriers can reduce the likelihood that even insured children will get the care they need. (General Accounting Office 1997)

Lack of insurance may affect the most helpless of people, newborn babies. Uninsured women are less likely to receive prenatal care than are privately insured women and more likely to have underweight children and premature births (Families USA 2010; Oberg et al. 1990). Private health insurance coverage for pregnant women is spotty. Prior to the Affordable Care Act, insurers could refuse to cover pregnant women, treating it as a preexisting condition, or could charge higher premiums for pregnant women. One estimate is more than two-thirds of corporations do not provide health insurance for dependents of employees (Andrews 2012b).

There are public programs to cover pregnancy, especially for low-income women. Federal law requires states under Medicaid to cover pregnant women with incomes under 133 percent of the federal poverty line. There is also an option to cover women with incomes under 185 percent of that indicator. As a result, Medicaid pays for about 40 percent of all births in the United States (Centers for Medicare and Medicaid Services n.d.).

Legislation in 2009 and 2010 extended insurance coverage for pregnant women. In 2009, the Children's Health Insurance Program (CHIP) was reauthorized, allowing states to cover pregnant women over the age of eighteen. The law provides for three options. The newest option is called the Pregnant Woman State Plan Amendments. It provides prenatal care and up to sixty days of care after delivery. Fifteen states make use of the Unborn Child State Plan Amendment, which originated with an administrative decision in 2002 by the Department of Health and Human Services to define a child from the point of conception and therefore eligible for benefits under the CHIP program. This program covers only the child and not the mother for non–pregnancy-related health problems. The third option is Section 1115 waivers, also a result of administrative action, in this case in 2000. Six states took part in this program as of 2010. States can design their own benefit programs, which could match those in the Pregnant Woman State Plan Amendments (Families USA 2010).

The Affordable Care Act provides new benefits for pregnant women, though some did not start until 2014. One example is that coverage of pregnancy will be part of the package of essential benefits for state health exchanges. Further, insurers will not be able to charge higher premiuns to pregnant women nor be able to refuse them coverage. The ACA also provides for a new program of home visitations for pregnant women by nurse practitioners and others (Andrews 2010).

The presence of health insurance also has an impact on the diagnosis of breast cancer. Women who have no health insurance or are covered by Medicaid are more likely to have breast cancer diagnosed later in the progression of the disease and are more likely to die as a result than women with breast cancer who have private health insurance (Committee on Health Insurance Status and Its Consequences 2009).

Those without health insurance also perceive themselves as less healthy than those with insurance. Death rates may be higher for those who lack health insurance than for those with it. This may be caused by both lack of access to medical care and lower quality of care when it is received (Committee on the Consequences of Uninsurance 2002).

Further, the lack of health insurance coverage results in low-income families having to make difficult choices in how to allocate their budgets. The competing demands of housing, food, clothing, and so forth lead lower-income families to forgo purchasing health insurance (Long 2003). Healthcare is expensive, but lack of healthcare coverage can be brutal on families.

Ironically, those without insurance are often charged more for healthcare services than those with coverage. This especially happens compared to employer-sponsored insurance, because employers can negotiate with providers for lower prices (discounts). The uninsured do not have that kind of leverage. The uninsured are often asked to pay prior to receiving services or make arrangements to pay (say, via credit cards) ("The Uninsured: A Primer" 2011a). The combination of delaying treatment and lack of insurance coverage often results in the incursion of large amounts of debt and bankruptcy (see Seifert and Rukavina 2006).

Uninsurance and underinsurance have impacts beyond those of the individual. In 1986, Congress passed the Emergency Medical Treatment and Active Labor Act (EMTALA). The legislation was passed, at least partially, in response to instances of what were known as "dumping," whereby hospitals would either refuse to treat uninsured patients or transfer them to other hospitals. Under EMTALA, hospitals receiving federal funds (through programs such as Medicare and Medicaid) are required to screen and treat anyone showing up at an emergency room with threatening health-care conditions. Hospitals are required to, at a minimum, stabilize the patient before releasing him or her (Furrow 1995; Rosenbaum 2013). The legislation has sometimes been used to show that people can get care even if uninsured. For example, President Bush in July 2007 said: "The immediate goal is to make sure there are more people on private insurance plans. I mean, people have access to health care in America. After all, you just go to an emergency room" (quoted in Froomkin 2007).

The law has been somewhat limited. Its penalties are fairly light. And in 2003, the Bush administration issued regulations loosening the requirements and downsizing enforcement ("Emergency Medical Treatment and Active Labor Act" n.d.; Rosenbaum et al. 2012). Rosenbaum et al. (2012) document several instances of violations of the EMTALA and suggest that a better system of reporting and monitoring is necessary.

Because uninsured people are more likely to use expensive emergency rooms than a regular physician, the cost of that care is shifted to others. Indeed, hospitals in particular engage in considerable cost shifting, given service to the uninsured and the low reimbursement rates for Medicaid patients. Those with private insurance are charged more (and pay higher premiums) because of such cost shifting. Because of the Medicare hospital Prospective Payment System (PPS), discussed in chapter 4, shifting costs to Medicare patients is virtually impossible. Given this cost shifting, portions of the community pay for uninsured care, but not on an explicit basis. Further, the use of underwriting creates a situation where those who most need the help are least likely to get it. That runs against the grain of the purpose of insurance.

Another aspect of the uninsurance problem is the consequences for communities where a significant percentage of the population lack health insurance. Such communities have what are called "negative spillover effects" (Gresenz and Escarce 2011). Gresenz and Escarce (2011) note that people who were insured, but lived in communities with high insurance rates, had difficulty accessing the system and lower satisfaction with access to care. This appeared to be the case even among seniors who have Medicare.

INSURANCE AND THE IDEA OF COMMUNITY

This brings us back to the issue of equity. Many health insurance provisions are put in place regardless of income. Consider a company that offers a health insurance plan covering dependents. The premiums are $350 a month for family coverage, and there are cost-sharing provisions. All employees are offered the same plan. The general manager of the company makes $215,000 a year (before taxes) and the janitor makes $20,000 (before taxes). Both have to pay the $350 monthly premium. The premium is only 2.8 percent of the general manager's income, but is 21 percent of the janitor's income. Now extend this example to those who try to buy health insurance as individuals rather than as part of a group. Typically, premiums for individual policies are not as high as family group policies but are also not as generous. Further, in the case of individual plans, the holder pays all the cost of the premiums, whereas in group (employer-based) plans, the employer will pay some of the premium costs. Cost-sharing provisions (deductibles, copayments) tend to be larger for individual policies (Kaiser Family Foundation 2004a; Pollack and Kronebusch 2004). The result is that, from 2004 to 2007, about 73 percent of those shopping on the individual health insurance market either could not afford the plan or were turned down because of a preexisting condition (Doty et al. 2007).

There is another way in which ethical issues play a role in the uninsurance and underinsurance problem. This is the problem of changes in insurance company policies. To simplify, health insurance policies can take two forms. On the one hand is community rating, by which everybody in the insurance pool pays the same premiums (though there may be differences based on age and other such factors, a practice known as risk adjustment). That way, the risk of using the insurance (needing healthcare) is spread over a larger population. Larger firms are more likely than smaller firms to have a community rating. Because the pool of employees is larger, there is a larger group of workers over which to spread the risk. Smaller firms, with fewer workers, have a smaller group over which to spread the risk. Insurance companies could handle the problem by treating all those it insures as the community, so it would not matter whether the firm was large or small, or the policy was for an individual or a group. Note that pooling risk for individual policies by definition cannot be done.

There has been an increasing tendency for insurance companies to write policies based on experience rating, under which the premiums are adjusted based on the likely risk of needing healthcare. A person with a chronic heart problem, for example, is more likely to need healthcare than one in good health with no chronic problems. Automobile insurance is written on this basis. Premiums are higher for those in the highest-risk groups, which includes those who have been in accidents and those in groups most likely to have accidents. For example, young single males have the highest auto insurance premiums of any group.

Such a practice makes sense from the standpoint of the insurance company, as well as policyholders in low-risk groups. Those more likely to need the service should pay more. Having community rating in auto insurance would mean higher rates for those in the low-risk groups and lower rates for those in the high-risk groups, pretty much what we see with the Affordable Care Act (see chapter 10).

But healthcare and health insurance are not automobile insurance. People in good health can do more, can realize more of their potential, than those in poor health. Healthcare is instrumental in the sense that it enables one to do other things. If there is a systematic bias through experience rating, then it carries over into other areas.

Stone brings the debate of community versus experience rating out into the open, looking at its philosophical underpinnings:

> Actuarial fairness—each person paying for his own risk—is more than an idea about distributive justice. It is a method of organizing mutual aid by fragmenting communities into ever-smaller, more homogeneous groups and a method that leads ultimately to the destruction of mutual aid. This fragmentation must be accomplished by fostering in people a sense of their differences, rather than their commonalities, and their responsibility for themselves only, rather than their interdependence. Moreover, insurance necessarily operates on the logic of actuarial fairness when it, in turn, is organized as a competitive market. (Stone 1993)

Such a view was incorporated in President George W. Bush's "ownership society" perspective. Each person would buy his or her own health insurance using money put away in tax-deferred health savings accounts (Vieth 2004).

The important idea here is that the insurance practice of experience rating breaks down the idea of community. The community argument would support, at a minimum, insurance reform and, at a maximum, national health insurance. In-between policies might include tax subsidies and employer mandates.

There is another insurance practice, very much related to experience rating, that leads to some people being uninsured and others being underinsured. This is the practice of insurance underwriting. Underwriting occurs when an insurance company refuses to insure workers in an entire firm (a practice known as "redlining") or individuals with preexisting conditions. Examples of redlined firms include "those characterized by an older work force (over age fifty-five) or high employee turnover, those engaged in seasonal work or exposed to hazardous working conditions, those lacking an employer-employee relationship, and those 'known to present frequent claims submissions'" (Zellers, McLaughlin, and Frick 1992, 174–75). Those with preexisting conditions, such as cancer, diabetes, or AIDS, and those with conditions that are likely to result in costly claims in the future, may be denied insurance either permanently or during a specified time. In addition, limits may be placed on payments to such individuals. An alternative practice is to raise all the premiums for the groups significantly, sometimes to prohibitive levels. It is not just insurance companies that engage in this practice. Employers that self-insure, and thus do not come under state regulation as do insurance companies, can also deny claims. Another thing companies can do is simply fire workers with high healthcare costs. This is apparently happening with workers with disabilities as firms seek to limit their healthcare costs (see Pereira 2003).

A law passed in 1986, the Consolidated Omnibus Budget Reconciliation Act (COBRA), allows workers who lose their jobs to maintain their health insurance for up to eighteen months after their job ended (Kreidler, n.d.). While this does provide for some workers and their families, the insurance is expensive. Under COBRA, the displaced worker pays both the employee's and the employer's share of the costs, including any increases that might occur over the eighteen-month period. The costs are substantial. In 2011, an employer-covered family health insurance plan cost, on average, $15,073 of which the employee contributed $4,129 (Claxton et al. 2011). So the worker with family coverage who lost his or her job would be paying $15,073, more than three-and-a-half times what he or she previously paid, but without the job to pay for it.

Even those who are insured may be underinsured. Kinney and Steinmetz (1994, 637) provide a definition and estimate of underinsurance, based on the 1990 Pepper Commission report: "those at risk of spending more than 10 percent of their annual income for healthcare in the event of serious illness."

A CLOSER LOOK: THE POOR, MINORITIES, AND WOMEN

In this section, we consider the healthcare problems of the disadvantaged, focusing on the poor, minorities, and women. To some extent, the material in this section overlaps with that in the previous section on the uninsured and the underinsured. But as we have noted, a sizable portion of the uninsured are not poor and do work. There are thus other problems that need to be addressed.

Pollack and Kronebusch identify four factors or dimensions that make some groups likely to be uninsured (or underinsured) and therefore suffer the consequences that we have discussed above. These factors are: "needs that hinder access to insurance, general economic disadvantage, discrimination, and impaired and proxy decisionmaking" (2004, 206).

Minorities and Low-Income Groups

In general, minorities and low-income groups do not have the same access to healthcare, or do not compare in health statistics on the same level as those who are white and/or wealthier. This is not a new phenomenon, as Byrd and Clayton (2003) make clear in their historical discussion of disparities in healthcare. In drawing this portrait of low-income and minority groups, we should point out that this is a statistical portrait. It applies in general to the groups discussed.

In looking at the health status of minority and low-income groups, we should note several important features. First, minority groups tend to have lower educational achievement, higher unemployment rates, higher crime rates, lower incomes and therefore higher poverty rates, higher proportions of female-headed families, and higher proportions of out-of-wedlock births. All of this seems to be correlated with health status. One of the confusing aspects of these data is that they are very much related to income and education (Beckles and Truman 2011). That is, many of these characteristics may be a result of poverty (socioeconomic class) rather than ethnicity (race) (Committee on the Consequences of Uninsurance 2002; Patel and Rushefsky 2008).[4]

One issue related to low-income groups suggests that their poorer health status is largely attributable to "risky" behaviors that they engage in, such as smoking, drinking, being overweight, and not exercising. In a sense, this is an argument that can be labeled "blaming the victim" (Ryan 1971; see also the discussion in Levy and Meltzer 2004). That is, this hypothesis suggests that higher mortality rates are due to actions taken (or not taken) by each person. A study reported in the June 3, 1998, issue of the *Journal of the American Medical Association* (*JAMA*) found that even considering such behaviors, low-income groups had higher mortality rates than higher income groups. Changing the behaviors would certainly help some, but mortality differences would remain (Lantz, House, and Chen 1998).

African Americans

McBride argues that healthcare policy toward African Americans went through three stages. The first stage was engagement (mid-1960s to late 1970s), when healthcare services and financing to the black community were increased and discrimination was lessened. The second phase, submersion, from the late 1970s to the mid-1980s, saw a cutback in social programs. For example, as a result of the 1981 Omnibus Budget and Reconciliation Act, the working poor were taken off AFDC and Medicaid rolls. The third phase, crisis recognition, began in the mid-1980s. This is a recognition that there is a problem, particularly in the large urban cities. But McBride (1993) points out that this last phase has not yet resulted in changed policies. Thus the healthcare problems of minorities and low-income groups remained. Indeed, a study of Chicago, Houston, and Los Angeles noted "the progressive deterioration in the delivery of healthcare to the poor and the indigent since the beginnings of the 1980s" (Ginzberg 1994).

African Americans, like many ethnic and racial minorities, are more likely to be uninsured than the white population. For non-Hispanic whites, the uninsurance rate was 12 percent in 2009. The rate for African Americans was 21 percent (Russell 2010; Pollack and Kronebusch 2004). We should thus expect the consequences of uninsurance to be higher among minorities than among the white population (Agency for Healthcare Research and Quality 2010).

Age-adjusted death rates are higher for minorities than for whites. For whites, the number of deaths per 100,000 population in 2009 was 732.6, compared to 922.9 for blacks (Kaiser Family Foundation n.d.). Death rates due to a variety of factors, including diabetes, cardiovascular disease, cancer, infant mortality, and substance abuse, are higher among African Americans than among whites (Agency for Health Care Research and Quality 2003, 2010; Committee on the Consequences of Uninsurance 2002; Hogue, Hargraves, and Collins 2000). African Americans tend to have less access to prenatal care and to give birth at earlier ages (National Center for Health Statistics 2004). This tends to result in higher rates of premature and low-weight births (Agency for Health Care Research and Quality 2003). Infant, neonatal, and postneonatal death rates are much higher for blacks than for whites. Consider the infant mortality rate: 5.6 per 1,000 live births for whites, compared to 12.9 for blacks. There have been improvements (decreases) in these death rates. The infant death rate among African Americans decreased by over 32 percent from 1983 to 2007. The white/black gap in infant mortality rates declined about 26 percent over the same period (National Center for Health Statistics 2011). African American women had the highest rate of low-weight births (2012 data) (Maternal and Child Health Bureau 2012).

African Americans tend to have higher rates of chronic conditions or disability than other ethnic groups, even accounting for income. For example, 63 percent of blacks with incomes under 200 percent of the federal poverty have at least one chronic condition or disability, compared to half of whites. For those with incomes over 200 percent of the federal poverty line, 45 percent of blacks have at least one chronic disease or disability, compared to 32 percent of whites (Mead et al. 2008; Russell 2010). Doing a little bit of arithmetic, we see that for those under 200 percent of the federal poverty line, the gap between blacks and whites is 26 percent; at the higher level, the gap is even larger, 40 percent.

African Americans also have higher rates of adult obesity, with the rate for African American women at almost half that population. Almost twice as many blacks have chronic conditions such as hypertension and heart disease, asthma, and diabetes than other ethnic groups. Cancer rates are higher among African Americans, and mortality rates from cancer are higher than for whites. Survival rates of cancers of the breast, prostate, and lung are lower than for whites (Russell 2010; see also Agency for Healthcare Research and Quality 2010).

Another public health problem of African Americans, though it may not appear that way, is homicide. Homicide death rates of African American males are 637 percent higher than those of white males (using 2008 numbers). They are also higher for Latinos, though the difference is not as great (National Center for Health Statistics 2011). The role of firearms and gun control is about as politically contentious an issue as can be found. The pro-gun lobbies are immensely powerful and have been able to suppress much discussion about this public health issue (see Klein 2012; Murphy 2012). Absent any discussion or action, guns and violence will continue to be a plague, especially in the African American community (Levine et al. 2012).

AIDS is another health problem that affects ethnicity differently. While a majority of AIDS victims are whites, the relative proportion of AIDS victims is disproportionately much higher among African Americans and Latinos. The white proportion is 8.2 cases per 100,000, versus 26.6 per 100,000 for Latinos and 73.7 per 100,000 for African Americans (Agency for Healthcare Quality and Research 2011). To put it another way, whites are 69 percent of the population but accounted for 28 percent of new AIDS diagnoses in 2003, versus Latinos, who make up 14 percent of the population and accounted for 20 percent of new AIDS diagnoses, and African Americans, who make up 13 percent of the population but accounted for 49 percent of new AIDS diagnoses (Kates and Leggoe 2005a, b). In 2009, African Americans accounted for 44 percent of new infections and are disproportionately represented in all stages of the HIV/AIDS cycle. AIDS accounts for a significant proportion of deaths among blacks, the ninth-leading cause among males and the third-leading cause among females (Centers for Disease Control and Prevention 2011). The death rate from AIDS has decreased among all racial and ethnic groups, but disparities remain. The death rate for African Americans in 2007 was 17.3 per 100,000 population versus 1.9 per 100,000 among whites, over nine times higher for blacks than for whites. The decline in HIV-related deaths has been higher for whites than for blacks (Agency for Healthcare Quality and Research 2011).

The Centers for Disease Control and Prevention (CDC) (2011) suggests four reasons why HIV infections are so much higher among African Americans than other racial or ethnic groups; each of them presents challenges for reducing incidence and consequences. One set of reasons, almost tautological, is that there is a high prevalence of the disease in the African American community and so sex among African American partners creates high risks of contracting HIV. A second reason is socioeconomic: high incidence of poverty, lack of access to healthcare, poor housing, and lack of prevention information. The third reason is lack of awareness of one's HIV status. The CDC estimates that 20 percent of those infected with HIV in the United States (and not just the black community) do not know that they are carrying the infection. This creates a greater possibility of transmitting the virus as well as later diagnosis and thus poorer outcomes. The fourth reason is stigma. HIV is often associated with homosexuality, so that finding out or admitting that one has HIV implies that one is a homosexual. There is, also, fear that someone with HIV or AIDS will be discriminated against.

The data also show that African American women are more likely than either white women or Latinas to have acquired the virus through heterosexual sex. In urban centers, 32 percent of African American men who have had sex with other men are infected with the virus (Kates and Leggoe 2005a). Drug-related transmissions (i.e., by intravenous drug users) are also another major path of HIV infection, though this is more significant for white women than for African American women. Auerbach (2004) summarizes the factors responsible for this epidemic:

> The experience of women and girls in the HIV-AIDS epidemic in the United States and around the world highlights how social arrangements, cultural norms, laws, policies and institutions contribute to the unequal status of women in society and to the spread of disease. Together they undermine the capacity of women and girls to exercise power over their own lives and to control the circumstances that increase their vulnerability to HIV infection, particularly in the context of sexual relationships. For African American women, gender inequalities are exacerbated by persistent racism.

As we have seen, African American women are especially hard hit (see Auerbach 2004; Clemetson 2004; and Fears 2005). Indeed, a study released in 2012 suggests that the HIV/AIDS rate among African American women is about five times higher than the CDC has estimated ("HIV Among Black Women 5 Times Higher than Previously Thought" 2012). This became a bit of an issue during the 2004 vice presidential debates between Vice President Dick Cheney and his Democratic counterpart, Senator John Edwards of North Carolina. The moderator of the debate, Gwen Ifill, an African American woman, asked the two candidates what the federal government should do to help stem the increase in AIDS among African American women. Neither candidate had an answer, nor even appeared to be familiar with the problem (Auerbach 2004).

Quality of care for African Americans is lower than for whites. Blacks are less likely than whites to receive screenings for such possible health threats as colorectal cancer. As a result, when blacks are diagnosed with that cancer, the disease is more likely to be at an advanced stage than for whites. Whites with diabetes are more likely to receive various services for that chronic disease than blacks. As a result, blacks are much more likely than any other group to be admitted to a hospital with complications related to diabetes (Agency for Healthcare Research and Quality 2010). The pattern is quite clear: African Americans receive fewer services for various diseases and suffer higher rates of adverse effects from them than whites. It is no wonder that 13 percent of African Americans report they are not in good health (Russell 2010).

Latinos

There is much variation within the Latino population, coming from Puerto Rico, Mexico, Cuba, and Central America, and so their health issues vary somewhat. In general, 32 percent of Hispanics lacked health insurance coverage compared to 12 percent for whites. Over a third of Hispanics lacking insurance had chronic health conditions, and many of the uninsured did not have a family physician (2009 data) (Russell 2010). Hispanics have higher rates of obesity, diabetes, kidney failure, and cervical cancer than whites.

A major access problem for Latinos is language. Those who speak only Spanish have a more difficult time getting needed care (Patel and Rushefsky 2008; Russell 2010). Over 21 million people in the United States under the age of sixty-five have limited English proficiency (LEP). Of those, 66 percent are Latinos ("Overview of Health Coverage for Individuals with Limited English Proficiency" 2012). People with LEP are more likely than those who are proficient to live in poverty and also have lower educational levels. Forty-nine percent of those with LEP are uninsured compared to 18 percent of those who are proficient. Similarly, people with LEP are less likely than people with English proficiency to have employer-based or private insurance and more likely to be on Medicaid or other public insurance program. People with limited English proficiency have less access to care and less access to preventive services, and are more likely to be dissatisfied with the care they receive. And as with many of the factors we are discussing in this chapter, there is a cumulative effect of having many different barriers to care. These barriers or factors include "race/ethnicity, citizenship status, low education, and poverty" ("Overview of Health Coverage for Individuals with Limited English Proficiency" 2012). The LEP population experiences many of these problems.

One of the interesting findings in the disparities literature is what is known as the Hispanic paradox. Latinos have a longer life span and lower infant mortality rate than any other group, including whites (Patel and Rushefsky 2008; Russell 2010). No accepted explanation has been offered for this paradox, though a small number of possible explanations have been given. It may be that Latino migrants who come to the United States are healthier than those of other groups. Another possibility, which has been called the "salmon-bias," suggests that Latinos who are terminally ill return to their home country. A third possibility is that the available data are inadequate (Patel and Rushefsky 2008).

Latinas are less likely to receive early prenatal care than almost any other ethnic or racial group (Mead et al. 2008). Why do disadvantaged women not get full prenatal care? One reason is financial barriers. Minority and low-income women are less likely than the general population to have health insurance (Mead et al. 2008; Agency for Health Care Research and Quality 2010; Garner et al. 1996). Even if financial barriers did not exist, there are not enough doctors willing to work in low-income areas or with high-risk mothers. In 2001, only 62 percent of physicians accepted new Medicaid patients, and only 54 percent of primary care physicians did so (Zuckerman et al. 2004). Thus the services, even if affordable, might not be available.

American Indians/Alaska Natives

American Indians and Alaska Natives have some of the worst health indicators of any of the racial/ethnic groups we are considering. Thirty-two percent do not have health insurance. They have much highest rates of obesity and overweight, including among children (Russell 2010). They have a high percentage of smokers (Mead et al. 2008). Alaska Natives and American Indians (AI/AN) have high rates of diabetes, and are more likely to die of diabetes and more likely to have strokes than whites (Mead et al. 2008; Russell 2010).

Where homicide is a major health issue within the African American community, suicide is a very serious problem within the American Indian and Alaska Native communities. According to Russell (2010, 5), suicide "is the second leading cause of death for those age 10 to 34 years" (see also Agency for Healthcare Research and Quality 2010). As a related point, mental health problems, including the use of drugs, are also higher for this group than for any other. The infant mortality rate among American Indians and Alaska Natives is higher than for whites (Mead et al. 2008; Russell 2010). Rates of asthma are higher for this group than any other except for blacks (Mead et al. 2008). American Indian and Alaska Native women are the least likely of racial/ethnic groups to receive prenatal care in the first trimester of a pregnancy (Mead 2008).

Breast cancer incidence and mortality rates are lower for AI/AN than for any other group except Asian/Pacific Islanders (Mead et al. 2008). Fifty-three percent of American Indians and Alaskan Natives report their health condition as fair or poor compared to 42 percent among whites (Mead et al. 2008).

The Agency for Healthcare Quality and Research (2010) issues a periodic report on disparities among different ethnic racial groups. Among other things, the report looks at changes in core measures of quality of care from 2001–2002 to 2007–2008. For American Indians/Alaska Natives, only one of the core measures showed improvement, fifteen saw no change, and six got worse.

Women

> Research has shown that many diseases and conditions, including heart disease, smoking, and lung cancer, affect women and men very differently. There are also several diseases, such as breast cancer and osteoporosis, that primarily affect women, and another range of conditions, including pregnancy, menopause, and certain reproductive-related cancers, that only affect women. Sex-based differences have been identified on several levels, including treatment efficacy, medication side effects, prevention strategies, and disease etiology. (Kaiser Family Foundation 2004b)

The issues of women's health cannot be understood only in biological terms, as simply the ills of the female of the species. Women and men are different, but we are also similar—and we both are divided by the social relations of class and race/ethnicity. To begin to understand how our social constitution affects our health, we must ask, repeatedly, what is different and what is similar across the social divides of gender, color, and class. We cannot assume that biology alone will provide the answers we need; instead, we must reframe the issues in the context of the social shaping of our human lives—as both biological creatures and historical actors. Otherwise, we will continue to mistake—as many before us have done—what is for what must be, and leave unchallenged the social forces that continue to create vast inequalities in health. (Krieger and Fee 1996, 27)

To a degree, women's health issues overlap those of minorities (race/ethnicity) and low-income groups (class). To the extent that women's income is low, especially in families headed by women, all the health problems associated with low income show up here. For example, issues surrounding prenatal care, while obviously a concern for women, are generally associated with low income. If programs aimed at low-income people are cut, as was done in the early 1980s and is again being done in the 2000s, then women will be affected.

On the other hand, there are certain issues that are unique to women, though of concern to men as well:

> . . . the large body of evidence of sex and gender differences in both the prevalence of health conditions and the use of health services. Women have unique reproductive health care needs, have higher rates of chronic illnesses, and are greater users of the health care system. In addition, women take the lead on securing health care for their families and have lower incomes than men, both of which affect and shape their access to the health system. (James et al. 2009).

Women are also less well protected by health insurance, both public and private. Fewer working women (39.4 percent) have employer-based health insurance than men (51.5 percent) (Fronstin 2004; see also Salganicoff et al. 2002). The percentage of women with extended bouts of being uninsured has grown, likely related to the state of the economy. Twenty percent of women were uninsured for four years or more in 2004; by 2008, that number had increased to 27 percent. Minority women are more likely to be uninsured than white women (Ranji and Salganicoff 2011). Baird (1998) notes that married men have higher rates of employer-provided insurance than married women do. She also notes that divorce has a devastating effect on private health insurance for unemployed women. Women's employment careers tend to be intermittent (women may take time off for childbearing, or they may make job changes because their husbands move), and women are more often in lower-paying jobs that are less likely to offer health insurance. Medicaid coverage is sporadic. Fewer than half of those eligible are covered, and doctors do not have to accept Medicaid patients. Further, because women, on the average, live longer than men, issues of long-term care and chronic illnesses are critical (Salganicoff et al. 2002). Racial and ethnic minority women and low-income women (there is a considerable overlap here) are more likely to experience chronic health conditions than are white women (Ranji and Salganicoff 2011).

The above paragraph probably understates the problem. First, the percentage of workers covered by employer-based health insurance has declined. Further, there is a growing trend toward using part-time or temporary workers, also unlikely to have health insurance benefits. The result is that about 25 percent of woman have no health insurance for all or part of the year (Ranji and Salganicoff 2011).

The lack of insurance affects access to the healthcare system. Twenty-four percent of women have delayed getting care because of the costs, with higher percentages for those without insurance or with incomes below the federal poverty line. Even women on Medicaid found cost barriers sufficient to delay seeking care. Other barriers to obtaining care facing women include lack of transportation or lack of chld care or inability to take time off from work (Ranji and Salganicoff 2011).

Women, like others facing barriers to obtaining healthcare, make trade-offs. In 2004, 8 percent of women said that they cut back on other basic needs because of the costs of heath care. By 2008, that number had doubled (Ranji and Salganicoff 2011).

Women of whatever race or ethnic group face unique problems related to their role in the family. They are often the primary caregiver for their children. If a child becomes sick, they may have to take off from work because of lack of child care. Women are less likely then men to work in jobs that provide paid sick leave. Women also tend to be the primary caregiver for family members who are chronically ill or disabled (Ranji and Salganicoff 2011).

There have been changes in the workforce participation of women and in the family structure, where there are two-worker families or the family is headed by a female. Adjustments to these changes have been slow. The Family and Medical Leave Act is one adjustment, but it was enacted in 1993. While it provides for leave without losing one's job, the leave is upaid. Muller's words, written in 1990, still depict the problems facing women and health insurance coverage:

> Independent coverage, benefit content and duplication, and cost sharing are issues that af-
> fect women differently in different family situations. Employers have expanded their use
> of peripheral or contingent workers who have few or no benefit entitlements, drawing on
> a largely female labor supply. It is not feasible to count on workplace arrangements as the
> social instrument for protecting individuals against health care costs. (1990, 73)

RIGHT TO LIFE, RIGHT TO CHOOSE, AND
THE BATTLE OVER BIRTH CONTROL

Reproductive issues, such as abortion and family planning, are among the most controversial issues in healthcare or any policy field. In general, the availability of abortion, while not completely eliminated, has been greatly reduced beginning in the late 1970s. Some of this has come about because of legislative changes at both the federal and, especially, state level. Some is a result of court decisions that have allowed restrictions, such as waiting periods. From 1976 to 2007, the U.S. Supreme Court issued decisions that mostly upheld restrictions on abortion, though not addressing the fundamentals of *Roe v. Wade,* the 1973 decision that set the course for this divisive issue. Another element has been the strong right-to-life movement, which has picketed abortion clinics. Medical schools are less frequently teaching abortion procedures.

We can see the volatility, intensity, and controversy surrounding healthcare in the passage of the Affordable Care Act as well as the elections of 2012. The issues of abortion and reproductive rights touch upon the values of order, including the protection of traditional social values, and liberty, including the right of privacy.

Advances in the biological sciences produced new means of birth control, such as pills originally developed in the 1950s. A major court case, *Griswold v. Connecticut* (1965), addressed the question of whether the state, in this case Connecticut, could forbid the sale of birth control pills to married couples. The U.S. Supreme Court ruled that the state could not and in the process developed the doctrine of a "right to privacy." The next year, the Court ruled that bans on sales of oral contraceptives to unmarried people was also unconstitutional.

Griswold then formed the basis for the 1973 *Roe v. Wade* decision, as well as the companion, *Doe v. Bolton.* In *Roe,* the majority divided the pregnancy into trimesters (three-month periods), based on the viability of the fetus/unborn child, that is, after the time when a child could live outside the mother's womb on its own (at that time, after about six months). In the first trimester, the decision about terminating a pregnancy (an abortion) would be between the woman and her doctor. In the second trimester, states could limit abortions if they threatened the mother's health. In the third trimester, the Court ruled, the state did have a legitimate interest in protecting the life of the fetus and could place restraints on the availability of abortion (Rhoden 1986).

Congress took its first stance in 1976 with the passage of the Hyde Amendment, which forbade the use of the federal component of Medicaid funds to pay for abortions. It also gave the states the right to take similar action, most of which forbid the use of the state share of Medicaid funding to pay for abortions.

In response to state actions, cases were brought before the federal courts. In 1989, the Court held in *Webster v. Reproductive Health Services* that some state restrictions were acceptable. As more cases came before the Court, and the makeup of the Court became more conservative, more and more restrictions were upheld. Many state laws became more restrictive and, in some cases, more intrusive. State laws began to require waiting periods before an abortion could take place. Some laws required the mother to read literature about the developing fetus or to undergo an ultrasound procedure and listen to the heartbeat. In 2012, the Commonwealth of Virginia passed a law requiring a transvaginal procedure, a probe put in the vagina to do the ultrasound. Other states considered this requirement but backed off because of public backlash. By July 2012, some thirty-nine new restrictions were placed on abortion (Gold and Nash 2012).

The inclusion of abortion as a procedure covered by the Affordable Care Act became one of the barriers to passage of the ACA. Because all Republicans voted against the act, the issue was one among the majority Democrats. The Hyde amendment addressed Medicaid funding for abortions. What about the state health exchanges that would be set up for those who had to buy insurance on the individual market? Could insurance policies written through the exchanges cover abortion services? Bart Stupak, a Democratic member of the House of Representatives from Michigan, was opposed to permitting abortions through the Affordable Care Act, including selling policies through the exchanges, where many subscribers would be eligible for federal subsidies to help pay for abortions. Members of the Catholic Church were somewhat divided, but clearly the U.S. Conference of Catholic Bishops took the most pro-life/anti-abortion stance. The ultimate outcome was that President Obama would issue an executive order that would prohibit abortions under any provision of the Affordable Care Act. This did not satisfy the bishops, who argued that a future president could overturn the executive the order. But it did satisfy Stupak and other moderate/conservative Democrats (Kirsch 2011; Starr 2013).

But the issue of reproduction has extended beyond allowing abortions to the availability of birth control. This part of the issue again was related to the Affordable Care Act. Now the question was whether the insurance plans issued under the state exchanges were required to cover contraception pills, devices, etc. The Obama administration issued a rule that required the coverage of reproductive technologies as part of the "essential benefits" that all plans should cover. And that moved to the larger stage of whether to cover birth control in insurance policies at all, as well as the defunding of Planned Parenthood. Again, the pro-life forces squared against the pro-choice forces. In this case, the pro-life forces added the religious argument that requiring institutions that objected to birth control to fund it violated religious freedom. The administration's compromise was to allow companies to refuse to pay for birth control coverage, but to allow insurance plans to offer it. This did not satisfy the pro-life groups (Aizenman 2012). While a bill to this effect submitted to Congress failed, a number of states, including the authors' home state of Missouri, have passed such religious exemption bills.

The opposing sides broke down along party and ideological lines, with the Democratic Party in 2012 declaring that the Republicans had declared a "war on women" (see, for example, People for the American Way 2012). Efforts by the Republicans included the defunding of Planned Parenthood, which does provide some abortion services but spends most of its funding on providing healthcare, including breast cancer screenings, to low-income women.

Reproductive issues are more than about freedom of choice or moral or religious stances, the social issues. They are also about economics. The ability to control how many and when to have children has an impact on a woman's ability to help her family economically. A study by Frost and Lindberg (2012; see also Marcotte 2012) for the Guttmacher Institute makes this point very strongly. The study of over 2,000 women who used family planning clinics that were funded by tax dollars found many reasons why women used birth control. We quote the summary of the study's results:

> A majority of respondents reported that birth control use had allowed them to take better care of themselves or their families (63 percent), support themselves financially (56 percent), complete their education (51 percent), or keep or get a job (50 percent). Young women, unmarried women, and those without children reported more reasons for using contraception than others. Not being able to afford a baby, not being ready for children, feeling that having a baby would interrupt their goals, and wanting to maintain control in their lives were the most commonly reported very important reasons for using birth control. (Frost and Lindberg 2012, 2)

A University of Michigan study supports this result: a sizable percentage of the decreased income disparity between men and women is due to access to birth control (Lowder 2012).

Another element that must be considered is the linkage between availability of contraceptives and abortion. A 2012 study of women in St. Louis and Kansas City, Missouri, found that the availability of contraception at no cost to women led to a decrease in unintended pregnancies and abortions (Peipert et al. 2012). Further, having contraception covered by insurance would enable women to use the more expensive but more effective birth control technologies (Andrews 2012a). The federal nature of the issue comes in also, because twenty-two states require health insurance policies to cover contraception. Six of the state mandates were signed by Republican governors, including 2012 Republican presidential nominee Mitt Romney in Massachusetts (Geiger and Levey 2012). Further, much of the public supports the Obama rule, including many Catholics (Serafini 2012).

SOCIAL DETERMINANTS

The health of people, whether in the United States or elsewhere, is the result of a combination of factors, including genetic makeup, lifestyle, access to healthcare, and the surroundings in which they live. This last factor is what is known as the "social determinants of health." The argument is that there are factors beyond the control of an individual that will affect that person's health in the present and in the future. For example, children who suffer from child abuse or other adverse events often have effects that show up in poor quality of health in later life (see Flaherty et al. 2006; Wegman and Stetler 2009).

Table 6.2 lists the variety of social determinants that might affect the quality of one's health. Income is one of the major determinants. Combining it with education and occupation allows us to talk about socioeconomic differences. In the case of income, those at higher incomes experience better health than those at lower incomes. Interestingly, Woolf and Braveman (2011) note that the relationship holds beyond the obvious rich and poor. Those at middle-class levels have better health than those at lower-income levels, but worse than those at higher levels. Woolf and Braveman point to research suggesting that lower income is related to higher premature death rates. Similar results are found when considering education. Those with lower levels of education have higher premature death rates than those at higher levels of education.

Table 6.2

Social Determinants of Health

- Availability of resources to meet daily needs (e.g., safe housing and local food markets)
- Access to educational, economic, and job opportunities
- Access to healthcare services
- Quality of education and job training
- Availability of community-based resources in support of community living and opportunities for recreational and leisure-time activities
- Transportation options
- Public safety
- Social support
- Social norms and attitudes (e.g., discrimination, racism, and distrust of government)
- Exposure to crime, violence, and social disorder (e.g., presence of trash and lack of cooperation in a community)
- Socioeconomic conditions (e.g., concentrated poverty and the stressful conditions that accompany it)
- Residential segregation
- Language/literacy
- Access to mass media and emerging technologies (e.g., cell phones, the Internet, and social media)
- Culture

Source: U.S. Department of Health and Human Services 2012.

Woolf and Braveman (2011) also look at community effects on health. The quality of food available in low-income communities makes it difficult to lead a healthy lifestye. Low-income neighborhoods tend to have more environmental problems, such as exposure to lead and other toxic substances, than more affluent communities (see, for example, Zubrzycki 2012). Living in poor neighborhoods, which have multiple chronic problems (high unemployment, poverty and crime, for example), creates stresses on residents, especially children (Woolf and Braveman 2011). Woolf and Braveman strongly argue that improving the health of people and communities requires focusing on the social determinants. Healthcare reform such as the ACA by itself will not work. Budget cuts to programs that focus on determinants would likely make matters worse.

Geography Is Destiny

> "Where an individual chooses to live can have a profound effect on their short- and long-term health."

> (Institute of Medicine 2008)

While many of the determinants and disparities mentioned above (see Table 6.2) and in other places (see, for example, Patel and Rushefsky 2008) are intertwined, the issue of geography or place deserves a separate consideration. And in that spirit, we take a bit of exception to the quote that opened up this section. While many people choose to live in a particular place, many others do not. Children are a good example of this. But people who lack the resources to move also make up a certain percentage of the population. To that we can add people who cannot move to certain places because of discrimination or lack of income. America remains very much a segregated community. One way of looking at this is the idea that "a ZIP code is at least as important as race, age and genetics in determining a person's health" (Walker 2011). A study conducted by the Johns Hopkins Bloomberg School of Public Health found that whites who lived in racially integrated neighborhoods had pretty much the same health outcomes as blacks in those neighborhoods. A study by the U.S. Department of Housing and Urban Development found that when women moved from high-poverty to low-poverty neighborhoods with the help of federal housing vouchers, the levels of obesity fell (Walker 2011).

One way of looking at the importance of place is regions of the country. Some regions, especially in the South and in the Appalachian area, have higher rates of premature death than, say, the Upper Midwest (see, for example, Halverson and Bischak 2008).

Rural areas, in particular, tend to suffer from lack of appropriate healthcare facilities. Part of this is due to the small populations of rural areas. While primary care seems to be adequate, more specialized care and hospitals require larger populations to work with. Transportation is often a barrier to obtaining care. Rural residents are thus less likely to use the healthcare system and less likely to obtain use of preventive services than people in more populous areas. Rural residents also tend to be poorer and older than urban residents (Patel and Rushefsky 2008; Agency for Healthcare Research and Quality 2011). Using 2010 data, Probst et al. (2011) found that rural blacks and whites had higher rates of mortality than did their urban counterparts. While education and income were higher in urban than in rural areas, accounting for some of the disparities, access to health insurance was also greater in urban than in rural areas.

Some statistics will help make the point (data from National Rural Health Association 2012). Rural areas have almost one-quarter of the country's population, about 62 million people. But only 10 percent of all physicians are located in rural areas, and the number of specialists per 100,000 population in rural areas is less than one-third that in urban areas. Average per capita income levels in rural areas are about three-quarters of what they are in urban areas. The poverty rate in rural areas is 14 percent, compared to the 11 percent in urban areas. Sixty-four percent of rural residents are covered by private insurance, compared to 69 percent in urban areas. Medicare spending per capita in rural areas is 85 percent of the national average, compared to 106 percent in urban areas. Finally, only 45 percent of the rural poor are covered by Medicaid, compared to almost 50 percent in urban areas.

Residents of urban inner-city areas, where the makeup is mostly ethnic minorities, also face health access and outcome problems (Patel and Rushefsky 2008; Smedley et al. 2008). These problems include lack of insurance, lack of a regular provider, and exposure to environmental insults. Smedley et al. (2008) point, as an example, to the neighborhood of South Camden, New Jersey, a largely minority neighborhood, which has a disproportionate number of facilities that pollute, as well as abandoned waste sites. The prevalence of providers within urban areas depends on the type of community. Higher-income neighborhoods have a higher ratio of physicians to population than lower-income neighborhoods do. Hospitals in inner city areas tend to have more financial problems than those in more affluent areas. Even within urban areas, there are often transportation issues (Patel and Rushefsky 2008).

The Special Case of Dental Care

Most discussions of healthcare needs focus on the traditional idea of health and medicine but ignore dental care issues. Paradise (2012, 1) notes that cavities remain "the most common chronic disease among children 6–18." Further, this disease is completely preventable. The impact of chronic dental problems in children and adults goes beyond just the cavities. Dental issues are linked with diseases such as sinus infection, heart and lung disease, and diabetes. Dental disease can lead to poor school performance, developmental issues among children, and poor speech (Paradise 2012). Oral diseases can lead to poor work performance and chronic pain (Licata and Paradise 2012).

Access to good dental care for those at the lower end of the socioeconomic scale may be even less than for regular medical care. Interestingly, because of changes to programs such as Medicaid and the Children's Health Insurance Program, low-income children may have better dental coverage than higher-income children. However, as Paradise (2012) points out, insurance coverage and access are not the same things.

There are disparities in access to dental care based on income, race, and ethnicity. For example, 42 percent of those with income under the federal poverty line had untreated cavities compared to 12 percent of those with incomes greater than 400 percent of the federal poverty line. Hispanic adults were the least likely to have seen a dentist in 2010 (Licata and Paradise 2012).

There are also disparities in dental healthcare related to geography. Rural areas, in particular, tend to have a shortage of dentists. Further, there is a national shortage of dentists and especially the more specialized ones, such as pediatric dentists (Paradise 2012).

Coverage of dental services is an option under Medicaid. When facing difficult budget issues, and states have been in this position for more than a decade, these optional services are often the first to be eliminated when cutting Medicaid. Additionally, private health insurance may not include dental services, and when covered, it is often limited. Thus out-of-pocket expenses may be high. Even when covered by Medicaid, finding a dentist who will treat such patients is diffi-cult because the reimbursements are low. A sizable number of dentists will not take on Medicaid patients because of low reimbursements. It may take up to a year before a Medicaid patient can get in to see a dentist for the first time. Even dentists who do accept Medicaid patients may limit the number of such patients they treat (Paradise 2012). The Affordable Care Act includes dental coverage in the "essential health benefits" required for insurance policies participating in health exchanges for children, but not for adults (Licata and Paradise 2012).

SOLUTIONS TO THE PROBLEMS OF
UNINSURANCE AND UNDERINSURANCE

The simple but difficult solution to the problem of lack of health insurance (or lack of adequate health insurance) would be a national health insurance (NHI) system. As we explored in chapter 2, the twentieth century is marked by failures to enact NHI (Starr 1982, 2013). Mayes (2005) refers to this as "the elusive quest." Finally, in 2010, the Patient Protection and Affordable Care Act, formally known as the Affordable Care Act (ACA), created something akin to national health insurance, though not necessarily providing a single system (see chapter 10 for a thorough discus-sion of the legislation and its aftermath).

The Affordable Care Act expanded insurance coverage in several ways. One is the individual mandate that everyone purchase health insurance. That provision was upheld by the Supreme Court in 2012, in *National Federation of Independent Business, et al., v. Sebelius, Secretary of Health and Human Services, et al.*, though not in the way quite intended by the writers of the legislation (see chapter 10). The ACA also contained an employer mandate. Both provisions come with subsidies for lower-income individuals and families and for smaller businesses. In the case of individuals or families in the nongroup market, the legislation calls for setting up exchanges, virtual markets in which people can choose healthcare plans.

The other major way that ACA sought to expand insurance coverage focuses on Medicaid. Under the plan, states would have to extend eligibility to people with income up to 133 (or 138) percent of the federal poverty line. The federal government would pick up most of the costs of those covered under the extended policy. Currently, as we noted in chapter 3, states generally have their eligibility levels at less than the federal poverty line (for adults). However, the enforce-ment mechanism created by ACA, the withholding of all Medicaid funds from states that did not extend the eligibility levels, was cut out by the 2012 Supreme Court ruling as too coercive. The Obama administration will need to offer more incentives or be more persuasive to get the coverage. The failure to get the extended coverage might lead to up to 17 million people not being covered (Kiff 2012).

Of course, there are other proposals that have been circulating for years. Hacker (2001, 2009) proposed a public plan that would be based on Medicare. Hacker's 2001 proposal would create a new part to Medicare that would cover those not insured. It would have the same advantage as mentioned above concerning Medicaid: the structure is already in place. It would add two further advantages. First, Medicare is entirely a federal government program, so the fiscal impact on and program differences between states would not be a problem. Second, provider reimbursement is higher for Medicare than for Medicaid. Thus access to services would be greater.

Hacker's 2009 proposal fits into the debate over healthcare reform that took place in 2009 and 2010, which we discuss in detail in chapter 10. One of the much talked about provisions during this time was state exchanges, where individuals and families who did not have or could not obtain health insurance through some other program, could purchase healthcare. For liberal Democrats, one of the big issues was whether the exchanges would contain a "public option" that would compete with private plans in the exchanges. Hacker's proposal suggested such a plan based on Medicare. The public option, whether Hacker's version or other versions, was not included in the ACA.

Another alternative, though it has gotten less consideration from the political system than Medicare expansion, looks to the Veterans Health Administration hospitals (see chapter 5). While there have been some issues of access, Padua (2009) argues that the quality of care at VHA facilities has been quite good once it has been accessed (but there is a problem of waiting time to get into the system). Further, costs have been kept under control. Padua (2009) notes that costs per patient served have remained pretty much the same from 1996 to 2005, while similar costs for patients in private plans rose dramtically during that same time period.

Another proposal, more typical of conservative and Republican proposals as opposed to the more liberal and Democratic Medicaid and Medicare proposals discussed above, would make use of tax credits and tax deductions. Presidents Nixon and George H.W. Bush offered variations of these proposals. Tax credits would be available to the poor, and deductions would be available to middle-income families (including the self-employed). Such tax incentives would be provided to both individuals and employers. One early proposal would offer individuals a $1,000 tax credit and families a $3,000 tax credit (Connolly 2005). This would help alleviate the cost of health insurance but would be substantially less than the cost of nongroup health insurance. A related and more reform-minded proposal would make use of tax-sheltered health savings accounts and high-deductible (i.e., "catastrophic") insurance policies (Alonso-Zaldivar 2005).

One problem that would have to be faced with the tax deduction/credit approach is that healthcare and, concomitantly, insurance premiums would rise faster than the deduction or credit, even if they were indexed to cost-of-living changes (Pear 1992). Another problem with the proposal is that it does not guarantee coverage. Further, to make any appreciable impact on reducing the number of uninsured, the tax credit would have to be much larger than is typically proposed (see Reschovsky and Hadley 2004).

An example of such a tax-credit-based bill was the plan offered by the conservative Heritage Foundation. Butler (1991) argues that the major problem of the healthcare system, at least as concerns the problem of the uninsured, is the tax code. The tax code allows employers to treat health insurance as a business expense eligible for a tax deduction. This leads to three major problems, two of which are relevant to the uninsurance problem.

The first problem is that the system is inequitable. Assume that health insurance as a fringe benefit is part of the total employee compensation package. If this is so, then the cost of the health insurance if given as salary would be taxed at the highest marginal tax rate. Because high-wage workers are taxed at higher marginal rates than low-wage workers, the benefit would be highest for high-wage workers. For those who must pay their own health insurance, the inequity is greater because they have only a limited tax deduction and thus must pay more from after-tax dollars (Butler 1991).

The second problem mentioned by Butler is "job lock," in which people keep their jobs for fear of losing health insurance coverage. By tying health insurance to employment, the tax code creates strong bonds between worker and job, a problem presumably dealt with by the Kassebaum-Kennedy bill (the Health Insurance Portability and Accountability Act). The final problem created by the tax code, though it is not directly related to the uninsurance problem, is that it creates inflationary pressures by severing the link between paying for the service and receiving it (Butler 1991).

The Heritage Foundation plan would eliminate the employer tax deduction for healthcare and replace it with a refundable tax credit for individuals. The tax credit would be available even to those who do not itemize their tax returns. If the healthcare tax credit were greater than the individual's tax obligation, the difference would be refunded to that individual. The credit would be geared toward the portion of family income spent on healthcare (insurance and out-of-pocket costs). If a family spent 10 percent of its income on healthcare, it would be eligible for a 20 percent tax credit (Butler 1991).

One interesting part of the proposal is the "healthcare social contract." Under the contract, all families would be required to join a health plan with a minimum package of benefits. Though Butler does not use the term, this plan is an individual mandate rather than an employer mandate. The federal government would be part of the contract by guaranteeing the fiscal viability of the individual mandate, either through tax credits or through access to Medicaid and/or Medicare (Butler 1991). The individual mandate became an important component of the ACA and one of its more controversial elements (see chapter 10).

The plan has important advantages. It severs the tie between work and health insurance (see Enthoven 2003). Employers would no longer have to worry about the increasing costs of healthcare, and workers would not be tied to a job just because of the health insurance benefit. A second advantage is that it is equitable because it focuses on percentage of income regardless of size of income and would provide more help for those who need it more, such as low-income workers and those with chronic health problems. A third advantage is that the program would reduce the costs of Medicaid for both federal and state governments, thus reducing the strain on federal and state budgets or enabling the provision of somewhat more generous programs (Butler 1991).

Like all policy proposals, this one has its disadvantages as well. One is the equity consideration. The argument that Butler makes that the current tax deduction system is inequitable because those with higher incomes would pay at a higher tax rate than those with lower incomes is an assumption. The numbers, on the face of it, are correct. Consider the following:

Let us assume two families with the heads of household filing joint income taxes, one with a taxable income of $30,000 a year and the other with a taxable income of $90,000 a year. The families are the same size, and the primary workers for the two families work for the same company and get the same health insurance package from the employer. The employer contribution to both families' health insurance is the same, say $3,000 a year. If the tax deduction were removed and the employer kept the total compensation package the same, the workers would each receive, in theory (though perhaps not in reality), an additional $3,000 in salary. This would increase their taxable incomes to $33,000 and $93,000, respectively. The tax for the lower-income family would increase by $450, an increase of about 12 percent (using 2003 tax rates) in tax obligations and a marginal tax rate of 15 percent. The tax for the higher-income family would increase by $840, an increase of about 5.2 percent in tax obligations and a marginal tax rate of about 28 percent. Thus the equity consideration, if it is a consideration at all, would apply only to those whose income was too low to pay federal income taxes. Otherwise, the current system, as Butler explains it, actually favors lower-income families as long as they pay income taxes, if one looks at the actual increase in tax obligations versus marginal tax rates. So, in that sense, Butler is partially correct.

But he is incorrect in two other senses. First, workers get the health insurance but not the money. This is a "let us assume" proposition rather than the real world. That is, the employers under such a system might retain some of the $3,000 of health insurance costs rather than give it all to the employee. Second, consider how the tax credit system would work. Let us take our families from the above example, the $30,000 income family and the $90,000 income family. Under the new system, both pay the same percentage of their income on healthcare. For the first family, that amounts to $3,000; for the second family it amounts to $9,000. These are the same in percentage terms, but the impacts on the two families are much different, given the original sizes of their incomes. Both would be eligible for a 20 percent tax credit, but that would amount to $600 for the lower-income family (a cut of 13.3 percent in tax obligation). For the upper-income family, the 20 percent tax credit would amount to $1,800 (a tax cut of 8.9 percent in tax obligation). While the percentage decrease of tax obligation would be lower for the higher-income family, thus seeming to be equitable, its tax credit would be three times as large as for the low-income family. It would be proportional at best.

A final problem with the tax credit plan is that while it may guarantee insurance coverage, it does not deal with the other problems discussed: risk rating and so forth. It also does not guarantee access to healthcare in inner cities and rural areas.

In at least one respect and for one racial group, Native Americans, healthcare access has improved. The Indian Health Service (IHS) is tasked with the goal of improving the health of the American Indian and Alaska Native population. This group, as we saw above and also in chapter 5, has some of the worst access to the healthcare system and poorest health outcomes of any racial/ethnic group. As a result of the services offered by IHS, life expectancy has increased and infant mortality has decreased within this population. Tuberculosis and injury have declined, and treatment for diabetes has increased (Sequist, Cullen, and Acton 2011). The healthcare problems of this group remain, but are less serious than two decades ago. As we discussed in chapter 5, perhaps there are lessons that can be drawn from the Indian Health Service.

CONCLUSION

In this chapter we have considered one of the major problems of the U.S. healthcare system, that of the disadvantaged. The uniquely American mix of public and private insurance programs, a post–World War II development, covers about 85 percent of the population but leaves over 40 million people without any insurance at all. Especially in the case of private insurance, it also leaves a portion of the population underinsured and vulnerable to catastrophic medical expenses.

One reason why the issue of access and the safety net has been so difficult is that perceptions about the problem differ. White Americans are less likely than African Americans or Latinos to think there are disparities in coverage, quality, and access. The lack of awareness of disparities exists even within the minority communities (Benz et al. 2011; Lillie-Blanton et al. 2000). The importance of this is that differential perceptions on lack of access make it difficult to deal with a problem and get it on the policy agenda.

An important consideration in the debate about expanding coverage is what the costs would be. The United States has been and is facing considerable health cost pressures, a topic we address in the next two chapters.

Incremental reforms, the kind that generally characterize public policy in the United States, have begun to address some of these problems. The CHIP program focuses on children. The Health Insurance Portability and Accountability Act addresses the "job lock" issue.

The passage of the ACA potentially could address the issue of insurance coverage. However, the 2012 Supreme Court decision that upheld most of the act called into question the reliance on the expansion of Medicaid. Already we have seen that Republican governors have rejected the idea of the expansion, at least partly on the additional costs they would eventually incur. Time will tell whether there will be sufficient incentives or political pressure to move the recalcitrant states to expansion.

Even if the ACA meets its objectives, the problems of the disadvantaged would remain. Having insurance coverage is important. We know from a considerable body of evidence that those without health insurance have more health problems and receive less and poorer-quality service than those with health insurance. But if the providers are not in the geographical area, such as inner cities or rural areas, having insurance by itself is insufficient.

We also know that poverty, ethnicity, and gender play important and intermixing roles in health outcomes. We know that blacks and Latinos on the average have poorer health outcomes than whites. We know that minority women and their babies have poorer health outcomes: more troubling pregnancies, low birth weights, and so forth. Additionally, one concern about the ACA, if it meets its access goals, is whether there would be a sufficient increase in the number of providers to meet the anticipated increased demand for services. Even with the comprehensive reform promised by the new legislation, it is likely that the problems of the disadvantaged will remain.

STUDY QUESTIONS

1. The policy process begins with the problem-identification stage. This means getting the political system to recognize that a problem exists. This stage, perhaps the most important in the policy process, is very contentious. There are disagreements over whether a problem that should be addressed by the political system exists, and, if so, what the nature of the problem is. This chapter focuses on the disadvantaged, people and families who lack health insurance. There are estimates that as many as 50 million people in the United States lack health insurance. Do you think this is a problem that should be addressed by the political system? Why? Republicans and Democrats disagree on both points (whether it is a problem and the nature of the problem). What are their positions? Why do they take those positions?

2. There are an estimated 10–12 million undocumented immigrants in the United States. While the president and Congress have considered immigration reform legislation, the fact remains that these immigrants do not have health insurance or a regular source of healthcare. When they do need healthcare, they go to hospital emergency departments, though they cannot pay. Hospitals shift some of those costs to insured payers. The Affordable Care Act does not covered the undocumented. Given the impact that they have, should undocumented immigrants be covered? Why or why not?

3. Having a federal system means that some states have a higher percentage of uninsured people than other states do. States with high percentages of uninsured people also tend to be the least generous in their safety net policies. Do you think a more national system would be an appropriate response to this? Or should we just leave it up to the states to decide how much to cover the uninsured?

4. As we note in the chapter, not all disparities are income-based. Some are geographically based. People in inner cities and rural areas have less access to healthcare providers than do those in suburban areas and more affluent parts of cities. Why do you think this is the case? What policies, if any, have been adopted to address these disparities? What additional policies, if any, do you think should be adopted?

5. A major goal of the Affordable Care Act is to cover more of the uninsured. What are the mechanisms for doing so? How well do you think it will work? To what extent are perspectives on this question influenced by ideology?

NOTES

1. Aday (1993b) briefly discusses the liberal, individual rights tradition and the communitarian tradition that underlies the notion of the common good. See also Aday (1993a).

2. For critiques of Jecker's argument, see Ruttenberg (1993) and Rochefort (1993).

3. For a discussion of what is known and not known about the issue of uninsurance, largely from an economics standpoint, see McLaughlin (2004).

4. For a discussion of the class-versus-race issue, see Wilson (1978, 1987).

REFERENCES

Abelson, Reed. 2005. "Wal-Mart's Health Care Struggle Is Corporate America's, Too." *New York Times,* October 29.

Aday, Lu Ann. 1993a. *At Risk in America: The Health and Health Care Needs of Vulnerable Populations in the United States.* San Francisco: Jossey-Bass.

————. 1993b. "Equity, Accessibility, and Ethical Issues: Is the U.S. Health Care Reform Debate Asking the Right Questions?" *American Behavioral Scientist* 36, no. 6 (July/August): 724–40.

Agency for Health Care Research and Quality. 2003. "National Healthcare Disparities Report." Washington, DC: U.S. Department of Health and Human Services.

————. 2010. "National Healthcare Disparities Report." Washington, DC: U.S. Department of Health and Human Services.

————. 2011. "National Healthcare Disparities Report." Washington, DC: U.S. Department of Health and Human Services.

Aizenman, N.C. 2012. New Front in Birth Control Rule Battle: The Courts." *Washington Post,* March 7.

Alonso-Zaldivar, Ricardo. 2005. "Healthcare Overhaul Is Quietly Underway." *Los Angeles Times,* January 31.

Andrews, Michelle. 2010. "Pregnant Women and New Mothers Will Get Benefits, Services Under Health Care Law." *Kaiser Health News,* June 8.

————. 2012a. "Insurance Coverage Might Steer Women to Costlier—But More Effective—Birth Control." *Kaiser Health News,* February 20.

————. 2012b. "Some Plans Deny Pregnancy Coverage for Dependent Children." *Kaiser Health News,* August 6.

Auerbach, Judith D. 2004. "The Overlooked Victims of AIDS." *Washington Post,* October 14.

Baird, Karen L. 1998. *Gender Justice and the Health Care System.* New York: Garland Publishing.

Beckles, Gloria, and Benedict I. Truman. 2011. "Education and Income—United States, 2005 and 2009." *Morbidity and Mortality Weekly Report, Special Supplement* 60 (January 14): 13–17.

Benz, Jennifer, et al. 2011. "Awareness of Racial and Ethnic Health Disparities Has Improved Only Modestly Over a Decade." *Health Affairs* 30, no. 10 (October): 1860–67.

Berk, Marc L., and Claudia L. Schur. 1998. "Access to Care: How Much Difference Does Medicaid Make?" *Health Affairs* 17, no. 3 (May/June): 169–80.

Butler, Stuart M. 1991. "A Tax Reform Strategy to Deal with the Uninsured." *Journal of the American Medical Association* 265, no. 19 (May 15): 2541–43.

Byrd, W. Michael; and Linda A. Clayton. 2003. "Racial and Ethnic Disparities in Healthcare: A Background and History." In *Unequal Treatment,* ed. Brian D. Smedley, Adrienne Y. Stith, and Alan R. Nelson, 455–527. Washington, DC: National Academies Press.

Centers for Disease Control and Prevention. 2011. "HIV Among African Americans." Washington, DC: U.S. Department of Health and Human Services.

Centers for Medicare and Medicaid Services. n.d. "Pregnant Women." Online at www.medicaid.gov/Medicaid-CHIP-Program-Information/By-Population/Pregnant-Women/Pregnant-Women.html.

Chapman, Audry R. 1994. "Introduction." In *Health Care Reform: A Human Rights Approach,* ed. Audrey R. Chapman, 1–32. Washington, DC: Georgetown University Press.

Children's Defense Fund. 1998. *The State of America's Children.* Washington, DC: Children's Defense Fund.

Claxton, Gary; Isadora Gil; Ben Finder; and Erin Holve. 2004. "Employer Health Benefits 2004 Annual Survey." Menlo Park, CA: Henry J. Kaiser Family Foundation, and Chicago, IL: Health Research and Educational Trust.

Claxton, Gary, et al. 2011. "Employer Health Benefits 2011 Annual Survey." Menlo Park, CA: Henry J. Kaiser Family Foundation, and Chicago, IL: Health Research and Educational Trust.

Clemetson, Lynette. 2004. "Links Between Prison and AIDS Affecting Blacks Inside and Out." *New York Times,* August 6.

Committee on the Consequences of Uninsurance, Institute of Medicine. 2002. *Care Without Coverage: Too Little, Too Late.* Washington, DC: National Academy Press.

Committee on Health Insurance Status and Its Consequences. 2009. *America's Uninsured Crisis: Consequences for Health and Health Care.* Washington, DC: National Academy Press.

Connolly, Ceci. 2005. "Bush Plans to Broaden Health Care." *Washington Post,* February 4.

Cust, Kenneth F.T. 1997. *A Just Minimum of Health Care.* New York: University Press of America.

Daniels, Norman; Donald W. Light; and Ronald L. Caplan. 1996. *Benchmarks of Fairness for Health Care Reform.* New York: Oxford University Press.

Dorn, Stan. 2008. "Uninsured and Dying Because of It: Updating the Institute of Medicine Analysis on the Impact of Uninsurance on Mortality." Washington, DC: Urban Institute.

Doty, Michelle, et al. 2007. "Failure to Protect: Why the Individual Insurance Market Is Not a Viable Option for Most U.S. Families." Washington, DC: Commonwealth Fund.

"Emergency Medical Treatment and Active Labor Act (EMTALA)" n.d. Ascension Health. Online at www.ascensionhealth.org/index.php?option=com_content&view=article&id=146&Itemid=172.

Enthoven, Alain C. 2003. "Employment-Based Health Insurance Is Failing: Now What?" *Health Affairs* (May 23): W3-237–W3-249.

Families USA. 2010. "Covering Pregnant Women: CHIPRA Offers New Option." Washington, DC: Families USA, July.

Fears, Darryl. 2005. "U.S. HIV Cases Soar Among Black Women." *Washington Post,* February 7.

Flaherty, E.G., et al. 2006. "Effect of Early Childhood Adversity on Child Health." *Archives of Pediatric and Adolescent Medicine* 160, no. 12 (December): 1232–38.

Fox, Maggie. 2010. "Nearly 59 Million Lack Health Insurance: CDC." Reuters, November 10.

Fronstin, Paul. 2004. "Sources of Health Insurance and Characteristics of the Uninsured: Analysis of the March 2004 Current Population Survey." Washington, DC: Employee Benefit Research Institute.

———. 2011. "Sources of Health Insurance and Characteristics of the Uninsured: Analysis of the March 2011 Current Population Survey." Washington, DC: Employee Benefit Research Institute.

Froomkin, Dan. 2007. "Mock the Press." *Washington Post,* July 11.

Frost, Jennifer, and Laura Duberstein Lindberg. 2012. "Reasons for Using Contraception: Perspectives of U.S. Women Seeking Care at Specialized Family Planning Clinics." *Contraception* 87, no. 4 (September 27): 1–8. Online at www.contraceptionjournal.org.

Furrow, Barry R. 1995. "An Overview and Analysis of the Impact of the Emergency Medical Treatment and Active Labor Act." *Journal of Legal Medicine* 16 (September): 357–52.

Garcia, Tamyra, Amy B. Bernstein, and Mary Ann Bush. 2010. "Emergency Department Visitors and Visits: Who Used the Emergency Room in 2007?" Hyattsville, MD: U.S. Department of Health and Human Services, National Center for Health Statistics.

Garner, M.O.; S.P. Cliver; S.F. McNeal; and R.L. Goldenberg. 1996. "Ethnicity and Sources of Prenatal Care; Findings from a National Survey." *Birth* 23, no. 2: 84–87.

Geiger, Kim, and Noam N. Levey. 2012. "Before Birth-Control Fight, Republicans Backed Mandates." *Los Angeles Times*, February 15.

General Accounting Office. 1997. *Health Insurance: Coverage Leads to Increased Health Care Access for Children.* Washington, DC: General Accounting Office.

Ginzberg, Eli. 1994. "Improving Health Care for the Poor." *Journal of the American Medical Association* 271, no. 6 (February): 464–65.

Gold, Rachel Benson, and Elizabeth Nash. 2012. "States Have Enacted 39 New Abortion Restrictions This Year Alone." Truthout.org, July 13.

Gould, Elise. 2004. "The Chronic Problem of Declining Health Coverage." EPI Issue Brief #202 (September 16). Washington, DC: Economic Policy Institute.

Graig, Laurene A. 1999. *Health of Nations: An International Perspective on U.S. Health Care Reform.* Washington, DC: CQ Press.

Greene, Jay. 2011. "Report: Uninsured Patients 3 Times More Likely to Use Emergency Departments, Are Sicker." *Crain's Detroit Business*, June 19.

Greenhouse, Steven, and Reed Abelson. 2011. "Wal-Mart Cuts Some Health Care Benefits." *New York Times*, October 20.

Gresenz, Carole Roan, and Jose J. Escarce. 2011. "Spillover Effects of Community Uninsurance on Working-Age Adults and Seniors." *Medical Care* 49, no. 9 (September): e14–e21.

Hacker, Jacob S. 2001. "Medicare Plus: Increasing Health Coverage by Expanding Medicare." In *Covering America: Real Remedies for the Uninsured, vol. 1: Proposal Summaries,* ed. Elliot K. Wicks, 73–100. Washington, DC: Economic and Social Research Institute.

———. 2002. *The Divided Welfare State: The Battle Over Public and Private Social Benefits in the United States.* New York: Cambridge University Press.

———. 2009. "Healthy Competition: How to Structure Public Health Insurance Plan Choice to Ensure Risk-Sharing, Cost Control, and Quality Improvement." Berkeley: Berkeley Center on Health, Economic & Family Security, University of California Berkeley School of Law.

Halverson, Joel A., and Greg Bischak. 2008. "Underlying Socioeconomic Factors Influencing Health Disparities in the Appalachian Region." Washington, DC: Appalachian Regional Commission.

"HIV Among Black Women 5 Times Higher than Previously Thought." 2012. *Huffington Post*, March 10.

Hoffman, Catherine, and Karyn Schwartz. 2008. "Eroding Access Among Nonelderly U.S. Adults with Chronic Conditions: Ten Years of Change." *Health Affairs* 27, no. 5 (July 22): w340–w348.

Hogue, Carol J.R.; Martha A. Hargraves; and Karen Scott Collins, eds. 2000. *Minority Health in America:*

Findings and Policy Implications from the Commonwealth Fund Minority Health Survey. Baltimore, MD: Johns Hopkins University Press.

Holahan, John, and Arunabh Ghosh. 2004. "The Economic Downturn and Changes in Health Insurance Coverage, 2000–2003. " Washington, DC: Kaiser Commission on Medicaid and the Uninsured.

Institute of Medicine. 2008. *Challenges and Successes in Reducing Health Disparities: Workshop Summary.* Washington, DC: National Academy Press.

James, Cara V., et al. 2009. "Putting Women's Health Care Disparities on the Map: Examining Racial and Ethnic Disparities at the State Level." Menlo Park, CA: Kaiser Family Foundation.

Jecker, Nancy S. 1993. "Can an Employer-Based Health Insurance System Be Just?" *Journal of Health Care Politics, Policy and Law* 18, no. 3 (Fall): 657–73.

Kaiser Commission on Medicaid and the Uninsured. 2012. "Health Coverage of Children: The Role of Medicaid and CHIP." Washington, DC: Kaiser Commision on Medicaid and the Uninsured.

Kaiser Family Foundation. 2004a. "Update on Individual Health Insurance." Menlo Park, CA: Kaiser Family Foundation.

———. 2004b. "Health Care & the 2004 Elections: Women's Health Policy." Menlo Park, CA: Kaiser Family Foundation.

———. n.d. "Number of Deaths per 100,000 Population by Race/Ethnicity, 2009." Menlo Park, CA: Kaiser Family Foundation.

Kari, Nancy; Harry C. Boyte; and Bruce Jennings. 1994. "Health as a Civic Question." Prepared for the American Civic Forum Madison, WI. Online at www.cpn.org/topics/health/healthquestion.html.

Kates, Jennifer, and Alyssa Wilson Leggoe. 2005a. "African Americans and HIV/AIDS." Menlo Park, CA: Henry J. Kaiser Family Foundation.

———. 2005b. "Latinos and HIV/AIDS." Menlo Park, CA: Henry J. Kaiser Family Foundation.

Kiff, Sarah. 2012. "The Supreme Court Surprise: Medicaid Ruling Could Reduce Coverage." *Washington Post*, June 28.

Kinney, Eleanor D., and Suzanne K. Steinmetz. 1994. "Notes from the Insurance Underground: How the Chronically Ill Cope." *Journal of Health Politics, Policy and Law* 19, no. 3 (Fall): 637–41.

Kirsch, Richard. 2011. *Fight for Our Health: The Epic Battle to Make Health Care a Right in the United States.* Albany, NY: Rockefeller Institute Press.

Klein, Joel. 2012. "How the Gun Won." *Time*, August 4, 26–32.

Krause, Elliott A. 1977. *Power and Illness: The Political Sociology of Health and Medical Care.* New York: Elsevier.

Kreidler, Mike. n.d. "Your Rights Under the U.S. COBRA Law." Olympia, WA: Office of the Insurance Commissioner.

Krieger, Nancy, and Elizabeth Fee. 1996. "Man-Made Medicine and Women's Health." In *Man-Made Medicine,* ed. Kary L. Moss, 17–35. Durham, NC: Duke University Press.

LaCalle, Eduardo, and Elaine Rabin. 2010. "Frequent Uses of Emergency Departments: The Myths, the Data, and the Policy Implications." *Annals of Emergency Medicine* 56, no. 1 (July): 42–48.

Lantz, Paul M.; J.S. House; and J. Chen. 1998. "Socioeconomic Factors, Health Behaviors, and Mortality." *Journal of the American Medical Association* 279, no. 21 (June): 1703–08.

Levine, Robert S., et al. 2012. "Firearms, Youth Homicide, and Public Health." *Journal of Health Care for the Poor and Underserved* 23, no. 1 (February): 7–19.

Levy, Helen, and David Meltzer. 2004. "What Do We Really Know About Whether Health Insurance Affects Health?" In *Health Policy and the Uninsured,* ed. Catherine G. McLaughlin, 179–204. Washington, DC: Urban Institute Press.

Licata, Rachel, and Julia Paradise. 2012. "Oral Health and Low-Income Nonelderly Adults: A Review of Coverage and Access." Menlo Park, CA: Kaiser Commission on Medicaid and the Uninsured.

Lillie-Blanton, Marsha, et al. 2000. "Race, Ethnicity, and the Health Care System: Public Perceptions and Experiences." *Medicare Care Research and Review* 57, supplement 1: 218–35.

Long, Sharon K. 2003. "Hardship Among the Uninsured: Choosing Among Food, Housing and Health Insurance." *New Federalism* Series B, no. B-54. Washington, DC: Urban Institute.

Lowder, J. Bryan. 2012. "Study Finds that Access to Birth Control Increases Women's Wages, but Do Conservative Women Care?" Salon.com, March 29.

Marcotte, Amanda. 2012. "Contraception Is an Economic Issue." *USA Today*, September 28.

Maternal and Child Health Bureau. 2012. "Low Birth Weight." Washington, DC: Health Resources and Services Administration, U.S. Department of Health and Human Services.

Mayes, Rick. 2005. *Universal Coverage: The Elusive Quest for National Health Insurance.* Ann Arbor: University of Michigan Press.

McBride, David. 1993. "Black America: From Community Health Care to Crisis Medicine." *Journal of Health Politics, Policy and Law* 18, no. 2 (Summer): 319–37.

McLaughlin, Catherine G. ed. 2004. *Health Policy and the Uninsured.* Washington, DC: Urban Institute Press.

Mead, Holly, et al. 2008. "Racial and Ethnic Disparities in U.S. Health Care: A Chartbook." Washington, DC: Commonwealth Fund.

Muller, Charlotte. 1990. *Health Care and Gender.* New York: Russell Sage Foundation.

Murphy, Jarrett. 2012. "Fear: The NRA's Real Firepower." *The Nation* 295, no. 11 (September 10): 11–15.

National Center for Health Statistics. 2004. "Health, United States, 2004." Hyattsville, MD: Centers for Disease Control and Prevention, U.S. Department of Health and Human Services.

———. 2011. "Health, United States, 2011." Hyattsville, MD: Centers for Disease Control and Prevention, U.S. Department of Health and Human Services.

National Rural Health Association. 2012. "What's Different About Rural Health Care?" Washington, DC: National Rural Health Association.

Oberg, Charles; Betty Lia-Hoagberg; Ellen Hodkinson; Catherine Skovholt; and Renee Vanman. 1990. "Prenatal Care Comparisons Among Privately Insured, Uninsured, and Medicaid-Enrolled Women." *Public Health Reports* 105, no. 5 (September/October): 533–35.

"Overview of Health Coverage for Individuals with Limited English Proficiency." 2012. Menlo Park, CA: Kaiser Family Foundation.

Padua, Joe. 2009. "Medicare for All: The Wrong Answer to the Right Question." Washington, DC: Campaign for America's Future.

Paradise, Julia. 2012. "Children and Oral Health: Assessing Needs, Coverage, and Access." Menlo Park, CA: Kaiser Commission on Medicaid and the Uninsured.

Patel, Kant, and Mark E. Rushefsky. 2008. *Health Care in America: Separate and Unequal.* Armonk, NY: M.E. Sharpe.

Pear, Robert. 1992. "President Leaves Many Areas Gray." *New York Times,* February 7.

———. 2005. "Governors Prepare to Fight Medicaid Cuts." *New York Times,* February 27.

People for the American Way. 2012. "How the War on Women Became Mainstream: Turning Back the Clock in Tea Party America." Washington, DC: People for the American Way.

Peipert, Jeffrey F., et al. 2012. "Preventing Unintended Pregnancies by Providing No-Cost Contraception." *Obstetrics and Gynecology* 120, no. 6 (December): 1291–97.

Pereira, Joseph. 2003. "To Save on Health-Care Costs, Firms Fire Disabled Workers." *Wall Street Journal,* July 14.

Pollack, Harold, and Karl Kronebusch. 2004. "Health Insurance and Vulnerable Populations." In *Health Policy and the Uninsured,* ed. Catherine G. McLaughlin, 205–55. Washington, DC: Urban Institute Press.

Probst, Janice, et al. 2011. "Higher Risk of Death in Rural Blacks and Whites than Urbanities Is Related to Lower Incomes, Education and Health Coverage." *Health Affairs* 30, no. 10 (October): 1872–79.

Quintana, J.M.; D. Goldmann; and C. Homer. 1997. "Social Disparities in the Use of Diagnostic Tests for Children with Gastroenteritis." *International Journal of Quality of Health Care* 9, no. 6 (December): 419–25.

Ranji, Usha, and Alina Salganicoff. 2011. "Women's Health Care Chartbook." Menlo Park, CA: Kaiser Family Foundation.

Reid, T.R. 2009. *The Healing of America: A Global Quest for Better, Cheaper and Fairer Health.* Farmington Hills, MI: Gale Group.

Reschovsky, James D., and Jack Hadley. 2004. "The Effects of Tax Credits for Nongroup Insurance on Health Spending by the Uninsured." *Health Affairs* (February 25): W4-113–W4-127.

Rhoden, Nancy K. 1986. "Trimesters and Technology: Revamping Roe v. Wade." *Yale Law Journal* 95, no. 4 (March): 639–97.

Rochefort, David A. 1993. "Commentary—The Pragmatic Appeal of Employment-Based Health Care Reform." *Journal of Health Care Politics, Policy and Law* 18, no. 3 (Fall): 683–93.

Rosenbaum, Sara, et al. 2012. "Case Studies at Denver Health: 'Patient Dumping' in the Emergency Department Despite EMTALA, the Law that Banned It." *Health Affairs* 31, no. 8 (August): 1749–56.

Rosenbaum, Sara. 2013. "The Enduring Role of the Emergency Medical Treatment and Active Labor Act. *Health Affairs* 32, no. 12 (December): 2075–81.

Russell, Lesley. 2010. "Fact Sheet: Health Disparities by Race and Ethnicity." Washington, DC: Center for American Progress.

Ruttenberg, Joan E. 1993. "Commentary—Revisiting the Employment-Insurance Link." *Journal of Health Care Politics, Policy and Law* 18, no. 3 (Fall): 675–81.

Ryan, William F. 1971. *Blaming the Victim.* New York: Pantheon Books.

Salganicoff, Alina; J. Zoe Beckerman; Roberta Wyn; and Victoria D. Ojeda. 2002. "Women's Health in the United States: Health Coverage and Access to Care." Menlo Park, CA: Henry J. Kaiser Family Foundation.

Schoen, Cathy, et al. 2011. "Affordable Care Act Reforms Could Reduce the Number of Underinsured U.S. Adults by 70 Percent." *Health Affairs* 30, no. 9 (September): 1762–71.

Seifert, Robert W., and Mark Rukavina. 2006. "Bankruptcy Is the Tip of a Medical-Debt Iceberg." *Health Affairs* 25 (February 28): W89–W92.

Sequist, Thomas D.; Theresa Cullen; and Kelly J. Acton. 2011. "Indian Health Service Innovations Have Helped Reduce Health Disparities Affecting American Indian and Alaska Native People." *Health Affairs* 30, no. 10 (October): 1965–73.

Serafini, Marilyn Werber. 2012. "Poll: Most Americans Support Contraception Rule." *Kaiser Health News*, March 1.

Smedley, Brian D., et al. 2008. "Unequal Health Outcomes in the United States: Racial and Ethnic Disparities in Health Care Treatment and Access, the Role of Social and Environmental Determinants of Health, and the Responsibility of the State." New York: Opportunity Agenda.

Starr, Paul. 1982. *The Social Transformation of American Medicine*. New York: Basic Books.

———. 2013. *Remedy and Reaction: The Peculiar American Struggle over Health Care Reform*, rev. ed. New Haven, CT: Yale University Press.

Stoddard, Jeffrey J.; Robert F. St. Peter; and Paul W. Newacheck. 1994. "Health Insurance Status and Ambulatory Care for Children." *New England Journal of Medicine* 330, no. 20 (May 19): 1421–25.

Stone, Deborah A. 1993. "The Struggle for the Soul of Health Insurance." *Journal of Health Politics, Policy and Law* 18, no. 2 (Summer): 287–317.

Thorpe, Kenneth E. 1997. *The Rising Number of Uninsured Workers: An Approaching Crisis in Health Care Financing*. Washington, DC: National Coalition on Health Care.

"The Uninsured: A Primer." 2011a. Menlo Park, CA: Kaiser Family Foundation.

"The Uninsured: A Primer. Supplemental Data Tables." 2011b. Menlo Park, CA: Kaiser Family Foundation.

U.S. Bureau of the Census. 1997. *Statistical Abstract of the United States 1997*. Washington, DC: U.S. Department of Commerce, Economics, and Statistics Administration.

———. 2004. "Historical Health Insurance Tables." Washington, DC: U.S. Department of Commerce, Economics, and Statistics Administration.

———. 2011. "Historical Health Insurance Tables." Washington, DC: U.S. Department of Commerce.

———. 2012. *Statistical Abstract of the United States 2012*. Washington, DC: U.S. Department of Commerce.

U.S. Department of Health and Human Services. 2012. "Social Determinants of Health." *Healthy People 2020*. Washington, DC: U.S. Department of Health and Human Services.

Vieth, Warren. 2004. "Bush Makes His Pitch for 'Ownership Society.'" *Los Angeles Times*, September 5.

Walker, Andrea K. 2011. "Where You Live Can Help Determine Your Health, Studies Say." *Baltimore Sun*, November 18.

"Wal-Mart Conference on Wal-Mart Draws Critics of Pay, Benefits." 2005. Bloomberg News, November 4.

Watson, Sidney Dean. 1994. "Minority Access and Health Reform: A Civil Right to Health Care." *Journal of Law, Medicine and Ethics* 22, no. 2 (Summer): 127–37.

Wegman, Holly, and Cinnamon Stetler. 2009. "A Meta-Analytic Review of the Effects of Childhood Abuse on Medical Outcomes in Adulthood." *Psychosomatic Medicine* 71, no. 8 (October): 805–12.

White, Joseph. 1995. *Competing Solutions: American Health Care Proposals and International Experience*. Washington, DC: Brookings Institution.

Wilson, William J. 1978. *The Declining Significance of Race: Blacks and Changing American Institutions*. Chicago: University of Chicago Press.

———. 1987. *The Truly Disadvantaged: The Inner City, the Underclass, and Public Policy*. Chicago: University of Chicago Press.

Woolf, Steven H., and Paula Braveman. 2011. "Where Health Disparities Begin: The Role of Social and Economic Determinants—And Why Current Policies May Make Matters Worse." *Health Affairs* 30, no. 10 (October): 1852–59.

Zellers, Wendy K.; Catherine G. McLaughlin; and Kevin D. Frick. 1992. "Small-Business Health Insurance: Only Healthy Need Apply." *Health Affairs* 11, no. 1 (Spring): 174–75.

Zubrzycki, Jaclyn. 2012. "Detroit Studies Illuminate Problem of Lead Exposure." *Education Week* 32, no. 5 (September 26): 6.

Zuckerman, Stephen; Joshua McFeeters; Peter Cunningham; and Len Nichols. 2004. "Changes in Medicaid Physician Fees, 1998–2003: Implications for Physician Participation." *Health Affairs* (June 23): W4-374–W4-384.

7

PROBLEM OF RISING
HEALTHCARE COSTS AND SPENDING

The 1960s saw a dramatic expansion in social programs. Civil rights, women's rights, educational opportunities, and improved housing and healthcare for citizens were the battle cries of a social revolution as the federal government attempted to enlarge individual opportunities. In the health field, providing access to decent healthcare became the primary goal of the federal government. The role of the government—that is, the public sector—in healthcare expanded considerably as it created public health insurance programs as a social safety net to provide coverage to those who lacked health insurance in the private sector for one reason or another.

In 1965, the federal government established Medicare and Medicaid to provide increased access to healthcare for the elderly and the poor. These programs were very successful in increasing healthcare access for large numbers of people (Davis and Schoen 1978). The creation and implementation of such programs was made possible by a healthy economy. Additionally, the Comprehensive Health Planning Act and Public Health Services Amendments of 1966 (PL 89–749) established the goal of providing the highest level of healthcare attainable to every person. Between 1985 and 1990, via congressional mandates, health coverage was expanded significantly in the Medicaid program, especially for women and children. Following the failure of healthcare reform during the Clinton administration in 1993–1994, Congress passed several incremental reforms to further increase access to healthcare. The Health Insurance Portability and Accountability Act (HIPPA) placed some limits on insurance companies' authority to deny coverage or to impose preexisting-condition exclusions and guaranteed portability of insurance coverage. In 1997, Congress created the State Children's Health Insurance Program (SCHIP), now called Children's Health Insurance Program (CHIP), to extend health insurance coverage to uninsured children. The Medicare Modernization Act (MMA), created in 2003 and implemented in 2006, added prescription drug benefits for Medicare recipients.

With the establishment of public health insurance programs, the total national healthcare expenditures have increased dramatically since the 1960s and have become a major area of concern for policymakers. In this chapter we examine the problem of healthcare costs and factors that have contributed to their escalation. In the next chapter we examine efforts undertaken by the federal and state governments and the private sector to contain rising healthcare costs.

RISING HEALTHCARE COSTS/EXPENDITURES

Healthcare expenditures in the United States have been rising faster than the general growth rate of the economy. Table 7.1 provides data on national healthcare expenditures for selected categories from 1960 to 2010 based on five-year intervals. The top part of the table provides data on sources of funds, while the bottom provides data on expenditures/spending for types of healthcare services.

Several observations about healthcare expenditures can be made from the data in Table 7.1. National healthcare expenditures have increased dramatically, from $27.3 billion in 1960 to $2.5 trillion in 2010.

236

Table 7.1

Selected National Healthcare Expenditures by Sources of Funds and Types of Services: 1960 to 2010 (in $ millions)

	1960	1965	1970	1975	1980	1985	1990	1995	2000	2005	2010
Total national health expenditures	27,359.4	41,957.4	74,853.5	133,584.9	255,782.5	444,623.3	724,282.3	1,027,457	1,377,185	2,029,148	2,593,644
Sources of Funds											
Out of pocket	13,051.4	18,262.2	25,014.7	37,372	58,438.8	96,002.1	138,657.7	146,366.6	201,815.5	263,379.1	299,694.6
% of total NHE	47.7%	43.5%	33.4%	28.0%	22.8%	21.6%	19.1%	14.2%	14.7%	13.0%	11.6%
Medicare	0	0	7,672.5	16,336.4	37,387	71,828.7	110,181.7	184,393.1	224,336.9	338,772.3	524,551
% of total NHE			10.3%	12.2%	14.6%	16.2%	15.2%	17.9%	16.3%	16.7%	20.2%
Medicaid (Title XIX)	0	0	5,289.7	13,445.6	26,032.5	40,937.4	73,660.8	144,862.2	200,482.8	309,538.5	401,417.7
% of total NHE			7.1%	10.1%	10.2%	9.2%	10.2%	14.1%	14.6%	15.3%	15.5%
CHIP (Title XIX and Title XXI)	0	0	0	0	0	0	0	0	3,015.4	7,549.2	11,667.8
% of total NHE									0.2%	0.4%	0.4%
Department of Veterans Affairs	897.4	1,119.5	1,719.5	3,380.5	5,739.9	8,332	10,939.1	14,839.7	19,082.2	29,802.5	46,016.5
% of total NHE	3.28%	2.67%	2.30%	2.53%	2.24%	1.87%	1.51%	1.44%	1.39%	1.47%	1.77%
Indian Health Services	0	0	0	196.7	448	721.3	996.1	1,654	1,982.5	2,488	3,578.8
% of total NHE				0.1%	0.2%	0.2%	0.1%	0.2%	0.1%	0.1%	0.1%

Types of Services

Hospital										
8,985.3	13,544.7	27,168.4	51,233.6	100,516.8	164,581.1	250,439	339,311.7	415,529.6	609,357.7	814,045.4
% of total NHE 32.8%	32.3%	36.3%	38.4%	39.3%	37.0%	34.6%	33.0%	30.2%	30.0%	31.4%
Physician and clinical										
5,630.3	8,587.2	1,4331.3	25,308.8	47,714.2	90,857	158,944.6	222,279.1	290,882.6	416,934	515,482.9
% of total NHE 20.6%	20.5%	19.1%	18.9%	18.7%	20.4%	21.9%	21.6%	21.1%	20.5%	19.9%
Prescription drug										
2,676	3,715	5,497	8,052	12,049	21,794.7	40,290.3	59,808.2	120,896.6	204,779.3	259,061.4
% of total NHE 9.8%	8.9%	7.3%	6.0%	4.7%	4.9%	5.6%	5.8%	8.8%	10.1%	10.0%
Nursing care facilities and CCRC										
810.6	1,407.9	4,033.8	8,021.9	15,269.6	26,253.5	44,890.3	64,478	85,119.9	112,454.8	143,077.6
% of total NHE 3.0%	3.4%	5.4%	6.0%	6.0%	5.9%	6.2%	6.3%	6.2%	5.5%	5.5%
Dental Services										
1,986.7	2,817.7	4,711	8,023	13,426.4	21,819.5	31,742.4	44,774.5	62,270.7	87,016.6	104,785.3
% of total NHE 7.3%	6.7%	6.3%	6.0%	5.2%	4.9%	4.4%	4.4%	4.5%	4.3%	4.0%
Home health care										
56.5	89.5	219.5	622.6	2,378.1	5,647.3	12,566.9	32,358.1	32,425.1	48,709.6	70,172.3
% of total NHE 0.2%	0.2%	0.3%	0.5%	0.9%	1.3%	1.7%	3.1%	2.4%	2.4%	2.7%

NHE = National Health Expenditures.

CCRC = Continuing Care Retirement Facilities.

Source: National Center for Health Statistics, Centers for Medicare & Medicaid Services, Baltimore, MD. 2012. Online at www.cms.gov/Research-Statistics-Data-and-Systems/Statistics-Trends-and-Reports/NationalHealthExpendData/NationalHealthAccountsHistorical.html.

The significant increase in national healthcare expenditures from $41.9 billion in 1965 to $133.5 billion in 1975 can be explained by the establishment of Medicare and Medicaid in 1965, which provided health insurance coverage to millions of elderly and poor people. By 1970 Medicare and Medicaid accounted for 17.4 percent of the total national healthcare expenditures. By 1975, they accounted for 22.4 percent of national healthcare expenditures. By 2010, Medicare and Medicaid accounted for 35.6 percent of national healthcare expenditures. In fact, Medicare expenditures as a percent of national healthcare costs doubled from 10.3 percent in 1970 to 20.2 percent in 2010. Similarly, Medicaid expenditures as a percent of the national total more than doubled, from 7.1 percent in 1970 to 15.5 percent in 2010.

Compared to private insurance, both Medicare and Medicaid have a higher percentage of expenditures dedicated to chronic health conditions. Medicaid also has a higher percentage than private insurance in spending for dedicated health services related to pregnancy and birth (Conway et al. 2011). This is not surprising, considering that most of the expansion of the Medicaid program over the years has been designed to provide coverage to poor women who are pregnant or have children.

Both Medicare and Medicaid expenditures are likely to continue to rise for a number of reasons. Medicaid's increase will be the result of its extended eligibility, under the Affordable Care Act (ACA), for health insurance coverage by as many as an additional 15 million currently uninsured individuals (see chapters 3 and 11). The ultimate number may depend on how many states opt out of Medicaid expansion under the ACA. However, compared to Medicare, Medicaid has more expenditure restrictions because of very low reimbursement payments to providers, as well as paying for fewer services (Moon 2005). Compared to private insurance, Medicare was more successful in holding the line on growth in healthcare costs during the 1980s and 1990s (Moon 2005). But Medicare expenditures are likely to continue to rise for two primary reasons. First, since Medicare recipients are elderly and/or disabled, they suffer from not only more health problems but also more serious ones. In addition, many have multiple chronic conditions requiring continual medical care. Second, the number of people eligible for Medicare is expected to increase significantly as more individuals from the baby-boom generation reach retirement age over the next decade. In addition, because of better medical care, people are also living longer. It is estimated that healthcare for the elderly alone could consume 10 percent of the nation's gross domestic product (GDP) by 2020 ("Technology and Longer Lives Leading to Higher Health Bills" 1998).

The public sector's role in providing health coverage to individuals has expanded considerably since the 1960s. In 1970, public sector health programs constituted about 19.7 percent of the national health expenditures. In 2010, public sector health programs—Medicare, Medicaid, the Children's Health Insurance Program, the Medicare Part D prescription drug program, the veterans health program, and the health program for the American Indians/Alaska natives (AI/AN)—accounted for about 37.6 percent of the national healthcare expenditures, with Medicare and Medicaid responsible for 35.6 percent.

Table 7.2 provides annual data about the sources of funds and expenditures by types of services from 2001 to 2010. It provides some insight about trends in healthcare expenditures in recent years. Out-of-pocket expenditures as a percentage of total national health expenditures have dropped every year from a high of 14 percent in 2001 to 11.6 percent in 2010. Medicare expenditures as a percent of national health expenditures have risen from 16.5 percent in 2001 to 20.2 percent in 2010. In contrast, Medicaid expenditures as a percent of national health expenditures have remained relatively stable, around 15 percent between 2001 and 2010. Expenditures for CHIP, veterans, American Indians, and Alaska Natives continue to be a very small percentage of national health expenditures.

Expenditures by Type of Health Services

Table 7.1 also provides data on healthcare expenditures by type of services. Again, several observations are warranted. Slightly over half of the total national healthcare expenditures in 1960

Table 7.2

Selected National Healthcare Expenditures by Sources of Funds and Types of Services: 2001 to 2010 (in $ millions)

	2001	2002	2003	2004	2005	2006	2007	2008	2009	2010
Total national health expenditures	1,494,116	1,636,416	1,774,297	1,900,045	2,029,148	2,162,410	2,297,098	2,403,938	2,495,842	2,593,644
Sources of Funds										
Out of pocket	209,122.3	222,194	236,815.5	248,894.5	263,379.1	271,944.2	287,276.8	293,986.5	294,430.1	299,694.6
% of total NHE	14.0%	13.6%	13.3%	13.1%	13.0%	12.6%	12.5%	12.2%	11.8%	11.6%
Medicare	247,114.5	264,587	282,010.8	310,473.5	338,772.3	403,108.1	432,257.9	466,907.1	499,770.5	524,551
% of total NHE	16.5%	16.2%	15.9%	16.3%	16.7%	18.6%	18.8%	19.4%	20.0%	20.2%
Medicaid (Title XIX)	224,236.4	248,217.6	269,104.8	290,916.8	309,538.5	306,839.9	326,370.8	343,813.5	374,433.4	401,417.7
% of total NHE	15.0%	15.2%	15.2%	15.3%	15.3%	14.2%	14.2%	14.3%	15.0%	15.5%
CHIP (Title XIX and Title XXI)	4,169.4	5,474.6	6,282.8	7,145.9	7,549.2	8,334.1	9,116.1	10,208.4	11,122.4	11,667.8
% of total NHE	0.3%	0.3%	0.4%	0.4%	0.4%	0.4%	0.4%	0.4%	0.4%	0.4%
Department of Veterans Affairs	21,082.5	22,782.4	26,516.7	27,951.3	29,802.5	31,860.8	33,959.1	38,243.3	42,379.3	46,016.5
% of total NHE	1.4%	1.4%	1.5%	1.5%	1.5%	1.5%	1.5%	1.6%	1.7%	1.8%
Indian Health Services	2,200.7	2,196.2	2,333.3	2,458.4	2,488	2,591.3	2,686.2	2,825.9	3,155.7	3,578.8
% of total NHE	0.1%	0.1%	0.1%	0.1%	0.1%	0.1%	0.1%	0.1%	0.1%	0.1%

(continued)

Table 7.2 (continued)

Types of Services	2001	2002	2003	2004	2005	2006	2007	2008	2009	2010
Hospital	449,356.5	486,477.4	526,159.4	566,006	609,357.7	651,907.1	692,489.5	729,257.5	776,089.5	814,045.4
% of total NHE	30.1%	29.7%	29.7%	29.8%	30.0%	30.1%	30.1%	30.3%	31.1%	31.4%
Physician and Clinical	315,717.3	340,852	368,080.6	393,102	416,934	438,797.9	461,803.8	486,601.1	502,749	515,482.9
% of total NHE	21.1%	20.8%	20.7%	20.7%	20.5%	20.3%	20.1%	20.2%	20.1%	19.9%
Prescription Drug	138,694.1	158,174.4	176,029.2	192,203.8	204,779.3	224,212.6	236,201.4	243,584	256,106.3	259,061.4
% of total NHE	9.3%	9.7%	9.9%	10.1%	10.1%	10.4%	10.3%	10.1%	10.3%	10.0%
Nursing care facilities and CCRC	90,780.8	94,479.8	100,307.7	105,745.6	112,454.8	117,283.1	126,437.3	132,660.5	138,670	143,077.6
% of total NHE	6.1%	5.8%	5.7%	5.6%	5.5%	5.4%	5.5%	5.5%	5.6%	5.5%
Dental services	67,821.4	73,684.4	76,278.7	82,053.1	87,016.6	91,441.9	97,337.9	102,368.8	102,474.4	104,785.3
% of total NHE	4.5%	4.5%	4.3%	4.3%	4.3%	4.2%	4.2%	4.3%	4.1%	4.0%
Home health care	34,419.6	36,628	39,797.6	43,808.5	48,709.6	52,591.1	57,771.7	61,463.4	66,103.7	70,172.3
% of total NHE	2.3%	2.2%	2.2%	2.3%	2.4%	2.4%	2.5%	2.6%	2.6%	2.7%

NHE = National Health Expenditures.

CCRC = Continuing Care Retirement Communities.

Source: National Center for Health Statistics, Centers for Medicare and Medicaid Services, Baltimore, MD. 2012. Online at www.cms.gov/Research-Statistics-Data-and-Systems/Statistics-Trends-and-Reports/NationalHealthExpendData/NationalHealthAccountsHistorical.html

occurred in two service areas—hospital and physician/clinical services. Together these services accounted for the majority of healthcare spending—53.4 percent, with 32.8 percent for hospital services and 20.6 percent for physician/clinical services. The overall expenditure patterns for these two services have pretty much remained the same over the years. In 2010, hospital and physician/ clinical services expenditures accounted for about 51.3 percent of national healthcare expenditures, slightly lower than in 1960. The highest expenditures for hospital and physician\clinical services were almost 56 percent of the national total, in 1980 and 1985. Hospital services have consistently remained the top expenditure category, followed by physician/clinical services. Their relative percentages have fluctuated a little over the years, and the growth in these two areas has slowed slightly from the high of the 1980s, but their rates of increase have generally outstripped the rate of inflation (Siegel, Mead, and Burke 2008). Expenditures for inpatient hospital services increased 89 percent between 1997 and 2005 despite the increase in outpatient care. Medicare paid about 47 percent of the cost of hospital inpatient services ("Hospital Charges Still Rising Despite More Outpatient Care" 2007).

The higher expenditures for physician services are generally attributed to greater administrative costs, higher physician income, more facilities/amenities, and low-capacity utilization of physicians and equipment for specialized diagnostic and therapeutic procedures (Fuchs 2005). Ironically, the Association of American Medical Colleges (AAMC) has been predicting a shortage of physicians over the upcoming decades due to demographic changes' leading to a dramatic increase in demand and reduction in physician supply through retirement. The AAMC has called for a 30 percent increase in U.S. medical school enrollment, an expansion of graduate medical education (GME) positions to accommodate increased enrollment, and more federal funding for GME (Latham 2005). However, the real problem is the geographic maldistribution of physicians in the country. In fact, the increased supply of physicians may exacerbate the problem because research shows that physician supply follows an "inverse care law," that is, supply of physicians being lowest in highest need areas, because most newly trained physicians end up practicing in areas that already have the most physicians (Latham 2005). Also, a higher supply of physicians could also lead to increased spending on healthcare. While it is true that regions with proportionately more general practitioners seem to enjoy lower healthcare costs, it does not necessarily follow that a bigger physician supply will reduce healthcare costs further or even slow the rate of growth. The reason is that primary care could be provided more economically by foreign medical school graduates, nurses, physician assistants, and other allied health professionals (Latham 2005).

Expenditures for prescription drugs have been the third largest category of national healthcare expenditures over the years. The percent of national healthcare expenditures spent on prescription drugs has varied from a low of 4.7 percent in 1980 to a high of 10 percent in 2010. Since the 1980s, expenditures on prescription drugs have almost doubled and likely will continue to grow due to the aging of the population. The fastest increase in healthcare expenditures in 2006 was an 8.5 percent increase in prescription drug expenditures, because of the addition of the new Medicare Part D benefits, which added prescription drug coverage to 25 million Medicare beneficiaries (Siegel, Mead, and Burke 2008).

In 2010, spending on hospital and physician/clinical services and prescription drugs accounted for 61.2 percent of overall national healthcare expenditures. Another 12.2 percent of spending was for nursing home, dental, and home healthcare services. The remainder consisted of administrative costs, durable and nondurable medical products and devices, public health services, research, and other professional services.

Table 7.2 provides data about the sources of funds and expenditures by types of services from 2001 to 2010. During this time period, expenditures for hospital services, physicians/clinical services, and prescription drugs as a percent of total national health expenditures has remained relative stable around 30, 20, and 10 percent respectively. Between 2001 and 2010, expenditures for nursing and continuing care facilities declined slightly, while expenditures for home healthcare have increased slightly as a percent of total national health expenditures. This is not too surprising given the emphasis on a policy of deinstitutionalization with respect to long-term care.

Growth in Public Sector Expenditures and Decline in Out-of-Pocket Expenditures

Expansion of third-party payers as a result of an increase in government and other private health insurance programs has resulted in a dramatic reduction in out-of-pocket payments by consumers. In 1960, prior to the introduction of Medicare and Medicaid, 47.7 percent of all personal healthcare spending was paid out-of-pocket by the patient. In 2010, that percentage had dropped to only 11.6 percent (see Tables 7.1 and 7.2). The introduction of Medicare and Medicaid in 1965, combined with expansion of private health insurance coverage, led to a dramatic decline in out-of-pocket expenditure by the patient (Baicker and Goldman 2011).

Healthcare Expenditures and GDP

Tables 7.3 and 7.4 provide some additional data on the growth of national health expenditures, per capita expenditures, U.S. population, GDP, and national health expenditures as a percent of GDP. Table 7.3 provides data for every five-year interval from 1960 to 2010, while Table 7.4 provides annual figures from 2001 to 2010.

Total national healthcare expenditures have increased steadily over the last fifty years in the United States. The rate of growth in national healthcare expenditures has been much higher than the growth in GDP over the same time period, and it has been dramatically higher than growth in the U.S. population. Between 1960 and 2010, the growth in the U.S. population ranged from the high of 7.5 percent to a low of 4.5. Similarly, the GDP growth has ranged from a high of 70.2 percent to a low of 15.1 percent. During the same time frame, the growth in national healthcare expenditures has ranged from a high of 91 percent to a low of 27.5 percent.

Per capita expenditures on healthcare have increased from $147 in 1960 to $8,402 in 2010. During the same time period, per capita expenditure growth rate measured at five-year intervals has ranged from a high of 82.9 percent to a low of 22.3 percent in 2010.

In 1960, national healthcare expenditures accounted for only 5.2 percent of the GDP, but by 2010 it had increased to 17.9 percent. The United States spends more money on healthcare overall and per capita than any other country in the world. Similarly, no other country even comes close to the United States in spending 17.9 percent of its GDP on healthcare. Yet, many of these countries rank higher on several indicators of health status and/or outcomes than does the United States.

Healthcare expenditures refers to the prices multiplied by the quantity or volume of consumption of healthcare services. Rising growth in healthcare expenditures relative to GDP can be explained by two factors. Either prices are rising faster in the healthcare sector than in any other sectors of the economy, or the volume of healthcare produced (quantity/volume of consumption) is rising more rapidly than output in other sectors of the economy (McGuire and Serra 2005). In the United States, both of these factors—higher prices and increased consumption—have contributed to increased healthcare expenditures.

As the data in Table 7.4 show, there is some good news with respect to rising healthcare expenditures. They have been growing at a much slower rate since 2002. The annual growth rate in national healthcare expenditures has dropped every year since 2002 from a high of 9.5 percent in 2002 to 3.9 percent in 2010. The same has been true of the annual growth rate in per capita expenditures, which has dropped from a high of 8.5 percent in 2002 to 3.1 percent in 2010. These drops in annual growth rate of national healthcare expenditures and per capita expenditures coincide with a drop in the GDP growth rate. The national healthcare expenditure growth rate has been double the rate of inflation except in 2008.

Table 7.3

National Healthcare Expenditures Summary and GDP: 1960–2010

	1960	1965	1970	1975	1980	1985	1990	1995	2000	2005	2010
National healthcare expenditures in $ billions	27	42	75	134	256	445	724	1,027	1,377	2,029	2,594
% Change from previous year listed		55.6%	78.6%	78.7%	91.0%	73.8%	62.7%	41.9%	34.1%	47.3%	27.8%
National healthcare expenditures per capita	147	210	356	607	1,110	1,840	2,854	3,825	4,878	6,868	8,402
% Change from previous year listed		42.9%	69.5%	70.5%	82.9%	65.8%	55.1%	34.0%	27.5%	40.8%	22.3%
U.S. population in millions	186	200	210	220	230	242	254	269	282	295	309
% Change from previous year listed		7.5%	5.0%	4.8%	4.5%	5.2%	5.0%	5.9%	4.8%	4.6%	4.7%
GDP in billions	526	719	1,038	1,638	2,788	4,218	5,801	7,415	9,952	12,623	14,527
% Change from previous year listed		36.7%	44.4%	57.8%	70.2%	37.5%	37.5%	27.8%	34.2%	26.8%	15.1%
National healthcare expenditures as share of GDP	5.2	5.8	7.2	8.2	9.2	10.5	12.5	13.9	13.8	16.1	17.9
Inflation rate[1]	1.5%	1.6%	5.8%	9.2%	13.6%	3.6%	5.4%	2.8%	3.4%	3.4%	1.6%

[1]The inflation rate is calculated from the Consumer Price Index (CPI) compiled by the Bureau of Labor Statistics and is based upon a 1982 base of 100. http://inflationdata.com/Inflation/Inflation_Rate/HistoricalInflation.aspx.

Sources: Centers for Medicare & Medicaid Services, Office of the Actuary, National Health Statistics Group; 2012. U.S. Department of Commerce, Bureau of Economic Analysis; and U.S. Bureau of the Census. 2012.

Table 7.4

National Healthcare Expenditures Summary of Selected Data: 2001–2010

	2001	2002	2003	2004	2005	2006	2007	2008	2009	2010
National health expenditures in $ billions	1,494	1,636	1,774	1,900	2,029	2,162	2,297	2,404	2,496	2,594
% change from previous year listed		9.5%	8.4%	7.1%	6.8%	6.6%	6.2%	4.7%	3.8%	3.9%
National health expenditures per capita	5,241	5,687	6,114	6,488	6,868	7,251	7,628	7,911	8,149	8,402
% change from previous year listed		8.5%	7.5%	6.1%	5.9%	5.6%	5.2%	3.7%	3.0%	3.1%
Medicare	247,114.5	264,587	282,010.8	310,473.5	338,772.3	403,108.1	432,257.9	466,907.1	499,770.5	524,551
% change from previous year		6.6%	6.2%	9.2%	8.4%	16.0%	6.7%	7.4%	6.6%	4.7%
Medicaid (Title XIX)	224,236.4	248,217.6	269,104.8	290,916.8	309,538.5	306,839.9	326,370.8	343,813.5	374,433.4	401,417.7
% change from previous year		9.7%	7.8%	7.5%	6.0%	-0.9%	6.0%	5.1%	8.2%	6.7%
Federal	132,288.1	145,339.4	160,894.8	172,437.3	177,639.2	174,035.3	185,857	202,856.9	247,456.5	269,504.5
% change from previous year		9.0%	9.7%	6.7%	2.9%	-2.1%	6.4%	8.4%	18.0%	8.2%
State and local	91,948.3	102,878.2	108,210	118,479.5	131,899.3	132,804.6	140,513.8	140,956.7	126,976.9	131913.2
% change from previous year		10.6%	4.9%	8.7%	10.2%	0.7%	5.5%	0.3%	-11.0%	3.7%

244

CHIP (Title XIX and Title XXI)	4,169.4	5,474.6	6,282.8	7,145.9	7,549.2	8,334.1	9,116.1	10,208.4	11,122.4	11,667.8
% change from previous year		23.8%	12.9%	12.1%	5.3%	9.4%	8.6%	10.7%	8.2%	4.7%
Federal	2,915.2	3,825.1	4,397.4	4,966.9	5,241.7	5,731.7	6,315.8	7,124.6	7,825.1	8,147.2
% change from previous year		23.8%	13.0%	11.5%	5.2%	8.5%	9.2%	11.4%	9.0%	4.0%
State and local	1,254.1	1,649.5	1,885.4	2,179	2,307.5	2,602.5	2,800.3	3,083.8	3,297.3	3520.6
% change from previous year		24.0%	12.5%	13.5%	5.6%	11.3%	7.1%	9.2%	6.5%	6.3%
U.S. population in millions	285	288	290	293	295	298	301	304	306	309
% change from previous year listed		1.1%	0.7%	1.0%	0.7%	1.0%	1.0%	1.0%	0.7%	1.0%
GDP in billions	10,286	10,642	11,142	11,853	12,623	13,377	14,029	14,292	13,939	14,527
% change from previous year listed		3.5%	4.7%	6.4%	6.5%	6.0%	4.9%	1.9%	-2.5%	4.2%
National health expenditures share of GDP	14.5	15.4	15.9	16	16.1	16.2	16.4	16.8	17.9	17.9
Inflation rate[1]	2.8%	1.6%	2.3%	2.7%	3.4%	3.2%	2.9%	3.9%	-0.3%	1.6%

[1]The inflation rate is calculated from the Consumer Price Index (CPI) compiled by the Bureau of Labor Statistics and is based upon a 1982 base of 100. http://inflationdata.com/Inflation/Inflation_Rate/HistoricalInflation.aspx.

Sources: Centers for Medicare & Medicaid Services, Office of the Actuary, National Health Statistics Group; U.S. Department of Commerce, Bureau of Economic Analysis; and U.S. Bureau of the Census.

However, it is important to keep in mind that lower spending on healthcare in recent years (short-term trends) cannot say anything about long-term trends. Often economic downturn and recession tends to depress health spending for several years. Thus, it is reasonable to assume that the recession of 2007–2009 contributed to the recent decline in healthcare spending.

Concentration of Expenditures by Certain Populations

When discussing national healthcare expenditures, it is important to note that they are concentrated heavily among certain segments of the population. For example, the sickest 1 percent of the population accounted for a little over 22 percent of all national healthcare expenditures; the sickest 5 percent accounted for over 48 percent of expenditures; and the sickest 50 percent of accounted for almost 97 percent of all expenditures on healthcare (Kaiser Family Foundation n.d.). These percentages have been fairly stable over the years (Berk and Monheit 2001).

Age-specific expenditures have also been on the rise. For example, healthcare costs of the average seventy-three-year-old are considerably higher than they were for the average seventy-three-year-old twenty years ago. Declining health after the age of sixty-five results in significant increases in the use of prescription drugs, hospital admissions, repair and replacement of body parts, and rehabilitative and physical therapy ("Technology and Longer Lives Leading to Higher Health Bills" 1998). In addition, costs at the end of life disproportionately contribute to healthcare expenditures in the United States (Greer and Danis 2011). Two factors—an aging population and healthcare technology—are likely to continue to drive healthcare expenditures higher (McGuire and Serra 2005). As the elderly develop more health problems, their use of healthcare services increases. The elderly's higher use of services is also related not just to the number of treatments but also to the type and complexity of healthcare services, that is, intense use of new medical technologies that drive healthcare costs upward (Moon 2005).

Concentration of Costs by Medical Condition

Leading Causes of Death

Similar to the concentration of health expenditures among the population, there is a concentration of health expenditures among medical conditions. The top ten causes of death in the United States accounted for 75 percent of the nearly 2.5 million deaths in 2010. In 2007, overall costs of the ten leading causes of death were over $1.1 trillion ("$1.1 Trillion: What the Top 10 Leading Causes of Death Cost the U.S. Economy" 2012).

Table 7.5 provides a list of the top ten leading causes of death in the United States in 1980 and 2010. As can be observed, not much has changed since 1980. Diseases of the heart and cancer were the top two leading causes of death in 1980 and remained so in 2010. Diabetes mellitus was ranked as the number seven leading cause of death in 1980 and again in 2010. One major change to note is that in 2010 Alzheimer's disease ranked as number six among leading causes of death, while it was not in the top ten in 1980.

Between 2000 and 2010, the biggest increase in death rate was from Alzheimer's disease (50 percent), followed by pneumonia and the flu (32 percent), strokes (31 percent), heart disease (25 percent), renal disease (21 percent), suicide (15 percent), diabetes (11 percent), accidents (7.6 percent), cancer (7.5 percent), and chronic lung disease (less than 1 percent) ("$1.1 Trillion: What the Top 10 Leading Causes of Death Cost the U.S. Economy" 2012).

While data about the cost of the 2010 leading causes of death have not been available from the Centers for Disease Control and Prevention at present, *24/7 Wall St* reviewed the leading causes of death to determine how much each of them cost the U.S. economy. It is important to note that

Table 7.5

Top Ten Leading Causes of Death and the Number of Deaths in the U.S.: 1980 and 2010

Rank	Cause of Death[1]	1980	Rank	Cause of Death[1]	2010[2]
1	Diseases of the heart	761,095	1	Diseases of the heart	595,444
2	Malignant neoplasms (Cancer)	416,509	2	Malignant neoplasms (Cancer)	573,855
3	Cerebrovascular disease	170,225	3	Lower respiratory disease (Chronic lung disease)	137,789
4	Unintentional injuries	105,718	4	Cerebrovascular disease (Strokes)	129,180
5	Chronic obstructive pulmonary disease	56,050	5	Accidents (Unintentional injuries)	118,043
6	Pneumonia and influenza	54,619	6	Alzheimer's disease	83,308
7	Diabetes mellitus	34,851	7	Diabetes mellitus	68,905
8	Chronic level disease and cirrhosis	30,583	8	Nephritis, nephrotic syndrome, nephrosis (Renal disease)	50,472
9	Atherosclerosis	29,449	9	Influenza and pneumonia	50,003
10	Suicide	26,869	10	Intentional self-harm (Suicide)	37,793

[1]Some of the categories for causes of death have changed from 1980 to 2010.
[2]Data for 2010 are preliminary.
Sources: Vital Statistics of the United States, vol. II, *Mortality, Part A,* 1980, Centers for Disease Control and Prevention, Atlanta, Georgia. 2011; Murphy et al., "Deaths: Preliminary Data for 2010." Centers for Disease Control and Prevention, National Vital Statistics Report, 60, no. 4, January 2012; *National Vital Statistics Reports,* 50, no. 4: 1–8. National Center for Health Statistics, Washington, DC. 2012.

the figures provided are for costs to the U.S. economy and not necessarily just health-related costs. Thus, these figures also include indirect costs associated with diseases, such as lost wages, productivity, and the like. The breakdown is as follows: heart disease ($190 billion); cancer ($227 billion); chronic lung disease ($65 billion); stroke ($34 billion); accidents ($308 billion); Alzheimer's ($70 billion); diabetes mellitus ($112 billion); renal disease ($61 billion); pneumonia and flu ($40 billion); and suicide ($36 billion). The total cost to the U. S. economy in 2010 was estimated to be slightly over $1 trillion dollars ("$1.1 Trillion: What the Top 10 Leading Causes of Death Cost the U.S. Economy" 2012).

Obviously, healthcare costs are heavily concentrated among the top ten leading causes of death in the United States. The age-adjusted suicide rate in American has been increasing steadily and so is the cost associated with successful and unsuccessful suicide attempts. Also, between 2000 and 2009, according to the U. S. Renal Data System, the direct cost of kidney disease doubled in the Medicare budget, and we should expect the cost to rise as diabetes and obesity rates continue to rise. Similarly, according to the Alzheimer's Association, Alzheimer's is a very expensive disease that involves high direct medical costs.

If present trends continue, cancer is likely to become the number one leading cause of death in the next five to ten years. On the positive side, while heart disease remains the number one leading cause of death, deaths caused by this disease are declining at a rapid rate, resulting in declining costs. Similarly, costs attributable to strokes have also decreased due to increased awareness and better treatment of risk factors such as high blood pressure, smoking, and improvement in acute stroke care ("$1.1 Trillion: What the Top 10 Leading Causes of Death Cost the U.S. Economy" 2012).

Chronic Health Conditions

In 2004, 44 percent of Americans or 133 million people experienced at least one chronic condition. This number has been climbing and is expected to reach 171 million by 2030 (Ameringer 2012). More than 25 percent of Americans suffer from two or more chronic health conditions requiring continuous care. Such conditions include heart disease, diabetes, high blood pressure, kidney disease, lung disease, hypertension, arthritis, asthma, HIV, mental illness, and dementia (Brody 2011). The prevalence of multiple chronic conditions increases with age and is very high among older Americans even though many Americans with multiple chronic conditions are under the age of sixty-five (U. S. Department of Health and Human Services 2010). About two-thirds of those over the age of sixty-four are afflicted with two or more chronic conditions (Ameringer 2012). The resources required to treat and manage chronic health conditions are immense. For example, 66 percent of total healthcare spending is directed toward care for about 27 percent of Americans with multiple chronic health conditions. Increased spending on chronic diseases among Medicare beneficiaries is one of the major reasons for driving the overall growth of expenditures in the Medicare program (U.S. Department of Health and Human Services 2010). Rising obesity rates are likely to influence increased healthcare spending on treatment of obesity-related chronic diseases such as diabetes, high blood pressure, and hypertension (Thorpe and Philyaw 2012).

The management and treatment of chronic health conditions is made difficult and more costly by the fact that the great majority of American physicians specialize in a specific body part or health condition. The highly specialized nature of American healthcare system works well in treating acute symptoms but is poorly situated to manage long-term illnesses. Experts generally are in agreement that primary care physicians are better than specialists in managing patients' chronic conditions. Lack of attention to primary care also leads to poor management and coordination of chronic disease symptoms. More medical students settle on fields other than primary care because specialties are more lucrative than primary care. Consequently, the American healthcare system produces many more specialists and fewer primary care physicians, and a highly specialized healthcare care system is more expensive (Ameringer 2012).

In the United States, the traditional method of reporting healthcare costs is reporting costs by healthcare setting or by healthcare payer. Another way to examine healthcare costs is to categorize national medical expenditures into patient-centered care categories such as chronic conditions, acute illness, trauma/poisoning, and the like. A study that analyzed data from the 2007 Medical Expenditure Panel Survey (MEPS) collected by the Agency for Healthcare Research and Quality (AHRQ) and categorized into patient-centered categories of care concluded that nearly half of expenditures were for chronic conditions and another 25 percent were for acute care categories (Conway et al. 2011).

Healthcare Expenditures in the United States Compared to Other Countries

How do healthcare expenditures in the United States compare with other industrialized countries? The United States spends more money on healthcare than any other member country in the Organization for Economic Cooperation and Development (OECD) (Congressional Research Service 2007). In 2010, the United States spent $8,233 per person on healthcare, while the average spending on healthcare per person among the thirty-three other industrialized countries of the OECD was $3,268. The United States spent 17.6 percent of GDP on healthcare compared to an average of 9.5 percent of GDP spent on health by OECD countries (Kane 2012).

Three things stand out with respect to healthcare costs when we compare the United States with other OECD countries. First, most OECD countries use a common fee schedule under which hospitals, doctors, and health services are paid similar rates for most of the patients they see. In the

United States, how much a healthcare service is paid depends on the kind of insurance a patient carries. Second, payment rates in OECD countries are continuously monitored and more flexible. It is easier to lower payment rates if prices are rising too fast. In the United States payment rates are less flexible. Third, in the United States there are fewer methods for lowering rising costs in the private sector than in the OECD countries (Kane 2012). The United States also uses more of the newest medical technologies and performs several invasive surgeries more frequently than in other OECD countries (Congressional Research Service 2007).

Despite the United States' spending so much more money on healthcare, some have argued that the health status of Americans trails that of other industrialized countries. Comparing the most highly industrialized countries, the United States ranks twelfth overall and at the bottom on the important indicators of low birth rate and neonatal and infant mortality (see Kawachi 2005). A survey of adults with recent healthcare problems in six countries found that "The United States often stands out with high medical errors and inefficient care and has the worst performance for access/cost barriers and financial burdens" (Schoen et al. 2005).

AMERICANS' VIEWS ABOUT HEALTHCARE COSTS/EXPENDITURES

As we have just seen, the United States spends more money on healthcare (total amount, per capita, and share of the GDP) than any other country in the world. Yet, in a 2006 survey of Americans, 57 percent of respondents thought that the United States was spending too little on healthcare in the aggregate (as a nation), and 70 percent said that the government in specifics was spending too little. Only 26 percent thought that the nation was spending too much, and 11 percent thought government was spending too much (Pew Research Center for the People and the Press 2006). This opinion is partly influenced by what Americans perceive as the negative economic impact on their families caused by their direct payments for healthcare services such as insurance premiums, copays, deductibles, and the general cost of services and products. In the same poll, when asked about average American spending on healthcare, 65 percent indicated that they spend too much. In addition, 32 percent of Americans indicated that they worried about not being able to afford healthcare services they thought they needed (Pew Research Center for the People and the Press 2006).

In another poll, conducted in 2009, 54 percent of respondents said their household had cut back on healthcare due to cost concerns in the previous twelve months ("More than Half Americans Say Family Skimped on Medical Care Due to Costs" 2009). Statistics show that Americans' concern about rising healthcare costs is well justified. A decade of healthcare cost growth has wiped out real income gains for the average U.S. family. For example, although a median-income U.S. family of four with employer-based health insurance saw its gross annual income increase from $76,000 in 1999 to $99,000 in 2009 (in current dollars), this gain was largely offset by increased spending to pay for healthcare. During the same time period, monthly spending for the family's health insurance premium increased from $490 to $1,115; out-of-pocket health spending increased from $135 to $235; and taxes devoted to healthcare increased from $345 to $440 (Auerbach and Kellermann 2011).

Healthcare costs particularly present a heavy burden for families where someone has a chronic illness. In a 2005 survey, 56 percent of Americans reported that they or someone else in their household had been diagnosed with a chronic illness. Another 29 percent of adults from households where someone had a chronic illness reported having had problems paying their medical bills during the past year (USA Today/Kaiser Family Foundation/Harvard School of Public Health 2005). As to who to blame for the problem of the high cost of healthcare, Americans do not blame themselves. They tend to blame the problem of high costs on profits made by the drug and insurance companies. In the same 2005 poll, thirty-five percent of Americans expressed the belief that excessive profits were the most important cause of rising healthcare costs; another nineteen percent placed the blame on malpractice lawsuits; fourteen percent blamed greed and waste in the healthcare system and only eight percent blamed the problem on the high cost of medical technology and drugs (USA Today/Kaiser Family Foundation/Harvard School of Public Health 2005). This is ironic in light of the fact that most experts agree that medical technology and prescription drugs are the major drivers of higher healthcare costs in the United States.

Overall, it seems that Americans are both dissatisfied with the current healthcare system and relatively satisfied with their own healthcare arrangements. Often there is wide gap between the public's support for a set of principles regarding what needs to be done about the problems of the healthcare system and their support for specific policies to achieve those goals (Blendon et al. 2006). Americans show a clear set of priorities. For example, they rate cancer, HIV, AIDS, heart disease, and medical research to address these conditions as top priorities. However, they do not rank many leading causes of death such as kidney disease, accidents and injuries, pneumonia, and influenza very high as serious problems. Americans' rating of the top ten serious health problems do not always match the CDC's list of leading causes of death (Blendon et al. 2001).

Where Americans do seem to be in agreement is on the need for more use of information technology. In a survey conducted between August and November 2009, 78 percent favored use of electronic medical records (EMRs), 78 percent believed that EMRs could improve quality of care, and 59 percent believed that they could help reduce healthcare costs. In fact, 64 percent believed that the benefits of EMR use outweigh privacy risks, and 72 percent support healthcare information sharing among providers (Gaylin et al. 2011). In another study conducted by the Institute of Medicine, a majority want their clinician to offer choices for tests and treatments, and 97 percent of those suffering from chronic illness indicated that they wanted their care to be coordinated. Only 54 percent said their care was coordinated (Novelli, Halvorson, and Santa 2012).

FACTORS RESPONSIBLE FOR RISING
HEALTHCARE COSTS/EXPENDITURES

There are many causes for increases in healthcare costs. To some, the increases are the result of higher public expectations about the healthcare system, advances in healthcare technology and their success, and the prevailing sentiment that healthcare is a right (McGregor 1981). Others see healthcare-cost increases in the fee-for-service reimbursement system, a medical arms race among hospitals, insurance companies and third-party payers, and the purchasers of healthcare, such as the federal government and industries, that for a long time ignored the cost problem (Latham 1983). Others argue that virtually all the medical-care price inflation can be accounted for by general inflation, the labor intensity of health industries, the behavior of wage rates during inflation, and the pattern of labor-productivity changes (Virts and Wilson 1984). Still others attribute rising healthcare costs to an aging population; unhealthy behavior and lifestyle choices such as tobacco consumption, sedentary lifestyle, and being overweight leading to diseases that are preventable; costs of caring for uninsured; and the practice of defensive medicine (Siegel, Mead, and Burke 2008).

The problem of rising healthcare costs is not a new one. The Committee on the Costs of Medical Care (CCMC) was formed in the late 1920s because of the high cost of hospital care at a time when health insurance had not yet come into existence (Ross 2002; Starr 1982). If there is any agreement among policymakers, healthcare practitioners, researchers, and healthcare consumers and purchasers, it is that healthcare costs too much. Healthcare costs continue to rise despite numerous efforts made by both the public and private sectors to contain them (see next chapter). Over the years, healthcare costs have risen at a much higher rate than the general rate of inflation and rate of growth in GDP. The key question is why spending on healthcare is consistently rising more rapidly than spending on other goods and services. What factors are most responsible for the problem of rising healthcare costs?

As mentioned above, several explanations have been offered. Given the highly interactive nature of factors that contribute to healthcare cost increases, sometimes it may not be possible to isolate each factor and calculate the precise contribution of each. However, there does appear to be a consensus among many healthcare experts and economists that one of the most important factors responsible for driving healthcare costs upward is the rapid development and spread of medical technology (Goyen and Debatin 2009; Hobson 2009; "How Changes in Medical Technology Affect Health Care Costs" 2007; Kumar 2011; Moon 2005; Siegel, Mead, and Burke 2008; Valletta 2008).

Role and Growth of Medical Technology

In this section we discuss the role of technology in the U.S. healthcare system, focusing on the cost of medical technology and its relation to overall healthcare costs. Medical technology is defined as the procedures, equipment, and processes by which medical care is delivered. Thus, it can include new medical/surgical procedures such as angioplasty and joint replacements; drugs such as biologic agents; and medical devices such as CT scanners and implantable defibrillators ("How Changes in Medical Technology Affect Health Care Costs" 2007).

Americans in general adore technology—iPods, iPads, Kindles, TiVos, Xboxes, smartphones, and so on. Thus, it is not surprising that Americans' infatuation with technology extends to the healthcare system (Hobson 2009). Medicine in the twenty-first century has become increasingly dependent on technology, more so than any other area (Kumar 2011). Today the scope of medical intervention includes kidney dialysis, organ transplantation, laser surgery, arthroscopic surgical techniques, computerized tomography scanners, nuclear magnetic resonators, and much more.

Surgical techniques have undergone dramatic changes in the past forty to fifty years. Organ transplants have become increasingly common, especially with respect to the heart, liver, and kidney. Replacement of human body parts with artificial parts has become a reality. Today it is possible to replace a human arm or hand with a realistic artificial arm or hand that can perform almost the same functions. Soon it may be possible to replace eyes, ears, bones, and other vital organs.

The new digital age is transforming American medicine as well as the practice of medicine. Telemedicine is acting as a bridge between doctors and hospitals, making geographic distances irrelevant (Belluck 2012). Medicine and its practice are being redefined with apps and iPads (Hafner 2012; Richtel 2012). The digital age is making e-health opportunities available to seniors to live well (Brody 2012).

New miracle drugs are being marketed each year. Progress in genetic science has created the potential to customize pharmacotherapy: for example, genetic tests could be routinely given to patients and a drug therapy tailored to a patient's drug-response profile. Pharmacogenetics will raise a host of legal, ethical, and policy challenges for major actors in the healthcare system (Patel and Rushefsky 2002; Robertson et al. 2002).

Three emerging technologies—personalized medicine, regenerative medicine, and remote patient monitoring—will significantly alter the role of hospitals in the healthcare delivery system (Goldsmith 2004).

In addition, the practice of online medicine, because of advances in communications and information technologies, will also change medical practice (Miller and Derse 2002). Computerized physician-order entry systems (physicians can prescribe medications by computer) will have the potential to reduce medical errors in hospitals (Doolan and Bates 2002).

Lewis Thomas (1975) provides another useful way of classifying technology in medicine. "Non-technology" is offered to patients with diseases that are not well understood. It mainly involves reassuring patients and providing nursing and hospital care, but offers little hope for recovery. Nontechnology is applied in cases such as intractable cancer, multiple sclerosis, and stroke. The second level of technology is called "halfway technology." This represents the "kinds of things that must be done after the fact, as efforts to compensate for the incapacitating effects of certain diseases whose course one is unable to do very much about. It is a technology designed to make up for disease or to postpone death" (Thomas 1975, 37). Examples include organ transplants and the use of artificial organs. Halfway technology for chronic kidney failure means dialysis or kidney transplant. For heart disease, the halfway technology can mean open heart surgery, a pacemaker, a transplant, or an artificial heart. Such halfway technologies are generally very expensive (Morris 1984). The final level of technology, "high technology," is exemplified by immunization, antibiotics for bacterial infections, and prevention of nutritional disorders. High technology "comes as a result of genuine understanding of disease mechanisms, and when it becomes available it is relatively inexpensive to deliver" (Thomas 1975, 40).

What accounts for the growth of medical technology in general and halfway technologies in particular? Many factors have influenced the dramatic growth in medical technologies in the United States. They include increased public and private sector funding for biomedical research, an increase in medical specialties, the third-party insurance payment system, competition among hospitals to attract the best physicians by stocking hospitals with the best technology, physicians' overuse of medical technology, lack of technology assessment and regulation, a culture that values technology, consumer awareness of and demand for new technologies, and the commercial/economic interests of the biotechnology industry (Bozic, Pierce, and Herndon 2004; Davidson 2010; Ernst & Young 2012; Goyen and Debatin 2009; Hobson 2009; "How Changes in Medical Technology Affect Health Care Costs" 2007; Pauly and Burns 2008; Schur and Berk 2008). All parties in healthcare—hospitals, clinics, physicians, consumers, insurers/payers, and manufacturers of medical devices—have a stake in the development and diffusion of medical technology.

The rapid proliferation of healthcare technologies has raised concerns in many quarters about their cost and the strain they put on the nation's resources. It also raises issues about the cost-effectiveness of such technologies.

Medical Technology and Costs/Expenditures

A great deal of modern technology—medical equipment, medical techniques, and pharmaceuticals—is very expensive. More important, the overuse of such technologies and continuous use of some technologies that have shown to be not very effective has helped drive healthcare costs upward (McClellan 1996; Nitzkin 1996). One of the most significant advances in medical technology, and one of the most costly, is the spread and increased use of such diagnostic tools as magnetic resonance imaging (MRI), computed tomography (CT), and positron emission tomography (PET) scans. Since such new diagnostic therapies are simpler and safer than exploratory surgery, they are used at a much higher rate, adding to healthcare costs. MRI, CT, and PET scan equipment costs between $1 million and $2.5 million, and hospital MRI and CT scan procedures cost $1,100 and $1,500 respectively, compared to a PET scan fee of $3,000 ("Positron Emission Tomography" 2003). On average, CT, MRI, and PET scans cost about $700, $800, and $2,000 respectively. In contrast X-ray costs average about $100 ("Health Plans Strain to Contain Rapidly Rising Cost of Imaging" 2005).

It is estimated that about 80 million advanced diagnostic radiology exams are conducted annually in the United States. The total cost of these exams/procedures in 2005 was estimated to be around $100 billion, up from $75 billion in 2000 ("Health Plans Strain" 2005). Annual spending on CT imaging alone more than doubled to $2.17 billion in 2007 from $975 million in 2000.

Patients in 2007 were 3.43 times more likely to receive a CT scan than those in 1998. Increased use of CT scan and other imaging procedures is linked to higher healthcare costs, longer emergency department stays, and more radiation exposure. From 2000 to 2010, the use of advanced radiology increased about threefold in emergency departments (Ostrow 2010). The volume of CT procedures conducted in the Medicare population increased 82 percent from 1999 to 2003 (Siegel, Mead, and Burke 2008). Another study, which tracked 2 million patients enrolled in six large integrated healthcare systems, found that between 1996 and 2010, the number of MRIs quadrupled, CT scans tripled, and PET scans increased 57 percent (Smith-Bindman et al. 2012). MRI equipment has proved to be so popular that today it is available not only in hospitals and doctors' offices but also in roadside facilities and shopping centers. From the very beginning, critics of CT scans had voiced concern that this technology was proliferating more rapidly than it should (Fineberg 1977).

The field of neonatology is another example of how technology has allowed us to save lives at increased cost. Due to numerous medical breakthroughs—incubators, intravenous feeding, advances in caesarean sections, controls for infection—that were made during the 1950s and 1960s, doctors have succeeded in saving the lives of babies with increasingly lower birth weights. However, the cost has been very high.

According to Henry Aaron, medical technologies account for most of the rise in healthcare spending in the United States (Aaron 1991). He argues that developments in medical technology affect outlays in two ways: new technology adds new treatments, and because of its less intrusive nature, many more patients benefit from it, resulting in increased use and costs (Aaron 1991). Cutler and McClellan (2001) have argued that medical technology affects the healthcare system in different ways. Some new technologies often substitute for older ones in therapy of established patients, which is called the treatment substitution effect. Such new technologies often bring health improvements and are valued highly, leading to more people being treated for diseases. This is called the treatment expansion effect. A study that examined the relationship between the supply of new technologies, healthcare utilization, and spending for diagnostic imaging and cardiac, cancer, and newborn care technologies concluded that more availability of medical technology is associated with higher use and more spending (Baker et al. 2003). Of course, it can also be argued that new medical technologies also lead to over-diagnosis and over-treatment that drive up healthcare costs (Brownlee 2007; Welch, Schwartz, and Woloshin 2011).

The hospital is the major center of high-tech medicine, and hospital care constitutes the single largest component of our healthcare spending, about 31.4 percent in 2010 (see Table 7.2). The most important factor stimulating hospital cost increases is the rapid adoption of new medical technology. Competition among hospitals combined with a third-party reimbursement system provides incentives for rapid installment of new technologies in hospitals. Since hospitals do not compete for patients on the basis of price, they try to gain market advantage by offering the most up-to-date services, and the cost of these technologies is passed on to the third-party payers—insurance companies.

Efforts at healthcare-cost containment produce a conflict with the nation's commitment to medical innovation, which receives widespread support from both elites and the general public (Goyen and Debatin 2009; Hobson 2009; "How Changes in Medical Technology Affect Health Care Costs" 2007; Rettig 1994; Schur and Berk 2008). Furthermore, attempts to control costs associated with medical technology immediately produce a confrontation between two powerful interests in the healthcare system: insurance companies and manufacturers of medical devices. The manufacturers argue that they are unfairly singled out and that many new inventions provide less costly alternatives for diagnosis and treatment. They argue that any technology that allows us to produce existing goods or services at a lower cost while maintaining or increasing quality is to be welcomed. Nevertheless, rapid cost escalation related to wasteful technologies deserves scrutiny.

Insurance companies generally try to limit coverage to care that is "reasonably necessary" or "medically necessary." These terms are generally interpreted broadly to cover any nonexperimental technology accepted by the medical community that is not considered unsafe or ineffective. Furthermore, courts have often expanded the scope of insurance coverage by relying on the notion that all ambiguities should be interpreted against the insurer and in favor of the beneficiary. Courts have often forced insurance companies to cover technologies and treatments still considered to be in an experimental stage.

Of course, not all technology is completely good or bad. On the positive side, technology can play a significant role in supporting the provision of adequate care in the areas of prevention and rehabilitation. Mobile healthcare units can help overcome the challenge of geographic maldistribution by helping to extend service areas and making medical service distribution more equitable (Jaros and Boonzaier 1993). On the negative side, technology can be unsafe, ineffective, and inefficient.

The relationship between healthcare technology and healthcare costs is a complex one because technology affects costs in many different ways. Part of the difficulty in determining the precise relationship between medical technology and healthcare costs lies in the many ambiguities surrounding such a discussion. Sometimes it is clear whether a new technology reduces the cost of treating a particular illness (e.g., polio vaccines). However, the impact of an innovation on healthcare costs is often not clear. In addition, it is not easy to measure whether a new technology is reducing costs or increasing them. Also, defining what constitutes a healthcare cost is difficult (Weisbrod and LaMay 1999). It is very difficult to directly measure the impact of medical technology on total healthcare spending because medical innovations happen continuously and the impacts of different changes tend to interrelate with one another. Thus, indirect approaches are often used to measure the cost impact of new technology by first estimating the impact of factors that can be accounted for, such as aging of the population, increased income, supplier-induced demand, and spread of insurance ("How Changes in Medical Technology Affect Health Care Costs" 2007). Thus, it is not too surprising that cost estimates of the impact of medical technology on overall healthcare spending vary considerably among researchers.

Most healthcare economists and other healthcare experts do seem to agree that medical technology is the largest factor driving up annual healthcare cost in the United States (Aaron 1991; Baker et al. 2003; Cutler and McClellan 2001; Fuchs 1993; Gelijns and Rosenberg 1994; Goyen and Debatin 2009; Hobson 2009; "How Changes in Medical Technology Affect Health Care Costs" 2007; Newhouse 1992; Schwartz 1987; Weisbrod 1991). There also appears to be a general consensus among health policy experts that new medical technology has been the largest contributor to the rapid increase in healthcare costs since the 1960s (Valletta 2008).

Some have argued that new medical technology may account for about one-half or more of real long-term growth in healthcare spending ("How Changes in Medical Technology Affect Health Care Costs" 2007). Lubitz (2005) has argued that as a percentage of GDP, health spending rose from 5.7 percent in 1965 to 14.9 percent in 2002, with medical technological changes accounting for at least half of the growth. Smith et al. (2009) estimated that medical technology explains 27–48 percent of health spending growth since the 1960s.

Others have argued that spending on new health technology—machines/devices, drugs, procedures—makes up as much as two-thirds of the more than 6 percent annual increases in healthcare costs (Hobson 2009). A study by the Advanced Medical Technology Association placed medical technology's share of national health expenditures for 2010 at 6 percent (McCarthy 2012).

However, just because technological change may contribute to growth in healthcare spending, it does not follow that all such changes are bad, because they can bring benefits in addition to costs. Thus, the real question is this: Are the benefits derived from new technological innovations worth the costs? Do the benefits outweigh the costs? If so, technological change is good, despite the fact that it brings increased costs. Similarly, if the costs outweigh the few marginal benefits produced by a new technology, one can argue that the cost is not worthwhile. Cutler and McClellan (2001) analyzed technological change in five medical conditions—heart attacks, low-birth-weight infants, depression, cataracts, and breast cancer. They concluded that in four of the five conditions examined—heart attacks, low-birth-weight infants, depression, and cataracts—the estimated benefits of technological change were far greater than the costs. In the fifth condition, breast cancer, costs and benefits were about equal in magnitude. Thus, they concluded that medical spending as a whole is worth the increased cost of care.

The introduction of new diagnostic or treatment therapy can increase costs considerably but result in improved health. In other words, some technologies are both high cost and high benefit. Some technologies may decrease costs by allowing care to be given in a lower-cost setting, replacing expensive procedures, keeping people healthier, reducing hospital stay and recovery time, and returning people to work sooner. Such technologies may be both low cost and high benefit. In contrast, some technologies may be very costly but produce only marginal benefits. It is these technologies—the high-cost and low-benefit technologies—that raise serious concerns among critics of the U.S. healthcare system. Some technologies are unsafe, while others are ineffective. Some technologies are medically effective, but are not cost effective. Technologies that are unsafe, ineffective, or not cost effective are called "wasteful technologies" (Kalb 1990).

Furthermore, the diffusion of these technologies has outpaced our ability to evaluate their value and their cost-effectiveness. Despite regulatory and competitive strategies to control the diffusion of technology, excessive supply and overuse exists.

Prescription Drugs and Costs/Expenditures

According to a comprehensive report on the nation's health issued by the federal government in December 2004, more than 44 percent of Americans take at least one prescription drug, while 16.5 percent take at least three (Pear 2004; Schmid 2004). The use of antidepressant drugs among U.S. adults has also soared (Vedantam 2004). The report documented the growing use of medication in the last decade. Prescription drugs, which make up around one-tenth of the total U.S. medical bill, were the fastest-growing expenditures, having risen at least 15 percent every year since 1998 (Schmid 2004).

During the 1980s and 1990s, the medical community came to recognize that patients in pain were undertreated. The result of this awareness was threefold. One, doctors were encouraged to think about their patients' pain severity. Second, medical students and staffs were instructed that if narcotics were prescribed for legitimate pain, patients could never become dependent on narcotics. Third, opioid pain medications like oxycodone and hydrocodone were framed as safer alternatives to nonsteroidal anti-inflammatory drugs. Consequently, the amount of opioid narcotics prescribed by American doctors tripled between 1999 and 2010. By 2011, enough hydrocodone was being prescribed to medicate every American around the clock for a month (Meisel and Perrone 2012).

According to an estimate by the Institute of Medicine (2012), 100 million Americans suffer from chronic pain. Excluding children, it means that almost one in two Americans has chronic pain (Meisel and Perrone 2012). Chronic pain is one of the costliest health problems in the United States, with an estimated price tag of $50 billion a year (Oz 2011). According to the U.S. Centers for Disease Control and Prevention, the number of pain prescriptions increased 600 percent between 1997 and 2007 (Gupta 2012). According to 2011 congressional testimony by the American Society of Interventional Pain Physicians, 80 percent of the world's pain killers are consumed in the United States (Gupta 2012).

Prescription drug overdoses are now the number one cause of accidental deaths in the United States, surpassing deaths from car crashes and accounting for more than 20,000 deaths per year (Gupta 2012). Since 1990, deaths from unintentional drug overdoses in the United States have increased over 500 percent. Most of this increase is attributed to prescription pain killers, which now kill more people than heroin and cocaine combined (Meisel and Perrone 2012).

Increased prescription drug consumption in the United States automatically increases spending on prescription drugs. Table 7.6 presents data on national prescription drug expenditures by sources of funds from 1960 to 2010 at five-year intervals. As the data show, national expenditures for prescription drugs have increased from $3 billion in 1965 to $259 billion in 2010. The five-year expenditure growth rate for prescription drugs reached a high of a 102 percent increase from 1995 to 2000, while the lowest increase of 27.8 percent occurred from 2005 to 2010. The data also show that the growth rate in consumers' out-of-pocket share of prescription drug expenditures has declined during this period as the health insurance market started growing considerably the 1960s, and prescription drug coverage was added as a benefit in private as well as government health insurance programs over the years.

Table 7.7 provides data on prescription drug expenditures from 2001 to 2010. Several trends are discernible from the data. First, the growth rate in prescription drug expenditures declined every year from 9.5 percent in 2002 to 3.9 percent in 2010. Second, the growth rate in prescription drug expenditures has slowed considerably since 2008. Third, the overall growth rate for prescription drug expenditures has declined for out-of-pocket expenses as well as for private and public health insurance expenses. Fourth, the prescription drug expenditures growth rate has remained twice as much as rate of growth in overall national spending on healthcare. Fifth, prescription drug expenditures have increased two to three times more than the annual inflation rate.

Rapidly rising prescription drug costs, growing concern about the affordability of needed drugs due to high prices, and high profits earned by drug manufacturers have helped to elevate this issue onto the national policy agenda. Although prescription drug spending is a relatively small proportion of total national healthcare spending, about 10 percent in 2010, it is one of the fastest-growing components. Expenditures for prescription drugs as a percent of total national healthcare spending have doubled from 4.7 percent in 1980 to 10 percent in 2010 (see Tables 7.1 and 7.2).

During the 1990s the rapid growth of spending on pharmaceuticals resulted in drugs' share of total health spending rising from 5.6 percent in 1990 to 8.8 percent by 2000, and it increased to 10 percent by 2010 (see Table 7.1).

The Medicare and Medicaid programs were created in 1965. Medicare did not provide prescription drug coverage for the first forty years of its existence, except for drugs administered in hospitals and other institutional settings and selected drugs administered in doctors' offices (largely for cancer therapy). In contrast, prescription drugs have been a very important and widely used benefit in the Medicaid program from the beginning of its creation. Prescription drugs play an important role in the treatment of chronic health conditions suffered by Medicaid patients. The data in Tables 7.6 and 7.7 reflect each program's share of prescription drug expenditures.

The Medicare Prescription Drug Improvement and Modernization Act of 2003 created a voluntary outpatient prescription drug benefit known as Medicare Part D (see chapter 4). The program took effect in 2006. As Table 7.7 shows, Medicare's prescription drug expenditures grew 90 percent between 2005 and 2006 and began to level off beginning in 2008 to single-digit percentage increases. It should also be noted that this 90 percent increase between 2005 and 2006 paralleled an almost 92 percent decline in Medicaid's expenditures for prescription drugs because Medicaid enrollees over the age of sixty-five (dual eligible) started receiving prescription drug coverage through Medicare Part D. Similarly, as Table 7.4 shows, in 2006 overall Medicare expenditures

Table 7.6

National Prescription Drug Expenditures by Sources of Funds: 1965—2010 (in $ millions)

	1965	1970	1975	1980	1985	1990	1995	2000	2005	2010
Total national health expenditures	41,957.4	74,853.5	133,584.9	255,782.5	444,623.3	724,282.3	1,027,457	1,377,185	2,029,148	2,593,644
% increase from previous year listed		78.4%	78.5%	91.5%	73.8%	62.9%	41.9%	34.0%	47.3%	27.8%
Total prescription drug expenditures	3,715	5,497	8,052	12,049	21,794.7	40,290.3	59,808.2	120,896.6	204,779.3	259,061.4
% increase from previous year listed		48.0%	46.5%	49.6%	80.9%	84.9%	48.4%	102.1%	69.4%	26.5%
Out of pocket	3,441.5	4,531	6,092.5	8,592.3	13,856.1	22,871.2	23,357.8	33,992.5	51,621.3	48,752.6
% increase from previous year listed		31.7%	34.5%	41.0%	61.3%	65.1%	2.1%	45.5%	51.9%	-5.6%
Health insurance	133.2	907	1,855.5	3,241.8	7,443.3	16,218.5	35,104.2	84,654.1	14,9323.5	206,903.1
% increase from previous year listed		580.9%	104.6%	74.7%	129.6%	117.9%	116.4%	141.2%	76.4%	38.6%
Private health insurance	130	483.7	967.2	1,810	5,047.2	10,862.1	24,383.9	60,679.9	101,645.3	117,002.7
% increase from previous year listed		272.1%	100.0%	87.1%	178.9%	115.2%	124.5%	148.9%	67.5%	15.1%
Medicare	0	0	0	0	20.5	185.4	721.5	2095.8	3936.7	59475.5
% increase from previous year listed						88.9%	74.3%	65.6%	46.8%	93.4%
Medicaid (Title XIX)	0	417	870.6	1,408.1	2,332	5,076.9	9,699.5	19,760.2	36,284.4	20,165
% increase from previous year listed			52.1%	38.2%	39.6%	54.1%	47.7%	50.9%	45.5%	-79.9%
CHIP (Title XIX and Title XXI)	0	0	0	0	0	0	0	302.5	1,112.2	1,613.6
% increase from previous year listed									72.8%	31.1%

Note: Other third-party payers/programs include things such as worker's compensation, general assistance, federal and state maternal/child health, Indian Health Service, and school health programs.

Source: National Center for Health Statistics, Centers for Medicare and Medicaid Services, Baltimore, MD. 2012. Online at www.cms.gov/Research-Statistics-Data-and-Systems/Statistics-Trends-and-Reports/NationalHealthExpendData/NationalHealthAccountsHistorical.html

Table 7.7

National Prescription Drug Expenditures by Sources of Funds: 2001–2010 (in $ millions)

	2001	2002	2003	2004	2005	2006	2007	2008	2009	2010
Total national health expenditures	1,494,116	1,636,416	1,774,297	1,900,045	2,029,148	2,162,410	2,297,098	2,403,938	2,495,842	2,593,644
% increase from previous year		9.5%	8.4%	7.1%	6.8%	6.6%	6.2%	4.7%	3.8%	3.9%
Total prescription drug expenditures	138,694.1	158,174.4	176,029.2	192,203.8	204,779.3	224,212.6	236,201.4	243,584	256,106.3	259,061.4
% increase from previous year		14.0%	11.3%	9.2%	6.5%	9.5%	5.3%	3.1%	5.1%	1.2%
Out of pocket	36,706.3	41,196	45,566.4	48,344.8	51,621.3	51,270.6	53,038.1	51,033.3	50,842.4	48,752.6
% increase from previous year		12.2%	10.6%	6.1%	6.8%	-0.7%	3.4%	-3.8%	-0.4%	-4.1%
Health insurance	99,304.4	113,899.7	126,903.2	140,202.7	149,323.5	168,897.2	179,403.3	188,925.9	201,737.9	206,903.1
% increase from previous year		14.7%	11.4%	10.5%	6.5%	13.1%	6.2%	5.3%	6.8%	2.6%
Private health insurance	70,598.4	79,649.3	86,273.1	94,364.1	101,645.3	102,159.7	106,767.1	110,131.2	117,194.7	117,002.7
% increase from previous year		12.8%	8.3%	9.4%	7.7%	0.5%	4.5%	3.2%	6.4%	-0.2%
Medicare	2,447.4	2,471.8	2,477.8	3,378.8	3,936.7	39,641.7	45,947.8	50,645.3	54,545.7	59,475.5
% increase from previous year		1.0%	0.2%	26.7%	14.2%	90.1%	13.7%	9.3%	7.2%	8.3%
Medicaid (Title XIX)	23,316.2	27,442.9	32,121	35,719	36,284.4	18,918.9	18,127.3	18,946.8	20,101.5	20,165
% increase from previous year		15.0%	14.6%	10.1%	1.6%	-91.8%	-4.4%	4.3%	5.7%	0.3%
Overall annual inflation rate[1]	2.8%	1.6%	2.3%	2.7%	3.4%	3.2%	2.9%	3.9%	-0.3%	1.6%

[1]The inflation rate is calculated from the Consumer Price Index (CPI) compiled by the U.S. Bureau of Labor Statistics and is based upon a1982 base of 100. To view the actual Consumer Price Index data from which this inflation rate is calculated, go to: ftp://ftp.bls.gov/pub/special.requests/cpi/cpiai.txt.

Note: Other third-party payers/programs include things such as worker's compensation, general assistance, federal and state maternal/child health, Indian Health Service, and school health programs.

Source: National Center for Health Statistics, Centers for Medicare and Medicaid Services, Baltimore, MD.2012. Online at http://www.cms.gov/Research-Statistics-Data-and-Systems/Statistics-Trends-and-Reports/NationalHealthExpendData/NationalHealthAccountsHistorical.html

grew 16 percent from the previous year while overall Medicaid expenditures in 2006 dropped to −0.9 percent from the previous year.

In 2007, the program provided drug benefits to 29 million beneficiaries, costing the federal government $39 billion for an average of $1,600 per individual enrolled in the program. The cost is expected to grow as per capita healthcare costs continue to outpace GDP growth and as the baby boom generation reaches retirement age and more individuals are enrolled in the program (Duggan, Healy, and Morton 2008). Thus, Part D has significantly increased government spending on healthcare. In the long run, it is hoped that Medicare Part D will control spending by allowing private insurance plans to compete with the traditional Medicare program for enrollees by negotiating with drug manufacturers for lower prices, covering treatments valued by Medicare recipients, and empowering consumers to select the most economical plan that best fits their healthcare needs by giving them a large menu of plans to choose from. However, critics are pessimistic about cost controls because they argue that under the plan, the government is not allowed to negotiate drug prices with manufacturers as the VHA does, that the program is too large and generous, and that the profusion of plan options is so large and complex that the elderly are unable to understand their choices and select the most economical plan (Duggan, Healy, and Morton 2008).

With respect to Medicaid, prescription drug expenditures are consuming a larger share of the state Medicaid budgets, reflected in the fact that total expenditures for prescription drugs by Medicaid enrollees increased 104 percent from $11.6 billion in 1996–1997 to 23.7 billion in 2001–2002, and the total number of prescriptions written increased from 201 million to 429 million. During the same time period, expenditures per user increased from $517 to $946 (Banthin and Miller 2006). Some of the factors that explain these increases are the introduction of new drugs, expansion in Medicaid eligibility, and the creation of CHIP in 1997. Disabled adults and elderly Medicaid recipients saw significant increases in total as well as per capita expenditures for prescription drugs, with disabled adults being the most intensive users of prescribed medicine. Medicaid also witnessed a rapid growth in expenditures for new drugs and therapies such as antidepressants, antipsychotics, anti-diabetic agents, and COX-2 inhibitors (Banthin and Miller 2006). Finally, it should be noted that the national expenditures on prescription drugs grew at a much slower pace, at rates of 4.7 percent, 3.8 percent, and 3.9 percent in 2008, 2009, and 2010 respectively.

The biggest factor in slowing the drug spending growth rate has been the increased use of generic drugs in the United States since many of the most prescribed brand-name drugs lost their patent protections starting in mid-2000s. The cost of generic prescription drugs averages about one-fourth that of an equivalent name-brand drug. As of 2011, 80 percent of prescriptions in the United States were filled by generic drugs, compared with 63 percent in 2006. Thus, aggressive generic substitutions helped bring down total drug expenditures (Hoadley 2012). According to an analysis by the generic drug industry, the use of generic drugs saved the U.S. healthcare system about $1.07 trillion between 2002 and 2011, with savings of about $193 billion in 2011 alone (Generic Pharmaceutical Association 2012). The Congressional Budget Office has estimated that the use of generic drugs in Medicare Part D generated $33 billion in savings in 2007, and costs would have been 55 percent higher without them (Congressional Budget Office 2010). The second factor that helped slow down the rate of growth in prescription drug spending was that relatively few new drugs with the potential for large market share and high costs have been approved by the FDA in recent years (Hoadley 2012).

The slower rate of growth in prescription spending is likely to continue in the short run because many other most prescribed brand-name drugs have already lost or will lose patent protection over the next few years, making generic equivalents available in the market. For five of the top ten drugs— Lipitor, Nexium, Abilify, Seroquel, and Crestor—generics were already available in 2010. Of the other five drugs, Actos, Singulair, and Plavix lost their patent in 2012, making generics available as substitutes (Hoadley 2012). The use of generic drugs in prevention of chronic diseases has been found to be far more cost-effective than previously thought. Increased access to essential generic medication can be an effective tool in controlling prescription drug costs (Shrank et al. 2011).

In fact, according to the study by IMS Institute for Healthcare Informatics (2013), for the first time in fifty-eight years, total spending on medicine dropped to $325.8 billion in 2012 from $329.2 billion in 2011—a decline of 1 percent. The reasons for the decline included availability of inexpensive generic versions of widely used drugs for chronic conditions and consumers/patients' rationing their own healthcare. However, this masks the real problem of the rising costs of complex specialty medicines that treat cancer and other diseases. In the long run, prescription drug prices are going to rise again (Thomas 2013).

In recent years, private third-party insurers have also attempted to control rising drug expenditures by steering patients toward preferred drugs on the insurer's list of approved medications, imposing higher copayments for a branded drug in the same therapeutic class, implementing differential copayments among the various branded drugs within a given therapeutic class under "three tier" formularies, and providing a more attractive copayment structure to encourage mail order dispensing for certain drugs (Berndt 2002).

However, there is no reason to believe that the slower rate of growth in prescription expenditures will continue. Federal actuaries project the growth rate to accelerate modestly over the next decade and again exceed overall healthcare spending growth due to higher use resulting from expansion of prescription drug coverage (Keehan et al. 2012).

What Accounts for Increased Costs and Expenditures on Prescription Drugs?

According to the Kaiser Family Foundation (2004), three factors have contributed to the increased spending for prescription drugs. One is increased use. The second is the proliferation of different kinds of drugs, with newer and higher-priced drugs replacing older ones. The third factor is the almost 25 percent increases in manufacturers' prices for existing drugs. Others have pointed to an aging population, growth in obesity rates in the country, and an increase in real income as additional contributors to increased spending on drugs during the 1990s. For example, Vandegrift and Datta (2006) have argued that about 8 percent of the increase in spending on prescription drugs during 1990–1998 can be explained by the increase in obesity, as obesity is associated with high-risk factors for cardiovascular disease such as hypertension, elevated cholesterol, and type-II diabetes as well as an increased risk of cancer, stroke, osteoarthritis, and other diseases. Rising real income accounted for another 55 percent of the increase in prescription drug expenditures. They have also argued that the higher percentage of the population over sixty-five and new drugs exert an influence on increases in per capita prescription drug expenditures.

Price increases and the large profits of the pharmaceutical industry have contributed to increased expenditures on prescription drugs. Price increases on popular branded drugs in 2011 were more than six times the overall rate of inflation for consumer goods, and spending for specialty drugs was up 23 percent. Prices on a collection of the most widely used brand-name prescription drugs increased 13 percent from September 2011 to September 2012, easily outpacing the overall economic inflation rate of 2 percent. These higher prices were partially offset by a 21.9 percent drop in prices for generic drugs (Berkrot 2012). Critics have argued that the drug industry makes too high a profit at the expense of patients. The U.S. pharmaceutical market is the world's largest market and was estimated to be at $300 billion in 2009. The top ten pharmaceutical companies, half of which are headquartered in the United States, account for 40 percent of the world market. The five largest U.S. companies ranked by revenue—Pfizer, Merck, Johnson and Johnson, Eli Lilly, and Bristol-Myers Squibb—had a combined revenue of $161.9 billion in 2009 ("Pharmaceutical Industry Profile" 2010). The pharmaceutical industry's profits skyrocketed in the 1980s and 1990s. In the 2001 Fortune 500 list, ten America drug companies ranked far above all other

American industries in average return measured as a percentage of sales (18.5 percent), of assets (15.3 percent), or of shareholders' equity (33.2 percent). In contrast, the median return for all other industries in the Fortune 500 was only 3.3 percent of sales. The pharmaceutical industry's average return is extraordinarily high compared to other industries (Angell 2004).

Another reason for the increased use and spending on prescription drugs is aggressive advertising and marketing by the pharmaceutical industry. For every dollar spent on basic research, $19 is spent by the drug companies for self-promotion and marketing (Eichler 2012). In 1985 the FDA lifted its moratorium on direct-to-consumer (DTC) advertising but emphasized that DTC advertising must include a detailed "brief summary" of risks and other information, while the broadcast advertisements are required to have a much shorter "major statement" of risks. In 1997, the FDA issued final guidance on DTC advertising: that in addition to being nondeceptive, prescription drug advertising must present fair and balanced information about effectiveness as well as risks, include a "major" statement conveying the most important risk information and all relevant information about the product's indication and limitations for use in consumer-friendly language.

In the wake of the FDA's 1997 guidelines, DTC advertising accelerated from $1.3 billion in 1998 to $2.7 billion in 2001 (Calfee 2002). By 2005, spending on DTC advertising had reached $4.2 billion and made up about 40 percent of total promotional spending by the pharmaceutical industry (Donohue 2006). In 2006, spending on drug advertising reached $4.8 billion (Appleby 2008). Between 1996 and 2000, aggressive annual marketing in relation to sales ratios ranged between 13.6 and 15.3 percent in the pharmaceutical industry, while the DTC marketing-sales ratio jumped from 1.2 percent to 2.2 percent between 1996 and 2000 (Berndt 2002).

Research on the pharmaceutical industry's advertising expenditures also shows that DTC advertising is highly concentrated on a small subset of new drugs. Furthermore, the decision to advertise a specific product to the public is not based on the superior safety or efficacy of a drug but rather more on the basis of likely returns on investment (Lexchin and Mintzes 2002). Other studies of drug advertising have shown that very few advertisers presented any quantitative data to support claims of benefits—87 percent described the benefits of medication with vague, qualitative terms and only 13 percent used data. Thus, patients have no way to judge a medication's effectiveness for themselves (Lexchin and Mintzes 2002). The rise of drug marketing throughout the pharmaceutical industry has been blamed on the integration of pharmaceutical firms' marketing efforts with their formerly semiautonomous research and development divisions, starting in the 1990s (Applbaum 2009).

Jerry Avron, a Harvard Medical School researcher and clinician and chief of the division of pharmacoepidemiology and pharmacoeconomics at Brigham and Women's Hospital in Boston, argues that millions of dollars a year are wasted on prescription drugs that are excessively priced, poorly prescribed, or improperly taken (Avron 2004). According to John Abramson (2004), a former family practitioner who teaches at Harvard Medical School, Americans are overmedicated and overmedicalized as a result of the commercialization of healthcare. Jerome Kassirer (2005), a former editor-in-chief of the *New England Journal of Medicine,* has argued that the U.S. healthcare system has been turned into a commercial enterprise because of the drug industry's huge expenditures for courting doctors to use their products and for recruiting physicians to tout their drugs. Marcia Angell (2004), another former editor-in-chief of the *New England Journal of Medicine,* has argued that prescription drugs are very expensive because the pharmaceutical industry is fraught with corruption. She contends that a huge portion of the revenue generated by big drug companies goes not into research and development (R&D) but into aggressive marketing campaigns to sell their products, while most of the actual R&D work is done by universities funded by the government. Drug companies offer high-priced junkets to doctors as educational opportunities, but in reality they are nothing more than bribes to get doctors to prescribe their drugs (Angell 2004).

A number of critics have questioned the honesty and integrity of the pharmaceutical industry (Goozner 2004; Greider 2003; Harris 2004a, 2004b; Harris and Berenson 2005; Kitsis 2009; Maier 1997). Even when drug companies are found guilty of criminal conduct and fines are levied against them, their profits far outweigh the penalties (Evans 2010; Lipton and Sack 2013).

Another major factor cited for increased spending on drugs is the growth of health insurance and prescription drug coverage. An unprecedented spread of insurance coverage for outpatient drugs occurred in the 1990s. Danzon and Pauly (2002) placed the direct effect of the growth in insurance coverage somewhere around one-fourth to one-half of total drug spending during the 1990s. The significant expansion of the Medicaid program under the Affordable Care Act will also contribute to higher prescription drug expenditures.

Also responsible for increased spending on drugs is patent protection and the lack of market competition in the pharmaceutical industry. The patent system enables protection from price competition. The Food and Drug Administration, a federal agency, is responsible for approving all drugs to make sure they are safe and effective before they are allowed to be sold in the marketplace. After successful clinical trials are completed, the drug company typically files an application for patent certification and exclusivity. The U.S. Patent and Trademark Office grants a patent, which typically expires twenty years from the date of the filing. "Exclusivity" means the FDA grants an exclusive marketing right to a drug company upon FDA approval of the drug, and it can run concurrently or not with a patent ("Development and Approval Process: Drugs." n.d.). Thus, a drug company essentially gets a monopoly on marketing and selling that drug in the marketplace until its patent runs out, at which point other drug manufacturers can enter the market by offering the generic equivalent of that drug. The pharmaceutical industry justifies the patent/exclusivity system on the grounds that they take high investment risks in research and development to discover new drugs.

A further factor attributed to increased spending on drugs is public opinion. Polls suggest that DTC advertising by drug manufacturers works. In a nationwide survey conducted in 2008 by USA Today/Kaiser Family Foundation and the Harvard School of Public Health (2008), one-third of respondents stated that prescription drug ads prompted them to ask their doctor about the advertised medicine, and 82 percent of those who asked said their physicians recommended a prescription; 44 percent of this segment said their physician gave them a prescription for the drug they asked about, while slightly more than half said their doctor prescribed a different drug. According to the survey, the percentage of people getting a drug after asking about an ad is on the increase.

The same survey (2008) demonstrated that Americans love the pharmaceutical companies' products, but they also blame the industry's high profits for high drug prices. Among those with an unfavorable opinion of drug companies, 68 percent gave their reasons as high prices, high profits, or greed. Among all Americans, almost eight in ten (79 percent), say the cost of prescription drugs is unreasonable, and seven in ten (70 percent) say that pharmaceutical companies are too concerned about making profits and are not concerned about helping people. Seventy-nine percent saw profits made by the drug companies as the biggest driver of the cost of drugs, while 72 percent listed the cost of medical research, 62 percent the cost of advertising, and 56 percent the cost of lawsuits as major drivers of the cost of drugs. Seventy-six percent of the American public think they are being charged unfairly compared to people in other countries and that people in the United States pay higher prices than do people in Canada, Mexico, and Western European countries for the same prescription drugs.

Finally, the high price of drugs in the United States is also blamed on the lack of regulation of the pharmaceutical industry in the United States compared to European countries. The reason Americans pay more than their counterparts in Europe for the same prescription drugs is that in the United States, government does not regulate prescription drug prices and profits made by pharmaceutical companies. As we have discussed previously, the Centers for Medicare and Medicaid

Services (CMS) is prohibited by law from negotiating drug prices with drug companies for their patients. Only the Department of Defense and the Veterans Administration negotiate drug prices with drug companies. Thus, veterans pay much less for the same prescription drugs than do other Americans, including Medicare and Medicaid beneficiaries.

In contrast, European governments not only regulate drug pricing, they also regulate and control drug manufacturers' profits, using a variety of tactics including reference pricing, negative lists, price freezes, price cuts, regulation of profits, general practitioner budgets, pharmaceutical expenditure ceilings, and promotion of generic drugs (Jonsson 2001; Nuijten et al. 2001). Also, all Western European countries have some form of universal health insurance system. As a result, about 75 percent of pharmaceutical expenditures are publicly reimbursed. This gives the governments of these countries an opportunity to impose a wide range of pricing policies on drug companies (Ess, Schneeweiss, and Szucs 2003). None of these strategies are used in the United States, where instead the efforts to control rising prescription drug spending are instead focused more on consumers via tools such as patient copayments and cost-sharing, medical practice guidelines, and formularies.

Medical Errors, Malpractice, Defensive Medicine, and Costs/Expenditures

Another factor often cited for rising healthcare spending is the cost of medical errors, medical malpractice lawsuits, and the practice of defensive medicine. The argument goes something like this: First, medical errors drive up healthcare costs and thus healthcare spending. Second, medical errors lead to many medical malpractice lawsuits that add to healthcare spending because of high financial awards handed out by juries and the high cost of medical malpractice insurance that physicians have to pay. Thus, the high cost of malpractice premiums leads to higher healthcare costs. Third, the fear of malpractice lawsuits leads many physicians to engage in the practice of defensive medicine, further driving up spending on healthcare. In this section we examine these arguments to see how much they contribute to increased healthcare costs and spending.

Medical Errors and Costs

According to the Institute of Medicine's (2000) report *To Err Is Human,* as many as 98,000 people die in hospitals each year as a result of medical errors that could have been prevented. In addition, thousands more are injured because of mistakes made in doctors' offices, nursing homes, and outpatient clinics in a complex system of care that is designed for efficiency and not necessarily patient safety (Lieberman 2004). The Institute of Medicine (IOM) defines medical error as the failure to complete a planned action as intended or the use of a wrong plan to achieve a given goal. According to the IOM report, medical errors typically include such mistakes as wrong or delayed diagnosis, an adverse drug event (prescribing the wrong drug, inaccurate dosage, etc.), improper transfusion, surgical injuries (including wrong site surgery), restraint-related injuries or deaths, falls, burns, and mistaken medical identities. Medical errors are generally divided into three categories—preventable and negligent, preventable but not negligent, and other adverse events.

More recent analysis suggests that adverse events happen in one-third of hospital admissions and thus adverse events may be ten times greater than previously measured (Classen et al. 2011). Another analysis suggests that medical interventions that harm or injure patients separate from the underlying medical condition may cause as many as 187,000 deaths in hospitals each year and 6.1 million injuries (Goodman, Villarreal, and Jones 2011).

There have been several attempts to measure the cost of medical errors. Aside from the cost in human life, the Institute of Medicine's (2000) report placed the cost of preventable medical errors between $17 billion and $29 billion per year in hospitals nationwide. A more recent analysis placed the total cost of measurable medical errors in the United States at $17.1 billion in 2008. This figure amounts to only about 0.72 percent of the total $2.4 trillion spent on healthcare in 2008 (Van Den Bos et al. 2011). Thus, the cost of medical errors as a percentage of total national spending on healthcare is rather very minor. Of course, when medical error causes the death of a patient, the cost of human life is not easy to measure, since it raises the question how much a human life is worth. According to Goodman, Villarreal, and Jones (2011), a patient's risk of dying in a U.S. hospital from an adverse medical event is 1 in 200. They estimated that the "social cost" of an adverse medical event, that is, what Americans would be willing to pay to avoid injuries and death caused by adverse medical events, was very large. Using the low and high estimates for the annual number of deaths from adverse medical events to calculate the age-adjusted social cost, they estimated that in 2006, the social cost of all inpatient medical adverse events—both death and injuries—was between $348 billion and $913 billion. When they used the actuarial study's estimate of total injuries—occurring both in and out of hospitals—they placed the total social costs of adverse medical events to between $393 billion and $958 billion, an amount equivalent to 18–45 percent of total healthcare spending in 2006.

Regardless of the wide variance in cost measurement of medical errors, it is clear that the problem has received considerable attention, including several books, such as Goldhill's (2013) *Catastrophic Care,* Charney's (2012), *Epidemic* of *Medical Errors and Hospital-Acquired Infections,* Kalra's (2011) *Medical Errors and Patient Safety: Strategies to Reduce and Disclose Medical Errors and Improve Patient Safety,* Banja's (2005) *Medical Errors and Medical Narcissism,* Wachter and Shojania's (2004) *Internal Bleeding: The Truth Behind America's Terrifying Epidemic of Medical Mistakes*, Gibson and Singh's (2003) *Wall of Silence: The Untold Story of the Medical Mistakes That Kill and Injure Millions of Americans,* and Rosenthal and Sutcliffe's (2002) *Medical Error: What Do We Know? What Do We Do?*

However, meaningful reforms designed to reduce medical errors are often difficult to achieve because of politics ("Politics Keeps Real Remedies Off Radar" 2004). If medical errors are as widespread as many of the recent reports and publications suggest, compensating patients who have suffered as a result of medical errors is important, whether it is done through the current tort litigation system or some other mechanism (Sage 2004).

Medical Malpractice Liability and Costs

Medical malpractice can be defined in a broad sense as "any unjustified act or failure to act on the part of a doctor or other healthcare professional that results in harm to the patient" (Stauch 1996, 247). Within the legal framework of medical injury, negligence is a conduct that fails to achieve accepted standards of professional healthcare, and malpractice is negligent conduct that does harm to a patient. Under the current tort system, negligence is treated as a civil wrong (tort), not a crime or breach of contract (Mullis 1995). In order for a patient (plaintiff) to win a malpractice case in a court, it must be reasonably demonstrated that (1) the healthcare provider deviated from generally accepted medical practice, and (2) the medical injury/harm caused to the patient was the result of the healthcare provider's action or failure to act. It must be shown that the patient's injury resulted from negligence and not from other causes such as the normal risk of medical treatment or the patient's prior health condition (Eastburn 1999; Farber and White 1991; Fielding 1995).

The defenders of the present fault-based system argue that the system promotes values of fairness and acts as a deterrent, because the prospect of being sued and having to pay for losses deters physicians from providing substandard care (Weiler et al. 1993). Critics argue that the current fault-based tort system leaves too many victims of medical malpractice uncompensated or undercompensated (Sugarman 1985) and it fails to act as a deterrent because very few victims of medical injury actually file lawsuits, and of those who do, only about half have any chance of success. Also, very few cases actually go to trial because many cases are dropped by plaintiffs, dismissed by judges, or settled out of court (Golann 2011; Pickert 2009). Critics of the current system also argue that part of the problem is that lawyers often file frivolous lawsuits—that is, malpractice cases that have no merit—because when they win a case, they generally receive 30 percent of the jury award as contingency fees. Thus, lawyers have an incentive for filing lawsuits.

The current tort system is criticized for contributing to rising healthcare costs. Critics point to the high costs of medical malpractice insurance premiums, the current tort system, and the practice of defensive medicine (Brennan and Howard 2004; Howard 2002, 2003) as major factors that contribute to rising healthcare costs. However, it is not easy to estimate the costs of the medical liability system. This is demonstrated by the fact that the U.S. Chamber of Commerce claims that meaningful medical malpractice reform can save from $120 billion to $500 billion over a decade ("Medical Liability Reform Must Have Teeth to Be Effective" 2009). This is a rather large range of estimates, amounting to a savings of anywhere from about $12 billion per year to $50 billion a year, but a rather small percent of total national healthcare spending of $2.6 trillion in 2010.

The Practice of Defensive Medicine and Costs

Physicians often argue that the fear of medical malpractice suits forces them to practice defensive medicine, which in turn drives up the cost of healthcare. Thus they often argue for tort reform (Carrier et al. 2010). Practitioners of defensive medicine are physicians who, in order to protect themselves from potential malpractice lawsuits, overtreat a patient. They often overprescribe diagnostic and treatment procedures as a defense against possible malpractice lawsuits. The most commonly used definition of defensive medicine was proposed by the now-defunct Office of Technology Assessment (OTA). It defined defensive medicine as occurring when "doctors order tests, procedures, or visits, or avoid certain high-risk patients or procedures, primarily (but not solely) because of concern about malpractice liability."

Recent surveys of healthcare professionals do lend some credence to the argument that fear of medical liability lawsuits leads to the practice of defensive medicine, impairs the doctor-patient relationship, and lowers job satisfaction among doctors. In a nationwide Harris Interactive survey of 300 practicing physicians, 100 hospital administrators, and 100 nurses, health professionals said that fear of malpractice leads to defensive medicine and lack of openness in discussing medical errors, and has had a negative impact on their practice. A majority of physicians (94 percent), hospital administrators (84 percent), and nurses (66 percent) believed that unnecessary or excessive care is provided to patients because of fear of malpractice lawsuits. The survey also found that 43 percent of doctors in active practice had considered leaving medicine because of the malpractice liability system. Fifty-nine percent of doctors indicated that liability concerns were a significant factor in discouraging medical professionals from openly discussing and thinking about ways to reduce medical errors and in discouraging hospitals from sharing the results of inquiring into patient injury cases ("Doctors and Other Health Professionals Report" 2003).

A study based on a sample of 824 physician specialists most affected by the malpractice insurance crisis in Pennsylvania concluded that it has led to a decrease in specialist physicians' satisfaction with their own medical practice in ways that may affect quality of care (Mello et al. 2004). In a more recent national survey of U.S. physicians, a majority believed that unnecessary procedures and testing can result from fear of malpractice issues (Bishop, Federman, and Keyhani 2010). Another survey reported an increase in the number of physicians practicing defensive medicine; 92.5 percent of surgeons indicated that they had ordered imaging tests to protect themselves from lawsuits, and they attributed 34 percent of overall healthcare costs to defensive medicine (Hettrich et al. 2010). According to a survey of 3,344 practicing members of the American Association of

Neurological Surgeons, 72 percent ordered additional imaging tests, 67 percent ordered laboratory tests, and 66 percent referred patients to consultants. Sixty-four percent of respondents considered malpractice premiums a major or extreme burden, and 45 percent stated that the fear of malpractice led them to eliminate high-risk procedures from their practice (Nahed et al. 2012). Finally, in an informal survey on the *Urology Times* website, 93 percent of respondents said they believe urologists practice defensive medicine (Nash 2012).

The estimates of how much the practice of defensive medicine adds to the overall cost of healthcare and the rise in healthcare spending vary considerably because of the difficulty of precise measurement. Some estimates include the cost of the medical malpractice system and the cost of defensive medicine in their calculations, while some have tried to calculate the cost separately.

Some of the critics of defensive medicine have claimed its cost to be in excess of $100 billion (Howard 2003). However, others have questioned that figure (Hyman and Silver 2004). Harvard researchers estimated that the nation's medical liability system accounted for $55.6 billion or 2.4 percent of the total healthcare spending in 2008, with almost $45.6 billion of that figure being spent on the practice of defensive medicine (Robeznicks 2010). Others have concluded that defensive medicine costs account for 5–9 percent of the total healthcare costs (Dove et al. 2010), while others have placed the number in the range of only 1–2 percent (Hermer and Brody 2010).

It is pretty clear from the above discussion that results of studies seeking to quantify the cost of defensive medicine vary considerably and no definitive answer exists about its cost.

Would Tort Reforms Help Reduce Healthcare Spending?

The criticisms of the current tort system have generated a great deal of debate about the reform of the current system and/or alternatives in order to reduce healthcare costs. Such reforms include placing a cap on noneconomic damages; rapidly compensating victims for medical injury with fair compensation without the need to prove negligence; offsetting payments received by the plaintiff from collateral sources; shortening the statute of limitations; limiting attorney contingency fees; using expert panels or special courts; using alternate dispute resolution methods; establishing medical practice guidelines; and moving to enterprise liability or a no-fault-based system (Greene 1996; McMillen 1996; Sage 2003; Struve 2004; Thorpe 2004).

Would tort reform lead to a reduction in healthcare spending? Proponents argue that it would. This argument is based on the notion that the threat of lawsuits has made medical care more costly (Sloan and Shadle 2009).

However, a great deal of the literature suggests that the impact of savings on overall healthcare cost/spending from tort reform may be overstated (Thomas, Ziller, and Thayer 2012). The Congressional Budget Office in 2008 indicated that it had not found sufficient evidence to conclude that practicing defensive medicine has a significant effect on spending (Pickert 2009). A panel on discussion of tort reform at the Georgetown University School of Law in 2009 concluded that a change in the current tort system is likely to have very little impact on the overall cost of healthcare because medical malpractice, including defensive medicine, adds at most very few percentage points in spending, and medical torts do not make a significant contribution to the annual rate of increase in healthcare costs (McCarthy 2009). According to one of the panelists, David Hyman, there is a mismatch between what we actually know about medical malpractice and the political and public perceptions about it. He further stated that the claim that vast sums are to be saved by enacting tort reform is not borne out (McCarthy 2009). Finally, as Amitabh Chandra of Harvard's Kennedy School of Government, one of the participants in a study that highlighted the $55 billion cost impact of medical malpractice liability on the U.S. healthcare system, stated, the amount of defensive medicine is not trivial but it is also unlikely to be a source of significant savings (Fox 2010).

Overpriced American Healthcare System

Critics of the American healthcare system have often argued that one of the reasons for the rising spending on healthcare is that it is overpriced, charging too much for health services compared to what other countries charge for similar services. Not only do we spend more on healthcare, our healthcare system also costs more and charges more for services than any other country. Spending in almost every area of healthcare is higher in the United States than any other countries. In recent years, many studies have documented these trends.

Evidence suggests that both higher prices and the provision of more services are important factors, but higher prices have greater influence on higher healthcare spending in the United States (Lind 2012). In fact, it is argued that the central problem with healthcare in the United States is not that it spends too much in general or spends too much on the elderly in particular but that it spends far more than other industrialized countries for similar services and results. The most important cause of America's healthcare inflation is the overcharging of nonelderly Americans by physicians, hospitals, and drug companies (Lind 2012).

U.S. primary care physicians receive higher fees than their counterparts in other countries due to a shortage of primary care physicians in the United States. For example, public and private payers paid much higher fees to U.S. primary care physicians for office visits—27 percent more by public and 70 percent more by private payers. U.S. primary physicians also earned a higher average income—$186,582—than their counterparts (Laugesen and Glied 2011). Similarly, the average U.S. physician specialist earns 78 percent above the average in other countries (Cutler and Ly 2011). U.S. orthopedic physicians earn a much higher income than their counterparts in other countries (Laugesen and Glied 2011). For example, the average income (adjusted for differences in cost of living) for orthopedic physicians in the United States is around $442,450 compared to $324,138 in Great Britain, $208,634 in Canada, $202,771 in Germany, $187,609 in Australia, and $154,380 in France (Squires 2012). According to a report by the International Federation of Health Plans (2011), physicians' fees per routine office visit in the United States (in U.S. dollars) are $162 on average compared to $64 in Switzerland, $45 in Chile, $40 in Germany, $30 in Canada, and $23 in France. Similar differences are found in physicians' fees for a variety of medical procedures. For example, physicians' fees for a normal delivery in the United States is around $7,222 compared to $1,639 in Australia, $1,048 in Chile, $460 in Canada, $449 in France, $340 in Spain, and $226 in Germany. For more highly specialized medical services, the differences are even more striking. Physicians' fees for hip replacement in the United States are about $5,379 compared to $2,513 in Australia, $2,500 in Chile, $1,123 in Spain, $1,011 in France, $872 in Canada, and $644 in Germany.

The United States also has higher overall hospital spending because of higher health services cost, that is, they charge more for services. According to the Organization for Economic Cooperation and Development (OECD), the United States spends 60 percent more on hospitalization than other comparable countries (Lind 2012). The average price for hospital services (both medical and surgical) in the United States is about 85 percent higher than the average in other OECD countries. For example, a hospital stay in the United States costs over $18,000 on average, compared to the OECD average of $6,200 (Kane 2012). In 2009, hospital spending per discharge, adjusted for differences in cost of living, was $18,142 in the United States compared to $13,483 in Canada, $11,112 in Denmark, $8,350 in Australia, $5,204 in France, and $5,072 in Germany (Squires 2012). Average cost per hospital stay in the United States is about $15,734, compared to $5,004 in Germany, $3,396 in France, and $2,479 in Australia (International Federation of Health Plans 2011).

With respect to specific surgical procedures, hospital costs also vary considerably among countries. For example, hip and knee replacements are cheaper in OECD countries than in the United

States. The total hospital and physician average costs for a hip replacement (in U.S. dollars) are $38,017 in the United States compared to $25,604 in Australia, $17,521 in Switzerland, $16,945 in Canada, $11,418 in Germany, and $11,353 in France. The average total facility and physician costs (in U.S. dollars) for angioplasty in the United States is around $26,524 compared to $12,212 in Switzerland, $10,559 in Chile, $10,060 in Canada, $6,189 in Germany, and $5,857 in France (International Federation of Health Plans 2011).

Hospital costs are also much higher in the United States for a variety of scanning and imaging services. The average cost of an MRI scan in the United States is about $1,080 in the United States compared to $903 in Switzerland, $599 in Germany, $478 in Chile, $281 in France, and $245 in Spain (International Federation of Health Plans 2011).

Not only hospital costs are higher in the United States compared to other countries, the cost for the same medical procedures also varies widely within the United States. For example, according to the hospital Medicare data released by the Centers for Medicare and Medicaid Services, average inpatient charges for services that hospitals provide in connection with a joint replacement range from a low of $5,300 at a hospital in Ada, Oklahoma, to a high of $223,000 at a hospital in Monterey Park, California. Hospital charges for similar services vary significantly within the same geographic area. For example, Bayfront Medical Center in downtown St. Petersburg, Florida, charges $75,739 for a hip replacement, but a patient can pay 30 percent of that amount at St. Anthony's Hospital less than two miles away (Stein 2013). Similarly, Beth Israel Medical Center in New York charges $51,580 to treat a blood clot in a lung, while just down the street, New York University Hospital Center charges $29,869 for the same treatment (Cass and Neergaard 2013).

Finally, prescription drug prices are much higher in the United States compared to most other countries. The average price for Nexium in the United States is about $176 compared to $69 in Switzerland, $52 in Spain, $36 in Canada, and $23 in France. The average price for Plavix in the United States is about $160 compared to $109 in Germany, $74 in Canada, $61 in Switzerland, and $49 in France. The average price for Lipitor in the United States is about $95 compared to $74 in Germany, $44 in Canada, $37 in France, and $14 in Spain (International Federation of Health Plans 2011).

The above discussion clearly documents much higher physicians' fees and income, hospital prices, and prescription drug prices in the United States compared to many other countries. These are major factors for the higher level of healthcare spending in the United States. However, as we mentioned above, another factor could be that the United States provides more healthcare services—diagnostic services and medical procedures—and has more medical technology compared to other countries. How does the United States compare with other countries with respect to these factors?

The results here are mixed. While it is true that, overall, the United States does provide more health services than many other countries, it is not true with respect to all healthcare services. For example, in the United States hip and knee replacements are performed almost entirely for the elderly. The United States performs 184 such operations per 100,000 residents compared to 296 in Germany, 287 in Switzerland, 236 in Denmark, 232 in Norway, 224 in France, and 214 in Sweden. On the other hand, the United States leads the world in advanced diagnostic tests—91.2 per 1,000 compared to 55.2 in France and 43 in Canada (Lind 2012).

The United States' health system also does less than other countries in certain other areas—practicing physicians (2.4 per 1,000 in the United States compared to the OECD average of 3.1); hospital beds (3.1 per 1,000 population compared to the OECD average of 4.9); average length of hospital stay (4.9 days in the United States compared to the OECD average of 7.1 days); and doctor consultations (3.9 per capita in the United States compared to the OECD average of 6.4 per capita) (Kane 2012).

In other areas, the United States does more than OECD countries. The U.S. health system has more MRI units and CT scanners (31.6 and 40.7 per 1 million population respectively) compared to the OECD average of 12.5 MRI units and 22.6 CT scanners per 1 million population. The United States also performs more MRI exams (97.7 per 1,000 population) and CT exams (265 per 1,000 population) compared to the OECD average of 46.3 MRI exams and 123.8 CT exams per 1,000 population. Also, the U.S. health system performs 254.4 tonsillectomies, 79 coronary bypasses, and 32.9 caesarean sections per 100,000 population, compared to the OECD average of 130.1 tonsillectomies, 47.3 coronary bypasses, and 26.1 caesarean sections per 100,000 population (Kane 2012).

What factors explain higher prices and spending on healthcare in the United States compared to other countries? There are at least ten possible explanations for this. First, in the United States health services are overpriced and patients are charged more for similar services than in other countries. Second, other countries have a system for rationing care. For example, in countries such as Great Britain, Australia, and New Zealand, the government decides not to pay for certain services (Lind 2012). Third, the United States has been slow to embrace the advantages of information and communication technology in improving administration of its systems and cutting down waste (Freudenheim 2012). In the United States, about $900 per person per year goes toward administrative costs, compared to $300 per person per year in France (Kane 2012). Fourth, many OECD countries use strong regulations to set/control prices that hospitals can charge for different services. This is not the case in the United States.

Fifth, in America's private health sector, medical providers are allowed to charge different prices for the same goods or services to different customers or insurers in order to maintain predetermined incomes or sales revenues. Such a privilege is not enjoyed by physicians, hospitals, and drug companies in other countries (Lind 2012). Sixth, since most OECD countries have some form of universal health coverage, the government is able to negotiate drug prices. In the United States only the VHA and Defense Department do so. In fact, the Centers for Medicare and Medicaid Services is prohibited by congressional legislation from negotiating drug prices for Medicare and Medicaid patients. Seventh, the market for many medical goods and services in the United States is inherently monopolistic or oligopolistic (for example the drug industry) and thus "market competition" often does not work to reduce costs except in few areas (Lind 2012).

Eight, there is a fundamental lack of price transparency in the U.S. healthcare system that often acts as an impediment to understanding price and cost differences (Laugesen and Glied 2011). Ninth, in several OECD countries, medical professions and health policymakers have developed "clinical guidelines" to promote more rational use of MRI and CT exams. In the United States, medical procedures and use of expensive diagnostic tests are all largely based on individual physicians' opinions/judgments about desirable procedures and tests. Physicians in the United States are more likely to order more procedures and diagnostic tests to avoid blame and to protect themselves against potential medical malpractice lawsuits. Tenth, since in the United States physicians are paid for the services and procedures they provide regardless of medical necessity or medical outcome, it creates an incentive to provide more services and surgical procedures.

In summary, the old saying that you get what you pay for does not necessarily apply to the U.S. health system (McLaughlin 2011). As we have stated before, the United States spends more money on healthcare (total and per capita), performs more diagnostic tests and medical procedures, and charges more for health services than any other country in the world, yet it does not rank very high on several indicators of healthcare access, health status, and health outcomes.

Costs of Waste, Fraud, and Abuse in the U.S. Healthcare System

Another explanation proffered for the high costs and spending on healthcare in the United States is that there is a considerable amount of waste in the system and eliminating waste can help reduce healthcare spending. Waste is often defined as healthcare spending that can be eliminated without reducing the quality of care (Kelley 2009). Waste in the healthcare system can result from over-treatment, failure to coordinate care, failure to execute care processes, administrative complexity/inefficiency, pricing failure, and fraud and abuse (Berwick and Hackbarth 2012). Others have categorized waste into administrative, operational, and clinical waste (Bentley et al. 2008).

In addition, misuse, overuse, and underuse of medical services can directly or indirectly add to healthcare costs. Misuse refers to the inappropriate use of services, while overuse refers to providing services that, while appropriate, may not provide much value for a specific patient. Underuse of services can result when a failure to diagnose an illness early and provide preventive and maintenance services can lead to a medical condition becoming more severe/complex, resulting in higher spending to treat the condition. Fraud and abuse are situations in which reimbursement claims are made by providers to third-party payers for services that are not provided and include providers receiving kickbacks, patients seeking treatment that are potentially harmful to them, and physicians prescribing services that are known to be unnecessary (Kelley 2009).

Federal regulators have aggressively prosecuted healthcare fraud since the early 1990s (Kesselheim and Studdert 2008). Patterns of fraud and abuse are strongly connected to the fee-for-service nature of most third-party payment programs. Under such a system, healthcare providers are compensated for each service or product they supply. This gives fiscal incentives to providers to bill for as much as possible. Examples of fraud and abuse that have resulted from such a system include a physician billing Medicaid for services that actually were sexual liaisons, another doctor billing for abortion services on a woman who was not pregnant, and a doctor who charged the program $3,000 for an office visit while he was on an African safari (Jesilow, Geis, and Harris 1995).

In the public sector, both Medicare and Medicaid are highly susceptible to waste, fraud, and abuse since they are governed by a very complex and interlocking array of state, federal, civil, criminal, and administrative antifraud laws, administered by multiple investigative and enforcement agencies (Hyman 2001). Medicare providers are reimbursed per units of service provided, and because the "medical necessity" concept triggers Medicare coverage, providers have an incentive to not only increase service volume but also to increase service intensity. Since Medicare payment is proportional to the complexity of the service, providers also have an incentive to give more complex and thus more remunerative services (Rai 2001). According to Etzioni (2012), bilking Medicare is much easier and the risk of getting caught and punished is much smaller than selling controlled substances.

In 1997, Medicare alone lost $20 billion to waste, fraud, and abuse, translating to a loss of 11 cents of every dollar spent on Medicare (Cruise 2002). Audits of the Medicare program have estimated that improper payment rates amount to 7–14 percent of total Medicare fee-for-service payments (Hyman 2001). In 2008, government-wide "improper payments" cost the federal government $72 billion (Iglehart 2009). In 2009, "improper payments" to service providers in Medicare and Medicaid by the U.S. government combined reached $98 billion (Iglehart 2010). These numbers have continued to climb. A very recent study suggests that spending in both Medicare and Medicaid programs, including state and federal costs, contributed to almost one-third of the total wasteful healthcare spending in the country, amounting to about somewhere between $166 billion and $304 billion (Lallemand 2012).

The federal government's war on healthcare fraud began in 1993 when then attorney general Janet Reno made pursuing healthcare-fraud perpetrators a top priority through aggressive use of the False Claims Act. The law made filing whistleblower suits much easier (Cruise 2002). In 1995, the Clinton administration launched a new initiative called Operation Restore Trust (Cruise 2002; Hyman 2001). The antifraud efforts were enhanced by the Health Insurance Portability and Accountability Act (HIPAA) of 1996, which created a national Health Care Fraud and Abuse Control Program and provided dedicated funding to pursue healthcare fraud.

Three specific fraud control provisions added were anti-kickback, self-referrals, and civil false claims. The anti-kickback provision criminalizes the solicitation or receipt of remuneration in connection with items or services for which payment could be made under Medicare or Medicaid. Self-referral provisions prohibit physicians from referring Medicare and Medicaid patients to ancillary providers in which they or their families hold financial interests and also prohibit service providers from billing for services performed as a result of such referrals. The civil false claims provision creates a cause of action against individuals or entities who knowingly present a false claim to the government (Rabecs 2006; Hyman 2001).

Under the Health Care Fraud and Abuse Control program, the federal government won or negotiated $605 million in judgments and settlements in 2004 related to Medicare and Medicaid (Rabecs 2006). Funds recovered through healthcare fraud enforcement are distributed to the Medicare Trust Fund, to other federal agencies that investigate and prosecute healthcare fraud, as well as to private parties who initiate suits on the government's behalf under the False Claims Act. However, patients who may have been harmed by such conduct do not receive any benefits (Krause 2006).

Despite some success, many obstacles hinder the successful investigation, prosecution, and sanctioning of healthcare providers who engage in fraudulent activities. One of the major obstacles is the hidden nature of the offenses. The old practice of insurance payers mailing to patients copies of bills that healthcare providers submit to third-party payers has been largely abandoned. Thus, the patients rarely know what healthcare providers submit for healthcare services for reimbursement. Second, when medical procedures are carried out on a patient while he/she is unconscious or heavily medicated, the patient is not in a position to determine whether services were actually performed. Third, few patients examine the bills, let alone understand them. Fourth, it is often difficult, even when a fraud is discovered, to obtain the cooperation of prosecutors, given their heavy caseload. Finally, the very nature of medicine effectively limits the possibility of catching a criminally errant practitioner because it is left up to each individual physician to diagnose illness and prescribe remedies, making it difficult to question a physician's diagnosis or treatment decisions (Jesilow et al. 1995). Thus, despite the best efforts, healthcare fraud has continued to grow. As healthcare expenditures have risen over time, so has the amount of fraud and abuse (Iglehart 2010).

Thus far our discussion has focused only on the fraud and abuse in the U.S. healthcare system. The estimate of the cost of total waste in the U.S. healthcare system and how much it contributes to total healthcare spending is considerably higher. A white paper by Robert Kelley (2009), vice president of Healthcare Analytics, estimates the total waste in the healthcare system to be around $700 billion annually, with $600 billion as a lower range and $800 billion as the higher. The author breaks down this total amount of waste by different categories/types of waste: administrative system inefficiencies—$100 billion to $150 billion; provider inefficiency and errors—$75 billion to $100 billion; lack of care coordination—$25 billion to $50 billion; unwarranted use of diagnostic and treatment services—$250 billion to $325 billion; preventable conditions and avoidable care—$25 billion to $50 billion; fraud and abuse—$125 billion to $175 billion. A more recent study by the Robert Wood Johnson Foundation (2012) placed the range of total waste in the U.S. healthcare system between $558 billion and $1,263 trillion annually. This study breaks down the categories of waste amount as following: failure of care delivery—$102 billion to $154 billion; failure of care coordination—$25 billion to $45 billion; overtreatment—$158 billion to $226 billion; administrative complexity—$107 billion to $389 billion; pricing failure—$84 billion to $178 billion; fraud and abuse—$82 billion to $272 billion. If we were to take the average of the low and high amounts of the total waste estimate in both studies, waste in the U.S. healthcare system contributes to about one-third of the total spending on healthcare.

Lifestyle Choices and Costs/Expenditures

Some observers attribute skyrocketing employee healthcare costs to poor health caused by unhealthy lifestyle choices and argue that almost 87.5 percent of healthcare claims are due to an individual's lifestyle, and thus, these costs are potentially preventable ("Primary Reason Why Health Care Costs Continue to Rise" 2012). By developing healthy habits, Americans can avoid largely preventable diseases such as diabetes, high blood pressure, and heart disease, and billions of dollars can be saved (Mendoza 2009).

According to this view, unhealthy lifestyle choices and behavior by Americans contribute to overall healthcare spending as well as increases in healthcare spending. The argument here is that while some illnesses are unavoidable, other illnesses are caused by unhealthy choices and behaviors and can be prevented by following a healthy lifestyle. Thus, illnesses/diseases caused by unhealthy choices and lifestyle unnecessarily add to spending on health. Circulatory diseases, diabetes, and certain cancers are linked to unhealthy eating, obesity, smoking, drinking, physical inactivity, and psychological stress. For example, the epidemic of obesity, particularly among young people, is related to diabetes and circulatory diseases. Similarly, the consequences of tobacco smoking include chronic obstructive pulmonary disease; coronary, cerebral, and peripheral pulmonary disease; and a variety of cancers. Lack of physical activity/exercise is related to obesity, risk of coronary heart disease, risk of stroke, and hypertension (Phillip 2002).

As mentioned earlier in this chapter, diseases of the heart, cancer, and diabetes are three of the leading causes of death in the United States. Obesity is closely related to diabetes. Obesity levels in the United States have increased significantly over many years and represent a substantial health burden. Obesity leads to 36 percent more total healthcare consumption and 77 percent more pharmaceutical consumption. It is estimated that 9.1 percent of total U.S. medical expenditures are due to obesity and/or being overweight (Comanor, Freech, and Miller 2006). Obesity is also associated with a 36 percent increase in inpatient and outpatient spending and a 7.7 percent increase in medication (Sturm 2002). It is estimated that the increased prevalence of obesity was responsible for almost $40 billion of increased medical spending through 2006, including $7 billion in Medicare prescription drug costs (Kelley 2009). The good news is that after the number of obese children more than tripled since the 1980s, the epidemic of obesity among children may have begun to decline. Childhood obesity rates have been dropping in several U.S. cities (Harmon 2012). Also, according to new data from the Centers for Disease Control and Prevention, the number of low-income preschoolers who qualify as obese or extremely obese has dropped over the last decade (Pittman 2012).

The impact of cigarette smoking on morbidity and mortality is well established. The socioeconomic status or material position, and lifestyle choices such as cigarette smoking, have an independent influence on health in the United States. Smoking inflicts greater harm among disadvantaged groups (Pampel and Rogers 2004). According to one analysis, smoking costs the country $150 billion each year in health costs and lost productivity (Kelley 2009). The good news here is that U.S. smoking rates are lower than those found in most other countries (Comanor, Freech, and Miller 2006).

Overall, while the United States is the wealthiest nation in the world, it is not the healthiest. According to a recent study by the Institute of Medicine (2013), although Americans' life expectancy and health have improved, those gains have lagged behind those in other high-income countries. According to the study, the reasons why Americans are unhealthy compared to other affluent countries include a large number of uninsured people, unhealthy behavior and lifestyle choices, a higher level of poverty, and a built-in physical environment that discourages physical activity.

Both the public and private sector can help reduce their healthcare spending by addressing problems related to unhealthy lifestyle choices of their employees by offering more health and wellness promotion programs (Heinen and Darling 2009). However, it is important to keep in mind that because of the complex pattern of interaction between lifestyle choices, environment, and genetics, it is difficult to separate out the individual contribution of each of these factors to some of the leading causes of morbidity and mortality in the United States. Thus, health and wellness promotion programs may help but not completely solve these problems.

CONCLUSION

Rising healthcare costs and correspondingly rising healthcare spending are two of the biggest problems confronting the American healthcare system. The United States spends more money on healthcare (overall, per capita, share of the GDP), prescription drugs, and biomedical technology than any other country in the world. Yet, the United States does not rank high on many of the healthcare indicators, and healthcare products and services cost more compared to other OECD countries. Over the years, national healthcare spending, medical inflation, and increases in prescription drugs have outpaced general inflation by a margin of 2–1 to 3–1. One hopeful sign is that the annual rate of increase on healthcare spending seems to have slowed considerably in the last three years. Whether this slow growth rate in healthcare spending is simply a temporary bleep on the radar screen or a long-term trend remains to be seen.

Government—that is, public sector—healthcare spending has continued to climb upward. Spending for the public sector healthcare programs for the elderly (Medicare), poor and disabled (Medicaid), children (CHIP), veterans' care, and American Indians and Alaska Natives, designed to serve as a social safety net, continues to rise but still leaves close to 50 million Americans without a health insurance. These programs combined accounted for about 38 percent of the national healthcare spending in 2010. Two of the largest programs—Medicare and Medicaid—alone accounted for 35.7 percent of national healthcare spending in 2010. In 1970, these programs accounted for only about 17.4 percent of national healthcare spending. Spending for both programs is growing at an unsustainable rate. The Affordable Care Act (ACA) of 2010 is designed to address both the problems of the uninsured and rising healthcare cost. It remains to be seen how successful the ACA is in addressing these problems, since many of the major provisions of the law do not go into effect until 2014.

The major culprits in the rising healthcare costs and rising healthcare spending in the United States appear to be frequent and intensive use of biomedical technology, high costs and high consumption rates of prescription drugs, waste including fraud and abuse, unhealthy lifestyle choices and behavior patterns, fear of medical malpractice lawsuits, and the practice of defensive medicine along with changing demographics. Of these, biomedical technology, prescription drug costs, and waste are the biggest contributors to increased spending. Others individually do not contribute a great deal to the overall healthcare spending, but combined they do make some difference. If the United States is serious about addressing the problem of rising healthcare costs and spending, cost containment efforts need to be focused on these factors. In the next chapter we discuss efforts made by both the public and the private sectors in the United States to contain rising health costs and spending through a mix of public policies and strategies involving varied approaches.

STUDY QUESTIONS

1. Discuss the problem of rising healthcare costs and expenditures in the United States. How have sources of healthcare expenditures changed over the years? In what specific areas do we find a high concentration of healthcare expenditures?
2. Discuss the concentration of healthcare expenditures by population characteristics, medical conditions, chronic health conditions, and major causes of deaths in the United States.
3. How do U.S. national healthcare expenditures compare to expenditures in other countries, especially member countries of the Organization for Economic Cooperation and Development (OECD)?
4. What do public opinion polls show about Americans' views and attitudes about healthcare expenditures and costs in the United States?

5. Discuss the major factors that have contributed to high and rising healthcare expenditures and costs in the United States.
6. What role has medical technology played in rising healthcare expenditures in the United States? Explain different types of medical technologies and which have contributed to rising costs and expenditures.
7. What factors have contributed to growth of medical technologies in the United States?
8. Discuss the history and current state of medical technology assessment in the United States. What are some of the problems with medical technology assessment in the United States?
9. What factors explain the [a] increased use of prescription drugs and [b] increased spending on prescription drugs in the United States?
10. How does the regulation of the pharmaceutical industry in the European countries differ from that in the United States?
11. How do medical errors, the practice of defensive medicine, and medical liability insurance contribute to rising healthcare costs?
12. Compare and contrast costs of healthcare services in the United States and OECD countries.
13. Discuss how waste, fraud, and abuse contribute to excessive healthcare expenditures and costs in the United States.
14. Discuss the role of lifestyle choices in contributing to healthcare expenditures and costs.

REFERENCES

Aaron, Henry J. 1991. *Serious and Unstable Condition: Financing America's Health Care.* Washington, DC: Brookings Institution.

Abramson, John. 2004. *Overdosed America: The Broken Promise of American Medicine.* New York: HarperCollins.

Ameringer, Carl F. 2012. "Chronic Diseases and the High Price of U.S. Healthcare." *Phi Kappa Phi Forum* 92, no. 1 (Spring): 4–6.

Angell, Marcia. 2004. *The Truth About the Drug Companies: How They Deceive Us and What to Do About It.* New York: Random House.

Applbaum, Kalman. 2009. "Is Marketing the Enemy of Pharmaceutical Innovation?" *Hastings Center Report* 39, no. 4 (August): 13–17.

Appleby, Julie. 2008. "As Drug Ads Surge, More Get Rx's Filled." *USA Today,* March 4. Online at http://usatoday30.usatoday.com/news/health/2008–02–29-drugs-main_N.htm.

Auerbach, David I., and Arthur L. Kellermann. 2011. "A Decade of Health Care Cost Growth Wiped Out Real Income Gain for an Average U.S. Family." *Health Affairs* 30, no. 9 (September): 1630–36.

Avron, Jerry. 2004. *Powerful Medicine: The Benefits, Risks, and Costs of Prescription Drugs.* New York: Alfred A. Knopf.

Baicker, Katherine, and Dana Goldman. 2011. "Patient Cost-Sharing and Healthcare Spending Growth." *Journal of Economic Perspectives* 25, no. 2 (Spring): 47–68.

Baker, Laurence; Howard Birnbaum; Jeffrey Geppert; David Mishol; and Erick Moyneur. 2003. "The Relationship Between Technology Availability and Health Care Spending." *Health Affairs,* Web Exclusive (November 5): W3-537–W3-551.

Banja, John D. 2005. *Medical Errors and Medical Narcissism.* Sudbury, MA: Jones and Bartlett.

Banthin, Jessica S., and Edward Miller. 2006. "Trends in Prescription Drug Expenditures by Medicaid Enrollees." *Medical Care* 44, no. 5 Supplement (May): 127–35.

Belluck, Pam. 2012. "With Telemedicine as Bridge, No Hospital Is an Island." *New York Times,* October 8. Online at www.nytimes.com/2012/10/09/health/nantucket-hospital-uses-telemedicine-as-bridge-to-mainland.html?.

Bentley, Tanya G.K.; Rachel M. Effros; Kartika Palar; and Emmett B. Keeler. 2008. "Waste in the U.S. Health Care System: A Conceptual Framework." *Milbank Quarterly* 86, no. 4 (December): 629–59.

Berk, Marc L., and Alan C. Monheit. 2001. "The Concentration of Health Care Expenditures, Revisited." *Health Affairs* 20, no. 2 (March/April): 9–18.

Berkrot, Bill. 2012. "U.S. Price Hikes on Branded Drugs Far Outpace 2012 Inflation." Online at www.reuters. com/article/2012/11/28/us-expressscripts-drugs-idUSBRE8AR04V20121128.

Berndt, Ernst R. 2002. "Pharmaceuticals in U.S. Health Care: Determinants of Quality and Price." *Journal of Economic Perspectives* 16, no. 4 (Autumn): 45–66.

Berwick, Donald M., and Andrew D. Hackbarth. 2012. "Eliminating Waste in U.S. Health Care." *Journal of the American Medical Association* 307, no. 14 (April): 1513–16.

Bishop, Tara F.; Alex D. Federman; and Salomeh Keyhani. 2010. "Physicians' Views on Defensive Medicine: A National Survey." *Archives of Internal Medicine* 170, no. 12 (June): 1081–83.

Blendon, Robert J; Kimberly Scoles; Catherine DesRoches; John T. Young; Melissa J. Herrmann; Jennifer L. Schmidt; and Minah Kim. 2001. "Americans' Health Priorities: Curing Cancer and Controlling Costs." *Health Affairs* 20, no. 6: 222–32.

Blendon, Robert J.; Mollyann Brodie; John M. Benson; Drew E. Altman; and Tami Buhr. 2006. "Americans' View of Health Care Costs, Access, and Quality." *Milbank Quarterly* 84, no. 4: 623–57.

Bozic, Kevin J.; Read G. Pierce; and James H. Herndon. 2004. "Health Care Technology Assessment." *Journal of Bone and Joint Surgery* 86, no. 6 (June): 1305–14.

Brennan, Troyen A., and Philip K. Howard. 2004. "Heal the Law, Then Health Care." *Washington Post,* January 25.

Brody, Jane E. 2011. "Tackling Care as Chronic Ailments Pile Up." *New York Times,* February 21. Online at www.nytimes.com/2011/02/22/health/22brody.html?_r=0.

———. 2012. "E-Health Opportunities for Seniors." *New York Times.* October 8. Online at http://well.blogs. nytimes.com/2012/10/08/e-health-opportunities-for-seniors/.

Brownlee, Shannon. 2007. *Overtreated: Why Too Much Medicine Is Making Us Sicker and Poorer.* New York: Bloomsbury.

Calfee, John E. 2002. "Public Policy Issues in Direct-to-Consumer Advertising of Prescription Drugs." *Journal of Public Policy & Marketing* 21, no. 2 (Fall).

Carrier, Emily R.; James D. Reschovsky; Michelle M. Mello; Ralph C. Mayrell; and David Katz. 2010. "Physicians' Fear of Malpractice Lawsuits Are Not Assuaged by Tort Reform." *Health Affairs* 29, no. 9: 1585–92.

Cass, Connie, and Lauran Neergaard. 2013. "High Hospital Bills Go Public, but Will It Help?" Associated Press, May 8. Online at http://news.yahoo.com/high-hospital-bills-public-help-211625086.html.

Charney, William. 2012. *Epidemic of Medical Errors and Hospital-Acquired Infections: System and Social Causes.* Boca Raton, FL: Taylor & Francis.

Classen, David C.; Roger Resar; Frances Griffin; Frank Federico; Terri Frankel; Nancy Kimmel; John C. Whittington; Allan Frankel; Andrew Seger; and Brent C. James. 2011. "'Global Trigger Tool' Shows that Adverse Events in Hospitals May Be Ten Times Greater than Previously Measured." *Health Affairs* 30, no. 4: 581–89.

Comanor, William S.; H.E. Freech III; and Richard D. Miller. 2006. "Is the United States an Outlier in Healthcare and Health Outcomes? A Preliminary Analysis." *International Journal of Health Care Finance and Economics* 6, no. 1 (March): 3–23.

Congressional Budget Office. 2010. *Effects of Using Generic Drugs on Medicare's Prescription Drug Spending.* Washington, DC: Congressional Budget Office. Online at www.cbo.gov/publication/21800.

Congressional Research Service. 2007. *U.S. Health Care Spending: Comparison with Other OECD Countries.* CRS Report for Congress. Washington, DC: Congressional Research Service.

Conway, Patrick; Kate Goodrich; Steven Machlin; Benjamin Sasse; and Joel Cohen. 2011. "Patient-Centered Care Categorization of U.S. Health Care Expenditures." *Health Research Services* 46, no. 2 (April): 479–90.

Cruise, Peter L. 2002. "Are There Virtues in Whistleblowing? Perspectives from Health Care Organizations." *Public Administration Quarterly* 25, no. 4 (Winter): 413–35.

Cutler, David M., and Dan P. Ly. 2011. "The (Paper) Work of Medicine: Understanding International Medical Costs." *Journal of Economic Perspectives* 25, no. 2 (Spring): 3–25.

Cutler, David M., and Mark McClellan. 2001. "Is Technological Change in Medicine Worth It?" *Health Affairs* 20, no. 5 (September–October): 11–29.

Danzon, Patricia M., and Mark V. Pauly. 2002. "Health Insurance and the Growth in Pharmaceutical Expenditures." *Journal of Law and Economics* 45, no. 52 (October): 587–613.

Davidson, Stephen M. 2010. *Still Broken: Understanding the U.S. Health Care System.* Stanford, CA: Stanford Business Books.

Davis, Karen, and Cathy Schoen. 1978. *Health and the War on Poverty: A Ten-Year Proposal.* Washington, DC: Brookings Institution.

"Development and Approval Process: Drugs." n.d. Washington, DC: Food and Drug Administration. Online at http://www.fda.gov/Drugs/DevelopmentApprovalProcess/default.htm.

"Doctors and Other Health Professionals Report that Fear of Malpractice Has a Big, and Mostly Negative, Impact on Medical Practice, Unnecessary Defensive Medicine, and Openness in Discussing Medical Errors." 2003. *Health Care News* 3, no. 2 (February 7): 1–5. Online at www.kff.org/kaiserpolls.

Donohue, Julie. 2006. "A History of Drug Advertising: The Evolving Roles of Consumers and Consumer Protection." *Milbank Quarterly* 84, no. 4: 659–99.

Doolan, David F., and David W. Bates. 2002. "Computerized Physician Order Entry System in Hospitals: Mandates and Incentives." *Health Affairs* 21, no. 4 (July–August): 180–88.

Dove, James T.; John E. Brush; Richard A. Chazal; and William J. Oetgen. 2010. "Medical Professional Liability and Health Care System Reform." *Journal of the American College of Cardiology* 55, no. 25 (June): 2801–3.

Duggan, Mark; Patrick Healy; and Fiona S. Morton. 2008. "Providing Prescription Drug Coverage to the Elderly: America's Experiment with Medicare Part D." *Journal of Economic Perspectives* 22, no. 4 (Fall): 69–92.

Eastburn, Larry. 1999. "Medical Malpractice Update." *Modern Medicine* 67, no. 7 (July): 58–62.

Eichler, Alexander. 2012. "Pharmaceutical Companies Spent 19 Times more on Self-Promotion than Basic Research: Report." *Huffington Post*, August 8. Online at www.huffingtonpost.com/2012/08/09/pharmaceutical-companies-marketing_n_1760380.html.

Ernst & Young. 2012. *Beyond Borders: Global Biotechnology Report 2011*. Washington, DC: Ernst & Young.

Ess, Silvia M.; Sebastian Schneeweiss; and Thomas D. Szucs. 2003. "European Healthcare Policies for Controlling Drug Expenditures." *Pharmacoeconomics* 21, no. 2: 89–103.

Etzioni, Amitai. 2012. "Cut Medicare? Cut Fraud." *Huffington Post*, December 12. Online at www.huffingtonpost.com/amitai-etzioni/cut-medicare-cut-fraud_b_2270848.html.

Evans, David. 2010. "When Drug Makers' Profits Outweigh Penalties." *Washington Post*, March 21. Online at www.washingtonpost.com/wp-dyn/content/article/2010/03/19/AR2010031905578.html.

Farber, Henry S., and Michelle J. White. 1991. "Medical Malpractice: An Empirical Examination of the Litigation Process." *RAND Journal of Economics* 22, no. 2 (Summer): 199–217.

Fielding, Stephen L. 1995. "Changing Medical Practice and Medical Malpractice Claims." *Social Problems* 42, no. 1 (February 1): 38–55.

Fineberg, H.V. 1977. "Computerized Tomography: Dilemma of Health Care Technology." *Pediatrics* 59, no. 2 (February): 147–49.

Fox, Maggie. 2010. "Malpractice Liability Costs U.S. $55.6 Billion: Study." *Romanian Journal of Medical Practice* 5, no. 3: 191.

Freudenheim, Milt. 2012. *"The Ups and Downs of Electronic Medical Records." New York Times*, October 8. Online at www.nytimes.com/2012/10/09/health/the-ups-and-downs-of-electronic-medical-records-the-digital-doctor.html?.

Fuchs, Victor R. 1986. *The Health Economy*. Cambridge, MA: Harvard University Press.

———. 1993. *The Future of Health Care Policy*. Cambridge, MA: Harvard University Press.

———. 2005. "Health Care Expenditures Reexamined." *Annals of Internal Medicine* 143, no. 1 (July): 76–78.

Gaylin, Daniel S.; Adil Maiduddin; Shamis Mohamoud; Katie Lundeen; and Jennifer A. Kelly. 2011. "Public Attitude About Health Information Technology and Its Relationship to Health Care Quality, Costs, and Privacy." *Health Services Research* 46, no. 3 (June): 920–38.

Gelijns, Annetine C., and Nathan Rosenberg. 1994. "The Dynamics of Technological Change in Medicine." *Health Affairs* 13, no. 3 (Summer): 28–46.

Gelijns, Annetine C; Lawrence D. Brown; Corey Magnell; Elettra Ronchi; and Alan J. Moskowitz. 2005. "Evidence, Politics, and Technological Change." *Health Affairs* 24, no. 1 (January–February): 29–40.

Generic Pharmaceutical Association. 2012. *Savings $1 Trillion Over 10 Years: Generic Drug Savings in the U.S.* Washington, DC: Generic Pharmaceutical Association. Online at www.fdalawyersblog.com/GPhA%202012%20Generic%20Drug%20Savings%20Study.pdf.

Gibson, Rosemary, and Janardan Prasad Singh. 2003. *Wall of Silence: The Untold Story of the Medical Mistakes that Kill and Injure Millions of Americans*. Washington, DC: LifeLine Press.

Golann, Dwight. 2011. "Dropped Medical Malpractice Claims: Their Surprising Frequency, Apparent Causes, and Potential Remedies." *Health Affairs* 30, no. 7: 1343–50.

Goldhill, David. 2013. *Catastrophic Care: How American Health Killed My Father—And How to Fix It.* New York: Alfred A. Knopf.

Goldsmith, Jeff. 2004. "Technology and the Boundaries of the Hospital: Three Emerging Technologies." *Health Affairs* 23, no. 6: 149–56.

Goodman, John S.; Pamela Villarreal; and Biff Jones. 2011. "The Social Cost of Adverse Medical Events, and What We Can Do About It?" *Health Affairs* 30, no. 4: 590–95.

Goozner, Merrill. 2004. *The $800 Million Pill: The Truth Behind the Cost of New Drugs.* Berkeley: University of California Press.

Goyen, Mathias, and Jorg F. Debatin. 2009. "Healthcare Costs for New Technologies." *European Journal of Nuclear Medicine & Molecular Imaging* 36, Supplement no. 1 (March): 139–43.

Greene, Risa B. 1996. "Federal Legislative Proposals for Medical Malpractice Reform: Treating the Symptom or Effecting a Cure?" *Cornell Journal of Law and Public Policy* 4, no. 2: 563–607.

Greer, Donley, and Marion Danis. 2011. "Making the Case for Talking to Patients About the Costs of End-of-Life Care." *Journal of Law, Medicine, and Ethics* 39, no. 2 (Summer): 183–93.

Greider, Katharine. 2003. *The Big Fix: How the Pharmaceutical Industry Rips Off American Consumers.* New York: Public Affairs.

Gupta, Sanjay. 2012. "Let's End the Prescription Drug Death Epidemic." *CNN,* November 15. Online at www.cnn.com/2012/11/14/health/gupta-accidental-overdose/index.html.

Hafner, Katie. 2012. "Redefining Medicine with Apps and iPads." *New York Times,* October 8. Online at www.nytimes.com/2012/10/09/science/redefining-medicine-with-apps-and-ipads-the-digital-doctor.html?.

Harmon, Katherine. 2012. "Early Childhood Obesity Rates Might Be Slowing Nation-Wide." *Scientific American,* December 25. Online at http://blogs.scientificamerican.com/observations/2012/12/25/early-childhood-obesity-rates-might-be-slowing-nation-wide/.

Harris, Gardiner. 2004a. "F.D.A. Failing in Drug Safety, Official Asserts." *New York Times,* November 19.

———. 2004b. "At F.D.A., Strong Drug Ties and Less Monitoring." *New York Times,* December 6.

———. 2005. "F.D.A. to Create Advisory Board on Drug Safety." *New York Times,* February 16.

Harris, Gardiner, and Alex Berenson. 2005. "10 Voters on Panel Backing Pain Pills Had Industry Ties." *New York Times,* February 25.

"Health Plans Strain to Contain Rapidly Rising Cost of Imaging." 2005. *Managed Care Magazine Online.* Online at www.managedcaremag.com/archives/0501/0501.imaging.html.

Heinen, Luann, and Helen Darling. 2009. "Addressing Obesity in the Workplace: The Role of Employers." *Milbank Quarterly* 87, no. 1 (March): 101–22.

Hermer, Laura D., and Howard Brody. 2010. "Defensive Medicine, Cost Containment, and Reform." *Journal of General Internal Medicine* 25, no. 5 (May): 470–73.

Hettrich, Carolyn M.; Richard C. Mather III; Manish K. Sethi; Ryan M. Nunley; and Amir A. Jahangir. 2010. "The Cost of Defensive Medicine." *American Academy of Orthopedic Surgeons Now* 4, no. 12 (December): 29.

Hoadley, Jack. 2012. *Adapting Tools from Other Nations to Slow U.S. Prescription Drug Spending.* Washington, DC: Center for Studying Health System Change, National Institute for Health Care Reform. Online at www.nihcr.org/Drug_Spending.

Hobson, Katherine. 2009. "Critics Take Aim at High-Tech Care." *U.S. News & World Report* 146, no. 7 (August): 76–78.

"Hospital Charges Still Rising Despite More Outpatient Care." 2007. *Medical Device Daily* 11, no. 230 (December 19): 3.

Howard, Philip K. 2002. *The Collapse of the Common Good: How America's Lawsuit Culture Undermines Our Freedom.* New York: Ballantine Books.

———. 2003. "Legal Malpractice." *Wall Street Journal,* January 27.

"How Changes in Medical Technology Affect Health Care Costs." 2007. Washington, DC: Kaiser Family Foundation. Online at www.kff.org/insurance/snapshot/chcm030807oth.cfm.

Hyman, David A. 2001. "Health Care Fraud and Abuse: Market Change, Social Norms, and the 'Trust Reposed in the Workmen.'" *Journal of Legal Studies* 30, no. S2 (June): 531–67.

Hyman, David A., and Charles Silver. 2004. "Believing Six Impossible Things: Medical Malpractice and Legal Fear." *Harvard Journal of Law and Public Policy* 28, no. 1 (Fall): 107–18.

Iglehart, John K. 2009. "Finding Money for Health Care Reform—Rooting Out Waste, Fraud, and Abuse." *New England Journal of Medicine* 363, no. 3 (July): 229–31.

———. 2010. "The Supercharged Federal Effort to Crack Down on Fraud and Abuse." *Health Affairs* 29, 6: 1093–95.

IMS Institute for Healthcare Informatics. 2013. *Declining Medicine Use and Costs: For Better or Worse?* Parsippany, NJ: IMS Institute for Healthcare Informatics. Online at www.imshealth.com/deployedfiles/ims/Global/Content/Insights/IMS%20Institute%20for%20Healthcare%20Informatics/2012%20U.S.%20Medicines%20Report/2012_U.S.Medicines_Report.pdf.

Institute of Medicine. 2000. *To Err Is Human: Building a Safer Health System.* Washington, DC: National Academy Press.

————. 2012. Institute of Medicine. *Relieving Pain in America: A Blue print for Transforming Prevention, Care, Education, and Research.* Washington, DC: The National Academies Press.

————. 2013. *U.S. Health in International Perspective: Shorter Lives, Poorer Health.* Washington, DC: National Academies Press.

International Federation of Health Plans. 2011. *Comparative Price Report: Medical and Hospital Fees by Country.* London: International Federation of Health Plans.

Jaros, G.G., and D.A. Boonzaier. 1993. "Cost Escalation in Health-Care Technology—Possible Solutions." *South African Medical Journal* 83, no. 6 (June 1): 420–22.

Jesilow, Paul; Gilbert Geis; and John C. Harris. 1995. "Doomed to Repeat Our Errors: Fraud in Emerging Health-Care System." *Social Justice* 22, no. 2 (Summer): 1995: 125–38.

Jonsson, B. 2001. ""Flat or Monotonic Pricing of Pharmaceuticals: Practice and Consequences." *European Journal of Health Economics* 2, no. 3: 104–12.

Kaiser Family Foundation. 2004. "Prescription Drug Trends." Fact sheet #3057–03. Washington, DC: Henry J. Kaiser Family Foundation. Online at www.kff.org/rxdrugs/upload/Prescription-Drug-Trends-October-2004-UPDATE.pdf.

————. n.d. "Trends and Indicators in the Changing Health Care Marketplace." Menlo Park, CA: Kaiser Family Foundation. Online at www.kff.org/insurance/7031/index.cfm.

Kalb, Paul E. 1990. "Controlling Health Care Costs by Controlling Technology: A Private Contractual Approach." *Yale Law Journal* 99, no. 4 (March): 1109–26.

Kalra, Jay. 2011. *Medical Errors and Patient Safety: Strategies to Reduce and Disclose Medical Errors and Improve Patient Safety.* Berlin: De Gruyter.

Kane, Jason. 2012. "Health Costs: How the U.S. Compares with Other Countries." Arlington, VA: Public Broadcasting Corporation. Online at www.pbs.org/newshour/rundown/2012/10/health-costs-how-the-us-compares-with-other-countries.html.

Kassirer, Jerome P. 2005. *On the Take: How America's Complicity with Big Business Can Endanger Your Health.* New York: Oxford University Press.

Kawachi, Ichiro. 2005. "Why the United States Is Not Number One in Health." In *Healthy, Wealthy, & Fair,* ed. James A. Morone and Lawrence R. Jacobs, 19–35. New York: Oxford University Press.

Keehan, Sean P.; Gigi A. Cuckler; Andrea M. Sisko; Andrew M. Madison; Sheila D. Smith; Joseph M. Lizonitz; John A. Poisal; and Christian J. Wolfe. 2012. "National Health Expenditure Projections: Modest Annual Growth Until Coverage Expands and Economic Growth Accelerates." *Health Affairs* 31, no. 7 (July): 1600–12.

Kelley, Robert. 2009. *Where Can $700 Billion in Waste Be Cut Annually from the U.S. Healthcare System?* New York: Thomson Reuters. Online at www.ncrponline.org/PDFs/2009/Thomson_Reuters_White_Paper_on_Healthcare_Waste.pdf.

Kesselheim, Aaron S., and David M. Studdert. 2008. "Whistleblower-Initiated Enforcement Actions." *Annals of Internal Medicine* 149, no. 5 (September): 342–50.

Kitsis, Elizabeth A. 2009. "Rx for the Pharmaceutical Industry: Call Your Doctors." *Hastings Center Report* 39, no. 4 (August): 18–21.

Krause, John H. 2006. "A Patient-Centered Approach to Health Care Fraud Recovery." *Journal of Criminal Law and Criminology* 96, no. 2 (Winter): 579–619.

Kumar, Krishna R. 2011. "Technology and Healthcare Costs." *Annals of Pediatric Cardiology* 4, no. 1 (January–June): 84–86.

Lallemand, Nicole C. 2012. "Reducing Waste in Health Care." Health Policy Brief, Washington, DC: Robert Wood Johnson Foundation. Online at www.healthaffairs.org/healthpolicybriefs/brief.php?brief_id=82.

Latham, Bryan W. 1983. *Health Care Costs: There Are Solutions.* New York: American Management Association.

Latham, Stephen R. 2005. "Two Few Physicians, or Too Many?" *Hastings Center Report* 40, no. 1 (January/February): 11–12.

Laugesen, Miriam J., and Sherry A. Glied. 2011. "Higher Fees Paid to U.S. Physicians Drive Higher Spending for Physician Services Compared to Other Countries." *Health Affairs* 30, no. 9 (September): 1647–56.

Lexchin, Joel, and Barbara Mintzes. 2002. "Direct-to-Consumer Advertising of Prescription Drugs: The Evidence Says No." *Journal of Public Policy and Marketing* 21, no. 2 (Fall): 194–201.

Lieberman, Trudy. 2004. "Your Health: Fatal Mistakes." *AARP Bulletin Online.* Online at www.aarp.org/bulletin/yourhealth/Articles/a2004–10–27-fatal_mistakes.html.

Lind, Michael. 2012. "America Doesn't Need Health Care Rationing." Salon.com, October 2. Online at www.salon.com/2012/10/02/america_doesnt_need_health_care_rationing.

Lipton, Eric, and Kevin Sack. 2013. "Fiscal Footnote: Big Senate Gift to Drug Maker." *New York Times,* January 19. Online at www.nytimes.com/2013/01/20/us/medicare-pricing-delay-is-political-win-for-amgen-drug-maker.html?

Lubitz, James. 2005. "Health, Technology, and Medical Care Spending." *Health Affairs,* Web Exclusive 24, no. 2 (Supplement): R81–R85.

Maier, Timothy W. 1997. "Pharmaceuticals: What Do They Buy?" *Insight on the News* 13, no. 25 (July 7): 14–15.

McCarthy, Mark. 2009. "Panel: Tort Reform Is Likely to Have Very Little Effect on Cost." *Medical Device Daily* 13, no. 193 (October): 1, 7.

———. 2012. "Study Says Med Tech Inflation at 1% Share of NHE Still 6%." *Medical Device Daily* 16, no. 207 (October): 1–8.

McClellan, Mark. 1996. "Are the Returns to Technological Change in Health Care Declining?" *Proceedings of the National Academy of Sciences of the United States* 93, no. 23 (November 12): 12701–709.

McGregor, Maurice. 1981. "Hospital Costs: Can They Be Cut?" *Milbank Memorial Fund Quarterly/Health and Society* 59, no. 1 (Winter): 89–98.

McGuire, Alistair, and Victoria Serra. 2005. "The Cost of Care: Is There an Optimal Level of Expenditure?" *Harvard International Review* 27, no. 1 (Spring): 70–73.

McLaughlin, Neil. 2011. "Pricey Healthcare: Studies Show U.S. Costs Are Higher, Benefits Lower—with Blame for All." *Modern Healthcare* 41, no. 39 (September): 17.

McMillen, Scott R. 1996. "The Medical Malpractice Statute of Limitations: Some Answers and Some Questions." *Trial Lawyers Forum* 70, no. 2: 44–47.

"Medical Liability Reform Must Have Teeth to Be Effective." 2009. Press release, September 17. Washington, DC: U.S. Chamber of Commerce. Online at www.uschamber.com/press/releases/2009/september/us-chamber-medical-liability-reform-must-have-teeth-be-effective.

Meisel, Zachary F., and Jeanmarie Perrone. 2012. "The Pain Game: Are Doctors to Blame for Prescription-Drug Abuse?" *Time* 180, no. 24, December 10. Online at http://ideas.time.com/2012/11/26/viewpoint-prescription-drug-abuse-is-fueled-by-doctors/.

Mello, Michelle M.; David M. Studdert; Catherine M. DesRoches; Jordan Peugh; Kinga Zapert; Troyen A. Brennan; and William M. Sage. 2004. "Caring for Patients in a Malpractice Crisis: Physician Satisfaction and Quality of Care." *Health Affairs* 23, no. 4 (July–August): 42–53.

Mendoza, Allie. 2009. "Staggering Health Care Costs Due to Unhealthy Lifestyle Pose a Major Threat to U.S. Economy." Examiner.com, July 2. Online at www.examiner.com/article/staggering-health-care-costs-due-to-unhealthy-lifestyle-pose-major-threat-to-u-s-economy.

Miller, Tracy E., and Arthur R. Derse. 2002. "Between Strangers: The Practice of Medicine Online." *Health Affairs* 21, no. 4 (July–August): 168–79.

Moon, Marilyn. 2005. "Confronting the Rising Costs of Healthcare in Medicare and Medicaid." *Generations* 29, no. 1 (Spring): 59–64.

"More than Half Americans Say Family Skimped on Medical Care Due to Costs." 2009. *Kaiser Health Tracking Poll,* February 2009. Washington, DC: Kaiser Family Foundation. Online at www.kff.org/kaiserpolls/kaiserpolls022509nr.cfm.

Morris, Jonas. 1984. *Searching for a Cure: National Health Policy Considered.* New York: Pica Press.

Mullis, Jeffrey. 1995. "Medical Malpractice, Social Structure, and Social Control." *Sociological Forum* 10, no. 1 (March 1): 135–63.

Nahed, Brian V.; Maya A. Babu; Timothy R. Smith; and Robert F. Heary. 2012. "Malpractice Liability and Defensive Medicine: A National Survey of Neurosurgeons." *Public Library of Science One* 7, no. 6 (June): 1–7.

Nash, Karen. 2012. "Urologists Often on the 'Defensive' When Ordering Tests." *Urology Times,* June 12: 59–60.

National Center for Health Statistics, Centers for Medicare & Medicaid Services, Baltimore, MD. 2012. Online at www.cms.gov/Research-Statistics-Data-and-Systems/Statistics-Trends-and-Reports.

Newhouse, Joseph P. 1992. "Medical Care Costs: How Much Welfare Loss?" *Journal of Economic Perspectives* 6, no. 3: 3–21.

Nitzkin, Joel L. 1996. "Technology and Health Care—Driving Costs Up, Not Down." *IEEE Technology and Society Magazine* 15, no. 3 (Fall): 40–46.

Novelli, William D.; George C. Halvorson; and John Santa. 2012. "Recognizing an Opinion: Findings from the IOM Evidence Communication Innovation Collaborative." *Journal of the American Medical Association* 308, no. 15 (October): 1531–32.

Nuijten, M.J.C; P. Berto; G. Berdeaux; J. Hutton; F.U. Fricke; and F.A. Villar. 2001. "Trends in Decision-Making Process for Pharmaceuticals in Western European Countries: A Focus on Emerging Hurdles for Obtaining Reimbursement and a Price." *European Journal of Health Economics* 2, no. 4: 162–69.

"$1.1 Trillion: What the Top 10 Leading Causes of Death Cost the U. S. Economy." 2012. New York: 24/7 Wall St. Online at http://247wallst.com/2012/01/18/1-1-trillion-what-the-10-leading-causes-of-death-cost-the-u-s-economy.

Ostrow, Nicole. 2010. "CT Scan Increases Threefold in Emergency Rooms, Raising Costs." Bloomberg. com. Online at www.bloomberg.com/news/2010–10–05/ct-scan-use-rises-threefold-in-emergency-rooms-raising-costs-study-shows.html.

Oz, Mehmet. 2011. "The End of Ouch?" *Time Magazine*, March 11. Online at http://content.time.com/time/specials/packages/article/0,28804,2053382_2053599,00.htm.

Pampel, Fred C., and Richard G. Rogers. 2004. "Socioeconomic Status, Smoking, and Health: A Test of Competing Theories of Cumulative Advantage." *Journal of Health and Social Behavior* 45, no. 3 (September): 306–21.

Patel, Kant, and Mark Rushefsky. 2002. *Health Care Policy in an Age of New Technologies.* New York: M.E. Sharpe.

Pauly, Mark V., and Lawton R. Burns. 2008. "Price Transparency for Medical Devices." *Health Affairs* 27, no. 6: 1544–53.

Pear, Robert. 2004. "Americans Relying More on Prescription Drugs, Report Says." *New York Times,* December 3.

Pew Research Center for the People and the Press. 2006. Poll conducted March 8–12, 2006. Online at www.people-press.org/files/legacy-questionnaires/273.pdf.

"Pharmaceutical Industry Profile." 2010. Washington, DC: International Trade Association, U.S. Department of Commerce. Online at http://ita.doc.gov/td/health/PharmaceuticalIndustryProfile2010.pdf.

Phillip, Peter. 2002. "The Rising Cost of Health Care: Can Demand Be Reduced Through More Effective Health Promotion?" *Journal of Evaluation in Clinical Practice* 8, no. 4: 415–19.

Pickert, Kate. 2009. "Malpractice Reform." *Time* 174, no. 12 (September 28): 16.

Pittman, Genevra. 2012. "Obesity Declining in Young, Poorer Kids: Study." *Huffington Post,* December 26. Online at www.huffingtonpost.com/2012/12/26/childhood-obesity-rate_n_2365422.html.

"Politics Keeps Real Remedies Off Radar" 2004. *USA Today,* September 14.

"Positron Emission Tomography (PET) Scan, PET/CT & Vitamin B-12." 2003. San Jose, CA: Bay Area Breast Cancer Network On Line. Online at www.babcn.org/images/news/petscan.htm.

"Prescription Drug Trends." 2010 (May). Washington, DC: Kaiser Family Foundation. Online at www.kff.org/rxdrugs/upload/3057–08.pdf.

"Primary Reason Why Health Care Costs Continue to Rise." 2012. Gaithersburg, MD: Potomac Companies, May 2. Online at www.potomacco.com/general/wellness-general/primary-reason-why-health-care-costs-continue-to-rise-employee-lifestyle-choices/.

Rabecs, Robert N. 2006. "Health Care Fraud Under the New Medicare Part D Prescription Drug Program." *Journal of Criminal Law and Criminology* 96, no. 2 (Winter): 727–56.

Rai, Arti K. 2001. "Health Care Fraud and Abuse: A Tale of Behavior Induced by Payment Structure." *Journal of Legal Studies* 30, no. S2 (June): 579–87.

Rettig, Richard A. 1994. "Medical Innovation Duels Cost Containment." *Health Affairs* 13, no. 3 (Summer): 7–27.

Richtel, Matt. 2012. "Apps Alert the Doctor When Trouble Looms." *New York Times,* October 8. Online at http://well.blogs.nytimes.com/2012/10/08/apps-alert-the-doctor-when-trouble-looms.

Robertson, John A.; Baruch Brody; Allen Buchanan; Jeffrey Kahn; and Elizabeth McPherson. 2002. "Pharmacogenetic Challenges for the Health Care System." *Health Affairs* 21, no. 4 (July–August): 155–67.

Robert Wood Johnson Foundation. 2012. *Health Policy Brief: Reducing Waste in Health Care.* Princeton, NJ: Robert Wood Johnson Foundation. Online at www.rwjf.org/content/dam/farm/reports/issue_briefs/2012/rwjf403314.

Robeznicks, Andis. 2010. "The Fear Factor." *Modern Healthcare* 40, no. 37 (September): 6–7.

Rosenthal, Marilyn M., and Kathleen M. Sutcliffe, eds. 2002. *Medical Error: What Do We Know? What Do We Do?* San Francisco: Jossey-Bass.

Ross, James S. 2002. "The Committee on the Costs of Medical Care and the History of Health Insurance in the United States." *Einstein Quarterly Journal of Biological Medicine* 19: 129–34.

Sage, William M. 2003. "Medical Liability and Patient Safety." *Health Affairs* 22, no. 4 (July–August): 26–36.

———. 2004. "The Forgotten Third: Liability Insurance and the Medical Malpractice Crisis. *Health Affairs* 23, no. 4 (July–August): 10–21.

Schmid, Randolph E. 2004. "40 Percent in U.S. Use Prescription Drugs." *Washington Post,* December 2.

Schoen, Cathy, et al. 2005. "Taking the Pulse of Health Care Systems: Experiences of Patients with Health Problems in Six Countries." *Health Affairs* (November 3): W5-509–W5-525. Online at healthaffairs.org.

Schur, Claudia L., and Marc L. Berk. 2008. "Views on Health Care Technology: Americans Consider the Risks and Sources of Information." *Health Affairs* 27, no. 6 (November/December): 1654–64.

Schwartz, William B. 1987. "The Inevitable Failure of Current Cost-Containment Strategies: Why They Can Provide Only Temporary Relief." *Journal of the American Medical Association* 257, no. 2 (January 9): 220–24.

Shrank, William H.; Niteesh K. Choudhry; Joshua N. Liberman; and Troyen A. Brennan. 2011. "The Use of Generic Drugs in Prevention of Chronic Disease Is Far More Cost-Effective than Thought, and May Save Money." *Health Affairs* 30, no. 7 (July): 1351–57.

Siegel, Bruce; Holly Mead; and Robert Burke. 2008. "Private Gain and Public Pain: Financing American Health Care." *Journal of Law, Medicine, and Ethics* 36, no. 4 (Winter): 644–51.

Sloan, Frank A., and John H. Shadle. 2009. "Is There Empirical Evidence for "Defensive Medicine"? A Reassessment." *Journal of Health Economics* 28, no. 2 (March): 481–91.

Smith-Bindman, Rebecca; Diana L. Miglioretti; Eric Johnson; Choonsik Lee; Heather S. Feigelson; Michael Flynn; Robert T. Greenlee; Rendell L. Kruger; Mark C. Hornbrook; Douglas Roblin; Leif I. Solberg; Nicholas Vanneman; Sheila Weinmann; and Andrew E. William. 2012. "Use of Diagnostic Imaging Studies and Associated Radiation Exposure for Patients Enrolled in Large Integrated Health Care Systems." *Journal of American Medical Association* 307, 22 (June13): 2400–09.

Smith, Sheila; Joseph P. Newhouse; and Mark S. Freeland. 2009. "Income, Insurance, ad Technology: Why Does Health Spending Outpace Economic Growth?" *Health Affairs* 28, no. 5 (September/October): 1276–84.

Squires, David A. 2012. *Explaining High Health Care Spending in the United States: An International Comparison of Supply, Utilization, Prices, and Quality.* Washington, DC: Commonwealth Fund.

Starr, Paul. 1982. *The Social Transformation of American Medicine.* New York: Basic Books.

Stauch, Marc S. 1996. "Causation Issues in Medical Malpractice: A United Kingdom Perspective." *Annals of Health Law* 5: 247–58.

Stein, Letitia. 2013. "Tampa Bay Hospital Charges Vary Widely, Medicare Data Shows." *Tampa Bay Times*, May 8. Online at www.tampabay.com/news/health/tampa-bay-hospital-charges-vary-widely-medicare-data-show/2119958.

Steinberg, Earl P., and Bryan R. Luce. 2005. "Evidence Based? Caveat Emptor!" *Health Affairs* 24, no. 1 (January–February): 80–92.

Struve, Catherine T. 2004. "Improving the Medical Malpractice Litigation Process." *Health Affairs* 23, no. 4 (July–August): 33–41.

Sturm, Roland. 2002. "The Effects of Obesity, Smoking, and Drinking on Medical Problems and Costs." *Health Affairs* 21, no. 2: 245–53.

Sugarman, Stephen D. 1985. "Doing Away with Tort Law." *California Law Review* 73: 555–664.

"Technology and Longer Lives Leading to Higher Health Bills." 1998. *USA Today* 127, no. 2643 (December): 10.

Thomas, Katie. 2013. "U.S. Drug Costs Dropped in 2012, but Rises Loom." *New York Times*, March 18. Online at www.nytimes.com/2013/03/19/business/use-of-generics-produces-an-unusual-drop-in-drug-spending.html?pagewanted=all&_r=0.

Thomas, J. William; Erika C. Ziller; and Deborah A. Thayer. 2012. "Low Costs of Defensive Medicine, Small Savings from Tort Reform." *Health Affairs* 29, no. 9: 1578–84.

Thomas, Lewis. 1975. *The Lives of a Cell.* New York: Bantam Books.

Thorpe, Kenneth E. 2004. "The Medical Malpractice 'Crisis': Recent Trends and the Impact of State Tort Reforms." *Health Affairs,* Web Exclusive W-4 (January–June): 20–30.

Thorpe, Kenneth E., and Meredith Philyaw. 2012. "The Medicalization of Chronic Disease and Costs." *Annual Review of Public Health* 33 (April): 409–23.

U.S. Department of Health and Human Services. 2010. *Multiple Chronic Conditions: A Strategic Framework.* Washington, DC.

USA Today/Kaiser Family Foundation/Harvard School of Public Health. 2005. Poll conducted April 25–June 9, 2005. Storrs, CT: Roper Center for Public Opinion Research.

———. 2008. *The Public on Prescription Drugs and Pharmaceutical Companies.* Washington, DC: Kaiser Family Foundation. Online at www.kff.org/kaiserpolls/upload/7748.pdf.

Vale, Luke. 2010. "Health Technology Assessment and Economic Evaluation: Arguments for a National Approach." *Value in Health* 13, no. 6 (September/October): 859–61.

Valletta, Robert G. 2008. "The Cost and Value of New Medical Technologies: Symposium Summary." *Federal Reserve Bank of San Francisco Economic Letter* 2007, no. 18 (July): 1–3.

Vandegrift, Donald, and Anusua Datta. 2006. "Prescription Drug Expenditures in the United States: The Effects of Obesity, Demographics, and New Pharmaceutical Products." *Southern Economic Journal* 73, no. 2 (October): 515–29.

Van Den Bos, Jill; Karan Rustagi; Travis Gray; Michael Halford; Eva Ziemkiewicz; and Jonathan Shreve. 2011. "The $17.1 Billion Problem: The Annual Cost of Measurable Medical Errors." *Health Affairs* 30, no. 4: 596–603.

Vedantam, Shankar. 2004. "Antidepressant Use by U.S. Adults Soars." *Washington Post,* December 3, A15.

Virts, John R., and George W. Wilson. 1984. "Inflation and Health Care Prices." *Health Affairs* 3, no. 1 (Spring): 88–100.

Wachter, Robert M., and Kaveh G. Shojania. 2004. *Internal Bleeding: The Truth Behind America's Terrifying Epidemic of Medical Mistakes.* New York: RuggedLand.

Weiler, Paul C.; Howard H. Hiatt; Joseph P. Newhouse; William G. Johnson; Troyen A. Brennan; and Lucian I. Leape. 1993. *A Measure of Malpractice: Medical Injury, Malpractice Litigation and Patient Compensation.* Cambridge, MA: Harvard University Press.

Weisbrod, Burton A. 1991. "The Health Care Quadrilemma: An Essay on Technological Change, Insurance, Quality of Care, and Cost Containment." *Journal of Economic Literature* 29 (June): 523–55.

Weisbrod, Burton A., and C.L. LaMay. 1999. "Mixed Signals: Public Policy and the Future of Health Care R&D." *Health Affairs* 18, no. 2 (March–April): 112–25.

Welch, Gilbert H.; Lisa M. Schwartz; and Steven Woloshin. 2011. *Overdiagnosed: Making People Sick in the Pursuit of Health.* Boston: Beacon Press.

8

HEALTHCARE COST CONTAINMENT

Bending the Cost Curve

As we saw in the previous chapter, the cost of healthcare and its continued growth underlie much of the other problems of the healthcare system. Increasing the percentage of the population with insurance, one part of the access issue discussed in chapter 6, is relatively easy. But all efforts to expand access, whether to insurance or to providers in underserved areas, is costly. If more people have access to the system, more people will use the system, and expenditures will rise even more.

The cost issues affect individuals and families, providers, insurers, employers, and governments at all levels. Healthcare, especially Medicaid, costs the states as least as much as education, one of the core functions of state governments. Medicare's trust fund, which affects some but not all parts of Medicare, is projected to run out by 2020. Entitlements, such as Medicare, Medicaid, and Social Security, are a significant portion of the federal budget. Reducing the federal budget deficits from the expenditure or spending side means addressing healthcare costs. The healthcare sector takes up more and more of our country's economy, as measured by gross domestic product (GDP). Clearly there is a problem, really a set of problems, that needs to be addressed.

One way of understanding what many think should be done is to consider the phrase that is the subtitle of this chapter, "bending the cost curve," a metaphor that lends itself to graphs and pictures (Safire 2009). An illustration of bending the curve can be seen in Figure 8.1. As the figure shows, we are talking about reducing increases in spending, not reducing spending, which is a much more difficult proposition. One could ask the question of whose cost curve should be bent (Elmendorf 2009): overall health expenditures, government health expenditures, insurance premiums, etc. A related point is that a certain proportion of cost containment is really cost shifting, moving costs from government or the private sector to consumers/beneficiaries. The question in that case becomes whether costs are really contained.

In the last chapter we carefully examined the cost problem. In this chapter we look at past and present efforts to control costs, and we consider future proposals. We end the chapter suggesting that there has already been some moderation in cost increases and with an intriguing view suggesting that perhaps we should not worry about it.

The 1960s saw a dramatic expansion in social programs. Civil rights, women's rights, educational opportunities, and improved housing and healthcare for citizens were the battle cries of a social revolution as the federal government attempted to expand individual opportunities. In the health field, healthcare came to be viewed as a right rather than a privilege. Providing access to decent healthcare became an important goal of the federal government.

In 1965, the federal government established Medicare and Medicaid to provide increased access to healthcare for the elderly and the poor. These programs were dramatically successful for large numbers of people (Davis and Schoen 1978). The creation and implementation of such programs was made possible by a healthy economy. Additionally, the Comprehensive Health Planning Act and Public Health Services Amendments of 1966 (PL 89–749) established the goal of providing the highest level of healthcare attainable to every person. By the late 1960s and early 1970s, however, the focus began to shift from providing access to concern about rising healthcare costs.

Figure 8.1   **Bending the Cost Curve**

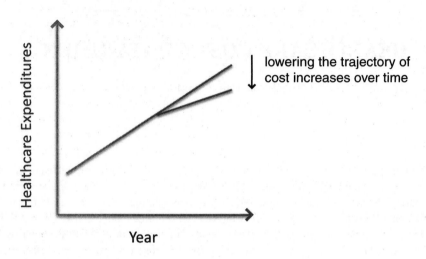

THEORETICAL FRAMEWORK: GOVERNMENT
REGULATION AND MARKET COMPETITION

The debate over how to contain rising healthcare costs centers on two broad approaches or strategies. One strategy relies on government regulation, while the other relies on increasing competition
in the healthcare market (see, for example, Enthoven and Singer 1997; Etheredge 1997; Evans
1997; Goldhill 2013; Goodman 2012; Moran 1997; Rice 1997; and Zatkin 1997). During the
decades of the 1970s, the 1980s, and the 1990s, the federal government tried both regulatory and
competitive strategies to contain health costs. Similarly, state governments and the private sector
have undertaken many initiatives in an attempt to contain rising healthcare costs. In the 2000s,
policymakers once again turned to a variety of approaches.

The Regulatory Strategy

One of the most important assumptions of the regulatory strategy is that the healthcare market
suffers from too many shortcomings, that it does not follow the model of perfect competition. The
seminal work in this field is an article published by economist Kenneth Arrow (1963; see also
Relman 2005; Stone 2012, 2005). For a retrospective discussion of Arrow's article, see "Special
Issue" 2001). Government regulation, it could be argued, can therefore help improve the performance of the market. Thus, one motivation for economic regulation of the system is the premise
that the system suffers from serious market failures, including information disparities, or asymmetries, between providers and consumers of health services and an insurance system (third-party
financing) that masks the costs of health services (Arrow 1963). This situation in turn produces
excessive expenditures, inefficiency, and maldistribution of labor power and resources. A related
market failure is that the healthcare system has a severe equity problem in differential access to
services and financing (see Morone and Jacobs 2005 and chapter 6). Thus the government must
play a role, under this assumption, in providing greater access to the healthcare market for those
who cannot afford it (McClure 1981).

The second assumption of the regulatory strategy is that the healthcare market is different from
other economic markets (Relman 2005). In healthcare, physicians control both supply and demand
because the physician is both the patient's consultant on what services are needed and the provider

of these services. Physicians are not trained to think in terms of aggregate costs. Physicians influence not only cost decisions regarding individual patients but also the growth and expansion of healthcare institutions, thus affecting hospital costs. In addition, the third-party-payment system, based on private health insurance and government payment, tends to remove the patient from the effects of healthcare costs, a perspective that colors some of the policy proposals of the twenty-first century (see chapters 10 and 11).

Another important potential difference between medical care and other goods and services is the absence of consumer information about appropriate price and quality levels (Arrow 1963; Pauly 1978). The role of information in facilitating choices about healthcare goods and services is crucial (Varner and Christy 1986). Some have argued that the medical market is on the verge of remedying the information deficit and that the determination of whether medical care is different from other goods and services is ultimately a political question (Pauly 1978). It might be argued that with the advent of the Internet, more medical information is available to consumers through Websites such as WebMD.

The third assumption of the regulatory strategy is that public regulation promotes important values of political accountability, public access to information, and public participation (Weiner 1982). The regulatory process is characterized by a high degree of formal due process. The requirements of public notices, public meetings, adversary procedures, formal recordkeeping, and limits on appeals help inform consumers by providing access to information and extending to them an opportunity to participate in the policymaking process (Eisner, Worsham, and Ringquest 2006).

Thus, government regulation of the healthcare system is justified on many grounds: as a way of improving the workings of the healthcare market, increasing equity, and promoting crucial public values with the hope that it will help contain healthcare costs. Some advocates of a regulatory strategy argue that a pure market in healthcare is unattainable and thus regulation is the second-best choice (Altman and Weiner 1978). Others argue for a more tightly regulated healthcare system as the best policy (Vladeck 1981, 1984).

Critics of the regulatory strategy charge that examples of past regulatory failures suggest that government regulation does not work (see, for example, Breyer 1979). These critics argue that too many fundamental structural and incentive problems are stacked against good regulatory performance (McClure 1981) and that comprehensive regulation will raise, not lower, the true cost of medical care (Davidson 2010; Goodman 1980, 2012), thus contributing to healthcare cost inflation (Durenberger 1982). Regulation, it is asserted, is not cost effective; it produces inefficiency and prevents technological innovations. Regulation often produces a cartel-like situation resulting in a monopoly on prices because regulatory agencies become captured by the regulated industry (Noll 1975). Wolf (1979) has argued that government programs, including regulation, are also subject to failure, analogous to market failures. To the critics of a regulatory strategy the answer is a competitive market strategy. "Competition" and market reform are the buzzwords for many health policymakers and healthcare providers (see, for example, Antos, Pauly, and Wilensky 2012; Cannon and Tanner 2005; Herzlinger 1997).

The Market Strategy

Those who support a market/competitive strategy argue that all three assumptions that underlie the regulatory strategy can be addressed.

The market strategy begins with a consideration of some classic works in economics. The "bible" of economics is Adam Smith's *The Wealth of Nations,* published in 1776. Smith argued that unfettered markets, free from government or monopoly interference, would produce the greatest benefits for humankind. Such markets were the most efficient, producing precisely the amounts of a good or service that producers want to sell and that consumers want to buy through the price mechanism. Anything that impeded the price mechanism would lower efficiency.

Smith's work formed the basis for classical (and neoclassical) economics and remains an important part of American ideology. The American bias has always been toward free markets and away from government control, though, as we saw above, in healthcare (as in other areas) the viability of free, competitive markets is questionable.

Frederich Hayek (1944), writing near the end of World War II, warned the country of moving toward more government control. Most influential was Milton Friedman's (1962) *Capitalism and Freedom*. Friedman argued that economic freedom supported political freedom. He discussed a number of policy issues showing how free markets would work better than government intervention or control.

The fundamental premise of the economic critique of the healthcare system is that the incentive structure of healthcare moves the system toward inefficiencies. It does this in several ways. Consider the traditional fee-for-service, third-party payment system.

There are four parts to the transaction: the patient with health insurance seeks a service; the patient sees a doctor, who provides that service; the doctor's charges depend on the amount of services provided; the more services, the higher the charge (that is why it is called fee-for-service). The doctor knows that the patient is covered by health insurance provided by the employer through an insurance company. The patient pays the bill and then files a claim with the insurance company for reimbursement. In some instances (but rarer than it used to be), the health insurance policy is so generous that the patient does not have to pay anything. In other cases, the doctor's office files the claim and bills the patient for the balance after the claim is paid. Depending on the policy, the patient may have met the deductible (the amount the patient has to pay before the insurance pays) for the year and may have limited copayments (the percentage of the remaining part of the bill, after the deductible, that the patient pays). The insurance company processes the claim and either pays the provider or reimburses the patient. The employer may pay the premiums on the employee's health insurance and may also (if the policy is especially generous) pay premiums for dependents. If not, then the employee pays the premiums, but at a group rate.

Who is concerned about the cost of care and the quality and efficiency of care (whether a particular test or treatment is really necessary) under such a system? If the doctor and the patient both know that third-party insurance will cover the cost, they have little concern. As long as the premiums cover the reimbursements (plus a profit), the insurer does not care. As long as premium costs are reasonable, and the federal government allows a business tax deduction for premiums (an incentive to cover or continue coverage), the employer does not care. The same situation is true for hospital care.

That is exactly the point that economic reformers seek to make. Under this kind of situation, typical up through most of the 1980s, the cost and the price of service are irrelevant. Economists argue that in the absence of paying the true cost of care, consumers will demand more healthcare than they really need, a problem labeled *moral hazard* (Davidson 2010; Goodman 2012; Pauly 1978).

Healthcare suffers from another problem that impedes the operation of free, competitive markets: *imperfect information.* Providers have considerable information and expertise (though not complete information) and are in a power position compared to other actors, especially consumers, or patients. Thus additional treatments, so the critique goes, are not the result of consumer demand for them but of provider requests. In that sense, healthcare is provider driven rather than consumer driven. Furthermore, consumers do not shop around comparing service and price at critical times (e.g., during a heart attack). Imperfect information, power asymmetries, and lack of a clear price mechanism work together to create market failures in healthcare. The classic discussion of these asymmetries in healthcare was by the Nobel Prize–winning economist Kenneth Arrow (1963). The question is how to solve these problems.

Not everyone agrees that Arrow's analysis still holds. Roy (2012) argues that Arrow's discussion of the healthcare system's problems is not unique to healthcare. Arrow mentioned five problems or distortions in that system: unpredictability, barriers to entry, importance of trust, asymmetrical information, and idiosyncrasies of payment (patients do not see the full costs of services provided) (Roy 2012). Roy states that each of these distortions is antiquated and, again, not unique to healthcare. Insurance, warranties, and other mechanisms have been created to deal with the problem of unpredictability in various markets (consumer electronics, homeowners' insurance, etc.). There are also barriers to entry in other fields, such as law and airlines. Other industries or transactions involve trust. When we eat a food product, we trust that it is safe and that it contains the ingredients listed on the label. Auto mechanics know more about cars than most of us do, especially as cars have become more electronically sophisticated. Finally, Roy notes that the Internet has websites that provide information about medical conditions.

Roy (2012) then looks at liberals' argument that shopping for healthcare is different from shopping for other items. For example, someone suffering a heart attack is not going to shop around for the best cardiologist; he or she will want and need rapid treatment. But Roy points out that much healthcare is not needed on this immediate basis. Those needing knee replacement surgery or routine examinations and care can shop around. Thus Roy's suggestion is a hybrid system:

> So, it seems to me, those who strongly believe in the shopping argument for socialized medicine should adopt a hybrid approach. Let's have a free market for the 70-plus percent of healthcare where market forces can most directly apply, and let's have universal catastrophic insurance for those situations where market forces work less well.
>
> This way, we might get the best of both worlds: an efficient, affordable, high-quality market for chronic and routine healthcare, and a universal system for those who get hit by a bus, or have a stroke, or get cancer. Such a system would leave no one behind. But it would also allow our health-care system to benefit, as much as possible, from the forces of choice, competition, and innovation. (Roy 2012)

Goodman likewise provides an economic critique of the healthcare system. He argues that the reason the system is more complex than other markets is that it is "institutionalized, bureaucratized, and extensively regulated" (2012, 1). A major problem for Goodman is that insurance covers so much of the costs that patients/consumers do not realize or experience the true expense of their healthcare. Indeed, Goodman (2012) makes the important point that the purpose of insurance, whether public or private, is to reduce the burden of costs on consumers. Further, he points to the transparency issue: that it is difficult to find out what something actually costs (on the problem of transparency in healthcare, see Makary 2012).

On the side of the exchange, Goodman notes that providers are paid based on various reimbursement schedules, which are different depending on the payer: Medicare, Medicaid, various health insurance plans, and so forth. Therefore, markets cannot work as they are supposed to, and the economic incentives are all wrong. Consumers would use the healthcare system more than necessary because costs to them were low; in some cases there were none at all. Providers made more money by doing more for their patients, knowing that someone else would be footing much of the bill.

Perverse incentives are the focus of Stephen Davidson's 2010 book, *Still Broken.* The incentives facing all elements of the healthcare system—providers, payers, consumers, employers—all move toward creating conditions that allow high healthcare costs, and thus higher healthcare spending, and access problems (individuals and families increasingly unable to afford healthcare coverage and services).What follows from this economic critique is market reforms. The purpose of the reforms is to change the incentives that face all those involved in receiving, delivering, and paying for healthcare services.

According to market reform advocates, new, alternative mechanisms of healthcare delivery must be found to provide healthcare consumers with multiple choices having cost consequences.

Creating conditions for fair market competition will produce that competition, which will help contain healthcare costs (Antos, Pauly, and Wilensky 2012; Cannon and Tanner 2005; Enthoven 1980). New incentives should be created. To make businesses more conscious of healthcare costs, tax laws should be altered to place a ceiling on the total amount of health insurance premiums that employers can deduct as a business expense. To make consumers more conscious of healthcare costs, insurance plans should rely on coinsurance and deductibles (Enthoven 1978a, 1978b). What is needed, some have argued, is to combine markets with a minimal but necessary amount of government regulation. This combination is known as managed competition (Enthoven 1988; Frech and Ginsburg 1988). Examples of programs or policies that rely on combining market-oriented competitive strategy with some government regulations include the Medicare Prospective Payment System (PPS), also known as diagnosis-related groups (DRGs), and the use of organizations such as HMOs and PPOs to provide managed care on a capitation basis to enrollees.

Some pro-competition advocates, such as Clark Havighurst (1982), have argued that one of the most effective and least intrusive methods for assuring fair competition is enforcement of antitrust laws. Antitrust principles are based on the assumptions that competition promotes efficiency and innovation and encourages diversity through decentralization, and that competitive markets are more stable than noncompetitive markets because the former adjust continuously to market conditions. These assumptions, in turn, are based on social values of individual initiative, individual freedom of choice, and the dangers of big business and big government (Pollard 1981). This does not mean that a competitive market would be unregulated; any competitive market requires monitoring and intervention from time to time to ensure that competition is fair and open. According to antitrust enforcement advocates, given the potential for exercise of monopoly power by physicians, hospitals, and other healthcare providers, policing healthcare markets must be an integral part of reforms designed to enhance competition (Pollard 1981).

In summary, advocates of the competitive strategy argue that improving structural mechanisms and changing incentives through introduction of competition in the healthcare market will result in better economic performance and reduced healthcare costs. Critics of the competitive strategy are skeptical of the results of market competition. To some, the prospects of a competitive strategy are promising but uncertain technically and politically (McClure 1983). Others argue that markets in healthcare are usually pseudo-markets dominated by one side of the transaction (Evans 1983), and that the supporters of competition may be grossly overemphasizing the beneficial results (Ginzberg 1982). It would take more than the stimulus from increased consumer cost-sharing or reduced tax subsidies to produce competitive behavior on the part of healthcare providers (Gabel and Monheit 1983). Opponents of an antitrust enforcement strategy argue that professional autonomy and self-regulation produce significant social benefits. In addition, physicians are likely to oppose antitrust enforcement because a free market could be worse for physicians' economic well-being than government regulation. Physicians often reap substantial economic benefits from regulations they control and from the government programs that pay the bills (Starr 1980).

In the pages that follow, we examine and evaluate various attempts to control healthcare costs and spending employing different combinations of the regulatory and competitive strategies by the federal government, state governments, and the private sector. We follow that up with looking at cost-containment efforts in the twenty-first century.

PAST EFFORTS AT CONTROLLING HEALTHCARE COSTS

Healthcare Planning and Cost Containment

During the late 1960s and early 1970s, the federal government responded to the concerns of rising healthcare costs by adopting various regulatory mechanisms. Health planning emerged as one of the major methods for controlling healthcare costs. While the federal government had always engaged in some planning, not until the late 1960s and early 1970s did healthcare planning become a dominant theme. Planning relies on a regulatory strategy and uses centralized decision making to guide the allocation of resources and ensure access to services.

The rationale for healthcare planning is based on the argument of excess capacity in the healthcare system in general, and in the hospital industry in particular, as a significant contributor to rising healthcare costs. The argument was that there were too many hospitals, beds, and medical equipment, which not only created unnecessary expansion and duplication of expensive resources but also led to overutilization of medical facilities (Goodman 1980). Supply creates its own demand, following Roemer's (1961) argument that hospital beds tend to be filled (for a dissenting opinion on the validity of what is called Roemer's law, see Scandlen 2011). This excess capacity, expansion, and duplication were encouraged by factors such as the third-party-payment system, the inability of the market to induce inefficient hospitals to reduce the number of beds or go out of business altogether, and competition among hospitals for prestige and physicians (Havighurst 1973).

While early approaches to planning were aimed at ensuring high-quality healthcare for everyone, health planning in the 1960s and 1970s focused explicitly on the problem of rising costs. One of the significant regulatory developments in the area of healthcare planning was certificate-of-need (CON) legislation. By 1973, twenty-three states had adopted such laws. The federal government got into the act with the passage of the 1972 amendments to the Social Security Act of 1935. This created the Section 1122 program, which called for review of hospital expansion proposals when Medicare funding might be involved.

Two years later, the federal government assumed control of the entire CON process. The National Health Planning and Resource Development Act of 1974 (PL 93–641) provided an institutional framework for healthcare planning. It replaced three previous federal programs: Comprehensive Health Planning, the Regional Medical Program, and the Hill-Burton Hospital Construction Program (Kennedy and Baruch 1980–81). The law required all states to adopt CON laws by 1980. It also established a network of state and local health planning agencies to shape local health systems based on national priorities. More than 200 local health systems agencies (HSAs) were established, each responsible for governing a specific area, to administer the CON laws. State health planning development agencies roughly paralleled the roles and responsibilities of local HSAs. The law provided for the representation of consumer and provider interests in the HSAs. Federal efforts at creating CON legislation ended during the Reagan administration, which was opposed to federal intervention.

CON laws required hospitals to document community need to obtain approval for major capital expenditures for expansion of physical plants, equipment, and services. The primary purpose of these laws was to prevent unnecessary investment in facilities and services. The laws were also designed to prevent the entry of new providers in the healthcare market unless a clear need was demonstrated.

Did the CON laws and the HSAs help contain overall growth of hospital costs in particular and healthcare costs in general? The available empirical evidence overwhelmingly points to the failure of healthcare planning to control healthcare costs. Research findings show little evidence that CON constrained investment or had any significant effect on the total level of investment (Gelman 1982; see also Salkever and Bice 1976). CON laws may have changed the composition of investment, but they may, in fact, also have led to increased overall hospital costs (Salkever and Bice 1979). There was some evidence that programs that focused on hospital beds alone may have had more success than those dealing with review of expansion of facilities, equipment, and services. Nevertheless, the effects of these narrowly focused programs were very weak. The investment in anticipation of regulation, rather than the effect of the CON laws, explains some initial decline in investment after adoption of the CON programs.

What accounts for the failure of CON laws and HSAs? One possible explanation is the capture theory of regulation (see, for example, Etzioni 2009; Laffont and Tirole 1991; McConnell 1970; Stigler 1971). This is the theory that regulatory agencies may adopt policies similar to the ones desired by the regulated industry, resulting in a cartel or monopoly situation. This occurs when a regulated industry subverts or captures the regulatory agency through politically inspired appointments, lucrative employment prospects in the industry for cooperative regulators, a regulated industry's ability to outspend the regulatory agency, and industry's influence with the elected officials who control a regulatory agency's appropriations. The fact that the American Hospital Association supported CON laws—and a fairly close correlation exists between the attitudes of the hospital industry and the regulators—may lend some legitimacy to this argument, even though it would be difficult to prove (Goodman 1980; Havighurst 1973).

A second explanation is that, despite consumer representation in the HSAs, provider interests had many more advantages in terms of information, expertise, and legal counsel (Bicknell and Walsh 1976; Salkever and Bice 1979). In addition, consistent political participation by consumers in the form of attending public hearings was difficult to achieve because it required time, effort, and money (Marmor and Morone 1979). Representatives of the healthcare providers dominated most public meetings (Lewin and Associates 1975). It has also been argued that pluralist interest-group representation, as occurred within HSAs, leads to bargaining, log-rolling, and collusive competition among narrowly defined special interests in which the interest of the general public is not well served (Vladeck 1977).

A third explanation for the failure of the CON laws and HSAs lies in the lack of public support. A nationwide public opinion poll in 1978 revealed that the public had very little confidence in, and recognition of, HSAs and had little support for hospital cost-containment strategies and their consequences. There was also little support for the goals and consequences of cost-containment strategies among groups traditionally underrepresented in health planning activities (Mick and Thompson 1984).

Within less than a decade, health planning, as established under the National Health Planning and Resource Development Act of 1974, was dismantled by the Reagan administration. Congress reduced health planning funding from $167 million in 1980 to $58 million in 1983 (Etheredge 1983). Most of the states eliminated local HSAs, though some states maintain CON programs (the authors' home state of Missouri is one example).

Professional Standards Review

One of the factors often cited as responsible for rising healthcare costs is overutilization of healthcare resources. The rise in healthcare costs since the enactment of Medicare and Medicaid programs in the mid-1960s created concern in Congress about the cost and quality of these programs, concerns that are still present nearly fifty years after those two programs were created. The Social Security Amendments of 1972 established the Professional Standards Review Organization (PSRO) program. The PSRO was designed as a peer-review mechanism to promote effective yet efficient and economical delivery of healthcare services for government-financed programs such as Medicare and Medicaid. Under the law, more than 200 local PSROs were created and staffed by local physicians to review and monitor care provided to Medicare and Medicaid patients by hospitals, extended-care facilities, and skilled nursing homes. The PSROs were responsible for determining whether the care provided was medically necessary, of professional quality, and delivered in an appropriate healthcare facility. They also had the authority to deny approval of payment for services to physicians who provide care to Medicaid and Medicare patients. Two of the stated goals of the program were to eliminate unnecessary medical treatment and unnecessary institutionalization. Thus, the PSRO program was created as a regulatory mechanism for reducing the cost of federal healthcare programs.

Did the PSRO succeed in achieving cost reductions? The majority of evidence suggests that it did not. A 1981 study by the Congressional Budget Office concluded that the cost of the program exceeded its benefits. Although the program slightly reduced Medicare utilization overall, it consumed more resources than it saved. It had very little impact on the federal budget (Congressional Budget Office 1981).

Many explanations are offered for this. One is that PSROs controlled by local physicians had no incentives to reduce utilization because such reduction would lead to reduced federal payments to the locality. Second, the program suffered from potential conflict between quality-enhancing and cost-reducing goals, a persistent problem (Ginzberg 1977). Third, the PSRO program could be used to advance the cartel objectives of healthcare providers (Goodman 1980). Doctor-policing laws such as PSRO or hospital peer review committees aimed at self-policing are generally ineffective because of a reluctance to speak out against colleagues, concern over libel lawsuits, and problems of due process safeguards (see Cassidy 1984; Rosenberg 1984; Varlova 1984).

The Reagan administration came to office in 1981 strongly supporting the elimination of federal regulatory programs. The PSRO program was on the administration's target list, but it failed to eliminate the program because of opposition in Congress. Federal funding for the PSRO program was cut from $58 million in 1980 to $15 million in 1983 (Etheredge 1983). Congress, through the Tax Equity and Fiscal Responsibility Act of 1982 (PL 97–248), renamed the program Peer Review Organizations (PROs). Today, PROs are responsible for reviewing the appropriateness and quality of healthcare provided to Medicare beneficiaries. The Medicare program has relied on the PROs to safeguard against inadequate medical treatment for individual patients. In 1987 the scope of the program was expanded beyond hospital-based care to include review of outpatient care. The program eventually evolved into a focus on quality improvement (see Bhatia 2000 and Centers for Medicare and Medicaid Services 2006). Utilization review became part of a newer strategy that developed in the 1990s, managed care.

Price Regulation

The most interventionist of cost containment strategies is price regulation. Here a government agency reviews prices and particular requests for increases, or sets them. Price regulation can include setting hospital rates, reviewing requests for increases in premiums on the part of health insurance companies, or, in some cases, setting levels that are charged by different providers. There has been experience with this at both the state and federal level.

At the state level, an example of price regulation is approvals required by states for health insurance companies' premium increases. Indeed, states have exercised considerable regulatory authority over health insurance companies beyond prices, such as quality and access. Price regulation encompasses some of the things we discussed in chapter 6 on access. For example, and these apply mainly to the individual or small market plans, health insurance companies may charge higher premiums for people with preexisting conditions (a practice that will be eliminated beginning in 2014 under the Affordable Care Act). States might require community rating, where premiums may not be charged according to health status (Fish-Parcham 2006; Kofman and Pollitz 2006).

Here we are referring to overall regulation of health insurance premiums. A few states require approval from the states before higher premiums can be imposed. In other states, premium increases can be enacted unless the states explicitly disapprove. A third set of states require filing of premium-increase requests, which then may be reviewed. In those states, regulators may require that increases be rolled back (Fish-Parcham 2006). Under the Affordable Care Act (chapter 10), insurance companies will have to submit their requests for rate increases to the federal government. The legislation requires a certain percentage of premiums gathered to be spent on healthcare (the medical loss ratio) and prohibits higher premiums for people with preexisting conditions.

Another element that states could regulate are hospital charges. Seven states enacted such programs, though only two remain, in Maryland and West Virginia (Atkinson 2009). Atkinson's

(2009) review found that when states regulated hospital rates, costs went up less than the national average. Such hospital rate regulation is politically difficult to maintain. And mandates to increase access tend to drive up costs. New (2005) found that the more mandates states imposed on health insurers, the higher the premiums.

States have also attempted to restrain costs through provider reimbursements in Medicaid. Under Medicaid, as we discussed in chapter 3, states set the levels of reimbursements for physicians, hospitals, nursing homes, and so forth. This kind of control on provider reimbursements does have its tradeoffs. Physicians are not required to take Medicaid patients, so may choose not to serve such patients or may limit the percentage of their practice dedicated to Medicaid patients. It can also cause financial distress to hospitals that find that the cost of treating patients is considerable higher than the reimbusements.

The federal government briefly engaged in price regulation. In 1971, in response to what was considered high inflation, the Nixon administration imposed a wage-and-price control program. For that period of time, costs, though not necessarily spending, slowed down. The difference is that in response to the controls, providers, especially physicians, began to unbundle their services. Rather than charge for treating the patient during a visit, the health services delivered were broken down into its components: a blood test, an injection, etc., with each service billed separately. Thus, the more services delivered, the more income even if prices and costs remained the same.

In 1974, the price control program was eliminated, with the healthcare industry promising to keep costs down. That did not happen, and the Carter administration proposed legislation in 1977 and 1979 that focused on hospital costs, the single largest component of healthcare spending (see chapter 7). The industry then proposed a "voluntary effort" as a substitute for government controls. When the Carter administration was unable to get such legislation passed, the voluntary effort had no volunteers and costs continued to rise (Altman and Levitt 2003; Davis and Stremikis 2009).

Davis and Stremikis (2009) argue that had measures proposed by presidents Nixon, Carter, and Clinton been effective (the key problem in their analysis), we would be spending much less on healthcare than we do today:

> Each set out regulatory restraints on the growth in provider payment or insurance premiums, or both. All had significant mechanisms to control costs, including changing provider payment, increasing competition in the insurance market, and controlling the growth in private insurance premiums. (2009, 2)

Assuming the programs would have worked, if the Nixon proposals had been adopted and there had been a 1.5 percent annual decrease in the rate of healthcare spending (for example, if spending increases in a given year were equal to 5 percent of GDP, under this scenario spending increases as a percent of GDP would have been 3.5 percent), we would be spending 10.7 percent of our GDP on healthcare in 2010 instead of the 17.7 percent it turned out to be. If we started with the Carter proposal, then healthcare spending as a percentage of GDP in 2010 would have been an estimated 11.5 percent; if we had adopted the Clinton Health Security proposal, it would have been 14.2 percent (Davis and Stremikis 2009). Of course, that is assuming effectiveness of the proposals.

HEALTH MAINTENANCE ORGANIZATIONS, HEALTHCARE RATIONING, MANAGED CARE, AND COST CONTAINMENT

Health Maintenance Organizations

The CON, HSA, and PSRO programs were examples of behavioral regulations. These programs were designed to scrutinize decisions about utilization, expansion, and acquisition of healthcare resources by providers. They were based on the assumption that changing behavior and cutting waste could contain healthcare costs (Brown 1986). They were not very successful. There was somewhat more success with the prospective payment system. The Maryland rate regulation system also seems to have successfully restrained cost increases in that state. But overall healthcare costs and spending continued to increase.

During the early 1970s, the federal government also tried a competitive market strategy to contain healthcare costs through prepaid group plans (PGPs), commonly known as health maintenance organizations (HMOs). The concept of PGPs was not new. Such plans had existed in the healthcare system without any federal assistance since the 1920s. During the early 1970s, the number of HMOs grew as a result of favorable market conditions and the rhetorical support provided by the Nixon administration. According to one estimate, the number of HMOs increased from 41 in 1970 to 133 in 1973 (McNeil and Schlenker 1975).

Dr. Paul M. Ellwood Jr., a key health adviser to President Richard Nixon, is credited with bringing the competitive market strategy in the form of HMOs to the attention of national health policymakers (Falkson 1980). In 1970 the Nixon administration asked Congress to create a new HMO option for Medicare recipients. In 1971 the administration began to use discretionary funds to plan the development of about a hundred HMOs around the country and asked Congress to create a special HMO development plan. The Department of Health, Education, and Welfare (now the Department of Health and Human Services) argued that there could be as many as 1,700 HMOs within a few years, with perhaps as many as 40 million people enrolled (U.S. Department of Health, Education, and Welfare 1971). After long debate, Congress passed the Health Maintenance Organization Act (PL 93–222) of 1973.

The federal government assumed the role of venture capitalist (Iglehart 1980). It encouraged the development of HMOs in an attempt to induce competition in the healthcare market with the hope of containing health costs. This market strategy was designed to eliminate, or at least reduce, centralized healthcare bureaucracy and replace it with decentralized market building. This was to be accomplished through the use of federal funds to support efforts in developing new healthcare organizations and alternative means of healthcare delivery. It promised pluralism, choice, efficiency, and reorganization through competition, markets, and incentives (Ellwood 1971; Havighurst 1970). The expectation was that HMOs would contain costs by (1) creating incentives for channeling health service utilization from costly inpatient settings (hospitals, skilled nursing homes, etc.) to less costly outpatient settings (visits to doctors' offices), (2) promoting competition with traditional healthcare delivery systems, and (3) exercising market power by obtaining preferential prices from various healthcare providers (Falkson 1980–81).

An HMO is a prepaid medical practice delivering a comprehensive set of healthcare services to enrollees for a fixed fee (capitation) paid in advance. The Health Maintenance Organization Act of 1973 provided for an expenditure of $375 million over five years. Most of these funds were used to encourage development of HMOs by providing start-up costs. The law offered federally qualified HMOs three basic benefits: (1) money for development of HMOs; (2) overriding of certain restrictive state laws; and (3) a mandate to employers, covered by the Fair Labor Standards Act of 1938, that employ twenty-five or more employees to offer HMO coverage as an alternative to whatever other health plans they provide. This was designed to provide healthcare consumers with at least a dual choice in health plans. In return, to qualify for federal funds, HMOs were to deliver a comprehensive package of benefits to a broadly representative population on an equitable basis with consumer participation. This was to be done at the same price as or a lower price than traditional forms of health insurance (Rosoff 1975).

The original legislation so heavily burdened HMOs with special services (comprehensive benefits, open enrollment, dual choice, and limits on copayments) and pricing requirements (same premiums to be charged to all enrollees, that is, "community rating" as opposed to "experience rating") (Rosoff 1975) that very few developers applied for federal support. By 1975, only five

HMOs had qualified for federal support. Between 1974 and 1976, the growth in the number of federally supported HMOs was very slow.

To remedy this problem the HMO amendments of 1976 and 1978 deregulated service and pricing requirements, including a reduction in service requirements and the elimination of open enrollment with the exception of large and established programs. In 1981 the federal government stopped providing new grants to HMOs. Since then, the federal government has focused its attention on the promotion of competition in general, incentives designed to increase private-sector involvement in HMO development, and risk contracts to HMOs that agree to enroll Medicare beneficiaries. The health maintenance strategy morphed or transformed into the managed care strategy.

Healthcare Rationing

One way of addressing rising healthcare costs is rationing. The major concept behind rationing is that there are limits to what we can expect and afford in the way of healthcare. It is based on the notion that healthcare costs are rising disproportionately compared to the small or marginal gains in overall national health. Therefore, we must establish priorities in health services and become more rational in our healthcare spending.

Advocates of this school of thought argue that healthcare costs are out of control and that regulatory controls on spending or competitive approaches based on economic incentives are doomed to fail. Regulatory approaches are, it is asserted, based on the faulty assumption that medical care produces health, and more care produces more health. The only realistic solution, therefore, is the rationing of healthcare resources. If the United States is serious about containing healthcare costs, society will have to forgo some medical benefits, and patients should not expect to receive all the care they want regardless of the costs (Aaron and Schwartz 1984, 1990). Proponents argue that healthcare rationing already exists in the actions of insurance companies, legislatures, hospitals, physicians, and individual premium payers, and we need to get on with the public business of determining how healthcare rationing should be carried out ethically (Menzel 1990). Observers call the existing de facto rationing "silent rationing," "under-the-table rationing," "rationing by finance," or "rationing by wallet" (Mechanic 1997).

Hoffman (2013) examines rationing in the United States and notes that the term is rarely used, and when it is, it is in a perjorative sense. The disputes over so-called "death panels" and comparative effectiveness analysis in the debate over the Affordable Care Act underscore Hoffman's observation. But she also notes that in the United States there is no right to healthcare, and healthcare is rationed on the basis of price. We have done this kind of rationing since 1930.

All countries engage in some form of rationing (Patel and Rushefsky 2002). In the United States, the major example of rationing is in organ transplantation. There are many more people who need new lungs, kidneys, hearts, and so forth than there are available organs. Both state and federal laws govern the process of deciding who will receive the organs (see President's Council on Bioethics 2003). These include the Uniform Anatomical Gift Act of 1968 and the Organ Transplantation Act of 1984.

Rationing can be explicit or implicit. *Implicit rationing* refers to discretionary decisions made by professionals, managers, and other healthcare personnel within the established budgetary guidelines. *Explicit rationing* refers to decisions made by an administrative authority regarding the amount of resources and types of resources to be made available, eligible populations, and specific rules for allocation. Explicit rationing is effected through constraining levels of available technology, locations of facilities and programs, expenditure levels, and the like (Mechanic 1997). The effort in the Medicaid program to establish treatment priorities represents one of the most explicit forms of rationing in the United States (Mechanic 1997).

In Oregon, healthcare rationing moved beyond the talking point, and the state took action to change the way in which healthcare programs were structured (see chapter 3). The state provoked a national debate in 1987 when it decided to stop financing most organ transplants for Medicaid patients and use the money instead for prenatal care for pregnant women. In 1990 it produced a revolutionary Medicaid plan. Rather than offer a minority of the poor a comparatively full package of services, the state proposed to give all its poor access to healthcare but with a reduced level of services. The state ranked most medical conditions as least or most economically worthwhile to treat under the plan. If money ran out before all services were covered, the lowest-priority services would not be covered. Faced with intense criticism of the listed priorities, in 1991 Oregon health officials overhauled the ranking and produced a new list. The George H.W. Bush administration turned down Oregon's request for a Medicaid waiver, necessary to implement rationing, partly on the grounds that it might conflict with the Americans with Disabilities Act. The Clinton administration, however, did issue the waiver in 1993, and the program began operation in 1994 (Guglielmo 2004). Despite the state's best efforts, Oregon had to resort to the more common means of rationing: reducing Medicaid rolls (from 90,000 to 54,000) (Guglielmo 2004). In 2002, Oregon received another waiver to increase Medicaid enrollments, along with reduction in plan benefits. But because of the increased cost-sharing that was part of the plan and difficult economic conditions, enrollment actually decreased. To use Jonathan Oberlander's (2007) phrase, the Oregon Health Plan unraveled. No other state has sought to engage in the kind of explicit rationing and public discussion seen in the Oregon model (Yegian 2004).

David Mechanic (1997) provides five reasons to be skeptical about explicit rationing. One is that once bureaucratic decisions have been made and put in place (i.e., once explicit standards are established), they are resistant to change because constituencies develop to preserve the status quo. Developing explicit standards is difficult and often impossible. It is not a science. Second, medical care involves a process of discovery and negotiation between a patient and a healthcare provider, not simply application of technical means. Third, patients have different experiences, needs, tastes, preferences, and values. Two patients in comparable medical situations may require different treatments. Fourth, explicit rationing will result in inflexibility in responding to the contingencies of people's real lives. Fifth, explicit rationing will be susceptible to political manipulation. Once decisions are removed from a dialogue between patient and doctor to the public arena, they become subject to political, social, moral, and legal turf battles (Mechanic 1997).

As Porter (2012) points out, rationing is inevitable because of limited resources (such as the number of providers). In the United States, we tend to ration depending on financial capability: "You get care if you have the money to pay for it; if not, you probably won't" (Porter 2012). Porter notes that various healthcare proposals from different sides of the political spectrum include, implicitly, some type of rationing. Paul Ryan (R-WI), the chair of the House Budget Committee and the Republican vice presidential candidate in 2012, offered a plan that would limit spending on Medicare but give seniors money to purchase their own health insurance plans.

The Affordable Care Act, Porter (2012) notes (see also Nix 2012), also contains provisions that are effectively a form of rationing

> by levying a tax on "Cadillac" insurance plans, and in turn pushing employers to seek cheaper options and lower costs. It creates an advisory board to cut costs from Medicare if spending rises above a set rate. And it finances an institute to evaluate which therapies are most clinically effective. Careful to avoid political blowback, the president's plan forbids Medicare to base its reimbursement decisions on the institute's findings. (Porter 2012)

Another experiment with rationing came in the late 1990s. This is the managed care revolution.

Managed Competition

The simplest way to reform healthcare markets is to focus on the consumer and insurance. The more generous the insurance policy, the less likely it is that costs are a consideration. The obvious solution would be to make health insurance less generous. Insurance may contain what is known as *first-dollar coverage,* beginning coverage with the smallest illnesses. Rather than cover everything, a *catastrophic health insurance policy* might be substituted. Such a policy would go into effect after a rather high deductible was met, perhaps as a percentage of family income. This is part of the system that Roy (2012) would support.

A typical health insurance policy might have a $300 deductible (some have no deductibles). After the first $300 of medical expenses, 80 percent or more of further medical expenses might be covered by insurance. But what if the policy were changed so that the deductible was $2,000 or higher, or 10 percent of a family's income? Then the consumer, or patient, would have to bear the expenses of further care and might not go to the doctor for every cold or sniffle. Only truly needed care would be undertaken. Further, the family would be protected from very high medical expenses (such as a cancer operation and treatment) after the deductible was met. Moreover, as we know with automobile insurance, the higher the deductible, the lower the premium to the worker and/or the employer.

There is an element of simplicity to such plans, which were proposed in the late 1970s and early 1980s and have reappeared in the 2000s under the guise of consumer-driven healthcare. Such analysis largely underlies the advocacy of medical savings accounts (MSAs), as they were originally known, and, more recently, health savings accounts (HSAs). These policies were first included in Medicare in 1996 on an experimental basis and then in the larger population, also on an experimental basis in 1997. MSAs were replaced by HSAs as a result of the 2003 Medicare legislation discussed in chapter 4. Goodman (2012) and Goldhill (2013), among others, advocated high-deductible plans coupled with health savings accounts.

Such catastrophic plans concentrated on what could be called the *demand side* of healthcare, the consumer, but most reform plans focused on the *supply side* of healthcare, the provider. This would mean changing the incentives built into the traditional system and trying to create more competitive markets.

The first attempt at a supply-side, market-reform solution came in the 1960s and 1970s. This was the health maintenance strategy mentioned in chapters 2 and 8. The strategy, the brainchild of Dr. Paul Ellwood, was an elegant concept (Bauman 1976; Falkson 1980). Based on already existing prepaid group plans (PGPs), the idea was to limit the money available to providers through a capitation system. The health maintenance organization (HMO) enrolls subscribers, who pay a monthly premium. The premiums constitute the total budget for the HMO. Providing more services does not produce more revenues. So the incentive was not to overtreat, as market reformers argue is done in the fee-for-service system, but to treat only as necessary. The HMO became the prototype of a *managed care organization* (in 1990s language), one that would review services and try to eliminate unnecessary care.

There was a further hope behind the HMO strategy: HMOs would create competitive pressures on the fee-for-service system so that all providers and insurers would begin to look at costs. As HMOs penetrated a market, competitive pressures would increase. This idea was embodied in the 1973 Health Maintenance Organization Act to promote, with federal assistance, the development of HMOs. Into the 1980s, at least, the competitive impact of the strategy was questionable.

The second stage came in the late 1970s and early 1980s. Alain Enthoven (1978a, 1978b, 1980) took the competitive strategy a step further by suggesting a complete reorganization of the healthcare system, in essence national health insurance. Originally writing in the 1970s in the *New*

England Journal of Medicine (and other journals) and then in his book *Health Plan,* Enthoven wanted to eliminate the employment–insurance connection.

The Consumer-Choice Health Plan (CCHP) was a form of national health insurance that would work as follows (Rushefsky 1981): Providers and insurers would organize into competitive health-care plans. Each plan would then determine what its premiums would be. The federal government would estimate the average cost of care in various geographical areas and pay a percentage of that average cost through tax credits or 100 percent of the average cost for the poor via vouchers. CCHP featured an open-enrollment period, community rating (see chapter 6), and a limit on out-of-pocket costs. Consumers would then choose among the competing plans, which could include a traditional fee-for-service plan, an HMO, a plan with a very high deductible, and so forth. Each plan would charge a different premium, but the federal government would pay the same amount regardless of the plan chosen. Thus, consumers would face the decision of what plan to choose depending on the financial consequences for them. The newly regained place of price signals plus open enrollments would create the competition among the plans and (it was hoped) restrain costs. Thus healthcare would be consumer driven rather than cost driven.

A somewhat less ambitious version of CCHP built on the employment-based insurance system already in place. For those with work-based insurance, the employer would pay the same premium for each employee regardless of which plan was chosen. Employees would have a choice of plans, with similar features, as mentioned above. For the poor or those without employment-based insurance, vouchers from the federal government could be used.

Competition plans created a great deal of interest in the late 1970s and early 1980s (Demkovich 1979; Wehr 1979). Congressmen Richard Schweiker (R-PA) and David Stockman (R-MI) offered bills based on the CCHP. In 1981 Schweiker became the secretary of the Department of Health and Human Services (HHS) and Stockman became director of the Office of Management and Budget (OMB) in the Reagan administration. A task force within HHS was created to investigate competitive ideas; however, nothing further came of the effort, perhaps because CCHP or a variant was essentially a form of national health insurance at a time when the Reagan administration was seeking to reduce the federal government's role.

In addition, several practical developments began to move toward competitive plans. One was a focus on deregulating the healthcare industry but engaging in vigorous anticompetitive regulation (Havighurst 1982). For example, the American Medical Association (AMA) had for a long time opposed the group practice of medicine, arguing that it trespassed on the traditional autonomy of the individual practitioner (Starr 1982). Over time, this opposition lessened, though the AMA still has some problems with managed care organizations.

Two developments among public employers provided some experience with choosing among competitive plans. The Federal Employees Health Benefits Program (FEHBP) allows federal employees to choose among competing plans, while the federal government provides level premium contributions. A similar program established in California, the California Public Employees' Retirement System (CalPERS), enrolls nearly a million public employees at all levels of government. CalPERS is a purchasing cooperative that negotiates with a number of different plans, such as HMOs, preferred provider organizations (PPOs), and traditional fee-for-service plans.

In the late 1980s and early 1990s, Ellwood, who had moved from Minnesota to Jackson Hole, Wyoming, formed a working group to develop a strategy for change based on the idea of managed competition. The working group and guests "included academics, public officials and leaders of the insurance and health industries" (Reinhold 1993; see also Enthoven 1993).

Enthoven, perhaps the chief theorist of the Jackson Hole group, began advocating managed competition in the late 1980s and continued into the 1990s Enthoven and Kronick 1989a, 1989b, 1992). Managed competition is an attempt to marry several different ideas—national health insurance, insurance reform, managed care, organization of providers and purchasers, and choice for consumers—while building on the present system.

The managed competition proposal was designed, according to Enthoven and Kronick (1989a, 31), to meet two major goals: "to provide financial protection from healthcare expenses for all . . . and to promote the development of economical financing and delivery arrangements." This would be done by enabling those not already in Medicare or Medicaid to purchase health insurance either through their employer or through a public sponsor organized by the states. The purpose of aggregating purchasers of insurance, either through employment or through sponsors (healthcare alliances), would be to allow them to bargain and contract with provider organizations such as HMOs and PPOs or the traditional fee-for-service system (or some of the other many possibilities).

Employers would pay a specific amount for full-time employees and dependents and would pay a payroll tax for those not covered. An employer's contribution would be 80 percent of the average price of plans offered (a defined contribution regardless of the plan chosen); subscribers would pay the difference. The tax laws would be changed to limit contributions by employers beyond the specified amount. Those not covered by an employer plan, such as the self-employed, would pay into the public sponsor plans, up to an income ceiling. The program would also include subsidies to pay for the premiums of the poor (not covered by Medicaid) and for small businesses.

Employers and sponsors would then negotiate with qualified health plans, made up of some combination of providers and insurers, who would offer a variety of plans. Subscribers would elect a plan each year. The federal government would collect the funds and make determinations about average costs of plans. The program could be run entirely by the federal government or by both the states and the federal government. Medicaid and Medicare would be left alone, at least at first, though recipients would be encouraged to join HMOs.

Like the earlier CCHP, the intent is to promote efficient organization of health providers and provide competition among those organizations. The major difference between the earlier and later plans is that purchasers would also be aggregated and would be in a position to bargain with providers, not at the time of the occurrence of an illness but at the point of purchasing coverage. While the plan does not attempt radical surgery on the healthcare system, the hope is that forces put into place would create significant changes, cover virtually the entire population, and cost less than the present system.

Managed Care

> By managed care, we mean forms of coverage that integrate financing and delivery, as well as the organizations that provide this coverage—health maintenance organizations (HMOs), preferred provider organizations (PPOs), and point-of-service (POS) plans. (Gold and Hurley 1997, 29)

> The bottom line is that the American public doesn't want to give too much power to *any bureaucrats*. It doesn't matter whether they work for the federal government or for the insurance industry. (Schneider 1998)

Definitions

One important and confusing aspect of policy debates and experiences with managed care is definitional. In this section, we offer some definitions so that we will all know what we are talking about.

We define *managed care* broadly as any health insurance plan that seeks to restrain the use of healthcare services. Such restraint can be as simple as requiring preauthorization for a nonemergency hospital stay (Weinder and de Lissovoy 1993; for a discussion of the symbolic significance of definitions, particularly in regard to managed care, see Hacker and Marmor 1999). Plans can also encompass more organized forms of provider delivery.

The classic type of managed care organization is the *health maintenance organization* (HMO), which we discussed above. An HMO is an organization whose providers, generally primary care physicians, are prepaid through monthly subscriber premiums (known as *capitation*) to deliver a comprehensive set of services. The HMO assumes the financial risk of providing those services. The original label for such an organization was prepaid group plan (PGP). PGPs were developed to provide healthcare services to employees in areas where medical services were thin. Kaiser-Permanente is typical of such plans.

HMOs come in various forms. A *staff-model HMO* is one in which the physicians are on a salary and members obtain services primarily from the HMO. In a *group-model HMO,* a multi-specialty group of doctors works primarily for the HMO's members. There are hybrid versions of these HMOs.

Another type of managed care organization is the *preferred provider organization* (PPO). Here the employer or insurer contracts with physicians for discount rates on services. Consumers can use providers outside the PPO but must pay higher copayments.

As physicians have been losing power and autonomy to managed care plans, they have some-times sought to sponsor their own plans, known as *provider-sponsored organizations* (PSOs). One last type of managed care plan, which was incorporated in the Balanced Budget Act of 1997 with Medicare, is the *point-of-service* (POS) plan. Here the consumer chooses the provider at the time the service is needed.

The Development of Managed Care

While managed care has been increasingly a part of Medicaid, and to a lesser extent Medicare, the push in the 1980s and 1990s came from the private sector, particularly large employers. The impetus was partly the drastically increasing cost of health insurance and partly the decreases in corporate profits and a weak economy (Bodenheimer and Sullivan 1998; Leyerle 1994). For example, the cost of employee healthcare for General Motors in the mid-1980s was twice the cost of steel, a problem that remains, twenty years later, for the giant corporation (Brink and Shute 1997; Lazarus 2005).

Health maintenance organizations became the major cost-containment strategy for the Nixon administration, culminating in the 1973 Health Maintenance Organization Act. The purpose was to provide a financial boost for the development of this type of alternative organization. The act was terminated during the Reagan administration. HMOs and the prepaid plans based on them became the prototype for what later came to be labeled managed care organizations (MCOs).

The fundamental concept behind HMOs was that they would enroll subscribers who would pay a monthly premium, similar to traditional health insurance plans. The difference is that cost-sharing for HMO subscribers is either nonexistent or minimal. What subscribers were doing was prepaying for their medical needs. Those prepayments then became the vast majority of the budget for HMOs to work with. In this way, many HMOs were risk-based. This means that if the cost of delivering medical care to their subscribers exceeded the budget, the HMO and the providers would lose money. On the other hand, if the HMO delivered services for less than the prepayments, they would make money. The incentive, therefore, would be to provide only needed, cost-effective services, including a range of preventive services. The early HMOs, such as the Kaiser Permanente and HIP plans in New York City, operated in this manner. Eventually, those ideas morphed into a cost-containment strategy as managed care.

Buchanan (1998) has outlined five cost-containment techniques that are commonly identified with the concept of managed care. One technique is payment limits. An example of such a technique is the use of DRGs by the federal government to reimburse hospitals for Medicare patient fees. A second technique is a requirement of preauthorization for medical services, such as surgeries. A third technique is the use of primary care physicians as "gatekeepers" to control access to specialists. A fourth technique is "de-skilling" (i.e., using less trained providers to provide certain services). A fifth technique is to provide financial incentives to physicians to limit utilization of care. Managed care is a fancy name for rationing.

The first significant move by a large employer into managed care came in 1988, when Allied-Signal canceled its healthcare plans and transferred its employees into Cigna's HMO (Bodenheimer and Sullivan 1998a; see also Anders 1996). Other large companies soon followed. The trend toward managed care can be easily shown. In 1988, 73 percent of workers who had employer-based health insurance were enrolled in conventional fee-for-service plans. Sixteen percent were enrolled in health maintenance organizations, and another 11 percent in preferred provider organizations. By 2012, less than 1 percent of covered workers were in conventional plans, while about 82 percent of covered workers were in some form of managed care plan (Claxton et al. 2012).

The public plans, Medicare and Medicaid, as discussed in chapters 3 and 4, have also seen growth in enrollment in managed care organizations. In the case of Medicare, recipients can choose whether to enroll in private plans through the Medicare Advantage (Part C) program. In 2013, 14.4 million Medicare recipients (28 percent of enrollees) were enrolled in such plans. Much of the increase in enrollment began in 2005 (Gold et al. 2013).

Medicaid recipients often do not have the luxury of choosing whether to enroll in a managed care plan. Thus, such enrollment is higher for Medicaid than for Medicare. In 2010, 65 percent of Medicaid recipients were so enrolled (Gifford et al. 2011).

One of the important changes in managed care is the rise of preferred provider organizations (PPOs). Part of this change was due to a backlash on the part of consumers and doctors against more stringent, controlling managed plans. PPOs differ from traditional health insurance plans in two ways. In PPOs, the insurer takes an active role in negotiating payment rates or selecting providers, and the providers are on notice to comply with aggressive utilization review procedures.

PPOs also differ from HMOs. PPO providers are paid on a fee-for-service basis and thus are not at financial risk for services they provide, nor do they have incentives to reduce utilization. Under PPOs, beneficiaries can use providers outside the PPO plan, which is not the case with HMOs. Unlike HMOs, PPOs do not generally practice in a common location or in group practices (Davis et al. 1990). PPOs are mainly sponsored by healthcare providers such as hospitals and physicians and by insurance companies.

The peak period for HMO market penetration was 1996, when 31 percent of covered workers were in HMOs. By 2012, that number had declined to 16 percent. By contrast, the market penetration of PPOs was 16 percent in 1988 and 56 percent by 2012 (Claxton et al. 2012).

Evaluating Managed Care

Has the use of managed care helped to contain healthcare costs? The success of such a strategy depends on the creation of healthcare delivery systems that are more efficient than the traditional system, and that are able to compete on price, benefits, access, style of medical care, and the existence of sufficient numbers of such systems throughout the country (Moran 1981). A review of the literature on HMO performance by Miller and Luft (2002) suggests that HMOs, the type of managed care plan most likely to control costs, have not been very successful at doing so.

One way that HMOs try to restrain costs is by lowering utilization. Miller and Luft (2002) found mixed results here, with some studies showing lower use of ambulatory services by HMO members over conventional plans, but the overall evidence is weak.

We can also consider changes in employer health plan premiums over time. In the 1996–2004 period, premiums increased by an average of 8.5 percent per year overall. From 2004 to 2012, when managed care organizations loosened up in response to consumer and provider complaints, premiums increased by an average of 5.8 percent. By comparison, Medicare average spending overall for the same period was higher, at 8.6 percent (data derived from Claxton et al. 2012; Centers for Medicare and Medicaid Services 2011).

On the other hand, there is some evidence that the healthcare sector will respond to real and possible pressure for change (Altman and Levitt 2003). When the Nixon administration was ready to lift price controls in 1974, some thought was given to leaving them on for hospitals. The hospital industry promised to control prices, and we can see what happened beginning in 1975. A similar sequence of events occurred in the late 1970s. The Carter administration strongly considered controls over hospital pricing and uniform accounting for hospitals. The industry promised that, through its voluntary efforts, it would restrain increases. The next decline came in the early and mid-1990s, with the Clinton Health Security Act proposal and the advent of managed care. The Clinton proposal failed, but managed care did seem to restrain spending increases for a while. But as we moved to the late 1990s, the managed care revolution faltered, and costs started increasing again. The Balanced Budget Act of 1997 brought about another change, as spending increases dipped at the end of the twentieth century.

Bodenheimer (2003) points out that while private spending increases show a wavelike, up-and-down appearance over time (see also Altman and Levitt 2003), Medicare spending shows consistent declines on a per capita basis. So, public-sector actions, if there is a political will to withstand the pain of cuts/restraints and the pressure of affected interests, can be effective.

COST-SHARING

A major strategy for reducing employer healthcare costs, in both the public and private sectors, is cost-sharing or cost-shifting.The patient shares in the direct cost of healthcare services for his or her own coverage or that of dependents. Cost-sharing includes deductibles, coinsurance, or copayments, as well as increased premiums. A deductible is the fixed amount that must be paid by the patient before the insurance benefits begin. Coinsurance is the percentage contribution that patients pay once the deductible is exceeded. Copayments are generally a fixed contribution, rather than a percentage contribution, toward each unit of service. This strategy helps reduce the cost to the employers by shifting part of the cost to the patient. It is based on the belief that when patients are made to share a higher cost for treatment (negative incentive), they will reduce health service utilization. Some studies have demonstrated that cost-sharing in the form of deductibles or coinsurance reduces the use of healthcare services (Lee and Tollen 2002; Newhouse et al. 1981; Robinson 2002). Others have argued that increased cost-shifting is not in the best interest of the workers, that some of the cost savings are illusory, and that such savings are likely to be one-time savings (Davis et al. 1990). Whatever the case, more and more employers are seeking to reduce costs through cost-sharing.

Cost-sharing is more likely in smaller companies than in larger ones, but for all size companies, cost-sharing is increasing. In 2006, 16 percent of small firms (3–199 workers) had a deductible of a least $1,000 for single coverage compared to just 6 percent for larger firms (220+ workers). By 2012, the numbers had climbed to 49 pecent and 26 percent, respectively (Claxton et al. 2012).

The amount of the deductibles varies by type of plan. HMOs are the least likely to have an annual deductible, with 70 percent of plans not requiring any deductible. When a deductible is charged, the average amount for family coverage is $1,329. Preferred provider organizations tend to require their subscribers to have a deductible; the average amount is $1,770. For those enrolled in high-deductible health plans (HDHP), all members pay a deductible; the average deductible amount is $3,924 (Claxton et al. 2012). In the 2006–2012 period, HMOs experienced the largest annual average increase in deductibles, 12.8 percent, and high-deductible health plans saw the smallest average increase in deductibles, 2 percent (calculated from Claxton et al. 2012). Premiums are also lower for HDHP plans than for the other types (Claxton et al. 2012). That is the tradeoff the high-deductible health plans make, lower premiums but higher deductibles.

Public employers are also increasingly engaging in cost-sharing/shifting. This is partly because of fiscal issues facing governments and because Republican governors have been increasingly successful in cutting back on benefits to state employees (Cauchon 2012).

WELLNESS PROGRAMS

Another set of initiatives consists of employee wellness programs. Larger employers are increasingly promoting programs designed to encourage healthier lifestyles and behavior. The emphasis is on preventive care to reduce the need for healthcare services. The assumption here is that prevention will lead to healthier workers and therefore reduced healthcare costs. The focus is on such lifestyle issues as smoking and obesity, as well as disease management related to chronic diseases (see Fleming 2005). Wellness programs can include financial incentives to join a fitness club and encouraging employees to provide biometrics testing (for example, of cholesterol and blood-sugar levels). The Affordable Care Act contains incentives for employers to offer such programs. Some states have also adopted wellness programs (Appleby 2012).

Such employee wellness programs penalize workers with unhealthy lifestyles by reducing their healthcare benefits, usually by raising the employee cost of those benefits. Some healthcare experts express concern over such meddling by employers because some of the healthcare problems of workers may be related to hereditary, environmental, or socioeconomic factors over which they have very little control. Some firms have also begun to consider lifestyles in hiring and firing decisions. This led the American Civil Liberties Union to charge that some employers are overstepping their bounds. It argued that if employers are allowed to refuse to hire workers, or to fire them, because of something they do in their private lives, workers will not have any private lives left (American Civil Liberties Union 1998; Miller and Bradburn 1991).

As with other programs, the big question is whether they produce cost savings. In one sense it is difficult to tell because the results of preventive activities are often not apparent for decades (smoking cessation programs are a good example). Given that it is much rarer that an employee will stay with the same company for all of her worklife, employers may not actually experience any benefits. The evidence overall is unclear, though the impact on the larger healthcare system could be dramtic (Appleby 2012; Draper, Tynan, and Christianson 2012).

COST CONTAINMENT IN THE TWENTY-FIRST CENTURY

The cost of health care in the United States is certainly of pressing concern. Some of the policies enacted in the twentieth century had an impact but, for various reasons, were not sustainable. The large, though decreasing, federal deficits are driven, in part, by the huge Medicare and Medicaid programs (Baker 2012; National Institute for Health Care Management Foundation 2012). Employers are looking for ways to decrease the cost of health benefits for their employees. Medicaid takes a big bite out of state budgets (Kliff 2012). Healthcare costs are a signficant portion of family budgets (Cohen, Gindi, and Kirzinger 2012).

A study by the Urban Institute (Holahan et al. 2011) examined different strategies for cost containment and estimated their impact. One strategy that they examined was to cap the tax exclusion for health insurance premiums paid by employers. The argument here is that insurance protects consumers from the cost of their care, which is, of course, the point of insurance.

By lowering the cost at the point of service, the argument goes, consumers will utilize more healthcare than if they had to pay the full cost or more of the cost. This is the moral hazard argument. Holahan et al. (2011) estimate that reducing the tax exclusion would lower national health expenditures in the 2014–2023 period by about 1.5 percent. This would also have an impact on federal deficits, as it would lower a tax expenditure (income excused from taxation), resulting in increased revenue.

Malpractice reform (see chapter 7), such as limiting the amount of noneconomic damages, would reduce spending during the 2014–2023 period by an estimated 0.7 percent. Holahan et al. (2011) point out that the evidence on other possible reforms is limited.

Several of the strategies focus on patient care. These include disease prevention, coordination of care, and end-of-life care. Disease-prevention strategies include raising taxes on cigarettes as a means of reducing consumption, a set of strategies to reduce the onset of asthma attacks at home (such as reducing the amount of dust in homes, plus education), and taxing sweetened beverages (again to reduce consumption and the obesity that may result at least partially from such consumption). Holahan et al. (2011) estimate that such actions could save more than $224 billion over the ten-year period, about 0.6 percent of national health expenditures.

The second patient care strategy is better coordination of care. This is especially important for those with chronic conditions, such as asthma, diabetes, disabilities, and so on. Patients may have multiple chronic conditions. Medicaid and Medicare fund many patients with these conditions and the costs are high. Holahan et al. (2011) estimate that people in these categories account for about 30 percent of healthcare spending. Another estimate is that 84 percent of the population have at least one chronic disease (Ginsburg 2012).

Goetzel et al. (2012) found that there is a significant relationship between health risks and healthcare spending. The ten health risks are depression, high blood glucose levels, high blood pressure, high body weight, tobacco use, physical inactivity, stress, high cholesterol levels, poor nutrition and eating habits, and high alcohol consumption. They argue that workplace programs to reduce the risks from these factors could reduce healthcare spending.

The U.S. healthcare system is fragmented. Patients with multiple chronic conditions will see different providers for each of their chronic conditions. No single provider or provider organization may be in charge or responsible for patient care. Medicare and Medicaid share patients (dual eligibles) but pay for different aspects of healthcare (Medicare focuses more on short-term care and Medicaid more on long-term care). While the cost savings from care coordination are uncertain, Holahan et al. (2011, 16) note that the more successful programs have the following characteristics:

> Targeting interventions to those most likely to benefit, in-person contact, access to timely information on hospital admissions and emergency room visits, close interaction between care coordinators and primary care physicians, and emphasis on teaching self-management skills.

Savings from care coordination would come from reductions in spending on long-term care and from less use of hospitals and pharmaceuticals (Holahan et al. 2011). Holahan et al. (2011) estimate that coordination based on these principles and better coordination between the two giant public insurance programs would save an estimated 0.9 percent on national health expenditures over a ten-year period. It is important to note the uncertainty in this estimate. The estimate of savings could be as much as $331.1 billion over this period, but the low estimate of savings is close to zero.

An important strategy for cost containment focuses on end-of-life care. As we discussed in the previous chapter, one of the cost issues is the concentration of expenditures (Berk and Monheit

2001). A small proportion of the population accounts for a very large percentage of national health-care expenditures. This is as true within Medicare as in the overall healthcare system. Holahan et al. (2011) observe that as much as 30 percent of Medicare spending was for those in the last year of their life, about 5 percent of the Medicare population. Further, much of the healthcare given to those near the end of their life is unwanted by patients and family and often reduces the quality of the patient's life (see chapter 9). So one solution is not to engage in undesired or undesirable heroic but futile treatment.

The alternative is to provide palliative care, care that eases the discomfort of the dying patient, either at home or in a hospice setting. Here is where end-of-life counseling would come in. Holahan et al. (2011) estimate modest savings from focusing on end-of-life care, about 0.3 percent of healthcare spending.

Of course, there are ethical issues related to these kinds of considerations. Physicians have an inbred desire to do all to help their patients. We certainly should not allow people to die just to save money. And end-of-life counseling became part of the debate over the Affordable Care Act as critics asserted, falsely, that the proposed legislation required so-called "death panels" for Medicare patients (see chapter 10; Starr 2013).

Some proposals focus on the payment system. One example is bundled payments, which the Centers for Medicare and Medicaid Services is experimenting with through Medicare and is also part of the Affordable Care Act. The problem that bundled payment addresses is the fragmented fee-for-service system, in which each service is charged separately. For example, consider knee-replacement surgery. The surgeon gets paid separately, the anaesthesiologist gets paid separately, the hospital gets paid separately. Postsurgical therapy is paid for separately. Under bundled payment, there is "global payment," a single payment that covers all the services and providers (Emanuel et al. 2012; Holahan et al. 2011).

In some ways this is similar to the DRG system that Medicare uses to pay for hospital visits and, in some ways, similar to the original idea of health maintenance organizations. If the providers can deliver the service for less than the global payment, then they can keep the rest of the payment as profit. If the resulting cost is more, than the providers absorb the loss. There will be a great deal of analysis and politics surrounding how the global payments are determined and what the levels are. And there need to be quality controls so that the service provided is appropriate. Holahan et al. (2011) estimate that the savings from bundled payments over the 2014–2023 period will amount to about 0.3 percent of healthcare spending. They do point out that their estimates do not included bundled payments for treating chronic diseases. Those estimates are more difficult to make because they do not deal with a single, discrete episode, such as bypass or knee-replacement surgery, but a lifetime of treatment.

Fraud, Waste, and Cost Control

One of the interesting targets for controlling costs is fraud and waste in healthcare spending. Shortly after the demise of the Clinton plan in 1994, the authors conducted a survey of health policy experts about the problems of the healthcare system and appropriate remedies (Patel and Rushefsky 1998). The policy experts saw problems such as the fee-for-service payment system and overall fragmentation of the healthcare system. We then compared our findings with public opinion polls and found disagreement between the experts and the general public. For the public, the major problem was fraud and waste in the healthcare system. As a side note, we should point out that the public's view of the problems of the healthcare system required virtually no changes on their part, unlike those of the experts.

To a certain extent, the public's view on waste and abuse was fairly accurate. Recent studies, as mentioned in chapter 7, attribute much of U.S. spending to waste and abuse of the system (Goldman 2012; Lallemand 2012). One estimate is that waste, separate from fraud and abuse, can cost as much as $650 billion a year, much higher than the savings estimated by Holahan et al. (2011) for all their strategies. The Institute of Medicine (Smith et al. 2012) estimates that waste in the American healthcare system is about $765 billion a year.

Waste can be defined as

> spending on services that lack evidence of producing better health outcomes compared to less-expensive alternatives; inefficiencies in the provision of healthcare goods and services; and costs incurred while treating avoidable medical injuries, such as preventable infections and hospitals. (Lallemand 2012, 1)

Fraud and abuse may be defined as

> "Fraud" refers to illegal activities in which someone gets something of value without having to pay for it or earn it, such as kickbacks or billing for services that were not provided. "Abuse" occurs when a provider or supplier bends rules or doesn't follow good medical practices, resulting in unnecessary costs or improper payments. Examples include the overuse of services or providing unnecessary tests. (Goldman 2012, 1)

In addressing the waste, fraud, and abuse issues, and indeed constraining costs in general, it is highly useful to remember that every dollar spent on healthcare is a dollar of revenue for someone. Reducing payments to providers, as we have done in Medicare and Medicaid, means less revenue for those providers. Cutting back on waste or profits means less revenue for someone.

Let us address the waste issue first. Earlier we mentioned the malpractice issue and tort reform (see also chapter 7). The study by Holahan et al. (2011) and others (Kelly 2009; Kelly and Fabious 2010; Van Den Bos et al. 2011) suggests more can be saved by reducing medical error than by tort reform. For example, hospital-acquired infections cost over $4 billion a year (Van Den Bos et al. 2011; "Medical Errors Cost Health Care System Billions" 2011; Wachter and Shojania 2004). Van Den Bos et al. (2011) found that most of the medical errors, including hospital-based infections, could be accounted for by ten types, suggesting that preventive efforts should be focused on those.

One way to reduce the number of medical errors (and increase the quality of care) is to develop systems and processes that focus on areas where medical errors are likely to occur. Goodman, Villarreal, and Jones (2011) offer an intriguing, market-based idea. They write that patients should be offered voluntary no-fault insurance against the possibility of an error. By doing so, patients would give up their rights to sue. Patients could also enhance the insurance policy by making additional payments. The premiums would be paid by physicians and hospitals and be experienced-rated. That is, providers with a record of medical errors would pay higher premiums. Providers would naturally wish to avoid the higher premiums and thus put the appropriate systems into place. These include "electronic health records, error-reducing software, and other safety innovations" (Goodman, Villarreal, and Jones 2011, 594).

Goodman, Villarreal, and Jones (2011) state that quality would be overseen by insurance companies and that the higher premiums paid would lead consumers to search for alternative providers; here is the use of prices and markets to achieve a goal. Goodman, Villarreal, and Jones point out the benefits of such a plan:

> The immediate consequence of offering no-fault compensation insurance to patients would be peace of mind: They would know in advance that any injury would be compensated and any harm would be acknowledged. Further, such a system would provide equity—something surely lacking in the current malpractice system. (2011, 594)

Another set of policies in this area focuses on overuse or overdiagnosis (Brawley and Gold-berg 2011; Brownlee 2007; Welch, Schwartz, and Woloshin 2011). Lallemand (2012) estimates that overdiagnosis or overtreatment costs as much as $226 billion in unnecesaary spending. She defines overtreatment as "care that is rooted in outmoded habits, that is driven by providers' prefer-ences rather than those of informed patients, that ignores scientific findings, or that is motivated by something other than provision of optimal care for a patient" (2). One example Lallemand provides is defensive medicine, based on the medical error/malpractice problem. Providers may do additional testing of patients to ensure that all that could possibly be done has been done and to avoid a lawsuit.

Welch, Schwartz, and Woloshin (2011) attribute much of the problem of overtreatment/over-diagnosis to a paradigm of early prevention and diagnostic screening. They argue that by doing early screenings, using advances in technology, more people are categorized as having a condi-tion or potential condition that requires some kind of treatment (on this point, see the discussion of numbers in Stone 2012). Two of their examples are screenings for prostate and breast cancer. Their recommendation is a paradigm shift away from early screening.

This brings us to the use of evidence-based medicine and comparative effectiveness analysis. The idea behind both concepts is that medical decisions would be based on scientific findings of the efficacy of a treatment (evidence-based medicine) and how well that treatment works compared to other treatments (comparative effectiveness analysis).

While the idea behind these concepts is fairly straightforward and should be noncontrover-sial, in fact it is not. Practitioners see themselves as already utilizing evidence-based medicine based on experiences with their patients, as well as keeping up with the scientific literature. Timble et al. (2012) suggest five sets of reasons why the results of such research may not be adopted or might be delayed in clinical practice. The first is financial incentives that discour-age such adoption. As one example, insurance coverage of various treatments may vary. More traditional treatments may be covered, while alternatives or even counseling about alternatives may not be. The following quote will give a taste of the problems that comparative effective and evidence-based medicine face:

> Under fee-for-service payment systems, however, invasive treatments . . . are generously reimbursed, while counseling patients about treatment options goes most unreimbursed. Meanwhile, most payers impose few coverage or payment obstacles for many invasive procedures, either because their approppriateness cannot be monitored or because payers are likely to face organized challenges from pharmaceutical or device manufacturers, profes-sional societies, or patient advocates when they attempt to use comparative effectiveness evidence to modify coverage policies. (Timble et al. 2012, 2169)

Even something like the interpretation of evidence from scientific trials is subject to economic incentives. Pharmaceutical companies will take measures to control the message or frame the meaning of the results of scientific studies, including television advertising, educating practitioners, and so forth (Timble et al. 2012; on framing and interpretation, see Stone 2012. George Lakoff has written about the importance of framing in politics (for an analysis of Lakoff and framing, see Bai 2005). Pharmaceutical companies have a financial stake in promoting the efficacy of their products over alternatives (see Abramson 2004).

A second problem is the ambiguity of evidence (Timble et al. 2012). Because scientific evidence is frequently nonconclusive or problematical, it lends itself to interpretation and criticism. Much of this takes the form of a methodological critique, focusing on the methods used in a particular study. This is often the case in scientific disputes, say over global warming (for a discussion of this, see Patel and Rushefsky 2005).

The third barrier is cognitive biases. Timble et al. (2012) point to several such biases. One is confirmation bias: favoring evidence that confirms what someone believes and then rejecting alternative studies. A second bias is to prefer doing something, even if the effectiveness of that something is limited, to doing nothing. A third is a bias in favor of newer over older technology.

The fourth barrier is the failure to think about how and when practitioners need and want the information and for what purpose. The final barrier is limited use of tools, particularly information technologies, to support the use of evidence-based medicine and comparative effective research.

Such research faces other barriers. Comparative effectiveness research has been linked to rationing. For example, Nix (2012) argues that comparative effectiveness research can be used by government bureaucrats to affect decisions made by practitioners and their patients. Nix states, for example, that in an effort to control the costs of Medicare, rationing is occurring through "so-called improvements in value and efficiency" (2012, 5). Indeed, Nix takes exception to the whole idea of quality measures. For one thing, she notes that providers cannot by themselves improve patient outcomes. At least some of the outcome is based on patient behavior (a lesson that those who would put all the responsibility for student achievement on teachers might wish to pay attention to).

On the other hand, Volsky (2009) argues that comparative effectiveness research will not lead to rationing. Rather, the government will provide information and, recognizing the ambiguity of such research, not impose guidelines on doctors. He also notes that the Affordable Care Act prohibits the government agency that examines comparative effectiveness research, the Center for Health Outcomes, from mandating changes in practice or coverage.

Another possible place for savings, in theory anyway, is in administrative costs. The fragmented American healthcare system has numerous payers. Think of medical practice in the 1950s. The family doctor was a solo practitioner who may have had a secretary. Many doctors did not have any administrative assistance. Now move forward to the present day. Not only are there fewer physicians in solo practice, but their offices have become more complex. The administrative staff may be as large as the provider component. One reason for this is the different ways providers get paid: Medicare, Medicaid, various private insurers, etc., each with their own guidelines, forms, and reimbursement policies. Then there are the payers with their administrative staff. For private insurers, that includes the cost of advertising. The result is that a much higher percentage of healthcare spending is accounted for by administrative costs in the United States than in countries with national healthcare systems. Woolhandler, Campbell, and Himmelstein (2003) found that administrative costs in the United States were about three times as much as in Canada (see also Bartlett 2012).

A related point is whether Medicare's administrative costs are lower than those of private insurance companies. This turns out to be very much of an ideological debate. Tyson (2012), for example, makes the argument that they are. She points out, additionally, that Medicare can negotiate for prices better than private insurance because of the size of the program and the number of enrollees. Private insurance also garners profits, which Medicare obviously does not.

Part of the debate is how one measures administrative costs. Liberals such as Krugman (2009) and Hacker (2009) point to the lower overhead costs and use as their measure of administrative costs the ratio of such costs to overall expenditures. In that case, Medicare wins: 3 percent compared to as much as 40 percent in the individual insurance market.

Conservatives take great exception to this. For example, Roy (2011) argues that Medicare is assisted by other agencies, such as the Internal Revenue Service, the Social Security Administration, and the Department of Health and Human Services. Roy also points out that private insurers pay state taxes on the premiums collected, which Medicare does not. He also notes the importance of the size of Medicare with its economies of scale that give it an advantage (a point also made by Klein 2009). Roy (2011) asserts that the appropriate measure for comparing administrative costs is cost per patient. In that case, Medicare's administrative costs are higher than private insurance.

Klein (2009) argues that there are difficulties in measuring administrative costs. In any event, he thinks that any savings from reducing administrative costs would be fairly small and not touch upon the real drivers of overall healthcare costs.

The Federal Budget and Healthcare Costs

Medicare and Medicaid are two of the largest federal programs (along with Social Security and defense spending). The two public programs, if their costs are not constrained, will continue to put pressure on federal spending and make deficit reduction more difficult. We address some of these issues in chapters 3, 4, and 10. Here we look at two related proposals that likely would reduce spending increases, in this case by cost-shifting.

A good example of this is the budget proposal by House Budget Committee Chair Paul Ryan (R-WI). The healthcare-related portion of the budget proposal has three major components ("How Paul Ryan's New Budget Would Transform Health Care" 2013).

The first part would repeal most of the Affordable Care Act, maintaining Medicare savings. The second part would transform Medicaid from a categorical program to a block grant program. As currently run, Medicaid expenditures depend on benefit packages set by states, the number of beneficiaries, and beneficiary use of healthcare services. Spending on Medicaid does not depend on funds that go through the regular federal budgeting process. It is, therefore, an uncontrollable expense (see chapter 3).

This was the same situation for the federal welfare program, Aid to Families with Dependent Children (AFDC), until 1996. But welfare was turned into a block grant: states receive a specific amount of money regardless of the number of welfare recipients or the state of the economy. Under welfare reform (see Rushefsky 2013), the amount of money was decreased with the idea that fewer people would remain on welfare.

Others have suggested such changes. President Reagan made such a proposal in 1981; Speaker of the House Newt Gingrich (R-GA) made a somewhat similar proposal in 1995. In 2003, President George W. Bush proposed giving states the option of making their Medicaid programs a block grant (Lambrew 2005).

The attraction of the block grant proposals is twofold. First, it would turn power and authority over to the states. As we saw in chapter 3 (and will see again in chapter 10), Medicaid is very much shaped by state policies. It is fair to say that there is no such thing as a single Medicaid program; rather, there are fifty-three Medicaid programs (fifty states plus three territories). While states have the authority to shape the program, they still have to meet federal requirements. States are also thought to more accountable to their populations because they are closer to them than the federal government (Lambrew 2005).

Second is the budget aspect. As with welfare reform, it would turn Medicaid from an uncontrollable expense to a controllable one for the federal government. The block grant would give the states a specific amount of money, again regardless of the number of recipients, recipient use of services, economic conditions, or healthcare inflation. Block grants would grow based only on the growth of the population. The Ryan proposal states that it would reduce federal spending by an average of $75 billion a year over a ten-year period ("How Paul Ryan's New Budget Plan Would Transform Health Care" 2013).

The third proposal focuses on Medicare. As we have seen in chapter 4, Medicare, unlike Medicaid, is a fully federally funded and federally administered program. Ryan's proposal would set up a premium support (or voucher) proposal. Beneficiaries, beginning in 2024, would get a subsidy (the premium support or voucher) from which they would purchase either traditional Medicare or a private plan (Medicare Advantage). This would have a budget effect similar to the Medicaid block grant. Medicare would become a controllable expense: the cost of the vouchers.

The subsidy would be manipulated if healthcare costs rose at a high rate, shifting costs from the federal government to beneficiaries.

The Ryan budget, a Republican plan, had no chance of being adopted in 2013 or 2014. But it does represent a way to reduce the growth of federal spending on healthcare. And it might become more politically viable if Republicans regain control of the presidency and the Senate and maintain their majority in the House.

The Price Is Right?

One important driver of healthcare costs, discussed in the previous chapter, is the price of healthcare, essentially meaning the prices charged by providers, pharmaceutical companies, and so forth. Mahar (2006) argues that the prices charged for goods and services on the part of corporate medicine in the search for profits are the major driving force in increasing and high costs and spending. Conover (2012) reaches the same conclusion about prices, though drawing different implications. He finds that if one adjusts for the higher costs in the United States, differences in per capita healthcare spending between us and other Western industrialized countries with national healthcare systems shrinks, though it does not disappear. But that, of course, could be the problem. Adjusting for higher costs acknowledges, in an obvious way, that costs are higher in the United States than in other Western industrialized countries.

If prices are a major problem, what is to be done? To some extent, we have already employed controls on prices. Provider reimbursements are controlled by states and the federal government in Medicaid and Medicare. Medicaid and the Department of Veterans Affairs negotiate drug prices with pharmaceutical companies, though Medicare is forbidden to do so by the 2003 Medicare Modernization Act (see chapter 4).

Reid (2009) finds that one reason healthcare systems in other countries spend less than we do is that provider salaries are limited and profits, especially for insurance companies, are prohibited. Physicians in particular are more likely to be paid a salary rather than on the basis of services delivered. This tends to be the case with health maintenance organizations and community health centers.

We could do things like that. But the reality is that the American political system will limit our ability to control prices. The political will is just not there. Even the Affordable Care Act, which we examine in chapter 10, is limited in what it does.

One important limitation in trying to control prices is the lack of transparency in pricing and the variation in pricing from one place to another. If consumers do not know how much something costs, it is difficult to shop around. Two cases exemplify this problem.

In the first case, an Arizona woman was stung by a scorpion and needed several antivenom serum injections (Alltucker 2011). The serum, which is produced by a Mexican company, costs around $100 per treatment. But it is a rare (called orphan) drug, and the cost of it is heavily inflated when it crosses the border into the United States and has to go through all the linkages and approval steps in the American healthcare system. The hospital involved charged the woman over $15,000 per dose, so the cost to the patient could have been as much as $75,000. But there is also variation in the prices charged even in one locale, in this case Phoenix. Prices varied from $7,900 to more than $15,000. In some cases, hospitals refused to say what they charged. Hospitals reported that they do not and have not recovered the full charges (Alltucker 2011).

A similar, though a bit different, incident occurred to a colleague of ours (Oakeson 2012). A baby was born to his wife and him. States mandate a series of blood tests of the newborn for a variety of possible conditions. When the tests came back, there was a positive finding for cystic fibrosis. That necessitated a second screening, which was negative. The family was charged $665 for each test, most of which was covered by the employer's health insurance costs. But the wife was curious and angered by the charges. She inquired and found that the test, conducted by a state laboratory, cost $65. So the charge to them and their insurance was ten times the actual cost of the test. The hospital stated that there are other costs involved, such as taking the blood, sending it to the state laboratory on the other side of the state, getting and interpreting results, and then billing. The wife complained, and the hospital agreed to reduce some of the costs.

One interesting part of this story is the variation in charges for the test. The other major hospital system in the city charges $531. A system about ninety minutes away charges $149, and another system about thirty minutes away charges $96 for the same procedure (Oakeson 2012).

A Competitive Strategy

An alternative strategy, with linkages to some of the policy proposals in the twentieth century, focuses on the greater use of markets (Rushefsky 2008). Goodman (2012), the president of the National Center for Policy Analysis, has long argued that the healthcare system contains perverse incentives that have led to the kind of system we currently have. For Goodman, a system that allows patients/consumers to make their own choices and to self-insure, along with changes that would make pricing transparent, would modify the incentives in the system. Examples of such plans are health savings accounts (HSAs), similar to individual retirement accounts. People would put money into those accounts to help pay for their healthcare costs and then take out a high-deductible health insurance policy to cover the more expensive needs. This would, to use Goodman's phrase, "empower patients" (2012, 143).

Goodman further suggests changes in insurance policies depending on the healthcare needs. For example, for the less expensive primary care needs, patients would assume full costs (which could be paid from the patient's health savings account). Another example he uses is cancer. He suggests that people pay for their own cancer screenings. If cancer is found, then the insurance policy would pay. This is somewhat similar to an idea put forth by Luft (2008). Goodman's basic point is to get the incentives right, to allow markets to work, to use price indicators, and to give both patients and providers the freedom to make decisions.

A STRATEGY FOR CONTROLLING COSTS

Controlling healthcare costs is never going to be easy, nor, like the "global war on terror," is there an end in sight. But there are some promising strategies. One such strategy has been offered by Davis (2005), president of the Commonwealth Fund. She suggests ten steps that concentrate on the supply side of health, which, she argues, have been successfully implemented in other countries.

The first step is better management of people with chronic conditions. One of several examples she provides is that better management of people with diabetes could reduce hospitalizations. The second step is to note that there is strong regional variation in how medical conditions are treated. Reducing the variations could save considerable funds. It would require better record keeping and sharing of data about such things as provider charges and patient outcomes.

Third, Davis suggests that there is overuse of medical procedures. More education for both providers and patients would help. The fourth step is very intriguing: Davis recommends that insurers and public programs stop reimbursing providers for medical errors, what she calls "comorbidity adjustments." This could save billions of dollars and also signal the need to providers to be more careful.

The fifth step is a simple one, which we have briefly mentioned in this chapter and in chapter 4: negotiate prices for pharmaceuticals. Davis recommends allowing Medicare to negotiate prices. Sixth is to reduce administrative costs by standardizing insurance procedures. She writes:

Private insurance companies have "overhead" of about 12 to 15 percent of revenues. Simplifying and standardizing private insurance could reduce administrative expenses. Hospitals, physicians, and other healthcare providers incur major administrative expenses as a result of variations across insurers and public programs in terms of benefits covered, payment regulations, conditions of provider participation, and coverage policies. Standardizing products and promoting common practices across all private and public insurers could save hospital and physician administrative costs. (Davis 2005)

The seventh recommendation, which follows from some of the earlier ones, is to make use of evidence-based medicine in making medical decisions. The eighth step is to make sure that every person has a regular provider who will be responsible for the care of the patient. This is known as primary care management, and Davis cites studies indicating savings from such programs.

The ninth step, again related to some of the earlier recommendations, is to reduce duplication of tests and paperwork. And the last recommendation is to implement information technology that would help avoid duplication and errors and assist in continuity of care.

Davis notes that the changes would save money while at the same time reducing provider income and possibly reducing jobs. This statement suggests, again, one of the major problems of reform in the healthcare field: every dollar spent on healthcare is a dollar of revenue or income for someone. Nevertheless, Davis suggests that the savings from these changes could be used to improve the system: cover the uninsured, pay for new information technology, expand screening programs, and so forth. Perhaps some combination of demand and supply controls might be the way to go.

CONCLUSION

This chapter has examined various regulatory and competitive strategies by the federal and state governments and the private sector to contain healthcare costs. Federal strategies aimed at health planning and peer reviews have proved to be failures. There is some evidence that the competitive strategy of HMOs has lowered costs to enrollees and reduced their hospitalization rates. However, the impact of Medicare managed care on containment of overall healthcare costs has been very limited, though perhaps the Medicare Advantage program will have more success. The changeover from a retrospective payment to a prospective payment system for Medicare reimbursements to hospitals, through the DRGs, has reduced the average length of hospital stays and has slowed the growth rate in hospital costs for the initial years of PPS. Medicare costs have continued to climb upward, however, and the PPS has had a limited impact on overall healthcare costs. The growth rate in the Medicare program has not shown any decline or slowdown.

State efforts in cost containment have had a limited impact on overall healthcare costs. State rate-setting programs have shown mixed results. States' attempts to replace the fee-for-service system with a negotiated or competitively bid fixed-price arrangement for Medicaid services, as in California and Arizona, have shown some success in reducing costs. There is no denying the fact that state governments' push in the direction of Medicaid managed care has paid some dividends, as reflected in savings materialized and a slowed growth rate in spending for the Medicaid program. Ever-increasing Medicaid costs have led states to cut back their programs, but the impact of such changes is that fewer people will be covered.

Private-sector innovations have also resulted in some healthcare cost containment. However, cost-shifting, utilization reviews, and increased reliance on HMOs and PPOs present a potential concern about access and equity. Wellness programs are increasing but are still not widespread among all industries.

Overall, a combination of regulatory and competitive strategies has produced some success in slowing the growth rate of healthcare spending. A number of factors are likely to influence its future direction.

First, government efforts to formulate health policies directed toward cost containment must be made in a political environment. Just as in any other public policy area, the interplay between various interest groups and partisan conflicts leads to the formulation of policies built on compromises, bargaining, and consensus building, which fail to produce the desired results.

Second, the value of cost containment inevitably comes into conflict with the cherished values of access and high-quality care in American culture. Almost all government programs aimed at cost containment have also attempted to ensure access and quality of care. Public opposition is likely to be high in any program that attempts to reduce access or lower the quality or number of services provided. Furthermore, many healthcare providers are likely to oppose rationing of health services.

Third, demographic changes are likely to create further pressures for more, not less, spending. The baby boom generation began to reach retirement age in 2010, resulting in a dramatic increase in the number of elderly people in our society. This is going to accelerate demand for healthcare resources.

Finally, technological advances in medicine are likely to continue at a rapid pace. Medical technology is very expensive, and it is one of the major contributors to increases in healthcare costs. We, as a society, have come to value medical technology regardless of the cost and regardless of the benefits it brings. Advances in medical technology have helped prolong life, and in some instances have eased pain and suffering, but they cannot cure many major illnesses. Nevertheless, the general public clings to the glimmer of hope offered by medical technology, and society's notions of health, life span, and life itself have changed. Until we as a society learn to resolve these value conflicts, future prospects for healthcare cost containment remain tenuous.

One change that might have an impact is to look at the incentives in the system. While the evidence on the perverse incentives of health insurance is perhaps more mixed than Goodman (2012) and others acknowledge, incentives are important. One reform would be to change the payment mechanism to a more bundled or global system and away from fee-for-service. Another change is to take to heart the findings of the Institute of Medicine study (Smith et al. 2012) and find ways to reduce waste, fraud, and abuse in the system. This might create a more efficient, high-quality system with fewer adverse events.

We leave this chapter by considering what Baumol (2012) calls the "cost disease." He compares healthcare (and education) to products such as computers and automobiles. The latter have seen great productivity increases and consequently decreases in costs. Consider the abilities of computers in the 1970s and compare them to computers in the 2000s. In the latter period, computers have much more capability, but the costs are lower than thirty years prior. Healthcare has certainly seen some productivity increases, but the costs have certainly not come down. What is the difference?

Healthcare and education, much more than the manufacturing of computers, requires personal service. It is difficult, though in some cases not impossible, to replace humans with machines in the delivery of healthcare services. Healthcare and education are part of what Baumol calls the "stagnant sector" (2012, 24–25). He argues that increases in the real price of healthcare services will continue, and continue to evade meaningful cost controls.

But this is not necessarily bad news, Baumol argues. He states that continued improvements in the sectors where prices are falling will allow us to afford the continued increased cost of healthcare. We will be spending less money in some sectors and more in others. The two will balance out. Baumol (2012) does not see this as a pessimistic perspective. Yes, healthcare costs will continue to rise, but we can afford it. Perhaps, he might say, we should just relax.

One last observation. Increases in healthcare spending have slowed dramatically in the 2009–2012 period, with decreases being seen before 2009. In 2009–2011, healthcare spending per capita grew at an annual rate of 3.1 percent. This compares to 7.4 percent for the 1980–2009 period (Ryu et al. 2013). The question becomes why.

One possibility is the recession that began in 2007 and the slow recovery that began in 2009. With more people out of jobs and out of health insurance, the use of healthcare would decline. If this is the case, then the slowdown would be temporary (Ryu et al. 2013). Another possibility is that, as we have seen, employers are increasingly engaged in cost-shifting to employees. That would also depress healthcare spending.

Ryu et al.'s (2013) analysis suggests that other factors were involved, and therefore it is possible that the slowdown could be more lasting. While their evidence is limited, they suggest that health reform may have had an impact, as changes in payment and organization may also have been a factor. It leads them to be cautiously optimistic.

What if cautiously optimistic turns out to be correct. The implications could be profound. Cutler and Sahni (2013) estimate that if the slowdown continues, we would spend about $770 billion less on healthcare in the 2013–2022 period than is being projected. That would mean less pressure on federal and state budgets and businesses and that households would have more money to spend on other things or to save, which would also positively affect the overall economy.

So if Baumol is correct, then we should not worry about healthcare costs. If healthcare spending per capita and overall continues to increase at a slower rate, then we have less to be concerned about. In the words of that famous philosopher, Alfred E. Neuman, "What, me worry?"

STUDY QUESTIONS

1. What do you think are the most important drivers or causes of increased spending on healthcare in the United States?
2. Which policies discussed in this chapter do you think have been the most effective in restraining cost increases? Which have been the least effective? Why?
3. How effective do you think the Affordable Care Act will be in restraining cost increases? Why? To what extent are perspectives on this question influenced by ideology?
4. To what extent do you think the private sector has done a better job of controlling costs than the public sector? Why?
5. In recent years healthcare spending increases have slowed down. Why do think that has happened? Will this trend continue? Why or why not? If it does continue, what are the implications?

REFERENCES

Aaron, Henry J., and William B. Schwartz. 1984. *The Painful Prescription: Rationing Hospital Care.* Washington, DC: Brookings Institution.
———. 1990. "Rationing Health Care: The Choice Before Us." *Science* 247, no. 4941 (Jan. 26): 418–22.
Abramson, John. 2004. *Overdo$ed America: The Broken Promise of American Medicine.* New York: HarperCollins.
Alltucker, Ken. 2011. "Scorpion Antivenom Has Stinging Cost." *Arizona Republic*, November 11.
Altman, Drew E., and Larry Levitt. 2003. "The Sad History of Health Care Cost Containment as Told in One Chart." *Health Affairs* (October 25): W83–W84.
Altman, Stuart H., and Sanford L. Weiner. 1978. "Regulation as a Second Best Choice." In *Competition in the Health Care Sector: Past, Present, and Future,* Bureau of Economics, U.S. Federal Trade Commission, 421–27. Washington, DC: Government Printing Office.
American Civil Liberties Union. 1998. "Legislative Briefing Kit: Lifestyle Discrimination in the Workplace." Washington, DC: American Civil Liberties Union.

Anders, George. 1996. *Health against Wealth: HMOs and the Breakdown of Medical Trust.* Boston: Houghton Mifflin.

Antos, Joseph R.; Mark V. Pauly; and Gail R. Wilensky. 2012. "Bending the Cost Curve Through Market-Based Incentives." *New England Journal of Medicine* 367, no. 10 (September 6): 954–58.

Appleby, Julie. 2012. "Employers Tie Financial Rewards, Penalties to Health Tests, Lifestyle Choices." *Kaiser Health News,* April 2.

Arrow, Kenneth J. 1963. "Uncertainty and the Welfare Economics of Medical Care." *American Economic Review* 53, no. 5 (December): 851–83.

Atkinson, Graham. 2009. "State Hospital Rate-Setting Revisited." New York: Commonwealth Fund.

Bai, Matt. 2005. "The Framing Wars." *New York Times,* July 17.

Baker, Sam. 2012. "CBO: Federal Healthcare Costs Skyrocketing." *The Hill,* November 8. Online at http://thehill.com/blogs/healthwatch/medicare/266955-cbo-federal-healthcare-costs-skyrocketing.

Bartlett, Bruce. 2012. "A Conservative Case for the Welfare State." *New York Times,* December 25.

Bauman, Patricia. 1976. "The Formulation and Evolution of the Health Maintenance Organization Policy, 1970–1973." *Social Science and Medicine* 10, nos. 3–4 (March–April): 129–142.

Baumol, William J. 2012. *The Cost Disease: Why Computers Get Cheaper and Health Care Doesn't.* New Haven, CT: Yale University Press.

Berk, Marc L., and Alan C. Monheit. 2001. "The Concentration of Health Care Expenditures, Revisited." *Health Affairs* 20, no. 2 (March/April): 9–18.

Bhatia, Anita J. 2000. "Evolution of Quality Review Programs for Medicare: Quality Assurance to Quality Improvement." *Health Care Financing Review* 22, no. 1 (Fall): 69–74.

Bicknell, William J., and Diana C. Walsh. 1976. "Critical Experiences in Organizing and Administering a State Certificate-of-Need Program." *Public Health Reports* 91 (January/February): 29–45.

Bodenheimer, Thomas. 2003. "The Not-So-Sad History of Medicare Cost Containment as Told in One Chart." *Health Affairs* (October 25): W88–W90. Online at healthaffairs.org.

Bodenheimer, Thomas, and Kip Sullivan. 1998, "How Large Employers are Shaping the Health Care Marketplace." *New England Journal of Medicine.* 338, no. 14 (April 12): 1003–1007.

Brawley, Otis Webb, and Paul Goldberg. 2011. *How We Do Harm: A Doctor Breaks Ranks About Being Sick in America.* New York: St. Martin's Press.

Breyer, S. 1979. "Analyzing Regulatory Failure: Mismatches, Less Restrictive Alternatives and Reform." *Harvard Law Review* 92, no. 1: 549–609.

Brink, Susan, and Nancy Shute. 1997. "Are HMOs the Right Prescription?" *U.S. News and World Report* 123, no. 14 (October 13): 60–64.

Brown, Lawrence D. 1986. "Introduction to a Decade of Transition." *Journal of Health Politics, Policy and Law* 11, no. 4 (Winter): 569–83.

Brownlee, Shannon. 2007. *Overtreated: Why Too Much Medicine Is Making Us Sicker and Poorer.* New York: Bloomsbury.

Buchanan, Allen. 1998. "Managed Care: Rationing Without Justice, but Not Unjustly." *Journal of Health Politics, Policy and Law* 23, no. 4 (Winter): 617–34.

Cannon, Michael F., and Michael D. Tanner. 2005. *Healthy Competition: What's Holding Back Health Care and How to Free It.* Washington, DC: Cato Institute.

Cassidy, Robert. 1984. "Can You Really Speak Your Mind in Peer Review?" *Medical Economics* 61 (January 23): 246–62.

Cauchon, Dennis. 2012. "States Rein in Health Insurance Expenses." *USA Today,* October 24.

Centers for Medicare and Medicaid Services. 2006. "Report to Congress: Improving the Medicare Quality Improvement Organization Program—Response to the Institute of Medicine Study." Washington, DC: Centers for Medicare and Medicaid Service.

———. 2011. "Medicare and Medicaid Statistical Supplement 2011." Washington, DC: U.S. Department of Health and Human Services.

Claxton, Gary, et al. 2011. "Employer Health Benefits, 2011 Annual Survey." Menlo Park, CA: Kaiser Family Foundation and Health Research & Education Trust.

———. 2012. "Employer Health Benefits, 2012 Annual Survey." Menlo Park, CA: Kaiser Family Foundation and Health Research & Education Trust.

Cohen, Robin A.; Renee M. Gindi; and Whitney K. Kirzinger. 2012. "Financial Burden of Medical Care: Early Release of Estimates from the Naitonal Health Interview Survey, January–June 2011." Washington, DC: U.S. Department of Health and Human Services, Centers for Disease Control and Prevention.

Congressional Budget Office. 1981. *The Impact of PSROs on Health-Care Costs: Update of CBO's 1979 Evaluation.* Washington, DC: U.S. Government Printing Office.

Conover, Christopher J. 2012. *American Health Economy Illustrated.* Washington, DC: AEI Press.

Cutler, David M., and Nikhil R. Sahni. 2013. "If Slow Rate of Health Care Spending Growth Persists, Projections May Be Off by $770 Billion." *Health Affairs* 32, no. 5 (May): 841–50.

Davidson, Stephen M. 2010. *Still Broken: Understanding the U.S. Health Care System.* Stanford, CA: Stanford Business Books.

Davis, Karen. 2005. "Taking a Walk on the Supply Side: 10 Steps to Control Health Care Costs." New York: Commonwealth Fund.

Davis, Karen; Gerard F. Anderson; Diane Rowland; and Earl P. Steinberg. 1990. *Health Care Cost Containment.* Baltimore, MD: Johns Hopkins University Press.

Davis, Karen, and Cathy Schoen. 1978. *Health and the War on Poverty: A Ten-Year Proposal.* Washington, DC: Brookings Institution.

Davis, Karen, and Kristof Stremikis. 2009. "The Costs of Failure: Economic Consequences of Failure to Enact Nixon, Carter, and Clinton Health Reforms." New York: Commonwealth Fund. Online at www.commonwealthfund.org/Blog/The-Costs-of-Failure.aspx.

Demkovich, Linda E. 1979. "Adding Competition to the Health Industry." *National Journal* 11 (October 27): 1797–1800.

Draper, Debra A., Ann Tynan, and Jon B. Christianson. 2012. "Health and Wellness: The Shift from Managing Illness to Promoting Health." Brief no. 121, June. Washington, DC: Center for Health System Change.

Durenberger, David F. 1982. "The Politics of Health." In *Competition in the Marketplace: Health Care in the 1980s,* ed. James R. Gay and Barbara J. Sax Jacobs, 4. New York: Spectrum Publications.

Eisner, Marc Allen; Jeff Worsham; and Evan J. Ringquest. 2006. *Contemporary Regulatory Policy,* 2d ed. Boulder, CO: Lynne Rienner.

Ellwood, Paul M., Jr. 1971. "Health Maintenance Strategy." *Medical Care* 9 (May/June): 291–98.

Elmendorf, Douglas W. 2009. "Letter to Honorable Max Baucas, Chairman, Committee on Finance, United States Senate." Washington, DC: Congressional Budget Office.

Emanuel, Ezekiel, et al. 2012. "A Systemic Approach to Containing Health Care Spending." *New England Journal of Medicine* 367, no. 10 (September 6): 949–54.

Enthoven, Alain C. 1978a. "Consumer Choice Health Plans" (first of two parts). *New England Journal of Medicine* 298 (March 23): 650–58.

———. 1978b. "Consumer Choice Health Plans" (second of two parts). *New England Journal of Medicine* 298 (March 30): 709–20.

———. 1980. *Health Plan: The Only Practical Solution to the Soaring Cost of Medicare Care.* Reading, MA: Addison-Wesley.

———. 1988. "Managed Competition of Alternate Delivery System." *Journal of Health Politics, Policy and Law* 13, no. 2 (Summer): 305–21.

———. 1993. "The History and Principles of Management Competition." *Health Affairs* 12: 24–48.

Enthoven, Alain C., and Richard Kronick. 1989a. "A Consumer-Choice Health Plan for the 1990s: Universal Health Insurance in a System Designed to Promote Quality and Economy" (first of two parts). *New England Journal of Medicine* 320, no. 1 (January): 29–37.

———. 1989b. "A Consumer-Choice Health Plan for the 1990s: Universal Health Insurance in a System Designed to Promote Quality and Economy" (second of two parts). *New England Journal of Medicine* 320, no. 2 (January 12): 94–101.

———. 1992. "Will Managed Competition Work? Better Care at Lower Cost." *New York Times,* Jan. 25.

Enthoven, Alain C., and Sara J. Singer. 1997. "Markets and Collective Action in Regulating Managed Care." *Health Affairs* 16, no. 6 (November/December): 26–32.

Etheredge, Lynn. 1983. "Reagan, Congress and Health Spending." *Health Affairs* 2, no. 1 (Spring): 14–24.

———. 1997. "Promarket Regulation: An SEC-FASB Model." *Health Affairs* 16, no. 6 (Nov/Dec): 22–25.

Etzioni, Amitai. 2009. "The Capture Theory of Regulation-Revisited." *Society* 46, no. 4 (July): 319–23.

Evans, Robert G. 1983. "Incomplete Vertical Integration in the Health Care Industry: Pseudomarkets and Pseudopolicies." *Annals of the American Academy of Political and Social Science* 468 (July): 60–87.

———. 1997. "Going for the Gold: The Redistributive Agenda Behind Market-Based Health Care Reform." *Journal of Health Politics, Policy and Law* 22, no. 2 (Summer): 427–66.

Falkson, Joseph L. 1980. *HMOs and the Politics of Health Service Reform.* Chicago: American Hospital Association and Robert J. Brady.

———. 1980–81. "Market Reform, Health Systems, and HMOs." *Policy Studies Journal* 9, no. 2: 213–20.

Fish-Parcham, Cheryl. 2006. "Understanding How Health Insurance Prmeiums Are Regulated." Washington, DC: Families USA.

Fleming, Sibley. 2005. "Wellness Programs Lighten Health Costs." *American City & County* 120, no. 3 (March): 8–10.

Frech, H.E., III, and Paul B. Ginsburg. 1988. "Competition Among Health Insurers, Revisited." *Journal of Health Politics, Policy and Law* 13, no. 2 (Summer): 279–91.

Friedman, Milton (with the assistance of Rose D. Friedman). 1962. *Capitalism and Freedom.* Chicago: University of Chicago Press.

Gabel, Jon R., and Alan C. Monheit. 1983. "Will Competition Plans Change Insurer-Provider Relationships?" *Milbank Memorial Fund Quarterly/Health and Society* 61, no. 4 (Fall): 614–40.

Gelman, Judith. 1982. *Competition and Health Planning. An Issue Paper.* Bureau of Economics, U.S. Federal Trade Commission. Washington, DC: Government Printing Office.

Gifford, Kathleen et al. 2011. "A Profile of Medicaid Managed Care Programs in 2010: Findings from a 50-State Survey." Washington, DC: Kaiser Commision on Medicaid and the Uninsured.

Ginsburg, Paul. 2012. "What Is Driving U.S. Health Care Spending? America's Unsustainble Health Care Cost Growth." Washington, DC: Bipartisan Policy Center.

Ginzberg, Eli. 1977. *The Limits of Health Reform: The Search for Realism.* New York: Basic Books.

———. 1982. "Procompetition in Health Care: Policy or Fantasy?" *Milbank Memorial Fund Quarterly/ Health and Society* 60, no. 3 (Summer): 386–98.

Goetzel, Roy Z., et al. 2012. "Ten Modifiable Health Risk Factors Are Linked to More Than One-Fifth of Employer-Employee Health Care Spending." *Health Affairs* 31, no. 11 (November): 2474–84.

Gold, Marsha, et al. 2013 (June). "Medicare Advantage 2013 Spotlight: Enrollment Market Update." Menlo Park, CA: Kaiser Family Foundation.

Gold, Marsha, and Robert Hurley. 1997. "The Role of Managed Care 'Products' in Managed Care Plans." *Inquiry* 34, no. 1 (Spring): 29–37.

Goldhill, David. 2013. *Catastrophic Care: How American Health Care Killed My Father and How We Can Fix It.* New York: Alfred A. Knopf.

Goldman, T.R. 2012. "Health Policy Brief: Eliminating Fraud and Abuse." *Health Affairs,* July 31. Online at http://www.healthaffairs.org/healthpolicybriefs/brief.php?brief_id=72.

Goodman, John C. 1980. *The Regulation of Medical Care: Is the Price Too High?* San Francisco: Cato Institute.

———. 2012. *Priceless: Curing the Healthcare Crisis.* Oakland, CA: Independent Institute.

Goodman, John C., Pamela Villarreal, and Biff Jones. 2011. "The Social Cost of Adverse Medical Events, and What We Can Do About It." *Health Affairs* 30, no. 4 (April): 590–95.

Guglielmo, Wayne J. 2004. "Why Oregon's Rationing Plan Is Gasping for Air." *Medical Economics,* April 19. Online at www.memag.com/memag/article/articleDetail.jsp?id=127172 &pageID=1.

Hacker, Jacob S. 2009. "The Case for Public Plan Choice in National Health Reform: Key to Cost Control and Quality Coverage." Berkeley, CA: Institute for America's Future, Center on Health Economic & Family Security, University of California, Berkeley School of Law.

Hacker, Jacob S., and Theodore R. Marmor. 1999. "The Misleading Language of Managed Care." *Journal of Health Politics, Policy and Law* 24, no. 5 (October): 1033–43.

Havighurst, Clark C. 1970. "Health Maintenance Organizations and the Market for Health Services." *Law and Contemporary Problems* 35, no. 1 (Autumn): 716–95.

———. 1973. "Regulation of Health Facilities and Services by 'Certificate of Need.'" *Virginia Law Review* 59, no. 7 (October): 1143–1233.

———. 1982. *Deregulating the Health Care Industry: Planning for Competition.* Cambridge, MA: Ballinger.

Hayek, Friedrich A. 1944. *The Road to Serfdom.* Chicago: University of Chicago Press.

Herzlinger, Regina. 1997. *Market Drive Health Care: Who Wins, Who Loses in the Transformation of America's Largest Service Industry.* Cambridge, MA: Perseus Books.

Hoffman, Beatrix. 2013. *Health Care for Some: Rights and Rationing in the United States Since 1930.* Chicago: University of Chicago Press.

Holahan, John, et al. 2011. "Containing the Growth of Spending in the U.S. Health System." Washington, DC: Urban Institute.

"How Paul Ryan's New Budget Plan Would Transform Health Care." 2013. Online at www.advisory.com/ Daily-Briefing/2013/03/13/How-Paul-Ryan-latest-budget-plan-would-transform-health-care.

Iglehart, John K. 1980. "The Federal Government as Venture Capitalist: How Does It Fare?" *Milbank Memorial Fund Quarterly/Health and Society* 59, no. 4 (Fall): 656–66.

Kelly, Robert. 2009. "Where Can $700 Billion in Waste Be Cut Annually from the U.S. Healthcare System?" Ann Arbor, MI: Thomson Reuters.

Kelly, Robert, and Raymond Fabius. 2010. "A Path to Eliminating $3.6 Trillion in Wasteful Healthcare Spending." Ann Arbor, MI: Thomson Reuters.

Kennedy, Louanne, and Bernard M. Baruch. 1980–81. "Health Planning in an Age of Austerity." *Policy Studies Journal* 9, no. 2 (Special #1): 232–41.

Klein, Ezra. 2009. "Administrative Costs in Health Care: A Primer." *Washington Post*, July 7.

Kliff, Sarah. 2012. "Graph of the Day: States Are Spending More on Medicaid, Less on Education." *Washington Post*, December 14.

Kofman, Mila, and Karen Pollitz. 2006. "Health Insurance Regulation by States and the Federal Government: A Review of Current Approaches and Proposals for Change." Washington, DC: Health Policy Institute, Georgetown University.

Krugman, Paul. 2009. "Administrative Costs." *New York Times*, July 6.

Laffont, Jean-Jacques, and Jean Tirole. 1991. "The Politics of Government Decision-Making: A Theory of Regulatory Capture." *Quarterly Journal of Economics* 106, no. 4 (November): 1089–1127.

Lallemand, Nicole Cafarella. 2012. "Health Policy Brief: Reducing Waste in Health Care." *Health Affairs,* December 13.

Lambrew, Jeanne M. 2005. "Making Medicaid a Block Grant Program: An Analysis of the Implications of Past Proposals." *Milbank Quarterly* 83, no. 1 (March): 41–63.

Lazarus, David. 2005. "Costs of Health Care Drag America Down." *San Francisco Chronicle,* June 8.

Lee, Jason S., and Laura Tollen. 2002. "How Low Can You Go? The Impact of Reduced Benefits and Increased Cost-Sharing." *Health Affairs,* June 19: W229–W241. Online at http://content.healthaffairs.org/content/early/2002/06/19/hlthaff.w2.229.full.pdf+html.

Leeds, Helen. 1996. *Health Care Cost Containment in the States: Strategies from the 1990s.* Washington, DC: Intergovernmental Health Policy Project.

Lewin and Associates. 1975. *Evaluation of the Efficiency and Effectiveness of the Section 1122 Review Process.* Springfield, VA: National Technical Information Service.

Leyerle, Betty. 1994. *The Private Regulation of American Health Care.* Armonk, NY: M.E. Sharpe.

Luft, Harold S. 2008. *Total Cure: The Antidote to the Health Care Crisis.* Cambridge, MA: Harvard University Press.

Mahar, Maggie. 2006. *Money-Driven Medicine: The Real Reason Health Care Costs So Much.* Boston: HarperCollins.

Makary, Marty. 2012. *Unaccountable: What Hospitals Won't Tell You and How Transparency Can Revolutionize Health Care.* New York: Bloomsbury Press.

Marmor, Theodore, and James Morone. 1979. "HSAs and the Representation of Consumer Interests: Conceptual Issues and Litigation Problems." *Health Law Project Library Bulletin* 4 (April): 117–28.

McClure, Walter. 1981. "Structural and Incentive Problems in Economic Regulation of Medical Care." *Milbank Memorial Quarterly/Health and Society* 59, no. 2 (Spring): 107–44.

———. 1983. "The Competitive Strategy for Medical Care." *Annals of the American Academy of Political and Social Science* 469 (July): 30–47.

McConnell, Grant. 1970. *Private Power & American Democracy.* New York: Vintage Books.

McGregor, Maurice. 1981. "Hospital Costs: Can They Be Cut?" *Milbank Memorial Fund Quarterly/Health and Society* 59, no. 1 (Winter): 89–98.

McNeil, Richard, Jr., and Robert E. Schlenker. 1975. "HMOs, Competition and Government." *Milbank Memorial Fund Quarterly/Health and Society* 53, no. 1 (Spring): 195–224.

Mechanic, David. 1997. "Muddling Through Elegantly: Finding the Proper Balance in Rationing." *Health Affairs* 16, no. 5 (September/October): 83–92.

"Medical Errors Cost Health Care System Billions." 2011. *National Journal,* April 7. Online at http://nationaljournal.com/healthcare/medical-errors-cost-health-care-system-billions-20110407.

Menzel, Paul T. 1990. *Strong Medicine: The Ethical Rationing of Health Care.* New York: Oxford University Press.

Mick, Stephen S., and John D. Thompson. 1984. "Public Attitude Toward Health Planning Under the Health Systems Agencies." *Journal of Health Politics, Policy and Law* 9, no. 4 (Winter): 783–800.

Miller, Annetta, and Elizabeth Bradburn. 1991. "Shape Up—or Else." *Newsweek*, July 1, 42–43.

Miller, Robert H., and Harold S. Luft. 2002. "HMO Plan Performance Update: Analysis of the Literature, 1997–2001." *Health Affairs* 21, no. 4 (July/August): 63–86.

Moran, Donald W. 1981. "HMOs, Competition, and the Politics of Minimum Benefits." *Milbank Memorial Fund Quarterly/Health and Society* 59, no. 2 (Spring): 190–208.

———. 1997. "Federal Regulation of Managed Care: An Impulse in Search of a Theory?" *Health Affairs* 16, no. 6 (November/December): 7–21.

Morone, James A., and Lawrence R. Jacobs, eds. 2005. *Healthy, Wealthy, & Fair: Health Care and the Good Society.* New York: Oxford University Press.

National Institute for Health Care Management Foundation. 2012 (June). "Government Spending for Health Entitlement Programs." Washington, DC: National Institute for Health Care Management.

New, Michael J. 2005. "The Effect of State Regulations on Health Insurance Premiums: A Preliminary Analysis." Washington, DC: Center for Data Analysis, Heritage Foundation.

Newhouse, Joseph P., et al. 1981. "Some Interim Results from a Controlled Trial of Cost-Sharing in Health Insurance." *New England Journal of Medicine* 305, no. 25 (December): 1501–7.

Nix, Kathryn. 2012. "Comparative Effectiveness Research Under Obamacare: A Slippery Slope to Health Care Rationing." Backgrounder no. 2679. April 12. Washington, DC: Heritage Foundation.

Noll, Roger G. 1975. "The Consequences of Public Utility Regulation of Hospitals." In *Controls on Health Care,* ed. Institute of Medicine, 32–48. Washington, DC: National Academy of Sciences.

Oakeson, Sarah. 2012. "Parents Protest Cost of Newborn's State-Mandated Blood Test." *Springfield News-Leader*, May 27.

Oberlander, Jonathan. 2007. "Health Reform Interrupted: The Unraveling of the Oregon Health Plan." *Health Affairs* 26, no. 1 (December 19): W96–W105.

Patel, Kant, and Mark E. Rushefsky. 1998: "The Health Policy Community and Health Care Reform in the United States." *Health: An Interdisciplinary Journal for the Social Study of Health, Illness and Medicine* 2, no. 4 (October): 459–84.

———. 2002. *Health Care Policy in an Age of New Technologies.* Armonk, NY: M.E. Sharpe.

———. 2005. *The Politics of Public Health in the United States.* Armonk, NY: M.E. Sharpe.

Pauly, Mark V. 1978. "Is Medical Care Different?" In *Competition in the Health Care Sector: Past, Present and Future,* ed. Bureau of Economics, U.S. Federal Trade Commission, 19–48. Washington, DC: Government Printing Office.

Pollard, Michael R. 1981. "The Essential Role of Antitrust in a Competitive Market for Health Services." *Milbank Memorial Fund Quarterly/Health and Society* 59, no. 2 (Spring): 256–68.

Porter, Eduardo. 2012. "Rationing Health Care More Fairly." *New York Times*, August 21.

President's Council on Bioethics. 2003. "Organ Transplantation: Ethical Dilemmas and Policy Choices." Staff background paper. Washington, DC: Executive Office of the President. Online at www.bioethics.gov/background/org_transplant.html.

Reid, T.R. 2009. *The Healing of America: A Global Quest for Better, Cheaper, and Fairer Health Care.* New York: Penguin Press.

Reinhold, Robert. 1993. "A Health-Care Theory Hatched in Fireside Chats." *New York Times,* February 10.

Relman, Arnold S. 2005. "The Health of Nations." *New Republic* 232, no. 4703 (March 7): 23–30.

Rice, Thomas. 1997. "Can Markets Give Us the Health System We Want?" *Journal of Health Politics, Policy and Law* 22, no. 2 (1997): 383–426.

Robinson, James. 2002. "Renewed Emphasis on Consumer Cost Sharing in Health Insurance Benefit Design." *Health Affairs,* March 20: W139–W154. Online at http://content.healthaffairs.org/content/early/2002/03/20/hlthaff.w2.139.full.pdf+html?sid=22e66a47-4233-40d0-913e-be6f60a76555.

Roemer, Milton I. 1961. "Hospital Utilization and the Supply of Physicians." *Journal of the American Medical Association* 178, no. 1 (December): 933–89.

Rosenberg, Charlotte L. 1984. "Why Doctor-Policing Laws Don't Work." *Medical Economics* 61 (March 5): 84–96.

Rosoff, Arnold J. 1975. "Phase Two of the Federal HMO Development Program: New Directions After a Shaky Start." *American Journal of Law and Medicine* 1, no. 2 (Fall): 209–43.

Roy, Avik. 2011. "The Myth of Medicare's 'Low Administrative Costs.'" *Forbes*, June 30. Online at www.forbes.com/sites/aroy/2011/06/30/the-myth-of-medicares-low-administrative-costs/.

———. 2012. "Liberals Are Wrong: Free Market Health Care Is Possible." *The Atlantic*, May 18. Online at www.theatlantic.com/business/archive/2012/03/liberals-are-wrong-free-market-health-care-is-possible/254648.

Rushefsky, Mark E. 1981. "A Critique of Market Reform in Health Care: The Consumer-Choice Health Plan," *Journal of Health Politics, Policy and Law,* 5 (August): 720–41.

———. 2008."Shaping the Demand for Health Care: Consumer-Choice Versus Consumer-Driven." Paper prepared for the 2008 Annual Meeting of the American Political Science Association, Boston, MA.

———. 2013. *Public Policy in the United States,* 5th ed. Armonk, N.Y.: M.E. Sharpe.

Ryu, Alexander, et al. 2013. "The Slowdown in Health Care Spending in 2009–2011 Reflected Factors Other Than the Weak Economy and Thus May Persist." *Health Affairs* 32, no. 5 (May): 835–40.

Safire, William. 2009. " Bending the Curve." *New York Times,* September 11.

Salkever, David S., and Thomas W. Bice. 1976. "The Impact of Certificate of Need Controls on Hospital Investment." *Milbank Memorial Fund Quarterly/Health and Society* 54, no. 1 (Spring): 185–214.

———. 1979. *Hospital Certificate-of-Need Controls: Impact on Investment, Costs and Use.* Washington, DC: American Enterprise Institute for Public Policy Research.

Scandlen, Greg. 2011. "Myth Busters #1: Roemer's Law." Online at http://healthblog.ncpa.org/myth-busters-1-roemer%E2%80%99s-law/.

Schneider, William. 1998. "Fear of Bureaucrats Strikes Again." *National Journal* 30, no. 29 (July 18): 1714.

Smith, Mark, et al., eds. 2012. "Best Care at Lower Cost: The Path to Continuously Learning Health Care in America." Washington, DC: Institute of Medicine, National Academy of Sciences.

"Special Issue: Kenneth Arrow and the Changing Economics of Health Care." 2001. *Journal of Health Politics, Policy, and Law* 26, no. 5 (October): 823–1204.

Starr, Paul. 1980. "Changing the Balance of Power in American Medicine." *Milbank Memorial Fund Quarterly/Health and Society* 58, no. 1 (Winter): 166–72.

———. 1982. *The Social Transformation of American Medicine.* New York: Basic Books.

———. 2013. *Remedy and Reaction: The Peculiar American Struggle over Health Care Reform.* New Haven, CT: Yale University Press.

Stigler, George. 1971. The Theory of Economic Regulation. *Bell Journal of Economics* 2, no. 1 (Spring): 3–21.

Stone, Deborah. 2012. *Policy Paradox: The Art of Political Decision Making,* 3d ed. New York: W.W. Norton.

———. 2005. "How Market Ideology Guarantees Racial Inequality." In *Wealthy, Healthy, & Fair,* ed. James A. Morone and Lawrence R. Jacobs, 65–89. New York: Oxford University Press.

Timble, Justin W., et al. 2012. "Five Reasons that Many Comparative Effectiveness Studies Fail to Change Patient Care and Clinical Practice." *Health Affairs* 31, no. 10 (October): 2168–75.

Tyson, Laura D'Andrea. 2012. "Evidence vs. Ideology in the Medicare Debate." *New York Times*, August 24.

U.S. Department of Health, Education, and Welfare. 1971. *Toward a Comprehensive Health Policy for the 1970s: A White Paper.* Washington, DC: U. S. Government Printing Office.

Van Den Bos, Jill, et al. 2011. "The $17.1 Billion Problem: The Annual Cost of Measurable Medical Errors." *Health Affairs* 30, no. 4 (April): 596–603.

Varlova, John. 1984. "A $2.2 Million Lesson in the Perils of Peer Review." *Medical Economics* 61 (December 24): 56–61.

Varner, Theresa, and Jack Christy. 1986. "Consumer Information Needs in a Competitive Health Care Environment." *Health Care Financing Review* (Annual Supplement): 99–104.

Vladeck, Bruce C. 1977. "Interest Group Representation and the HSAs: Health Planning and Political Theory." *American Journal of Public Health* 67, no. 1 (January): 23–29.

———. 1981. "The Market vs. Regulation: The Case for Regulation." *Milbank Memorial Fund Quarterly/Health and Society* 59, no. 2 (Spring): 209–23.

———. 1984. "Variation Data and the Regulatory Rationale." *Health Affairs* 3, no. 2 (Summer): 102–9.

Volsky, Igor. 2009. "Why Comparative Effectiveness Research Will Not Ration Care." Online at http://thinkprogress.org/health/2009/06/19/170836/republicans-offer-redundant-cer-amendments/?mobile=nc.

Wachter, Robert M., and Kaveh G. Shojania. 2004. *Internal Bleeding: The Truth Behind America's Epidemic of Medical Mistakes.* New York: Rugged Land.

Wehr, Elizabeth. 1979. "Competition in Health Care: Would it Bring Costs Down?" *Congressional Quarterly* 37, no. 31 (August 4): 1587–95.

Weinder, Jonathan P., and Gregory de Lissovoy. 1993. "Razing a Tower of Babel: A Taxonomy for Managed Care and Health Insurance Plans." *Journal of Health Politics, Policy and Law* 18, no. 1 (Spring): 75–103.

Weiner, Stephen M. 1982. "On Public Values and Private Regulation: Some Reflections on Cost Containment Strategies." *Milbank Memorial Fund Quarterly/Health and Society* 59, no. 2 (Spring): 269–96.

Welch, H. Gilbert, Lisa M. Schwartz, and Steven Woloshin. 2011. *Overdiagnosed: Making People Sick in the Pursuit of Health.* Boston: Beacon Press.

Wolf, Charles, Jr. 1979. "A Theory of Non-Market Failures." *Public Interest* 55 (Spring): 114–23.

Woolhandler, Steffie, Terry Campbell, and David U. Himmelstein. 2003. "Costs of Health Care Administration in the United States and Canada." *New England Journal of Medicine* 349, no. 8 (August 21): 768–75.

Yegian, Jill Matthews. 2004. "Conference Summary: Setting Priorities in Medical Care Through Benefit Design and Medical Management." *Health Affairs,* May 19: W4-300–W4-304. Online at healthaffairs. org. content/early2004/05/19/hlthalff.w4.300.citation.

Zatkin, Steve. 1997. "A Health Plan's View of Government Regulation." *Health Affairs* 16, no. 6 (November/December): 33–35.

9

CONTEMPORARY ISSUES IN HEALTH POLICY

MEDICAL TECHNOLOGIES: LAW, POLITICS, RELIGION, AND ETHICS

Technology assessment has been highly fragmented and sporadic in the United States. As a society, we have failed to make systematic decisions about research and development of medical technologies such as: Who should determine whether a particular technology should be developed and funded? On what basis should individuals be provided access once a technology is available in the marketplace? What level of technological intervention is appropriate for a specific medical problem? What is the total impact of the rapid spread of high-cost medical technologies on society in general and on the U.S. healthcare system in particular (Blank 1989)?

The rapid proliferation of halfway technologies and spiraling healthcare costs also raises many legal and ethical dilemmas that we as a society must confront and address through public policies related to healthcare. The term "dilemma" in the popular sense is understood to mean a difficult choice between two or more alternatives. An ethical dilemma refers to a situation in which all the alternatives are morally problematic, that is, each alternative seems to involve a wrong act or action (Van DeVeer 1987).

Advancements in medical technology and ethical concerns raised by such technologies have given rise to the field of bioethics. "Bioethics is the application of ethical analysis to issues of health care" (Pillar 1992, 419). Debates about ethical issues raised by medical technology start during the developmental stage and continue through the experimental and implementation stages. Arthur Caplan (1989) has argued that society's obligation to provide healthcare exists if four conditions are present. One is that the person is clearly in need of help. The second condition is that help exists and is available. Third, the person in need wants help, and our obligation to help is stronger if such help does not harm others. Finally, there is a reasonable chance of actually providing some help, that is, doing some good.

Any discussion of the ethical uses of medical technology must also take into consideration special concerns about respecting the patient's dignity. Threats to a patient's dignity can arise from a variety of sources, such as substandard conditions of treatment (inadequate space, equipment, etc.), healthcare providers' decisions and behaviors, and the clash of innovative technology with traditional standards (Pillar 1992).

Unfortunately, the use of many new medical technologies raises a complex set of legal, ethical, policy, and political issues that are not easily resolved. The discussion about medical technology is never purely a matter of science. Political beliefs and ideologies, along with religious values, constantly enter into debates about assisted reproductive and life-sustaining technologies. Assisted reproductive technologies raise some fundamental questions about who is a parent, what is informed consent, what is contractual surrogacy, who is legally and financially responsible for a child conceived through assisted reproductive technologies, especially when a child does not have any genetic connection to his/her parents. Similarly, life-sustaining technologies raise questions such as what is life, what is quality of life, when does life begin, does an individual have the right to refuse the use of life-sustaining technologies to prolong his/her life, that is, whether persons have a right to die with dignity. Can religious beliefs and healthcare needs or necessities coexist? The current healthcare market has seen an unprecedented growth in the size and influence of religious health systems, which can affect access to assisted reproductive health services and end-of-life decisions. Religious hospitals are the fastest-growing type of hospital system in the United States. There has also been an expansion of religiously affiliated managed care plans (Fogel and Rivera 2003). Religiously sponsored managed care plans often do not provide certain services, such as contraception. Refusal clauses, such as the 1973 Church amendment, allow healthcare providers to opt out of providing abortion or sterilization services (Fogel and Rivera 2003).

In the following pages, we discuss some of the ethical dilemmas raised by medical technology in two areas. First, we look at the ethical dilemmas raised by assisted reproductive and life-sustaining technologies. Second, we end this section with a broad discussion of the issue of healthcare rationing and the ethical concerns it raises.

THE BEGINNING OF LIFE: ASSISTED REPRODUCTIVE TECHNOLOGIES

The growth of assisted reproductive technologies (ARTs) has raised a host of legal and ethical issues regarding decision making and the use of such technologies. ARTs are noncoital methods of conception involving manipulation of both eggs and sperm. Such technologies challenge people's basic values and create intense controversy. "Reproductive technologies include drugs, devices, and medical interventions that control reproduction and/or prevent sexually transmitted infections (STIs), such as contraceptives and products used to enhance fertility, as well as techniques for in vitro and in vivo fertilization" (Woodsong and Severy 2005, 194). In other words, reproductive technologies include those designed to prevent unwanted pregnancies and births as well as those aimed at enabling a couple to conceive and bear children (Beckman and Harvey 2005).

During 2006–2010, among all U.S. women ages fifteen to forty-four (in all marital statuses), 10.9 percent suffered from impaired fecundity, according to the Centers for Disease Control and Prevention (CDC). During the same period and in the same age group, 7.4 million women or 11.9 percent received fertility services ("Key Statistics from the National Survey of Family Growth" 2011). According to the CDC's 2010 ART success rates, 147,260 ART cycles were performed at 443 reporting clinics in the United States during 2010, resulting in 47,090 live births (deliveries of one or more living infants) and 61,564 infants ("Assisted Reproductive Technology [ART]" n.d.). Only about 1 percent of pregnancies in the United States originate from artificial insemination or in vitro fertilization (Northup 2011). However, they often raise complex legal and ethical issues.

According to the Centers for Disease Control and Prevention (2004), ARTs include all fertility treatments in which both eggs and sperm are manipulated. In general, ART procedures involve surgically removing eggs from a woman's ovary, combining them with sperm in the laboratory, and returning them to a woman's body or donating them to another woman. The three types of ART are: (1) in vitro fertilization (IVF), (2) gamete intrafallopian transfer (GIFT), and (3) zygote intrafallopian transfer (ZIFT). In an IVF procedure, eggs are removed from the ovary and fertilized with semen in a laboratory. The resulting embryos are transferred back into the woman's uterus through the cervix. GIFT uses a fiber-optic instrument called a laparoscope to guide the transfer of fertilized eggs and sperm (gametes) to the woman's fallopian tubes through a small incision. ZIFT involves fertilizing a woman's eggs in the laboratory and then using a laparoscope to guide the transfer of the fertilized eggs (zygotes) to the woman's fallopian tubes.

Procedures that involve only the use of fertility drugs or intrauterine insemination (IUI), generally known as artificial insemination (AI), are not considered ARTs. In this procedure a woman takes medicine to stimulate egg production without the intention of having the eggs retrieved. Both IVF and IUI allow a couple to contract with a third-party woman (a surrogate) who carries the child. The child is genetically linked to one or both partners (a couple). The third-party woman relinquishes the child to the couple after the child is born (Beckman and Harvey 2005).

Since the birth of the first test-tube baby, about a million children have been conceived with high-tech help. Some studies have suggested that babies born through ARTs might be at higher risk of birth defects and genetic disorders. However, a comparative study of the health of ART babies and naturally conceived babies by a panel of experts from Johns Hopkins University, the American Society for Reproductive Medicine, and the American Academy of Pediatrics found that ART babies do not have a greater risk of birth defects, cancer, or problems with growth or psychological development (Stenson 2005).

It is important to understand the role of consent and contract with respect to ARTs. In their context, consent forms serve a dual purpose. First, the consent form provides information about the medical risks, benefits, and alternatives. Second, it provides for selection of options regarding the disposition of any excess embryos that may be created. It is this duality and the enforceability of the terms of the consent that have often led to legal disputes between divorcing couples who no longer agree about the disposition of excess embryos remaining after the fertility treatment. In most cases, courts have viewed such consent agreements as contracts between both members of the couple (Elster 2005).

In contractual parenting (surrogacy), the intended parents (couple) contract with a woman to carry a child for them and to relinquish that child after birth. In traditional surrogacy, the surrogate is impregnated with the sperm of the male partner of the intended parents through artificial insemination. This is also called AI surrogacy. In this situation, the impregnated woman is both the genetic and birth mother and the intended father is the genetic father. Gestational surrogacy is the term used when the female partner of the intended parents has viable eggs but is unable to successfully carry a pregnancy to term. Here, the intended mother's eggs are fertilized with her male partner's sperm in a laboratory using IVF, and the embryo is then implanted into the surrogate mother's uterus. In this case, the surrogate has no genetic connection to the child and the intended parents are the genetic parents (Ciccarelli and Ciccarelli 2005).

The use of ART produces complicated policy dilemmas that often challenge social, political, and legal understanding of family, property, and reproductive rights. ARTs have created many challenges to traditional notions of family building and the legal construction of parenthood. Medical technology in this area has advanced much more rapidly than the law's ability to address questions of rights and responsibilities that arise between the parties. It raises questions such as who should control stored embryos when the couple who created them no longer agree on their disposition. Who should be recognized as a child's legal parent or parents when donated gametes or a surrogate are involved in the child's conception? How do we define motherhood when one woman provides an egg to be gestated by another woman once it has been fertilized? Can an intended parent escape liability for child support when a child has been conceived through third-party assisted reproduction if the couple eventually get a divorce? When a couple has divorced, who has the right to determine if preserved embryos will be used to create a baby after the embryos have been frozen but before they have been implanted (Ciccarelli and Ciccarelli 2005; Elster 2005)?

Reproductive Technologies, Courts, and Right to Conceive and Bear Children

Courts have tended to support the premise that intent, as reflected in consent forms or contracts, should define the relationships created through collaborative reproductive arrangements. In the case of *Davis v. Davis* in 1992 in Tennessee, where the issue involved was who should have control over stored embryos in the case of a divorcing couple, the court determined that the party seeking to avoid procreation (in this case the husband) should prevail. *Kass v. Kass,* a 1998 New York case, involved a situation in which seven embryos remained frozen when a couple divorced. The wife wanted control over the embryos so she could continue her attempts to have a child, but the husband objected on the ground that he did not want to have a child with his ex-wife. The appellate court enforced a written directive signed by the couple at the time the embryos were created that specified that the embryos should be donated for scientific research. However, in the 2000 case of *A.Z. v. B.Z.* in Massachusetts, the court refused to enforce a prior written disposition agreement, arguing that the consent form did not state that the husband and wife intended it to act as a binding agreement. In a 2001 New Jersey case, *J.B. v. M.B.,* where a husband in a divorce case wanted, over the wife's objection, to exercise control over the stored embryos, the court concluded that the party choosing not to become a biological parent should prevail (Daar 2001; Elster 2005).

With respect to contract and surrogacy, one of the most well-known cases is that of Baby M in 1988. This case involved a surrogacy arrangement in which the surrogate not only gestated the child but was also the genetic contributor. The surrogate, Mrs. Whitehead, turned over the baby to the intended parents (Mr. and Mrs. Stern). However, the very next day, she changed her mind. Fearing she might commit suicide, the intended parents gave the child back to Mrs. Whitehead. Four months later, the baby was forcibly taken by the police from a home where Mrs. Whitehead was hiding the baby. Mr. Stern filed a complaint seeking possession and custody of the child and enforcement of the terms of the surrogacy contract. The trial court found that the surrogacy contract was valid and granted sole custody to Mr. Stern. The appellate court argued that the surrogacy contract was equal to baby selling and found the contract to be void and unenforceable. However, the court also concluded that the surrogate was the mother of the child. The court granted custody of the child to Mr. Stern but remanded the case back to the lower court for determination of the nature and extent of Mrs. Whitehead's visitation rights (Ciccarelli and Ciccarelli 2005; Foote, Reibstein, and Figueroa 1998).

In the 1989 case of *In re Marriage of Buzzanca,* a couple—John and LuAnne Buzzanca—had selected an egg donor and a sperm donor and contracted with a gestational surrogate party to carry the resultant embryo. The couple was divorced before the child was born, and the husband argued that he had no child support obligation. The trial court ruled that the child had no legal parents, since neither John nor LuAnne had any genetic or biological link to the child nor had they adopted the child. The appellate court, however, reversed the decision on the ground that the child would never have been born without the actions undertaken by the Buzzancas and thus determined that they were the legal parents (Elster 2005).

Judicial resolutions of some issues raised by ARTs is incomplete because courts have addressed specific legal issues raised in specific cases. However, not all issues raised by such technologies have been addressed. There exists a wide gap between the incomplete nature of judicial resolutions and the lack of comprehensive public policy in this area at either the national or state levels. For example, the U.S. Supreme Court's due process jurisdiction has firmly established the right to avoid bearing children via its decisions announcing the right to contraceptive use and right to abortion. However, courts have said little about the right to have children. Often women who have been convicted of a crime and sentenced are required, as a part of probationary conditions, to use specific forms of birth control or to simply avoid procreating, restricting their reproductive rights. In recent years there is an increased trend toward appellate court acceptance of such probationary conditions by focusing not on the constitutionality of these conditions but rather on their reasonableness in the particular case. This in turn has created inconsistencies across courts (Nairn 2010).

Another issue raised is whether children born through ARTS are entitled to information about their biological origins. Child-focused research has begun to address the psychological implications for children conceived through ARTs. The psychological issues related to assisted human reproduction have not been addressed adequately, demonstrating the gap between emerging technologies and law. Some have called for a uniform legal approach that will recognize the right of all children to have access to information about their identity and conception for their psychological well-being (Moyal and Shelley 2010).

Another area where laws are needed is embryo donation. When a person or couple uses in vitro fertilization to create embryos, they often end up with more embryos than they need. Most fertility clinics require such people to specify what they want done with the remaining embryos. They can elect to destroy them, store them, donate for research, or donate to other persons for artificial reproduction. Yet, there are still hundreds of thousands of frozen embryos in fertilization clinics in the United States. Litigation related to embryo donations is limited. As embryo donations increase, the need for legislation that would help predictability for parents and guidance for courts becomes all the more necessary (Miller 2010).

Also, current laws are inadequate to allocate the paternal obligations between two men involved in the artificial insemination process. If a man is financially responsible for a child during his lifetime, that child is generally classified as his heir if he dies intestate. Once an artificially conceived child is allowed to inherit from his/her father, the issue to be resolved becomes, from which father does the child have the legal right to inherit? The child may have the right to inherit from the husband of his/her mother or from the man who donated the sperm that resulted in his/her conception (Lewis 2009). There is also a controversy over whether a child conceived by way of ARTs after the death of one parent is considered a child of that parent for inheritance purposes (Suppon 2010).

Under current laws relating to child support, it is typically presumed that it is in the "child's best interest" to receive financial support from mothers as well as fathers. Thus, those men who never consented to the sexual act that caused the pregnancy are nevertheless liable for the support of the resulting child. These include men who become fathers as a result of statutory rape and also adult males who become fathers as a result of a sexual assault or having their sperm stolen and used by a woman for the purposes of self-insemination.

Consider the following two examples. In the first case, an Alabama man attended a party at the home of a female friend. He arrived at the party intoxicated and shortly thereafter passed out in a bed at the female friend's house. After several months, his female friend boasted to several people that she had engaged in sexual intercourse with this man while he was unconscious and how the evening saved her a trip to the sperm bank. The women gave birth to a child, and genetic testing confirmed the biological paternity of the man she had intercourse with. Another case involved a Louisiana man who, in 1983, was visiting his sick parents at the hospital. One evening a nurse offered to perform oral sex on him, but only if he wore a condom. At the end of their encounter, the nurse had agreed to dispose of the used condom, but the man never saw her actually do it. Nine months later, the nurse gave birth to a child, and genetic testing revealed a 99.9994 percent probability that the man she had performed oral sex on was the father. In both these cases, courts ordered each man to pay child support for the resulting child. These are examples of men who had been forced into fatherhood and were forced to pay child support despite not having consented to the act that led to insemination. Under the child's best interest standard, fathers are strictly liable for any biological child regardless of wrongful conduct by the mother, and courts have been unwilling to allow fathers to even raise lack of consent as a defense against liability (Higdon 2012).

However, this notion of child's best interest is undermined by laws regulating artificial insemination. In the context of artificial insemination, a man becomes the legal father of an artificially inseminated child only if he affirmatively consents to fatherhood. Few states have comprehensive laws to establish parentage of children born using ARTs, even though thousands of such children are born each year and courts are forced to apply antiquated laws. In 2008, the Uniform Probate Code (UPC) added two sections in complicated parentage and inheritance issues that arise in the field of ARTs. These sections address donation of all reproductive material; apply to all participants in ARTs; address ARTs, assisted insemination, maternity, and also situations in which the intended parents have divorced or one parent has died before the pre-embryos are implanted. However, it is not clear whether states will enact these new UPC sections, because earlier efforts to enact uniform laws (the Uniform Parentage Act) dealing with the parentage of children born through the use of ARTs have met with very little success. Very few states have enacted comparable provisions of the Uniform Parentage Act (Knaplund, 2012).

Courts and Reproductive Technologies and Preventing Unwanted Pregnancies and Births

As mentioned previously, reproductive technologies include those aimed at enabling a couple to conceive and bear children as well as those designed to prevent unwanted pregnancies and births. Medical interventions that help control reproduction include contraceptives and abortion. In 1943, the U.S. Supreme Court—in the first reproductive rights case, *Skinner v. Oklahoma*—struck down vasectomies as criminal punishment and recognized the right to have offspring as a sensitive and important area of human rights (Northup 2011). However, as we noted earlier, often women who have been convicted of a crime and sentenced are required as a probationary condition to use specific forms of birth control or to simply avoid procreating, restricting their reproductive rights. In individual cases, courts have often declared such probationary conditions/restrictions to be reasonable. Thus, courts have been inconsistent in this area.

In 1965, in *Griswold v. Connecticut,* the U.S. Supreme Court recognized that married couples have a constitutional right to use contraception within a "zone of privacy" that encompasses marital relationship. The Court's decision focused on the special nature of the marital relationship (Northup 2011). In 1972, in *Eisenstadt v. Baird,* the U.S. Supreme Court extended the right to use contraceptives to unmarried individuals and justified it on the ground that the "right of privacy" includes the right of an individual, married or single, to be free from unwarranted governmental intrusion into matters that fundamentally affect a person such as a decision whether to have a child. Thus, the Supreme Court made a transition from a zone of privacy based on a marital relationship to zone of privacy protecting all individuals from unwarranted government intrusion into the most private decisions.

The U.S. Supreme Court in 1977, in *Casey v. Population Services International,* relying on the same reasoning, struck down New York State's ban on the sale of contraceptive to minors under sixteen years of age. However, the Court did not recognize a right for minors to engage in sexual activity and validated the state's interest in curbing teenage promiscuity. The Court found it unreasonable for the state to prescribe pregnancy (by denying contraceptive) and the birth of an unwanted child as a punishment for fornication (Northup 2011). The Affordable Care Act requires health insurance plans to cover contraceptive services. This has created much controversy and objections by religious organizations that argue that requiring them to provide and/or pay for contraceptive services goes against their religious beliefs and violates their First Amendment right to freedom of religion. The controversy surrounding this issue is discussed more extensively in the chapter on the Affordable Care Act (chapter 11.)

In the 1973 landmark case, *Roe v. Wade,* the U.S. Supreme Court made abortion legal for women in the United States. The Court's decision recognized a woman's right to choose an abortion under the constitutional right to privacy (Farmer 2008). The Court stated that not only does the right to privacy include activities related to marriage, family relationships, and childbearing and education, but also it is broad enough to include a woman's decision to terminate pregnancy (Northup 2011). Ever since the establishment of abortion rights, the political controversy has continued, as opponents of abortion rights have continuously sought either to get the Supreme Court to overturn the *Roe v. Wade* decision or to at least impose more restrictions on access to abortion (Gerber Fried 2008). While opponents have failed thus far to get the Supreme Court to overturn *Roe v. Wade*, they have succeeded in getting the courts to impose more restrictions on abortion rights. In a major setback to *Roe v. Wade*, the U.S. Supreme Court in 1992, in *Planned Parenthood v. Casey,* adopted an undue burden test under which the plaintiffs have the burden of proof and have to show that they faced a substantial obstacle to get an abortion in order to win or prevail in their challenge to an abortion restriction (Farmer 2008). In 2003, President George W. Bush signed into law the Partial-Birth Abortion Ban Act. The law was found unconstitutional in the U.S. District Courts for the Northern District of California, the Southern District of New York, and the District of Nebraska. The attorney general of the United States, Alberto Gonzales, appealed the decisions to the U.S. Court of Appeals and ultimately to the U.S. Supreme Court. The Supreme Court in 2007 in *Gonzales v. Carhart* and its companion case, *Gonzales v. Planned Parenthood,* overturned the U.S. District Court decisions and upheld the constitutionality of the Partial-Birth Abortion Ban Act of 2003. This was the first time that the court upheld a specific abortion-ban procedure. Writing for the majority, Justice Kennedy further ruled that the law did not impose an undue burden on the due process right of women to obtain an abortion despite the fact that the law did not provide an exception for when a woman's health was in danger. Justice Kennedy also discussed the potential for women to experience "psychological harm" following an abortion (Farmer 2008).

During its eight years (2001–2009), the George W. Bush administration appointed many conservative judges to the federal courts. According to Sylvia Law, leading scholar in the field of law and women's right at New York University School of Law, reproductive rights litigators mostly lost in the last two decades (Farmer 2008). Opponents of abortion have succeeded in initially turning abortion and reproductive healthcare issues into a moral issue and in the last decade or so arguing that women need more protection from their own decision making (Farmer 2008).

As a result of several court rulings and state legislative actions, women seeking abortions today are required to undergo a state-mandated sonogram, counseling, and waiting periods (Farmer 2008). As of February 2012, thirty-five states required counseling, eleven states required ultrasound services, thirty states have established a twenty-four-hour waiting period, and twenty-eight states required parental consent involving a minor, while another nineteen required parental notification ("Abortion Laws" 2012). These actions have led some proponents of abortion rights to argue that continuing to rely on the *Roe v. Wade* decision to protect abortion rights with an increasingly unsympathetic Supreme Court is a losing strategy and that advocates of abortion rights instead should focus more on state constitutional law, as many state constitutions are textually broader and suggest a broader intent to protect autonomy or gender equality (Moss 2008).

ARTs, Religion, and Politics

Most state laws in general consider the husband or male partner, with his consent to insemination, to be the legal father of any child born of the procedure. However, only eight states specifically address the issue of egg donation by women. These statutes recognize the recipient couple as the legal parents of any child born through such an arrangement but do not confer parental rights or obligations upon the donor of the eggs (Elster 2005). Fourteen states have amended their constitutions to prevent gay couples from having the right to marry. However, hundreds of gay couples are finding ways to create families with or without marriage through surrogates. The definition of "parent" varies considerably from state to state ("Definition of 'Parent' and Related Variations in Child Welfare" n.d.). Most state laws also vary with respect to embryo and gamete disposition ("Embryo and Gamete Disposition Laws" 2007).

In addition to technologies that help overcome infertility problems, a host of technologies make it possible for a woman to prevent unwanted pregnancies and limit unwanted births. These include female hormones delivered via injection or pill, mechanical devices placed in the uterus, and surgical procedures (Beckman and Harvey 2005). These technologies are not high-tech like the ones that help conceive children. Of course, the 1973 *Roe v. Wade* decision established the right to legalized abortion in the United States.

Religious groups have been very active in influencing the public regarding issues such as procreation, infertility treatments, and abortion (Schenker 2005). Birth control technologies such as contraceptives and abortions have been very controversial. Some religious groups view many of these technologies as unacceptable. For example, the Catholic Church characterizes abortion and contraception as immoral (Beckman and Harvey 2005).

Reproductive technologies have received a great deal of public attention and debate because politics and religious belief systems have become intertwined in public policymaking. This is reflected in a very mobilized and well-funded prolife movement that advocates that legal personhood be conferred at conception (Solinger 1998). Social conservatives have also pushed for more restrictive policies with respect to fertility treatments as well as stem cell research (see chapter 2).

The fact that these new technologies are often viewed by some as "playing God" brings religious interests to the policy debate (Russo and Denious 2005). Pro-life advocates have lobbied for defunding organizations such as family planning clinics that provide abortions, and pro-life advocates also have pushed for extending the gag rule, which prohibited medical professionals from discussing abortion as an alternative in family planning counseling. Even appointments to scientific advisory panels have become political, and there has been unprecedented interference by politicians, policymakers, and ideological groups with the peer-review process used by government agencies such as NIH, combined with attempts to distort, misrepresent, and/or suppress scientific findings that run counter to the conservative social agenda (Russo and Denious 2005). The politics of reproductive technologies is characterized by conservative religious groups promoting policies that attempt to limit women's access to these technologies. On the other side of the political spectrum, advocates for women's rights have lobbied for public policies designed to increase access to reproductive technologies (Beckman and Harvey 2005).

In the field of bioethics, a philosophical consensus called the Great Bioethics Compromise was developed in 1970 to keep a close eye on scientific innovations and their social implications, and to apply the brakes now and then through regulations and guidelines (Moreno 2005). The President's Council on Bioethics was founded in November 2001, and as science became politicized, there was a breakdown of this consensus on the council (Moreno 2005). This is reflected in several of the council's reports on cloning, stem cell research, and reproductive technologies, in which it has taken a much more conservative position. The council's report on reproductive technologies recommended that Congress impose unspecified penalties on clinics for not reporting assisted reproduction as required under federal statute. It urged professional societies to create unspecified enforcement mechanisms to force compliance with ethics and practice guidelines. Furthermore, it recommended that Congress enact eight prohibitions on the practice and research related to assisted reproduction and called for a temporary moratorium on these practices and research but, ironically, proposed no time limit or sunset provisions (President's Council on Bioethics 2004). In effect, the indefinite duration of these prohibitions would make them functionally a permanent ban. However, the council failed to provide any meaningful analysis for its recommendations, and the report failed to address important ethical and policy questions (Wolf 2004). The council's work reflected a shift in balance toward using law to ban and penalize and away from a more moderate and rights-oriented approach (Wolf 2004).

The President's Council on Bioethics ceased to exist when, in November 2009, President Barack Obama created a new commission by an executive order, the Presidential Commission for the Study of Bioethical Issues ("History of Bioethics Commissions" n.d.). The commission acts as an advisory panel for the nation's leaders in medicine, science, ethics, religion, law, and engineering. It advises the president on bioethical issues arising from advances in biomedicine and related areas of science and technology ("About the Commission" n.d.). The commission has not issued any new reports or studies on the subject of reproductive health since its creation.

ARTs, Ethics, and Law

Aside from the legal and political issues, ARTs raise a host of ethical issues, reflected in a plethora of literature on this topic (Baruch, D'Adamo, and Seager 1988; Bayles 1984; Beck and Cowley 1994; Cohen 1996; Cohen and Taub 1989; Devine 2004; Feinberg and Feinberg 2010; Garrett, Baillie, and Garrett 1989; Gilbert, Tyler, and Zackin 2005; Harwood 2007; Henifin 1993; Hoffman, D'Adamo, and Seager 1988; Kolata 1994; Nichols 1993; Pollard 2009; Raymond 1993; Robertson 1994; Ryan 2001; Salzman and Lawler 2012; Shannon 2004; Strathern 1992).

The ethical and legal issues are likely to get only more complicated in the future because of several new trends. First, there is a growing movement of surrogate mothers who are choosing to carry children for gay couples over traditional families. Second, many surrogates, whether for heterosexual or gay couples, work as gestational carriers, meaning that they bring children to term but not with their own genetic material (Bellafante 2005). Finally, there is a growing trend of harvesting sperm from cadavers. Ethicists seem to be in agreement that whatever is done should reflect what the dead person would have wanted. When a wife makes the request to extract sperm from the deceased husband because she wants to conceive a child, it raises few questions. But, even in such a case, the issue can get very complex, as demonstrated by an example that arose in Florida. In this case, two weeks after the wedding, the husband was killed in an automobile accident. At the request of the widow and her mother, physicians extracted a sperm sample from the deceased husband. Soon after, the wife met someone new, and she decided not to use her husband's sperm to conceive. However, her mother wanted to carry the child herself, that is, she wanted to give birth to her own grandchild! The sperm bank refused to release the sample (Bauman 1997).

Ethical issues of fertility and reproduction can be examined from two perspectives—that of the infertile individual who wants to have a child and that of perspective of a community—and these two perspectives do not always coincide. ARTs raise issues not only of autonomy and personal choice but also of malfeasance and justice (Baird 1996). Some of the ethical issues raised by ARTs are the following.

In the United States the private marketplace plays a major role in this field. One of the important issues is how to control and balance private commercial activity to protect vulnerable consumer interests, since commercial organizations, which are solely interested in making money, have no reason or incentive to balance conflicting interests. What role should government play in protecting consumer interests through regulations and a system of accountability? How should collective resources be allocated in a society? Is there a danger of devaluing human dignity if the process of having children and creating families becomes commercialized? Are ARTs luxury items, or services that should be underwritten by a society? How do we ensure that everyone in society has equal access to ARTs (Baird 1996; Shanner and Nisker 2001)?

Other ethical questions raised by ARTs: What constitutes informed consent, specifically when it is applied to posthumous assisted reproduction? Is it ethical to retrieve spermatozoa from patients who are in a coma? What is the best way to respect the wishes of the deceased donor and to protect the interests of the unborn child? Could gametes be considered property, and what is the definition of paternity in cases of children born in such circumstances (Bahadur 2004; Benagiano 2003)? Are embryos persons, property, objects, or a unique category (Shanner and Nisker 2001)?

Since, in some ARTs, as many as five adults may play a parenting role (genetic mother and father—ovum and sperm provider; the gestational mother; and the intended social parents) and each operating in his or her best interest, how do we protect the offspring, who could not consent to an arrangement that may significantly shape their developing identities? In such arrangements, donor anonymity protects the privacy of donors and recipients, but what about the rights of the offspring with regard to having access to his or her genetic medical history (Shanner and Nisker 2001)?

Finally, one of the most important issues is ensuring equal access to medically necessary and appropriate ARTs and avoiding overuse, both at the micro and macro level. At the macro level, issues of accountability, cost-effectiveness, and justice become important in the distribution of resources. At the micro level, issues of autonomy, personal choice, and responsibility play an important role.

Advocates for ARTs argue that many factors, such as lack of uniform laws governing surrogacy, lack of health insurance coverage for expensive infertility treatment, lack of information about available options, and the like restrict women's access to ARTs. Furthermore, acceptability of ARTs is influenced by factors such as culture, social class, ethnicity, age, and sexual preference. Some analysts suggest that only a group of well-off non-Hispanic white women have access to many of the available options, but not disadvantaged women (Beckman and Harvey 2005). Approximately 12 percent of U.S. women of childbearing age have received assistance for infertility. Since 1980s, only fifteen states have passed laws that require insurers to either cover or offer coverage for infertility diagnosis and treatment ("State Laws Related to Insurance Coverage for Infertility Treatment" 2012).

THE END OF LIFE: LIFE-SUSTAINING TECHNOLOGIES AND THE RIGHT TO DIE

Courts and the Right to Die

Today's life-support technologies are capable of keeping patients alive for a long time, even when they have no chance of regaining consciousness. Mechanical ventilators can keep patients breathing, and artificial nutrition and hydration can sustain severely debilitated and dying individuals for many years. This raises the specter of individuals being kept alive in a vegetative, helpless state, sustained by a host of tubes and machines (Cantor 1993). The questions of who shall live, who shall die, and who shall decide raise difficult ethical and legal issues (Buckley 1990). Some well-publicized court cases help illustrate the complexities involved in such situations.

The Karen Quinlan Case

One of the early cases to highlight the ethical and legal dilemmas involved a New Jersey woman named Karen Quinlan who, at the age of twenty-one, slipped into a deep coma. She was hooked up to a respirator in a hospital. Her doctor informed her parents that their daughter was never going to come out of her coma because her brain was severely damaged. She might not necessarily die and, kept on a life-support system, might live for many years. Quinlan's parents asked the doctor to turn off the respirator. The doctor refused, and they went to court. The judge in the lower court disagreed with the parents. They then appealed the decision to the New Jersey Supreme Court and, on March 31, 1976, the parents won the right to have the respirator turned off. The state supreme court ruled that Karen had a constitutional right of privacy, which her guardian could assert on her behalf (Peters 1990). Ironically, it turned out that Karen Quinlan was able to breathe on her own. She was moved from a hospital to a nursing home, where she died in June 1985.

The Elizabeth Bouvia Case

A different dilemma was presented in the case of twenty-six-year-old Elizabeth Bouvia, who in September 1983 admitted herself to the psychiatric unit of California's Riverside General Hospital.

She had had a very difficult life and was almost totally paralyzed from cerebral palsy. Once admitted, she asked for assistance in starving herself to death. What was unique about this case is that Ms. Bouvia was not terminally ill but wanted the hospital staff to provide her with pain-killing drugs and hygienic care while she waited to die. The hospital refused. Elizabeth Bouvia went to court and lost; the court ordered that she be force-fed. On April 7, 1984, she left the hospital. The hospital bill for 217 days, excluding physicians' fees, was more than $56,000; it was paid by the hospital and the state of California. After repeated court appeals, the California Court of Appeals found in her favor. The court said that she could refuse life-sustaining medical treatment. The court ruled that the right of a competent adult patient to refuse treatment is a constitutionally guaranteed right. After her victory, Bouvia changed her mind and did not kill herself (Pence 1995; Shreve and Kailes 1990).

The Nancy Cruzan Case

Another case involved thirty-two-year-old Nancy Cruzan of Missouri. She had been in a persistent vegetative state for seven years since a car accident. Her prognosis was hopeless. Her cerebral cortex had atrophied, but she was not dead, and she could have lived in such a vegetative state for many more years. The cost of her medical treatment was about $130,000 a year, paid by the state. In 1987 her parents requested that Nancy's feeding tube be removed so she could die. A lower court granted the request in July 1988, but the state supreme court in November 1988 reversed the decision, agreeing with the state's argument that the state of Missouri had an "unqualified" interest in preserving life. According to the court, the state's interest was not in the "quality" of life; the state's interest was in "life" (Angell 1990).

Nancy's parents appealed the decision to the U.S. Supreme Court. In June 1990, the court, in a five-to-four decision, agreed with the decision of the Missouri Supreme Court. The court found that a competent person has a constitutionally protected right to refuse life-saving hydration and nutrition. If the person is incompetent, the court ruled, the state is entitled to require rigorous proof that this person, when competent, would have requested removal of a feeding tube in the event of his or her future incompetence. According to the court, the state of Missouri was entitled to require clear and convincing proof that a surrogate decision maker was choosing what Ms. Cruzan herself, when competent, desired (Meilaender 1990).

It is interesting to note that the court based its ruling not on the ground of a fundamental privacy right, as was the case with Quinlan, but on the ground of a liberty interest. The court argued that the state's interests must be balanced against the interests of the patient (McCormick 1990; Peters 1990). On December 14, 1990, the Circuit Court of Jasper County, Missouri, declared that there was clear and convincing evidence that if Nancy Cruzan were mentally able, she would want to terminate her nutrition and hydration and she would not want to continue her present existence. Her parents were authorized to remove the nutrition and hydration tube. After the removal of the feeding tube, Nancy Cruzan died on December 26, 1990.

On the other side of the ledger was a case in Minnesota in which a public hospital sought permission to remove a respirator from an eighty-seven-year-old woman who was in a persistent vegetative state. The hospital argued that continuing treatment was not in the woman's best medical or personal interest; however, the family of the woman opposed the request. The family won, and the woman died a year later (Kamisar 1991).

The Barbara Howe Case

The case of Barbara Howe, who suffered from Lou Gehrig's disease, reflects the complexities involved in such cases. She was admitted to Massachusetts General Hospital in November 1999.

She had told her daughter, doctors, and nurses to do whatever was necessary to keep her alive as long as she could appreciate her family. Over the years, Barbara Howe continued to lose control of her body. A ventilator breathed for her and a feeding tube nourished her. She was no longer able to communicate with her caregivers what she wanted. Blue Cross and Blue Shield of Massachusetts had stopped covering her hospital stay in 2003. Howe's longtime doctor and nurses believed that she was in pain and that keeping her alive was tantamount to torture. However, Barbara Howe's oldest daughter, Carol Carvitt, who was her healthcare proxy, disagreed. Barbara Howe had become stuck in a limbo that no one foresaw. Howe's doctors and nurses wanted to withdraw life support, but the probate and family court in February 2005 found that there was no sufficient cause to overturn Carol Carvitt as her mother's healthcare proxy (Kowalczyk 2005a). However, the judge urged Carvitt to think about her mother's best interest. Finally, in March 2005, Carol Carvitt agreed to terminate life support to her mother by June 30, 2005 (Belluck 2005). Barbara Howe passed away on Saturday, June 4, twenty-six days before a court settlement that would have allowed the hospital to turn off her life support (Kowalczyk 2005b).

One subtle change that has occurred in right-to-die cases is that most of the earlier cases involved a conflict between family members and hospitals in which the families pressed to let their loved ones die, while the hospitals tried to keep the patient alive. However, in the past decade or so, in instances when family members and hospitals have clashed, it is often the family members who want to continue life support and aggressive medical treatment while the doctors believe it is time to stop. This is the case partly because extraordinary medical advances have given hope to families. Patients and families are often skeptical or suspicious of doctors' and hospitals' intentions and believe that a life-support system may be terminated for economic reasons (Belluck 2005). The technology of artificial hydration and nutrition (AHN) that helps prolong life has become common practice. The question has become who decides when technology actually stops benefiting and becomes harmful to the patient. Drs. Jeffrey Ponsky and Michael Gauderer, who created the current techniques for inserting feeding tubes into patients in 1979, recently stated that the procedure has gone too far, because the feeding tubes are often used for patients who do not have any potential for recovery. They never imagined that their procedure would lead to such a massive ethical dilemma. Feeding tubes are used 250,000 times a year and have become a routine part of end-of-life care (Milicia 2005).

The Terri Schiavo Case

No right-to-die case received more national attention and generated more political maneuvering than the tragic case of Terri Schiavo in Florida. On February 25, 1990, she suffered a cardiac arrest, apparently caused by a potassium imbalance. Her heart stopped temporarily, cutting off oxygen to her brain and causing brain damage. In June 1990, a court appointed Terri's husband, Michael Schiavo, her guardian. Terri's parents, the Schindlers, did not object, because, according to all the reports, Michael and the Schindlers got along splendidly. In November 1992, Michael Schiavo won a malpractice case against one of Terri's doctors for misdiagnosing Terri's medical condition. He was awarded $750,000 for Terri's care and $300,000 for himself.

It is at this point that the relationship between Michael Schiavo and his in-laws, the Schindlers, started to turn sour, and they began to have disagreements over the use of this money and Terri's treatment. In 1993, the Schindlers attempted to remove Michael as Terri's legal guardian, but the state district court refused. On March 1994, a court-appointed guardian said that Michael Schiavo had acted appropriately and attentively toward his wife. In May 1998, Michael Schiavo filed a petition to remove Terri Schiavo's feeding tube. The Schindlers were strongly opposed to the removal. A second court-appointed guardian, in December 1998, reported that Terri Schiavo was in a persistent vegetative state with no chance for improvement. However, he also indicated that

Michael Schiavo's decision making might be influenced by the potential to inherit the remainder of Terri's estate.

The court trial began on January 20, 2000. Terri Schiavo had not left a living will. Her husband Michael testified that in their past conversations, Terri had indicated that she would not want to live her life this way. Based on the testimony of her husband and two other individuals, Judge George Greer ruled on February 11, 2000, that Terri would have chosen to have her feeding tube removed. He ordered the removal of the feeding tube but later stayed his order to give the Schindlers an opportunity to appeal. On January 24, 2001, the Florida Second District Court of Appeals upheld Judge Greer's ruling permitting removal of Terri's feeding tube. On April 18, 2001, the Florida Supreme Court elected not to review the decision of the second district court of appeals (Cerminara and Goodman 2005; "Indepth: Terri Schiavo, Schiavo Timeline" 2005; "Key Dates in Schiavo Right-to-Die Case" 2005; "Terri Schiavo Timeline" 2005).

For the next several years, the struggle between Michael Schiavo and the Schindlers continued, as appeal after appeal was filed by the two sides. After many appeals, Judge Greer ordered the removal of the feeding tube to take place on October 15, 2003. On October 7, 2003, Florida Governor Jeb Bush filed a brief in federal district court supporting the Schindlers' efforts to stop the removal of the feeding tube. On October 10, 2003, a federal judge ruled that he lacked jurisdiction to hear the case. Terri Schiavo's feeding tube was removed on October 15, 2003 (Cerminara and Goodman 2005).

It was at this point that politics took over. As the Schindlers' legal options dwindled, Catholic, evangelical, and anti-abortion groups seized on their cause, helping to publicize it and fund it. Starting in 2001, the anti-abortion Life Legal Defense Foundation paid for the Schindlers' legal costs. All this helped get the attention of politicians eager to show off their pro-life credentials (Campo-Flores 2005).

Within days of the feeding tube removal, the Florida legislature passed a special law, referred to as "Terri's Law," that gave Governor Jeb Bush the power to issue a "one-time stay" in certain cases ("Can States Intervene in Medical Decisions?" 2004). On October 21, 2003, Governor Bush issued an executive order to reinstate the feeding tube. On October 29, 2003, Michael Schiavo, joined by the American Civil Liberties Union, filed a lawsuit in state court arguing that "Terri's Law" was unconstitutional. In September 2004, a unanimous Florida Supreme Court declared "Terri's Law" unconstitutional on the grounds that it violated the principle of separation of powers between the executive, legislative, and judicial branches of government (Hallifax 2004; Sutton 2004). Governor Bush filed a petition seeking U.S. Supreme Court review of the Florida Supreme Court's decision. On January 24, 2005, the U.S. Supreme Court refused to grant such a review (Roig-Franzia 2005).

At this point, conservatives decided to nationalize the issue. Representative Dave Weldon (R-FL) and Senator Mel Martinez (R-FL) pushed for Congress to pass a broadly worded law aimed at due process law for disabled people like Terri. House Majority Leader Tom DeLay (R-TX) and Senate Majority Leader Bill Frist (R-TN) provided the leadership. The U.S. Senate wanted a narrowly worded bill specifically addressing Terri Schiavo's situation. After compromises, on March 21, 2005, Congress passed a narrowly crafted law that applied only to Terri Schiavo. The law, called "An Act of the Relief of the Parents of Theresa Marie Schiavo," gave the U.S. District Court for the Middle District of Florida jurisdiction to hear and review the Schiavo case. President Bush signed it into law the same day (Hulse 2005). This set in motion a series of lawsuits filed by the Schindlers in federal district courts and appeals to the U.S. Court of Appeals and the U.S. Supreme Court in an effort to have the feeding tube reinserted in Terri Schiavo. The federal courts consistently rejected the Schindlers' various constitutional claims and refused to reinstate the feeding tube. The U.S. Court of Appeals and the U.S. Supreme Court similarly denied such requests on several appeals (Goodnough 2005a, 2005b; Goodnough and Liptak 2005a, Goodnough and Liptak 2005b; Long 2005).

The feeding tube was removed on March 18, 2005. The parents of Terri Schiavo appealed to Governor Bush to intervene further in the case (Lyman 2005). Responding to political pressure from the conservatives, Governor Bush asked the Florida Department of Children and Families (FDCF) to obtain custody of Terri Schiavo in light of allegations of spousal abuse brought against Michael Schiavo. After holding a hearing, Judge Greer on March 24, 2005, issued a restraining order prohibiting the FDCF from removing Terri Schiavo from the hospice or reinstating the feeding tube. The Schindlers decided to end their federal appeals (Associated Press 2005). Terri Schiavo died on March 31, 2005. President Bush called upon the nation to build a culture of life. The Vatican issued a statement calling Ms. Schiavo's death a violation of the sacred nature of life that shocked the conscience (Goodnough 2005c).

An autopsy of Terri Schiavo backed her husband's contention that she was in a persistent vegetative state. The medical examiner's office stated that Terri Schiavo had suffered massive and irreversible brain damage and was blind. It also found no evidence that she was strangled or otherwise abused as had been alleged by her parents and others ("Schiavo Autopsy Finds No Sign of Trauma" 2005; "Schiavo Autopsy Shows Irreversible Brain Damage" 2005). Senator Mel Martinez, who had pressed Terri Schiavo's case in Congress the most, stated that he had since had second thoughts about Congress's involvement in the case. Senate Majority Leader Bill Frist, an M.D., voiced his opinion on the Senate floor on March 17, 2005, that after viewing videotape of Ms. Schiavo, it was clear to him that she was responsive. Democrats cited the autopsy results as proof that Ms. Schiavo's husband and critics of federal government intervention in the case had been vindicated. Dr. Frist angrily stated that he had never made a formal diagnosis and had nothing to retract, and he did not respond to questions about the autopsy findings (Kornblut 2005b).

For the social conservatives who argue that sanctity of life trumps everything else, Terri Schiavo's case came along at the right time—their ascendancy in U.S. politics. The election of November 2004 had resulted in the reelection of George W. Bush to the presidency and strengthened Republican control of both houses of Congress (Stolberg 2005a). They did not like the outcome in Schiavo's case. Pat Robertson called the removal of the feeding tube "judicial murder," while Tom DeLay called it "an act of medical terrorism" (Eisenberg 2005). DeLay threatened retribution against judges who had refused to intercede in the case (Hulse and Kirkpatrick 2005).

It is ironic that, in the fall of 1988, when his own father, Charles Ray DeLay, was in a coma and kept alive by intravenous lines and oxygen equipment, Tom DeLay had joined his family in a difficult decision to let his father die (Roche and Verhovek 2005). It is also interesting to note that President Bush, who flew into the nation's capital from a vacation in Crawford, Texas, to sign the law that allowed federal review of the Terri Schiavo case, had signed a law in 1999, while he was governor of Texas, that allowed attending physicians, in consultation with a hospital bioethics committee, to discontinue life-support efforts when a patient's condition was hopeless. In fact, only about two weeks prior to Terri Schiavo's death, a hospital in Houston, Texas, acting under this law with the concurrence of a judge, disconnected a critically ill baby from life support over his mother's objections. According to medical ethicists, this was the first such case in the United States (Nichols 2005).

Representative Christopher Shays (R-CT), one of the only five Republicans in the House who had voted against Congress's emergency legislation throwing the Terri Schiavo case into the federal courts, declared that "this Republican Party of Lincoln has become a party of theocracy" (Eisenberg 2005, 23).

Since the Terry Schiavo case there has not been any other major case that has reached the U.S. Supreme Court dealing with the right-to-die issue.

Public Opinion and the Right to Die

The tragic case of Terri Schiavo also resonated with the public, as they found themselves contemplating difficult philosophical issues and matters of trust, such as what constitutes a life worth living? To whom should I delegate my own end-of-life decisions? How should I face death

(Mehren and Verhovek 2005)? A number of polls suggested that Americans had strong feelings about the Terri Schiavo case and that social conservatives had miscalculated public opinion. In a CBS poll of a nationwide random sample of 737 adults (interviewed by telephone between March 21 and 22, 2005), 66 percent said that the feeding tube should not be reinserted into Terri Schiavo. Sixty-one percent said that the case should not be heard by the U.S. Supreme Court. A larger number, 82 percent, indicated that Congress and the president should not be involved in the Schiavo matter. Seventy-two percent said that members of Congress got involved to advance their own political agenda and not because they really cared about Terri Schiavo. Only 34 percent said that they approved of Congress's job performance—the lowest rating Congress had received since December 1997. A strong majority of 75 percent said that the government should stay out of deciding life-support cases ("Poll: Keep Feeding Tube Out" 2005).

What is even more interesting is that, according to a 2005 poll conducted by *Time* magazine, most Americans, including those who call themselves born-again or evangelical Christians, supported the decision to remove Terri Schiavo's feeding tube. Overall, 59 percent of all respondents and 53 percent of those who called themselves evangelical Christians supported removal of the feeding tube. Seventy-five percent said that it was wrong for Congress to get involved while 70 percent said that it was wrong for President Bush to get involved. Sixty-five percent said that the president's and Congress's involvement in the case had more to do with politics than values. In fact, 51 percent indicated that they were more likely to vote against their representative/senator if he/she had voted in favor of moving the case to the federal courts ("*Time* Poll: The Schiavo Case" 2005). Of course, for the Senate that would mean voting against all incumbent senators, since the Senate had passed the measure by unanimous consent!

The Legacy of Terri Schiavo

Terri Schiavo's case has spurred debate in statehouses across the country, and many states are taking a new look at end-of-life legislation. All fifty states already have laws that allow people to write advance directives or a living will that specifies their healthcare preferences if they are incapacitated or designates a healthcare proxy to make decisions for them. The new proposed legislations are designed to address situations like Terri Schiavo's, in which the incapacitated person has not left a living will or designated a healthcare proxy. End-of-life legislation has been introduced in at least ten states (Dewan 2005). A new coalition of disability rights activists and right-to-life individuals has emerged to push new laws in the area of right-to-die (Tanner 2005).

Thus, the broader legal battle over the laws that govern when and how a person dies has restarted as states consider measures that will change standards for letting patients die (Kornblut 2005a). The forces of politics, religion, and medicine are on a collision course (Goodnough 2005b). The outcome is uncertain because, depending on the nature of politics and the coalition of these forces, different states may craft different policies. The Schiavo case has also created a tension between social and economic conservatives within the Republican Party. High-profile economic conservatives such as Grover Norquist and Stephen Moore who have generally supported President Bush and the congressional Republican leadership were very critical of them for turning what would normally be considered a state issue over to the federal courts (Feldman and Richey 2005).

The Right-to-Die Movement

The cases discussed above illustrate the legal and ethical complexities created by today's life-sustaining technologies. Who should live and who should die? Who decides? When is life worth preserving? Who determines what quality of life is? How does one measure a person's quality of life? Should the courts be involved in making such decisions? Does a patient have a right to demand unending medical treatment in a hopeless case? Does a patient have a right to seek assistance of a physician to help end his or her own life? Can euthanasia ethically be justified? What should be the ethical role of the physician and other caregivers? Is every life precious no matter how disabled? Do human beings have the right to self-determination and to decide when life has value?

These are the ultimate questions that have been debated throughout the history of Western thought. The answers depend on our understanding of what makes us human beings. Aristotle argued that existence itself is inviolable. Thus, the plea to continue feeding Terri Schiavo against the wishes of her husband or the courts' determination of her expressed inclination is consistent with Aristotle's teaching. On the other side, René Descartes, a philosopher of the Enlightenment, defined human life not as biological existence (an inviolable gift of life from God) but as consciousness about which people can make judgments. The argument in favor of removing the feeding tube on the ground that Terri Schiavo's quality of life had deteriorated to such an extent that it was not worth living would be consistent with Descartes's thinking (Leland 2005).

Two Oscar-winning films, *Million Dollar Baby* and *The Sea Inside,* which provided sympathetic views of people seeking to end their own lives, have brought issues of assisted suicide once again to center stage.

Approximately 10,000 patients live in a vegetative state in the United States. The complexities created by the life-sustaining technologies have given rise to the "right-to-die" movement across the country. Proponents of the right to die assert that individuals have a right to die with dignity and to determine when to end their lives. They argue that passive as well as active euthanasia is justified. Passive euthanasia refers to a situation in which death results from omitting or terminating treatment. Active euthanasia—that is, actively assisted suicide—refers to a situation in which the healthcare provider gives the patient a means to kill himself or herself, or assists in the administration of the means. The publicity surrounding pathologist Jack Kevorkian of Michigan, who assisted terminally ill patients in killing themselves, heightened the debate over the issue of the right to die. It has led the Michigan state legislature to pass a law making it a crime to assist someone in euthanasia.

Opposition to the right-to-die movement has come from many sources, including the right-to-life movement. These opponents argue that suicide is wrong on religious and theological grounds, as well as being harmful to the community and the common good, and that it produces harmful consequences for other individuals in society (Garrett, Baillie, and Garrett 1989). Others have argued that no human being has a right to decide, for himself/herself or for others, when life is no longer worth living. They posit that there is a danger that such decisions may be based on wrong or ulterior motives. An example would be an agreement to end the life of a patient whose continual stay in the hospital was a financial burden to the family, or of a patient whose family members stood to benefit financially by inheritance. It can be argued that, once a society agrees that at some stage a life is not worth sustaining, the society is on a "slippery slope." Once passive euthanasia becomes acceptable, the next step will be active euthanasia, which in turn can easily lead to forced or involuntary euthanasia. Another worry is that if active euthanasia became a common practice, it could undermine the role of doctors as healers and caregivers (Gibbs and Sachs 1990).

Public sentiment seems to favor the right-to-die movement. A poll conducted in 1990 for Time/CNN by Yankelovich Clancy Shulman revealed that 80 percent of those surveyed said decisions about ending the lives of terminally ill patients should be made by their families and doctors and not by lawmakers. Eighty-one percent believed that if a patient is terminally ill and unconscious but has left instructions in a living will, the doctor should be allowed to withdraw life-sustaining treatment—passive euthanasia. Fifty-seven percent went even further and said that in such cases it is all right for a doctor to administer a lethal injection or provide a lethal pill—active euthanasia (Gibbs and Sachs 1990). A more recent poll suggests that Americans' views have not changed on the subject. In a 2004 Gallup poll, 65 percent agreed that a doctor should be allowed to assist a suicide when a person has a disease that cannot be cured and that person is living in pain, while 41 percent opposed physician-assisted suicide on moral or religious grounds. The support for physician-assisted suicide in this 2004 survey actually rose from 52 percent who supported physician-assisted suicide in a 1996 survey (Schwartz 2005). In a survey by *Time* magazine in March 2005, 52 percent of Americans said that they agreed with Oregon's physician-assisted-suicide law, while 41 percent disagreed (Eisenberg 2005). In fact, according to a Harris/BBC World News America poll conducted in August 2010, a majority of Americans, 58 percent, favor physician-assisted suicide for those terminally ill in great pain who want to end their lives ("Large Majorities Support Physician Assisted Suicide for Terminally Ill Patients in Great Pain" 2011).

Oregon's Death with Dignity Act

On November 8, 1994, Oregon voters approved the Death with Dignity Act by a margin of 52 percent to 48 percent. Known as Ballot Measure 16, the act allows physicians in the state to write lethal drug prescriptions for terminally ill patients who are expected to die within six months. Opponents of the law took the issue to the federal courts and lost. The Ninth U.S. Circuit Court of Appeals rejected the argument that depressed terminally ill adults would be prevented under the law from making informed decisions. The court stated that the specter of involuntary suicides was merely speculative. The U.S. Supreme Court, in October 1997, refused to hear the challenge and, without comment, issued an order letting the ruling of the Ninth U.S. Circuit Court of Appeals decision stand (Biskupic 1997). On June 9, 1997, the Oregon legislature, declining to either amend or repeal the act, placed it on the ballot for a second vote. In the November 4, 1997, election 60 percent of voters voted against repeal of the law, while 40 percent voted in favor ("Oregon's Right to Die Movement" 1995).

In March 2005, the U.S. Supreme Court agreed to hear the George W. Bush administration's challenge to Oregon's law. The Bush administration wanted to revoke the license of doctors who prescribe a lethal prescription on the ground that federal drug laws trump states' rights to regulate medical practice (Eisenberg 2005). However, in a stinging rebuke to the Bush administration, the U.S. Supreme Court in January 2006, in *Gonzales v. Oregon*, by a majority of 6–3, sided with the state of Oregon and upheld the state's Death with Dignity Act and ruled that the federal government did not have the authority to prosecute physicians under the federal drug laws ("Oregon's Right-to-Die Law Upheld by Supreme Court" 2006).

According to the Oregon Public Health Division, since 1997, under the Oregon's Death with Dignity Act, a total of 1,050 people had a lethal dose prescription written to end their own lives, and of these, 673 individuals died ingesting prescriptions written under the law ("Oregon's Death with Dignity Act—2012" 2013). Thus, contrary to opponents' fears, only a handful of terminally ill patients have requested and received assistance in ending their lives.

Individual healthcare providers and society have tried to address some of the problems arising out of life-sustaining technologies in a variety of ways. Many hospitals have established ethics committees to help with ethical and related issues arising out of treatment of terminally ill patients. They often perform the functions of educating the hospital staff, developing policies in problem areas, and acting as advisory consultants to healthcare providers and occasionally to family members. Some have expressed concerns that the committees' decisions, instead of being advisory, may turn into de facto binding decisions, diminishing the role and rights of patients, family members, and healthcare providers (Garrett, Baillie, and Garrett 1989).

Physician-Assisted-Suicide Laws in Other States

In 2008, voters in Washington State approved a public "Initiative 1000," which established Washington State's Death with Dignity Act, which went into effect on March 5, 2009. Thus, Washington became the second state to legalize physician-assisted suicide. Many of the law's provisions are modeled after the Oregon law, requiring that the patient be an adult (eighteen years and over), be mentally competent as verified by two physicians, be terminally ill with less than six months to live, and must make a voluntary request without any coercion. Also required are a fifteen-day waiting period between the oral and written request and the written request must be witnessed and signed by two independent witnesses before patient's wishes are granted ("Death with Dignity Act" n.d.). According to the data collected by Washington State's Department of Health, between 2009 and 2012 a total of 304 individuals had submitted a written request for medication to end their own lives, and in 271 cases physicians had written prescriptions for a lethal dose of medication under the law ("Death with Dignity Data" 2012).

In 2009, the Supreme Court of the State of Montana handed down a decision in which for the first time a state high court gave the green light for doctors to prescribe a lethal dose of drugs for their patients. In contrast, in both Oregon and Washington, physician-assisted suicide was approved as a result of citizen initiative in a popular vote. The Montana case had originated when Robert Baxter, a terminally ill retired truck driver, four physicians, and Compassion and Choices, a national end-of-life advocacy group, filed a lawsuit in state district court challenging the constitutionality of the application of the state's homicide statutes to physicians who provide drugs for assisted suicide to mentally competent and terminally ill patients. In December 2008, a district court judge ruled that Montana's constitutional provision ensuring the right to privacy and human dignity, taken together, did encompass the right of a competent terminally ill patient to die with dignity, and ruled that a patient may use the assistance of a physician for a lethal dose of prescription and physicians would be protected from prosecution under Montana's homicide statues (Marker 2010; Bostrom 2010).

As of this writing, legalizing assisted suicide has been on the agenda of about half a dozen states. This issue has become more prominent in recent years because of the large number of baby boomers who are facing end-of-life issues themselves, and organizations such as Compassion and Choices have been working hard to advance the cause (Haigh 2013).

Living Wills and Durable Power of Attorney

As a result of intense media publicity surrounding major court cases, there has also been an increase in the public's interest in "living wills" and "durable power of attorney." A living will is signed by a competent person in good health and gives permission to his or her doctor to turn off life-support systems in the case of terminal illness or a permanent coma. Thus the living will gives the person some control over his/her last few days or weeks of life. Because both the National Conference of Commissioners of Uniform State Laws and the American Bar Association have given their stamp of approval to the Uniform Rights of the Terminally Ill Act, the number of persons signing living wills is expected to increase. To prevent abuse, state laws in the area of living wills often stipulate specific conditions that must be met. For example, some states require that at least two physicians certify that the patient's illness is terminal. Some states require that the living will be witnessed by people who are not healthcare providers or beneficiaries of the person's last will. A Harris/BBC World News America poll conducted in August 2010 shows that 28 percent of adult Americans and 63 percent of Americans over the age of sixty-five have living wills and/or written directives for themselves ("Large Majorities Support Physician Assisted Suicide for Terminally Ill Patients in Great Pain" 2011).

An alternative to a living will is for an individual to assign a permanent power of attorney to another person. In this scheme, another person (for example, a spouse, a family member, or a friend) is designated as a surrogate healthcare decision maker in case a person is unable or incompetent to make decisions for herself/himself due to serious illness.

EMERGENCY CONTRACEPTION

A contemporary controversial issue related to reproductive rights is the issue of emergency contraceptives, often referred to as the "morning after pill." This is a pill that has hormones similar to regular birth control pills and prevents pregnancy by keeping the ovaries from releasing eggs. It also works by causing the cervical mucus to thicken and thus block sperm from meeting with and fertilizing an egg. Emergency contraception can be used up to 120 hours or five days after unprotected sex to prevent pregnancy. The pills are more effective the sooner one takes them after unprotected sexual intercourse. Three brands of emergency contraception sold in the United States are Plan B One-Step, Ella, and Next Choice (Office of Population Affairs n.d.). The Plan B (or the generic "Next Choice One Dose") reduces the risk of pregnancy by up to 89 percent if taken within seventy-two hours of unprotected sex. Within twenty-four hours, it is about 95 percent effective ("Judge Orders FDA to Remove Restrictions on Morning-After Pill" 2013). Emergency contraception is not intended to be used as a regular form of birth control.

In 1996, the American College of Obstetricians and Gynecologists published practice guidelines for its members on the use of emergency contraception. In 1997, the Food and Drug Administration (FDA) declared that emergency contraceptive pills were safe and effective.

Emergency contraception has received a great deal of attention from consumer advocates, public policy experts, the mass media, and health professionals ("Emergency Contraception: Is the Secret Getting Out?" 1997). As a result of this publicity, there was an increased awareness about emergency contraception among consumers as well as healthcare professionals. A survey conducted in 1997 showed that 59 percent of women and men, 99 percent of obstetricians/ gynecologists, 90 percent of family practice physicians, and 98 percent of nurse practitioners/ physician assistants had heard of or were familiar with emergency contraception ("Emergency Contraception: Is the Secret Getting Out?" 1997). A 2004 survey found that 64 percent of women of reproductive age correctly stated that it is something a woman can do to prevent pregnancy in the few days following unprotected sexual intercourse. This was up from 51 percent in 2000 ("Emergency Contraception" 2004).

In 1999, the FDA approved the emergency contraceptive Plan B as a prescription drug. A citizen petition was filed to sell the drug over the counter without a prescription. The FDA's own advisory panel of experts agreed that such a change made sense to increase access. However, under the George W. Bush administration, FDA officials refused to grant an approval because they feared that if they did, they would be fired (Bazelon 2013). The Bush administration was accused by high-level officials of engaging in ideological meddling for political reasons and ignoring science.

In 2003, an FDA Advisory Panel overwhelmingly voted for the FDA to allow the product to be sold without a prescription (Dooren 2011). That same year, Plan B manufacturer Women's Capital Corporation submitted an application to the FDA to have the status of emergency contraceptive Plan B changed from by-prescription-only to over-the-counter (OTC). In 2004, the FDA overruled the panel recommendation, and Plan B was refused OTC status on the ground of lack of data on the effects that accessible emergency contraceptive would have on the behavior of teenagers; that is, teenagers might engage in more risky sex behavior if they had easy access to emergency contraception. It had very little to do with safety and efficacy of the pill itself. The administration was again accused of stonewalling the review process of emergency contraceptive Plan B for almost two years (2003–2005) to appease the administration's religious base and of ignoring the agency's own procedures and trampling on science (Spencer 2005).

In 2006, the FDA under the Bush administration made a partial concession by allowing sale of Plan B over the counter to women eighteen or older while keeping the drug available by prescription-only for girls seventeen and younger (Bazelon 2013). In 2009, the FDA lowered to seventeen the age at which the pill can be sold without a prescription (Dooren 2011). This means that a girl under seventeen has to go through added steps of getting a prescription from a physician for the emergency contraception and asking the pharmacist for the drug. In addition, some physicians may refuse to write such a prescription or a pharmacist may refuse to dispense emergency contraception on grounds of conscience or ethics. There have been many recorded instances of girls with prescriptions turned away at the pharmacy. Some have called for a common law "duty to dispense" that could serve as a foundation for a wrongful pregnancy action against a dissenting pharmacist (Spreng 2008). Others have also rejected the claim of the right of pharmacists to refuse to dispense an emergency contraceptive for conscience's sake (Card 2011; Kelleher 2010; Lewis and Sullivan 2012).

In 2011, FDA Commissioner Margaret Hamburg was ready to approve a request by the drug's manufacturer, Teva Pharmaceutical Industries, Ltd., to remove the current requirement that girls under age seventeen needed a prescription for the emergency contraceptive drug. She stated that the agency found the drug to be safe and effective in adolescent females. She also stated that younger women could properly use the drug without the intervention of a doctor. However, Health and Human Services Secretary Kathleen Sebelius overrode the decision by the FDA commissioner on the ground that the data submitted by the agency did not prove it was appropriate for girls under the age of seventeen to take Plan B without a prescription. She argued that there were significant behavioral and cognitive differences between older adolescent girls and the youngest girls of reproductive age that should be taken into consideration in making such a determination (Dooren 2011). She further stated that the studies submitted by the FDA did not show that girls of all ages understand the drug's use, and the fact that 10 percent of eleven-year-olds have gotten their periods was enough to back up her concerns. President Obama issued a statement supporting Secretary Sebelius's decision (Bazelon 2013).

Sebelius's action met with much negative feedback from the medical and scientific communities as well as supporters of women's rights. Erin Matson, vice president of the National Organization for Women, the largest feminist advocacy group in the United States, criticized the decision and argued that Obama's and Sebelius's statements had no medical evidence to offer against the scientifically based opinion the FDA had about the health effects of Plan B on girls of all ages (Lu 2012). Three scientists writing in the *New England Journal of Medicine* (Bazelon 2013), including the journal's editor, questioned the soundness of Secretary Sebelius's reasoning by pointing out that a twelve-year-old girl can buy a lethal dose of acetaminophen (Tylenol) without any prescription and no questions asked. Swallowing a bottle of Tylenol could cause death. The side effects of Plan B by comparison are nausea and delayed menstruation. They pointed out that if one were to really apply the reasoning that Secretary Sebelius set, laxatives, cough suppressants, and analgesics would have to be taken off the over-the-counter market (Bazelon 2013).

Left-leaning women's health advocates accused the Obama administration of allowing election year politics to interfere with a decision the FDA typically makes based on scientific evidence. The FDA's timing was politically bad because it preceded President Obama reelection, and the administration showed a lack of courage by overruling FDA's decision. On the other hand, right-leaning organizations praised Secretary Sebelius's decision (Dooren 2011).

In the aftermath of this controversy, several health professional groups publicly took the position that emergency contraceptives should be available over the counter. In November 2012, the nation's largest group of obstetricians and gynecologists stated that birth control pills should be sold over the counter, like condoms. The American College of Obstetricians and Gynecologists declared that birth control pills are safe, women can easily tell if they have risk factors, other over-the-counter drugs are sold despite the fact that they have serious side effects, and there was no need for a pap smear or pelvic exam before using birth control pills (Neergaard 2012). Also in November 2012, the American Academy of Pediatrics (AAP), after examining the risks and benefits based on available data, called on the nation's pediatricians to counsel all of their adolescent patients about emergency contraception and make advance prescriptions for it available to girls under the age of seventeen (Begely 2012; American College of Obstetricians and Gynecologists 2012).

Following such endorsements, Kristen Moor, president and CEO of the Reproductive Health Technologies Project, urged the secretary of Health and Human Services to reconsider her decision based on science and the medical evidence and to come up with an agreement to make emergency contraceptives more easily available to the women who need it (Rovner 2012). However, the help in this area came from a different direction.

On April 5, 2013, U.S. District Judge Edward Korman, in his latest ruling in a lawsuit filed back in 2005 by the Center for Reproductive Rights to push for unfettered over-the-counter access to Plan B, ruled that the FDA must remove all age restrictions on the sale of emergency contraception without a doctor's prescription and declared that Plan B would be among the safest drug sold over the counter. He further stated that the FDA's argument that young people could misuse the drug as a rationale for its age restriction was unpersuasive (Koebler 2013). He also argued that the case was not about the potential misuse of Plan B by eleven-year-olds and said the number using emergency contraception was likely to be minuscule since less than 3 percent of girls under age of thirteen were sexually active (Neumeister and Neergaard 2013).

In a scathing rebuke accusing the Obama administration of letting election-year politics trump science, Judge Korman indicated that it was unclear whether Secretary Sebelius had the power to issue an order overruling FDA decision. He further argued that even if she did have the power, her decision was arbitrary, capricious, and unreasonable. The judge ordered an end to age restriction within thirty days. On April 30, 2013, the FDA announced that it was approving Plan B One-Step—the morning-after pill—to be sold without a prescription to girls fifteen and over, in retail aisle next to other over-the-counter medications. However, girls will have to show an ID to prove their age to purchase Plan B One-Step. The FDA spokesperson insisted that the decision to drop the age to fifteen from seventeen was made independent of Judge Korman's ruling and was not intended to address the court's ruling.

The Planned Parenthood Federation of America officials praised the FDA's decision and urged it to remove all age restrictions on emergency contraception (Szabo 2013). However, the very next day, on May 1, 2013, the Obama administration angered women's groups by announcing its decision to appeal judge Korman's ruling, seeking to overturn it. The Justice Department asked for a delay of the judge's order that the pills be available within thirty days of his ruling and argued that the court did not have jurisdiction over prescription drug policy decisions (Smith 2013). Ironically, the Justice Department's decision to appeal the ruling is in line with the views of many conservative anti-abortion groups who do not want contraceptives made available to young girls (Belluck and Shear 2013). The conservatives praised the administration for its decision to appeal but at the same time faulted it for making the pill available to girls as young as fifteen (Smith 2013). Others called the Obama administration's action laughable and accused it of trying to have it both ways on the morning-after pill and taking an anti-scientific stand for irrationality (Weigant 2013). It remains to be seen how this issue will play out in the courts.

Unintended Pregnancies and the Use of Emergency Contraception

Overall, half of all pregnancies in the United States are unintended—either mistimed or unwanted. Some are the result of contraceptive failure (e.g. a condom breaks, a diaphragm slips), or inconsistent or incorrect use of birth control. The problem of unintended pregnancy cuts across couples of all ages, ethnic groups, and socioeconomic backgrounds ("Emergency Contraception: Is the Secret Getting Out?" 1997). According to experts, as many as 1.5 million of the over 3 million unintended pregnancies occurring annually in the United States can be prevented by the use of emergency contraception, including as many as 700,000 pregnancies that result in induced abortions ("Emergency Contraceptive Pills" 2004).

According to the National Center of Health Statistics of the Centers for Disease Control and Prevention, approximately 10 percent of women in the United States have used emergency contraception ("Emergency Contraception State Laws" 2012). In 2000, only 2 percent reported using emergency contraceptives. This number was up to 6 percent in 2003. The increased use of emergency contraception may have accounted for up to 43 percent of the total decline in abortion rates in the United States between 1994 and 2000 ("Emergency Contraceptive Pills" 2004). Ten percent of women between the ages of fifteen and forty-four reported using emergency contraception at least once between 2006 and 2008 ("Emergency Contraception" 2010).

The federal Emergency Contraception Education Act of 2010 was designed to fund a national campaign to educate women and healthcare providers and has been credited with increasing awareness of emergency contraception and its use ("Emergency Contraception" 2010). The use of emergency contraception has been on the rise particularly among women in their early twenties. It was used by 11 percent of sexually active women from 2006 to 2010. However, nearly one in four women (25 percent) between the age of twenty and twenty-four had used the emergency contraceptive pill at some point during the same time period (Tavernise 2013). Half the women who used the pill said they did it because they had unprotected sex, with white women and more educated women using it the most. Also about one in five never-married women had taken the morning-after pill compared to just one in twenty married women ("Report Finds More U.S. Women Are Using the Morning-After Pill" 2013).

The Politics of Emergency Contraception

As can be seen from the above discussion, the administrations of both George W. Bush and Barack Obama have been accused by critics of playing politics with public policy dealing with emergency contraception and letting political considerations triumph over medical and scientific evidence. The use of and easy access to emergency contraception have been advocated by liberal women's rights groups as well as several groups of health professionals. Morning-after pills are particularly controversial among conservative groups that contend they can cause abortion by interfering with the implantation of a fertilized egg that they regard as a person (Tavernise 2013). However, conservative groups have had a harder time making their case since morning-after pills are designed to prevent a pregnancy rather than to abort a pregnancy. Advocates of emergency contraception view the issue as one of empowerment of women and as a sensible public policy to prevent unwanted pregnancies and thus reduce the need for abortion.

RU-486 and Abortion

Emergency contraception and morning-after pills should not to be confused with the RU-486 (mifepristone) drug or pill. Emergency contraception such as Plan B and Ella are designed to prevent a pregnancy. It does not terminate a pregnancy. In contrast, RU-486 is taken after a pregnancy is confirmed to induce an abortion (Kaye 1986). RU-486 is actually taken at the end of the cycle, before the expected menstrual period. The drug, developed by French pharmaceutical company Roussel Uclaf, is a steroid compound that blocks the uterine from receiving progesterone, causing the fertilized ovum to discharge. RU-486 is considered to be an effective method for termination of a pregnancy in the first seven to eight weeks of pregnancy (Banwell and Paxman 1992; Klein, Raymond, and Dumble 2013; Raymond, Klein, and Dumble 1991; Stulac 1991).

Consequently, RU-486 has generated a considerable amount of controversy in the United States. On the one side are doctors and patients who see RU-486 as a safe, effective, and private method for terminating pregnancy and thus consider it to be a major medical breakthrough. RU 486 has been touted as "the gentle abortion" by its supporters (Ebert 2002). On the other side are conservatives who view RU-486 as a "death pill" and an easy way to terminate even more unborn lives. The primary concern of opponents is that easy access to RU-486 discourages self-critical abortion decisions and that abortion will be trivialized by a pill taken at home (Stulac 1991).

The decision by the manufacturer of RU-486, Roussel Uclaf, to relinquish its U.S. patent rights on RU-486 in 1994 was a major victory for feminist organizations in the United States who had sought the introduction of the drug in the U.S. market since 1988. The intervention by the Clinton administration at the pleading of the feminist groups was instrumental in helping transfer patent rights for RU-486 to the United States (Jackman 2002). In 2000, the FDA approved the use of mifepristone as a safe and effective medical method for terminating pregnancy. It is marketed in the United States under the name of Mifeprex. The protocol established by the FDA requires that a doctor administer 600 mg of mifepristone to a patient within seven weeks of her last menstrual period and then administer misoprostol two days later in the clinic. (Misoprostol is a prostaglandin medicine used to terminate a pregnancy by starting labor.) After additional clinical trials, the FDA developed a new protocol under which a much lower dose of mifepristone—200 mg—could be used and the follow-up misoprostol would be self-administered by the patient at home (Colb 2013).

The availability of RU-486 in the U.S. market has introduced the term "medical abortion" as opposed to "surgical abortion." In a surgical abortion, women go to a clinic and submit to a surgical procedure performed by a medical professional to terminate a pregnancy. In contrast, in a medical abortion, in theory a woman who wants to terminate her pregnancy can take pills and bring about her own abortion. The medical provider simply provides the means for performing abortion, that is, the pill, but it is the woman herself who takes the crucial step in terminating her pregnancy. Thus, in medical abortion, the role of medical professionals is significantly reduced (Colb 2013).

Medical abortion has made it more difficult for opponents of abortions to use traditional methods/strategies to protest and to promote their anti-abortion agenda. For example, in the past, the pro-life movement has tended to focus its condemnation on abortion providers—doctors and clinics. In medical abortion, the perpetrator of abortion is no longer the provider but the pregnant woman herself. The pro-life movement would need to change its legal strategy of trying to criminalize actions of abortion providers to trying to vilify and criminalize the actions of the pregnant woman herself. Also, it is difficult to focus demonstrations and picket lines at abortion clinics since medical abortion can take place within the privacy of a woman's own home (Colb 2013). In summary, access to medical abortion has made it more difficult for pro-life groups to use some of the traditional tools to oppose abortions in the United States. Nevertheless, abortion continues to remain a very controversial issue in the United States.

A total of 784,507 abortions were reported to CDC in 2009, of which 16.5 percent were performed by early medical abortion. The use of early medical abortions increased 10 percent from 2008 to 2009 (Pazol et al. 2012). From the time of its introduction in the U.S. market, September 2000, to April 2011, about 1.52 million women have used mifepristone. During the same period, 2,207 cases with an adverse event have been reported among patients who took the drug, including fourteen deaths ("Mifepristone U.S. Postmarketing Adverse Events Summary Through 04/30/2011" 2011).

IMMIGRANTS AND HEALTHCARE

In 2011, about 39.9 million immigrants were living in the United States, accounting for 13 percent of the total population. Immigrants are defined as foreign-born individuals living in the United States, including naturalized citizens, lawfully present noncitizens, and undocumented immigrants. Of the 39.9 million immigrants, about 17.9 million (5.8 percent of the U.S. population) were naturalized citizens, while another 22 million (7.2 percent of the U.S. population) were made up of two categories of individuals. One category is lawfully present noncitizens (11 million) who have been granted permission to remain in the United States because they are permanent residents (have a green card) or work authorization or refugee status or political asylum, etc. The second category includes undocumented immigrants (about 11 million) who entered the United States without permission or who initially entered with permission but subsequently lost their lawful status (e.g., foreign students who entered the United States on student visa and stayed past their student visa expiration date) ("Immigration Reform and Access to Health Coverage" 2013).

Many of the immigrants live in mixed immigrant status families that include lawfully present or citizen family members as well as undocumented immigrants. For example, in 2010, there were an estimated 4.5 million U.S.-born children whose parents were undocumented ("Immigration Reform and Access to Health Coverage" 2013). Thus immigrants as a group constitute a very complex mix of individuals who vary by country of origin, number of years they have stayed in the United States, ethnicity/race, socioeconomic and health status, as well as acculturation and assimilation ("How Does Health Coverage and Access to Care for Immigrants Vary by Length of Time in the U.S.?" 2009).

A majority of immigrants who are naturalized citizens of the United States receive their healthcare the same way native citizens do—through their employer or through other private coverage. Those who are low-income and meet eligibility criteria can receive healthcare through safety net programs such as Medicaid or the Children's Health Insurance Program (SCHIP).

In general, immigrants are more likely to be uninsured than U.S.-born citizens, and they face increased barriers to accessing needed healthcare. Even immigrants who have lived in the United States for a longer period of time are significantly less likely to be insured than recent immigrants. Given the fact that immigrants have a greater problem accessing care and obtain less physician care, they are more likely to utilize emergency care in hospitals, which is much more expensive. Noncitizen immigrants are more likely than U.S. natives to have a healthcare visit classified as uncompensated care (Stipson, Wilson, and Eschbach 2010). The higher uninsured rate among immigrants is due to their limited access to private coverage because they work in low-wage jobs and firms that often do not offer health coverage ("How Does Health Coverage and Access to Care for Immigrants Vary by Length of Time in the U.S.?" 2009).

In 2011, over half of immigrants in the United States were from the Western Hemisphere—Canada, Mexico, Central and South America, and the Caribbean. A quarter of immigrants were born in Asia or the Pacific Islands, and the remaining quarter were of European, African, and Middle Eastern descent ("Key Facts on Health Coverage for Low-Income Immigrants Today and Under the Affordable Care Act" 2013). In contrast to immigrants from Europe, Canada, and Australia, who not only have higher educational attainment but also are culturally more similar to citizens of the United States, Hispanics generally enjoy a lower socioeconomic status and have lower levels of employment due to their young age, language difficulty, and lower levels of education. They are also more likely to be employed in sectors such as agricultural, construction, and industries that employ contract and seasonal workers, and thus increase their chances of job loss ("How Does Health Coverage and Access to Care for Immigrants Vary by Length of Time in the U.S?" 2009).

Lawful Noncitizen Immigrants and Healthcare

Lawfully present noncitizen immigrants can obtain health insurance coverage in the United States either through their employer or through private insurance. However, when it comes to public health programs, they are subject to Medicaid and CHIP eligibility restrictions. The Personal Responsibility and Work Opportunity Reconciliation Act (PRWORA) of 1996 decoupled social welfare benefits from health insurance safety-net programs such as Medicaid. The law placed complex restrictions on social welfare and health insurance benefits for legal immigrants who are not citizens, placing a five-year waiting period before they can access many social safety-net programs such as Medicaid and CHIP (Scotch and Loganathan 2011).

Under the Children's Health Insurance Program Reauthorization Act (CHIPRA) of 2009, state governments were given the option to eliminate this five-year waiting period for lawfully residing noncitizens who are pregnant women or children. Since 2002, states have also had the option to use federal CHIP funds to cover prenatal care for pregnant women regardless of their immigration status ("Immigrants' Health Coverage and Health Reform: Key Questions and Answers" 2009). As of January 2013, twenty-five states had elected the CHIPRA option for lawfully present immigrant children and twenty had elected the option for lawfully residing pregnant women ("Key Facts on Health Coverage for Low-Income Immigrants Today and Under the Affordable Care Act" 2013).

Under the Affordable Care Act (ACA) of 2010, lawfully present noncitizen immigrants will continue to face the five-year waiting period for Medicaid. They will, however, be able to purchase health insurance coverage in the healthcare exchanges and receive tax credit without a waiting period, which could significantly help to expand their coverage and access to healthcare ("Key Facts on Health Coverage for Low-Income Immigrants Today and Under the Affordable Care Act" 2013).

Under the immigration reform proposals presented by both President Obama and a bipartisan group of eight senators, individuals who are granted provisional lawful status will not be eligible for federal public assistance benefits, including health coverage. This is similar to when in June 2012 the Obama administration announced a new program referred to as Deferred Action for Childhood Arrivals (DACA) under which certain undocumented youths would be given temporary permission to stay in the United States. However, in August 2012, the Department of Health and Human Services (DHHS) announced policy that would exclude these youths from the health coverage options that are available to other lawfully present immigrants ("Immigration Reform and Access to Health Coverage" 2013). It remains to be seen if Congress will pass a comprehensive immigration reform bill, and even if it does, what provisions would be included in the final legislation.

Undocumented Immigrants and Healthcare

An estimated 11.1 million immigrants living in the United States are undocumented ("Unauthorized Immigrants" 2013). They represent the biggest challenge to the U.S. healthcare system. They are ineligible for most of the federal social and health benefits programs, yet they cost the U.S. healthcare system in numerous ways.

Under federal law, undocumented immigrants are prohibited from enrolling in Medicaid and CHIP programs. However, Medicaid payment for emergency services may be made on behalf of undocumented immigrants who would otherwise qualify for Medicaid. Since 2002, state governments also have had the option to use federal CHIP funds to cover prenatal care for pregnant women regardless of their immigration status ("Immigrants' Health Coverage and Health Reform: Key Questions and Answers" 2009). As of January 2013, fifteen states had elected this option ("Key Facts on Health Coverage for Low-Income Immigrants Today and Under the Affordable Care Act" 2013). Under the ACA, undocumented immigrants will continue to remain ineligible for Medicaid and will be prohibited from purchasing health insurance coverage through state exchanges and to receive tax credits ("Immigration Reform and Access to Health Coverage: Key Issues to Consider" 2013).

According to the Pew Hispanic Center, most undocumented immigrants in the United States are employed in the service industry (31 percent) followed by construction (19 percent), production (15 percent), and farming (4 percent) (Pew Hispanic Center 2006). Most undocumented immigrants given their immigration status and employment concentration in certain sectors of the economy earn close to minimum wage and fall below the federal poverty line. However, given their status as undocumented immigrants they are ineligible for Medicaid and CHIP (Pew Hispanic Center 2006).

In 1986, Congress barred undocumented immigrants from the federal health benefits generally available to the poor with one major exception—emergencies (Zarembo and Gorman 2008). The Emergency Medical Treatment and Active Labor Act of 1986 guarantees emergency medical treatment to anyone, regardless of their legal status or ability to pay. In return, hospitals receive federal reimbursement for care provided to undocumented immigrants in emergency rooms. Since undocumented immigrants are otherwise ineligible for federal health benefits and are more likely to be uninsured, chronic care for undocumented immigrants often turn into emergency room visits for dialysis or diuretics. Such treatments in hospital emergency rooms are much more expensive compared to outpatient clinics. Acute care services of emergency rooms are among the most expensive way to pay for healthcare services (Garg 2010). In addition, the federal definition of what constitutes an emergency as well as when an emergency starts and ends is open to interpretation, leaving in place an ambiguous federal policy (Zarembo and Gorman 2008). The result is an irrational public policy that, on the one hand, prohibits federal health benefits such as Medicaid and CHIP to undocumented immigrants, but on the other hand, pays for more expensive emergency room services to the same undocumented immigrants. Dialysis offers a striking example. The U.S. taxpayers covered the entire cost of dialysis treatment (about 2,000 times over a seventeen-year period) of Marguerita Toribio, an undocumented immigrant from Mexico, including a kidney transplant in 1993. In California alone, undocumented immigrants account for about 1,350 of the 61,000 people on dialysis, costing the taxpayer $51 million in 2007 (Zarembo and Gorman 2008).

Health services and other benefits available to illegal immigrants can vary from state to state. Local government and local public hospitals are often responsible for implementing the provision of health services to the medically indigent and uninsured. Many public and private hospitals bear the burden of substantial costs in providing undocumented immigrants care that is often uncompensated (Scotch and Loganathan 2011). State and local governments are generally the ones that bear the cost of undocumented immigrants. During the recession of 2007–2009, many states and local governments facing state budget deficits cut back on health services provided to the uninsured and the indigent, and undocumented immigrants often constitute a sizable portion of such populations (Wood 2009).

Communities with large numbers of undocumented immigrants face considerable financial strain in trying to meet the healthcare needs of the undocumented immigrants. For example, California, which has the nation's largest population of undocumented immigrants, spent an estimated $1.2 billion in 2011 through Medicaid to care for 822,500 undocumented immigrants. The New Jersey Hospital Association in 2010 estimated it cost between $600 million and $650 million annually to treat 550,000 undocumented immigrants. Texas, in 2010, had provided $96 million in benefits to undocumented immigrants (Sherman and Plushnick-Masti 2012). Presented with a high financial burden, public hospitals are often faced with the option of closing down clinics and services. For example, in 2010, two large public hospitals—Grady Hospital in Atlanta, Georgia, and Jackson Memorial Hospital in Miami, Florida—closed the doors of their outpatient dialysis clinics to nonpaying patients, most of whom were undocumented immigrants, due to inability to cover the costs. Ironically, many of these same patients now access dialysis in the emergency room of the same hospitals, even though it is a more expensive way to treat the same patients, because hospitals get federal dollars for care provided in the emergency room (Garg 2010).

The often confusing, contradictory, and ambiguous federal healthcare policy toward immigrants in general and undocumented immigrants in particular perhaps reflects the ambivalent attitudes Americans have about immigration. The plight of undocumented immigrants elicits strong feelings on both sides of the debate. On the one side are those who strictly take an anti-immigration policy position and oppose undocumented immigrants' being able to access publicly financed social welfare and healthcare programs. Those who favor providing access to health services for the undocumented immigrants justify their position from a social justice and human rights perspective, that every human being is entitled to basic rights and social justice demands that everyone have access to healthcare. This argument has generally failed to win over many converts (Okolec 2009).

Another perspective that advocates providing undocumented immigrants access to healthcare takes a public health approach. Here, advocates argue for framing healthcare from an individual level to a community level by appealing to the larger community to take preventive action to avoid disease. This view helps move health from a personal, individual arena to the arena of healthcare as a social good. The reason for this is that Americans are often described as compassionate people when thinking about community as a whole. Framing healthcare as a public, that is, common or social good rather than an individual good also acknowledges the role of public health to monitor community health, prevent illness, and live up to one of its ethical principles, which is to advocate for the empowerment of the disenfranchised community members and ensure that resources and conditions necessary for health are accessible to everyone (Okolec 2009). Whether such a perspective takes hold in the long run in the United States remains to be seen. What is clear in the short term is that the current confusing, ambiguous, and irrational healthcare policy with respect to undocumented immigrants is likely to continue. Progress in this area, if any, is likely to come in small, incremental steps.

CONCLUSION

The discussion of reproductive and life-sustaining technologies in this chapter exemplifies the complexities of legal and ethical issues raised by modern medical technology. Similar complex issues are raised by healthcare technology in areas such as organ transplants (Garrett, Baillie, and Garrett 1989; General Accounting Office 1989; Shaw et al. 1991). Organ transplants raise many ethical issues for donors, recipients, healthcare providers, and society as a whole. When is it ethical to donate organs? What criteria should be used in deciding who gets an organ transplant and who does not? Is it ethical to sell organs? Since it is reasonable to assume that there will always be more demand than supply of available organs, would allowing the selling of organs produce an economic market, in which organs would be bought and sold as are other goods and services? What are the ethical issues related to the living donor versus the living but terminal donor? Is it ethical to end the life of a terminal patient in order to make an organ available?

Healthcare technology has also produced a revolution in reproductive processes that raises many difficult ethical problems. Ethical objections to artificial insemination are often raised on religious or theological grounds. Objections are also raised on the ground that artificial insemination produces harmful consequences for society when the woman is not married, when the donor is not screened, or when the identity of the donor is concealed. Similar ethical concerns are raised with in vitro fertilization (i.e., test-tube fertilization), surrogate parenthood, embryo transfers, and the use of frozen embryos and sperm banks.

End-of-life technologies have produced many legal and ethical concerns as reflected in the right-to-die cases discussed in this chapter. The case of Terri Schiavo also highlights the clash of science, religion, and politics when it comes to policy making.

Healthcare technology is developing at a rapid pace, while our capacity and our ability to comprehend and deal with the legal and ethical issues raised by medical technology are lagging behind. Now that we have entered the twenty-first century, policymakers will be increasingly confronted with the challenge of formulating public policies that require an understanding of the legal and ethical implications of rapidly emerging new technologies. Developments in the United States can be best characterized as a patchwork approach to bioethics. Most initiatives have tended to be private rather than government-sponsored. This has the advantage of producing multiple or pluralistic approaches that foster diversity.

Private bodies also are under less political pressure (Cohen and McCloskey 1994). But such approaches often lack the necessary authority to produce meaningful and timely responses. Kathi E. Hanna, Robert M. Cook-Deegan, and Robyn Y. Nishimi (1993) have advocated that the United States adopt a new approach to addressing issues of bioethics. They have called for the establishment of a centralized national forum, along the lines of a presidential commission, that would conduct research, hold hearings, and address issues of broad public interest dealing with, for example, assisted-suicide and life-sustaining and reproductive technologies. They have also recommended creation of an entity within the Department of Health and Human Services to establish protocols for federally funded biomedical experiments and research. Such proposals have come under criticism from some quarters. For example, Ira H. Carmen (1994) argues that "good" or "ethical" biomedicine cannot be defined in the abstract. According to Carmen, our constitutional and political order requires a delicate weighing and balancing of competing interests by policymakers. The Madisonian model that underlies our political system requires that the people's representatives, not some presidential commission, work through the political branches to formulate national policies. Whether Congress is up to the task remains to be seen.

The same notion is applicable to controversies surrounding issues of emergency contraceptives, RU-486, and healthcare for immigrants, especially for undocumented immigrants. Legal and ethical issues are also present in these issues, though perhaps not as intense as in other reproductive technologies and end-of-life issues. The controversy surrounding emergency contraceptives and RU-486 reflects a clash of moral and religious values in American society, which plays out in the political process along ideological and partisan lines about how such issues are defined and perceived. Low-level ideological and partisan divides sometimes make it possible to arrive at a policy consensus through bargaining and compromises. Under conditions of intense partisan and ideological conflicts, it is much more difficult to achieve policy consensus, resulting in policy paralysis. However, more often than not, policy decisions are based more on partisan and electoral calculations than on science or facts. Ideological and partisan conflicts combined with the American public's ambivalence about immigrants have failed to produce a comprehensive immigration reform policy over the last decade. Whether the changed and more receptive political climate in the wake of the 2012 presidential and congressional elections, in which the Republican Party lost a large majority of immigrant, and more specifically Hispanic (the largest and the fastest growing minority in the United States), votes to the Democratic Party, leads to the passage of the proposed bipartisan immigration reform remains to be seen. Even if such an effort is successful and comprehensive immigration reform becomes a reality, it is unlikely, at least in the short run, to significantly impact healthcare for undocumented immigrants. A path to citizenship for undocumented immigrants, proposed in the reform, in the long run would make healthcare more accessible to them as they become legal residents and ultimately achieve U.S. citizenship.

STUDY QUESTIONS

1. What is bioethics, and how does it relate to medical technology? Give specific examples.
2. What are different types of assisted reproductive technologies (ARTs)? What kinds of ethical issues do such technologies raise?
3. Discuss some of the major court cases dealing with the right to conceive and bear children, parenthood, and surrogacy.

4. Discuss some of the major court cases dealing with preventing unwanted pregnancy and birth.

5. Discuss major cases dealing with right to die and the constitutional principles the courts have established.

6. Discuss the intersection of politics, religion, political ideology, and ethics with reproductive technologies and the right-to-die issues.

7. How have state governments responded to the issue of right to die?

8. Discuss the evolution of the right-to-die movement in the United States. What do public opinion polls show about Americans' views on this issue?

9. How did the policy about the use of emergency contraception evolve in the United States? What role did religion, political ideology, and partisanship play in shaping policy making in this field? Do you agree with the current policy? Why?

10. How does the availability of RU-486 change debate about abortion?

11. Discuss different categories of immigrant population in the United States and the health services available to them.

REFERENCES

"Abortion Laws." 2012. Washington DC: National Conference of State Legislatures. Online at http://www. ncsl.org/issues-research/health/abortion-laws.aspx.

"About the Commission." n.d. Presidential Commission for the Study of Bioethical Issues. Online at http:// bioethics.gov/cms/about.

American College of Obstetricians and Gynecologists. 2012. "Over-the-Counter Access to Oral Contraceptives." *Committee Opinion*, no. 544 (December): 1–5.

Angell, Marcia. 1990. "Prisoners of Technology: The Case of Nancy Cruzan." *New England Journal of Medicine* 322, no. 17 (April 26): 1226–28.

"Assisted Reproductive Technology (ART)." n.d. Centers for Disease Control and Prevention. Online at http://www.cdc.gov/ART/index.htm.

Associated Press. 2005. "Schiavo's Parents Give Up Their Federal Appeal." *New York Times,* March 27.

Bahadur, G. 2004. "Ethical Challenges in Reproductive Medicine: Posthumous Reproduction." *International Congress Series* 1266 (April): 295–302.

Baird, P.A. 1996. "Ethical Issues of Fertility and Reproduction." *Annual Review of Medicine* 47, no. 1: 107–16.

Banwell, Suzanna., and John M. Paxman. 1992. "The Search for Meaning: RU 486 and the Law of Abortion." *American Journal of Public Health* 82, no. 10 (October): 1406–14.

Baruch, Elaine H.; Amadeo F. D'Adamo Jr.; and Joni Seager, eds. 1988. *Embryos, Ethics, and Women's Rights: Exploring the New Reproductive Technologies.* New York: Haworth Press.

Bauman, Norman. 1997. "Dead Men Conceiving: Trend Raises Ethical, Legal Questions." *Urology Times* 25, no. 2 (February): 4–5.

Bayles, Michael D. 1984. *Reproductive Ethics.* Englewood Cliffs, NJ: Prentice Hall.

Bazelon, Emily. 2013. "The Politics of Prude." Online at www.slate.com/articles/news_and_politics/jurisprudence/2013/04/plan_b_if_you_liked_bush_s_war_on_science_you_ll_love_obama_s_cowardice.html.

Beck, Melinda, and Geoffrey Cowley. 1994. "Mother Nature?" *Newsweek,* January 17.

Beckman, Linda J., and S. Marie Harvey. 2005. "Current Reproductive Technologies: Increased Access and Choice?" *Journal of Social Issues* 61, no. 1 (March): 1–20.

Begeley, Sharon. 2012. "Prescribe Morning-After Pill in Advance, Say Pediatricians." Reuters News, November 26. Online at www.reuters.com/article/2012/11/26/us-contraception-emergency-idUS-BRE8AP04420121126.

Bellafante, Ginia. 2005. "Surrogate Mothers' New Niche: Bearing Children for Gay Couples." *New York Times,* May 27.

Belluck, Pam. 2005. "Tide Has Turned When Hospitals, Families Clash Over Patient Care." *San Diego Union Tribune,* March 27.

Belluck, Pam, and Michael Sheer. 2013. "U.S. to Defend Age Limits on Morning-After Pill Sales." *New York Times,* May 1. Online at www.nytimes.com/2013/05/02/health/us-will-appeal-order-on-morning-after-pill.html.

Benagiano, G. 2003. ""Public Health and Infertility." *Reproductive Medicine Online* 7, no. 6 (December): 606–14.

Biskupic, Joan. 1997. "Oregon's Assisted Suicide Law Leaves On." *Washington Post*, October 15: A03.

Blank, Robert H. 1989. Introduction. In *Biomedical Technology and Public Policy*, ed. Robert H. Blank and Miriam K. Mills, vii–xv. New York: Greenwood Press.

Bostrom, Barry A. 2010. "*Baxter v. State of Montana.*" *Issues in Law and Medicine* 26, no. 1 (Summer): 79–82.

Buckley, Jerry. 1990. "How Doctors Decide: Who Shall Live, Who Shall Die." *U.S. News & World Report*, January 11.

Campo-Flores, Arian. 2005. "The Legacy of Terri Schiavo." *Newsweek*, April 4.

"Can States Intervene in Medical Decisions?" 2004. *Christian Science Monitor*, August 3.

Cantor, Norman L. 1993. *Advance Directives and the Pursuit of Death with Dignity*. Indianapolis: Indiana University Press.

Caplan, Arthur. 1989. "Hard Data on Efficacy: The Prerequisite to Hard Choices in Health Care." *Mount Sinai Journal of Medicine* 56, no. 3: 185–90.

Card, Robert F. 2011. "Conscientious Objection, Emergency Contraception, and Public Policy." *Journal of Medicine and Philosophy* 36, no. 1 (January): 53–68.

Carmen, Ira H. 1994. "Bioethics, Public Policy and Political Science." *Politics and Life Sciences* 13, no. 1 (February 1): 79–81.

Centers for Disease Control and Prevention. 2004. *Assisted Reproductive Technology Success Rates: National Summary and Fertility Clinic Report 2002*. Online at www.cdc.gov/reproductivehealth/ART02/index.htm.

Cerminara, Kathy, and Kenneth Goodman. 2005. "Key Events in the Case of Theresa Marie Schiavo." Joint Project of the University of Miami Ethics Programs and the Shepard Broad Law Center at Nova Southeastern University. Online at www.miami.edu/ethics2/schiavo/timeline.htm.

Ciccarelli, John K., and Janice C. Ciccarelli. 2005. "The Legal Aspects of Parental Rights in Assisted Reproductive Technology." *Journal of Social Issues* 61, no. 1: 127–37.

Cohen, Cynthia B., ed. 1996. *New Ways of Making Babies: The Case of Egg Donation*. Bloomington: Indiana University Press.

Cohen, Cynthia B., and Elizabeth L. McCloskey. 1994. "Private Bioethics Forums: Counterpoint to Government Bodies." *Kennedy Institute of Ethics Journal* 4, no. 2 (September 1): 283–89.

Cohen, Sherrill, and Nadine Taub, eds. 1989. *Reproductive Laws for the 1990s*. Clifton, NJ: Humana Press.

Colb, Sherry F. 2013. "The U.S. Court of Appeals for the Sixth Circuit Upholds Restrictions on Medical Abortion: Why Should Anyone Care?" *Verdict*, January 9. Online at http://verdict.justia.com/2013/01/09/the-u-s-court-of-appeals-for-the-sixth-circuit-upholds-restrictions-on-medical-abortion.

Daar, Judith F. 2001. "Frozen Embryo Disputes Revisited: A Trilogy of Procreation-Avoidance Approaches." *Journal of Law, Medicine and Ethics* 29, no. 2 (summer): 197–202.

"Death with Dignity Act." n.d. Washington State Department of Health. Online at www.doh.wa.gov/YouandYourFamily/IllnessandDisease/DeathwithDignityAct.aspx.

"Death with Dignity Data." 2012. Washington State Department of Health. Online at www.doh.wa.gov/YouandYourFamily/IllnessandDisease/DeathwithDignityAct/DeathwithDignityData.aspx.

"Definition of 'Parent' and Related Variations in Child Welfare." n.d. Washington, DC: National Conference of State Legislatures. Online at www.ncsl.org/documents/cyf/definitions_of_parent.pdf.

Devine, Richard J. 2004. *Good Care, Painful Choices: Medical Ethics for Ordinary People*. New York: Paulist Press.

Dewan, Shaila. 2005. "States Taking a New Look at End-of-Life Legislation." *New York Times*, March 31.

Dooren, Jennifer C. 2011. "Obama Health Chief Blocks FDA on 'Morning After' Pill." *Wall Street Journal*, December 8. Online at http://online.wsj.com/article/SB10001424052970203413304577084560710472558.html.

Ebert, Martina. 2002. "RU 486 and Abortion Practices in Europe: From Legalization to Access." *Women and Politics* 24, no. 3: 13–34.

Eisenberg, Daniel. 2005. "Lessons of the Schiavo Battle." *Time*, April 4, 22–30.

Elster, Nanette R. 2005. "Assisted Reproductive Technologies: Contracts, Consents, and Controversies." *American Journal of Family Law* 18, no. 4 (Winter): 193–99.

"Embryo and Gamete Disposition Laws." 2007. Washington, DC: National Conference of State Legislatures. Online at www.ncsl.org/issues-research/health/embryo-and-gamete-disposition-laws.aspx.

"Emergency Contraception." 2004. Washington, DC: Henry J. Kaiser Family Foundation. Online at www.kff.org/womenshealth/upload/3344–03.pdf.

———. 2010. Washington, DC: Henry J. Kaiser Family Foundation. Online at www.kff.org/womenshealth/upload/3344–04.pdf.

"Emergency Contraception: Is the Secret Getting Out?" 1997. Washington, DC: Henry J. Kaiser Family Foundation. Publication no. 1352. Online at www.kff.org/womenshealth/1352-contraception.cfm.

"Emergency Contraceptive Pills." 2004. Washington, DC: Henry J. Kaiser Family Foundation. Online at www.kff.org/womenshealth/upload/Emergency-Contraceptive-Pills.pdf.

"Emergency Contraception State Laws." 2012. Washington, DC: National Conference of State Legislatures. Online at www.ncsl.org/issues-research/health/emergency-contraception-state-laws.aspx.

Farmer, Ann. 2008. "Roe's Mid-Life Crisis Protecting Reproductive Health Rights." *Perspectives* 17, no. 2 (Fall): 4–7.

Feinberg, John S., and Paul D. Feinberg. 2010. *Ethics for a Brave New World.* Wheaton, IL: Crossway.

Feldman, Linda, and Warren Richey. 2005. "The Terri Schiavo Legacy." *Christian Science Monitor,* April 1.

Fogel, Susan B., and Lourdes A. Rivera. 2003. "Religious Beliefs and Healthcare Necessities." *Human Rights: Journal of the Section of Individual Rights and Responsibilities* 30, no. 2 (Spring): 8–11.

Foote, Donna; Larry Reibstein; and Ana Figueroa. 1998. "And Baby Makes One." *Newsweek,* 131, no. 5: (February 2): 68–69.

Garg, Megha. 2010. "It Pays to Provide Health Care: A Case for Including Undocumented Immigrants." *Kennedy School Review* vol. 10: 25–28.

Garrett, Thomas M.; Harold W. Baillie; and Rosellen M. Garrett. 1989. *Health Care Ethics: Principles and Problems.* Englewood Cliffs, NJ: Prentice Hall.

General Accounting Office. 1989. *Heart Transplants: Concerns About Cost, Access, and Availability of Donor Organs.* Washington, DC: Government Printing Office.

Gerber Fried, Marlene. 2008. "Thirty-Five Years of Legal Abortion: The U.S. Experience." *IDS Bulletin* 39, no. 3: (July): 88–94.

Gibbs, Nancy, and Andrea Sachs. 1990. "Love and Let Die: In an Era of Medical Technology, How Are Patients and Families to Decide Whether to Halt Treatment—or Even to Help Death Along?" *Time,* March 19.

Gilbert, Scott F.; Anna L. Tyler; and Emily J. Zackin. 2005. *Bioethics and the New Embryology: Springboards for Debate.* Sunderland, MA: W.H. Freeman and Sinauer Associates.

Goodnough, Abby. 2005a. "Appeals Court Refuses to Order Schiavo's Feeding Reinstated." *New York Times,* March 23.

———. 2005b. "Few Options for Schiavo's Parents as U.S. Judge Denies Request." *New York Times,* March 25.

———. 2005c. "Schiavo Dies, Ending Bitter Case Over Feeding Tube." *New York Times,* April 1.

Goodnough, Abby, and Adam Liptak. 2005a. "Schiavo's Parents Appeal to the Supreme Court on Feeding Tube." *New York Times,* March 24.

———. 2005b. "Supreme Court Rejects Request to Reinsert Feeding Tube." *New York Times,* March 24.

Haigh, Susan. 2013. "Assisted Suicide on Legal Agenda in Several States." Associated Press, February 8. Online at http://news.yahoo.com/assisted-suicide-legal-agenda-several-states-084111046.html.

Hallifax, Jackie. 2004. "Fla. Court Nixes Law Keeping Woman Alive." Associated Press, September 23. Online at story.news.yahoo.com.

Hanna, Kathi E.; Robert M. Cook-Deegan; and Robyn Y. Nishimi. 1993. "Finding a Forum for Bioethics in U.S. Public Policy." *Politics and Life Sciences* 12, no. 2: 205–19.

Harwood, Karey. 2007. *The Infertility Treadmill: Feminist Ethics, Personal Choice, and the Use of Reproductive Technologies.* Chapel Hill: University of North Carolina Press.

Henifin, Mary S. 1993. "New Reproductive Technologies: Equity and Access to Reproductive Health Care." *Journal of Social Issues* 49, no. 2 (Summer): 61–74.

Higdon, Michael J. 2012. "Fatherhood by Conscription: Nonconsensual Insemination and the Duty of Child Support." *Georgia Law Review* 46, no. 2 (Winter): 407–57.

"History of Bioethics Commissions." n.d. Online at http://bioethics.gov/cms/history.

Hoffman, Elaine; Amadeo F. D'Adamo; and Joni Seager, eds. 1988. *Embryos, Ethics, and Women's Rights: Exploring the New Reproductive Technologies.* New York: Harrington Park Press.

"How Does Health Coverage and Access to Care for Immigrants Vary by Length of Time in the U.S?" 2009. Washington, DC: Kaiser Commission on Medicaid and the Uninsured. Henry J. Kaiser Family Foundation. Online at www.kff.org/uninsured/upload/7916.pdf.

Hulse, Carl. 2005. "Congress Passes and Bush Signs Legislation on Schiavo Case." *New York Times,* March 21.

Hulse, Carl, and David D. Kirkpatrick. 2005. "Even Death Does Not Quiet Harsh Political Fight." *New York Times,* April 1.

"Immigrants' Health Coverage and Health Reform: Key Questions and Answers." 2009. Focus on Health Reform. Washington, DC: Henry J. Kaiser Family Foundation. Online at www.kff.org/healthreform/upload/7982.pdf.

"Immigration Reform and Access to Health Coverage: Key Issues to Consider." 2013. Washington, DC: Kaiser Commission on Medicaid and the Uninsured. Henry J. Kaiser Family Foundation. Online at www.kff.org/uninsured/upload/8420.pdf.

"Indepth: Terri Schiavo, Schiavo Timeline." 2005. *CBC News,* March 31. Online at www.cbc.ca.

International Anti-Euthanasia Task Force. n.d. "The Facts About Oregon 'Death With Dignity Act' Initiative." Online at www.iaetf.org.

Jackman, Jennifer. 2002. "Anatomy of a Feminist Victory: Winning the Transfer of RU 486 Patent Right to the United States, 1988–1994." *Women and Politics* 24, no. 3: 81–100.

"Judge Orders FDA to Remove Restrictions on Morning-After Pill." 2013. CBS New York, April 5. Online at www.newyork.cbslocal.com/2013/04/05.

Kamisar, Yale. 1991. "Who Should Live—or Die? Who Should Decide?" An Interview with Professor Kamisar at the University of Michigan Law School. *Trial* 27, no. 12 (December 1): 20–26.

Kaye, Tony. 1986. "Are You for RU 486?" *New Republic* 194, no. 4 (January 27): 13–15.

Kelleher, Paul J. 2010. "Emergency Contraception and Conscientious Objection." *Journal of Applied Philosophy* 27, no. 3 (August): 290–304.

"Key Dates in Schiavo Right-to-Die Case." 2005. Associated Press, May 23. Online at news.yahoo.com.

"Key Facts on Health Coverage for Low-Income Immigrants Today and Under the Affordable Care Act." 2013. Washington, DC: Kaiser Commission on the Uninsured. Henry J. Kaiser Family Foundation. Online at www.kff.org/uninsured/upload/8279–02.pdf.

"Key Statistics from the National Survey of Family Growth." 2011. Centers for Disease Control and Prevention. Online at www.cdc.gov/nchs/nsfg/abc_list_i.htm#infertility.

Klein, Renate; Janice G. Raymond; and Lynnette Dumble. 2013. *RU 486: Misconception, Myths, and Morals.* 2d ed. North Melbourne, Australia: Spinifex Press.

Knaplund, Kristine S. 2012. "Children of Assisted Reproduction." *University of Michigan Journal of Law Reform* 45, no. 4 (Summer): 899–935.

Koebler, Jason. 2013. "Federal Judge Order FDA to Remove Age Restriction on the Over the Counter Morning After Pill." *U.S. News and World Report,* April 15. Online at www.usnews.com/news/articles/2013/04/05/federal-judge-orders-fda-to-remove-age-restriction-on-over-the-counter-morning-after-pill.

Kolata, Gina. 1994. "Reproductive Revolution Is Jolting Old Views." *New York Times,* January 11.

Kornblut, Anne E. 2005a. "A Next Step: Making Rules to Die By." *New York Times,* April 1.

———. 2005b. "Schiavo Autopsy Renews Debate on G.O.P. Actions." *New York Times,* June 16.

Kowalczyk, Liz. 2005a. "Hospital, Family Spar Over End-of-Life Care." *Boston Globe,* March 11.

———. 2005b. "Woman Dies at MHG After Battle Over Care." *Boston Globe,* June 8.

"Large Majorities Support Physician Assisted Suicide for Terminally Ill Patients in Great Pain." 2011. Harris/BBC World News America. Online at www.harrisinteractive.com/NewsRoom/HarrisPolls/tabid/447/mid/1508/articleId/677/ctl/ReadCustom%20Default/Default.aspx.

Leland, John. 2005. "Did Descartes Doom Terri Schiavo?" *New York Times,* March 27.

Lewis, Browne. 2009. "Two Fathers, One Dad: Allocating the Paternal Obligations Between the Men Involved in the Artificial Insemination Process." *Lewis and Clark Law Review* 13, no. 4 (Winter): 949–1006.

Lewis, Jeffrey D., and Dennis M. Sullivan. 2012. "Abortifacient Potential of Emergency Contraceptives." *Ethics and Medicine* 28, no. 3 (Fall): 113–20.

Long, Mark. 2005. "Federal Judge Nixes Schiavo's Feeding Tube." Associated Press, March 25. Online at news.yahoo.com.

Lu, Kerri. 2012. "Obama Administration Overrules FDA Decision—The Politics of Emergency Contraception." *Yale Journal of Medicine and Law,* May 21. Online at www.yalemedlaw.com/2012/05/obama-administration-overrules-fda-decision-%e2%80%93-the-politics-of-emergency-contraception/.

Lyman, Rick. 2005. "Governor Is Pressed on Schiavo as Legal Moves Dwindle." *New York Times,* March 27.

Marker, Rita L. 2010. "The Montana Supreme Court Says Yes." *Human Life Review* 36, no. 2 (Spring): 56–64.

McCormick, Richard A. 1990. "Clear and Convincing Evidence: The Case of Nancy Cruzan." *Midwest Medical Ethics* 6, no. 4 (Fall): 10–12.

Mehren, Elizabeth, and Sam H. Verhovek. 2005. "The Death of Terri Schiavo: A Very Private Issue Resonates with Public." *Los Angeles Times,* April 1.

Meilaender, Gilbert. 1990. "The Cruzan Decision: 9.5 Theses for Discussion." *Midwest Medical Ethics* 6, no. 4 (Fall): 3–5.

"Mifepristone U.S. Postmarketing Adverse Events Summary Through 04/30/2011." 2011. Washington, DC: Food and Drug Administration. Online at www.fda.gov/downloads/Drugs/DrugSafety/PostmarketDrugSafetyInformationforPatientsandProviders/UCM263353.pdf.

Milicia, Joe. 2005. "Doctors: Feeding Tube Goes Beyond Purpose." Associated Press, March 26. Online at news.yahoo.com.

Miller, Molly. 2010. "Embryo Adoption: The Solution to an Ambiguous Intent Standard." *Minnesota Law Review* 94, no. 3: 869–95.

Moreno, Jonathan D. 2005. "The End of the Great Bioethics Compromise." *Hastings Center Report* 35, no. 1 (January–February): 14–15.

Moss, Scott A. 2008. "The Intriguing Federalist Future of Reproductive Rights." *Boston University Law Review* 88, no. 1 (February): 175–225.

Moyal, Dena, and Carolyn Shelley. 2010. "Future Child's Rights in New Reproductive Technology: Thinking Outside the Tube and Maintaining the Connections." *Family Court Review* 48, no. 3 (July): 431–46.

Nairn, Joanna. 2010. "Is There a Right to Have Children? Substantive Due Process and Probation Conditions That Restrict Reproductive Rights." *Stanford Journal of Civil Rights and Civil Liberties* 6, no. 1 (April): 1–39.

Neergaard, Lauran. 2012. "OB/GYN Back Over-the-Counter Birth Control Pills." Associated Press, November 20. Online at http://news.yahoo.com/ob-gyns-back-over-counter-birth-control-pills-220213466—finance.html.

Neumeister, Larry, and Lauran Neergaard. 2013. "Judge Making Morning-After Pill Available to All." *U.S. News and World Report*, April 5. Online at http://health.usnews.com/health-news/news/articles/2013/04/05/ny-judge-makes-morning-after-pill-available-to-all.

Nichols, Bruce. 2005. "Hospital Ends Life Support of Baby." *Dallas Morning News,* March 15.

Nichols, Mark. 1993. "Tinkering with Mother Nature: A Controversial Report on Reproductive Technologies." *Maclean's* 106, no. 48 (November 29): 38–40.

Northup, Nancy. 2011. "Estranged Bedfellows." *Human Rights* 38, no. 2 (Spring): 2–22.

Office of Population Affairs. n.d. "Emergency Contraception Fact Sheet." Washington, DC: U.S. Department of Health and Human Services. Online at www.hhs.gov/opa/reproductive-health/contraception/emergency-contraception/

Okolec, Jeanne E. 2009. "Health Care for the Undocumented: Looking for a Rationale." *Journal of Poverty* 13, no. 3: 254–65.

"Oregon's Death with Dignity Act—2012." 2013. Oregon Public Health Division. Online at http://public.health.oregon.gov/ProviderPartnerResources/EvaluationResearch/DeathwithDignityAct/Documents/year15.pdf.

"Oregon's Right-to-Die Law Upheld by Supreme Court." 2006. ABC News, January 17. Online at http://abcnews.go.com/Politics/SupremeCourt/story?id=1514546.

"Oregon's Right to Die Movement." 1905. Denver, CO: The Hemlock Society, USA. Online at www.compassionandchoices.org/.

Pazol, Karen; Andreea A. Creanga; Suzanne B. Zane; Kim D. Burley; and Denise J. Jamieson. 2012. "Abortion Surveillance—United States, 2009." *Morbidity and Mortality Weekly Report* 61 (November): 1–44.

Pence, Gregory E. 1995. *Classic Cases in Medical Ethics.* 2nd edition. New York: McGraw Hill.

Peters, Philip G., Jr. 1990. "The Constitution and the Right to Die." *Midwest Medical Ethics* 6, no. 4 (Fall): 13–16.

Pew Hispanic Center. 2006. *The Size and Characteristics of the Unauthorized Immigrant Population Residing in the United States.* Washington, DC: Pew Hispanic Center.

Pillar, Barbara. 1992. "Bioethical Issues in the Use of Technology." *Nursing Economics* 10, no. 6 (November–December): 419–22.

"Poll: Keep Feeding Tube Out." 2005. March 21. Online at www.cbsnews.com/stories/2005/03/23/opinion/polls/main682674.shtml.

Pollard, Irina. 2009. *Bioscience Ethics.* New York: Cambridge University Press.

President's Council on Bioethics. 2004. *Reproduction and Responsibility: The Regulation of New Biotechnologies.* A Report of the President's Council on Bieoethics, Washington, DC. Online at www.bioethics.gov.

Raymond, Janice G. 1993. *Women as Wombs: Reproductive Technologies and the Battle Over Women's Freedom.* San Francisco: Harper.

Raymond, Janice G; Renate Klein; and Lynette Dumble. 1991. *RU 486: Misconceptions, Myths, and Morals.* Cambridge, MA: Institute on Women and Technology.

"Report Finds More U.S. Women Are Using the Morning-After Pill." 2013. Fox News, February 14. Online at www.foxnews.com/health/2013/02/14/report-finds-more-us-woman-are-using-morning-after-pill/.

Robertson, John A. 1994. *Children of Choice: Freedom and the New Reproductive Technologies.* Princeton, NJ: Princeton University Press.

Roche, Walter F., Jr., and Sam H. Verhovek. 2005. "DeLay's Own Tragic Crossroads." *Los Angeles Times,* March 27.

Roig-Franzia, Manuel. 2005. "Court Lets Right-to-Die Ruling Stand." *Washington Post,* January 25.

Rovner, Julie. 2012."Morning After Pill Advocates Seek Another Look at Age Rules." NPR News, December 7. Online at http://capsules.kaiserhealthnews.org/index.php/2012/12/morning-after-pill-advocates-seek-another-look-at-age-rules/.

Russo, Nancy F., and Jean E. Denious. 2005. "Controlling Birth: Science, Politics, and Public Policy." *Journal of Social Issues* 61, no. 1 (March): 181–91.

Ryan, Maura A. 2001. *Ethics and Economics of Assisted Reproduction: The Cost of Longing.* Washington, DC: Georgetown University Press.

Salzman, Todd A., and Michael G. Lawler. 2012. *Sexual Ethics: A Theological Introduction.* Washington, DC: Georgetown University Press.

Schenker, Joseph G. 2005. "Assisted Reproductive Practice: Religious Perspectives." *Reproductive BioMedicine Online* 10, no. 3 (March): 310–19.

"Schiavo Autopsy Finds No Sign of Trauma." 2005. CNN, June 15. Online at www.cnn.com.

"Schiavo Autopsy Shows Irreversible Brain Damage." 2005. Associated Press, June 15. Online at www.msnbc.msn.com.

Schwartz, John. 2005. "New Openness in Deciding When and How to Die." *New York Times.* March 21.

Scotch, Richard K., and Sai Loganathan. 2011. "Local Government's Role in Health Care for Undocumented Immigrants: Three Counties in North Texas." *Journal of Public Management & Social Policy* 17, no. 2 (Fall): 11–24.

Shanner, Laura, and Jeffrey Nisker. 2001. "Bioethics for Clinicians: 26. Assisted Reproductive Technologies." *Canadian Medical Association Journal* 164, no. 11 (May 29): 1589–94.

Shannon, Thomas A., ed. 2004. *Reproductive Technologies: A Reader.* Lanham, MD: Rowan & Littlefield.

Shaw, Linda R., et al. 1991. "Ethics of Lung Transplantation with Live Donors." *Lancet* 338, no. 8768 (September 14): 678–81.

Sherman, Christopher, and Ramit Plushnick-Masti. 2012. "Fewer Health Care Options for Illegal Immigrants." Associated Press, December 14. Online at http://news.yahoo.com/fewer-health-care-options-illegal-immigrants-081953393.html.

Shreve, Maggie, and June Isaacson Kailes. 1990. "The Right to Die or the Right to Community Support." *Midwest Medical Ethics* 6, nos. 2–3 (Spring/Summer): 11–15.

Smith, Kathryn. 2013. "Appeal of Morning After Pill Angers Women's Groups." Politico.com. Online at www.politico.com/story/2013/05/justice-department-appeals-morning-after-pill-ruling-90842.html.

Solinger, Rickie, ed. 1998. *Abortion Wars: A Half Century of Struggle, 1950–2000.* Berkeley: University of California Press.

Spencer, Naomi. 2005. "Bush Administration Plays to Religious Right in Delaying Contraceptive Approval." World Socialist Web Site. Online at www.wsws.org/en/articles/2005/11/plan-n26.html.

Spreng, Jennifer E. 2008. "Pharmacists and the 'Duty' to Dispense Emergency Contraceptives." *Issues in Law and Medicine* 23, no. 3 (Spring): 215–77.

"State Laws Related to Insurance Coverage for Infertility Treatment." 2012. Washington, DC: National Conference of State Legislatures. Online at www.ncsl.org/issues-research/health/insurance-coverage-for-infertility-laws.aspx.

Stenson, Jacqueline. 2005. "Viva in Vitro." *Health* 19, no. 2 (March): 77.

Stipson, Jim P.; Fernando A. Wilson; and Karl Eschbach. 2010. "Trends in Health Care Spending for Immigrants in the United States." *Health Affairs* 29, no. 3 (March): 544–50.

Stolberg, Sheryl G. 2005a. "A Cacophony of Epitaphs." *New York Times,* March 31.

———. 2005b. "Schiavo's Case May Reshape American Law." *New York Times,* April 2.

Strathern, Marilyn. 1992. *Reproducing the Future: Essays on Anthropology, Kinship and the New Reproductive Technologies.* New York: Routledge, Chapman and Hall.

Stulac, Francine. 1991. "RU 486: The Politics of Choice." *Health Matrix* 1, no. 1 (Spring); 77–100.

Suppon, Jenna M. 2010. "Life After Death: The Need to Address the Legal Status of Posthumously Conceived Children." *Family Court Review* 48, no. 1 (January): 228–45.

Sutton, Jane. 2004. "Florida Court Strikes Down Law in Right-to-Die Case." *Reuters News,* September 23. Online at news.yahoo.com.

Szabo, Liz. 2013. "FDA: Morning-After Pill to Move Over-the-Counter." *USA Today,* April 30. Online at www.usatoday.com/story/news/nation/2013/04/30/morning-after-plan-b-fda/2125109/.

Tanner, Robert. 2005. "Schiavo Case Spurring Statehouse Debate." Associated Press, April 4. Online at news.yahoo.com.

Tavernise, Sabrina. 2013. "Use of Morning-After Pill Rising, Report Says." *New York Times*, February 14. Online at www.nytimes.com/2013/02/14/health/use-of-morning-after-pill-is-rising-report-says.html.

"Terri Schiavo Timeline." 2005. CBS News, April 1. Online at www.cbs4.com/moreinfo/local_story_053154624.html.

"*Time* Poll: The Schiavo Case." 2005. *Time*, April 4, 26–27.

"Unauthorized Immigrants: How Pew Research Center Counts Them and What We Know About Them." 2013. Washington. DC: Pew Research Center. Online at www.pewresearch.org/2013/04/17/unauthorized-immigrants-how-pew-research-counts-them-and-what-we-know-about-them/.

Van DeVeer, Donald. 1987. "Introduction." In *Health Care Ethics: An Introduction,* ed. Donald Van DeVeer and Tom Regan, 3–57. Philadelphia: Temple University Press.

Weigant, Chris. 2013. "Plan B's Plan B." *Huffington Post*, May 1. Online at www.huffingtonpost.com/chris-weigant/plan-bs-plan-b_b_3196790.html.

Wolf, Susan M. 2004. "Law and Bioethics: From Values to Violence." *Journal of Law, Medicine & Ethics* 32, no. 2 (Summer): 293–306.

Wood, Daniel B. 2009. "In Hard Times, Illegal Immigrants Lose Healthcare." *Christian Science Monitor*, March 24. Online at www.csmonitor.com/Business/2009/0324/p01s01-usec.html.

Woodsong, Cynthia, and Lawrence J. Severy. 2005. "Generation of Knowledge for Reproductive Health Technologies: Constraints on Social and Behavioral Research." *Journal of Social Issues* 61, no. 1 (March): 193–205.

Zarembo, Alan, and Anna Gorman. 2008. "Dialysis Dilemma: Who Gets Free Care?" *Los Angeles Times*, October 29. Online at http://articles.latimes.com/2008/oct/29/local/me-dialysis29.

10

THE AFFORDABLE CARE ACT

Stumbling Toward Universal Health Insurance?

I am not the first President to take up this cause, but I am determined to be the last. It has now been nearly a century since Theodore Roosevelt first called for healthcare reform. And ever since, nearly every President and Congress, whether Democrat or Republican, has attempted to meet this challenge in some way. A bill for comprehensive health reform was first introduced by John Dingell Sr. in 1943. Sixty-five years later, his son continues to introduce that same bill at the beginning of each session.

Our collective failure to meet this challenge—year after year, decade after decade—has led us to a breaking point.

—Barack Obama 2009

The conditions in 2010 created a window for reform, but it was not a big one. To squeeze legislation through that window, Democrats had to work around the many constraints that might otherwise have doomed chances for passing a bill. And working around those constraints helped to shape the central choices they made, including the choices that left the law vulnerable to counterattack.

— Paul Starr 2013, 16–17

"What's past is prologue," William Shakespeare wrote—and it seems that's especially true when it comes to healthcare. The history of health reform in American spans a century of false starts, near misses, and historic advances that culminated when President Obama signed the Patient Protection and Affordable Care Act into law on March 23, 2010. It was a day that a lot of people thought would never come and a moment that almost didn't happen—and the story of how we got there is one of the most important stories in modern politics and public policy-making.

—John Kerry 2010, 7

As the above quotes suggest, getting comprehensive healthcare reform enacted would be exceptionally difficult and contentious. The process of passage through Congress was treacherous, with land mines placed all over the place. It took some "unorthodox," though hardly unknown, maneuverings (Sinclair 2012) to finally achieve passage. The law relied heavily on past Republican initiatives, yet it garnered no Republican support. It sought to reform a highly fragmented system, yet left much of it in place. It was less than liberals had hoped for and more than conservatives wanted.

This chapter focuses on healthcare reform that was enacted in 2010. We first look at the years preceding passage of the Affordable Care Act (ACA), 2006–2008. We follow that up with describing the process of passing the legislation and the controversies surrounding that passage. This is followed by an examination of threats to the act, such as court challenges and the 2012 election, and implementation of the act. We then look at Republican alternatives to health reform and conclude the chapter with some judgments about the legislation and its implementation and the future of healthcare reform.

THE ROAD TO THE AFFORDABLE CARE ACT (2006–2008)

Kingdon's Multiple Streams Model

One way of understanding the series of events leading up to the passage of the Patient Protection and Affordable Care Act (PPACA), more formally known as the Affordable Care Act (ACA), is to make use of a model of agenda building known as the multiple streams model (Kingdon 2010).

The model starts with three streams. The problems stream focuses on the problem-identification stage of the policy process (see Rushefsky 2013). In this stream, there is debate over whether a problem exists and, if so, what is the nature of the problem. Additionally, there is debate over whether a government response is necessary to address that problem. Different people and groups will have various perceptions about the nature of the problem and what to do about it. Further, there are often ideological differences that play a role in these perceptions. These ideological differences also play a strong role in perceptions about the Affordable Care Act.

The second stream is the policies stream. Here policy advocates or entrepreneurs push favored public policies and seek opportunities to get those policies adopted. As Kingdon (2010, 116) notes, policy solutions may stew in a "primeval soup," sometimes for decades, with some solutions emerging and others being cast aside.

The third stream is the politics stream. Here changes such as the results of elections or interest group activity provide an opportunity to seek innovative public policies.

An important aspect of this model is that these streams do not necessarily flow together. Problems can fester for years or decades in the case of healthcare. Policy entrepreneurs may have spent years finding the right time for their proposed solutions. Political change is independent of the other two streams.

But there are certain times when the three streams come together, with the political stream being the most important. When all three streams are in sync, there is what is called a "window of opportunity." Some big policy issues, such as healthcare reform, will assume a prominent place on the government agenda, and there is a real opportunity, though a brief one, for action (Kingdon 2010).

The Problems Stream

Cost

We have spent much of this book addressing the problems facing the American healthcare system. One problem that underlies all the rest is the cost of healthcare. We spend considerably more money on healthcare than does any other industrialized nation. Healthcare costs increase faster than inflation and faster than the growth of the economy, so that more and more of our economic activity is taken up in paying for healthcare. The two large government programs, Medicaid (chapter 3) and Medicare (chapter 4), have seen continual increases in costs and pressure put on state and federal budgets. Employers face ongoing increases in the cost of healthcare for their employees and have begun placing more of those costs on them. As Kingdon (2010) points out, this puts American companies, especially manufacturers, at a disadvantage with much of their foreign competition. In other Western industrialized countries, the government pays for healthcare rather than the companies and, thus, the products of companies such as Toyota and Honda cost less than if they had to pay for their workers' health insurance costs. According to some estimates, health insurance premiums account for as much as $2,000 of the cost of a domestically produced car (Johnson 2012). Insurance premiums continue their dramatic rise. Individuals have problems paying for the cost of their healthcare, especially if they lack insurance or adequate coverage. Healthcare costs are an important cause of individual bankruptcy (National Patient Advocate Foundation 2012).

Even individuals with health insurance face problems. Insurance policies often have lifetime caps on how much they will pay out, and catastrophic healthcare could exceed those limits. Insurance companies, especially in the small business and individual markets, engaged in practices that left subscribers exposed to the full cost of their medical expenses (see Potter 2010). Companies would deny coverage for a claim because of an alleged pre-existing condition, a practice known as recision (Potter 2010). These practices became so contentious that it led, in the late 1990s and early 2000s, to consideration of what was called "patient's bill of rights" legislation at both the state and federal level. While Congress did not enact such legislation (until 2010), many states did (Patel and Rushefsky 2006).

Access

The second major problem is one of access (chapter 6). An estimated 47–50 million people lack health insurance (though some have disputed the numbers). There are ethnic/racial dimensions to the access issue. Minorities, such as Hispanics and African Americans, are less likely to have health insurance than whites. Higher-income individuals and families are more likely to be covered than lower-income individuals and families. Lack of access to healthcare can also be a function of geography. People in rural areas and inner cities tend to have less access than people in suburbs. Employment-based insurance, the prime mechanism for insurance coverage in the United States, decreased throughout the twenty-first century. Lack of access to the healthcare system has health consequences (see chapter 6; Patel and Rushefsky 2008).

These problems, cost and access, have been captured on film, in books, and in articles. Three examples stand out. The first is Michael Moore's 2007 documentary *Sicko*. The documentary begins by stating that it is not going to explore the problem of the uninsured, but rather the problems that affect those with inadequate insurance (the underinsured). For example, one of his cases focused on a man who damaged two of his fingers in an accident. His insurance company said it would pay to fix only one of his fingers, so he had to choose which finger to keep. After looking at these kinds of cases and the American healthcare system, Moore examined other healthcare systems and noted that the problems he describes would be taken care of by other healthcare systems at little or no cost.

Jonathan Cohn's (2007) similarly titled *Sick* also critically examines the American healthcare system. He provides case studies of people struggling with the healthcare system and argues that the system is unraveling.

Wendell Potter (2010) worked in the health insurance industry for a quarter of a century. His book, *Deadly Spin,* uncovers practices such as recisions that are undercutting the country's healthcare system.

Of course, these critiques came from the left. The right also saw problems with the healthcare system, but rather than seeking a national health insurance policy, they have sought market reforms. For example, Herzlinger (2007, 1) casts her net widely in search of villains: "the health insurers, hospitals, government and doctors." Her solution is to have consumers take charge of their own healthcare through solutions like high-deductible health plans and health savings accounts (see below).

The Policies Stream

Types of Healthcare Systems

There is no dearth of possible policy alternatives or solutions for the healthcare system's problems. One source is the healthcare systems of other Western industrialized countries. Reid (2010) provides a useful typology of different healthcare systems as well as indicating a major problem with the U.S. healthcare system.

Reid distinguishes among four types of healthcare systems. The first and oldest is the Bismarck model, developed in the late nineteenth century under Prussian and then German chancellor Otto von Bismarck. This model keeps much of the healthcare system private, but utilizes a series of health insurance plans financed by workers and their employers. The plans are nonprofit, and costs and services are tightly regulated.

The second type is the Beveridge model, adopted in England after World War II. This model approximates what has been called in the United States socialized medicine. The government owns the facilities (such as hospitals), and the workers are government employees, though doctors can take private paying patients.

The third type is the national health insurance model, typified by the Canadian system. The facilities and workers are private, but there is a single payer, the government, which collects taxes (premiums) and pays the providers.

The final type is what Reid (2010) calls the out-of-pocket model, which has virtually no public system and patients pay for their own healthcare if they can afford to.

So we have these four models that can be drawn upon. One of Reid's (2010) most critical points is that there are elements of all four models in the United States. Employer-based health insurance is basically the Bismarck model. Veterans and military personnel are in a Beveridge type system (such as the VHA hospitals that we discuss in chapter 5). Those on Medicare are in a national health insurance model. And those without health insurance are in the out-of-pocket model.

Looking at healthcare in the United States this way provides an insight as to why it has been and is so difficult to reform the system: we have these different sets of systems. American healthcare is highly fragmented. The politics of healthcare in America suggests that we are very unlikely to adopt any of these systems as *the* one system. But looking at other healthcare systems does give us a picture of possibilities. Other countries have faced many of the same problems that the United States has but went in different directions. Ultimately, despite the models of what other countries have done, the United States chose none of the above.

Policy Proposals

Policy proposals have been flowing in Kingdon's (2010) primeval soup for decades. In general, liberals/Democrats have favored some type of national health insurance plan or public sector program. At a minimum, they have advocated expansion of current programs, such as the Children's Health Insurance Program (CHIP) and Medicaid. Conservatives/Republicans have, in general, opposed the comprehensive plans and resisted expansion of current programs, though this is not entirely the case; Richard Nixon proposed the Comprehensive Health Insurance Plan (CHIP), and President Bush proposed and Congress enacted an expansion of Medicare to cover prescription drugs.

Another way of thinking about policy proposals is to focus on the role of government. Liberals/Democrats tend to favor programs that expand the role of government, whereas conservatives/Republicans tend to pursue plans that rely more on the private sector (see, for example, Capretta and Dayaratna 2013; Goodman 2012). Republican and conservative proposals focused on cost control and market mechanisms. Democratic/liberal proposals tended to focus more on access issues and public sector solutions. Libertarians were mostly interested in government doing less.

We begin with Democratic proposals.

Democratic Reform Proposals

One popular proposal was offered by Hacker (2007). Entitled "Health Care for America," it would retain employer-sponsored insurance, with an employer mandate: either employers would provide health insurance for their workers or pay 6 percent of their payroll into a pool that would be used to finance another feature of the plan. In health insurance policy language, this is known as "play-or-pay." A second part would keep Medicare for those currently eligible for it. The third part would be a new program, the Health Care for America plan (a Medicare-style plan) that would enroll those who had neither Medicare nor employer-sponsored insurance. Employers, Hacker wrote, could enroll their employees in Health Care for America and save administrative costs.

A fourth part would be an individual mandate. Those who were uninsured would be required to enroll in Health Care for America or purchase a private plan. Those enrolled in Medicaid or CHIP would be moved to either Health Care for America or an employer-sponsored program. Thus Medicaid would be eliminated under Hacker's proposal. There would be subsidies, depending on income, for low-income individuals and family.

Hacker wrote that under his plan there would be substantial cost savings. First, Medicare has lower administrative costs than private insurance, 2 percent versus 14 percent for private insurance (Hacker 2007). Second, Health Care for America would be covering so many people—about half of the U.S. population according to Hacker—that there would be administrative efficiencies. Third, both Medicare and Health Care of America would have leverage to bargain with providers of services and equipment. Cost savings would also occur at both the federal and state levels with the termination of Medicaid and CHIP.

Hacker also described what changes would not take place. Here the contrast with conservative/Republican plans is set out very markedly:

> Equally important is what Health Care for America would not do. It would not eliminate private employment-based insurance. It would not allow employers to retreat from the financing of a reasonable share of the cost of health insurance. It would not leave Americans coping with ever-higher private insurance premiums with an inadequate voucher, or pressure them to enroll in HMOs that do not cover care from the doctors they know and trust. It would not break up the large insurance groups in the public and private sectors that are best capable of pooling risks today. And it certainly would not encourage individualized Health Savings Accounts that threaten to further fragment the insurance market and leave Americans even less protected against medical costs. (2007, 2)

Davis and Schoen (2008) proposed keeping much of the public programs (Medicare, Medicaid, and CHIP) and employer-based insurance. They suggested a series of reforms for the individual insurance market and the creation of what was called at that time an "insurance connector" (3), what is now known as health exchanges, for individuals and small businesses. They envisioned the connector as a single national system. The exchanges would include a "public option," a plan similar to Medicare that would compete with private insurance plans. The insurance reforms focused on the kinds of problems mentioned above, such as recisions.

The liberal think tank Institute for America's Future advocated a public option as part of healthcare reform (Clemente 2009). Its plan was based, in part, on work by Hacker (2009). The Institute argued that Medicare was a good model for such a plan, because it had controlled costs better than private insurance and, further, had taken action to cut back on what it called "excess growth" in health spending (Clemente 2009, 5). Another point for the public plan option was to provide competition to the private sector, which had become less competitive. Lower administrative costs and strong bargaining power were two other advantages of a public plan.

In 2008, Hillary Clinton, then a Democratic senator from New York and a candidate for the 2008 Democratic presidential nomination, offered the American Health Choices Plan (Hillary for President 2008). Her plan would first allow those who have health insurance and want to continue with that coverage to keep it. The plan promised those currently insured that their premiums would be lowered and it would reduce cost-shifting. Those who want to change, which includes employers, employees, and individuals, would have a choice of plans. The plan calls for enrolling these groups and people in the Federal Employees Health Benefit Program, which does have a large array of choices. Interestingly, the plan points out that this is the same program that members of Congress are enrolled in. The Clinton plan would include as one of the choices a public plan. The plan notes that neither the public option nor the health choices menu would require additional bureaucracy, because the implementing agencies were already in place.

The Clinton plan also called for insurance reform, such as guaranteed issue (prohibiting insurance companies from turning down someone because of a preexisting condition), restraints on premium increases, and requirements that health insurance companies spend most of their money on paying for services. The plan also called for an individual mandate and subsidies. It was, in fact, fairly close to what was included in the ACA.

The Clinton plan was important for two reasons. First, it was a specific plan proposed by a Democratic senator and a presidential aspirant. Second was Clinton's history of concern about health reform and her role in the deliberations over President Clinton's health reform proposal in 1993. Opponents of President Clinton's proposed Health Security Act referred to the bill as HillaryCare, a phrase later adapted to the ACA (ObamaCare).

Liberal/Democratic proposals in the 2006–2009 period went in various directions. They were offered by think tanks such as the Economic Policy Institute, the Center for American Programs, and Families USA. Some wanted to expand employer-based health insurance. Others focused on expanding Medicare and Medicaid. A few would have preferred a single-payer system, but, in the American political system, this was not possible.

Conservative/Republican Reform Proposals

Some Republican plans, such as those included in the 2012 Republican Party platform, focused on the two large public sector programs, Medicare and Medicaid. Medicare would be converted into a premium support or voucher program, a defined-benefits program as we discussed in chapter 4. Medicaid would be turned into a block grant program, similar to what happened with welfare reform in 1996 (see chapter 3; Kliff 2012; Rushefsky 2013). Both proposals would have the same effect of limiting the federal government's exposure to increases in healthcare costs. The size of the voucher and the block grant can be manipulated or remain the same in future years. Under current law, both are entitlements determined by the size of the recipient pool and their medical expenses.

Another set of health reform proposals came from, among other sources, Senator John McCain's (R-AZ) 2008 campaign. This one would end the decades-long tax treatment of employer-based insurance. Without the tax deduction, employers would likely end this benefit to workers. One of the interesting questions is whether, if such a proposal were enacted, employers would take the funds used to pay for their employees' insurance and add that to their salary or keep some or all to themselves. The McCain and similar plans would substitute an individual tax credit that could be used to purchase a healthcare plan. All three proposals would shift costs to consumers, and consumers/patients would have the responsibility for and choice of plans (Kliff 2012). Such proposals would rely more on private markets than is currently the case.

A related set of ideas would rely on consumer-driven or consumer-directed healthcare plans (CDHCP) and health savings accounts (see, for example, Goodman 2012; Grassley 2009; Rush-efsky 2013; Capretta and Dayaratna (2013)). Such healthcare plans, which are becoming more common, would have a much higher deductible than current employer-sponsored health insurance plans (an important feature to remember when Republicans criticized the Affordable Care Act; see below). The employee would establish a health savings account, similar to an individual retirement account, in which she would deposit money, tax free, that could be used to pay for healthcare. Such plans were virtually unknown prior to 2006. By 2012, 19 percent of all employer-sponsored health plans were the high-deductible type (Claxton et al. 2012).

In 2009, four Republican senators proposed "The Patients' Choice Act." The act provided for a refundable tax credit that would be invested in a health savings account and also be used to purchase insurance. The tax credit would be $5,700 per family and $2,300 per individual. A supplement up to $5,000 would be available for those at the lower end of the income scale (Turner and Antos 2009). Employers could still provide health insurance and receive a tax deduction. Under the proposal, states would set up health exchanges (virtual markets) from which consumers would choose.

Other Republican ideas included converting the health insurance market from individual state markets to a national market. Under current laws, states have the prime responsibility for regulating health insurance plans. Each plan has to, effectively, be registered in any state in which it wishes to do business. The idea behind such proposals is that a national market would create more competition for consumers and thus produce lower health insurance costs or at least restrain them.

Health Insurance Industry Reform Proposals

The interest group representing insurance companies, America's Health Insurance Plans (AHIP), also took part in the debate. Long an opponent of national health insurance (Starr 1982, 2013), the insurance industry had made a major effort to kill the Clinton healthcare plan. This included running a series of television spots, known as the "Harry and Louise" ads, which attacked various parts of the Clinton plan. But by the late 2008s, the healthcare problems had worsened, and AHIP could read the writing on the wall. Healthcare reform might very well succeed this time, and the industry wanted a seat at the table.

The AHIP proposals focused on access to health insurance and relying on the states more than the federal government. The plan, published in 2006, had five principles. First, the federal government should provide state incentives to cover adults and children. Second, states should be encouraged by the federal government to expand Medicaid coverage to 100 percent of the federal poverty line (FPL) and 200 percent for those in the CHIP program. Third, the federal government should provide subsidies for low-income adults and families up to 400 percent of the federal poverty line. Interestingly, this principle states that those in the individual or small business market should purchase insurance using "existing market mechanisms" (America's Health Insurance Plans 2006, 4). The fourth principle was to provide a tax deduction for those with incomes over 400 percent of the federal poverty line to encourage them to purchase insurance. Finally, employers should be "encouraged" (America's Health Insurance Plans 2006, 4) to provide insurance for their employees. Further, the plan stated that the current business tax deductions for health insurance should be maintained.

In 2007, AHIP developed a follow-up plan, called the "Guaranteed Access Plan" (America's Health Insurance Plans 2007). This plan would essentially be a high-risk pool plan. High-risk people are those with preexisting conditions or a history of high medical costs. If such a person applied for an individual policy (group plans, such as employer-sponsored plans generally allow all members or employees to be a member of the plan) and was turned down, then she or he would have access to this state-based plan. Eligibility would be based on how much a person's healthcare costs would be. The criteria would be twice the average of claims in a particular state. If the person could not get into a guaranteed access plan, then private health insurance would be the insurer of last resort. In both cases, the premiums charged would be limited to 150 percent of market rates.

The Massachusetts Model

Attempts at healthcare reform in the 1993–1994 period at the national level prompted some states, such as Massachusetts, to attempt its own reforms. The Massachusetts effort ultimately failed, but a later attempt in that state had a profound impact on the healthcare reform debates that began in 2008.

In 2006, the Massachusetts state legislature passed and Republican governor Mitt Romney signed an ambitious healthcare plan that was similar in many ways to the Affordable Care Act. The program contained the following elements (Long 2008): an individual mandate (all residents had to have health insurance), expansion of Medicaid, an employer mandate (play-or-pay), subsidies to pay for health insurance for low-income individuals and families, reform of the insurance market and a virtual online health insurance market, known as the connector. In the ACA, the connector became the state health exchanges.

The Political Stream

The third stream in the Kingdon (2010) model is the politics stream. Here we can see the impact of elections, changes of administration and/or control of Congress, interest group activity, and public opinion. We begin with elections.

The unpopularity of the Iraq war and the general decline in public opinion approval of the George W. Bush administration led to several key Democratic victories. The first came in 2006 when Democrats regained control of both houses of Congress for the first time since the 1994 elections. Democrats began anticipating successful elections at the congressional and presidential levels and started preparing to jump-start healthcare reform. The anticipation was fulfilled in 2008. Democrats won bigger majorities in both the House and the Senate, and Illinois Democratic Senator Barack Obama defeated Republican Senator John McCain (AZ). By the time Obama took office in January 2009, the chair of the Senate Finance Committee, Max Baucus (D-MT), offered a plan that was almost identical to what eventually passed Congress.

The 2008 Presidential Elections

The 2008 presidential campaign itself lent momentum to healthcare reform. All three Democratic candidates, Barack Obama, New York Senator Hillary Clinton, and former North Carolina senator and 2004 Democratic vice presidential candidate John Edwards, offered plans. They were fairly similar; for example, all had some type of health insurance exchange. The major difference between the two major candidates, Clinton and Obama, was that Clinton supported an individual mandate for all, whereas Obama supported it only for children (Jacobs and Skocpol 2010; Starr 2013). Of course, the Obama administration made healthcare reform a major priority for his first term.

Interest Groups

Interest group activity had certainly changed from the events of 1993–1994. Healthcare industry groups generally opposed the Clinton plan, though there were some exceptions, such as Physicians for a National Health Program. But 2009 was somewhat different. In May 2009, six healthcare industry associations indicated that it supported healthcare reform. The six were the Advanced Medical Technology Association (AdvaMed), the American Hospital Association (AHA), Pharmaceutical Researchers and Manufacturers of America (PhRMA), the American Medical Association (AMA), America's Health Insurance Plans (AHIP), and Service Employees International Union (SEIU) (Jacobs and Shapiro 2010, 12). Not all of the support was wholehearted. While AHIP, for example, overtly supported healthcare reform, it also worked covertly to change or defeat it (Starr 2013).

Public Opinion

Where was the public on all this? The number one issue on the public's mind in the months before the election was the economy, which at that time was in the midst of the worst recession since the Great Depression (Rushefsky 2013). Even so, 62 percent of respondents in a Kaiser Health Tracking Poll in October 2008 thought this was the right time to take on healthcare reform. The primary healthcare issue, according to the respondents, was costs. Overall support for healthcare reform was around the 50 percent mark (a percentage that remained fairly constant) with Democratic respondents much more supportive of change and Republican respondents much more supportive of keeping the system that currently existed (Kaiser Family Foundation 2008). This partisan divide would remain a key characteristic of debates over the Affordable Care Act before, during, and after enactment (see, for example, Weisman and Pear 2013).

An intriguing analysis of public opinion data in 2009 found that comparing it with 1993 was like watching the movie *Groundhog Day*, in which the day keeps repeating itself. Rivlin and Rivlin (2009) found that in 2008 about 82 percent of the public favored fundamental change compared to 92 percent in 1993. In 1993, 63 percent of the public supported reform versus 55 percent in 2008. Public support for reform was greater, at least initially, for the new Clinton administration than it would be for the new Obama administration.

THE LEGISLATIVE PROCESS: AN ORDEAL BY FIRE (2008–2010)

The Opening Moves

One of the lessons absorbed by the Obama administration from the failure of healthcare reform during the Clinton administration was not to make a specific policy proposal but to let Congress lead. President Obama would work for healthcare reform, often behind the scenes, sometimes very publicly. Late in the process the president would lobby members of his own party to support reform, offering deals when needed. But Congress would take the lead.

With Democrats anticipating a victory at the presidential level in 2008 as well as stronger legislative majorities, the party began to consider healthcare reform. This can be seen in the work of Senate Finance Chair Max Baucus (D-MT), who commenced meetings of Republicans and Democrats in the committee to garner support for healthcare reform and held numerous hearings (Starr 2013). In December 2008, Baucus issued a proposal that was very close to what the final legislation looked like. It called for national, rather that state, health insurance exchanges, allowing those age fifty-five to sixty-four to enroll in Medicare, income-based subsidies to purchase health insurance, an individual mandate, reducing (over)payments to Medicare providers, free preventive services, and tax code reform (Baucus 2008).

In the meantime, interest groups were working to gather support for reform. Families USA, a consumer-oriented group, spent much of its time working for health insurance reform and attacking insurance companies. A group that sprang up in 2008 was Health Care for Americans Now (HCAN), "a coalition launched by progressive organizers . . . bringing together labor unions, Moveon.org, Campaign for a New America, community organizations, and women's minority and faith-based groups" (Starr 2013, 191).

Industry interest groups played an important role in the 2009–2010 events as compared to the 1993–1994 period. During the Clinton administration, industry interest groups for the most part opposed the plan. As we have seen, during the Obama administration, those interest groups decided that some type of reform would pass, and they wanted to help shape it. In turn, the Obama administration and Congress made deals with various segments of the industry.

One such group was the pharmaceutical industry. The industry received protection from the federal government's negotiating pharmaceutical prices, a deal also made as part of the Medicare Modernization Act (see chapter 4). Additionally, the industry received protections against reimportation of cheaper drugs from foreign countries, such as Canada. In return, the industry promised to work to find $80 billion in savings, mostly related to closing the doughnut hole in the Medicare Modernization Act. However, the deal apparently cost the head of the industry association, former congressman Billy Tauzin, his job (Altman and Shactman 2011).

The insurance industry was another major player. It was unalterably opposed to the Clinton Health Security Act proposal. Again, this time was somewhat different. The head of the industry interest group (AHIP), Karen Ignagni, publicly committed to support healthcare reform. AHIP agreed to discontinue industry practices that rejected applicants or refused to cover treatments, in return for the promise that everyone would have health insurance (the individual mandate), though it never made a deal with congressional committees (Starr 2013).

But much of the Affordable Care Act was insurance reform, and the for-profit health insurance companies remained wary of the proposed legislation. The Obama administration, for its part, saw the insurance industry as the cause of many of its problems and denounced the industry as part of a strategy for garnering support for the legislation. Covertly, the insurance industry began to oppose the legislation (Starr 2013).

In August 2009, AHIP sent a check for $86.2 million to the U.S. Chamber of Commerce. The purpose was to fund a campaign against healthcare reform. The reason for doing it this way was that the opposition would be seen as coming from the Chamber and not AHIP. The Chamber was under no obligation to report the original source of funding. Further, AHIP was a middleman; the money was actually from the large for-profit insurance companies (Starr 2013). Thus the insurance industry was both for and against health insurance reform.

The Legislative Process: Ideal vs. Real

The legislative path to enactment itself was very complex. American government textbooks typically portray the legislative process as comprising a bill being sponsored by a congressional member; then being sent to a committee and subcommittee for hearings, discussions, and changes (known as markups); voted on and, if approved, sent to the floor of the legislative chamber; going through the Rules Committee in the House that places constraints on length of debate and the number and type of amendments; and then debated and voted on in the floor of the chamber. The Senate, with its looser rules, allows more debate and amendments and procedures (such as the filibuster or the threat of a filibuster) that can bog down the process. If the legislation passes both houses of Congress, it would then go to a House-Senate conference committee to iron out differences in the two bills. The conference committee report then goes back to the House and the Senate for an up-or-down vote, again subject to the peculiarities of Senate procedures. If approved by both houses, the bill then goes to the president for either a signature or a veto. If it is vetoed, Congress could override the veto, though that is a very infrequent result. That is the way it is supposed to happen.

But in recent years, changes in partisanship in Congress have made this normal process much more difficult. The minority party, especially in the Senate, has acted more like an opposition party in a parliamentary system than a minority party that may oppose the majority on many occasions but also shows a willingness to compromise and get things done. Mann and Ornstein (2012), two very close and careful observers of Congress in particular and American politics in general, have noted how a parliamentary-oriented party system (majority party controls the process and the minority party opposes) has been superimposed on the American constitutional system, leading to breakdowns. The failure of Congress, especially the Senate, to pass a budget resolution in recent years is one example of this (though the budget agreement reached after the October 2013 government shutdown is an exception to this; see below). The inability to pass the twelve appropriations bills every year and continual threats of government shutdowns because of the failure to resolve disagreements between the parties are two other examples.

The number of clotures filed (motions to end debate) has dramatically increased. From 2001–2006, when Republicans controlled the Senate and the Democrats were in the minority for most of this period, there were a total of 65 cloture votes attempted. During the 2007–2012 period, when Democrats were the majority in the Senate and Republicans were a minority, there were 127 cloture votes attempted, more than double the previous period (Ornstein et al. 2013). During the 1979–2012 period, the average number of cloture votes when Republicans were in the minority was more than thirty percent higher (57.25) than when Democrats were in the minority (41.63) (Dews 2013). At the same time, the number of conference committees has dropped (Sinclair 2012).

Political Parties at War

Mann and Ornstein (2012) note that while both parties have played the obstructionist game, they attribute most of the problems to the growing conservatism within the Republican Party (see also Kaiser 2012; Ornstein et al. 2013; Poole et al. 2012). The polarization is thus, in Poole et al.'s (2012) phrase, asymmetric.

One can see this polarization via three measures: party unity, ideology, and what can be called "outrage industry" (Berry and Sobieraj 2014). Party unity is the extent to which members of a particular party vote with that party. Looking at the 2009 through 2012 period, on average, 88.5 percent of House Democrats voted with their party compared to 89 percent of Republicans. The figures for the Senate were 91.5 percent (Democrats) and 84.3 percent (Republicans) (Ornstein et al. 2013. There was not much overlap in voting between the two parties.

The second measure is ideology. The Poole-Rosenthal ideological scale (Poole et al. 2012) measures ideology based on voting records in Congress. Looking at four years (1981, 1991, 2001, and 2011), we can see the changes in ideological makeup (see Table 10.1). Over this period of time, Democrats became more liberal and Republicans became more conservative. Not much of a surprise there. The important point, however, is that Republicans became much more conservative than Democrats became liberal. Indeed, the scores for Democrats in both the House and the Senate remained pretty close to each other (same scores for Senate Democrats) in 2001 and 2011, while Republicans became more conservative. This is consistent with Mann and Ornstein's (2012) conclusion.

As Roarty (2013) notes in the *National Journal's* annual rating of Congress, there is much less ideological overlap among the two parties than there was ten or twenty years ago. Both parties seem more like enemy camps in a military conflict. Compromise becomes difficult, though not

Table 10.1

Ideological Change in Congress (selected years)

House	Entire Chamber	Democrats	Republicans
1981	−0.044	−0.289	0.265
1991	−0.058	−0.317	0.359
2001	0.101	−0.374	0.542
2011	0.193	−0.394	0.675
Senate	Entire Chamber	Democrats	Republicans
1981	0.022	−0.286	0.275
1991	−0.049	−0.328	0.311
2001	0.013	−0.357	0.382
2011	0.038	−0.357	0.488

Note: A score of 0.0 would indicate a centrist ideology, a negative score indicates a more liberal ideology, and a positive score a more conservative ideology.
Source: Ornstein et al. (2013, Tables 8–9 and 8–10).

impossible. This enhanced partisanship also affects any attempts to improve the ACA (see below). These are some of the political issues that we discussed in chapter 1.

The third set of measures focuses on the "outrage industry." Berry and Sobieraj (2014) look at different types of media, such as cable news networks (Fox, MSNBC), talk radio, newspaper columns, and the blogosphere. The outrage industry employs some combination of thirteen modes of outrage: insulting language, name calling, emotional display, emotional language, verbal fighting/ sparring, character assassination, misrepresentative exaggeration, mockery/sarcasm, conflagration, ideologically extremizing language, slippery slope, belittling, and obscene language (Berry and Sobieraj 2014, p. 40). They find that conservatives engage in more outrage activities than liberals, consistent with voting records and ideology. One can see this in the rise of the Tea Party movement with the Republican Party. Berry and Sobieraj (2014) observe, as did Roarty (2013) mentioned above, that the outrage industry has an impact on political discourse, elections, and congressional policymaking. To the last point, they note that it becomes more difficult for the parties to collaborate and compromise in this atmosphere.

Summers (2013) argues that gridlock can be a good thing. He notes that there are not sufficient checks and balances in the system, referencing the Vietnam and Iraq wars. He also argues that even in periods of gridlock, where it seems that Congress cannot do anything, things can get done:

> The great mistake of the gridlock theorists is to suppose that progress comes from legislation, and that more legislation consistently represents more progress. While people think the nation is gripped by gridlock, consider what has happened in the past five years: Washington moved faster to contain a systemic financial crisis than any country facing such an episode has done in the past generation. Through all the fractiousness, enough change has taken place that, without further policy action, the ratio of debt to gross domestic product is expected to decline for the next five years. Beyond that, the outlook depends largely on health-care costs, but their growth has slowed to the rate of GDP growth for three years now, the first such slowdown in nearly half a century. At last, universal healthcare has been passed and is being implemented. Within a decade, it is likely that the United States no longer will be a net importer of fossil fuels. Financial regulation is not in a fully satisfactory place but has received its most substantial overhaul in 75 years. For the first time, most schools and teachers are being evaluated on objective metrics of performance. Same-sex marriage has become widely accepted.

While acknowledging Summers' point, all of the trends described above played out as the ACA wended its way through the House and, especially, the Senate.

Ornstein and Mann (2013) took objection to Summers' dismissal of the problems of gridlock. They noted that the ACA passed in spite of Republican opposition. But there was a price to pay for it. The legislation, Ornstein and Mann argued, was not as good as it could have been. Further, the lack of bipartisanship meant that about half the country would be opposed to the legislation and that opponents (Republicans) would continue efforts to hinder its implementation, repeal it, and delegitimize it.

Moving Through Congress

Healthcare reform bills were sent to two committees in the Senate (Finance; and Health, Education, Labor, and Pensions or HELP) and three committees in the House (Energy and Commerce; Ways and Means; and Education and Labor). The two Senate committees coordinated much of their work. But it would be up to the leadership in both the House and the Senate to cobble together a single bill from the multitude of committee actions.

One potential barrier to passage of healthcare reform was the need to get sixty senators to allow movement of the bill on the Senate. Republicans, it was clear, were going to oppose pretty much any effort at healthcare reform. Only Olympia Snowe (R-ME) would vote for healthcare reform in the Senate Finance Committee; even then she voted against it on the floor of the Senate. One of the most important tools of a minority in the Senate is the filibuster. It takes sixty votes to end debate (invoking cloture), and the Senate has adopted the "rule of sixty." If there are not sixty votes to end debate, then the bill will not come to the floor of the Senate. The threat of a filibuster is perhaps more important than the actual filibuster itself.

The 2008 elections gave Democrats a larger majority in the Senate, but not a filibuster-proof one. However, Bernie Sanders (I-VT) caucused with the Democrats, giving them fifty-nine votes. The sixtieth vote came when Arlen Specter (R-PA), who was originally a Democrat and then switched to the Republican side, switched back to the Democrats. He felt that he would not be able to win the primary campaign for his seat in 2010 as a Republican because of challenges from the more conservative Tea Party wing of the party. (As it turned out, while Specter's defection to the Democrats helped move the passage of the Affordable Care Act, it did not help keep his Senate seat—he lost it in the November 2010 elections.)

The Democrats had their sixty votes. But it was a tenuous hold. Not a single one could be lost. In the summer of 2009, Senator Ted Kennedy (D-MA), the Senate's foremost advocate of comprehensive healthcare reform, died. Massachusetts governor Duval Patrick appointed Paul Kirk to fill Kennedy's seat until a special election in January 2010. In that election, Republican Scott Brown defeated Martha Coakley. The Democrats had lost their sixtieth vote, and it would influence the process in 2010.

Making Sausage

But that was only part of the Democrats' problems. The Democratic Party contains a wide range of views on politics, and the more conservative members (known informally as Blue Dog Democrats) raised objections and asked for deals. It is an old saw that there are two things one should never watch being made: one is sausage, the other is legislation. The ACA fit this well. Most of the negotiations over the bill among congressional members came within the Democratic Party. While the Democratic Party in the House was sufficiently large (and does not have the procedural barriers that exist in the Senate) that the loss of a few Blue Dog Democrats would not threaten health reform, that was clearly not the case in the Senate. Two examples illustrate this problem.

Senator Ben Nelson (D-NE) was an opponent of abortion (see below) and wanted additional restrictions on abortion within the legislation. He agreed to a provision that would separate government and personal funds paying for abortions in policies obtained through the state health exchanges. He also got a concession that allowed states to prohibit abortions being paid for by state health exchange policies. In return for agreeing to this, he asked for and received a promise that Nebraska would receive full federal funding for Medicaid expansion. Under the ACA, the federal government would pay 100 percent of the costs of Medicaid expansion for three years, and 90 percent thereafter. Nelson's price for compromise was that the federal government would permanently pay the full costs. This was known as the "Cornhusker Kickback" (Altman and Shactman 2011). The deal made quite a stir, though in the end the bill that accompanied the ACA eliminated it.

The second example is Senator Mary Landrieu (D-LA). Landrieu was opposed to the public option, a part of the House bill. But she had other concerns. In 2005, Hurricane Katrina had devastated Louisiana and other Gulf Coast states. Her price for not supporting a filibuster was additional money for her home state. Senate Majority Leader Harry Reid (D-NV) inserted an amendment in his manager's bill (the bill that combined the two Senate committee versions) that would provide additional Medicaid money to "certain states recovering from a major disaster" (Altman and Shactman 2011, 296). This was known, more colorfully than the deal Nelson got, as the "Louisiana Purchase." Deals such as these characterized much of the deliberations over healthcare reform.

Abortion

There also were issues that were, in one sense, tangential to healthcare reform but impacted passage as well as implementation. The most important of these was abortion. Abortion has been a festering public policy issue since the 1973 *Roe v. Wade* U.S. Supreme Court decision. *Roe* effectively legalized abortion (though abortion was legal in some states prior to the decision). Following *Roe,* actions by the courts, the legislature, the executive branch, and the states limited the availability of abortion. In subsequent decades, states have enacted restrictions on abortion that, for the most part, have been upheld by the Supreme Court. In addition, in 1976 and every year thereafter, the Hyde Amendment, named after its sponsor, Representative Henry Hyde (R-IL), forbade the use of federal Medicaid funds to pay for an abortion. It also allowed states to prohibit the use of its contributions to Medicaid to pay for an abortion. There were limited exceptions for the health of the mother or in cases of rape and incest.

Some Democrats in the House were concerned that policies issued through the state health exchanges might allow abortions. Private health insurance plans frequently contained a provision that would pay for abortions. In the case of the state health exchanges, the federal government would provide assistance to the states in setting them up. But if states refused to set up a health exchange (as a number of states did; see the section on implementation), then the federal government would set them up using federal funds. Further, given the nature of the customers in the health exchanges, those not receiving employer-sponsored insurance or in one of the government programs would receive federal subsidies for purchase of the policies, depending on their income. Thus federal dollars were involved with the exchanges.

Pro-life groups, such as the U.S. Conference of Catholic Bishops, oppose abortion under any circumstances and certainly oppose public funding for abortion. There was, however, a split within the Catholic Church. The Leadership Conference of Women Religious (LCWR), though not necessarily all Catholic sisters, supported healthcare reform in opposition to the bishops' stance, though agreeing with the bishops on their abortion stance (Landsberg 2010). For the LCWR leaders, unlike the bishops, opposition to abortion did not lead to opposition to the ACA ("LCWR Stance on Healthcare Reform Draws Praise and Criticism" 2010).

In the House, Bart Stupak (D-MI) led the charge against inclusion of abortion coverage in any manner in the Affordable Care Act. One possible solution was to separate out the funding. A person wishing to have abortion paid for by her insurance company, under this proposal, would have to pay for a separate policy out of her own pocket. The Senate eventually went along with this Stupak amendment. Further, President Obama agreed to issue an executive order restating that federal dollars would not fund abortions. But this did not satisfy pro-life groups, and they continued to argue that the health reform bill would allow more abortions.

Misinformation Campaigns

Another problem that the Affordable Care Act and its sponsors faced was a misinformation campaign on the part of some its opponents. As an example, consider the charge that the bill contained so-called "death panels."

The provision that was in the legislation would pay doctors to provide end-of-life counseling and present options to the patient and the family. A bill outside of the health reform legislation would have permitted Medicare to pay for such counseling. It was introduced in 2009 by a bipartisan group of members of the House of Representatives. It was later incorporated into the healthcare reform legislation (Altman and Shactman 2011).

The idea that such counseling was a death panel came first from Betsy McCaughey. In 2009, on her radio show, McCaughey said: "Congress would make it mandatory—absolutely required—that every five years people in Medicare have a required counseling session that will tell them how to end their life sooner" (quoted in Starr 2013, 212). Other conservative/Republican opponents quickly picked up this call (part of the "outrage industry"; see Berry and Sobieraj 2014). The phrase "death panels" originated with a Facebook posting by former Alaska governor and 2008 Republican vice presidential candidate Sarah Palin, who wrote that Medicare recipients

> will have to stand in front of Obama's "death panel" so his bureaucrats can decide, based on a subjective judgment of their "level of productivity in society," whether they are worthy of healthcare. (quoted in Starr 2013, 213; see also Altman and Shactman 2011)

Similar comments were made about cost-effectiveness research (CER). The idea behind CER is to evaluate treatments and procedures based on biomedical research and then rely more on the more cost-effective ones. This was transformed by opponents of healthcare reform as a form of rationing and bureaucratic meddling. The argument was that some agency would determine which procedures could be used (Altman and Shactman 2011).

These kinds of misinformation campaigns were part of a strategy set forth by Frank Luntz to defeat healthcare reform (Luntz 2009; McDonough 2011; Starr 2013). Luntz, a GOP strategist, has spent much of his career looking at how to frame policy debates that would advantage his party. Such framing is not confined to Republicans. Westen (2007) has written about the importance of appealing to emotion to frame political and policy debates from a Democratic Party perspective, arguing that Republicans were much better at framing debates than Democrats.

Luntz is a communications specialist and pollster who has been involved in policy debates since the mid-1990s for the Republican Party. For example, in 1995, Luntz counseled Republicans on how they should talk about the cuts they wanted to make in Medicare (for a discussion of the politics around the proposed 1995 Medicare cuts, see Rushefsky and Patel 1998). For example, Luntz advised the party not to talk about "improving" Medicare, because that sounded to seniors as if it would mean additional benefits. Instead, Republicans should talk about "strengthening" Medicare (quoted in Boxer 1995).

In 2009, Luntz gave Republicans similar advice as to how to talk about healthcare reform. For example, here is Luntz's fourth talking point:

> *The arguments against the Democrats' healthcare plan must center around "politicians," "bureaucrats," and "Washington"* . . . *not the free market, tax incentives, or competition.* Stop talking economic theory and start personalizing the impact of a government takeover of healthcare. They don't want to hear that you're opposed to government healthcare because it's too expensive (any help from the government to lower costs will be embraced) or because it's anti-competitive (they don't know about or care about current limits to competition). But they are deathly afraid that a government takeover will lower their quality of care—so they are extremely receptive to the anti-Washington approach. It's not an *economic* issue. It's a *bureaucratic* issue. (2009, 1, emphasis in original)

Similarly, the first political use of the phrase "Obamacare," recalling how Republicans labeled the Clinton Health Security Act proposal as "Hillarycare," was by Mitt Romney (who would be the Republican presidential candidate in 2012) in 2007. Other Republicans picked up the phrase, and eventually even Democrats started calling the ACA Obamacare (Baker 2012).

Healthcare Reform and Public Opinion

An important reason why such messaging works is the nature of public opinion. Researchers have found that the public is not well informed about public policy issues, especially the details. For example, following the 2010 elections, less than half the country knew that the Republicans had gained control over only the House of Representatives. The same survey found much ignorance about the Troubled Assets Relief Program (TARP), part of the effort to help the housing industry recover from the recession (Rushefsky 2013). Only about 16 percent of those surveyed knew that more than half of the money lent had been repaid. Respondents in previous surveys tended to incorrectly identify the TARP program with the Obama administration rather than the Bush administration (Pew Research Center 2010).

A further important finding about public opinion is what might be called "policy ambivalence." The public is concerned about the size of government and high taxes and supports private markets and individual autonomy. At the same time, it likes much of what government does, but does not want to pay for it (Cantril and Cantril 1999).

These dynamics can be seen in the 1993–1994 debates over healthcare reform and the 2009–2010 debates. As we know, the Clinton Health Security proposal was defeated in Congress. What was interesting was an article appearing in the March 10, 1994, issue of the *Wall Street Journal* (Stout 1994). It found that a sizable majority liked the plan when presented with its features. That support diminished greatly when the participants were told that it was the Clinton plan. A similar dynamic was at work with the ACA. A majority of the public like much of the provisions of the act but disapprove of Obamacare (Kaiser Family Foundation 2011). Democrats and Independents tended to view the legislation much more favorably than Republicans, though Republicans like some of the provisions, such as guaranteed issue (prohibiting insurance companies from rejecting applications) and the closing of the Medicare doughnut hole. The Obama administration drew the lesson that Congress, rather than the president, should be out in front on healthcare reform. Thus proposals emanated from the legislature. The administration proposed only a general set of principles and only proposed a program in 2010. Even then, it mirrored the consensus among congressional Democrats.

Another reason the Obama administration hesitated to submit its own proposal was the effect of presidential leadership on conflicts within Congress. Lee (2009) found that when presidents take the lead on an issue, even a relatively noncontroversial one, it tends to exacerbate whatever partisanship exists in the U.S. Senate. It thus appeared to be good politics for the Obama administration not to be in the forefront. A 2013 public opinion poll (Rayfield 2013) found that when the law is referred to as Obamacare, supporters become even more supportive and opponents become even more opposed. In a time of hyper-partisanship, tying controversial legislation with a much-disliked president, as Republicans disliked Obama, can be politically effective.

One of the more interesting public opinion findings is that exposure to contradictory information does not necessarily change people's minds and may even reinforce their views. Paradoxically, those who are most informed about issues tend to hold on to their positions despite the contradictory information (Sunstein 2013). This suggests that disinformation campaigns are very powerful and hard to counter. This shows the importance of the "outrage industry" (Berry and Sobieraj 2014). Advocates of health reform faced this problem during the legislative and into the implementation stage.

Town Hall Meetings

Another important series of events that surrounded passage of the ACA began in August 2009. While neither house of Congress had yet passed a bill, committees had, and the general outlines of what the legislation would look like was readily apparent. Congress normally takes a month-long recess in August, which gives members a chance to get away from Washington, to refresh, to do some politicking back home, and to meet with constituents. An important way of doing this is with town hall meetings.

Senators and representatives, especially on the Democratic side, were taken by surprise at the town hall meetings that year. The meetings were packed with opponents of healthcare reform, especially against the requirement that everyone have health insurance—the individual mandate. In addition, the economy was in the midst of the Great Recession, and the federal government was spending billions of dollars bailing out financial institutions (begun under the Bush administration) and trying to stimulate/restart the economy (begun under the Obama administration). In the meantime, unemployment was rising and home owners were losing their homes.

In this context came the phenomenon known as the Tea Party, self-named after the Boston Tea Party protesting British taxes. While there were legitimate concerns raised by those at the town halls, the Tea Party was not a spontaneous eruption against an aggressive, overreaching federal government. At least three groups planned the protests at the town hall meetings (Starr 2013). While supporters of healthcare reform mobilized to counteract the opposition, the Tea Party wing of the Republican Party and the town hall demonstrations were perfect opportunities for media coverage. The town hall protests provided visuals that made the conventional news media and also the newer Internet social media such as YouTube (Starr 2013).

Starr (2013) notes that the protests and media coverage had two important effects. First, the opponents of healthcare reform had a bigger impact in the media than the supporters. This was especially true of those who watched or listened to conservative-oriented media outlets, such as Fox News (Berry and Sobieraj 2014). Starr (2013, 217) writes: "an NBC poll at the time found that 45 percent of the public—and 75 percent of Fox News viewers—believed the legislation would give the government power to cut off care for the elderly."

The other point was that the protests and media coverage galvanized the supporters. Beleaguered Democrats asked Health Care for Americans Now (HCAN) for help. The protests also tended to move congressional Democrats more to the left on healthcare reform (Starr 2013).

A More Favorable Climate for Reform

Two articles suggested that despite the problems of gridlock and increased partisanship, the political situation was actually favorable to Obama and congressional Democrats. Beaussier (2012) argued that two factors enabled passage of the ACA. One was centralization of control by the leadership of both political parties, especially the Democrats. They were thus able to overcome the massive resistance of Republicans by making use of unorthodox or unusual legislative mechanisms that Sinclair (2012) wrote about (see below). A second factor was that the Democrats, normally a messy, undisciplined political party, were able to hold together (with the help of deals) to provide all the votes the ACA would need. Beaussier (2012) makes the intriguing observation that increased political polarization made it less likely that the parties would negotiate and therefore there was little need for bipartisan negotiation and support (which would not be forthcoming anyway). All the negotiations occurred within the Democratic Party.

Peterson (2011), focusing on the problems and political streams (Kingdon 2010), compared the Obama period to earlier efforts to pass national health insurance. He found that the various problems (such as costs and insurance coverage) were worse than in any of the previous periods. Further, what he calls "contextual factors" (2011, 431–33) also were more favorable under Obama than in any previous administration. The public was more supportive of reform than in previous administrations, and interest groups were also more supportive, though not completely so. In other words, this time was different, more favorable, than past efforts.

The ACA Clears the Obstacles

Table 10.2 presents a timeline of major events in the passage of the Affordable Care Act. The House of Representatives passed its version of healthcare reform on November 7, 2009. The Senate passed its version on December 24, 2009. Senate Majority Leader Harry Reid (D-NV) wanted the Senate to pass a bill before the Christmas break while they still had their filibuster-proof majority, so he kept the Senate in session until the bill was passed on Christmas Eve. By January 15, 2010, congressional leaders of both houses were pretty close to an agreement that would enable a conference report. Four days later, however, Republican Scott Brown won the special election in Massachusetts to replace Ted Kennedy. Senate Democrats no longer had a filibuster-proof majority.

This then led to the use of an unorthodox technique, reconciliation (Sinclair 2012). Reconciliation is a process first put into place by the 1974 Congressional Budget and Impoundment Act. The original purpose of reconciliation was to order budget cuts felt necessary to stay within the congressional budget resolution (for a discussion of the federal budget process, see Mikesell 2013; Rubin 2009). One feature of reconciliation made it an ideal vehicle for those seeking to get legislation passed: by Senate rules, it was not subject to a filibuster. Thus, only a standard majority would be necessary to pass it. The reconciliation process has been used before. For example, the welfare reform legislation passed in 1996 made use of the process. The Bush-era tax cuts in 2001 and 2003 also employed the reconciliation path. The catch was that reconciliation legislation had to be related to the federal budget in some way, what is known as the "Byrd Rule," named after the late West Virginia Democratic senator Robert Byrd. The Senate parliamentarian would have to rule that the reconciliation bill was germane, related to the budget.

Because a conference committee was now out of the question, the House and the Senate resorted to a form of ping-pong, another example of unorthodox lawmaking (Sinclair 2012). President Obama and the House leadership worked to convince the more liberal House Democrats to accept the Senate bill, which had features that liberals did not like. For example, the House bill contained a public option for the state health exchanges, but the Senate bill did not. On March 21, 2010, the House voted to accept the Senate bill. Four days later, March 25, the Senate passed the Health Care and Education Reconciliation Act of 2010. Later that day, the House passed it as well. Healthcare reform had finally come to the United States.

Table 10.2

Affordable Care Act (ACA) Timeline

2006

(November)	Democrats regain control of both houses of Congress
	Massachusetts adopts healthcare reform that is a model for Affordable Care Act

2007   Interest groups begin thinking about working toward reform

2008   Democratic presidential primaries: all three major candidates support reform
Democratic congressional staffers begin looking at reform proposals
Barack Obama defeats John McCain; Democrats win larger majorities in both houses of Congress
Senate Finance Committee chair Max Baucus (D-MT) issues "white paper" on reform containing most of the elements of what would be contained in the Affordable Care Act

2009   President Obama in State of the Union message calls for comprehensive healthcare reform
White House holds "summit" meeting with industry groups

July 15	Senate HELP Committee passes health reform bill
July 31	House Energy and Commerce Committee passes health reform bill
August	Town hall meetings demonstrate opposition to legislation
August 26	Senator Edward M. Kennedy dies
October 13	Senate Finance Committee passes health reform bill
November 7	House passes health reform bill by five votes
December 24	Senate passes health reform bill

2010

January 19	Scott Brown wins special election to fill remainder of Kennedy's term; Democrats lose their filibuster-proof majority
February 25	Obama holds cost containment summit
March 21	House passes Senate version of Affordable Care Act
March 23	Obama signs executive order banning federal funds from being used to pay for abortions; Obama signs Affordable Care Act
March 25	Congress passes Health Care and Education Reconciliation Act
March 30	Obama signs Health Care and Reconciliation Act
November	Republicans make gains in Senate and regain control of House

2012

March 26–28	U.S. Supreme Court hears oral argument in case challenging Affordable Care Act
June 28	U.S. Supreme Court rules on *NFIB v. Sebelius,* affirming part of Affordable Care Act but rejecting other parts
November	President Obama reelected; Democrats gain seats in House and Senate, but Republicans retain control of House

2013   Health exchanges open for enrollment

THE PATIENT PROTECTION AND AFFORDABLE CARE ACT

Goals and Purposes

The Affordable Care Act is a complex piece of legislation superimposed on a complex health-care system. A summary of the ACA by the Congressional Research Service was itself fifty-five pages (*Landmark: The Inside Story of America's New Health-Care Law* 2010). In this section we describe the basic elements of the legislation, noting that some change has occurred because of a 2012 U.S. Supreme Court decision (see below). The basic elements include expanded access, cost-sharing and subsidies, changes to the tax code, health insurance exchanges, benefit design,

Figure 10.1 **Healthcare Reform Implementation Timeline**

Keys

☐ = Coverage Provisions

⬚ (dotted) = Compliance Provisions

⬛ = Delivery System Provisions

▨ (hatched) = Payment Reduction Provisions

2010	2011	2012	2013	2014	2015	2016	2017	2018	2019

Medicaid Expansion

Insurance Reforms (Pre-existing conditions for adults, premium limits)

Insurance Reforms (Pre-existing conditions for children, no annual or lifetime limits, children on parents insurance until 26)

Individual Mandate

Waste, Fraud, and Abuse Provisions for Medicare and Medicaid

Disclosure of Industry Payments to Physicians and Teaching Hospitals

Accountable Care Organizations

Hospital Value–Based Purchasing

Bundled Payments Pilot

Hospital-Acquired Infections Penalties

Hospital Readmission Payment Reductions

Medicaid DSH Payment Reduction

Medical Device Tax

Hospital Market Basket Reductions

Independent Payment Advisory Board

Medicare DSH Payment Reduction

Hospital Productivity Adjustments

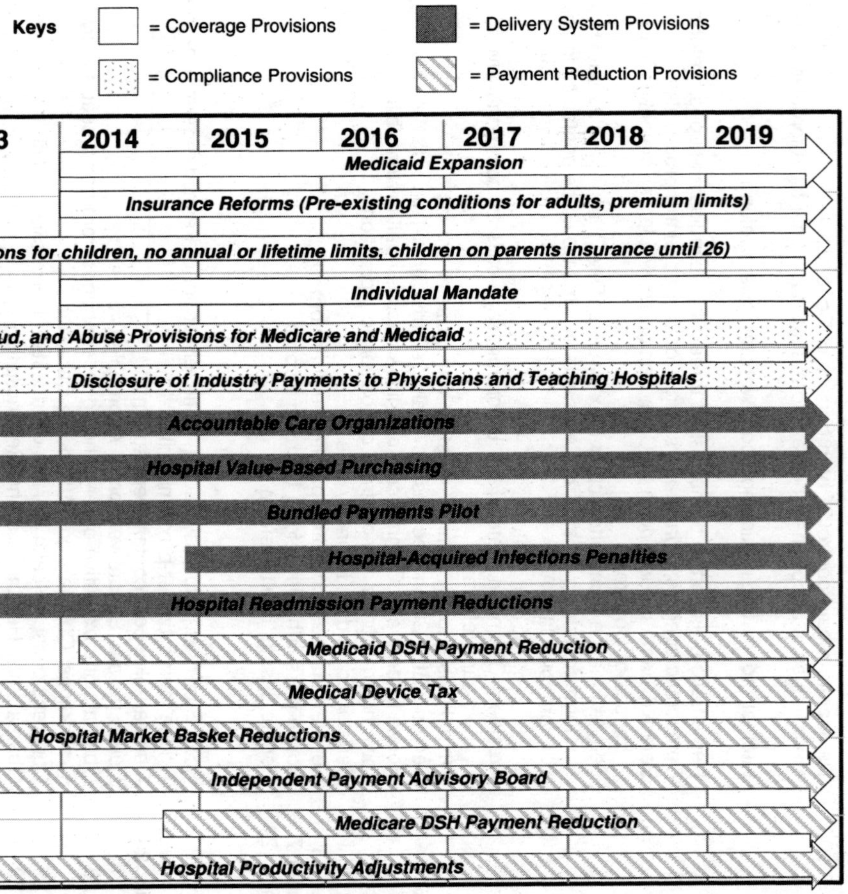

Source: Kaiser Family Foundation. 2010. "Healthcare Reform Implementation Timeline." Menlo Park, CA: Henry J. Kaiser Family Foundation.

private insurance, Medicaid expansion, cost containment, improving quality and performance, prevention and wellness, long-term care, and Medicare. Note that implementation takes place over a period of time (see Figure 10.1). We will discuss implementation issues below.

Major Provisions

Mandates

The most important goal of the ACA is to increase access to the healthcare system by increasing health insurance coverage. A key part of this, as noted above, is the *individual mandate*. Because insurance companies agreed to accept all applicants regardless of pre-existing conditions (guaranteed issue), the only way an insurance system would work under these conditions was if everyone had insurance. If only sick people bought health insurance, then the premiums would have to be so high as to be unaffordable. Failure to have insurance would result in a penalty. Some exemptions were made, for example, for people who had religious objections and for those with very low incomes (Kaiser Family Foundation 2010).

A second, related feature is a modified *employer mandate*. Employers with fifty employees or more would either have to provide health insurance or pay a fee into a pool that would help pay for the legislation. As in the case of the Massachusetts plan, the fee was considerably less than the cost of providing health insurance (Bernasek 2013). In addition, employers who have at least one employee receiving a tax credit to help pay for premiums would pay a fee.

Medicaid Expansion

A third element is Medicaid. As we observed in chapter 3, eligibility for Medicaid varies dramatically depending on the state and the category someone falls into. Eligibility for children is easier than for adults. Childless adults have effectively no chance of getting on Medicaid. In some states, such as the authors' home state of Missouri, the income cut-off line for childless adults is 20 percent of the federal poverty line. The federal poverty level per year for a single adult in 2013 was $11,490. Twenty percent of that is $2,298 annual income.

The Affordable Care Act required that states expand Medicaid eligibility for all persons up to 133 percent (or 138 percent of the federal poverty line, depending on how one reads the legislation). This would result in a significant increase in Medicaid enrollment. To ease the burden on states, the federal government would pay 100 percent of the costs of the expansion from 2014 through 2016; thereafter, the payments would be slightly reduced to 90 percent of the costs by 2020 and thereafter. Failure of states to expand as required would have meant the loss of a considerable portion of their Medicaid funds from the federal government. This last part was struck down by the U.S. Supreme Court (see below).

Health Insurance Exchanges

One of the major ways that the ACA provides for increased insurance coverage is through the creation of *health insurance exchanges*. An exchange may be defined as:

> a structured marketplace for the sale and purchase of health insurance. "Customers" can include individuals and businesses. The insurance companies ("issuers") that choose to sell their products through an exchange may be required to comply with consumer protections, such as offering insurance to every qualified applicant. Exchanges, however, are not issuers; rather, exchanges contract with issuers who will make insurance products available for

purchase through exchanges. Essentially, exchanges are designed to bring together buyers and sellers of insurance, with the goal of increasing access to coverage. (Fernandez and Mach 2013, 7)

The legislation calls on the states to create health exchanges, essentially a virtual market, for those seeking nongroup insurance. The legislation notes that if a state fails to set up a health insurance exchange, the federal government will do so. In some cases, the federal government and a state may jointly run an exchange, what is known as a partnership exchange (Fernandez and Mach 2013). This is another area that has undergone some modification (see the section below on implementation).

The exchanges, whether state or federal, have numerous tasks to carry out. These include determining eligibility for the exchanges, helping people find the best exchange, helping determine eligibility for subsidies, and so forth. The exchanges also determine whether an individual might be eligible for a public program, such as Medicaid, and then help the individual enroll in that program (Fernandez and Mach 2013). Exchanges also certify plans as qualified. Exchanges assist individuals in picking plans and determining what their financial responsibility is. Examples of consumer assistance include toll-free telephone hotlines, a website, a calculator to help compare plans, outreach programs, and a Navigator program to help consumers and businesses find their way around the exchanges. Exchanges are also to oversee the finances of plans, including collecting and distributing premiums (Fernandez and Mach 2013).

The legislation creates different categories of plans, also known as benefit tiers, which would be available in the exchanges. The four tiers, from most costly and generous to least costly and less generous, are platinum, gold, silver, and bronze. All plans would have virtually the same benefits, known as essential benefits, to be defined by regulations (see section on implementation below). The major difference is what percentage of the costs the plan would pay. Platinum plans would pay 90 percent of the benefits, versus the bronze plans that would pay 60 percent. This would give consumers a range of choices when deciding which health plan to pick. The more generous the plan (such as platinum), the higher the premiums. All plans would limit out-of-pocket costs, which are set at whatever the out-of-pocket limit is for health savings accounts. The limit for out-of-pocket costs as of 2010 was $5,950 for individuals and $11,900 for families. For those who have incomes below 400 percent of the federal poverty line, the out-of-pocket spending limits would be reduced (Kaiser Family Foundation 2010).

There are also different types of exchanges (Fernandez and Mach 2013). One type is the SHOP (small business health options program) exchange for small businesses (99 or fewer employees) that qualify. Another type is multistate plans. Businesses and consumers could enroll in these plans regardless of plan location. Companies that participate in the exchange have to offer a child-only plan. Some plans may be nonprofit, run by consumers; these are CO-OP (consumer-operated and oriented plan) plans. Insurance plans can also offer catastrophic plans. Such plans have limited coverage, lower premiums, and higher cost-sharing. Another type of plan would provide only dental benefits (Fernandez and Mach 2013). The different types of plans and the requirements for the plans indicate the complexity of the ACA.

Subsidies

The writers of the Affordable Care Act recognized that some individuals and families would have difficulty paying for health insurance premiums in the exchanges. As a result, the legislation put into place a series of tax credits to pay for premiums. The premiums are refundable and paid in advance of normal tax refunds and are based on a sliding income scale. The subsidies would be available for those with incomes up to and including 400 percent of the federal poverty line. To illustrate, the federal poverty line for a family of four in 2013 was $23,550. Therefore, families of that size with incomes up to $94,200 would be eligible for some subsidy. Subsidies would also be available to small businesses that provide health insurance for their employees (Kaiser Family Foundation 2010). Lesser subsidies are also available to help pay for the cost-sharing features of a plan.

Reforming Private Insurance Markets

An important series of provisions reforms the private insurance market. Two features stand out. First, the states have traditionally had the major responsibility for regulating insurance sold within the states. The ACA is, effectively, a partial preemption of this state responsibility on the part of the federal government. Second, this section of the law, the patient protection part, is effectively a patient's bill of rights, the subject of state and federal activity in the late 1990s and early 2000s (see Patel and Rushefsky 2006).

The law requires that insurance companies spend 80–85 percent of premiums collected on healthcare. This is known as the *medical loss ratio*, an interesting phrase and indicative of some of the issues with insurance companies. Payments made for claims are considered a loss to the insurer. From the standpoint of investors, the lower the medical loss ratio (paying out smaller percentage in claims), the better the company was doing (on the problems with insurance companies, see Potter 2010). The legislation also addresses increases in insurance plan premiums. It requires that plans submit their premium increases to the federal government with the rationales for the increases.

The law modifies health insurance practices. It eliminates lifetime ceilings on benefits. Prior to the law, plans might limit lifetime coverage to, for example, $1 million. While that may seem like a great deal of money, the reality is that catastrophic illnesses such as cancer or chronic illnesses can result in costs that exceed the ceiling.

Pre-existing condition exclusions for children are prohibited. Further, children up to the age of twenty-six can stay on their parents' health insurance plan even if they are not living at home and are working. Beginning in 2014 insurance companies are prohibited from turning down anyone for a pre-existing condition (see Figure 10.1).

The legislation also affects differences in pricing of insurance policies. As we explained in chapter 6, insurance companies have increasingly sold policies on the small group and individual market that are experience rated. That is, the price of policies would depend on risk factors of the subscriber, such as age or pre-existing condition. This was one of the practices insurance companies engaged in that led to increased numbers of the uninsured. Under the ACA, insurance plans are limited to differential or experience pricing based on such factors as age, size of family, whether the subscriber is in a group or individual/small market plan, and whether the subscriber uses tobacco.

High-Risk Pools

As we shall discuss below, the ACA will be implemented over a period of about ten years. Many of the insurance reforms/patient protections will not take place until 2014. Those in the individual market with pre-existing conditions faced alternatives—either they could purchase expensive policies that did not cover their pre-existing conditions or they could not get any insurance. The first state to address the issue of the uninsurables and therefore create a high-risk pool was Minnesota in 1976. By 2013, nearly a quarter of a million people were enrolled in state high-risk pools run by thirty-four states (Smith-Dewey 2013). That is a very small number compared to the size of the uninsured population.

ACA sought to address this transitional problem in a program called pre-existing condition insurance plan (PCIP). In eighteen states, the federal government ran the programs and lowered costs. In the District of Columbia and twenty-three states, the federal government lowered the standards for eligibility (Anderson 2013). The costs of the program were extremely high.

Because of the larger-than-expected enrollment and the high costs, the Obama administration ceased enrolling people into the pools in early 2013. The problem with high-risk pools is the same problem that led to the individual mandate. If the only people enrolled in a health insurance plan are sick people, premiums paid by enrollees will be very high and the costs of the program will be very high. These are not the characteristics of a sustainable program (Hall and Moore 2012; Lubell 2013).

Medicare

The Affordable Care Act also addresses Medicare. Two of the most important provisions affect Parts C and D (see chapter 4 for a discussion of Medicare). Part C is the Medicare Advantage (MA) portion. It allows Medicare recipients to enroll in alternative delivery plans, such as a health maintenance organization or a preferred provider organization. These plans would then provide all Medicare-covered services, and many would add additional services.

As we discussed in chapter 4, the 2003 Medicare Modernization Act provided that the MA plans be paid at 115 percent of the average per capita spending on Medicare recipients. This was to provide an incentive for plans to include Medicare recipients and for recipients to enroll in them. The political party division on this issue was pretty clear. Republicans wanted to transform Medicare into something else, and Democrats liked Medicare as it was and thought the plans were being overpaid. Democrats won on this issue. Over a period of time, payments to plans will be lowered to the Medicare average per capita payment.

The other important change to Medicare concerned prescription drugs (Part D). Recall from chapter 4 that the prescription drug benefit was the major portion of the Medicare Modernization Act. But it contains an oddity known as the doughnut hole. At the point at which $2,970 is spent on covered pharmaceuticals (combining patient out-of-pocket expenses and Medicare coverage), the recipient will have to pay 100 percent of the cost of pharmaceuticals until the out-of-pocket costs reach $4,750 per year. The ACA gradually eliminates the doughnut hole.

The ACA also establishes an Independent Payment Advisory Board that will submit recommendations to Congress for changes if Medicare spending on a per capita basis exceeds growth of inflation plus 1 percent. This is one of those areas that was subject to misinformation (see, for example, the critique of comments by the 2012 Republican vice presidential candidate and chair of the House Budget Committee, Paul Ryan [R-WI], in PolitiFact Florida 2012). The summary of the bill by the Kaiser Family Foundation states:

> The Board is prohibited from submitting proposals that would ration care, increase revenues or change benefits, eligibility or Medicare beneficiary cost sharing (including Parts A and B premiums), or would result in a change in the beneficiary premium percentage or low-income subsidies under Part D. (2010, 8)

The law also reduces disproportionate-share payments to hospitals. Medicare pays additional money to hospitals that have a large number of uncompensated claims, thus a disproportionate share. But if much more of the population will be covered, there should be fewer uncompensated claims. This feature was dramatically affected by a 2012 U.S. Supreme Court decision (see below).

The ACA eliminates patient cost-sharing for a number of preventive services and treatments. The law also increases payments to primary care services under Medicaid. This is one way to increase the likelihood that primary care physicians will be willing to take on Medicaid patients (see chapter 3).

Controlling Costs

The legislation also seeks ways to reduce costs. One way ACA attempts to do this is through the exchanges (Zuckerman and Holahan 2012). As with similar programs, such as Medicare Advantage, Part D of Medicare, the Federal Employees Health Benefits Program, and CalPERS (California Public Employee Retirement System), the exchanges are a form of managed competition. Consumers are faced with an array of plans and have to pay a portion of the premiums for the plan (with help from subsidies, depending on income). This will cause consumers to purchase the type of plan they want, and the competition for subscribers will keep prices low. That, at least, is the theory of managed competition.

Medicare is the focus of several cost-constraining provisions. The ACA calls for cuts in provider reimbursements and cuts DSH (disproportionate share hospital) payments, because if pretty much everyone has health insurance coverage, hospitals do not have to absorb losses from unreimbursed treatment (Zuckerman and Holahan 2012).

The legislation also includes some reforms in payment and reimbursement. For example, those hospitals treating Medicare patients with above-average hospital readmissions might find their Medicare payments reduced. A related provision calls for studies of "bundled" payments for those treating Medicare recipients. Under the fee-for-service system, providers are paid for each service rendered. Under a bundled system, similar in some ways to diagnostic-related groups (DRGs; see chapter 8), the providers are given a single amount to cover all services (Zuckerman and Holahan 2012).

Another method for constraining costs is to tax so-called "Cadillac plans" (Orszag and Emanuel 2010). These are plans with very high premiums that cover almost all healthcare service expenses. The point of this is to reverse or limit the incentives currently in the system that lead to excessive use of healthcare services (Zuckerman and Holahan 2012).

Other parts of the law include funding cost-effectiveness research on medical treatments. Such research would help those involved in the system, such as patients, providers, and payers, to use the treatments or procedures most likely to prove beneficial (Zuckerman and Holahan 2012).

Another provision is coverage of the preventive services mentioned. The idea behind this provision is that covering the cost of these services (such as mammograms) will encourage more people to get the services and, hopefully, catch health problems at an early stage.

The Independent Payment Advisory Board's task is to recommend changes if Medicare expenses exceed certain criteria. The law also seeks to reduce waste and fraud and create a somewhat less bureaucratic healthcare system (Orszag and Emanuel 2010).

Finally, the law promotes organizational changes. The Affordable Care Act encourages the creation of *accountable care organizations* that would better coordinate patient care and take responsibility for the full range of patient care. This is an attempt to create more efficiencies and decrease the fragmentation that characterizes the American healthcare system.

In short, there are a number of features of the ACA directed at cost control. But cost control is not the strongest component of ACA. Critics of Obamacare argue that these kinds of controls will not work (see, for example, Suderman 2012). Even those favorably disposed to the legislation have expressed some skepticism about the efficacy of ACA's cost-control features (see, for example, Zuckerman and Holahan 2012). But spending increases have grown smaller in recent years, and perhaps ACA has contributed at least a little to that slowdown (see chapter 8). Nevertheless, the access features are much stronger than the cost-control features.

CHALLENGING THE AFFORDABLE CARE ACT

> . . . the Affordable Care Act was both politically controversial and technically innovative, inviting constitutional challenge. (Whittington 2013, 275)

The Affordable Care Act, passed by very small margins in the House and the Senate and with no Republican support, was challenged almost immediately after its passage. The challenges were judicial, electoral, and legislative. We begin with the judicial challenges.

The Affordable Care Act on Trial

Almost immediately after President Obama signed the Affordable Care Act, it faced a myriad of legal challenges, which came mostly from state attorneys general in Republican states. The challenges were twofold. First were challenges to the constitutionality of the ACA, particularly the individual mandate. The second challenge was based on the Medicaid expansion required under the ACA and what it would do to state budgets. In total, twenty-seven states challenged the law (Stewart 2011). One private plaintiff was Liberty University in Virginia.

The cases went before federal district courts and then federal appellate courts. For the most part, the decisions were associated with political party. Those judges who had been appointed by Democratic presidents voted to uphold the law; those appointed by Republican presidents, with two exceptions, voted to deem the law unconstitutional. In a couple of instances, the judges ruled that if the individual mandate were unconstitutional, then the whole law was unconstitutional. This is the severability issue: would the ACA law hold up if a part of it (such as the individual mandate) was declared unconstitutional?

Because of the variety of issues and decisions, the U.S. Supreme Court combined the cases into one, *National Federation of Independent Business (NFIB) v. Sebelius* (2012). Generally speaking, oral argument before the Court takes sixty minutes, thirty minutes for the supporters and thirty minutes for the opposition. In this case, the Court broke the issues down into three parts and heard oral argument over three days.

The first issue had to do with standing. Because the penalty or tax would not take place until 2014, under the Anti-Injunction Act challenges could not be made until imposed. The Court ruled that the payment for not having health insurance was not a tax but a penalty, and therefore standing was not an issue.

The two other issues were the important ones. We start with the individual mandate. Recall that the purpose of the individual mandate, part of the concept of shared responsibility, was that if no one could be turned down for health insurance coverage regardless of their health situation, then everyone had to have health insurance. Otherwise, premiums would skyrocket because only the sick would take insurance. This was the experience with high-risk pools as well as the guaranteed issue reform in New York State (prohibiting insurers from turning down applications because of pre-existing conditions [Parente and Bragdon 2009]). The individual mandate was an important part of the Massachusetts plan, the model for the Affordable Care Act.

The arguments against the individual mandate were, first, that it infringed on personal liberty and, second, that it went beyond congressional authority. The constitutional basis for the individual mandate was Congress's power to regulate commerce between the states.

Opponents of the ACA and the individual mandate argued that if the federal government could compel this activity (purchasing health insurance), then it could compel pretty much anything. Some, including U.S. Supreme Court Associate Justice Antonin Scalia, used the "broccoli" argument: if Congress could compel purchase of insurance then it could compel eating of broccoli (Fried 2013). This was both a constitutional argument and a health policy argument (Hall 2013).

The third issue the Court faced was the extension of Medicaid. Under provisions of ACA, failure of a state to extend coverage to people up to 133 (or 138) percent of the federal poverty line could result in the state's losing all its federal Medicaid funding. The question was whether this was too coercive (Kaiser Family Foundation 2012).

In recent years, highly charged court cases have produced a series of 5–4 decisions from the Court. The array of justices is political, with the four more conservative judges on one side and the four more liberal justices on the other side (see Toobin 2008, 2012). The swing justice has been Anthony Kennedy. The fate of the ACA was thus likely up to Justice Kennedy.

The big surprise was not that the ACA survived the court challenge but who the swing vote was: Chief Justice John Roberts. The first decision, over standing, was easily dismissed. All sides agreed that the Court should rule on the constitutionality of the Affordable Care Act. The Court ruled that for purposes of the Anti-Injunction Act, the fee to be paid by those who refused to purchase health insurance was not a tax but a penalty.

The second issue, on the constitutionality of the individual mandate, was a bit of a reach. A majority of the Court ruled that basing the mandate on the commerce clause was not valid. The majority distinguished between regulating an activity and regulating an inactivity (failure to purchase health insurance). The conservative majority (including Justice Kennedy) also thought that the ACA was stretching the commerce clause beyond acceptable limits, though a number of scholars disagreed with this interpretation (see Fried 2013).

That ruling would seem to have doomed the Affordable Care Act. Indeed, CNN reported, based on reading only the beginning of the summary of the case, that the Court had ruled the legislation as unconstitutional (Fried 2013). But for whatever reason, Chief Justice Roberts then went in a different direction (Toobin 2012).

Roberts, now siding with the liberals, wrote the majority opinion that the fee charged persons for not purchasing a health insurance policy was not a penalty but a tax. This would be acceptable under Congress's authority to tax and spend. Thus, the individual mandate and the constitutionality of the Affordable Care Act was upheld (Fried 2013; Mashaw 2013).

It should be pointed out that the Court's rulings on the first two issues were a perfect example of what Stone (2012) calls a policy paradox. A paradox is when something can be two different things at the same time. For purposes of the Anti-Injunction Act, the individual mandate was a penalty rather than a tax. For purposes of the constitutionality of the mandate, it was a tax, rather than a penalty (Fried 2013).

The third issue was Medicaid expansion. The challenge from the states was that the penalty for noncompliance was too severe (Kaiser Family Foundation 2012). By a 7–2 majority, with two liberals joining the conservative justices, the Court ruled that the penalty was, indeed, too severe. There is no question that the federal government can attach conditions to grants it gives to state governments. But to the majority, the federal government had overreached.

In sum, the Affordable Care Act survived the court challenges, though lawsuits continued in 2013 and 2014. At the same time, the Court made it more difficult to meet the coverage expansion of the legislation. The Congressional Budget Office (CBO) predicted, after the Supreme Court decision, that "in 2022, about six million fewer people will be covered by Medicaid as a result of some states deciding against expansion. The forecast estimates that roughly half of those individuals (three million) will instead receive subsidies through the exchanges, while the other half will remain uninsured" (Barnes et al. 2012, 4).

Electoral Challenges

The other challenge to the Affordable Care came via elections in 2010 and 2012. If Republicans regained control of Congress and the presidency, they could repeal all or parts of the legislation.

The 2010 off-year elections produced mixed results. Republicans won (and Democrats lost) sixty-three seats in the House and thus did regain control. In the Senate, Republicans won (and Democrats lost) three seats, cutting into the Democratic majority. While the Republican House could set up roadblocks for implementation of the Affordable Care Act, a Democratic Senate and president ensured that the Act would survive.

In the 2012 elections, the presidency was at stake as well as Congress. While the economy was no longer in a recession, recovery was slow. The country was bitterly divided by party. The Republican presidential candidate was former Massachusetts governor Mitt Romney. Romney had worked with the Democratic-controlled Massachusetts legislature and Senator Kennedy to pass a health reform bill in 2006 that was a model for the Affordable Care Act. However, Romney insisted that while the 2006 legislation was good for the state, a similar piece of legislation was not good for the country as a whole. It was a difficult position to hold.

Obama won his reelection, and Democrats picked up seats in both the Senate and the House. Republicans retained control of the House and used that control to continually try to repeal all or parts of the ACA or to eliminate funding for implementation of it.

It is likely that the 2014 off-year elections will be another opportunity to fight over ACA. Republicans plan to link Obamacare with the IRS scandal that erupted in 2013 over scrutinizing conservative-oriented groups seeking nonprofit status. Their ultimate goal remains repealing Obamacare (Abdullah 2013). Democrats, for their part, plan to run supporting Obamacare (Isenstadt 2013). Of course, by the time the November 2014 elections come around, Obamacare will have been in place for four-and-half years, and the important and popular insurance reforms will have been implemented.

Legislative Challenges

Republicans, conservatives, and libertarians remain unalterably opposed to the ACA. By March 2013, the U.S. House of Representatives made thirty-seven attempts to fully or partially repeal the law or to defund it ("5 Key Points" 2013).

One example of such attempts was proposed on January 3, 2013, by Senate Republicans. The bill was entitled the "American Liberty Restoration Act." The extremely short legislation had the purpose of repealing the individual mandate. A second example, introduced in the House of Representatives about three weeks later, was entitled "Protecting Seniors' Access to Medicare Act." Also very short, the purpose of this bill was to repeal provisions related to the Independent Payment Advisory Board (Peters 2013). By one measure, the House has spent about 15 percent of its time on the floor since Republicans regained control in 2011 on trying to repeal the legislation (Mahar 2013; Peters 2013).

Apart from full or partial appeal, another legislative strategy deployed by Republicans was to defund the program. An example of this was the action of freshman senator Ted Cruz (R-TX). In early 2013, Cruz proposed an amendment to a continuing resolutions bill that would defund ACA until the economy recovers. Cruz stated that he was willing to risk a government shutdown if his amendment did not pass. House Republican leadership opposed the idea of a shutdown over Obamacare, and Cruz's amendment ultimately died (Kiene 2013). Despite that, Cruz engaged in a twenty-one-hour filibuster. The failure to pass some type of budget bill by October 1 (the beginning of the federal new year for budget purposes) led to a sixteen-day partial government shutdown fueled by Republican desire to repeal or defund the ACA. The backlash to the shutdown hurt Republicans, and in December 2013, Congress and the president agreed to a deal that allowed the budget process to continue for two years without shutdowns (Weisman 2013).

IMPLEMENTING THE AFFORDABLE CARE ACT

The Affordable Care Act is a complex piece of legislation. It seeks to extend health insurance coverage and at the same time tries to control costs. Implementation of it will be trying.

The first point to make about implementation is that it will take place over a six-year period (see Figure 10.1). Some parts took effect immediately, such as allowing children up to the age of twenty-six to remain covered under their parents' insurance policy. Also in 2010, insurance companies were prohibited from refusing coverage to children. The individual mandate takes effect in 2014, as does establishment of the state health exchanges.

A related point is that the legislation is complex and implementation of parts of the legislation (the exchanges) has been rough, a problem acknowledged by the Obama administration (see, for example, "Obama Acknowledges" 2013). One scenario for the course of implementation is that it starts off bumpy or poorly and then gradually improves as learning takes place (Sabatier and Mazmanian 1980). The Affordable Care Act is a complex piece of legislation, with many parts superimposed on top of a complex healthcare system

The complexity of the problems (including political problems) can also be seen in two of the rules issued by the Department of Health and Human Services (DHHS). The first rule focuses on Medicare accountable care organizations (ACO). One of the ways that the ACA seeks to control costs is through reorganization of the healthcare system. While the ACA does not mandate reorganization, it does encourage it.

In March 2011, Health and Human Services issued a proposed rule on ACOs, defining what they are, how they have to operate, and how they have to be structured. The complexity of the rule is indicated by the number of federal agencies involved in crafting it: the Centers for Medicare and Medicaid Services (CMS), the Department of Health and Human Services Office of Inspector General (OIG), the Department of Justice (DOJ), the Federal Trade Commission (FTC), and the Internal Revenue Service (Hastings 2011). Later in October 2011, HHS issued its final rule. Interest groups were able to change or water down some of the provisions of the rule. Timetables were moved back, and the number of quality measures for evaluating ACOs was reduced. Community health centers could not participate in ACOs (Galewitz and Gold 2011).

Another example of complexity and politics mixing together is *essential health benefits* (ESBs). Insurance companies offering plans in the exchanges are supposed to have the same essential benefits, including free preventive care. The following ten categories of items are required to be included:

> ambulatory patient services; emergency services; hospitalization; maternity and newborn care; mental health and substance use disorder services, including behavioral health treatment; prescription drugs; rehabilitative and habilitative services and devices; laboratory services; preventive and wellness services and chronic disease management; and pediatric services, including oral and vision care. (Office of the Assistant Secretary for Planning and Evaluation 2011)

One issue that arose over essential benefits was contraceptives as a covered preventive service. In July 2011, the Institute of Medicine, part of the National Academy of Sciences, recommended that contraceptive devices be included in the free provision of preventive services. In August of that year, the Department of Health and Human Services included them as part of the essential benefits (Pear 2011a, 2011b). Pro-life groups, such as Catholic bishops and Catholic institutions including universities and charities, immediately opposed including them (Pear 2011b) and urged the Obama administration to remove the benefit. Congressional Democrats opposed the change.

By early 2013, the Obama administration had made three compromises to try to appease religious organizations as well as Democrats. The administration exempted some businesses and organizations where there were religious objections to contraception. Instead the organizations would have a separate insurance policy that would cover contraceptives paid by insurance companies and beneficiaries. The compromise satisfied pretty much nobody (Pear 2013a). Indeed, Liberty University in Virginia, founded by Jerry Falwell, filed suit in federal court in 2013 challenging the new rule, arguing that it violated the university's religious freedoms (requiring the provision of contraceptives that the university's counsel argued were essentially abortion drugs) and challenging the employer mandate as unconstitutional and beyond Congress's commerce clause powers (Haberkorn 2013). While the Liberty University suit was dismissed by the Court, in a case to be decided in 2014, the Court may rule on whether corporations, as persons, have religious rights under the First Amendment, and can thus exempt contraception coverage from the plans offered to their employees ("High Court Ends Liberty University Lawsuit over ObamaCare" 2013).

Three more of the many issues that implementation of the Affordable Care Act faces are insurance company participation in the exchanges, efforts by businesses to avoid covering their employees and at the same time avoiding penalties, and the application forms for the exchanges. As of May 2013, a limited number of insurers in Illinois had expressed interest in participating in the exchange. In the authors' home state of Missouri, only two insurance companies, Anthem Blue Cross/Blue Shield and Coventry, are participating in the federally run exchanges (American Academy of HIV Medicine 2013). The problem here is that the small number of insurers would mean limited competition and possibly higher prices for the plans. Insurers were concerned that those likely to use the healthcare system (such as those with pre-existing conditions) will enroll, while those less likely to use the healthcare system might hesitate to enroll (Johnson 2012). This is the adverse selection problem in health insurance and undermines the whole point of having an individual mandate. If the trend in Illinois and Missouri is replicated elsewhere, this would undermine one of the major goals of the Affordable Care Act.

A second example of the complexity of implementation issues is determining eligibility for the exchanges and the subsidies. In March 2013, the Department of Health and Human Services unveiled its application form—twenty-one pages that could take up to three-quarters of an hour to complete. It led to numerable complaints, and the next month DHHS issued a shorter form. There was still a bit of confusion about the form, because all the pages needed to be completed, and the time necessary to complete them was pretty short for single people. Families, however, had to fill out more of the form, depending on their size (see Gold 2013).

The third example is employers' trying to avoid some of the coverage requirements of the ACA. Under the law, employers with over fifty employees must offer health insurance to those employees working more than thirty hours a week. Smaller businesses are trying to get Congress to raise the number of hours that trigger the requirement. Some businesses have begun to reduce workers' hours to avoid either providing health insurance or paying penalties. Even states and nonprofits are considering this means of avoiding the mandate (Radnofsky 2013b).

One part of the Affordable Care Act that died during the implementation stage is the CLASS Act (Glickman 2011). Long-term care, such as nursing homes and assisted living, is a problem that generally has not been well addressed in the United States (see chapter 4). Long-term care is expensive, and while private long-term care insurance is available, a relatively small percentage of the population has purchased such coverage, and the coverage itself is limited. The ACA attempted to remedy that problem. The CLASS (Community Living Assistance and Services and Supports) Act (part of ACA) sought to create a public insurance program that workers would purchase for later years. But in September 2011, the Senate Appropriations Committee deleted funding for the program, and the next month the administration abandoned the program completely. Questions were raised about the sustainability of the program, particularly since enrollment was voluntary. The ability of the Senate, with its Democratic majority, to form a conference committee with the House was limited by the lack of a filibuster-proof majority. The result was that while fixes were proposed by the Obama administration, the political support sufficient for passage and for an adequate program was never there (Glickman 2011).

The major and most publicized problems began in October 2013, though the origins of the problems precede that date. October 1, 2013 was the day when those eligible for insurance on the exchanges could enroll in them. Under the ACA, enrollees had until December 23, 2013 to enroll and get insurance coverage by the beginning of 2014. The exchanges are virtual markets. People had to sign up online. The first few days saw a tremendous number of people trying to enroll, almost all of whom failed in the attempt. Part of the problem was that the large number of people who attempted to enroll was beyond the capacity of the computer systems to handle.

But the major problems were with the computer systems. The systems were not completely pre-tested and the likelihood that they would work well at first was very small. Prospective enrollees would have to wait hours after initialing attempting to enroll; or they would be knocked off the system; or they would receive incorrect information. They could not see the available plans and the costs associated with them before they were signed up, and insurance companies were sent incorrect information. The problems went on and on and were fodder for Jon Stewart and *The Daily Show* and, especially, for those opposed to the ACA. The problems were more severe for federally run exchanges (see below), but some state exchanges also saw problems.

President Obama and the Department of Health and Human Services issued several delays and promised that the federal website, healthcare.gov, would be running more smoothly by the end of November 2013. By the end of December 2013, the federal website was handling about 40,000 people a day and nearly a million people had been enrolled. Better, but not nearly as many as originally predicted (about seven million people) (Korte and Locker 2013).

FEDERALISM AND THE AFFORDABLE CARE ACT

A critical feature of the Affordable Care Act is that it heavily involves the concept of federalism. States have an important role to play in the success or failure of healthcare reform. Two of the major roles that states have is setting up state health exchanges and expanding Medicaid cover-age. Both are mechanisms to expand the number of those with insurance coverage, and they have proved to be problematical. States are demonstrating varying perspectives on whether to cooperate, almost as if they were two different political systems, Republican or Democratic (Brownstein and Czekalinski 2013). The battle over healthcare reform is continuing at the state level.

Health Insurance Exchanges

Under the ACA, states are to set up state health exchanges, similar to the Health Connector es-tablished in Massachusetts in 2006 and Part D under the 2003 Medicare Modernization Act. The purpose of the exchanges is to provide a virtual market by which individuals and those in small business could purchase insurance at a reasonable cost. The ACA stated that if the states did not set up health exchanges, the federal government would. Presumably, states would prefer to set up the exchanges under their own rather than federal control.

However, many of the opponents of the ACA, including states that challenged the constitu-tionality of the legislation, refused to set up the exchanges. This reaction should be considered a continuation of the legislative and judicial battles, with Democrats supporting the law and Republicans opposing it. As of May 2013, eighteen states stated that they would set up state health exchanges, twenty-six states refused to set up exchanges (meaning the federal government would have to do so), and seven were considering what to do (the numbers add up to 51 because it includes the District of Columbia). Setting up the exchanges in the recalcitrant states becomes a task for the Department of Health and Human Services. Further, when the federal government has the responsibility for setting up the exchanges, it still will have to work with state agencies. As we saw above, the rollout of the exchanges in the fall of 2013 was a disaster.

Opponents raised another issue related to the exchanges. Under the ACA, those participating in the exchanges may be eligible for federal subsidies (refundable tax credits) to help purchase the policies. The question was raised whether those federal subsidies would be available if the federal government ran the exchanges. This then became another judicial challenge, not over the constitutionality of the law as in 2012, but over its implementation (Radnofsky 2013a; Savage 2013).

To complicate things even more, Republicans in Congress are trying to stop federal funding of the exchanges. Because blocking legislation, such as appropriations bills, is easier than passing legislation, this is potentially a very real threat to the success of the ACA (Pettypiece and Salant 2013). And, as we saw above, the defunding effort led to a government shutdown just as the exchanges were rolled out. DHHS secretary Kathleen Sebelius then went to industry group executives seeking funds for implementation, which Republicans challenged (Kliff 2013b).

Then there is the problem of getting the word out about the exchanges so that people will enroll. A poll released in April 2013 indicated some of the problems. According to the poll (Kliff 2013a), 42 percent of the public were unclear as to whether the law was still on the books; another 7 percent thought that the Supreme Court had declared the law unconstitutional; and another 12 percent thought that Congress had repealed it. One of the administration's tasks was to inform the public about the exchanges. In 2013, the Obama administration began a campaign to inform the public about the law and to prepare people for enrolling in the health exchanges and choosing the appropriate insurance policy (Shapiro 2013). Even that was challenged by Republicans ("House GOP Expands Investigation" 2013). One strategy was to ask help from the National Football League and other sports enterprises to get the word out about Obamacare and the exchanges (Galewitz 2013).

A related point has to do with navigators. Because of the complexity of the exchanges, navigators are employed to help people make their choices on the virtual marketplaces. States that oppose the Affordable Care Act and refuse to operate their own exchanges are also making it difficult for navigators. These can be labeled "navigator suppression measures" (Health Care for America Now 2013, 3). These measures include stringent course requirements and training, residency requirements, high fees, background checks, and bans on providing advice (Health Care for America Now 2013). These are measures designed to make it more difficult for people to enroll.

Assuming that the state exchanges, which in 2013 have had varied experience with their operation, do run smoothly, Obama and the Democrats may not get much credit for it. That is because the states that are running their own exchanges are giving them names that do not refer to the ACA. For example, Kentucky's plan is called "Kynect." California's is "Covered California." Connecticut's is "Access Health CT." The federal marketplace is "healthcare.gov" (Stephens, Artiga, and Gates 2013).

States are also engaged in considerable marketing to encourage eligible people to enroll in the marketplaces. The techniques utilized include informational videos, television commercials in English and Spanish, personal stories, and music and radio commercials (Stephens, Artiga, and Gates 2013).

For example, in Vermont a television commercial shows residents doing a variety of activities and then points to the marketplace (Vermont Health Connect) with the slogan "For Vermonters by Vermonters" (online at https://www.youtube.com/watch?v=yulTgIUERo4). An example of a personal story is "Ajay's Story," about a young woman with asthma who will now get coverage under Covered California (online at https://www.youtube.com/watch?v=Y7qQriEOu24).

Medicaid Expansion and the States

The Medicaid issue was the result of the 2012 Supreme Court decision. Recall that the Court ruled that the penalty imposed on states for not extending Medicaid coverage was too coercive. It would be up to each state whether to comply with the Affordable Care Act.

As with the issue of health exchanges, the state reactions split along party lines, though there was some division within the Republican Party on this. One factor was simply opposition, partisan and ideological, to the ACA. Another factor had to do with costs and federal payments.

The ACA called for states to extend Medicaid coverage to 133 percent (effectively 138 percent) of the federal poverty line. Eligibility for Medicaid varied by state and category of applicant. Coverage for children was greater than for parents and virtually zero for nonparental adults. Who would pay for the extension?

As we saw above, the ACA calls for the federal government to pay for 100 percent of the additional costs from 2014 to 2016. After that, the federal government would pay for 90 percent of the additional costs. States that hesitated or refused to expand had two concerns. One was whether the federal government would actually keep its part of the bargain, especially given the federal budget deficits and attempts to reduce them. The second concern was the cost of that 10 percent that states would have to cover after 2016. While that might seem like a small price, the impact on states, given their tight budgets, was not insignificant.

The calculations of the impacts of Medicaid expansion and the ACA on the state budgets (see Holohan et al. 2012) are complicated. States will gain from the ACA because fewer people would be uninsured even if the state does not extend Medicaid. Holohan et al. (2012) estimated that states would save about $10 billion through 2022 even without the extension.

The debate over Medicaid expansion has sometimes pitted Republicans against Republicans. Florida is a good example. The *Tampa Bay Times* noted that "Medicaid expansion is supported by the Florida Chamber of Commerce, Associated Industries, the healthcare industry and the majority of state voters" ("The Legislature's $51 Billion Failure" 2013; see also Campo-Flores 2013). Republican governor Rick Scott supported expansion in 2013, as did the Republican-controlled Florida Senate. But the Republican-controlled Florida House of Representatives did not, and the expansion bill died. Turning down the expansion meant giving up $51 billion in federal dollars and about a million residents without insurance ("The Legislature's $51 Billion Failure" 2013).

As of spring 2013, twenty states plus the nation's capital had agreed to the expansion. Thirteen states have declined, and seven had not yet decided. Failure to expand Medicaid has consequences for states and businesses and residents in those states (Alonso-Zaldivar 2013a). Obviously, it would leave millions of people uninsured. Pear (2013b) notes that 50 percent of those lacking health insurance live in the states that have refused to expand Medicaid. They are among the poorest in the country. Further, businesses in those states might face a combined penalty of $1 billion if at least one of their employees gets subsidized insurance through an exchange. If Medicaid were available, then there would be no penalty (Alonso-Zaldivar 2013a).

Perhaps the state facing the most wrenching problems related to Medicaid is Mississippi. Here the high-stakes politicking is a reversal of the defunding bill that Ted Cruz proposed in the U.S. Senate (see above). Republicans control both houses of the Mississippi state legislature as well as the governor's mansion. Both the governor and the majority Republicans opposed the Medicaid expansion. But the minority Democrats, strongly supporting Obamacare and the expansion, playing a game of chicken, did not allow a vote on reauthorizing Medicaid as a tactic to at least allow debate. The state legislature adjourned as normal in April. This puts those already in the program, about 700,000 people, in jeopardy of losing their Medicaid coverage (Hess 2013).

Another interesting, related quirk has to do with legal immigrants. Under the 1996 Personal Responsibility and Work Opportunities Reconciliation Act (welfare reform), legal immigrants were prohibited from enrolling in Medicaid for five years. Thus, poor legal immigrants cannot enroll in Medicaid, but under the ACA, they could enroll in the health exchanges, creating a situation where legal immigrants get health insurance but citizens do not (Alonso-Zaldavar 2013a).

A third issue that Alonso-Zaldavar (2013a) points to is the fairness issue. In states that reject Medicaid expansion, people with incomes just over the federal poverty line will be eligible for insurance and subsidies through the exchanges. Those with incomes just under the federal poverty line will not be covered.

One state that opposed Medicaid expansion, Arkansas, developed an intriguing proposal that might provide a way out of this political stalemate. Arkansas proposed that people who enroll under the expansion be allowed to participate in the state health exchanges, rather than in traditional Medicaid (Hancock 2013). This could meet Republican preferences by providing a private option rather than an expanded government program. This is similar reasoning to the prescription drug benefit (Part D) that was added to Medicare in 2003 (see chapter 4). The advantages of the plan, apart from garnering Republican support, include access to a wider group of plans and providers. As we saw in chapters 3 and 6, physicians do not have to accept Medicaid recipients as patients. Providers would be paid at higher rates than Medicaid pays, and that would expand access. As Hancock (2013) notes, having assured access means that treatments that would otherwise be delayed can start earlier, thus producing a healthier and less costly population (see also Davidson 2010; Patel and Rushefsky 2008).

There are some disadvantages to the Arkansas plan. The major one is cost. Insurance on the exchanges will be more costly than Medicaid, perhaps as much as 50 percent more, according to a Congressional Budget Office report (Hancock 2013). On the other hand, supporters of relying more on private markets argue that competition among plans will restrain and perhaps even lower costs (Hancock 2013). Another issue is synchronizing the health exchange with Medicaid. Policies purchased under the health exchanges will come with substantial cost-sharing provisions. But cost-sharing is limited under Medicaid. The Arkansas plan seems to be one alternative that reluctant states might consider.

States' refusal to expand Medicaid means that fewer people will be covered than if all the states expanded Medicaid. An estimated five million people will be left without any insurance. These are generally people whose income is too low ironically to be eligible for subsidies on the exchange. Texas, Florida, Georgia, North Carolina, Louisiana, Virginia, and Missouri will have the largest number of uninsured, with Texas leading the way with over one million residents who will remain uninsured (Kaiser Family Foundation n.d.; Levy 2013). Interestingly, the states that are not expanding Medicaid already have very low eligibility standards, lower than those who are expanding (Rudowitz and Stephens 2013).

Apart from the health consequences of remaining uninsured, the states that are not expanding Medicaid tend to be disproportionately in the south and also disproportionately affect people of color (Rudowitz and Stephens 2013). Additionally, these states will also not receive billions of dollars of assistance that would come with expansion. States not expanding will forego an estimated $346 billion over a ten-year period (2013–2022) (Rudowitz and Stephens 2013). Of course, one could argue that this will produce savings for the federal budget.

One other element of the refusal of many states to expand Medicaid must be mentioned. The ACA assumed that between the exchanges and Medicaid expansion, pretty much the entire population would be covered. If this were indeed the case, then the federal government would cut, under provisions of the ACA, disproportionate share hospital (DSH) payments, that is payments to hospitals with a large number of Medicaid and uninsured patients. But the 2012 Supreme Court decision effectively gave states the option on whether to expand Medicaid, and, as we have seen, many states, including the authors' home state of Missouri, declined to do so. But the DSH payment cuts remain. So hospitals in states that refuse to expand Medicaid will see a decrease in federal funding, while still treating the large number of uninsured patients that come to them. For this reason, among others, hospitals and their state associations lobbied state legislatures to expand Medicaid. Unfortunately for the hospitals, many legislatures refused to do so.

Yet even with all the problems of the rollout and the opposition to the Affordable Care Act, it is likely that one of the targets will be met in 2014. In 2013, the Congressional Budget Office predicted that the exchanges (federal and state) would have seven million enrollees in 2014 (Kliff 2013c). Based on the experience with initial enrollment in Medicare Part D (the prescription drug benefit), the 7 million figure appears plausible. There are two caveats to this. One is that the exchanges continue to improve. The other is getting the right mix of enrollees, such as younger, healthier people along with older and/or less healthy enrollees (Kliff 2013c).

PLSD: POST-LEGISLATIVE STRESS DISORDER

The bumpiness of implementation made Democrats nervous. Max Baucus (D-MT), chair of the Senate Finance Committee and one of the architects of the Affordable Care Act, declared the ACA a "train wreck." Other Democrats expressed their unease as well (see Cohn 2013a). Senate Majority Leader Harry Reid (D-NV) argued that there needed to be more funding to successfully implement the ACA and forestall the train wreck. Republicans were trying to reduce funding for the ACA (Bolton 2013). Indeed, Republicans were doing all they could in Congress, at the state level, and in the courts to either repeal or eviscerate it. President Obama noted that implementation would face some glitches ("Obama Acknowledges Possible 'Glitches' in ACA Implementation" 2013), a mild understatement as we have seen.

Ross Douthat, an influential Republican columnist for the *New York Times,* wrote that the train wreck was really the Republican Party. He noted that the Republicans do have a conservative alternative to Obamacare but are afraid to vote for it. As a result, he wrote:

> This, *this,* is the Republican Party's healthcare problem. It isn't that ideas about health policy don't exist, and it isn't that they won't work. It's that right now the feasibility question is purely academic, because even after five years of debating these issues, and despite Eric Cantor's best efforts, there still aren't enough Republican lawmakers willing to take even the smallest of steps toward putting those ideas to the test. This means that no matter how much of a "bureaucratic nightmare" the implementation of the current healthcare law turns out to be, liberals at least have this ace in the hole: When it comes to healthcare reform, there is still no *politically* realistic alternative to their approach. (Douthat 2013)

While the Affordable Care Act will faced a roller-coaster ride (Sabatier and Mazmanian 1980) and Republicans continue to try to either repeal it or thwart it, not everyone was so concerned. Drews Altman, responding to comments by Senator Baucus about the coming train wreck and by *New York Times* columnist David Brooks about chaos, wrote:

> There are always problems in big government programs and unintended consequences that could not be predicted in advance of implementation. The longer term question is not whether there will be problems—there will be glitches and there will be even more successes as people gain coverage and insurance is reformed—but whether the political system today has the capacity to learn from implementation, adapt and make improvements. (2013)

Altman mentions several things that can successfully affect implementation. He writes that as states become more familiar with the exchanges, changes will be made to improve how they are run. More flexibility given to the states might induce more to participate. The

Department of Health and Human Services made some minor changes administratively. The two implementation problems that Altman sees are the "hypertension" that exists in Congress between Republicans and Democrats and whether the two sides can reach an agreement to improve/change the ACA, and the media coverage that focuses on what is not working rather than what is working.

Cohn (2013a) also argues that the ACA is not a train wreck. He says the law is not perfect; it is the result of compromises and is complicated. He also notes that many of the problems (Medicaid and state health exchanges) are the result of what he calls a "broken" health insurance market that did not cover a substantial portion of the population. Cohn also observes that the ACA does not strongly address the cost issue, again because of compromises necessary to passage. But he also observes that the problems have been festering for decades, and it will take time to address them.

Cohn (2013a) points to other programs that got off to a slow or bumpy ride: These include Medicare Part D and the Children's Health Insurance Program. Both are now moving much more smoothly. The ultimate problem, Cohn states, is expectations. Parts of the law have already been implemented, and expectations are few. He concludes his piece: "These people may be a lot better off because of Obamacare or they may be only a little bit better off. Either way, they'll be better off—and, over time, their situation will improve. That's not bad for government work" (2013a).

CONCLUSION

It was big—the most ambitious effort in recent decades to reorganize a major institution on a basis that agrees more closely with principles of justice and efficiency. Yet it was also comparatively limited—compared, that is, with the health-care systems of other democracies or to the ideal remedies that many reluctant supporters of the legislation would have preferred.

This is the puzzle of the Affordable Care Act. It calls for major changes, but it is also notable for what it leaves unchanged. After four decades of rising inequality and insecurity, it provides a major boost to the living standards of low-wage workers and their families and increases economic protection for the middle class. The central thrust of the law is to change how health insurance works and to make it affordable, though it also includes measures to improve the quality of medical care and control its costs. But the law does not substantially alter how medical care is organized, and it may not change the long-term trajectory of health spending. Most Americans with secure, employment-based insurance will see little different in their own coverage or healthcare. (Starr 2013, 239)

The attempt at comprehensive healthcare reform was seemingly like the Hundred Years War (1337–1453) between England and France. Presidents and members of Congress have spent decades trying to rationalize the American healthcare system, making it more efficient, controlling costs, and covering more people. While we made a series of incremental steps (such as the development of private health insurance, the passage of Medicare, Medicaid, and CHIP), the development of the healthcare system made it difficult to make substantial changes without invoking opposition from various groups. This is the path dependency argument. Once we took a particular direction, it was very hard to move in a different direction. This is the argument, using slightly different language, that Starr (2013) makes, referring to the policy trap of incremental healthcare policymaking.

So what are we to make of the Affordable Care Act? There are many perspectives from which to view the ACA. Earlier in this chapter, we briefly examined the four major types of healthcare systems, following the scheme of Reid (2010). Reid distinguished among four models of healthcare systems: Bismarck, Beveridge, National Health Insurance, and Out-of-Pocket models. The authors of the ACA chose to pick none of the above and stay with our hybrid, fragmented system. The focus of the ACA was on limiting the Out-of-Pocket model. The legislation is mostly insurance reform, providing additional access to people who did not have health insurance and patient protections (patient's bill of rights) for the entire population.

A second perspective is the partisanship one, and it combines with an institutional perspective. Other major legislative achievements, such as Medicare, Medicaid, Social Security, welfare reform, and the Bush-era tax cuts had some supports from Republicans and Democrats. The ACA was not so fortunate.

Recall that in 1993–1994, Republicans, who were in the minority in both houses of Congress, opposed any kind of healthcare reform that could be attributable to the Democrats and the Clinton administration. This played out again in 2009 and 2010, and in the aftermath of enactment. Republicans, as Mann and Ornstein (2012) observe, acted pretty much in unison against healthcare reform. There were attempts on the part of Senate Democrats and the Obama administration to work with Republicans. Some of the changes to the legislation were the result of these attempts. Max Baucus (D-MT), the chair of the Senate Finance Committee, convened the gang of six (three Democrats including Baucus and three Republicans) to negotiate a compromise. In the end, not unexpectedly, the negotiations failed. But it did serve one purpose: it delayed action in the Senate. Had Senate Democrats, seeing that there would be no support from Republicans, moved ahead with their filibuster-proof majority, Congress would likely have passed a bill in 2009 rather than go through the convoluted process it went through in 2010.

It should also be noted that much of the Affordable Care Act relies on ideas that originated with Republicans: these include the individual mandate and the exchanges. An analysis of the legislation found that in the Senate "More than one-fourth of the linked ideas are found in bills sponsored by Republicans" (Wilkerson, Smith, and Stramp 2013, 25; Krugman 2011). The notion that Republicans had no input into the Affordable Care Act is not accurate.

There is also the related institutional factor. In 1993, two political scientists, Sven Steinmo and Jon Watts, presented a paper, later published in 1995, predicting the failure of the Clinton administration effort. The title of the paper was "It's the Institutions, Stupid!" (a play on the internal Clinton 1992 campaign motto to focus on the economy, "It's the economy, stupid!"). Their argument was that the institutional barriers, particularly in the Senate, would prove insurmountable. Despite majorities in both houses of Congress in 1993–1994, Democrats could barely move the legislation. While Republican resistance was certainly responsible for the policy failure during the Clinton administration, the Democrats also share some blame. There was disagreement within the party about the Clinton plan or any other plan. Thus there was no majority that supported healthcare reform.

Though comprehensive healthcare reform did pass in 2009, those institutional barriers remained difficult, though not impossible, to hurdle. In both 1993–1994 and 2009–2010, Republicans sought any means possible to thwart healthcare reform legislation. Part of the difficulty of getting anything passed was that in 2009–2010, as in the earlier period, most of the difficult negotiations occurred within the Democratic Party. Combine that with the difficulties of getting sixty votes in favor of reform, and the result was deals (Cornhusker Kickback, Louisiana Purchase) and unorthodox lawmaking (Sinclair 2012), such as the use of the reconciliation procedure, the absence of conference committees, and one House accepting what the other did (ping-pong).

Further, the institutional and political problems that made passage of the Affordable Care Act so difficult also will impede any efforts to improve it. House Republicans have spent a considerable amount of time trying to repeal it. By May 2013, the House attempted to repeal the ACA thirty-seven times (Mahar 2013). Most complex pieces of legislation have required subsequent changes to fix problems or make needed changes. As Weisman and Pear write:

But as they prowl Capitol Hill, business lobbyists like Mr. DeFife, healthcare providers and others seeking changes are finding, to their dismay, that in a polarized Congress, accomplishing them [needed corrections] has become all but impossible.

Republicans simply want to see the entire law go away and will not take part in adjusting it. Democrats are petrified of reopening a politically charged law that threatens to derail careers as the Republicans once again seize on it before an election year.

As a result, a landmark law that almost everyone agrees has flaws is likely to take effect unchanged. (Weisman and Pear 2013)

Ezra Klein (2013c) argues that the kind of gridlock described above effectively means that Congress defaults policy making to other elements of government, such as an agency or a court or the president. Those other bodies may not be as accountable as Congress. Klein writes, "Gridlock doesn't mean nothing moves. It means that American policy ends up taking some very unusual detours" (2013c).

The result of all this was legislation that pleased no one completely. Starr (2013) and Altman and Shactman (2011) assert that the Affordable Care Act was about as good as could be gotten from Congress. This sentiment is most picturesquely captured by Jacob Hacker. In 1997, Hacker published a book entitled *The Road to Nowhere* on the effort of the Clinton administration to pass the Health Security Act. During the subsequent debates beginning in 2007, Hacker advocated a more public role in the healthcare system, suggesting, first, that we use Medicare as the model, and then pushing for the public option in the exchanges. After the ACA was passed, he published an article (Hacker 2010) exploring why comprehensive healthcare reform passed this time, but expressing some unhappiness with the outcome. The article was entitled "The Road to Somewhere." And these were supporters of the law.

Republicans, conservatives, and libertarians remain unalterably opposed to the Affordable Care Act. They have filed lawsuits against it, continuing in 2013 and 2014. Republicans at the state level have refused to set up health exchanges, allowing the federal government to do so. Republicans, especially in state legislatures, have refused to expand Medicaid eligibility, an important component of the Affordable Care Act. Republicans in the U.S. House of Representatives repeatedly tried to repeal the ACA or limit or defund its implementation. This is pictured in a May 14, 2013, editorial cartoon by Steve Sacks for the *Minneapolis Star Tribune*. It shows an angry elephant (the symbol of the Republican Party) in the shower washing its head. The shampoo is "Repeal Obamacare Shampoo" and the directions read: "1) Work yourself into lather. 2) Rinse. 3) Repeat. And repeat. And repeat. . . ." The caption of the cartoon is "Gonna Wash that Law Right Out of My Hair?" The October 2013 partial government shutdown was at least to some extent due to attempts to defund/repeal the ACA. The continuing attacks and the incremental nature of policy making were nicely captured by Secretary of State George Schultz in 1986:

Nothing ever gets settled in this town. It's not like running a company or a university. It's a seething debating society in which the debate never stops, in which people never give up, including me, and that's the atmosphere in which you administer (quoted in Apple 1986).

In some ways, Republican opposition is hard to explain. The Affordable Care Act leaves much of the American healthcare system in place. It contains elements that have Republican origins, such as the individual mandate and the state health exchanges (Krugman 2011). Both of those elements are contained in the 2003 Medicare Modernization Act (MMA), proposed by a Republican president and passed by a Republican-majority Congress. The MMA (see chapter 4) requires all Medicare recipients to have a drug plan (the individual mandate) or pay a fine/tax when they finally buy one. For those not getting a drug benefit through a retirement plan, recipients go on a virtual market to compare plans and purchase (the exchanges). The Massachusetts plan, passed by a Democratic state legislature but negotiated with and signed by a Republican governor (Mitt Romney), was the model for the Affordable Care Act, though there certainly are differences between the ACA and the plan adopted in Massachusetts (see Jan 2013).

Republicans, for the most part, prefer smaller government, lower taxes, and less regulation. Their opposition to the ACA is to the expansion of the federal role, what they call a "government takeover." This was on top of the financial bailout and large federal deficits that were the result of the Great Depression (Rushefsky 2013).

To the extent that Republicans have a healthcare policy, it would include the following elements (Klein 2013a):

1. They want to end the tax bias in favor of employer-sponsored health insurance to create full portability (either through a tax credit, deductibility, or another method);
2. They want to reform medical malpractice laws (likely through carrot incentives to the states);
3. They want to allow for insurance purchases across state lines;
4. They want to support state-level pre-existing-condition pools;
5. They want to fully block-grant Medicaid;
6. They want to shift Medicare to premium support;
7. They want to speed up the FDA device and drug approval process; and
8. They want to maximize the health savings account model, one of the few avenues proved to lower healthcare spending, making these high deductible and HSA plans more attractive where Obamacare hamstrung them.

Questions can be raised as to whether the plan would cover much of the population and whether it would control costs, but it does represent an alternative vision to the Affordable Care Act.

While repeal may be difficult, there are other ways to stall implementation. Representative Michael Capuano (D-MA) (2013) describes this as effectively "death by a thousand cuts." This includes resisting funding for implementation, refusing to confirm officials appointed to oversee implementation (though that was limited in 2013 prohibiting filibustering of most presidential appointments), refusing to fund salaries of officials to run exchanges, and so forth. The IRS scandal that broke out in the spring of 2013 (when IRS agents targeted certain conservative/Republican groups that had filed for not-for-profit status, though it was later discovered that liberal and progressive groups were also targeted) became part of Republican opposition to Obamacare. Republicans argued that given the mistrust engendered by the scandal, the IRS could not be trusted to implement its part of healthcare (the tax penalty). The National Republican Congressional Committee (the Republican Party committee in the House of Representatives that seeks to get more Republicans elected) went so far as to claim that the IRS would be in control of our healthcare (see Hicks 2013; Kessler 2013). Republicans also see the 2014 off-year elections as a referendum on Obamacare. Of course, by that time, a good portion of the ACA will have been implemented, such as the insurance protections, and that might affect how voters feel about the law (Alonso-Zaldivar 2013b).

The same questions can be asked of the Affordable Care Act. The Supreme Court's 2012 decision concerning Medicaid expansion makes it less likely that important segments of the population will have health insurance coverage. The cost-control measures in the Affordable Care Act are weaker than the insurance features. Implementation in some cases has proved difficult and bumpy, made more difficult by opposition. The ACA was a compromise that ultimately did not completely satisfy its proponents.

Another issue that the ACA and its supporters face is the combination of public information (pretty low) and opposition (pretty high) (Carroll 2013). As we have seen, a good portion of the public is not certain that the ACA still exists. Some think that it was repealed, while others think the U.S. Supreme Court declared it unconstitutional. Additionally, according to a May 2013 poll, Obamacare had the support of only about 43 percent of the public. Interestingly, those opposed to the ACA were divided in their reasons for that opposition. Nearly a third of the opponents thought that the law does not go far enough.

Even supporters of the law are anxious about its survival and successes. Cohn (2013b) suggests five things that could derail the Affordable Care Act. The first is that there will not be a sufficient number of healthy people signing up for insurance. Second is that the computer systems may not be up to the task. Cohn describes the daunting but not impossible tasks ahead for programmers and systems:

> Consider what the new system has to do. First, it determines whether you're eligible for Medicaid or for subsidized private insurance. If it's the latter, it will figure out what subsidies, if any, you qualify for. To do that, it must verify your identity, residency, and income, which means communicating with the Social Security Administration, Homeland Security Department, and Internal Revenue Service. You'll be presented with insurance choices, based on a separate set of communications with the carriers. Finally, the system will calculate your premium, taking the subsidies into account.
>
> Ensuring all the different entities communicate seamlessly is a headache-inducing task—especially when some of the systems are old and idiosyncratic. Federal officials are particularly nervous about states that have asked Washington to run their exchanges but insist on determining Medicaid eligibility themselves. Many states already make Medicaid enrollment arduous. Under Obamacare, they could make it cumbersome to connect to Medicaid websites or force applicants to wait many weeks before hearing whether they qualify. On top of all this, the whole online operation has to run with ironclad security, given the sensitive nature of the data involved. (2013b, 32)

The Fall 2013 rollout of the exchanges, at least in the first few months, supported Cohn's anxieties.

Cohn's third concern is that insurance companies will raise prices and/or might not participate in the exchanges. The fourth concern is resistance of Republicans at the state level and Republicans in Congress. At the state level, the refusal to set up the exchanges or to expand Medicaid will mean insurance will be extended to fewer people. At the congressional level, Cohn points out that the ACA needs subsequent legislation to clear up some ambiguities in the law and to fix any problems. Cohn's final concern is that President Obama and Obamacare will be blamed for all the problems that will inevitably occur.

Another way to judge the Affordable Care Act is the extent to which it "bends the cost curve." If healthcare costs and insurance premiums continue to rise at a rapid rate, then the ACA will be labeled a failure. As we saw in chapter 8, in recent years cost increases have diminished. Some of that is due to the severe recession and the slow recovery. But at least some may be due to the ACA. Klein (2013b) suggests that the ACA will result in a decrease in cost increases.

We argue that there are two major problems with the Affordable Care Act, apart from arguments by those who oppose the legislation or any kind of healthcare reform or larger government role. First, the legislation leaves in place a very fragmented system. While there are provisions in the act that seek systemic changes, those changes are modest at best. It leaves in place much of what Michael Reagan (1999) calls "The Accidental System." The four types of healthcare systems that

Reid (2010) discusses pretty much remain. We understand that the ACA was a product of a difficult political process. Even supporters recognize that it was not what they wanted, and there are weaknesses to it that may be addressed in subsequent years.

The other, related, problem, discussed in some detail in this chapter, is the federal nature of the Affordable Care Act. It is not just that it requires states to do much of the heavy lifting in implementing the program (state health exchanges and Medicaid expansion, among others), but there is both opposition in many of the states to implementation and, equally as important, states will differ in how they shape their policies even when cooperating. Thus, it will continue to be the case that there really is no such thing as an American healthcare system, but a set of systems, differing by geography and category (employer-insured, Medicare, Medicaid, etc.). A national system would have been easier to implement and simpler. But American exceptionalism suggests that we work within the time-honored constitutional principle of federalism.

With Obama winning reelection in 2012 and the Democrats maintaining their majority in the Senate until at least 2015, the Affordable Care Act will continue to be implemented and become part of the healthcare scene; 2013 and 2014 are the crucial years for implementation. Changes will surely be made to the ACA; this is the normal course of events for legislation. The ACA will be no exception. The shape of the healthcare system(s) will continue to evolve.

STUDY QUESTIONS

1. There is an old saying that there are two things that one should never watch being made: one is sausage and the other is legislation. In what ways does the passage of the Affordable Care Act look like sausage making? Why were unorthodox congressional procedures utilized in getting the ACA passed?
2. The failed attempt at comprehensive reform during the Clinton administration provided lessons learned by the Obama administration and congressional Democrats in 2009 and 2010. What were those lessons?
3. What do you see as the strengths of the Affordable Care Act? What do you see as its weaknesses? Explain your answer. To what extent are answers to these questions influenced by ideology?
4. The most controversial part of the Affordable Care Act is the mandate that everyone purchase insurance. Why was this included in the legislation? Why was it so controversial? Do you agree with the mandate? Why or why not?
5. Since the passage of the Affordable Care Act, Republicans have continually tried to either repeal it in full or defund it. Why do they continually do this? In 2014, the major portions of the ACA will have been implemented. If Republicans regain control of the Senate in 2014 or 2016 and if a Republican becomes president in 2016, do you think they will be able to repeal the ACA? Why or why not?
6. A number of states have refused to expand Medicaid and/or set up their own health exchanges. Why is that the case? What are the impacts of the refusal to participate?
7. The chapter notes that other countries have adopted national health insurance systems and have controlled costs better than the United States. Yet none of the policies adopted by these countries were adopted here or even seriously considered. Why not?
8. Why did the Obama administration succeed in passing comprehensive health reform when all previous efforts had failed?
9. In what way did increased partisanship shape the Affordable Care Act?
10. In what ways does increased partisanship affect the ability to improve the Affordable Care Act?

REFERENCES

Abdullah, Halimah. 2013. "How the Next Battle Over Obamacare Could be the Ugliest Yet." CNN, May 31. Online at www.cnn.com.

Alonso-Zaldivar, Ricardo. 2013a. "Fallout for States Rejecting Medicaid Expansion." Associated Press, April 22. Online at http://bigstory.ap.org/article/fallout-states-rejecting-medicaid-expansion.

———. 2013b. "Republicans See 'Obamacare' Debacle as Key to 2014." Associated Press, May 26.

Apple, R.W., Jr. 1986. "A Lesson from Shultz." *New York Times*, December 9.

Altman, Drews. 2013. "Can We Learn from ACA Implementation and Improve the Law?" Menlo Park, CA: Kaiser Family Foundation. Online at http://kff.org/health-reform/perspective/can-we-learn-from-aca-implementation-and-improve-the-law/.

Altman, Stuart, and David Shactman. 2011. *Power, Politics, and Universal Health Care: The Inside Story of a Century-Long Battle.* Amherst, NY: Prometheus.

American Academy of HIV Medicine. 2013. "Missouri State Insurance Exchange." Online at http://www.aahivm.org/moexchange.

America's Health Insurance Plans. 2006. "We Believe Every American Should Have Access to Affordable Health Care Coverage: A Vision for Reform." Washington, DC: America's Health Insurance Plans.

———. 2007. "Guaranteed Access to Coverage for All Americans." Washington, DC: America's Health Insurance Plans.

Anderson, Steve. 2013. "Federal Reform: High-Risk Insurance Pools." Online at www.healthinsurance.org.

Baker, Peter. 2012. "Democrats Embrace Once Pejorative 'Obamacare' Tag." *New York Times*, August 3.

Barnes, Julie, et al. 2012. "Primer: Understanding the Effect of the Supreme Court Ruling on the Patient Protection and Affordable Care Act." Washington, DC: Bipartisan Policy Center (August).

Baucus, Max. 2008. "Call to Action: Health Reform 2009." Washington, DC: U.S. Senate Finance Committee.

Beaussier, Anne-Laure. 2012. "The Patient Protection and Affordable Care Act: The Victory of Unorthodox Lawmaking." *Journal of Health Politics, Policy and Law* 37, no. 5 (October): 741–78.

Bernasek, Anna. 2013. "Why a Health Insurance Penalty May Look Tempting." *New York Times*, June 22.

Berry, Jeffrey M., and Sarah Sobieraj. 2014. *The Outrage Industry: Political Opinion Media and the New Incivility.* New York: Oxford University Press.

Bolton, Alexander. 2013. "Reid: More Funding Needed to Prevent ObamaCare from becoming a 'Train Wreck.'" *New York Times*, May 1.

Boxer, Sarah. 1995. "Word for Word/Sweetening the Bitter Pill; How a Republican Should Break Bad News to Grandma." *New York Times*, September 17.

Brownstein, Ronald, and Stephanie Czekalinski. 2013. "Altered States." *National Journal* 45, no. 15 (April 13): 12–21.

Campo-Flores, Arian. 2013. "GOP Clashes Stymie Medicaid Expansion." *Wall Street Journal*, May 2.

Cantril, Albert H., and Susan Davis Cantril. 1999. *Reading Mixed Signals: Ambivalence in American Public Opinion About Government.* Washington, DC: Woodrow Wilson Center Press.

Capretta, James C., and Kevin D. Dayaratna. 2013. "Compelling Evidence Makes the Case for a Market-Driven Health Care System." *Heritage Foundation Backgrounder* no. 2867 (December 20).

Capuano, Michael E. 2013. "Obamacare Is Facing Death by a Thousand Cuts." *Boston Globe*, May 29.

Carroll, Aaron. 2013. "Myths About Obamacare." CNN, May 29. Online at www.cnn.com.

Claxton, Gary, et al. 2012. "Employer Health Benefits 2012 Annual Survey." Menlo Park, CA: Henry J. Kaiser Family Foundation, and Chicago, IL: Health Research and Educational Trust.

Clemente, Frank. 2009. "A Public Health Insurance Plan: Reducing Costs and Improving Quality." Washington, DC: Institute for American's Future.

Cohn, Jonathan. 2007. *Sick: The Untold Story of America's Health Care Crisis—And the People Who Pay the Price.* New York: Harper Collins.

———. 2013a. "Why Obamacare Is Not a 'Train Wreck' (Again)." *New Republic*, April 29.

———. 2013b. "My Obamacare Anxiety: The Five Scenarios That Keep This Reform Advocate Up at Night." *New Republic* 244, no. 8 (May 27): 30–33.

Davidson, Stephen M. 2010. *Still Broken: Understanding the U.S. Health Care System.* Stanford, CA: Stanford Business Books.

Davis, Karen, and Cathy Schoen. 2008. "Using What Works: Medicare, Medicaid, and the State Children's Health Insurance Program as a Base for Health Care Reform." Invited testimony before the House Committee on Energy and Commerce, Subcommittee on Health Hearing on "America's Need for Health Reform." September 18. Washington, DC: Commonwealth Fund.

Dews, Fred. 2013. "Chart: A Recent History of Senate Cloture Votes Taken to End Filibusters." Washington, DC: The Brookings Institution. Online at http://www.brookings.edu/blogs/brookings-now/posts/2013/11/chart-recent-history-of-senate-cloture-votes-to-end-filibusters#.

Douthat, Ross. 2012. "The Republican Health Policy Trainwreck." *New York Times*, April 30.

Fernandez, Bernadette, and Annie L. Mach. 2013. *Health Insurance Exchanges Under the Patient Protection and Affordable Care Act (ACA)*. Washington, DC: Congressional Research Service.

"5 Key Points to Know About the Health Care Overhaul Before Major Provisions of the Law Begin." Associated Press, June 19.

Fried, Charles. 2013. "The June Surprises: Balls, Strikes, and the Fog of War." *Journal of Health Politics, Policy and Law* 38, no. 2 (April): 225–41.

Galewitz, Phil. 2013. "NFL's Help Sought on Promoting Obamacare Insurance Plans." *Kaiser Health News,* June 24.

Galewitz, Phil, and Jenny Gold. 2011. "HHS Releases Final Regulations for ACOs." *Kaiser Health News,* October 20.

Glickman, Howard. 2011. "Requiem for the CLASS Act." *Health Affairs* 30, no. 12 (December): 2231–34.

Gold, Jenny. 2013. "A Shorter Exchange Application, but Is It Simpler?" *Kaiser Health News*, April 30.

Goodman, John C. 2012. *Priceless: Curing the Healthcare Crisis*. Oakland, CA: The Independent Institute.

Grassley, Chuck. 2009. "Heath Reform—A Republican View." *Health Affairs* 361, no. 25 (December 17): 2397–99.

Haberkorn, Jennifer. 2013. "Liberty University Pivots in Health Law Challenge." Politico, May 17. Online at www.politico.com.

Hacker, Jacob S. 1997. *The Road to Nowhere: The Genesis of President Clinton's Plan for Health Security.* Princeton, NJ: Princeton University Press.

———. 2007. "Health Care for America: A Proposal for Guaranteed, Affordable Health Care for All Americans Building on Medicare and Employment-Based Insurance." Washington, DC: Economic Policy Institute, January 11.

———. 2009. "The Case for Public Plan Choice in National Health Reform." Washington, DC: Institute for America's Future.

———. 2010. "The Road to Somewhere: Why Health Reform Happened." *Perspectives on Politics* 8, no. 3 (September): 861–76.

Hall, Jean P., and Janice M. Moore. 2012. "Realizing Health Reform's Potential." Washington, DC: Commonwealth Fund.

Hall, Mark A. 2013. "Health Care Law Versus Constitutional Law." *Journal of Health Politics, Policy and Law* 38, no. 2 (April): 267–72.

Hancock, Jay. 2013. "The Arkansas Medicaid Model: What You Need to Know About the 'Private Option.'" *Kaiser Health News*, May 1.

Hastings, Douglas. 2011. "The Medicare ACO Proposed Rule: Legal Structure, Governance, and Regulatory Sections." *HealthAffairs Blog*, April 5. Online at http://healthaffairs.org/blog/2011/04/05/the-medicare-aco-proposed-rule-legal-structure-governance-and-regulatory-sections/.

Health Care for Americans Now. 2013. "Anti-Obamacare States Try to Throw Navigators Off-Course." Washington, DC: Health Care for Americans Now.

Herzlinger, Regina. 2007. *Who Killed Health Care? America's $2 Trillion Medical Problem—And the Consumer-Driven Cure.* New York: McGraw-Hill.

Hess, Jeffrey. 2013. "Political Fight Jeopardizes Mississippi's Entire Medicaid Program." *Kaiser Health News*, June 22.

Hicks, Josh. 2013. "The IRS Role in Obamacare and How Republicans Are Using It." *Washington Post*, May 29.

"High Court Ends Liberty University Lawsuit over ObamaCare." Fox News, December 2. Online at www.foxnews.com/politics/2013/12/02/high-court-ends-liberty-u-lawsuit-over-health-law/.

Hillary for President. 2008. "The American Health Choices Plan." Online at www.hillaryclinton.com.

Holohan, John, et al. 2012. *The Cost and Coverage Implications of the ACA Medicaid Expansion: National and State-by-State Analysis.* Washington, DC: Kaiser Commission on Medicaid and the Uninsured.

"House GOP Expands Investigation of Sebelius' ACA Donation Requests." 2013. *California Healthline*, May 28. Online at www.californiahealthline.org.

Isenstadt, Alex. 2013. "Democrats' 2014 Strategy: Own Obamacare." Politico, June 4. Online at www.politico.com.

Jacobs, Lawrence R., and Theda Skocpol. 2010. *Health Care Reform and American Politics: What Everyone Needs to Know.* New York: Oxford University Press.

Jan, Tracy. 2013. "U.S. Won't Mirror Mass. on Health Exchanges." *Boston Globe*, May 20.

Johnson, Toni. 2012. "Healthcare Costs and U.S. Competitiveness: Backgrounder." Washington, DC: Council on Foreign Relations, March 26.

Kaiser, Robert G. 2012. "'It's Worse than It Looks: How the American Constitutional System Collided with the New Politics of Extremism' by Thomas E. Mann and Norman J. Ornstein." *Washington Post*, April 30.

Kaiser Family Foundation. 2008. "Kaiser Health Tracking Poll: Election 2008." Menlo Park, CA: Henry J. Kaiser Family Foundation.

———. 2010. "Summary of the Affordable Care Act." Menlo Park, CA: Henry J. Kaiser Foundation.

———. 2011. "Kaiser Health Tracking Poll: Public Opinion on Health Care Issues." Menlo Park, CA: Henry J. Kaiser Family Foundation, November.

———. 2012. "A Guide to the Supreme Court's Decision on the ACA's Medicaid Expansion." Menlo Park, CA: Henry J. Kaiser Family Foundation, August.

———. n.d. "Interactive: A State-by-State Look at How the Uninsured Fare Under the ACA." Online at http://kff.org/interactive/uninsured-gap/.

Kerry, John. 2010. "Foreword." In *Power, Politics, and Universal Health Care: The Inside Story of a Century-long Battle* by Stuart Altman and David Shactman, 7–9. Amherst, NY: Prometheus.

Kessler, Glenn. 2013. "The NRCC's Claim that the IRS Will Be 'In Charge of Your Health Care.'" *Washington Post*, May 29.

Kiene, Chelsea. 2013. "Ted Cruz: Defund Obamacare or Risk Government Shutdown." *Huffington Post*, March 13.

Kingdon, John. 2010. *Agendas, Alternatives, and Public Policies*. Updated 2nd ed. Glenview, IL: Longman.

Klein, Ezra. 2013a. "The Republican Plan for Replacing Obamacare Doesn't Replace Obamacare." *Washington Post*, April 3.

———. 2013b. "One Way Obamacare May Already Be Working." Bloomberg, May 29. Online at www.Bloomberg.com.

———. 2013c. "Congress, Today Is Your Fault." *Washington Post*, June 25.

Kliff, Sarah. 2012. "The Republican Plan to Overhaul Health Care." *Washington Post*, August 27.

———. 2013a. "Poll: 42 Percent of Americans Unsure if Obamacare Is Still Law." *Washington Post*, April 30.

———. 2013b. "Budget Request Denied, Sebelius Turns to Health Executives to Finance Obamacare." *Washington Post*, May 10.

———. 2013c. "Obamacare Just Might Net Its 7 Million." *Washington Post*, December 30.

Korte, Gregory, and Ray Locker. "Insurance Sign-Ups Surpasses 1 Million." 2013. *USA Today,* December 30.

Krugman, Paul. 2011. "Conservative Origins of Obamacare." *New York Times,* July 27.

Landmark: The Inside Story of America's New Health-Care Law and What It Means for Us All. 2010. New York: Public Affairs.

Landsberg, Mitchell. 2010. "Nuns in U.S. Back Healthcare Bill Despite Catholic Bishops' Opposition." *Los Angeles Times*, March 18.

"LCWR Stance on Healthcare Reform Draws Praise and Criticism." 2010. *Update: A Publication of the Leadership Conference of Women Religious* (April). Online at cwr.org/sites/default/files/publications/files/LCWRnewsletter4-10.pdf.

Lee, Frances E. 2009. *Beyond Ideology: Politics, Principles, and Partisanship in the U.S. Senate*. Chicago: University of Chicago Press.

"The Legislature's $51 Billion Failure." 2013. *Tampa Bay Times*, May 3.

Levy, Marc. 2013. "Gap Leaves 5 Million Uncovered." *Springfield News-Leader,* December 31.

Long, Sharon K. 2008. "On the Road to Universal Coverage: Impacts of Reform in Massachusetts at One Year." *Health Affairs* (June 3): w270–w284.

Lubell, Jennifer. 2013. "ACA High-Risk Pool Failings Offered as Cautionary Tale." American Medical News, April 15. Online at www.amednews.com/article/20130415/government/130419966/7.

Luntz, Frank. 2009. "The Language of Healthcare 2009." Campaign for America's Future. Online at http://thinkprogress.org/wp-content/uploads/2009/05/frank-luntz-the-language-of-healthcare-20091.pdf.

Mahar, Maggie. 2013. "The 37th Vote to Repeal Health Care Reform: Why?" Healthinsurance.org, May 21. Online at www.healthinsurance.org.

Mann, Thomas E., and Norman J. Ornstein. 2012. *It's Worse than It Looks: How the American Constitutional System Collided with the New Politics of Extremism.* New York: Basic Books.

Mashaw, Jerry L. 2013. "Legal, Imagined, and Real Worlds: Reflections on *National Federation of Independent Business v. Sebelius.*" *Journal of Health Politics, Policy and Law* 38, no. 2 (April): 257–66.

McDonough, John E. 2011. *Inside National Health Reform.* Berkeley: University of California Press.

Mikesell, John. 2013. *Fiscal Administration,* 9th ed. Farmington Hills, MI: Cengage.

National Patient Advocate Foundation. 2012. "Issue Brief: Medical Debt, Medical Bankruptcy and the Impact on Patients." Washington, DC: National Patient Advocate Foundation.

Obama, Barack. 2009. "Obama's Health Care Speech to Congress." 2013. *New York Times*, September 9.

"Obama Acknowledges Possible 'Glitches' in ACA Implementation." 2013. *California Healthline*, May 1.

Office of the Assistant Secretary for Planning and Evaluation. 2011. "Essential Health Benefits: Individual Market Coverage." Washington, DC: U.S. Department of Health and Human Services.

Ornstein, Norman J., et al. 2013. *Vital Statistics on Congress*. Washington, DC: American Enterprise Institute, The Campaign Finance Institute, and the Brookings Institution.

Ornstein, Norman J., and Thomas E. Mann. 2013. "Gridlock Is No Way to Govern." *Washington Post*, April 18.

Orszag, Peter R., and Ezekiel J. Emanuel. 2010. "Health Care Reform and Cost Control." *New England Journal of Medicine* 363 (August 12): 601–3.

Parente, Stephen T., and Tarren Bragdon. 2009. "Why Health Care Is So Expensive in New York." *Wall Street Journal*, October 16.

Patel, Kant, and Mark E. Rushefsky. 2006. *Health Care Politics and Policy in America,* 3rd ed. Armonk, NY: M.E. Sharpe.

———. 2008. *Health Care in America: Separate and Unequal.* Armonk, NY: M.E. Sharpe.

Pear, Robert. 2011a. "Panel Recommends Coverage for Contraception." *New York Times*, July 19.

———. 2011b. "Democrats Urge Obama to Protect Contraceptive Coverage in Health Plans." *New York Times*, November 19.

———. 2013a. "Birth Control Rule Altered to Allay Religious Objections." *New York Times*, February 1.

———. 2013b. "States' Policies on Health Care Exclude Some of the Poorest." *New York Times*, May 24.

Peters, Jeremy. 2013. "House to Vote Yet Again on Repealing Health Care Law." *New York Times*, May 14.

Peterson, Mark A. 2011. "It Was a Different Time: Obama and the Unique Opportunity for Health Care Reform." *Journal of Health Politics, Policy and Law* 36, no. 3 (June): 429–36.

Pettypiece, Shannon, and Jonathan D. Salant. 2013. "Health Law Critics Seek to Gut Program by Undermining Exchanges." *Bloomberg Businessweek*, May 28. Online at www.bloomberg.com.

Pew Research Center. 2010. "Public Knows Basic Facts About Politics, Economics, but Struggles with Specifics." Washington, DC: Pew Research Center, November 18. Online at www.pewresearch.org/2010/11/18/public-knows-basic-facts-about-politics-economics-but-struggles-with-specifics/.

PolitiFact Florida. 2012. "Paul Ryan Said '15 Unelected, Unaccountable Bureaucrats' Could 'Lead to Denied Care for Current Seniors.'" *Tampa Bay Times,* August 18. Online at http://www.politifact.com/florida/statements/2012/aug/23/paul-ryan/paul-ryan-said-15-unelected-unaccountable-bureaucr/.

Poole, Keith T., et al. 2012. "Polarization Is Real (and Asymmetric)." Voteview Blog, May 16. Online at http://voteview.com/blog/?p=494.

Potter, Wendell. 2010. *Deadly Spin: An Insurance Company Insider Speaks Out on How Corporate PR Is Killing Health Care and Deceiving Americans.* New York: Bloomsbury.

Radnofsky, Louise. 2013a. "Obamacare Gets New Court Challenge." *Wall Street Journal*, May 2.

———. 2013b. "Employers Push Back on Health Law's Insurance Trigger." *Wall Street Journal*, May 3.

Rayfield, Jillian. 2013. "Poll: Dems Like 'Obamacare' More than They Like 'Health Care Law.'" *Wall Street Journal*, June 19.

Reagan, Michael. 1999. *The Accidental System: Health Care Policy in America.* Boulder, CO: Westview.

Reid, T.R. 2010. *The Healing of America: A Global Quest for Better, Cheaper, and Fairer Health Care.* New York: Penguin.

Rivlin, Sheri, and Allan Rivlin. 2009. "Public Opinion on Healthcare Reform 2009 and 1993—Is This a New Day or 'Groundhog Day'?" *Huffington Post*, March 24.

Roarty, Alec. 2013. "Can This Congress Be Saved?" *National Journal*, February 21. Online at nationaljournal.com.

Rubin, Irene S. 2009. *The Politics of Public Budgeting: Getting and Spending, Borrowing and Balancing.* 6th ed. Washington, DC: Congressional Quarterly.

Rudowitz, Robin, and Jessica Stephens. 2013. "Analyzing the Impact of State Medicaid Decisions." Menlo Park, CA: The Kaiser Commission on Medicaid and the Uninsured.

Rushefsky, Mark E. 2008. "Shaping the Demand for Health Care: Consumer-Choice Versus Consumer Driven." Paper prepared for delivery at the 2008 Annual Meeting of the American Political Science Association, Boston.

———. 2013. *Public Policy in the United States,* 5th ed. Armonk, NY: M.E. Sharpe.

Rushefsky, Mark E., and Kant Patel. 1998. *Politics, Power & Policy Making: The Case of Health Care Reform in the 1990s.* Armonk, NY.: M.E. Sharpe.

Sabatier, Paul, and Daniel Mazmanian. 1980. "The Implementation of Public Policy: A Framework of Analysis." *Policy Studies Journal* 8, no. 4 (January): 538–60.

Savage, David G. 2013. "More Legal Troubles for Affordable Care Act." *Los Angeles Times,* October 25.

Shapiro, Ari. 2013. "Obama's Next Big Campaign: Selling Health Care to the Public." *Morning Edition*, National Public Radio, May 28. Online at http://www.npr.org/2013/05/28/186496205/obamas-next-big-campaign-selling-health-care-to-the-public.

Sinclair, Barbara. 2012. *Unorthodox Lawmaking: New Legislative Process in the U.S. Congress*. 4th ed. Washington, DC: CQ Press.

Smith-Dewey, Chuck. 2013. "Traditional State Health Risk Pools." Healthinsurance.org, January 3. Online at www.healthinsurance.org.

Starr, Paul. 1982. *The Social Transformation of American Medicine*. New York: Basic Books.

———. 2013. *Remedy and Reaction: The Peculiar American Struggle Over Health Care Reform*, rev ed. New Haven, CT: Yale University Press.

Steinmo, Sven, and Jon Watts. 1995. "It's the Institutions, Stupid! Why Comprehensive National Health Insurance Always Fails in America." *Journal of Health Politics, Policy and Law* 20, no. 2 (Summer): 329–72.

Stephens, Jessica, Samantha Artiga, and Alexandra Gates. 2013. "Getting into Gear for 2014: An Early Look at Branding and Marketing of New Health Insurance Marketplaces." Menlo Park, CA: Kaiser Family Foundation.

Stewart, Brandon. 2011. "List of 27 States Suing over Obamacare." *The Foundry,* January 17. Online at http://blog.heritage.org/2011/01/17/list-of-states-suing-over-obamacare/.

Stone, Deborah. 2012. *Policy Paradox: The Art of Political Decision Making*. 3rd ed. New York: Norton.

Stout, Hilary. 1994. "Many Don't Realize It's the Clinton Plan They Like." *Wall Street Journal*, March 10.

Suderman, Peter. 2012. "Why Obamacare's Health Care Cost Controls Won't Work." Reason.com, December 13. Online at http://reason.com/archives/2012/12/13/why-obamacares-health-care-cost-controls.

Summers, Lawrence. 2013. "When Gridlock Is Good." *Washington Post*, April 14.

Sunstein, Cass R. 2013. "Why Well-Informed People Are Also Close-Minded." Bloomberg View, April 15. Online at www.bloombergview.org.

Toobin, Jeffrey. 2008. *The Nine: Inside the Secret World of the Supreme Court*. New York: Knopf Doubleday.

———. 2012. *The Oath: The Obama White House and the Supreme Court*. New York: Knopf Doubleday.

Turner, Grace-Marie, and Joseph R. Antos. 2009. "The GOP's Health Alternative." *Wall Street Journal*, May 20.

Weisman, Jonathan. 2013. "Capitol Leaders Agree to a Deal on the Budget." *New York Times,* December 10.

Weisman, Jonathan, and Robert Pear. 2013. "Partisan Gridlock Thwarts Effort to Alter Health Law." *New York Times*, May 26.

Westen, Drew. 2007. *The Political Brain: The Role of Emotion in Deciding the Fate of the Nation*. New York: Public Affairs.

Whittington, Keith E. 2013. "'Our Own Limited Role in Policing Those Boundaries': Taking Small Steps on Health Care." *Journal of Health Politics, Policy and Law* 38, no. 2 (April): 272–82.

Wilkerson, John, David Smith, and Nick Stramp. 2013. "Tracing the Flow of Policy Idea in Legislatures: A Text Reuse Approach." September 17: 1–34. Online at http://www.kenbenoit.net/pdfs/NDATAD2013/PolicyIdeas2013TextasData.pdf.

Zuckerman, Stephen, and John Holahan. 2012. "Despite Criticism, the Affordable Care Act Does Much to Contain Health Care Costs." Washington, DC: Urban Policy Center, Urban Institute.

11

HEALTHCARE POLITICS AND POLICY IN AMERICA

A Never-Ending Story

The American healthcare system is product of innovations within the biomedical fields, organizational developments, and the political environment in which the system operates. As we have discussed in various chapters, it might be unfair to call American healthcare a system. Rather it is a series of systems, developed over a period, for various reasons. Whether we call it "accidental" (Reagan 1999) or employ terms such as path dependency (Oberlander 2003) or policy trap (Starr 2013), it is clear that no one person or group sat down and developed a plan that eventually was adopted. The result is a complex, fragmented, maze-like healthcare system.

These characteristics, combined with various features of the American political system such as separation of powers, divided government, and federalism created an atmosphere in which health policymaking was disjointed (Lindblom 1959). Private health insurance, with its beginnings in the 1930s, was started because patients had trouble paying providers (Starr 1982). A decision by the Internal Revenue Service (IRS) during World War II put us on the track for employer-based insurance. Medicare and Medicaid were enacted for different reasons; indeed, Medicaid seemed to appear, like some magic trick, in legislation that originally focused on hospital care for the elderly. The Children's Health Insurance Program (CHIP) and protections for workers changing jobs appeared as kind of a consolation prize for the failure to enact the Clinton Health Security Act. A drug benefit for Medicare recipients (Medicare Part D) was proposed by a Republican president and enacted by a Republican-controlled Congress. It provided a new benefit and was underfunded. These are all incremental reforms. Sometimes the times just have to be right for something big to happen, an idea that is known as "punctuated equilibrium" (Baumgartner and Jones 2009). That was the Affordable Care Act (ACA).

Healthcare is a policy area in which there has been considerable change and turmoil. And the problems have not disappeared. Costs and spending are problems that have not yet been resolved. Davidson (2010), writing in the aftermath of the passage of the Affordable Care Act, argued that the American healthcare system was still broken.

There are several dimensions to this situation. Medicaid is a costly program to both the states and the federal government and impacts both sets of government budgets. It is likely that even though not all states will expand Medicaid as called for by the ACA, enrollment will increase. Based on the experience with the Massachusetts plan adopted in 2006, the Medicaid enrollment expansion is effectively a "welcome-mat" (Sonier, Boudreaux, and Blewett 2013) for people who were eligible for Medicaid before the health reform legislation. The increase could be sizable, and as more enroll in the program, spending will increase.

The same things can be said about Medicare. Enrollment in Medicare is not affected by the ACA. But the baby boomer generation is beginning to retire. The boomers are some 79 million strong and about 10,000 turn sixty-five every day ("U.S. Faces 'Explosion of Senior Citizens'" 2011). While Medicare has made some strides in cutting spending per recipient, overall spending will continue to increase. Medicare and Medicaid will have major impacts on the federal budget and attempts to reduce federal deficits.

Other concerns about the healthcare system abound. Access remains a problem. The U.S. Supreme Court 2012 decision on the constitutionality of the Affordable Care Act, *NFIB v. Sebelius,* made one of the most important tools of expanded access to healthcare more difficult: Medicaid expansion. While the ACA does have financial incentives for states to broaden Medicaid eligibility, many states have refused to go along. These tend to be the states with the highest percentage of uninsured people and families. Their status in the healthcare system will stay the same or decrease.

Indeed, states that refuse to expand Medicaid eligibility may find that their hospitals will suffer. Hospitals provide a certain amount of uncompensated care. Under the 1986 Emergency Medical Treatment and Active Labor Act, hospitals are required to treat and stabilize everyone who comes to the emergency room, regardless of ability to pay. Federal law has compensated hospitals that provided a sizable amount of such services; this is the Disproportionate Share Hospital (DSH) program. However, under ACA, such payments are cut. Presumably, pretty much everyone will have health insurance (except illegal immigrants) and therefore the amount of uncompensated care will decrease. But this will be less so in states that do not expand Medicaid eligibility, so hospitals in those states may experience a cut in federal payments and thus revenue (Blau 2013).

Two other examples of issues: One is technology (chapter 9). Technology can and has improved the quality of care in our health system. But not all technology is beneficial, and most raises some concerns. One is overuse, or overdiagnosis. Related to that is that medical technology can increase costs and spending. New technology, for the most part, costs more than the technology it replaces or complements. An MRI can do much more than an X-ray, but it costs much more. Technology can prolong lives, and thus it raises ethical concerns about end-of-life care.

At the other end are controversies that continue to arise over abortion and contraception (chapter 9). The 1973 *Roe v. Wade* decision set off a firestorm of opposition that has hardly abated. Court decisions and federal and state legislation have restricted the availability of abortion. In some cases, states such as Texas and South Dakota have sought to make abortions illegal after the twentieth week of a pregnancy, directly challenging the trimester distinction created by the *Roe* majority. The abortion issue became a barrier to the ACA, nearly leading to its defeat in Congress. And pro-life groups still think that legislation in some ways funds abortions.

The availability of contraception became an implementation issue for the ACA. The Obama administration included coverage of contraception devices as part of the "essential benefits" that must be included in health insurance policies. Again, pro-life groups, such as Catholic bishops, took exception. Despite attempts to compromise on this by the Obama administration, pro-life groups were not satisfied.

What has increasingly characterized debates over healthcare policy are ideological and partisan divides. While Barack Obama may have claimed, as the keynote speaker at the 2004 Democratic National Convention, that there are no red states or blue states, just the United States, the states are not acting that way. Those with Democratic majorities in the state legislature and Democratic governors are expanding Medicaid and establishing health exchanges. Those with Republican leadership are resisting. It is almost as if we have two countries. These political divides, which we can see in Congress as well, combine with the federal nature of our political system to make implementation more problematical. Not impossible, but more difficult.

A final element that we wish to mention is the public. The public is as divided about Obamacare as the leadership. The public also has limited knowledge about the law, even among its supporters. Getting the public to participate in the exchanges and enroll in Medicaid is important to whatever success Obamacare will have. That may be our biggest challenge.

THE FUTURE

John Connor is the hero of the *Terminator* movie series. In the future, he is one of the leaders of the rebels (i.e., humans) fighting the machines that have taken over. He sends his friend Kyle Reese back in time to thwart the plan to kill Sarah Connor before John is born. The plan is to change the future. All the *Terminator* movies have the same plot: try to change the past so as to change the future. And in all those movies, the plan fails. The future does not change. John Connor's message to his mother, relayed by Kyle, is that "The future is not set, there is no fate but what we make for ourselves."

As we look to the future of healthcare policy and politics in America, three things should be kept in mind. First, making predictions is a tricky business, and humans are not very good at it. Few would have predicted that comprehensive healthcare reform would actually have passed in the United States, however limited and flawed that reform. Second, as John Connor says, we make our own future.

Third, the complexity of the healthcare system makes substantial changes difficult and tradeoffs are needed if we want to achieve our goals. Bernstam (2013) argues that the problem with the ACA (and health reform in general) is that it cannot be everything we want it to be at the same time: "It cannot simultaneously be 1) universal, 2) comprehensive, and 3) affordable. This is the impossible trinity of objectives. This is a point made decades ago by the economist Eli Ginzberg (1977). Increasing access and controlling costs are incompatible objectives. But this does not mean that we cannot or should not make an attempt to increase coverage, control costs and improve the delivery of health care. The old saying is that perfection is the enemy of the good. While no one would claim that the ACA is perfect, advocates, at least, argue that it is an improvement.

The ACA is likely to provide the framework for future policy changes. As the health insurance reforms take place and consumers begin to make choices among plans on the health exchanges in 2014, we do enter a somewhat new age. Resistance to the legislation remains strong, and implementation in the early years will be uneven. Republicans and Democrats see the 2014 off-year elections and 2016 presidential elections as a referendum on the ACA. The future of ACA is not set, but the longer the ACA stays in place, the harder it will be to dismantle.

STUDY QUESTIONS

1. This final chapter, indeed the entire text, makes the argument that the American healthcare system is highly fragmented. In what ways is the system fragmented? What are the impacts of such fragmentation? How well does the Affordable Care Act address the fragmentation problem?
2. Having gone through the entire text now, what do you see as the major problems facing the American healthcare system? What, if any, changes would you like to see?
3. How well does the Affordable Care Act address the problems of the American healthcare system? What changes would you like to see in the ACA to address those problems?
4. From your perspective, what would the perfect healthcare system look like?

REFERENCES

Baumgartner, Frank R., and Bryan D. Jones. 2009. *Agendas and Instability in American Politics,* 2nd ed. Chicago: University of Chicago Press.

Bernstam, Michael. 2013. "The Impossible Trinity of ObamaCare." Fox News, December 16. Online at http://www.foxnews.com/opinion/2013/12/16/impossible-trinity-obamacare/.

Blau, Max. 2013. "This Georgia Hospital Shows Why Rejecting Medicaid Isn't Easy." *Washington Post* June 26.

Davidson, Stephen M. 2010. *Still Broken: Understanding the U.S. Health Care System.* Stanford, CA: Stanford University Press.

Ginzberg, Eli. 1977. *The Limits of Health Reform: The Search for Realism.* New York: Basic Books.

Lindblom, Charles E. 1959. "The Science of 'Muddling Through.'" *Public Administration Review* 19, no. 2 (Spring): 79–88.

Oberlander, Jonathan B. 2003. *The Political Life of Medicare.* Chicago: University of Chicago Press.

Reagan, Michael E. 1999. *The Accidental System: Healthcare Policy in America.* New York: Westview Press.

Sonier, Julie; Michel H. Boudreaux; and Lynn A. Blewett. 2013. "Medicaid 'Welcome-Mat' Effect of Affordable Care Act Implementation Could Be Substantial." *Health Affairs* 32, no. 7 (July): 1–7.

Starr, Paul. 1982. *The Social Transformation of American Medicine.* New York: Basic Books.

———. 2013. *Remedy and Reaction: The Peculiar American Struggle Over Healthcare Reform,* rev ed. New Haven, CT: Yale University Press.

"U.S. Faces 'Explosion of Senior Citizens': Will Baby Boomers Strain Economy?" 2011. *PBS Newshour,* January 3. Online at www.pbs.org/newshour/bb/social_issues/jan-june11/boomer_01–03.html.

APPENDIX A

Important Health Policy–Related Web Sites

GOVERNMENT

Agency for Healthcare Research and Quality (AHRQ): www.ahrq.gov
(U.S. Department of Health and Human Services)

Bureau of Health Professions: www.bhpr.hrsa.gov
(U.S. Department of Health and Human Services)

Bureau of Labor Statistics: www.bls.gov
(U.S. Department of Labor)

Centers for Disease Control and Prevention (CDC): www/cdc.gov
(U.S. Department of Health and Human Services)

Centers for Medicare and Medicaid Services (CMS): www.cms.hhs.gov
(U.S. Department of Health and Human Services)

Congressional Budget Office: www.cbo.gov
(U.S. Congress)

Food and Drug Administration: www.fda.gov
(U.S. Department of Health and Human Services)

Government Accountability Office: www.gao.gov
(U.S. Congress)

Health Finder: www.healthfinder.gov
(National Health Information Center, U.S. Department of Health and Human Services)

Health Resources and Services Administration (HRSA): www.hrsa.gov
(U.S. Department of Health and Human Services)

Library of Congress: www.loc.gov
(U.S. Congress)

Medical Expenditure Panel Survey: www.meps.ahrq.gov
(Agency for Healthcare Research and Quality; U.S. DHHS)

Medicare Payment Advisory Commission: www.medpac.gov
(Independent Commission established by Congress in 1997 to advise Congress on Medicare program)

National Center for Health Statistics: www.cdc.gov/nchs
(Centers for Disease Control and Prevention)

National Institute on Aging: www.nia.gov
(National Institutes of Health)

National Institutes of Health: www.nih.gov
(U.S. Department of Health and Human Services)

National Mental Health Information System: www.mentalhealth.samhsa.gov/
(U.S. Department of Health and Human Services)

National Practitioner Data Bank: www.npdb-hipdb.com/search/index.html
(U.S. Department of Health and Human Services; Substance Abuse and Mental Health Services
Administration)

State of Oregon—Physician Assisted Suicide: http://oregon.gov/DHS/ph/pas/index.shtml
(Provides annual reports on physician-assisted suicide)

Statistical Abstract of the United States: www.census.gov/statab/www
(National data book contains statistics on social and economic conditions in U.S.)

U.S. Census Bureau: www.census.gov

U.S. Department of Health and Human Services: www.hhs.gov/

U.S. National Library of Medicine: www.nlm.nih.gov/nlmhome.html
(National Institutes of Health)

PRIVATE SECTOR

American Association of Retired Persons (AARP): www.aarp.org

America's Health Insurance Plans (AHIP): www.ahip.org

Harris Polls: www.harrisinteractive.com/Harris_polls
(Harris Interactive Market Research Firm)

Moving Ideas: The Electronic Policy Network: www.movingideas.org
(A Project of American Prospect—Progressive/liberal perspective)

National Association of Insurance Commissioners: www.naic.org/index.htm

THINK TANKS/RESEARCH ORGANIZATIONS

Brookings Institution: www.Brookings.org

Center on Budget and Policy Priorities: www.cbpp.org

Center for Studying Health System Change: www.hschange.com

Urban Institute: www.urban.org/
(A nonpartisan economic and social policy research organization)

ACADEMIC

Institute of Medicine: www.iom.org
(National Academy of Sciences)

Program for Health Systems Improvement: www.phsi.Harvard.edu
(Harvard University)

State Health Access Data Assistance Center: www.shadac.org/
(University of Minnesota—Funded by Robert Wood Johnson Foundation)

UCLA Center for Health Policy Research: www.healthpolicy.ucla.edu/

FOUNDATIONS/NOT-FOR-PROFIT ORGANIZATIONS

Carnegie Foundation for the Advancement of Teaching: www.carnegiefoundation.org/

Children's Defense Fund: www.childrensdefense.org

Commonwealth Fund: www.commonwealthfund.org/
(Supports independent research on issues and provides grants to improve practices and policy)

Cover the Uninsured Week: www.covertheuninsuredweek.org
(A project of the Robert Wood Johnson Foundation)

The Heritage Foundation: www.heritage.org/research/healthcare/index.cfm
(Conservative voice in health policy)

Institute for Health Policy Solutions: www.ihps.org

Kaiser Family Foundation: www.kff.org/statedata

National Academy of Social Insurance: www.nasi.org
(Nonprofit, nonpartisan organization made up of leading experts on social insurance)

National Academy of State Health Policy: www.nashp.org/index.cfm
(Nonprofit, non-artisan organization)

National Conference of State Legislatures: www.ncsl.org
(Bipartisan organization serving state legislators)

National Health Policy Forum: www.nhpf.org
(Nonpartisan information exchange program)

Public Health Foundation: www.phf.org
(Nonprofit organization that helps health agencies and community health organizations)

Robert Wood Johnson Foundation: www.rwjf.org/index.jsp
(Seeks to improve health of all Americans)

State Health Facts: www.statehealthfacts.org/cgi-bin/healthfacts.cgi
(Henry J. Kaiser Family Foundation)

United States Pharmacopeia (USP): www.usp.org
(The official public standards-setting authority for all prescription and over-the-counter medicines, dietary supplements, and other healthcare products manufactured and sold in the United States)

CONSUMER HEALTH ADVOCACY GROUPS

American Health Care Association (AHCA): www.ahcancal.org/

Center for Health Care Strategies (CHCS): www.chcs.org/

Children's Defense Fund (CDF): www.childrensdefense.org/

Families USA: www.familiesusa.org/

Health Consumer Alliance (HCA): www.healthconsumer.org/

Society for Healthcare Consumer Advocacy (SHCA): www.shca-aha.org

PRIVATE SECTOR

Alliance Cost Containment: www.alliancecost.com/

American College of Emergency Physicians: www.acep.org/

American Hospital Association (AHA): www.aha.org

American Medical Association (AMA): www.ama-assn.org

American Nurses Association (ANA): www.nursingworld.org

America's Health Insurance Plans (AHIP): www.ahip.org

Medical Device Manufacturers of America (MDMA): www.medicaldevices.org

National Coalition on Health Care: nchc.org/

Pharmaceutical Research and Manufacturers of America (PhRMA): www.phrma.org

USA Managed Care Organization (USAMCO): www.usamco.com/

Washington Business Group on Health: www.businessgrouphealth.org

INTERNATIONAL HEALTH

Global Health Reporting: www.globalhealthreporting.org
(Henry J. Kaiser Family Foundation, provides global health data)

Health Canada: www.hc-sc.gc.ca
(Canadian government)

Organization for Economic Cooperation and Development (OECD) www.oecd.org/home/

World Health Organization (WHO): www.who.int/en/
(United Nations' specialized agency for health)

World Health Organization Statistical Information System (WHOSIS): www3.who.int/whosis/
menu.cfm

IMPORTANT REPORTS

Flexner Report: http://www.carnegiefoundation.org/sites/default/files/elibrary/Carnegie_Flexner_
Report.pdf

APPENDIX B

Chronology of Significant Events and Legislation in U.S. Healthcare

1778 The first national pension law is passed for soldiers who fought in the American Revolution.

1797 The first recorded inoculation of an American Indian takes place.

1798 President John Adams signs into law an act providing for relief of sick and disabled seamen, which approved the establishment of the first Marine Hospital.

1799 The first Marine Hospital is established.

1811 The federal government authorizes the first domiciliary and medical facility for veterans.

1832 Congress appropriates $12,000 to hire physicians to provide vaccinations to American Indians. This was the first large-scale smallpox vaccination authorized by Congress.

1847 The American Medical Association (AMA) is founded.

1849 The Bureau of Indian Affairs (BIA) is transferred to the newly created Department of the Interior. The responsibility for Indian healthcare is transferred from military to civilian control.

1863 The National Academy of Sciences is established to assist in caring for the Union Army.

1865 The United States Soldiers and Sailors Protective Society is organized to help veterans.

1866 The Grand Army of the Republic (GAR) is formed as a political group to lobby for veterans benefits.

1870 First Reorganization Act federalizes the Marine Hospital Service.

1872 The American Public Health Association (APHA) is founded. This organization is concerned with the social and economic aspects of health problems.

1878 The National Quarantine Act is signed into law. This legislation is designed to prevent entry into the country of persons with communicable diseases.

1879 The Arrears Act specifies that veterans' benefits start from the time of discharge from the army and for dependents from the time of the death and not at the time of application, as was the case previous to the act.

1899   The National Hospital Superintendents Association is created. It later becomes the American Hospital Association (AHA).

1904   The Council on Medical Education is established by the AMA.

1908   Congress passes the Federal Employers Liability Act, preempting state tort law, designed to govern the liability claims brought by employees against railroads operating in interstate commerce.

1910   The Flexner Report is published, calling for the adoption of the German model of medicine, with scientifically based training, the strengthening of first-class medical schools, and the elimination of a great majority of inferior schools.

Congress starts to formally appropriate funds for Bureau of Indian Affairs healthcare services.

1912   The U.S. Public Health Service (USPHS) is formed from the Marine Hospital Service.

1921   The Sheppard-Towner Act is signed into law. It establishes the first federal grant-in-aid program for local child health clinics.

The Snyder Act provides formal legislative authorization for Indian healthcare and provides for regular congressional appropriations.

1928   The Sheppard-Towner Act is terminated.

1929   Blue Cross is established.

1930   The National Institutes of Health (NIH) is established for the purpose of discovering the causes, prevention, and cure of disease.

President Herbert Hoover establishes the Committee on the Cost of Medical Care.

President Hoover signs a law consolidating many separate veterans' programs into an independent federal agency called the Veterans Administration.

1934   The Federal Emergency Relief Administration (FERA) gives the first federal grants to local governments for public assistance to the poor, including financial support for healthcare.

1935   The Social Security Act is signed into law. The act provides for unemployment compensation, old-age benefits, and other benefits.

1937   The National Cancer Act is passed by Congress, establishing the National Cancer Institute (NCI).

1939   The Murray-Wagner-Dingell Bill is introduced, proposing national health insurance.

1943   The U.S. Supreme Court, in the first reproductive rights case, *Skinner v. Oklahoma,* strikes down vasectomies as criminal punishment and recognizes the right to have offspring as a sensitive and important area of human rights.

1944   The Servicemen's Readjustment Act, famously known as the "GI Bill of Rights," offers low-interest loans for veterans to purchase homes, farms, or small businesses, unemployment benefits, financial assistance for education, as well as healthcare and rehabilitation services.

1946   The National Hospital Survey and Construction Act (Hill-Burton Act) mandates the provision of federal funding to subsidize the construction of hospitals.

The National Mental Health Act is signed into law, providing federal grants to states for research, prevention, diagnosis, and treatment of mental disorders.

Congress passes and President Truman signs Public Law 293, formally creating the Veterans Health Administration (VHA) within the Veterans Administration.

1951   The Internal Revenue Service rules that employers' costs for healthcare insurance premiums are tax-deductible.

1952   The nongovernmental Joint Commission on Accreditation of Hospitals (JCAH) is established.

The Health Insurance Association of America (HIAA) is formed.

1954   The Transfer Act moves responsibility for Indian health to the Public Health Service, which at that time was part of the Department of Health, Education, and Welfare.

1955   The Indian Health Service (IHS) is established as an agency under the United States Public Health Service.

1956   The Dependents Medical Care Act is passed, providing the Department of Defense with the authority to provide civilian healthcare to eligible dependents of military service members.

1960   The Kerr-Mills Act (Medical Assistance Act) is signed into law, providing federal matching payments to states for vendor payments.

1965   Medicare and Medicaid are passed as amendments to the Social Security Act of 1935.

In *Griswold v. Connecticut,* the U.S. Supreme Court recognizes that married couples have a constitutional right to use contraception within a "zone of privacy" that encompasses marital relationship.

1966   The Comprehensive Health Planning Act is signed into law. This legislation is an attempt to implement healthcare facility planning through the states.

The Civilian Health and Medical Program of Uniformed Services (CHAMPUS) is established for active duty family members and is later extended to retired service members and their dependents.

1971   Ralph Nader's Health Research Group is founded.

Senator Edward Kennedy introduces the Health Security Act, which calls for a comprehensive program of free medical care.

1972   President Nixon, in response to Kennedy's plan, introduces the National Health Insurance Partnership Act.

The Professional Standards Review Organizations (PSROs) are created through the Social Security Amendments of 1972.

The Office of Technology Assessment (OTA) is established. This organization maintains, in part, a concern for medical technology assessment.

In *Eisenstadt v. Baird,* the U.S. Supreme Court extends the right to use contraceptives to unmarried individuals.

1973   The Health Maintenance Organization Act is signed into law.

The U.S. Supreme Court legalizes abortion in *Roe v. Wade.*

1974   The Congressional Budget and Impoundment Control Act is signed into law.

The National Health Planning and Resource Development Act is signed into law.

The Employee Retirement Income Security Act (ERISA) is signed into law.

1975   The State of California passes the Medical Injury Compensation Reform Act, which places a cap of $250,000 on jury awards for noneconomic damages.

The Indian Self-Determination and Education Assistance Act (ISDEAA) is passed.

1976   The Indian Health Care Improvement Act (IHCIA) is passed.

The New Jersey Supreme Court rules that Karen Quinlan has a constitutional right of privacy, which her guardian could assert on her behalf.

1977   In *Casey v. Population Services International,* the U.S. Supreme Court strikes down New York State's ban on the sale of contraceptive to minors under sixteen years of age.

1981   The Omnibus Budget Reconciliation Act (OBRA) is passed.

The Health Care Financing Administration (HCFA) grants waivers to states to pay for home healthcare.

1982   The Tax Equity and Fiscal Responsibility Act (TEFRA) is signed into law.

The National Center for Health Care Technology (NCHCT) is abolished.

1983   The Prospective Payment System (PPS), a mandate of the Deficit Reduction Act of 1982, begins.

1984   The Deficit Reduction Act requires Medicaid beneficiaries to assign to the states any rights they had to other health benefit programs.

1985   Congress creates the Physician Payment Review Commission (PPRC).

Congress passes the Medical Malpractice Immunity Act (MMIA).

1986   The Omnibus Budget Reconciliation Act (OBRA) of 1986 gives the states the option to extend Medicaid coverage to pregnant women and infants who are members of households with incomes as high as 100 percent of the federal poverty level.

Congress passes the Health Care Quality Improvement Act.

The Emergency Medical Treatment and Active Labor Act guarantees emergency medical treatment to anyone, regardless of their legal status or ability to pay.

1987   The Omnibus Budget Reconciliation Act increases the income requirements of pregnant women and infants to 185 percent of the federal poverty level.

1988   The Medicare Catastrophic Coverage Act is passed.

The Pepper Commission Report is released.

1989   President Reagan elevates Veterans Affairs to cabinet-level Department of Veterans Affairs.

The Omnibus Budget Reconciliation Act requires provision of all Medicaid-allowed treatment to correct problems identified during early and periodic screening, diagnosis, and treatment (EPSDT).

The Medicare Catastrophic Coverage Act is repealed.

The Office of Health Technology Assessment (OHTA) is established.

The Agency for Health Care Policy and Research (AHCPR) is created.

The U.S. Supreme Court, in *Webster v. Reproductive Health Services*, gives states the authority to regulate and thus restrict abortions in public clinics.

The Medicare Prospective Payment System is extended to physicians.

1990   The U.S. Supreme Court rules that a competent person has a constitutionally protected right to refuse life-saving hydration and nutrition (Nancy Cruzan case).

The Safe Medical Devices Act strengthens the FDA by controlling the entry of new products and monitoring the use of the marketplace.

1991   Harris Wofford wins special senatorial election in Pennsylvania, firmly placing healthcare on the policy agenda.

1992   Congress enacts the Prescription Drug Use Fee Act.

Amendments to the IHCIA of 1976 reauthorize the Indian Self-Determination Act and provides for tribal self-governance demonstration projects.

The U.S. Supreme Court in *Planned Parenthood v. Casey* adopts an undue burden test.

1993   President Bill Clinton unveils his Health Security Act.

CHAMPUS program is renamed TRICARE.

1994   Congress fails to pass any health reform bill.

President Clinton issues an executive order to facilitate tribal involvement in the administration of Indian programs.

Oregon voters approve the Death with Dignity Act.

1995   The Medicare Hospital Insurance Trust Fund is projected to go bankrupt by 2002.

Republicans adopt a balanced budget target of 2002, calling for reductions in spending for Medicare and Medicaid.

President Clinton announces a balanced budget target of 2005, with smaller reductions in Medicare and Medicaid.

President Clinton proposes federal regulation of private insurance.

Congress passes the Federally Supported Health Centers Assistance Act (FSHCAA).

The Office of Technology Assessment is abolished.

1996   Congress passes the Personal Responsibility and Work Opportunity Reconciliation Act, separating Medicaid from welfare.

Congress passes the Health Insurance Portability and Accountability Act (HIPAA).

Congress gives mental health the same status as physical health.

States begin passing patients' rights bills, regulating health maintenance organizations.

The Veterans Eligibility Reform Act is passed, expanding veterans' benefits.

1997   Congress passes the Balanced Budget Act creating the Medicare+Choice program and extends the prospective payment system to nursing homes, home healthcare agencies, and hospice agencies.

The Balanced Budget Act increases health insurance for children through the creation of the State Children's Health Insurance Program (SCHIP).

1997   President Clinton establishes the Advisory Commission on Consumer Protection and Quality in the Health Care Industry (also known as the Quality Commission).

Texas passes a patient's rights law allowing enterprise liability suits.

The Food and Drug Administration (FDA) declares that emergency contraceptive pills are safe and effective.

1998   President Clinton proposes to extend Medicare to those age fifty-five to sixty-four who are uninsured.

The House passes a patient's rights bill. The Senate fails to act.

The number of uninsured in United States exceeds 40 million people, almost 16 percent of the population.

Some HMOs drop out of the Medicare program, citing high costs and federal refusal to raise payments.

The Veterans Eligibility Reform Act goes into effect. It dramatically changes and reforms the VHA.

1999   The FDA approves the emergency contraceptive Plan B as a prescription drug.

The Agency for Health Care Policy and Research (AHCPR) is renamed the Agency for Healthcare Research and Quality (AHRQ)

2000   The FDA approves the use of mifepristone as a safe and effective medical method for terminating pregnancy.

2001   The President's Council on Bioethics is founded.

President George Bush announces his policy to restrict federal funding to stem cell lines already in existence at the time.

2003   President George W. Bush signs into law the Medicare Prescription Drug, Improvement, and Modernization Act.

The Florida legislature passes "Terri's Law," giving Governor Jeb Bush the power to issue a "one-time stay" of any court order directing the withdrawal of nutrition and hydration so long as certain conditions are met. Using this power, Governor Bush issues an executive order to reinstate the feeding tube in Terri Schiavo.

President Bush signs the Partial Birth Abortion Ban Act into law.

2004   The Medicare drug discount card program begins.

2005   Congress passes an Act of Relief of the Parents of Theresa Marie Schiavo.

2005   Judge George Greer issues a restraining order prohibiting the Florida Department of Children and Families (FDCF) from removing Terri Schiavo from the hospice or reinserting the feeding tube.

Terri Schiavo passes away.

The Base Realignment and Closure Commission (BRCC) recommends closing down the Walter Reed Army Medical Center in Washington, DC, and moving its staff and services to the U.S. National Naval Medical Center.

2006   The Medicare prescription drug benefit begins.

The U.S. Supreme Court in *Gonzales v. Oregon* upholds the state of Oregon's Death with Dignity Act.

2007   The U.S. Supreme Court in *Gonzales v. Carhart* and *Gonzales v. Planned Parenthood* upholds the constitutionality of the Partial Birth Abortion Ban Act of 2003.

2008   Voters in Washington State approve a public "Initiative 1000," which establishes the state's Death with Dignity Act. The law goes into effect in 2009.

2009   Congress passes the Children's Health Insurance Program Reauthorization Act (CHIPRA).

President Obama signs an executive order allowing federal tax dollars to be used for broadening federal support for embryonic stem cell research.

President Obama creates the Presidential Commission for the Study of Bioethical Issues. The President's Council on Bioethics is abolished.

Washington State's Death with Dignity Act goes into effect.

The Supreme Court of the State of Montana gives the green light for doctors to prescribe a lethal dose of drugs for their patients for the purpose of assisted suicide.

2010   The Affordable Care Act (ACA) is passed.

The Federal Emergency Contraception Education Act funds a national campaign to educate women and healthcare providers about emergency contraception.

2011   Walter Reed Army Medical Center is merged and integrated with the National Naval Medical Center and renamed Walter Reed Bethesda.

2012   The Obama administration creates a new program called Deferred Action for Childhood Arrivals (DACA) under which certain people who came to the United States as children and meet several key guidelines may request consideration of deferred action (removal of an individual from the U.S. is deferred as an act of prosecutorial discretion) for a period of two years, subject to renewal, and would then be eligible for work authorization.

U.S. Supreme Court decides *NFIB v. Sebelius*.

2013   U.S. District Court Judge Edward Korman rules that the FDA must remove all age restrictions on the sale of emergency contraception without a doctor's prescription.

The FDA lowers availability of Plan B One-Step morning after pill without a prescription to girls fifteen and over.

INDEX

Page numbers in *italics* indicate figures and tables

ABOUT THE AUTHORS

Kant Patel (Ph.D., University of Houston, 1976) is an emeritus professor of political science at Missouri State University. From 1977 to 2011 he taught health policy and politics, policy analysis, and intergovernmental relations. He has published articles in journals such as *Evaluation and Health Profession, Health Policy and Education, Political Methodology, Journal of Political Science, International Journal of Policy Analysis and Information Systems*, and *Journal of Health and Social Policy,* among others. He is coauthor (with Mark E. Rushefsky) of *Politics, Power, and Policy Making: The Case of Health Care Reform in the 1990s* (M.E. Sharpe, 1998); *Health Care Policy in an Age of New Technologies* (M.E. Sharpe, 2002); *The Politics of Public Health in the United States* (M.E. Sharpe, 2005); and *Health Care in America: Separate and Unequal* (M.E. Sharpe, 2008).

Mark E. Rushefsky (Ph.D., Binghamton University [State University of New York], 1977) is professor of political science at Missouri State University. He teaches and writes on public policy and public administration. He is the author of *Making Cancer Policy* (SUNY Press, 1986); and *Public Policy in the United States: At the Dawn of the Twenty-First Century*, 5th ed. (M.E. Sharpe, 2013); as well as articles and chapters on healthcare and the environment. He is coauthor (with Kant Patel) of *Politics, Power, and Policy Making: The Case of Health Care Reform in the 1990s* (M.E. Sharpe, 1998); *Health Care Policy in an Age of New Technologies* (M.E. Sharpe, 2002); *The Politics of Public Health in the United States* (M.E. Sharpe, 2005); and *Health Care in America: Separate and Unequal* (M.E. Sharpe, 2008).